Marketing Problem Solver

Marketing Problem Solver

Cochrane Chase & Kenneth L. Barasch

Edited by Edmund Van Deusen

Second Edition

Chilton Book Company · Radnor, Pennsylvania

The first edition of MARKETING PROBLEM SOLVER was published by Cochrane Chase & Co., Inc. This second edition is published by arrangement with that firm and with Kenneth L. Barasch.

Second Edition   *All Rights Reserved*
Published in Radnor, Pennsylvania 19089, by Chilton Book Company

Manufactured in the United States of America

Library of Congress Cataloging in Publication Data
Chase, Cochrane.
     Marketing problem solver.

     First ed. by K. L. Barasch.
       1.   Marketing—Handbooks, manuals, etc.
I.   Barasch, Kenneth L.   Marketing problem solver.
II.   Title.
HF5415.C4844   1976   658.8′002′02   76-57697
ISBN 0-8019-6496-2
ISBN 0-8019-6495-4 *pbk.*

8 9 0 1 2 3   8 7 6 5 4 3

Acknowledgment

This book bears the imprint of many persons who, in a formal review or in informal conversation, made a significant contribution to its development. We would like to express our appreciation to Edmund Van Deusen for his cooperation in editing the current edition of the Marketing Problem Solver, and to Forrest G. Allen and William Koelzer for editing the first edition. Thanks also to the 26 marketing practitioners from a wide variety of industries and job functions whose informal reviews helped MPS retain its practical, real-world orientation. The staff at Cochrane Chase & Company should also be congratulated for a variety of contributions. And most of all, a thank you goes to our wives, Donna B. and Janice C., for their patience and encouragement while preparation of this book was in progress.

Contents

Introduction

A number of textbooks have been written about the theory of marketing. The Marketing Problem Solver isn't one of them.

A number of books get caught up in the latest statistical advancements in marketing. The Marketing Problem Solver isn't one of them, either.

In fact, the Marketing Problem Solver isn't like any other book at all. It is, instead, a practical, how-to-do-it tool that does exactly what it was created to do—solve your marketing problems.

One thing, that's all—solve your real-world marketing problems. No hodge-podge of case histories, personal stories, irrelevant theories, or belabored narrative explanations. The Marketing Problem Solver breaks down marketing into easy-to-grasp subjects. It translates esoteric terminology into layman's language, and changes marketing theory into marketing action.

For virtually any marketing, advertising, and public relations task, MPS directs you through each stage of development on a step-by-step basis. It outlines responsibilities, schedules, and methods of measuring results, complete with procedures, check lists, reference sources, fill-in forms, facts, and examples.

Maybe you need to create a marketing plan, or calculate your break-even point on a new product, or figure the advertising budget, or evaluate the effectiveness of your sales force. Whatever the job, you solve it as you read the step-by-step guidelines, fill in the forms, consult the charts, ponder the examples, and arrive at conclusions. You actually create the plan, the calculation, the budgets, the evaluation, or whatever, as you go.

There is, however, one other reason why we created MPS. It is our observation that too many marketing decisions have always been based on the dubious foundation of intuition—also known as "gut feel," and "flying by the seat of the pants."

MPS uses the other end of the marketing man. Where decisions have been emotional, MPS attempts to be rational. Where decision factors have been subjective, MPS helps you to make them objective. Where variables have been poorly defined, MPS lets you ferret them out and assign numerical values.

In this respect, MPS moves marketing closer to the area of science. True, each marketing decision ultimately hinges on your judgement. The approach of MPS, however, is to give you as much information as possible to make the right decision.

MPS's twelve chapters can help you develop any portion or all of a marketing program. Together, they add up to everything you need to know in order to plan, implement, and monitor any marketing program. And to make MPS even easier to use, we've included a cross-reference index in the back of the book. With it, you can quickly locate any one of over 1500 specific entries.

Besides being an invaluable tool for marketing, advertising, public relations, and sales executives, MPS is also an excellent vehicle for those who work with those job functions—such as corporate officers, general management, financial, and manufacturing executives. And although it is oriented toward industrial marketing and communication, much of it could also apply to the marketing of consumer products and services.

Finally, MPS is also a great training tool for use in undergraduate and graduate study, as well as for special seminars and company training programs.

Marketing Problem Solver

CHAPTER

I

Marketing Research

Introduction

What Is Marketing Research?

Marketing research (MR) is the systematic and objective search for, and analysis of, information relevant to identifying and solving any marketing problem.

While MR helps identify and solve marketing problems, it is not a substitute for management decisions. It simply helps you make better decisions through predictions based on interpretation of gathered information.

Value of Marketing Research

The vital first step in any marketing effort, MR is valuable to you in several ways. Manufacturers are distant from their customers and markets, both geographically and mentally. Whereas marketing communications and the sales force communicate the manufacturer's message to customers, MR helps complete the cycle by communicating from customers to manufacturer.

MR makes two major contributions to top management. First, it helps the company recognize, establish priorities for, and seize profitable opportunities (e.g., new products, new channels).

Second, MR identifies problems. It tells where goals are met or not met (i.e., lets you know results of current marketing programs). MR also helps develop alternative solutions to problems, and verify informa-

tion on which decisions must be based. In short, MR increases your ability to draw meaningful conclusions and make decisions on alternative marketing approaches; it also gives some idea of risks and consequences associated with alternative strategies and plans.

The value of specific marketing intelligence must be determined in terms of the risks involved in making marketing decisions, including the degree of uncertainty, investments required, and potential profits at stake.

When to Do Marketing Research Projects

There is a great need for exchange of ideas between senior marketing personnel and MR staff. Senior marketing personnel should discuss with the research staff problem areas where key marketing decisions must be made. Concurrently, the research staff should present ideas for gathering information to improve management's decision-making capabilities.

Whether to conduct specific research projects depends on the costs and benefits of contemplated decisions and the risks and consequences of making a wrong decision. A specific research project should be undertaken if, and only if, the value of the information provided by the research will be greater than its cost. In short, a MR project

1

should be conducted only if the net expected payoff (long or short-term) of the research is positive.

Research Budget [1]

It's difficult to set a MR budget at the beginning of a fiscal period. However, the job is easier if you view research projects in these two ways:

First, some research can measure the effectiveness of various promotional campaigns, prices, products, etc., which are planned for at the beginning of the period. Since these projects are known, you can plan the research and determine associated costs.

The second type of research cannot be planned in advance because of new problems arising and new products being developed. Also, competitive maneuvering takes place. Many situations occur for which no research plans have been made. The best approach is to allocate a contingency budget, the size of which can be determined only by experience (e.g., 20% of total research budget).

Types of Research Projects

MR projects cover a broad variety of subjects. The most common include:

Business, economic, and corporate research (e.g., forecasting, trends analysis, diversification and acquisition studies, plant, personnel, and warehouse location studies, etc.). Such studies are routinely made.

Sales and market performance research (e.g., potentials, market share analysis, determine customer characteristics, sales analysis, establish quotas and territories, analyze channels of distribution, identify target markets, attitude surveys, motivation research, etc.). Such studies are routinely conducted.

Product research (e.g., development, modifications, acceptance, competitive analysis, testing, packaging studies, etc.). This is a prevalent form of MR.

Promotion research (e.g., copy, media, concept, motivations, effectiveness). Some research is being done in this area, but not as much or as well as it could be.

Distribution channels research (e.g., location, type, performance). Such research is not often done, although it can be very profitable if done properly.

Price research (e.g., which is the best price to maximize profits?). Price research is seldom conducted today, though more should be done.

Market test (e.g., testing of product, promotion, distribution channels, and price in a market segment or geographic area).

Chapter Plan

The purpose of this chapter is to familiarize you with the MR process and its uses. Specific tools of this process are then presented in a step-by-step format.

The two tools most often used in industrial marketing are (1) secondary research of available source information, and (2) primary research surveys. These tools are described in considerable detail. Consumer-oriented primary research tools, such as audits, use of recording devices, and people-watching, are not covered.

The reference guide at the end of the chapter contains an enormous amount of information that has been assembled from hundreds of sources. It provides references to basic marketing information sources relating to almost every aspect of industrial marketing research, and references to scores of directories as well as directories to directories.

The chapter is organized into five major sections, as shown in the flow chart. Each section contains a step-by-step, straight-

---

[1] Several studies have noted that industrial companies spend on the average 0.1% of sales on MR. This is far too little in light of the benefits from properly developed research.

forward approach. The steps, identified as a consecutive series of seventeen major tasks, are further divided into sub-tasks which contain specific directions for accomplishing the majority of work involved in industrial marketing research. This is done to provide a practical, rather than academic, approach to the subject of industrial marketing.

Marketing Research— Chapter Plan

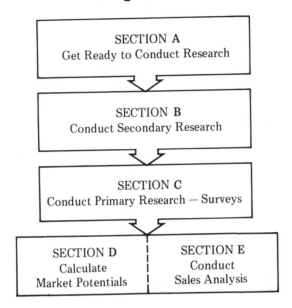

Section A

Get Ready to Conduct Research

This section prepares you to conduct MR projects and to do work with outside research firms. Two primary tasks are covered:

> TASK 1: Assignment of Responsibility
> TASK 2: Determining Research Objectives/Plan

When assigning responsibility, first decide if you should have your own internal research department or use an independent outside service. If you elect to establish an internal department, what should its reporting structure be? What type of personnel are needed?

If you plan to use an outside research service, where can you find one, how do you select the best one, and how should you work with one on the project? These subjects are covered in Task 1.

Task 2 includes problem/objective identification, a list of typical problems that can be approached through MR, and the procedures for approaching any project.

Task 1: Assign Responsibility

Should You Have Your Own Research Department?

MR is a technical activity using many specialized skills. It requires familiarity with information sources, obtaining information and analyzing and interpreting results. MR also requires a familiarity with the business, products, and markets being studied.

Because of skill and time requirements, most industrial companies cannot afford their own MR staff. Those who can generally have small ones. Consumer products companies, however, will frequently have research groups considerably larger than their industrial counterparts.

About half of all industrial companies have at least one person spending part or full time conducting or coordinating MR projects. With the growing appreciation of the value of MR, the size of departments and the number of projects conducted has grown immeasurably in recent years.

Reporting Structure

The MR department generally reports to the marketing manager, or other senior marketing personnel (e.g., vice-president, marketing) for actual problem solving tasks. In fewer cases (e.g., evaluation and identification problems), the research department reports to corporate management or to the research and development department. In any case, top management support of, exposure to, and demand for the research activity, is absolutely essential if the research is to be effective.

Personnel Requirements

Regardless of whether the research department pinpoints problems and uses outside firms to conduct the project or undertakes the project itself, similar skills and background are required. The department head and staff members need not have doctoral degrees, but should have a broad educational base. Primary emphasis should be upon hiring a generalist. Business and marketing backgrounds are essential; while experience in economics, psychology, sociology, statistics, accounting, industrial engineering, and mathematics are desirable.

In addition, research personnel should, ideally, possess these characteristics: imagination, creativity, knowledge of research techniques, sales skill, leadership ability, knowledge of your industry, administrative skill, and analytical ability.

Outside Research Services

The decision to conduct research projects in-house or to hire consultants depends on two key criteria. First, do you completely understand the problem and all operative factors and influences? Second, do you know how to use appropriate research techniques? (Good research is costly, but poor research is even more costly when information obtained leads to wrong decisions.)

Use of outside services often reduces the need for more full-time staff, and many projects are of such magnitude or technical difficulty that they exceed in-house resources. Results may be more professional, objective, and accurate than if projects were conducted in-house. Also, the reputation of a competent research organization often lends credibility to a report.

Where to Find Outside Services

Numerous types of research services are available (e.g., general consultants, specialized researchers, field interviewers, tabulators, product testers, etc.) for each research task, and for each marketing specialty.

If you choose a large general research firm offering diverse talents, they will assign a project director and specialists to work on your problem. Or, you can choose a smaller, more specialized research organization. The latter usually requires more searching before making your decision, but may result in lower cost and more personalized services.

If you are going to use outside research services for the first time, ask for recommendations from your associates, industry trade association, the American Marketing Association, or consult the reference guide to this chapter.

Also consider those research firms having completed assignments for you in the past. Was the work done on time? Did the firm's recommendations stimulate your own management's thinking in the area studied? To what extent did you accept and implement the firm's recommendations? Was the project completed within cost estimates?

How to Select Outside Researchers

Before engaging an outside consulting firm, you should have a clear idea of precisely what you expect of it. Allow adequate time for your search and evaluation of candidate firms. Don't overlook your own role in working with the firm to the extent required in arriving at a satisfactory solution to your problem. Don't make a selection based solely on the firm's presentation. You may wish to investigate several firms before making a final selection. When evaluating any firm, get specific answers to these questions:

How long has the firm been in business? What do previous clients think about the firm's work? Good credit?

What are the educational and experience backgrounds of the principals and staff to be assigned to your project? Do they have direct or indirect experience in the problem areas under consideration?

Does the firm's proposal reveal a clear and complete understanding of your problem?

Specifically, what information, assistance, and resources will the firm require from you in the course of the project?

Specifically, what does the firm commit itself to furnish you as evidence of project completion?

Are the firm's time and cost estimates specific and reasonable?

A Written Agreement as Basis for Outside Research Work

In addition to mutual cooperation between the research firm and your staff, a written agreement is required for a successful project. This agreement should cover:

The schedule for major steps of the project. Penalties for nonperformance (e.g., not completing study on time).

The desired quality (e.g., supervision required, validation that interviews were really conducted and not falsified, etc.).

What subcontractors will be used for what steps?

The form of interim progress reports and final presentation that will be made.

Who will hold full rights to publication of study results?

Fees (i.e., frequently stated as being within plus or minus ten percent), and when they will be paid.

Task 2: Determine Research Objectives/Plan [2]

Identify Problems/Objectives

The first step in any MR program is to identify and clearly define the fundamental nature of specific situations to be investigated. What are its key elements? What are the relationships involved? These should be defined in writing. The time and money spent on determining the exact nature of the situation frequently saves more time and money on the overall research project.

In planning research, management should think in terms of the uses and decisions that will be made with the research. This is their basic responsibility with regard to research projects. Management should tell the research deparment what they need to decide, and then let the researchers translate these uses into research terms.

Next, determine which problems to tackle first (within the priorities placed by senior marketing management), necessary time limits, qualified personnel, and cost constraints.

The problems (questions) arising differ depending on the stage in a product's life cycle. The following examples demonstrate types of problems you'll encounter.

Innovation Problems

Before new products are developed, several key questions must be answered. Do customers/prospects believe their wants and needs are being satisfied with existing product/service classes, brands, quality levels, prices, and channels of distribution? If not, what products and applications are needed in each market? What are the characteristics of each market? Where are they concentrated geographically? Who will decide what to buy? Who will actually buy? Who will use the product?

Some further questions must be answered. How large in units and dollars is the potential market? What market share can be expected? What profits can be expected? What are the strengths and weaknesses of your product vis-a-vis other direct and indirect competitive products?

Development Problems

During the period from the decision to go-ahead with production to actual product introduction and full-scale marketing, several key questions must be answered. In what ways will the product be valuable to customers? Which markets will most readily accept and offer the best sales potential for this new product? What sales levels/penetration

---

[2] "Plan" is used synonymously with research design.

can be expected during the market development stage of the product? What's the market trend?

After these questions are answered, competitive activities should be analyzed. Then you can develop a plan for promotional techniques and budgets, prices to be charged to maximize profit, and channels of distribution meeting current user buying habits.

Introduction/Pioneering Problems

During initial full-scale marketing of a product, performance-oriented questions need answering. For example, what product, price, channels, and promotion mix appears to be the most effective contributor to product sales? Is product increasing market share? How fast? What are current and expected break-even points? How much profit is expected over a specific time period?

Growth Problems

When the product is approaching the peak of its sales life, other types of questions must be answered. For example, are profit levels and market share increasing, holding their own, or starting to decrease? Why? Is the product demanding more management time than justified by profits? What maneuvers can be used to delay product decline?

Maturity Problems

When the product's sales have stabilized and are reaching decline, sustaining questions must be answered. Can sufficient product revisions or new uses be created to in-

crease demand? Are there new markets or customer groups where the product has additional applications?

Decline and Abandonment Problems

When product sales decline to the point where abandonment is being considered, the following questions need to be answered: Would another manufacturer be interested in buying the development rights? How can ill will be avoided with remaining customers when production ceases?

List Needed Data

Plan the project schedule, including a list of the quantitative and qualitative data needed, data sources, collection method, persons responsible, estimated timing, and estimated costs.

Make Preliminary Investigation

Now make an inexpensive, preliminary investigation to help better define and formulate problems, identify relevant variables, set a framework for the study, determine what data are available, and possibly produce some tentative solutions. This would include a review of secondary research (see Task 3), and interviews with experienced people to get practical aspects of the problem (e.g., executives, salesmen, and dealers). If additional data are required for problem solution, primary research studies may then be conducted (see Tasks 4–10).

Section B
Secondary Research

Task 3: How to Use Secondary Research Sources

Value of Secondary Research

As a general rule, no research project should be undertaken without a search of secondary research sources (i.e., that data already gathered for another purpose). This search should be done early in the problem investigation stage and prior to collecting any primary data.

Although gathered for purposes other than solving your immediate problems, secondary research sources are valuable for several reasons:

May solve your problem without having to do any primary research.

Secondary research costs are substantially lower than primary collection costs.

Searching secondary research sources is considerably quicker than conducting primary research.

It may help define the problem and formulate hypotheses about its solution.

Helps plan collection of primary data.

May be used in defining the population and selecting the sample for primary research.

How to Evaluate Secondary Research

Several criteria for evaluating data gained from secondary research sources include:

Was the data pertinent and relevant to the problem? Does it contain same measurements and definitions, and is it current?

Who collected the data? What was the purpose of publication? Check for bias.

What was the method of data collection? Was it stated? Was the research exhaustive? Was it from an original source?

Is there evidence of careful work? Are facts accurate?[3] Is the report objective?

Types of Secondary Research Sources

Secondary research sources may be internal or external to your company. Internal data sources include sales records, invoices, shipping statements, plus a variety of other documentation. If such materials are set up in the form of a library, it will facilitate making sales analyses. (See Section E.)

External data sources provide information free or at minimal cost. Many such sources make valuable additions to your company library, while others may be available at your local public or university library. There are seven major types of external secondary research sources discussed below: basic reference sources, trade publication reports and articles, trade associations, directories, re-

---

[3] Judging the accuracy of "facts" is not always easy. One test is to ask yourself if they make sense. Another is to review the logical basis of reasoning used by the primary investigator, and to judge whether he may have some reason to be biased. Was the research conducted by a recognized authority or expert? Or, has it been accepted by a recognized authority or expert? Do the facts result from perception (observation and experiment), or are they derived by inference? Do they fit logically into the existing pattern of facts already known? Do they exist as a consequence of some recognized and explainable cause? Are the facts consistent with the results of other, related investigations?

search organizations, government sources, and competitor analyses.

Basic Reference Sources

A great number of reference sources exist which provide information on specific subjects or references to other sources containing information on specific subjects. The reference guide to this chapter lists such materials. They can be purchased direct from the publisher or may be found in your local library. If the library is used, first see the reference librarian, then search the card catalog.

Trade Publication Reports and Articles

Hundreds of trade magazines are published by commercial organizations and associations. These publications, which generally cover specific industries or functions, are an excellent source of marketing information.

In addition to relevant articles contained in each issue, many publications compile and publish up-to-date statistics and market data paralleling their area of interest. Through surveys of subscribers and additional independent research, statistical analyses and forecasts are often presented on the industry's status, plants, expenditures for certain products, technology, production levels, and awareness and attitudes toward certain products and manufacturers.

Several handy references speed the finding of appropriate publishers to contact and magazines to peruse. The references are readily divided into two groups: (1) references to publishers and magazines; and (2) indexes to articles and reports.

References to Publishers and Magazines

A list of magazines and publishers, including addresses and phone numbers, broken down by industry or markets can be found in a number of sources. These reference sources can be purchased for use in your own office, or can be found at most college and major public libraries. Several of the major references are listed in the reference guide at the end of this chapter.

Indexes to Articles and Reports

In addition to reviewing articles in magazines to which you personally subscribe, you can increase your knowledge of published materials by glancing through one of many frequently published indexes which list titles, authors, publication, date, and page numbers for articles in a specific industry, market, or subject area. Once specific articles are identified, you can write direct to the publication for a copy or check the files of back issues at the library. These indexes can be purchased by individuals or companies, but their high price usually dictates a trip to the local library for their review. Several of the more useful indexes are listed in the reference guide.

Trade Associations

Trade associations are groups of people, or companies in the same industry, organized to improve their industry's and members' performance. To achieve this end, associations provide statistics and information on their industry and membership. In some cases, associations conduct their own research; in others, they interpret the research findings of other organizations.

Most public and college libraries have reference books listing selected associations by industry group. These books can also be purchased for use in your own office. After selecting key associations, you can request information via phone calls, letters, or personal visits. Sometimes information is made available only to members. The reference guide to this chapter includes a list of directories and encyclopedias to help you find the right association.

Directories

Directories generally list the names and related information about companies in a particular market, industry, or state. Thousands of directories are published each year by independent businesses, trade associations, and magazine publishers as special issues. By reviewing these, one can compile a list of customers and prospects for given products, determine whom specifically to call on, new market potentials, plant locations, and new sources of supply.

Most directories can be purchased for use in your own office, and many may be found in your local library. The reference guide to this chapter lists directories to directories, helpful in locating information on many markets. Also listed are some specific geographical and industrial directories. The list is by no means complete. It is only exemplary of those which are available.

Research Organizations

Many MR firms, management consultants, and advertising agencies provide clients with various MR services. In some cases they can refer you to sources of information. In other cases, this support takes the form of published or syndicated reports on markets, research projects on improving the marketing process, and customized research projects on a variety of subjects.

The reference guide to this chapter presents a list of directories referring to marketing firms that perform a variety of specialized research projects. Most include detailed information on the organization by location, size, nature of staff, area of specialization, and other pertinent data. The directories can be purchased for use in your office or can be perused in your local library.

Government Sources

Federal, state, and local governments also provide information on specific industries and economic conditions. Data are rarely broken down by companies or brands.

There are three ways to obtain government-published information: go to the local library; contact the publishing agency; or write to the Superintendent of Documents,

U.S. Government Printing Office, Washington, DC 20402. Some of the information is free, while most others are available at the cost of printing (from 10 cents to several dollars). You can pick up materials either at the agency's local field offices, or write direct to their main headquarters.

The discussion which follows includes using (1) library services; (2) the two primary government information bodies (Department of Commerce and Small Business Administration); (3) obtaining local and regional information; and (4) the Standard Industrial Classification System.

Libraries

Many libraries have a documents room and/or a government publications section which maintains files of government publications. There are approximately 500 so-called depository libraries in the United States. Through these libraries, federal government documents are made available to persons throughout the United States. Each library selects classes of publications of interest to its particular clientele. So in some cases, you may have to make special requests for selected materials. A list of depository libraries can be obtained from your local library or the U.S. Department of Commerce office.

U.S. Department of Commerce

The U.S. Department of Commerce (DOC) is one of the best sources of information in the business field. This department provides information on:

Business and industry—production, sales, raw material sources, trends, marketing practices, and locational factors.
Science and technology—discoveries, inventions, new products and processes, patents, standards, and applications of new technical knowledge and methods.
General economy—national income, national product, national and regional economic trends, markets, potentials, balance of payments, foreign aid programs, business indexes, indications, and other factors.

For specific information, write to the U.S. Department of Commerce, Washington, DC 20203, or check with the nearest local DOC office. The Washington office will send you a list of all their local offices.

In additon to the field offices listed, there are over 500 business organizations in the United States and its territories which serve their local areas as "cooperative offices" of the DOC. These include local and state chambers of commerce, manufacturers and trade associations, and state and local planning and development commissions. These offices generally provide a limited amount of the same type of data provided by the main DOC offices. Local field offices of the DOC, or the main office can provide a list of all local cooperative offices.

Small Business Administration

The Small Business Administration (SBA) is an independent agency of the federal government. It specializes in advising and assisting small business concerns through regional and branch offices. Further information on specific data available and a list of local SBA offices can be obtained by writing to the SBA, Washington, DC 20416.

Local and Regional Information Sources

The amount and type of data available from states and local governments varies from area to area. In some cases, overlaps occur while in others no data exists. The trend, however, has been toward improved data bases for decision-making.

Every state publishes a number of valuable market and economic analyses. Additional unpublished data are also available from the publishing agencies upon request. Data includes directories of companies within the state, statistical abstracts of current and historical data, including employment, cost of living, labor supply, production statistics, demand, supply, price information, movement, and storage of goods.

Local governments collect statistics in the course of their regulatory and administrative activities, but seldom publish them for general distribution. However, requests by individuals for information are often quickly answered.

Some excellent sources of information about local, state and regional areas are listed in the reference guide to this chapter.

In addition to the sources listed, you should check with chambers of commerce, local newspapers, commercial banks, and universities.

Chambers of commerce provide data (including directories) on companies, and the business environment in local areas. The Chamber of Commerce of the United States provides business analysis of federal policies, including bulletins, studies, etc., on economic, business, and governmental developments affecting American enterprise. State and local chambers of commerce try to promote and develop commercial, industrial, and other economic activities in their areas—and therefore, provide numerous useful publications.

Local newspapers often provide extensive amounts of information on their metropolitan areas. Major commercial banks frequently publish information on businesses and economic conditions in their local, state, and county areas. University bureaus often have ongoing programs to collect and disseminate business information about the local area.

Standard Industrial Classification System

A basic, useful research tool available to marketing management is the Standard Industrial Classification (SIC) system, developed by the federal government. The system is useful for gathering, organizing, consolidating, analyzing, comparing and disseminating industry information.

SIC is a numerical system which classifies the entire economy into broad industry segments, and then subdivides each segment into major groups, subgroups, and detailed groups. Numbers are assigned based on primary products produced or operations performed at specific plant locations.

Broad industry segments are assigned two-digit numbers (e.g., "35" refers to "Machinery, Except Electrical"). There are approximately 80 broad industry groups.

Additional digits are added to the two-digit number for further refinement (e.g., "351" refers to "Engines and Turbines" segment of the "Machinery, Except Electrical" group). There are approximately 400 three-digit subgroups.

The four-digit number "3519" refers to the "Internal Combustion Engines" segment of the "Engine and Turbines" segment of the "Machinery, Except Electrical" group. There are over 1,000 four-digit classifications. A great deal of published data is available by four-digit SIC on consumption, shipments, capital expenditures, employment, and so forth. This makes it the most common classification used for marketing purposes.

Industries are further classified to seven digits, although little statistical data exists at this level of refinement. Since information gathered about a sample of firms in a particular industry can be projected across the entire industry, SIC information breakdowns are valuable for a variety of purposes, including:

Aligning sales territories
Developing channels of distribution
Setting sales quota for territories
Allocating and measuring advertising/promotion efforts
Locating markets and usage patterns (potential)
Measuring your penetration (share)

A complete list of classifications, and definitions can be found in the government's *Standard Industrial Classification Manual*, which is published by the Executive Office of the President, Office of Management and Budget. For more information on SIC you can purchase a copy of the basic manual from any U.S. Department of Commerce field office, or the Superintendent of Documents, U.S. Government Printing Office, Washington, DC 20402.

Competitor Analyses

One of the most vital functions of the marketing executive is to know the competitive environment, and its impact on his own company's plans, products, and operations. This data should be gathered and recorded for each direct and indirect competitor. Data can be kept in a 3-ring binder, from which extracts and analyses can be made.

Data to Be Gathered on Competitors

Names and addresses
Products manufactured—SIC
Principal officers and executives (organization)
Geographical coverage
Total sales over past five years (and earnings)
Net worth
Inventory (i.e., in process, finished goods, etc.)
Plant and warehouse size
Number of salesmen, distributors, employees
Number and location of branches
Share of market
Selling methods
Competitive practices (i.e., allowances, terms, discounts, etc.)
Advertising and promotion methods, plans and apparent results
What your and their customers think of them
Quality, performance, and reliability of products
Shipment lead time
Deliveries on time
Field service capability
Costs: production, distribution, and service
Research and development capability
Strengths and weaknesses of competitive products
Operating advantages and disadvantages of products
Guarantees/warranties

Sources of Information on Competition

The sources listed throughout this section help conduct competitive analyses. In addition, take every opportunity to circle reader service cards related to competitors appearing in trade magazines. Request copies of brochures, literature, and annual reports. Also, clip all publicity and advertisements about the competition.

Conclusions

Clearly, an abundance of secondary source information is available from diverse sources throughout the nation and the world. With a little digging you can uncover almost any kind of business, marketing, and economic information.

There are situations, however, in which no amount of digging will uncover the information needed to satisfy a particular requirement—because the needed information simply doesn't exist. Then, and only then, should you consider developing information through a primary research project. Methods for doing this are described in Section C, which follows.

Section C

Conduct Primary Research–Surveys

Surveys: A Primary Form of Research

Primary research can take the form of surveys, observations, and experiments. The latter two forms are not prevalently used in industrial research. Therefore, this section of the book concentrates only on the survey method.

Surveys are a versatile, flexible, and relatively inexpensive tool for gathering data about a marketing problem. In short, surveys include the solicitation of suggestions, ideas, or comments from a representative sample of a target population. This enables you to make predictions as to how the overall population feels about any specific issue. The persons contacted are called respondents.

Disadvantages of Surveys

The primary disadvantage of surveys is that they are limited to the willingness and capability of people to help you. For example, people sometimes lie. Sometimes they don't even know they are lying. People often give answers that they feel the interviewer wants them to give. People some-

times refuse to cooperate. People sometimes can't be reached.

Survey Steps

In making a survey, it's always best not to start off with preconceived notions which might bias your study results. At this point, you should have already defined the problem, purpose, and objectives of the survey. After the plans for all of the tasks listed below are sufficiently developed, the survey can be conducted.

TASK 4: Select type of survey
TASK 5: Determine sample size and make-up
TASK 6: Prepare questionnaire
TASK 7: Conduct interviewing
TASK 8: Process data
TASK 9: Analyze data
TASK 10: Prepare report/present findings

Before conducting any survey, develop a written summary of exactly how each task will be accomplished. Include who will do each task and the deadline for completion of each. The "Research Schedule/Cost" form allows you to do this, along with a cost estimate. The form can be made more detailed by adding all required sub-tasks.

Task 4: Select Type of Survey

Three Basic Types

Select the survey method which provides the needed information in the most direct

and efficient way. Three basic methods are available: personal interview, mail questionnaire, and telephone interview. There is no one best technique for every research purpose. Review the descriptions of each technique and then make your decision based upon allowable time and money available, the characteristics of the product, the market under study, and the degree of accuracy desired. (See the "Types of Survey Methods" chart.)

Research Schedule/Costs

1. Decisions involved:

2. Information needed:

3. Research design summary:

OPERATION	SCHEDULE		COST (EST.)
	BEGIN	END	
1. Select type of survey			
2. Determine sample size and make-up			
3. Prepare questionnaire			
4. Conduct interviewing			
5. Process data			
6. Analyze data			
7. Write report/present findings			

Task 5: Determine Sample Size and Make-up

What Is Sampling?

Sampling is the everyday experience of making decisions concerning the characteristics of a large number of items based on an analysis of a limited number of items from that larger group. The larger group of items is called the population or universe, and the limited number of items selected from the larger group is called a sample. Everyday sampling examples include:

Taking a sip of wine before accepting the entire bottle at a restaurant.

Blood test—you can determine the type and quality of blood in your entire body simply by testing a small amount.

Dipping your toe into a swimming pool to check the temperature before diving.

Types of Survey Methods

TYPE	DESCRIPTION	ADVANTAGES	DISADVANTAGES
Personal Interview	Personal interviews are well-suited for complex product concepts requiring extensive explanations and new products (especially those having highly concentrated markets). Information is sought in face-to-face question-and-answer sessions between an interviewer and a respondent. The interviewer usually has a questionnaire to guide him, although this form is not necessarily shown to the respondent. Answers can be recorded during or after the interview. The interviewer can use a formal questionnaire with a pre-arranged ordering, or have a list of general discussion subjects, and make up questions as the interview progresses.	1. Allows interviewer to gain additional information from his own observations. (e.g., interviewer can classify age, etc. of respondent.) 2. Better control than other interviewing methods. 3. Allows more detailed information to be gathered. 4. Usually gets a higher percentage of completed answers, since interviewer is there to explain exactly what is wanted. 5. Can use visual aids (e.g., tables, schematics, samples, prototypes) to demonstrate concepts. 6. Allows in-depth exploration of product attributes and how to solve problems. 7. Is flexible to allow interviewer to adjust questions to respondent's greatest interests. 8. Personal contact often stimulates greater cooperation and interest by respondents.	1. Can be costly when compared to other methods, especially when wide geographic areas must be covered. 2. Interviewer bias can seriously cause misleading responses and misrecording of answers. 3. Requires detailed supervision of data-collection process. 4. Time-consuming to train interviewers, and to obtain data. 5. May distract respondent if interviewer is writing answers at the same time they are talking. 6. Different approaches by different interviewers makes it difficult to standardize conduct of surveys.
Telephone Survey	Telephone interviews are best suited for well-defined basic product concepts or specific product features. Questioning is done over the telephone. Information sought is usually well-defined, nonconfidential in nature and limited in amount. Telephone surveys should be used to	1. Fast (e.g., quicker than personal or mail). 2. Inexpensive (e.g., cost of an equal number of personal interviews would be substantially greater.) 3. Easier to call back again if respondent is busy at the time (personal is more difficult).	1. Limited to telephone subscriber locations (e.g., can't interview a man in the field; and many businessmen are out of the office most of the day.) 2. Can usually obtain only a small amount of information. 3. Can usually provide only limited classification data.

Method	Description	Advantages	Disadvantages
(continued)	supplement other research techniques. It is often best to employ a professional telephone interview service, rather than attempt the interviewing yourself.	4. Usually has only a small response bias because of closed-end questions. 5. Has wide geographical reach.	4. Difficult to obtain motivational, and attitudinal information. 5. Difficult for highly technical products or capital goods. 6. Can become expensive if long distance calls are involved, unless Wide Area Telephone Service (WATS) is available.
Mail Survey	Mail questionnaires can be used to broaden the base of an investigation or to supplement the first-hand knowledge acquired from personal interviews. They are most effective when well-defined concepts are involved and specific limited answers are called for. Questionnaires are sent through the mail to people familiar with a specific problem or market under investigation. If the group is small, a questionnaire can be sent to each member. If it is a large group, a representative sample must be selected for testing. The questionnaire is usually accompanied by a letter explaining the survey's purpose and requesting the respondent answer and return the questionnaire in an enclosed postage-paid envelope. Sometimes the questionnaire can be printed on the back of a post card to avoid the cost of envelopes and the chance of respondents misplacing envelopes and not being able to mail the completed questionnaire back. Variation: Warranty cards can include marketing-oriented questions. These questions must be answered and the card returned for the warranty to be valid.	1. Can get wide distribution at a relatively low cost per completed interview. 2. Helps avoid possible interviewer bias; absence of interviewer may lead to a more candid reply. 3. Can reach remote places (e.g., drilling engineer on site in Saudi Arabia). 4. Unless his name is requested, the respondent remains anonymous and, therefore may give confidential information that otherwise would be withheld. 5. Respondent may be more inclined to answer since he can do so at his leisure.	1. Accurate, up-to-date mailing lists are not always available to ensure successful distribution. 2. Returns may not be representative of the entire group being surveyed, since respondents may differ significantly in opinions, knowledge, etc. from those not replying. As many as 80-90% may not return questionnaires. Respondents generally have stronger feelings about the subject than nonrespondents. 3. Questionnaire length is limited. 4. Inability to insure that questions are understood fully and answers are properly recorded. 5. It is difficult to lead respondents through questions one at a time if this is essential, since the respondent can read the entire questionnaire before answering question 1. 6. Time consuming. 7. Troublesome with certain highly technical products.

Sampling enables making statements concerning population characteristics (i.e., parameters or properties), without looking at all the members. This is accomplished through statistical inference. A good sample is one having a systematic and unbiased method for selecting people to respond to your questions. It also requires that you reach people who are best qualified to give answers.

Why Sample?

It is often physically impossible to check all items in the population (e.g., all the fish in a lake).

Certain tests are destructive in nature (e.g., minimum tensile strength, blood test, quality control).

It may be prohibitive in cost and time to study entire population.

Sample results alone may be adequate in determining population characteristics. Increased data may not significantly improve the accuracy of results.

Develop Sampling Plan

Since it is impossible and unnecessary to interview all potential customers, selecting a representative sample of relatively few persons to contact is sufficient. If the sample is properly selected, what is discovered about the sample will usually be true of the entire market (within certain limits).

After reviewing this section, you can determine specifically:

Who to talk to (i.e., a miniature cross-section of the market). Make sure you reach the people in each plant who can give the most reliable answers.

How many people to talk to (e.g., larger numbers give increased reliability).

How to select respondents (e.g., random or nonprobability).

Types of Sampling Techniques

Basically, there are two kinds of samples: probability and nonprobability. Both are discussed below. Although there is no one best sampling method, your situation will undoubtedly call for preferred use of one technique or another. Whatever the technique, it should allow a sample to be drawn that is representative of population characteristics. To save time and money, it's best to realize the impossibilities of finding a "truly typical" person. Few researchers or managers know just what such a person is like. Although probability samples provide increased accuracy, nonprobability samples selected with good judgement, are better than "guestimates."

Probability Samples

In probability samples, every member of the population has a known chance of being selected (e.g., 10% chance). This fact generally provides greater accuracy than does nonprobability samples. There are various kinds of probability samples, four of which are discussed below:

Simple Random Sample—Items to be sampled are selected on a purely random basis. Each element has a known and equal chance of being selected. This unrestricted sampling procedure is similar to a lottery. You can put the names of each member of your study population (i.e., market) on slips of paper and put each in a fish bowl, thoroughly mix, then withdraw one at a time until the desired sample size is filled. Another method is to use a table of random numbers. In any case, this procedure is time-consuming and costly to develop, but usually allows increased accuracy. Primary difficulties arise because complete lists are often unobtainable and the composition of the market may be unknown.

Systematic Sample—Using a randomly chosen starting point, select every nth item in whatever order the population is available (e.g., alphabetical). For every 10th name, you would select the 10th, 20th, 30th, etc., until your sample was filled. This procedure can be used only if the population is organized in an orderly way (e.g., all invoices in numerical order in a drawer).

Stratified Random Sample—Imposes a design restriction by subdividing the population into homogeneous groups, called strata, from which independent random samples are selected. This assures that the sample will be proportionately similar in composition to the universe. It also permits greater emphasis on certain segments if desired (e.g., talk more to larger buyers). Strata might be company size, industry, number of employees, etc.

Cluster Sample—Randomly select natural population groupings or clusters, with use of any of the previous three methods to select sample items. For example, all metalworking companies in Anaheim, California.

Nonprobability Samples

In nonprobability (or purposive) sampling, each item has an unknown chance of selection. This method is generally less expensive, faster, and less accurate than probability sampling techniques. Three types of nonprobability samples are discussed below:

Judgement Sample—Arbitrary human judgement is used to select sample members. This technique departs from the theoretical model from which all mathematical statements of sampling reliability are derived. However, a judgement sample might produce valid results if, *and only if*, it happens to be a reasonably accurate model of the universe which it represents. This requires expert professional knowledge and intuition about the market. There is some risk of bias, but there is no way of knowing how much.

Quota Sample—The researcher selects a control characteristic (e.g., job function, industry, size of plant, etc.) and determines the percent of the population having each characteristic. Then he allocates a number in each population segment to be included in the sample.

Interviewers are given these quotas which they must fill by a certain time. This method is relatively quick and inexpensive, but lacks accuracy of random sampling. Too many controls may result in unfulfillment of sample.

Chunk/Convenience Sample—Office workers, fellow employees, friends, and other groups are often selected for the sole reason that it is convenient to use them.

How to Solve Sampling Problems

Sampling is estimating. The validity of estimates based on sample results depends on their accuracy (i.e., freedom from bias) and the precision of the estimates (i.e., limits within which they can be believed). Many researchers are satisfied with less than a perfect sample because they know that perfection is not possible within the time and budget normally allowed for research projects.[4]

This sub-task gives a rigorous description of sampling theory and statistical errors. Such precision is generally required for extremely important decisions (e.g., modifying an already successful product); but not so important for minor or preliminary decisions (e.g., getting a broad, firsthand market reaction to a new product concept, especially early in the brainstorming stage). If your applications do not require such strict reliability standards, or if you are not statistically inclined, turn to the Sample Size Calculator—a shorthand approach to sampling.

For simplicity of discussion, we shall consider only the probability (i.e., unrestricted) random sample. This type can be designed with no more effort than is needed to draw a random set of numbers from a comprehensive list of users. Thus, it is cheaper and faster than when extra efforts must be made to stratify the sample according to company size, location, etc. In fact, no knowledge is required about these factors. When strict

---

[4] Another main cause of inaccurate, nonpredictive results is inadequate questioning sequence and naive interpretation.

randomness is achieved, the cross-section of a large, unrestricted sample should closely parallel that of its universe.

There are dangers that, in a *small* sample, the cross-section of characteristics may deviate widely from those of the original universe. Therefore, when a small sample is used (e.g., less than 30 members), it would be advisable to verify that its composition is approximately proportional to the composition of the universe from which it was drawn.

The following discussion of mathematical methods for analyzing random samples should not be used to analyze a nonprobability (e.g., judgement) sample. In practice, however, this rule is often knowingly violated. This is because many researchers believe that the indications provided are better than none at all. Formula and mechanized approaches are shown, as well as a shortcut method—a nomograph for sample size calculation.

Formula for Solving Sampling Problems

The size of a random sample depends on five factors:

F = percent of FAVORABLE responses (e.g., 30%).

U = percent of UNFAVORABLE responses (e.g., 70%). F plus U must always equal 100%.

E = percent ERROR in the favorable responses, measured plus and minus (above and below) the percent favorable responses. If the latter were 30%, and the error 5%, the range of favorable responses would be from 25% to 35%.

N = NUMBER of individual members contained in the sample.

C = factor which determines the probability that the percent error can be relied on in a given percentage of cases:

When C = 1.96, the percent error (E) would not be exceeded in 95 samples out of 100. That is, the probability of being correct is 95%.[5]

When C = 3.0, the percent error would not be exceeded in 99.7 cases out of 100. The probability of being correct is *almost* certain.

Other values for C can be found in standard statistical texts. These factors are related by the following statistical formula:

$$E = C\sqrt{\frac{F \times U}{N}}$$

To illustrate the use of this formula, we shall first solve several sampling problems "the hard way." Then, we shall introduce a simple graphic calculating aid, called a "Sample Size Calculator," which—with the aid of a straightedge—enables you to get approximate answers to a variety of sampling survey problems. The formula and the Sample Size Calculator are for use only with unrestricted random samples.

Mechanized Version for Solving Sampling Problems

If the formula appears formidable, use the mechanized version below to take you through the calculations one step at a time. This version of the formula enables you to calculate the percent error, when the proba-

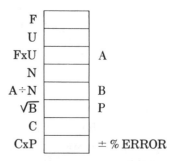

[5] For convenience this factor is sometimes rounded to 2.00, in which case the probability of being correct is 95.46%. If you use C = 2.00 instead of 1.96, the plus and minus error is increased 2.04%, and the size of sample calculated will be 7.62% smaller.

bility of being correct is determined by the factor, C.

Below are six examples that illustrate how to solve several sampling problems. These examples illustrate various trade-offs available to you in planning a sampling survey.

If you want extreme accuracy, you must pay for it in the form of a large sample (more time and money). But, if you can relax your requirements, it is possible to get good results with a much smaller sample. This boils down to two alternatives:

(1) Determine amount of money available; then the maximum reliability level achievable.
(2) Specify degree of reliability; then obtain this degree at minimum cost.

In this step we have only scratched the surface of statistical sampling theory as applied to some fairly simple types of sampling problems. If your problems are more complex than those illustrated, it would be advisable to engage a consultant who is qualified in statistical science.

Example (1): Determine Error in Favorable Response Rate

Suppose you demonstrate a new product to a sample of 50 purchasing agents selected at random from a universe of 4,200 potential users. You get a 30% favorable response—and, therefore, 70% unfavorable. With a 95% probability of being correct (i.e., C = 1.96), the mechanized calculations below show that the error in the 30% favorable responses is ±12.7%. That is, the *true* percent of favorable responses you would get if you had "sampled" the *whole population* of 4,200 users, would be somewhere between 17.3% and 42.7%.

F	30%	
U	70%	
FxU	2100	A
N	50	
A÷N	42	B
√B	6.48	P
C	1.96	
CxP	12.7%	± % ERROR

When you apply these percentages to the whole market of 4,200 potential users, you find the *true* number who would favor your product (with a 95% probability of being correct) lies somewhat between:

$$17.3\% \times 4{,}200 = 727 \text{ users, and,}$$
$$42.7\% \times 4{,}200 = 1793 \text{ users.}$$

This range of almost 2.5 to 1 is a measure of the uncertainty that exists because your sample included only 50 members. Obviously, any decision based on such a small sample would involve unusually high risks.

If the sample of 50 members was a judgement sample (i.e., not a random sample), then—to help make allowance for sampling bias—you should use C = 3.0. In this case, you will find the error in the 30% favorable response is ±19.4%. And the "true" number of the total population of 4,200 users favoring your product will lie somewhere between 445 (10.6% or 4,200) and 2,075 (49.4% of 4,200). With such a wide range of error, any time devoted to collecting the sampling data would be a total waste.

Example (2): Cut Error Level

The mathematics of sampling theory are such that to cut the error in half, you must increase the *size* of the sample by four times. In example (1), instead of a sample of only 50 members, you must increase it to 200 to reduce the error from 12.7% to 6.35%. In this case, with a 95% probability of being correct, you can determine for yourself that the probable number of favorable responses in the 4,200 user universe, will be between 993 and 1527 users.

Example (3): Determine Sample Size

Now let's use a variant of the formula to determine the *size* of a sample. If we square both sides of the above formula and solve for N (the number of members in the sample), we get—

$$N = C^2 \times \frac{F \times U}{E^2}$$

Suppose you are starting from scratch, and you have no idea as to the percent of favorable responses you might get. The safest thing to do in this case is to assume a 50% favorable and 50% unfavorable response when you survey your potential users. This will make the product of F × U the maximum it can ever be.

Further, let's assume that you want your results to be accurate within ±2.5%—with a probability of 99.7% of being correct (i.e., practically certain to be correct—in which case C = 3).

Now, you can substitute these values in the above formula, or you can use the mechanized program below—which will help you to solve the formula step-by-step.

C	3	
C²	9	G
E	2.5	
E²	6.25	H
G ÷ H	1.44	J
F	50%	
U	50%	
FxU	2500	K
JxK	3600	NUMBER

In this case, you find the sample size must be 3,600 members—which is almost 86% of the universe of 4,200 members. But remember, we used the ultra-conservative, "worst case" values for F and U in the formula—and we also required a 99.7% probability of being correct. The resulting large sample size is the price we must pay if we want highly accurate results.

Example (4): Reduce Sample to Reasonable Size

This example demonstrates how to reduce sample size to more reasonable proportions. The only reason we used a 50%—50% allocation in the previous example was because of ignorance of the probable distribution of responses in the actual sample population.

However, if you keep a sequential record of the number of favorable responses versus the total number of responses, you can calculate the cumulative percent of favorable

responses as the sampling operation proceeds. The table of "responses" shows how to do this. In the first column, record the total number of responses—both favorable and unfavorable. (In our example, we have shown these in batches of ten.) In the second column, keep a running record of the number of favorable responses in each batch of ten people sampled. Keep a running *cumulative* record of the favorable responses in the third column. Divide the third column total by the first column total, expressing the result as a percent, and list this number in the fourth column. In the table you will note that from the 80th to the 160th response in the first column, the cumulative percent of favorable responses in the fourth column tends to stabilize around 18%.

(1) CUMULATIVE NO. OF RESPONSES	(2) NO. OF FAVORABLE RESPONSES	(3) CUMULATIVE NO. OF FAVORABLE RESPONSES	(4) CUMULATIVE % FAVORABLE RESPONSES
10	2	2	20
20	3	5	25
30	2	7	23
40	1	8	20
50	0	8	16
60	2	10	17
70	2	12	17
80	3	15	19
90	1	16	18
100	2	18	18
110	2	20	18
120	3	23	19
130	1	24	18
140	0	24	17
150	3	27	18
160	2	29	18
—	—	—	—
—	—	—	—
—	—	—	—

Now, assume that this 18% favorable response trend is reasonably characteristic of the total population. The percent unfavorable response will then be 82%. Now repeat the calculations for the size of sample N, using the method of example (3)—as shown in the mechanized version of the formula for N, below.

In this calculation we see that by simply keeping a running record of the percent favorable responses we can reduce the size of the sample from 3600 to 2125.

C	3	
C²	9	G
E	2.5	
E²	6.25	H
G÷H	1.44	J
F	18%	
U	82%	
FxU	1476	K
JxK	2125	NUMBER

C	1.96	
C²	3.84	G
E	5%	
E²	25	H
G÷H	0.154	J
F	18%	
U	82%	
FxU	1476	K
JxK	227	NUMBER

Example (5): Narrowing Error Range

Suppose we used the smaller size sample, and when we completed the 2125 demonstrations, or interviews, we found that the actual percent of favorable responses turned out to be 17.6%. Therefore, the percent unfavorable responses is 82.4%. If you use the first formula—example (1)—you will find that the percent error, with a 99.7% probability of being correct, will now be ±2.48%.

Therefore, the true percent favorable responses will lie somewhere in the range bounded by 17.6% plus 2.48% (=20.08%), and 17.6% minus 2.48% (=15.12%). If we apply these percentage limits to the total population of 4,200 potential users, we can be *practically certain* (i.e., 99.7% probability of being correct) that the true number of users that will favor the product will be at least 635 (i.e., 15.12% of 4,200), and not more than 843 (20.08% of 4,200).

Example (6): Overview

In this example, we will again assume that the percent favorable responses will be about 18%—using the running record from the table in example (4). But we will relax the requirement for precision, so that we can be satisfied with an error of plus or minus 5%, and we will also relax the accuracy requirement to a 95% probability of being correct.

Using these values, we can calculate the size of sample needed to give us plus or minus 5% error, with a 95% probability of being right (see calculations in the mechanized version of the formula below). The result is 227 members in the sample.

Now, let's assume that we complete the sampling operations using this 227 member sample, and we find that the actual percent of favorable responses is 18.6%. The percent unfavorable responses is therefore 81.4%. With this information, we must again calculate the percent error, using the same formula used in example (1).

F	18.6%	
U	81.4%	
FxU	1514	A
N	227	
A÷N	6.67	B
√B	2.58	P
C	1.96	
CxP	5.06%	± % ERROR

The calculations are shown in the mechanized version of the formula above. You can see that the percent error is very close to the 5% that we established when we were calculating the size of the sample, above.

The true percent error in the total population is therefore somewhere in the range bounded by 18.6% plus 5.06% (=23.66%), and 18.6% minus 5.06% (=13.54%).

Finally, we can say—with a 95% probability of being correct—that the true number of potential users who will favor the product will be at least 569 (13.54% times 4,200), and not more than 994 (23.66% × 4,200).

Correction Factor for Sample Size

The sample size can obviously affect accuracy. To remedy this, the sampling error—as previously calculated—must be multiplied by a correction factor. For example, if the "sample" includes the whole population, the "error" due to sampling is zero.

Here is a table of correction factors:

SAMPLE SIZE AS A % OF THE POPULATION	SAMPLING ERROR CORRECTION FACTOR
100%	0
95	0.224
90	0.316
85	0.387
80	0.447
75	0.500
70	0.548
65	0.592
60	0.632
55	0.671
50	0.707
45	0.742
40	0.775
35	0.806
30	0.837
25	0.866
20	0.894
15	0.922
10	0.949
5	0.975
4	0.980
3	0.985
2	0.990
1	0.995

Example

From a population of 4,500 you draw a random sample of 900 members. On a survey, 30% of these members "favor" your product. At the 95% confidence level you can determine that the sampling error in this case is 3%. But the 900 member sample comprises 20% of the whole population. In the above table, opposite 20%, you find the sampling error correction factor to be 0.894. Multiplying the 3% error by 0.894, you find the corrected sampling error to be $3\% \times 0.894 = 2.68\%$. The "true" percent of favorable responses then will lie between 27.3% (30% minus 2.68%), and 32.68% (30% plus 2.68%). Applying these percentages to the 4,500 member population, you conclude that from 1230 to 1470 members of the population can be expected—at a 95% confidence level—to regard your product favorably.

The Sample Size Calculator Chart [6]

The Sample Size Calculator chart provides an approximate graphical solution to the sampling formula. The scale at left is graduated proportionally to the percent favorable responses received (or expected) in a sampling survey. Values from 1% to 50% are graduated on the left side of this scale, and values from 50% to 99% are graduated on the right side of the scale.

The middle scale is graduated proportionally to sample sizes ranging from thirty to ten thousand. The right-hand scale is graduated proportionally to the percent sampling error (plus or minus) in the percent favorable responses. Graduations on the left side of this scale are for 95% probability of being correct (i.e., 95% confidence), and graduations on the right side of the scale are for 99.7% confidence.

To use this chart, lay a straightedge (a ruler) to connect known values on any two of the scales, and read the third value where the straightedge intersects the third scale. You can use the chart to solve *all* but the first of the previous examples.

Try example (2): Lay the straightedge to connect 200 on the middle scale with 30% favorable response, on the *left* scale. Where the straightedge intersects the *right*-hand scale (on the 95% confidence side), read the error, which will be about 6.3%. The true number of favorable responses will be between 30% plus and minus 6.3%, or between 23.7% and 36.3% of the population.

In example (3): Connect 50% favorable response on left-hand scale, with 2.5% error (99.7% confidence scale) on the right-hand scale. Read about 3,600 on the middle scale.

For example (6): Connect 18% on left-hand scale with 5% (95% confidence) on the right-hand scale. Read about 230 on the middle scale.

---

[6] This calculator chart is based on the formula using C = 1.96. Some calculating aids have been published using C = 2.00, which give sample sizes about 7.6% smaller than those given in our chart.

Sample Size Calculator [7]

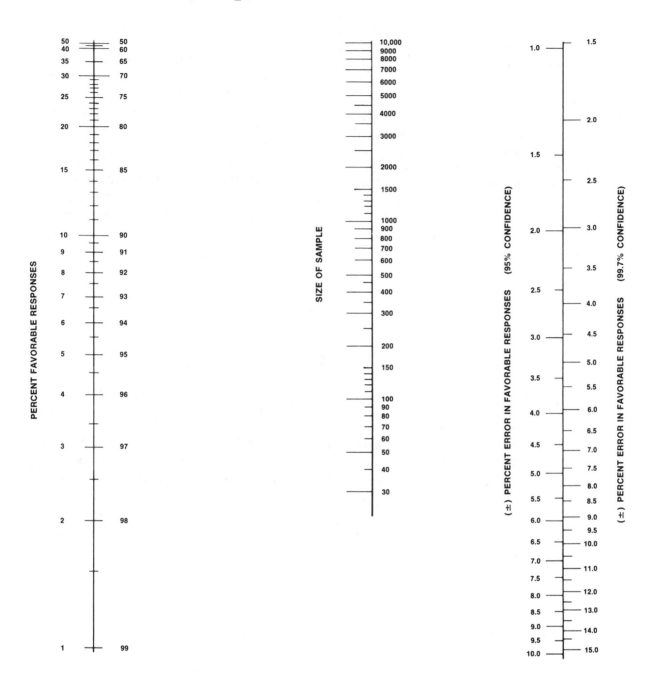

[7] © Cochrane Chase and Co., Fullerton, Ca. 1973.

Sampling Errors

There are two primary sampling errors which may occur: sampling and systematic. To begin with, it is difficult to obtain a truly representative sample—one with parameters exactly similar to those of the universe.

It is not unusual for a manager/researcher to specify 1,000 interviews be conducted in a certain fashion before having an appreciation for the non-sampling errors that occur (e.g., questionnaire design, interviewer bias, responding errors, recording errors, editing errors, etc.). To yield more reliable results, it may be better to do 500 interviews with the additional funds spent on better questionnaire development, field training, supervision, and other techniques.

Two points are frequently overlooked in industrial surveys:

You might not need a very large sample (as indicated by statistics shown earlier) since a small number of potential customers may account for a large percentage of purchases in a market. As long as you carefully weigh this data, it will probably be as accurate as a larger sample size.

Since industrial purchasing decisions involve many individuals (e.g., design engineer, production manager, purchasing agent, etc.), you may have to interview more than one person within each company.

Task 6: Prepare Questionnaire

Purpose of Questionnaire

A questionnaire is simply a series of questions. It serves as a means to obtain and record information pertinent to a research objective. It helps direct the questioning process, and simplifies clear and proper recording of information.

Preparation Procedure

In preparing a questionnaire, it generally is best to follow certain steps. First, you need a list of objectives; i.e., what data are needed. Then you can determine the type and form of the questionnaire, and the contents of individual questions.

From this, you can write all the questions you can think of which must be answered. Avoid unnecessary, redundant, or overlapping questions.[8] Determine the type of questions (e.g., open-end, multiple choice, etc.). Decide on the precise wording of each question. Develop a rough initial questionnaire in desired sequence (i.e., preferably with easy questions first; hard ones at the end); then you can determine the graphic layout.

The questionnaire should be pretested on a small sample of persons—drawn from the group to be surveyed—to determine the best way to talk with respondents, the best language to use, the best interview length, the question order and phrasing, and what technique works best (e.g., personal interview). Test until the questions and the order, etc., are 100% clear. This may be costly and time-consuming, but is mandatory. Even the simplest words and questions may be misinterpreted. Ten pretests are the minimum. If there isn't time for a pretest, have a colleague read the questionnaire after a brief explanation of its purpose. If each word is not crystal clear, go back to the drawing board. Then you can revise and develop the final questionnaire, and proceed with data collection.

---

[8] To check the consistency of respondent's answers, redundant questions are sometimes used. In such cases, the questions are worded differently, and designed to elicit responses which are related, but not specifically duplicative.

Parts of a Questionnaire

Questionnaires are generally composed of several basic parts: introduction, basic data, classification data, and identification data.

The introduction includes the name of the interviewer, the name of the research company for which the study is being conducted, the purpose of the survey, and how it will help the prospective respondent.

To help the interviewer, begin the written questionnaire with a boxed-off statement of how he should open the interview.

Basic questionnaire data includes the actual questions to be asked. Classification data includes such things as the respondent's type of company, plant description, products, and job function. Identification data include the respondent's name and address, interviewer's name, date and time of interview, and other desired items.

Types of Questionnaires

There are several types of questionnaire styles from which to choose. They can be direct or indirect; structured or unstructured. The structured-direct type is frequently used.

Structured questionnaires include a specific list of questions; whereas unstructured questionnaires list general topics. The direct questionnaire has no hidden meaning, while the indirect questionnaire attempts to get at inferences, motivations, and subconscious feelings.

Types of Questions

There is a wide variety of question types from which to choose. As with questionnaire types, individual questions can also be direct or indirect, structured or unstructured. Within each broad category of question types, there are various sub-categories. Each of these is listed in the "Questioning Techniques" chart, along with its advantages, disadvantages, and an example of each.

Questionnaire Guidelines

Although questionnaire development is an art primarily based on experience, there are several guidelines to follow. There are no formulas; the guides are presented only as rules of thumb. These cover: an overview, wording, question order, contents, and additional comments on mail questionnaires.

General Instructions

Develop questionnaires from respondent's point of view.

Prepare questionnaire so that it can be interpreted and used in the same way by each interviewer.

Always give the respondent adequate instructions.

Pretest questionnaire before using it.

Determine methods for tabulating results before a final questionnaire is drafted.

Make all questionnaires, especially for mail surveys, inviting and attractive (i.e., they appear to be easy to complete).

Wording

No question should be over 20 words. The words should correspond with the level of education, knowledge, and experience of respondents. In general, use simple everyday words and state questions in a specific, clear, direct manner. Avoid ambiguous words and those which may be difficult to define or interpret. Fully explain what you mean by such words as "quality," "taste," "appearance," "service," etc. There is often a variety of wording possibilities, none of which may be perfect. But, in any case, use good grammar.

Do not use confusing, embarrassing, or offensive questions. Avoid compounding two questions into one. Use mutually exclusive and exhaustive multiple choice questions (i.e., no overlapping answers, and all possible answers are listed).

Questioning Techniques

TECHNIQUE	ADVANTAGES	DISADVANTAGES	EXAMPLE
I. Direct-closed-end questions[9] A. Dichotomous (yes-no, true-false)	1. Is a good lead-in to more detailed questions. 2. Provides a specific answer. 3. Is quickly edited, tabulated, and analyzed. 4. Is relatively easy to answer. 5. Orderly and systematic. 6. Easy to pretest. 7. Less demanding of interviewer abilities. 8. Lower cost per interview.	1. Forces respondent to make a choice, even though he might be uncertain. 2. Provides no detailed information. 3. Difficult to word properly.	1. Are you responsible for the purchase of metal fasteners? ( ) Yes ( ) No
B. Closed Response.	1. Relatively short and easy to answer. 2. Is quickly edited, tabulated, and analyzed. 3. Provides a specific answer. 4. Orderly and systematic. 5. Easy to pretest. 6. Less demanding of interviewer abilities. 7. Lower cost per interview.	1. Presupposes researcher knows all relevant alternative answers. 2. Can often be an exhaustive list of answers. 3. Difficult to word properly.	1. What brand of fasteners do you usually buy? 2. List all brands of fasteners with which you are familiar.
C. Multiple Choice	1. Respondent will be less likely to make arbitrary choice than with dichotomous questions. 2. Easily edited, tabulated, and analyzed. 3. If constructed properly, lists all possible relevant alternatives. 4. Orderly and systematic. 5. Easy to pretest. 6. Less demanding of interviewer abilities. 7. Lower cost per interview.	1. Presupposes researcher knows all relevant alternative answers. 2. May not present clearly different alternatives; hard to make choices mutually exclusive (i.e., no overlapping answers). 3. Choices may have different meanings for different respondents. 4. Ordering of choices may bias answers (Note: to avoid this, use random ordering).	1. If you were to buy fasteners today, which of the following brands would you consider? ( ) Ramset ( ) Star ( ) Massey ( ) Other
D. Rating scales	1. Measures intensity of feelings toward an issue. 2. Provides relative precisions when intervals on scale are equal. 3. Easy to pretest.	1. Scale intervals may not provide clear distinctions in respondent's mind. 2. Scale intervals may not reflect respondent's knowledge levels. 3. Respondent may have different conceptions of different terms used (e.g., what does average really mean?) 4. Allows more than one brand to be	1. How would you rate the quality of Ramset's fasteners? ( ) Very Good ( ) Good ( ) Average ( ) Low ( ) Very low ( ) Don't know

28

Category	Advantages	Disadvantages	Example
			( ) Don't know
E. Preference Questions	1. Provides relatively quick responses on likes and dislikes. 2. Gives both direction and magnitude of feelings. 3. Relatively easy to pretest. 4. Must choose one brand as best, no "ties."	1. Answers may not reflect true action in real buying situation.	1. Which of these brands do you prefer? (i.e., which one of four; or present all possible pairs and ask which is liked best for four brands, this would be 12 different pairs.)
F. Ranking	1. Yields information quickly. 2. Gives information on rankings of products in respondent's mind. 3. Relatively easy to pretest.	1. Answers may not reflect true action in real buying situation, due to artificial research setting. 2. Ranking does not indicate degree of preference intervals between ranks. 3. Cannot have respondent rank too many items because of confusion created by the ability to discriminate between more than four or five items.	1. How would you rank these fasteners in regard to price? Rank Product A ( ) Product B ( ) Product C ( )
II. Open-end questions[10]			
A. Kick-off	1. Provides quick answers. 2. Generally little misunderstanding in explaining questions.	1. May be hard to code or combine answers.	1. What brand of hydraulic lifts do you usually purchase?
B. · Probing	1. Elicits further information on original question.	1. Difficult to record and interpret answers accurately.	1. Why do you like this particular brand?
III. Indirect Approach[11]			
A. Individual Interviews	1. Elicits preconscious attitudes and motives. 2. Can acquire information not obtainable from direct/structured questions. 3. Flexible; can adjust to individual interview.	1. Often difficult to interpret. 2. Usually difficult to record. 3. More time-consuming and costly than direct questions. 4. Difficult to summarize. 5. Somewhat demanding of interviewer abilities.	1. Please complete this sentence: "I believe that most industrial companies should spend more on group insurance because _____." 2. Show a picture and ask what it means to respondent (e.g., a trademark or company logo).
B. Group Interview	1. Group interaction may elicit reactions that otherwise remain hidden in individual interviews.	1. Presence of others may inhibit development of some individual's ideas. 2. Expensive; but not as costly as talking with each person individually. 3. Difficult to interpret and summarize. 4. Demanding of interviewer abilities.	1. Describe a product, and ask the group if they think the product will be successful and why.

---

[9] Used in personal, mail, and telephone interviews.

[10] Used primarily in personal interviews, with some usage in telephone, and only small usage in mail surveys.

[11] Usually restricted to personal interviews.

Do not lead respondent to desired conclusions or comments, or otherwise bias his response.

Question Order

When asking memory questions, try and lead respondent back time-wise (i.e., When did they start looking? How long ago? When did they buy? etc.). People tend to remember in order: things they do; things they see; things they hear.

Question order should help maintain a high level of interest among persons you are interviewing. Always start with a simple or general, yet interesting, question. End questionnaire with more difficult and specific questions.

Question sequence should avoid confusion and facilitate the respondent's flow of thought.

Contents

Use only questions pertinent to your objectives.

Cover all required subjects.

Subject matter should maintain high interest level among persons being interviewed.

There is no set number of questions to ask; it depends on the situation and the objectives of the survey.

Only ask questions which can be answered truthfully and accurately by the respondent.

If possible, one or more cross-checks can be included in the questionnaire to determine whether a respondent answered questions conscientiously. Include a question to check against some known fact. This helps test accuracy of results.

Request only that personal/confidential data that are *essential* for analysis purpose.

Encourage respondent to give additional information which may reflect his individual reaction, or to otherwise qualify his remarks.

Make questions easy to answer (e.g., answer boxes, check marks).

Mail Questionnaires—Additional Requirements

A short personal cover letter should convince respondent of importance of his answer and importance of the survey, and tell how he will benefit. Assure respondent of confidentiality.

Mail questionnaires must be attractive, look easy, interesting, and important. The appearance must persuade respondents to answer. Select paper, layout, and type accordingly. Use of white space gives questionnaire an "easy to complete" feeling. Always leave adequate space for replies.

Product illustrations often help increase the response rate.

Including a self-addressed, postage-paid envelope helps increase the response rate.

Premiums (e.g., gifts, money samples) often help increase the response rate, but may bias replies (e.g, may attract souvenir seekers). If a premium is used, be sure it is something the prospective respondent will find desirable, yet not bias his answers. Obviously the premium must be lightweight, and relatively inexpensive.

Questions must be easy to interpret and answer, since no researcher is there to help.

You can sometimes increase response rate by asking a few questions of great interest to respondent, but of no primary significance to researcher.

If you mail a questionnaire to subscribers of a certain publication, response rate may increase if the request comes directly from that publication. Responses as received are then mailed to researcher.

Do not ramble. Too many researchers attempt to cram every question into the mail survey. This usually decreases response rate.

If you ask respondents to rank items in order of importance, limit the number of items to five or less.

Develop procedure to correct nonresponse bias. If many recipients of your mail questionnaire do not respond, an attempt should be made to contact these nonrespondents via follow-up mail questionnaire, telephone, or personal interview to find out why they did not respond, and if their answers may be significantly different than those who did respond.

Task 7: Conduct Interviewing

Overview

Once the basic survey plan and questionnaire have been developed, you can collect information from the field. Gathering data by mail is discussed in Chapter IX-Direct Mail. For personal and telephone interviewing, you will need to select, train, and supervise the interviewers.

How Many Interviewers?

If you know how long the average telephone or personal interview takes, the desired sample size, and the time allowed for completion of interviewing, you can readily determine the number of interviewers needed.

Step 1: Multiply number of interviews times average interview time (e.g., 500 interviews times 12 minutes each equals 6,000 minutes).

Step 2: Divide total interview time (i.e., minutes) by 60 to determine required hours (e.g., 6000 divided by 60 equals 100 hours).

Step 3: If you're planning personal interviews, add travel, training, and supervision time (e.g., 30% more time yields 130 hours—100 + 30).

Step 4: Divide total time by the average working day—6½ hours or other figure based on your experience (e.g., 130 hours divided by 6½ hours is 20 working days).

Step 5: Divide number of days needed for interviewing by the number of days allotted to that task (e.g., 20 days divided by 4 days allotted for interviewing equals 5; therefore, 5 interviewers are needed).

Select Interviewers

Basically, there are two sources of interviewers: in-house or outside services. The latter is normally recommended except for smaller surveys.

Using Salesmen as Interviewers

Many companies use their salesmen (or staff) for interviewing purposes. The advantages and disadvantages of this procedure are discussed below. In most cases, disadvantages outweigh advantages.

Advantages

Many industrial salesmen have engineering or technical backgrounds which tend to increase the potential for accurate reporting, familiarity with statistics, and scientific research procedures.

Salesmen generally have an understanding of their firm's marketing problems and their customer's production problems.

Salesmen are already on your payroll, and readily available to receive instructions.

Salesmen's established contacts can facilitate data collection (i.e., better rapport exists with respondents if they are interviewed by someone they know).

Disadvantages

If salesmen conduct interviews without conducting normal sales functions, the cost of interviewing rapidly increases.

Salesmen may bias the interview by interjecting personal opinions into questionnaire.

Salesmen are often overly enthusiastic and optimistic, which may affect the reliability of the survey.

Outside Interviewing Services

Organizations providing skilled interviewers for a fee are available in most large cities. Consult your local Yellow Pages under "Marketing Research."

The American Marketing Association, Suite 606, 222 S. Riverside Plaza, Chicago, IL 60606, or the Marketing Research Trade Association, Inc., P.O. Box 1415, Grand Central Station, New York, N.Y. 10017, can provide a list of interview firms.

When using an interviewing service, make sure they have knowledge of, and are conversant with, terminology related to your products. Remember, interviewers will be talking with design engineers, technicians, management, purchasing agents, and a variety of other people.

Train Interviewers

Good interviewers have few refusals and make few technical errors. To achieve this skill, each must fully understand the survey objectives, the sampling plan, and the questionnaire itself. Give each interviewer complete written instructions on how to conduct the interview, how to classify respondents, the meaning of each question, the manner of recording the answers, and any other responsibilities. Also, give interviewers an adequate supply of questionnaires, directions to interviewing locations, identification cards, sheets on which to list interview data, time sheets, and an envelope in which to store all materials.

As part of the training period, check to see if all materials are accounted for. Have interviewers read over the questionnaires—and almost memorize them. Have each individual conduct a "test" interview in your presence. This test can be done on another interviewer, or on an actual prospect.

Ground Rules

Each interviewer should be given a written list of ground rules to follow. An example of such a list includes:

List names of all persons contacted who refused to be questioned.

Read questions exactly as worded on the questionnaire and in the same order. Small changes in wording or order can significantly alter answers. Ask every question. Do not omit one because it seems unimportant or has already been answered.

Always record an answer for every question. If nothing is recorded, the researcher will not know if you asked the question or if there simply was no response. Note if respondent refused to answer.

Always record answers in the proper space. Put all volunteered information in the margin. Record it at the time given, even if it answers a later question.

Do not explain, interpret, or add questions, unless otherwise directed.

Record answers exactly, even if you must use abbreviations and shorthand; even if they appear to be irrelevant. Always obtain clear, complete, and unambiguous answers; not vague ones.

Do not lead respondents to answer one way or another.

Probe for further responses only where directed. If probing is directed, clearly and slowly repeat respondent's answer as you write it down. This may lead to some more ideas. Never express approval or disapproval.

Conduct Interviews

The following suggestions are made to improve the interviewing process:

All interviewers should start by making a few practice interviews, possibly observed by the researcher or survey supervisor.

Always have a good appearance and pleasant manner. The initial impression in personal interviews is essential to developing required rapport. Be relaxed and self-confident.

In both personal and telephone surveys, the interviewer must introduce himself and state the name of the organization conducting the survey, objectives of the survey, and how it will help the prospective respondent.

Be prepared to meet resistance. If in person, the interviewer might show the respondent a letter or some identification proving who he is. The interviewer must assure that strictest confidence will prevail, and that there will be no sales follow-up. The interviewer might even offer the respondent a copy of the results in return for answering the questions.

If the respondent tells you that he is not familiar with the subject matter, ask him whom you can contact.

Win the prospective respondent's confidence. Give him a compliment, arouse his curiosity, and otherwise establish and maintain rapport. Tell respondent that his views are important. Encourage him to freely express ideas and give information. Focus your entire attention on him. Listen attentively. If the respondent gets too talkative, politely cut him off with, "We would be much more interested in some other points," and proceed with interview.

Try to minimize disruptions by conducting the interview in quiet surroundings with a minimum of interruptions, if this is at all possible. Avoid appearance of haste, nervousness, or uncertainty.

Always listen for what *isn't* being said.

Don't wear the respondent out. If he is unable to answer or expand, go on to next question. When the respondent is ready to quit (i.e., says so, gets fidgety, etc.), end the interview as soon as possible.

After interview completion, thank the respondent for his cooperation, check the questionnaire for total completion, legibility, ease of reading, and correct wording. Note any problems which occurred.

Supervise Interviewing

All interviews must be conducted and accurately reported. Ensure this is done by spot checking field work. Send a follow-up post card to the respondent, or telephone to ask if he was interviewed. Always tell each interviewer beforehand that all his work will be carefully checked.

Compare turndowns and question difficulty encountered by each interviewer. If significant discrepancies exist with individuals, possible falsification has occurred.

For studies over a long time period, list those errors commonly committed collectively by all interviewers. Send a copy of this list to each interviewer, calling out his individual errors. This helps him to correct those mistakes in the future. Also, point out the good aspects of his work as this information is equally valuable to him.

The supervisor may want to conduct some validating and editing of completed questionnaires early in the interviewing. (See Task 8.) If mistakes are being made, they can be corrected to eliminate future errors, and the consequent cost in time and money.

List of Materials Needed by Supervisor

Supervisors need a copy of all materials distributed to interviewers. They also need a list of interviewers' names, addresses, phone numbers, quotas, and assignments; a file for keeping completed interviews and validation forms; and a schedule showing when interviewing will begin, and the deadline for completion.

Task 8: Process the Data

Get Data Ready for Analysis

After survey information is gathered, the sample must be verified, questionnaires edited, and replies tabulated before analysis and a written report can be developed.

Verify the Sample

Information gathered in the field must be analyzed for sufficient size and representativeness of the sample. A quick check of the sample will ensure that each major class of people in the target universe being studied is represented in about the same proportion as they exist in the real world. Lack of similar representation in the sample may suggest bias in the survey.

The sample size can be checked for adequate size by using the techniques discussed in Task 5.

You may also wish to validate the sample by calling several respondents, checking to see if they were actually interviewed. This ensures against interviewer's falsification of answer forms. Some researchers suggest that ten percent of each interviewer's work be validated.

Classify Data

After the survey data have been collected, they must be organized under some system of classification to facilitate description and analysis. This requires defining one or more categories, or systems for classification of data, and determining the kind and number of items to be assigned to each class.

When to Develop Classes

Normally the system of classification of survey data should be developed in the early stages of the research project. However, when open-end questions and unstructured interviews are used, it won't be possible to decide upon the system of classifying data until the responses to questions have been analyzed.

There are advantages in establishing the data classes early in the project:

Compels researcher to consider types and ranges of responses in more detail. This may result in an improved questionnaire and answer sheet.

Having a well-planned system of data classification can make it possible to give interviewers more detailed instructions. This can result in a higher consistency of interpretation of responses and reduce editing problems.

A well-planned system of classification facilitates the orderly collection and tabulation of responses to questionnaires.

Guidelines for Developing Classes

The system of classification is governed by the purpose of the survey, the kind of problems being investigated, the use that will be made of the survey responses, and the types of responses required. Here are some guidelines to use in setting up your system of categories or classes of data:

The classes within the system must be mutually exclusive. There are no exceptions to this basic principle of classification.

A separate class should be established for each structured response to a question. For example: true, false, don't know. For unstructured responses, the entire possible range of relevant responses must be defined, and a class established for each response.

Each class should be designed to contain homogeneous responses; that is, responses having a common identifying characteristic such as price, color, shape, size, weight, length, width, location, age, sex, specific job function, and quantity of a specific product bought last year.

Each class should have only one dimension of the problem. Thus, don't combine "tool and die makers" with "machinists" if their separation is essential to the problem solution.

When a wide range of numerical data are to be accumulated, the range should be divided into class intervals to facilitate tabulation and statistical analysis of the data. For example, if a question concerns the number of engineers employed in various plants, class intervals might be established as follows (note that a separate class is provided for "None" and "No answer" in order to cover all possible cases):

None	( )
1 to 9	( )
10 to 19	( )
20 to 29	( )
30 or more	( )
No answer	( )

If the data collected in the survey are to be machine-processed, you should develop the classification system in cooperation with a data processing specialist. This will ensure that the classification system will lend itself to the standard coding systems used in machine-processing, as well as adapt to any limitations of the machine-processing system.

Edit Questionnaires

Now you must review data reported by interviewers on the questionnaires or answer sheets for accuracy and clarity. This should be done soon after data collection. Early editing permits questioning of interviewers, and catching of misunderstandings and recording errors while answers are relatively fresh in their minds.

Decide Who Should Edit

Use a central source to edit questionnaires. This ensures consistency and uniformity in handling of data. If the number of questionnaires and answers to be edited is not too large, the use of a single editor will reduce variations. As the number of questionnaires and data increases, it will be necessary to increase the number of editors if time is at a premium. If more than one edi-

tor is employed, assign each a different portion rather than have each edit an entire questionnaire.

What to Look for

Each questionnaire should be edited to ensure certain requirements are fulfilled.

Entries are legible
Answers are complete
Answers are consistent
Answers are accurate (i.e., no bias dishonesty or erroneous information)
No mistakes

If these are not met, set aside those questionnaires; do not include them in the analysis.

Code Questionnaire Responses

Now assign the responses to specific categories (i.e., coding). The discussion which follows covers pre- vs. post-coding, types of coding procedures, and what makes for good coding.

Pre- vs. Post-Coding

Pre-coding is used when codes are assigned to categories before data are collected. This is done primarily on structured questionnaires. The interviewer actually codes answers when he interprets the response, and decides on the category during the interview.

Post-coding is used when codes are assigned to responses after data collection. Post-coding is used for unstructured questionnaires, and is generally done at time of editing.

Types of Coding

The types of coding depend on how data are to be tabulated. The easiest method is the use of coding boxes printed on the questionnaire.

A second coding technique calls for data to be transferred to coding sheets. This may take more time, but the double checking often catches additional errors.

What Makes for Good Coding

Good coding requires considerable training and supervision. Explain the entire data collection process to your coders. Give written examples and instruction forms.

If you use more than one coder, it is often wise to compare results for inconsistencies. This latter practice may identify situations when category expansion or combinations must occur.

Coding for Machine-Processing

When the data are to be machine-processed, the individual data classes and subclasses are assigned machine code numbers, or letters, or combinations thereof. The method of coding for machine-processing is beyond the scope of this book. Assigning machine code symbols can be accomplished by, or in conjunction with, a specialist from your company's data processing section.

Tabulate Data

Now that editing and coding are completed, data can be tabulated. Tabulating is the counting of the number of responses in each data category. There are two aspects of data tabulation: the degree of sophistication required, and the method to be used.

Degree of Sophistication

The number of responses can be counted by simple tabulations or by cross-tabulations.

Basic (or simple) tabulation is merely a marginal tabulation or frequency distribution (i.e., tally). You simply count the number of responses given in each data category. A form similar to the one shown on this page typifies basic tabulation procedures (i.e., making tallies next to appropriate categories).

Cross-tabulations are often used, because of their expanded informational usefulness. Cross-tabulations are the simultaneous counting of the number of responses occurring in each data category in two or more information sets. An example of a cross-tabulation is shown on the next page. The two category classes are degree of ownership and size of company. The cross-tabulation shows that as company size increases, there is a greater tendency to own the facility.

Cross-tabulations are very useful for analytical purposes, but are more expensive to develop. For example, if there were 20 questions on a questionnaire, there would be 190 possible cross-tabulations (20 times 19 divided by 2). Normally however, you will not be interested in *all* of the possible cross-tabulations; so this should reduce the cost of development.

Hand vs. Mechanical Tabulation

Edited questionnaires can be tabulated by hand or computer (e.g., tape or punch cards, etc.). Either method can be faster and less expensive than the other, depending on the sample size, number of categories and type of analysis. The chart at the end of Task 8 identifies when to use each type.

QUESTION: "How many fasteners do you purchase per year?"		
CATEGORY	FREQUENCY	
None	|||	= 3
1 – 10,000	IIII IIII IIII IIII III	= 23
10,001 – 20,000	IIII IIII IIII IIII IIII I	= 26
20,001 – 30,000	IIII IIII IIII IIII	= 20
30,001 – 40,000	IIII IIII III	= 13
40,001 – 50,000	IIII III	= 8
Over 50,000	IIII	= 5
No Answer	II	= 2

Question: "Do you rent, lease, or own your current facility?"				
SIZE OF COMPANY BY SALES	RENT	LEASE	OWN	TOTAL
Under $100,000	ⵌ ⵌ l = 11	ⵌ llll = 9	llll = 4	24
$100,001-500,000	ⵌ ll = 7	ⵌ l = 6	lll = 3	16
$500,001-1,000,000	ⵌ l = 6	ⵌ ll = 7	ⵌ l = 6	19
$1,000,001-5,000,000	llll = 4	ⵌ = 5	ⵌ ll = 7	16
over $5,000,000	ll = 2	llll = 4	ⵌ llll = 9	15
No Answer	ll = 2	l = 1	ll = 2	5

Early in the process of designing your survey, it would be wise to consult with a specialist from your data processing section for advice on whether or not you should plan on using machine tabulation. If machine tabulation is to be used, the specialist can help you design the survey questionnaire to facilitate machine processing.

CONDITION	USE HAND TAB	USE COMPUTER TAB
Number of categories	Few	Many
Sample size	Small	Large
Amount and kinds of analyses(e.g., number of cross-tabulations)	Limited	Extensive or intricate

Task 9: Analyze the Data

Analysis Steps

Before plunging into statistical techniques, be sure that you (or the researcher) have the intuitive skills for drawing inferences and making sound analyses. This requires a knowledge of the problem, the industry, and what management wants to do with the data. With this essential background, analyses can be directly related to information required by management.

Now examine the tabulated data to develop a clear statement of facts (e.g., summarize the classified data), formulate additional working hypotheses, infer whether significant differences exist between categories, and draw some conclusions as to why differences exist. These distinct stages sometimes merge, do not always follow in sequence, and sometimes are not all needed.

Summarize Categorized Data

The simple tabulations and cross-tabulations developed in Task 8 may not be enough to adequately analyze data. Several descriptive measures may be used for drawing inferences, making decisions, or simply describing results. These descriptive measures include:

Measures of central tendency (i.e., averages)

Measures of dispersion (i.e., variation in a distribution)

Relative measures (i.e., percentages)

Measures of Central Tendency

Measures of central tendency refer to averages. There are three basic types of averages: arithmetic mean, median, and mode.

Arithmetic Mean

The arithmetic mean is the point around which values of distribution balance (i.e., the center of gravity). For a finite population (or sample) characteristic, the mean is the sum of the values (e.g., number of units) of the characteristic (e.g., product desired) for each unit in the population, divided by the total number of units. Examples for computing the mean for untabulated data, grouped data, and for probability distributions are shown below:

FOR UNTABULATED DATA—Add the value of the characteristic for each member of the sample and divide by the number of members. For example, assume there are five potential customers for your product, and they currently buy 500, 1,000, 1,000, 2,000, and 2,500 units respectively. The average units purchased by these five companies are:

$$\frac{500 + 1000 + 1000 + 2000 + 2500}{5} = \underline{\underline{1400}}$$

FOR GROUPED DATA—Weight or multiply the value of the characteristic for each group by the number of times it occurred (i.e., frequency).[12] Add these weighted numbers, and divide by the number in the sample. For example, assume there are one hundred utility companies in the United States interested in buying your generating plant. Forty companies need one unit each. Thirty companies need two units each. Fifteen companies need three units each. Ten companies need four units each. Five companies need five

units each. What does the average company want?

Units Desired By Each		Number of Companies		Total Units Desired
1	×	40	=	40
2	×	30	=	60
3	×	15	=	45
4	×	10	=	40
5	×	5	=	25
		100		210 units ÷ 100 companies =2.1 units each

FOR PROBABILITY DISTRIBUTION— Multiply the expected outcome by the probability of its occurring, and add the products. For example, assume that there is a 20% chance of selling no units, a 30% chance of selling one unit, a 20% chance of selling two units, a 15% chance of selling three units, a 10% chance of selling four units, and a 5% chance of selling 5 units. Then, the expected number of units to be sold is:

$$.20 \times 0 = 0.00$$
$$.30 \times 1 = 0.30$$
$$.20 \times 2 = 0.40$$
$$.15 \times 3 = 0.45$$
$$.10 \times 4 = 0.40$$
$$.05 \times 5 = \underline{0.25}$$
$$\underline{1.80} \text{ or}$$

approximately 2 units

Median

The median is the point at which the number of observations below it and above it are equal when data are ranked by size. In many cases, marketing data are not symmetrically distributed; these are called "skewed" distributions. The median then is a very revealing measure of central tendency (i.e., balance). If the distribution is skewed to the right, the median is lower than the mean, and is therefore a more accurate indication of central tendency.

---

[12] If categories have a range, use the midpoint of the range times the frequency of occurrence. For example, if the range is 80–90, use a midpoint of 85 [(80 + 90) ÷ 2].

Finding the median is a simple matter of counting the number of units, then recounting and stopping at the halfway point.

For example, the following list of numbers has a median of 8. It is found by counting the number of units in the sample (seven) dividing that number by two, and then recounting halfway down the list.

1, 2, 6, ⑧ 10, 15, 20
median

There are seven items in the list. Dividing by two equals 3½. That means that the median has three numbers above it and three below it. In the above example, the number 8 has three numbers above it and three below it.

If there is an even number in the sample, the median will be between two numbers. For example, take the following list:

1, 2, 3, 4

The sample size is 4. Dividing by 2 equals 2. That means that the median has two numbers above it and two below it. Logically, then, the median must be equally between the numbers 2 and 3, or 2½.

Mode

The mode is simply that value which occurs most frequently, and which is therefore most typical. For example, take the following list of numbers:

1, 2, 3, 3, 4, 4, 4, 5

The mode is 4, since it occurs three times, while no other number occurs more than twice.

Some distributions will have two or more modes. For example, take the distribution:

1, 1, 2, 3, 4, 4

This distribution is bimodal, with the numbers 1 and 4 each occurring twice.

Measures of Dispersion

Measures of dispersion are used to summarize categorized data. The range, standard deviation, and variance are three mea-

sures frequently used for this purpose. Most of the concepts are too complex to be adequately covered in a book of this scope. These and other statistical measures are described in "Statistical Methods," by Arkin and Colton, *Barnes and Noble College Outline Series (No. 27)*, Barnes & Noble, Inc., New York, NY 10022.

A brief comment about the range and standard deviation may be helpful. The range indicates extremes of distribution. For example, the range of prices might be $20 to $35; a range of units purchased might be 5,000 to 22,000.

Standard deviation and variance are abstract measures of dispersion which are difficult to define with any intuitive meaning. They do play an important role in the analysis of statistical distributions, and in the testing of statistical hypotheses. Consult a statistics text to get a better understanding of their uses and method of calculation.

Relative Measures

Percentages are widely used in marketing research. Unfortunately, the simplicity of percentages is often deceptive. When you see a percentage used, always ask, "Percentage of WHAT?" They are often misrepresented inadvertently or intentionally. In addition, percentages present several problems:

> In which direction should the percentage be computed?
> How do you interpret the percent of difference?
> Do you take the percent of the independent variable (cause) or the dependent variable (effect)?

Percentages are used in three ways to measure differences:

> Absolute difference in percentages
> Relative difference in percentages
> Percent of possible change (or difference)

Since the three concepts may conflict or otherwise cause misrepresentation, each is explored using the following example:

	Before Your Ads Appear In Magazine "X"	After Your Ads Appear In Magazine "X"
Subscribers to Magazine "X"	60.0%	80.0%
Nonsubscribers to Magazine "X"	30.0%	45.0%
TOTAL	48.0%	66.0%

Absolute Difference Method

The absolute difference method shows that the percent level increased 20% for subscribers and 15% for nonsubscribers. This shows a distinction must be made between percent and percentage points. This method is often used for its simplicity and speed of calculation, even though it suffers from possible misinterpretation.

Relative Difference Method

The relative difference method shows a 33% increase for subscribers, $[(80-60) \div 60] \times [100]$; and a 50% increase for nonsubscribers, $[(45-30) \div 30] \times [100]$. This method exaggerates the impression of a slight increase from a very low level.

Percent of Possible Difference

The percent of possible difference method shows a 50% increase for the subscribers, $[(20) \div (100-60)] \times [100]$; and a 21% increase for the nonsubscribers, $[(15) \div (100-30)] \times [100]$.

This method is the best measure from a research and interpretative standpoint, but it requires special explanations to enhance understanding.

The principal argument for using the percent of possible difference method is the "ceiling effect." Where causal relationships are involved, your goal is generally to convert unfavorable behavior to favorable behavior. The higher the proportion of favorable behavior to begin with, the greater the difficulty of getting significant increases in favorable responses.

Formulate Additional Hypotheses

During the course of virtually every study, regardless of how well-planned, new hypotheses may be suggested by the data. Tentative explanations of behavior or relationships among variables not originally considered may develop. Any new hypotheses must be carefully considered. Determine the cost of testing the new hypothesis. Remember, no hypothesis should be tested unless the expected value of additional information may be more than the cost of acquiring it.

Infer Whether Meaningful Differences Exist Between Categories

Now you can determine whether differences between categories resulted from chance variation in the sampling process, or whether they reflect actual differences in the population being studied.

Make these tests for differences in the mean, percentage, or other sample statistics, by using appropriate statistical tools, including standard error tests. The mathematical procedures for these tests are too complex to discuss here. Refer such problems to a statistician, or, if you have a technical background, refer to a standard college statistics text.

Infer Relationships Between Variables

Now, you can draw conclusions regarding relationships among variables involved. This is useful for predicting future behavior.

Inferring relationships between variables depends on two key factors: association and causation. The difference between these two terms is in kind and degree. Association means only that two or more variables (e.g., advertising budget and sales) tend to change together to a greater or lesser extent. The extent depends upon the degree of association involved.

If a mutual change in variables is evident (i.e., both variables change at same time) and persistent in both direction and degree, we still cannot conclude that there is a functional relationship that one variable is dependent (the effect) and the other variable or variables, are independent (the cause). In short, association does not necessarily imply causation; but causation does imply association. For example, if you add salesmen and sales go up, the two variables are associated, but the first did not cause the second merely by association. The increase in sales may have been caused by some other factor.

To determine whether causal relationships exist, you must control the effects of variables not to be analyzed. Try to isolate all other (suspected) causal associations. Unfortunately, there are no statistical techniques which determine extraneous variables (e.g., competitive actions)—the burden rests with the researcher.

Sometimes you need not determine whether an observed association is causal in nature. If substantial reason exists that the association is stable and persistent over the time period covered by the forecast, it may be sufficient simply to know the extent of association.

Two basic methods exist for analyzing relationships between variables:
Informal interpretation of arrays of data
Formal mathematical techniques

Arrays of Data

Analyzing arrays of data (i.e., arrangement of a series of terms) is one of the simplest ways to examine relationships among variables. Two basic tools are cross-tabulations and scatter diagrams. Cross-tabulations were covered earlier. Scatter diagrams are discussed in this section.

Scatter diagrams should be prepared prior to any mathematical analysis of relationships. They help you to gain a better understanding of the nature and the degree of association involved among variables.

Scatter diagrams graphically depict relationships between any two sets of data. First, in tabular form we'll present data for ten customers (e.g., the number of calls made on them, and the number of units purchased).

CUSTOMER	NUMBER OF CALLS ON THIS CUSTOMER	UNITS PURCHASED
1	1	2
2	6	24
3	2	5
4	0	3
5	8	30
6	5	27
7	4	22
8	7	31
9	3	15
10	3	11

This is useful data in its present form, but its usefulness is enhanced considerably if it is displayed graphically. Convention dictates that the independent variable be scaled on the horizontal axis, as shown on the next pg. Once all points are plotted, simply draw a freehand curve approximately through the center of all points. This tool is most useful for getting a broad picture of the relationships involved in many company activities.

Formal Mathematical Techniques

Mathematical models used for estimating and forecasting depend on having an exact, deterministic relationship between variables expressed in quantitative terms. Unfortunately, this is not always possible. Sometimes the relationships are obscured by use

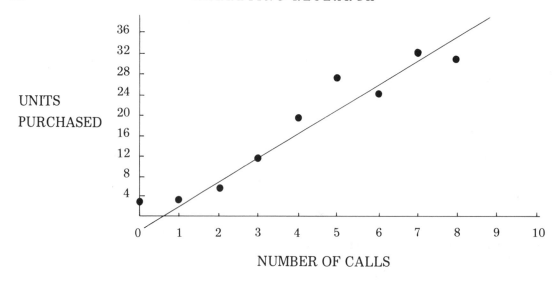

UNITS PURCHASED

NUMBER OF CALLS

of sample data. Some variables change rapidly over time. Sometimes the effects of extraneous variables are reflected in the data, but are not explicitly taken into account in the analysis.

Although there are limitations, quantitative tools are available to express relationships between marketing variables. Applications include sales forecasts, sales quotas, advertising budget determination, setting prices, measuring the effectiveness of promotional campaigns, etc. Some of the prevalent tools used in such analyses include regression, correlation, discrimination, and chi-square.

Regression analysis can improve prediction by measuring the degree of change in a dependent variable associated with changes in one or more independent variables. Regression analysis can be simple or multiple. With single (simple) regression, one dependent variable (e.g., sales), and one independent variable (e.g., promotion budget) may be analyzed. With multiple regression, one dependent variable (e.g., sales), and two or more independent variables (e.g., promotion budget, number of salesmen, and price) may be analyzed.

Correlation analysis measures the degree to which the regression line "explains" the original variance observed in data. It tells whether all variance is explained, or if the variance is not fully explained.

Discriminant analysis is useful for measuring non-quantitative variables (e.g., service). It's like regression analysis in use and interpretation, except that the dependent variable is classified dichotomously (i.e., "high potential" and "low potential"). The nature of the relationship is established between a dichotomously-classified dependent variable, and one or more independent variables.

Chi-square is used to verify the presence of association between sets of data (e.g., sample values and known theoretical parameters, or two or more samples). It attempts to rule out that association has occurred as a result of chance. If this is accomplished, then it can be assumed that a significant association exists.

Conclusions

The preceding descriptions of statistical tools of analysis are intended only to make you aware of the existence of such tools. Marketing research has drawn upon many highly sophisticated mathematical tools which are covered in standard college textbooks on the subject. In making statistical analyses, it is important to do so with a full understanding of the pitfalls and limitations of statistics, lest you be accused of the saying, "figures never lie, but liars figure."

Whatever your findings as the result of making a survey or other research studies, the next step is to organize your findings and present them in a formal report or presentation. This is covered in the next task.

Task 10: Prepare Reports/Present Findings

Culmination of Research Project

The report is the culmination of any research project. It makes research findings available in easily digestible form for further study by interested company executives. Basically, there are two types of reports: written and oral. These two types are discussed below, with comments on ways to present data.

Written Research Report

The written research report is generally composed of several basic parts, the contents and order of which depend on the purpose of the report. At a minimum, the report should include a title page, table of contents, foreword/summary, survey of objectives, major findings and conclusions, methodology of survey, research limitations, recommendations, and appendices (tables, data, computations, and detailed analyses).

Writing Hints

Good writing will increase chances that your report will be read, understood, and given serious consideration. The suggestions below may help you to improve your research writing.

Title should accurately describe report's contents.

Start with an outline of each heading and subheading. Then add major points. This outline procedure helps you write logically and sensibly.

Always think out what you're trying to say before writing anything. Use trial and error to put your thoughts into writing and revise it until it reads smoothly.

Always write for the audience, both in language and content. Express your ideas in clear, complete, and objective language.

Include all essential information needed to properly understand and interpret results. Don't tell more than the reader needs to know. Usefulness of a report is not measured by the pound. Errors of too long a report far exceed the number of instances of too short a report. Keep the report brief. Offer additional details on request.

Explain fully why and how research was done. What is it about? Who made the survey? When was it made? Where was it made?

Properly weight the results to compensate for possible distortions in the sample distribution.

Don't hide unpleasant results, weaknesses or limitations in the research. The report will be more believable if you admit these drawbacks.

Include a copy of the questions exactly as they appeared in the questionnaire, together with instructions to interviewers.

Use descriptive column headings for all statistical presentations.

Use headings and subheads where appropriate to break the text up into "bite size" pieces.

Use charts and visuals to increase emphasis on specific statistics.

State all sources of outside information used.

Always summarize at the end of long or involved sections.

Base conclusions only on material included in the report.

Prepare Oral Report

To support most written reports, a researcher may be called upon to make an oral presentation of his study results. Always rehearse before a final presentation. When the presentation begins, request that questions he held until the end of the presentation (one question may lead to others which may destroy a well-prepared presentation). Get to the point quickly—don't keep your audience in suspense. Don't read the report. Rather, rely on charts, graphs, photographs, diagrams, and drawings to illustrate and explain findings. Stick to the facts; don't ramble.

When completed, present final arguments and recommendations, and have sufficient copies of the report so that every attendee receives one. Then be prepared to answer questions. Try to anticipate questions, and cover these points during your talk. Bring any supportive materials needed to explain your findings, and answer questions.

Ways to Present Data [13]

In addition to straight narrative, there are two basic visual forms of data presentation: graphic and tabular. Some examples are presented below to help you think of the best ways to present your research data. If you use tables, always include the table number, title, headings, subheads, column heads, and data source. Data can be presented in rows and columns, by product, region, etc., over any desired time period. Some examples of ways to present data are presented here.

---

[13] An excellent book on making business charts is *How to Chart*, by Walter E. Weld, Codex Book Company, 74 Broadway, Norwood, MA 02062.

BAR CHARTS

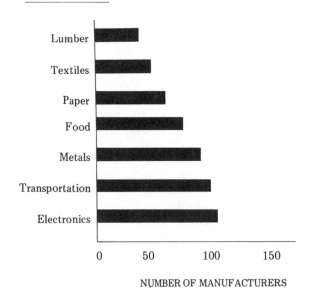

NUMBER OF MANUFACTURERS

MULTIPLE BAR

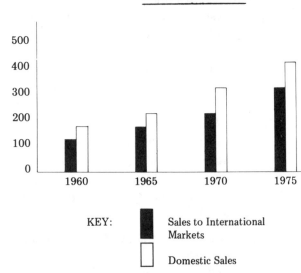

KEY: ■ Sales to International Markets
□ Domestic Sales

TWO-DIRECTION LINE CHART

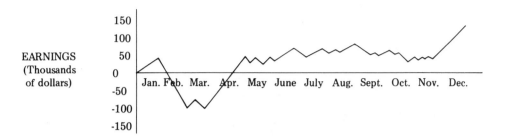

EARNINGS
(Thousands
of dollars)

PIE CHARTS

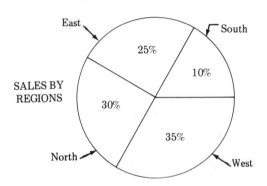

SALES BY
REGIONS

TWO-DIRECTIONAL BAR CHART

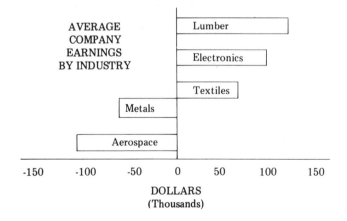

AVERAGE
COMPANY
EARNINGS
BY INDUSTRY

DOLLARS
(Thousands)

LINE CHARTS

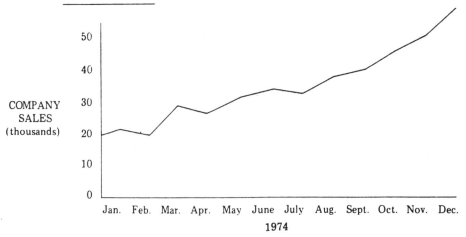

COMPANY
SALES
(thousands)

Jan. Feb. Mar. Apr. May June July Aug. Sept. Oct. Nov. Dec.

1974

COMPONENT BAR CHART

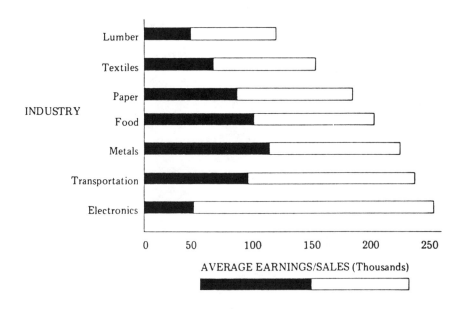

INDUSTRY

Lumber
Textiles
Paper
Food
Metals
Transportation
Electronics

0   50   100   150   200   250

AVERAGE EARNINGS/SALES (Thousands)

MULTIPLE LINE

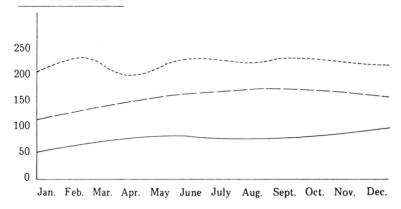

Jan. Feb. Mar. Apr. May June July Aug. Sept. Oct. Nov. Dec.

KEY: Inquiries = ------------
      Sales Calls = ___ ___ ___
      Orders = _____

46

Section D
Calculate Market Potentials [14]

What Are Potentials?

Market potentials are calculations representing the ability of a market area or industry to absorb a specific amount of a product's sales. Sales potentials are the share of the market potential which a firm can reasonably expect to capture.

Uses of Potentials

There are many uses for market potentials. The most prevalent ones include:

Determine areas with greatest sales potential for concentration by direct sales force.
Determine the number of salesmen or representatives required to cover an area adequately.
Identify boundaries for sales territories.
Establish quotas for salesmen, territories, and product-lines.
Chart direction for advertising and sales promotion coverage.
Check the effectiveness of individual salesmen or representatives.

Degree of Accuracy

There are several methods for calculating market potentials, none of which will be best in every situation. Some are complex and time consuming. Some are more accurate than others. However, use the method which best suits your objectives. For example, if salesmen are compensated with commissions based on quotas established via potentials, then high accuracy in calculating potentials is required. In contrast, if rough approximations are required to obtain a general idea of territorial ranking, then less perfection is required.

Information Sources

Data used for calculations include internal sales records, sale reports, etc., as well as external secondary research sources, and primary research surveys. These latter sources are discussed in detail in sections B and C of this chapter.

Factors Affecting Potentials

Accuracy of potentials depend on the industry, product, channels of distribution, the market, the competition, and so forth. Some general guidelines may be helpful:

It is generally easier to calculate accurate potentials for older, more established industries, particularly where the rate of growth or decline is relatively constant. Data are readily available on such markets.
Potentials are more reliable when calculated for products where unit sales are large, dollar value small, or side market exists for a standard product.
Potentials are more reliable when there is a large number of plants concentrated in few geographical areas, and where total market output is divided among many plants versus being concentrated in a few larger ones.
It is difficult to accurately develop potentials for new products or growth indus-

TASK 11: Calculate Market Potentials (Using Surveys)
TASK 12: Calculate Market Potentials (Using Company Records)
TASK 13: Calculate Market Potentials (Using Industry Data)
TASK 14: Calculate Market Potentials (Using a Census)

tries, especially where a small number of large companies dominate the industry output.

Four Primary Techniques

While there are numerous techniques for calculating market potentials, only four of the more widely used and accepted ones are discussed here:

Before selecting one of these approaches, review the advantages and disadvantages of each method as shown in the methods evaluation chart.

Task 11: Calculate Market Potentials (Using Surveys)

Use of Surveys as a Base

Market surveys of current and prospective users are a frequently used device for calculating potentials and for answering specific questions about your market. Survey results are readily projected to the entire market. Simply extrapolate them across published industry data, giving relative purchasing power of each market segment for the product under study.

This task presents the survey method for calculating potentials. Success of such calculations depends on accurate surveys and reliability of data used to represent the relative purchasing power of each market segment. Section C presents guidelines for the proper conduct of market surveys, while Section B describes sources of industry data. Therefore, we can get right to calculation of the potentials.

Two Approaches

Market potentials which are developed with the use of surveys can be developed around (1) a *buying* approach, or (2) a *possible use* approach. Each of these is discussed below. The buying approach method is most useful for standard industrial products, such as maintenance, repairs, or operating supplies.

The possible use approach is best suited for new industrial products, for highly technical products, or for existing products with extensive engineering changes.

Buying Approach

The buying approach requests information from respondents relative to past purchases (i.e., in units or dollars) of a particular type of product. Other information can be gathered at the same time (e.g., desired brands, seasonal requirements, how they purchase, number of employees, etc.). Purchases (either past or future intentions) are then projected across all plants in that particular industry in order to calculate total market potential.

This method assumes the survey was conducted within a representative cross-section of the total market and that sample results can be reliably projected to the entire market on the basis of plant employment. For data to be accurately interpreted, purchases must be weighted directly in proportion to the number of production workers employed.

Types of Data Requested for Buying Approach

The types of data gathered might be based on the following questions:

Evaluation of Methods for Calculating
Market Potentials

METHOD	ADVANTAGES	DISADVANTAGES
Survey Method	1. Allows researcher to gather attitudinal and behavioral data. 2. Prospective purchasers actually contribute to estimates. 3. Relies on published census data. 4. Is easily understood. 5. Useful for standard industrial products or for new products.	1. There is a question as to whether the right buying influence was contacted in each plant. 2. Only limited data can be gathered if mail is used. 3. Projection and interpretation may be subject to question. 4. Questions may be raised as to how accurate, and how current the data are. 5. Industries may not be sufficiently homogeneous for groupings to be made.
Company Records Method	1. Good approach for products having been sold for a minimum of two years. 2. Data are readily available. 3. Relies on published census data. 4. Allows calculation of market share in one easy step.	1. Reliance on past sales is not always a good indicator of future conditions. 2. Does not consider major changes in promotion budgets or direction. 3. Does not consider any changes in method of distribution.
Industry Data Method	1. Considers varying consumption rates in each industry having use for product. 2. By using published census data, market areas' ability to purchase are readily pinpointed. 3. The use of weighting tends to cancel out errors in data within various territories.	1. Data may not be current enough to provide a complete census of all firms in an area. 2. Requires use of SIC system for a purpose which it is normally not accustomed. 3. Relies on judgement in formulation of ratios. 4. Industrial concentrations in small areas may affect reliability adversely. 5. Certain products do not always have a consistent relationship with the statistical series used.
Census Method	1. Does not rely on possibility of projection or sampling errors. 2. Plants actually supply data since they are in best position to give past and expected purchases. 3. Including salesmen in your analysis forces them to think of business opportunities in their territory.	1. Not practical for wide industrial markets, due to high cost and time constraints. 2. Estimating requirements of nonrespondents may reduce overall accuracy. 3. Sales force participation may bias results, especially if potentials are intended for use in developing quotas. 4. There may be some response errors. 5. A complete list of firms in the market is often difficult to obtain.

1. Does your plant use (NAME OF PRODUCT)? ( ) Yes ( ) No

If "yes" to question 1, please answer the following questions; if "no" to question 1, please return questionnaire to us.

2. How many (NAME OF PRODUCT) were used in your plant last year?
3. For what applications?
4. Please list the names of your leading suppliers of this product.
5. Do you anticipate the use of more (NAME OF PRODUCT) in the next year? ( ) Yes ( ) No

6. If yes, when do you plan to buy (DATE)?

7. How many units do you expect to buy in the next year? _____

8. Also, please list your plant's:
   a. Total workers _____
   b. Number of employees directly engaged in work related to (PRODUCT)

   _____

   c. Principal product manufactured by your plant _____

How to Calculate National Potential (Buying Approach)

Once survey results are tabulated, you can calculate the national market potential (see form below).

In column 1, list all SIC numbers comprising the market for the product under study. In the example, SICs 34 through 37 were the prime segments. The analysis can be more refined by going to four-digit SICs. In column 2, write the industry descriptions.

In columns 3 through 5 record information obtained from the market survey. In column 3, enter total annual product purchases by industry, as reported by surveyed firms. In the example, surveyed firms purchased $210,000 worth of the subject product (all brands).

Column 4 is the total number of production workers employed by the surveyed firms. For example, there were 12,650 employees reported in firms surveyed from SIC 34.

Column 5 lists average annual purchases per worker. This is calculated by dividing column 3 by column 4, for each industry. For example, average annual purchases per worker in SIC 34 is $2.37 ($30,000 divided by 12,650 workers).

In column 6, enter the national number of

National Market Potential Calculation
for (PRODUCT) for (YEAR)

METHOD: BUYING APPROACH

(1) SIC NOS.	(2) KEY INDUSTRY DESCRIPTIONS	MARKET SURVEY RESULTS FROM REPORTING PLANTS			(6) NATIONAL NUMBER OF WORKERS	(7) NATIONAL MARKET POTENTIAL (Column 5 x Column 6)
		(3) TOTAL ANNUAL PRODUCT PURCHASES	(4) TOTAL NUMBER OF WORKERS	(5) AVERAGE ANNUAL PURCHASES PER WORKER (Column 3 ÷ Column 4)		
34	Fabricated Metal Products	$ 30,000	12,650	$ 2.37	1,275,902	$ 3,023,888
35	Machinery, Except Electrical	45,000	23,220	1.94	1,743,531	3,382,450
36	Electrical Eqpmt. and Supplies	75,000	17,500	4.29	1,660,498	7,123,536
37	Transportation Equipment	60,000	45,000	1.33	1,657,990	2,205,127
	TOTALS	$210,000				$15,735,001

workers in each industry (e.g., 1,275,902 workers in SIC 34). This number can be obtained from several secondary research sources listed earlier in this chapter. This particular figure was taken from the 1971 County Business Patterns.

In column 7, calculate and enter national market potential for each industry. This is done by multiplying column 5 by column 6. For example, the national market potential for SIC 34 is $3,023,888 (i.e., $2.37 times 1,275,902 workers).

As a final step, add national market potentials for each industry listed in column 7. The total is the estimated national market potential for the particular product under study.

How to Calculate Territory Potential/Market Share (Buying Approach)

Territory calculations are identical to national calculations. In columns 1 and 2, use the SICs and key industry descriptions from the national charts. In column 3, enter the national average annual purchases per worker, as calculated from the national table, column 5.

In column 4, enter the number of workers in a particular territory. This is found by reference to secondary literature. In the example, New York State is analyzed. The state has 86,203 workers in SIC 34, 131,380 workers in SIC 35, etc.[15]

Territory sales potential is then calculated by multiplying columns 3 and 4, and entering the product in column 5. For example, in SIC 34 for the state of New York, there are 86,203 workers times an average annual purchase per worker of $2.37. This yields a territory market potential of $204,301 for SIC 34. Then, summing the potentials for each SIC, total New York State territorial potential for all listed industries is $1,332,627.

[15] From U.S. County Business Patterns.

Territory Market Potential Calculation
for (PRODUCT) for (YEAR) for (AREA)

METHOD: BUYING APPROACH

(1) SIC NOS.	(2) KEY INDUSTRY DESCRIPTIONS	(3) NATIONAL AVERAGE ANNUAL PURCHASES PER WORKER	(4) TERRITORY NUMBER OF WORKERS	(5) TERRITORY MARKET POTENTIAL (COLUMN 3 x COLUMN 4)	(6) TERRITORY ANNUAL SALES OF YOUR COMPANY	(7) % TERRITORY SALES OF TERRITORY POTENTIAL: (Column 6 ÷ Column 5) (Your company's share of market)
34	Fabricated Metal Products	$2.37	86,203	$ 204,301	$ 42,000	20.6%
35	Machinery, Except Electrical	1.94	131,380	254,877	26,000	10.2
36	Electrical Eqpmt. and Supplies	4.29	178,637	766,353	70,000	9.1
37	Transportation Equipment	1.33	80,524	107,096	25,000	23.3
	TOTALS			$1,332,627	$163,000	12.2%

Now you are in a good position to analyze your company's market share. In column 6, enter your company's actual territory annual sales. To obtain share of market in each industry, divide column 6 by column 5. For example, current market share in SIC 34 in New York is 20.6% ($42,000 divided by $204,301). To determine your total market share across all listed industries in New York, divide the total of column 6 by the total of column 5. In the example, total market share is 12.2% ($163,000 divided by $1,332,627).

This territorial analysis allows you to compare territory performance in terms of market shares achieved in each area.

Possible Use Approach

The possible use method of calculating market potentials is not as reliable as other methods, but is one of the few methods used effectively for new products, existing products with major changes, or existing products being sold to distinctly new markets.

Types of Data Requested

This approach requires data on plant operations and products, rather than on past or expected purchases. It is designed to determine whether a particular plant can use a specific product in its operations or as part of one of its products, and if so, to what extent.

An attempt is made to determine interest levels. The questionnaire must include a complete product description, including what the product can do for the respondent. Types of questions might include:

1. Does your plant do any of the following functions?
   a. A list of functions which your product is part ( ) Yes ( ) No
   b. Another function ( ) Yes ( ) No
   c. Another function ( ) Yes ( ) No
   (and so on)

National Market Potential Calculation
for (PRODUCT) for (YEAR)

METHOD: POSSIBLE USE APPROACH

(1) SIC NOS.	(2) KEY INDUSTRY DESCRIPTIONS	MARKET SURVEY RESULTS (FROM REPORTING PLANTS — ADJUSTED)					(8) NATIONAL NUMBER OF WORKERS	ESTIMATED NATIONAL MARKET POTENTIAL	
		EXPECTED ANNUAL PRODUCT PURCHASES			ESTIMATED AVERAGE ANNUAL PURCHASES PER WORKER				
		(3) LOW	(4) HIGH	(5) NUMBER OF WORKERS	(6) LOW (Column 3 ÷ Column 5)	(7) HIGH (Column 4 ÷ Column 5)		(9) LOW (Column 6 x Column 8)	(10) HIGH (Column 7 x Column 8)
34	Fabricated Metal Products	$20,000	$50,000	12,650	$1.58	$3.95	1,275,902	$ 2,015,925	$ 5,039,813
35	Machinery, Except Electrical	30,000	60,000	23,220	1.29	2.58	1,743,531	2,249,155	4,498,310
36	Electrical Equipment and Supplies	55,000	90,000	17,500	3.14	5.14	1,660,498	5,213,964	8,534,960
37	Transportation Equipment	45,000	75,000	45,000	1.00	1.67	1,657,990	1,657,990	2,768,843
	TOTALS							$11,137,034	$20,841,926

2. Do you perform any of the above operations in?
   a. Your receiving
      area   ( ) Yes ( ) No
   b. Your production
      line   ( ) Yes ( ) No
   c. Your final inspec-
      tion   ( ) Yes ( ) No
   d. Your warehouse ( ) Yes ( ) No
      (*and so on*)
3. Do you use (PRODUCT) as a component in making your plant's end-product?
                           ( ) Yes ( ) No
4. Approximately how many (PRODUCT) do you buy annually?
5. Are you planning the purchase of additional (PRODUCT) this year? If yes, when?

How to Calculate National Potential (*Possible Use Approach*)

Now take the survey results and determine whether a respondent plant can be considered a prospect or not, and if so, to what extent. In addition to responses made by plants, find out about the manufacturing operations of each SIC. Then you can make a better judgement.

The "NATIONAL MARKET POTENTIAL CALCULATION—Possible Use Approach" form will help you calculate national market potentials using the possible use approach. Note that because of reliance on judgement, a *range* of expected product purchases is given. This range can be from conservative to optimistic, depending on the person making the analysis. Calculations on the form are essentially the same as for the buying approach method.

How to Calculate Territorial Potentials (*Possible Use Approach*)

Territorial potentials can be calculated using the possible use approach. The technique is identical to the buying approach method, except for addition of a low-high range.

Territory Market Potential Calculation
for (PRODUCT) for (YEAR) for (AREA)

METHOD: POSSIBLE USE APPROACH

(1) SIC NOS.	(2) KEY INDUSTRY DESCRIPTIONS	NATIONAL AVERAGE ANNUAL PURCHASES PER WORKER		(5) TERRITORY NUMBER OF WORKERS	TERRITORY MARKET POTENTIAL	
		(3) LOW	(4) HIGH		(6) LOW (Column 3 x Column 5)	(7) HIGH (Column 4 x Column 5)
34	Fabricated Metal Products	$1.58	$3.95	86,203	$136,201	$ 340,502
35	Machinery, Except Electrical	1.29	2.58	131,380	169,480	338,960
36	Electrical Eqpmt. and Supplies	3.14	5.14	178,637	560,920	918,194
37	Transportation Equipment	1.00	1.67	80,524	80,524	134,475
	TOTALS				$947,125	$1,732,131

Task 12: Calculate Market Potentials
(Using Company Records)

When to Use

Company sales records are ideal sources for calculating market potentials for existing products. Past sales results are projected to the entire industry. As long as there are no major changes in direction of promotion or distribution activities, these figures are adequate projectors of future sales. (Ensure that non-recurring single orders are not allowed to over influence your base sales records.)

How to Calculate

The "NATIONAL MARKET POTENTIAL CALCULATION—Company Sales Records" form gives an example of using company sales figures to project market po-

tential. Fill in columns 1 and 2 with key SIC numbers and descriptions. Then, from your company sales records, enter in column 3 the total annual sales to all customers in each listed SIC. In column 4 enter the total employment in customer plants. This can be determined from secondary research sources (e.g., Dun & Bradstreet, Standard & Poor's).

Calculate and enter in column 5 the average annual sales per employee. This is done by dividing column 3 by column 4. In the example for SIC 34, average annual sales per employee is $2.88 ($70,000 divided by 24,300 employees).

In column 6, enter national employment figures for each SIC. This is obtained through secondary literature sources (e.g.,

National Market Potential Calculation
for (PRODUCT) for (YEAR)

METHOD: COMPANY SALES RECORDS

(1) SIC NOS.	(2) KEY INDUSTRY DESCRIPTIONS	(3) TOTAL ANNUAL SALES TO CUSTOMERS	(4) TOTAL EMPLOYMENT IN CUSTOMER PLANTS	(5) AVERAGE ANNUAL SALES PER EMPLOYEE (Column 3 ÷ Column 4)	(6) NATIONAL EMPLOYMENT	(7) NATIONAL MARKET POTENTIAL (Column 5 x Column 6)	(8) % ANNUAL SALES OF NATIONAL MARKET POTENTIAL (Column 3 ÷ Column 7)
34	Fabricated Metal Products	$ 70,000	24,300	$2.88	1,275,902	$3,674,598	1.9%
35	Machinery, Except Electrical	90,000	45,200	1.99	1,743,531	3,469,627	2.6
36	Electrical Equip. and Supplies	120,000	30,000	4.00	1,660,498	6,641,992	1.8
37	Transportation Equipment	100,000	60,000	1.67	1,657,990	2,768,843	3.6
	TOTALS	$380,000				$16,555,060	2.3%

U.S. County Business Patterns). Then calculate and enter in column 7 the national market potential for each SIC. This is done by multiplying column 5 by column 6. For SIC 34, the national market potential is $3,674,598 ($2.88 times 1,275,902 employees). Summation of column 7 yields the national market potential across all listed SIC industries.

In column 8, calculate and enter the percent annual sales of national market potential. This is calculated by dividing column 3 by column 7. For SIC 34, this company has achieved a 1.9% share of market potential. Overall, the company has achieved a 2.3% share.

Calculate Territorial Potentials

Territorial potentials can be calculated in a manner similar to national ones. In the example form, we have transferred from the national form the average annual sales per employee, and entered it in column 3. Territory employment is determined from secondary research sources (e.g., U.S. County Business Patterns) and entered in column 4.

Territory potential can then be calculated and entered in column 5 by multiplying column 3 by column 4. For SIC 34, this yields $248,265 ($2.88 times 86,203 workers). Total market potential is determined by adding industry potentials in column 5. Total market potential for this product is $1,358,734.

The analysis can be taken one step further by computing the % territory sales of territory potential. This is done by dividing column 6 by column 5. For example, the percent for SIC 34 is 16.9% ($42,000 divided by $248,265).

Territory Market Potential Calculation
for (PRODUCT) for (YEAR) for (AREA)

METHOD: COMPANY SALES RECORDS

(1) SIC NOS.	(2) KEY INDUSTRY DESCRIPTIONS	(3) AVERAGE ANNUAL SALES PER EMPLOYEE	(4) TERRITORY EMPLOYMENT	(5) TERRITORY MARKET POTENTIAL (COLUMN 3 x COLUMN 4)	(6) TERRITORY ANNUAL SALES	(7) % TERRITORY SALES OF TERRITORY POTENTIAL (COLUMN 6 ÷ COLUMN 5)
34	Fabricated Metal Products	$2.88	86,203	$248,265	$ 42,000	16.9%
35	Machinery, Except Electrical	1.99	131,380	261,446	26,000	9.9
36	Electrical Eqpmt. and Supplies	4.00	178,637	714,548	70,000	9.8
37	Transportation Equipment	1.67	80,524	134,475	25,000	18.6
	TOTALS			$1,358,734	$163,000	12.0%

Task 13: Calculate Market Potentials
(Using Industry Data)

Five Step Approach

This method of calculating market potential for a product is based on correlating company sales with published industry data reflecting relative buying power of various market segments. The resulting index represents an area's share of purchasing strength for a product in terms of use or possible use.

Five Basic Steps

A certain degree of mathematical ability, combined with good judgement, increases the accuracy of this method of calculating potentials. There are five basic steps which must be completed:

Step 1—Gather Market Data
Step 2—Estimate Factors Influencing Market
Step 3—Assign Weights
Step 4—Select Representative Industry Data
Step 5—Calculate Index

Step 1: Gather Market Data

Study the available secondary research materials and review previous sales analyses to obtain the following data:

List of products manufactured and/or distributed in this market.
Key industries having use of particular product (by SIC)—separate list for each product class.
Industry percentages: proportion of plants in each industry having use for particular product.
Industry weights: relative value of each SIC as a portion of the total market; unadjusted for future market conditions; technological advances, etc.

These data should be entered on a Market Analysis Data Form, as shown. For example, from previous findings, it was determined that the product under study is sold primarily to four broad industry groups (i.e.,

SIC 34–37). All other industries comprise less than one percent of the market, and are therefore excluded from calculations. Approximately 40% of the firms in SIC 34 are users of the product. Also, it was found that companies in SIC 34 purchase 16% of all product sales in this category.

Step 2: Estimate Factors Influencing Market

Now study each key industry to estimate whether past relative purchasing requirements will continue in the future or increase or decrease. Consider both internal and external factors. Record data regarding all the below-listed points on the "Factors Affecting the Future Market" form.

Include internal factors such as new products and applications, new and expired patents, significant price changes, new advertising and promotion campaigns, changes in channels of distribution, addition of new sales staff, etc.

Also include external factors such as changes in purchasing patterns of large buyers, government legislation or policies, general business conditions, competitive actions, and wide growth or declines of specific industries, users, or manufacturers.

Step 3: Assign Weights for Key Industries

Values can now be assigned to purchasing requirements of each industry as a proportion of the total market. Based on the determination of factors which affect the future market for a product, each SIC's share of total market can be adjusted.

In the example (ASSIGN WEIGHTS BASED ON MARKET/COMPANY FACTORS form), for SIC 34, the percent of total market was adjusted upward from 16% to 25% to reflect favorable conditions projected in the previous step. All SICs are adjusted, but the total must' add to 100%.

Market Analysis Data Form for (PRODUCT) for (PERIOD COVERED)

METHOD: INDUSTRY DATA - STEP 1

(1) SIC NOS.	(2) KEY INDUSTRY DESCRIPTIONS	(3) PERCENT OF PLANTS WITHIN EACH INDUSTRY THAT USE THIS PRODUCT	(4) PERCENT THIS INDUSTRY IS OF THE TOTAL MARKET (unadjusted weight)
34	Fabricated Metal Products	40	16%
35	Machinery, Except Electrical	10	9
36	Electrical Eqpmt. and Supplies	100	45
37	Transportation Equipment	25	30
	TOTALS		100%

Factors Affecting the Future Market for (PRODUCT)

METHOD: INDUSTRY DATA - STEP 2

(1) SIC NOS. - KEY INDUSTRY DESCRIPTIONS	(2) UPWARD FACTORS	(3) DOWNWARD FACTORS
34 - Fabricated Metal Products	New product applications. Industry use of product increasing.	Patent expires on old model. Competition is using price cuts. Government standards on safety may require product modifications.
35 - Machinery, Except Electrical	New Product applications. Can afford to be more price competitive.	Industry business conditions are declining. Channels of distribution are not satisfied with current profit margin.
36 - Electrical Eqpmt. and Supplies	New product applications. Approved significant increase in promotion budget.	Government standards may be impossible to meet. Competition is offering significant service extras.
37 Transportation Equipment	New Product applications. New channels of distribution with new customer base.	User-industry may be declining. Industry is not very progressive.

Assign Weights Based on Market/Company Factors

METHOD: INDUSTRY DATA - STEP 3

(1) SIC NOS. - KEY INDUSTRY DESCRIPTIONS	(2) PERCENT THIS INDUSTRY IS OF TOTAL MARKET (unadjusted)	(3) PERCENT THIS INDUSTRY IS OF TOTAL MARKET (adjusted)[16]
34 - Fabricated Metal Products	16%	25%
35 - Machinery, Except Electrical	9	12
36 - Electrical Eqpmt. and Supplies	45	35
37 - Transportation Equipment	30	28
TOTALS	100%	100%

[16] The adjustments are made on an arbitrary basis, according to the marketing manager's knowledge and judgement.

Step 4: Select Representative Industry Data

Now select representative industry data against which company sales can be compared. The data must be accurate and complete, as well as current. Some types of industry data are (on a national or regional basis):

Number of plants
Number of production workers
Number of total employees
Value added by manufacture
Value of products shipped
Expenditures for new plant and equipment
Value of materials consumed
Value of fuels and electrical energy consumed

These data can be found in the secondary research sources presented in Section B of this chapter.

Single or Multiple Data

You can use one set of statistical data or two or more sets. The single set method (e.g., number of plants) is the easiest from a statistical standpoint, as well as being less time-consuming. The multiple data method (e.g., number of plants and number of production workers) strives for greater accuracy by using two or more sets of industry data weighted by SIC importance. For simplicity, the remainder of this discussion is based on using a single set of data.[17]

Which Set of Industry Data Should Be Used?

Two sets of data are predominantly used: number of production workers, and value added by manufacture.

[17] The multiple data approach requires the combination of each series into a single series by weighting the importance of each.

Production workers are most commonly employed for measuring the relative importance of various industries as markets for particular products. Theoretically, industrial purchases within each industry vary approximately proportional to the number of production workers employed by each company. Thus, a plant with 4,000 production workers is assumed to purchase about twice the amount of a particular product than a plant with 2,000 workers in the same industry.

Value added is a realistic measure of market activity and therefore of market potentials. Value added by manufacture is determined by subtracting the costs of materials, supplies, packaging, fuel and energy, utilities, and sub-contracted work from the value of shipments. Unfortunately, it is available only every five years from the government's U.S. Census, "Survey of Manufacturers."

In the example (GATHER INDUSTRY DATA form), we have gathered data on the number of workers in a territory (column 2) and in the nation (column 3). The percent of workers employed in the territory for each SIC industry is calculated by dividing column 2 by column 3 and entering the result in column 4. For example, in SIC 34, 6.8% of all workers are employed in New York (86,203 divided by 1,275,902).[18]

Step 5: Calculate Index

Finally, calculate the market potential index for a specific area (Market Potential Calculation—Step 5). In column 1, list the key industries. In column 2, enter the number of production workers in the territory from column 2 of the previous chart. Enter in column 3, the percent of national

---

[18] The data used in this example are taken from U.S. County Business Patterns.

Gather Industry Data for (AREA) for (YEAR)

METHOD: INDUSTRY DATA APPROACH - STEP 4

(1) SIC NOS. - KEY INDUSTRY DESCRIPTION	(2) TERRITORY NUMBER OF WORKERS	(3) TOTAL WORKERS IN U. S.	(4) PERCENT OF NATIONAL WORKERS IN AREA (Column 2 ÷ Column 3)
34 - Fabricated Metal Products	86,203	1,275,902	6.8%
35 - Machinery, Except Electrical	131,380	1,743,531	7.5
36 - Electrical Eqpmt. and Supplies	178,637	1,660,498	10.8
37 - Transportation Equipment	80,524	1,657,990	4.9

Market Potential Calculation for (PRODUCT) for (TERRITORY)

METHOD: INDUSTRY DATA APPROACH - STEP 5

(1) SIC NOS. - KEY INDUSTRY DESCRIPTIONS	(2) NUMBER PRODUCTION WORKERS IN TERRITORY	(3) PERCENT OF NATIONAL WORKERS IN AREA	(4) ADJUSTED PERCENT OF MARKET	(5) WEIGHTED PERCENT TOTAL WORKERS (Column 3 times Column 4 ÷ 100)
34 - Fabricated Metal Products	86,203	6.8%	25%	1.7%
35 - Machinery, Except Electrical	131,380	7.5	12	.9
36 - Electrical Eqpmt. and Supplies	178,637	10.8	35	3.8
37 - Transportation Equipment	80,524	4.9	28	1.4
				————
				7.8

workers based in each area, from column 4 of the previous chart.

In column 4, enter the adjusted percent of market for each industry, as determined in step 3 (see weighting chart, column 3). Now calculate the weighted percent of total workers, and enter the result in column 5 (column 3 times column 4) divided by 100.

In the example for SIC 34, the result is 1.7%. The summation of these weighted percentages for each industry yields the market potential for the territory as a per-cent of the national market potential. Thus, we estimate that the New York market could absorb approximately 7.8% of the volume of this product.

Once territory sales potentials are calculated for all of your sales territories, they can be listed in order of magnitude to determine strong vs. weak areas. This information may then be used as a rational basis for allocating your available sales resources (salesmen, travel budget, time, advertising, publicity, etc.).

Task 14: Calculate Market Potentials (Using a Census)

Uses

This method of estimating sales potentials is most adaptable to industrial products of high dollar value, low volume, concentrated markets, and where sales are made through the company's own sales force or through manufacturers' agents.

Data Needed for Census Approach

The census method requires that information on purchasing requirements be gathered on each plant in the market for your product. The information from each plant is then combined to derive a total market potential figure.

CALCULATE MARKET POTENTIALS

First, list all firms within the market area, including addresses. Now gather data from these plants on:

Plant name and location
Plant size
Type of product produced
Estimated purchases of your product (annual)
Estimate of your company's share of business
List of chief competitors for this business

These data should be recorded on a form which can be easily tabulated. Data should be segregated by market and geographical territory.

How to Collect Data

Data can be collected by making surveys, as explained in Section C, or your salesmen or distributors can be asked to make "guestimates" based on their experience and judgement. The latter approach may yield usable estimates, since salesmen should have an intimate familiarity with the customer's production facilities and operations. On the other hand, salesmen may inject bias, or correspondingly reduce their daily sales efforts if much time must be spent on paperwork, and may not know enough prospects.

Keep Data Current

After adding all estimates of plant purchases, this figure must be periodically checked and updated. Request salesmen or distributors to be alert for new accounts in their territories. Review trade journals and directories to make sure you have included all possible plants. And as a final check, compare your calculated potentials against industry data published in government sources, such as the U.S. Census, "Survey of Manufacturers."

Section E
Make Sales Analysis

Why Make Sales Analyses?

Sales analyses can yield valuable information on marketing factors such as performance of individual products, territories, and salesmen. Basically, such analyses show how the company got where it is today. Specific relationships between sales and other variables can then be identified, and extrapolated into the future. This helps pinpoint strengths and weaknesses in territories, products, salesmen, distributors, and other elements of the selling process.

Sources of Data

Secondary research sources and internal company records are the basic sources of data for making sales analyses. The most important and useful data are your company's order forms, sales, shipping, invoice records and salesmen call reports, warranty cards, etc. These can be used to arrange and relate data, to facilitate comparisons, and reveal strengths, weaknesses, and opportunities. If you're not currently making sales analyses, you should begin now to develop a system for collecting, organizing, and classifying the data needed for this purpose.

Types of Sales Analyses

Sales analyses can be made in four key areas. Each major area and some suggested sub-areas for analysis are listed below:

A. General Sales, Costs, and Profit Analysis 1. Annual sales (dollars or units) 2. Annual net profits 3. Distribution costs 4. Direct selling expenses 5. Seasonal, cyclical, irregular sales 6. Gross margin trends 7. Quotation analysis 8. Average order size (sales ÷ orders)	C. Geographical Sales Analysis 1. By state, city, zip code, etc. 2. Sales territory 3. Individual salesmen 4. Types of customers 5. Product types 6. Sales divided by quotas 7. Total sales/man/day 8. Sales/calls 9. Sales cost analyses
B. Customer Sales Analysis 1. Customer classes 2. New versus old customers 3. SIC of customers 4. Size of customer plants 5. Size of purchases 6. Frequency of purchase 7. Analysis of major customers' buying habits	D. Product Sales Analysis 1. Classes of products 2. Product lines within classes 3. Individual products within lines 4. Product attachments, accessories, repair parts, etc. 5. Packaging modes 6. Pricing analyses

Section Contents

The remainder of this section presents examples of some of the above analyses. Although the examples are not exhaustive, they demonstrate some of the many ways that sales data can be analyzed. The examples include:

Task 15: Make Share of Market Analysis

Types of Breakdowns

The share of market analysis can be made on a national basis or by territories. It can be broken down by "all customers," or can be segregated by industry, size of customer, or other ways that will suit your needs.

How to Calculate

To illustrate how this analysis is made, see the "Share of Each Industry Segment by SIC" form. The form analyzes major industries involved in a company's penetration of the market in terms of both small and large (over 500 workers) plants, and within various SICs.

In column 1, relevant SICs are listed. Columns 2 and 3 list the number of plants that have bought the company's products. Column 2 lists all plants, and column 3 lists only those plants having more than 500 workers (arbitrarily considered to be large plants). This information was taken directly from the company's sales records.

The total number of plants in the market

Share of Each Industry Segment by SIC

(1) SIC NOS. - KEY INDUSTRY DESCRIPTIONS	NUMBER OF PLANTS SOLD		NUMBER OF PLANTS IN MARKET		PERCENT OF MARKET SOLD	
	(2) ALL PLANTS	(3) PLANTS HAVING OVER 500 WORKERS	(4) ALL PLANTS	(5) PLANTS HAVING OVER 500 WORKERS	(6) ALL PLANTS (Column 2 ÷ Column 4)	(7) PLANTS HAVING OVER 500 WORKERS (Column 3 ÷ Column 5)
34 - Fabricated Metal Products	4,100	12	25,875	328	15.8%	3.7%
35 - Machinery, Except Electrical	3,605	20	36,778	612	9.8	3.3
36 - Electrical Equipment and Supplies	400	8	11,315	659	3.5	1.2
37 - Transportation Equipment	800	24	7,835	457	10.2	5.3

(column 4), and those employing more than 500 workers (column 5), are obtained from secondary data sources (in this case the data might be obtained from "U.S. County Business Patterns").

Then the percent of total market sold (column 6) is computed by dividing column 2 by column 4. The percent of market sold in the over 500 workers category (column 7) is determined by dividing column 3 by column 5. In each case, the figures have been multiplied by 100 to express them as percentages.

The entries in columns 6 and 7 show that this company is more successful in selling to smaller companies, and that it received a much smaller share of the market in selling to firms with 500 or more employees. Based on this knowledge, a company can direct its promotional and sales campaigns toward the larger market, which offers a source of untapped potential.

Task 16: Make Quotation Analysis

Purpose of Quotation Analysis

This tool is for companies that submit competitive bids (quotations) which may or may not be accepted by a prospective customer. Analysis of the successful versus unsuccessful quotations, by product and type of customer, can yield information that can be used in improving a company's competitive posture. The goal is to achieve a higher success ratio in competitive bidding.

How to Conduct

Quotations may be classified by customer industries, company size, new vs. old accounts, geography, product model, and so forth. Columns 2 and 3 on the "Quotation Analysis" form can be filled in from past quotation records. This shows the number of firms quoted and the number sold. Then divide column 3 by column 2 to determine the success ratio (column 4). This pinpoints those industries, territories, products, etc., in which you are not closing your sales effectively.

In the example by industry, the company is not performing as well in SIC 34 as it is in other SIC areas. Conversely, the success ratio in SIC 37 far exceeds other industrial customers.

It can be seen that this company does well in closing sales to smaller companies, but has some difficulty in closing sales to larger ones.

The company does well in submitting quotes to previous customers, but only half as well when submitting quotes to new prospects.

From a territorial standpoint, the firm appears to have a great deal of success in the East, but very little success in the South.

Finally, the company is very successful in selling unequipped models, but the success ratio decreases rapidly when extra equipment is added.

Each of these examples highlights areas where more research should be done to identify the reasons for poor vs. good performance. For example, take the level of equipment included on any model. It appears that as the company adds new accessories, the success ratio decreases. This fact can now be analyzed to determine reasons for the decrease. Surveys of non-buyers and buyers can be made. It might turn out that the pricing structure on accessories is far above that of the competition. Ways could then be explored to become more competitive in supplying and pricing accessory equipment.

Quotation Analysis

	(1) ANALYSIS CATEGORIES	(2) NUMBER QUOTED	(3) NUMBER SOLD	(4) SUCCESS RATIO (column 3 ÷ column 2)
A.	By SIC			
	No. 34 - Fab. Metal Prods	160	10	6.3%
	No. 35 - Mchy., Ex. Elect.	180	42	23.3
	No. 36 - Elect. Equip. & Supplies	200	28	14.0
	No. 37 - Transp. Equip.	60	20	33.0
	No. _____			
	No. _____			
	No. _____			
	No. _____			
B.	By Size of Customer's Company (employees)			
	1 - 49	180	50	27.8%
	50 - 99	150	25	16.7
	100 - 499	110	15	13.6
	500 - 999	70	6	8.6
	1,000 - 4,999	60	3	5.0
	5,000 and up	30	1	3.3
C.	New vs. Old Customers			
	New Customers	210	20	9.5%
	Previous customers	390	80	20.5
D.	Territory			
	1. North	130	20	15.4%
	2. South	90	5	5.6
	3. East	240	60	25.0
	4. West	140	15	10.7
	5. _____			
	6. _____			
	7. _____			
	8. _____			
E.	Product models			
	1. Unequipped	300	70	23.3%
	2. Partially equipped	180	20	11.1
	3. Fully Equipped	120	10	8.3
	4. _____			
	5. _____			

Task 17: Make Source of Sales Analysis

Usefulness of Source of Sales Analysis

Source of sales analyses allows a company to pinpoint the *best* sources of sales so it can direct more of its efforts toward developing leads from those sources. Conversely, analysis of the poor sales sources may uncover reasons that are within the power of the company to correct, and thus expand its sales base.

How to Conduct

To make a source of sales analysis, add to your sales order system an entry to show how each sale originated. For example, did the sale originate from an advertising lead, inquiry at a trade show, inquiry from articles about your company in the trade press, same application for present customers, new application, salesman contact, referral from present customer, or a combination of sources?

The source of sales form can be used to analyze the source of each sale. For any desired time period (e.g., a month, year, etc.), record the name and address of each customer sold, the date sold, and the amount sold (columns 1 through 3). Under column 4, place a check mark under the appropriate source of sale. Then, add the number of check marks in each column to determine where the greatest portion of sales are originated.

In the example, sales of a company are recorded for the first quarter of a year. Totals show that most sales came from present customers—same applications, and from a recently held trade show at which the company exhibited. The company can now investigate ways to increase leads in areas previously not productive and to increase leads from currently productive sources.

Source of Sales Analysis for (PERIOD)

(1) CUSTOMER AND LOCATION	(2) DATE SOLD	(3) AMOUNT SOLD	(4) SOURCE OF SALE						
			ADVG. LEAD	TRADE SHOW INQUIRY	PUBLICITY INQUIRY	PRES. CUSTOMER SAME APPLICATION	PRES. CUSTOMER NEW APPLICATION	NEW CUSTOMER SALESMAN CONTACT	REFERRAL FROM PRESENT CUSTOMER
Martin Tools, Calif.	1/15/73	$20,000				X			
ABC Fasteners, Calif.	1/20/73	15,000			X				
Diamond Mfg., Wash.	1/22/73	10,000	X						
Raymond, Inc., Oregon	1/26/73	12,000		X					
Andrews Bros., Calif.	1/28/73	15,000		X					
Johnson Tools, Arizona	1/31/73	18,000		X					
Barton Indus., Calif.	2/12/73	20,000					X		
Air Jet Machines, Nev.	2/20/73	6,000						X	
Ayer Machinery, Texas	2/28/73	12,000							X
Stannick Tool Co., Nev.	3/6/73	8,000	X						
Wise Industries, Calif.	3/10/73	14,000			X				
Smith Tool, Calif.	3/21/73	18,000				X			
Tyler Tool Co., Texas	3/28/73	20,000				X			
TOTALS	1st Qtr 1973		2	3	2	3	1	1	1

Marketing Research Reference Guide

General Reference Sources

Data Sources for Business and Market Analysis, The Scarecrow Press, Inc., 52 Liberty St., Box 656, Metuchen, NJ 08840. A guide to marketing information on a variety of business areas. It includes references to periodicals, trade associations, business firms, and other key sources.

Dun & Bradstreet Directories, Dun & Bradstreet, Inc., 99 Church St., New York, NY 10007. Annual lists of U.S. firms, including information on products, annual sales, number of employees, names, and titles of 75,000 key executives. Listing is cross-referenced by company name and product classification.

Encyclopedia of Business Information Sources, Gale Research Co., 700 Book Tower, Detroit, MI 48226. Lists up-to-date information sources on a variety of business problems. It includes references to encyclopedias, handbooks, bibliographies, periodicals, directories, and other useful sources.

Foreign Commerce Handbook, Chamber of Commerce of the United States, 1615 H Street, N.W., Washington, DC 20006. Lists over 100 local Chambers of Commerce in the United States which maintain departments, bureaus, and so forth, of foreign trade, and have compiled lists of importers and exporters in their area.

Fortune Plant and Product Directory Of The 1,000 Largest U.S. Industrial Corporations, Fortune, Time & Life Building, New York, NY 10020. An annual list of the 1,000 largest U.S. industrial companies, with addresses, sales, assets, profits, employment, and products.

Guide To Reference Books, American Library Assoc., 50 E. Huron St., Chicago, IL 60611. Lists reference books for all major fields of study, including bibliographies, government documents, dissertations, directories, and so forth.

How To Use The Business Library, H. Webster Johnson, South-Western Publishing Co., 5701 Madison Rd., Cincinnati, OH 45227.

Moody's Industrial Manual, Moody's Investor Service, 99 Church St., New York, NY 10007. An annual publication, with semi-weekly up-dates describing the operations, plants, subsidiaries, officers, directors, comparative income statements, long-term earnings record, and other financial and operating data on domestic and foreign industrial companies. Similar publications are also available on banking, utilities, government, and transportation.

Poor's Register Of Corporations, Directors & Executives, Standard & Poor's Corp., 345 Hudson St., New York, NY 10014. A multivolume service listing information on U.S. and Canadian corporations and key executives. Lists over 30,000 companies with addresses, products, services, sales, number of employees, and standard industrial classification. Lists over 260,000 prospects, including job titles, business addresses, and telephone numbers of 70,000 top-level officers and directors.

Sources Of Business Information, University of California Press, 2223 Fulton St., Berkeley, CA 94720. Contains 300 pages of references to management, foreign trade, marketing, and related categories.

Statistics Sources, Gale Research Co., 700 Book Tower, Detroit, MI 48226. A guide to data on industrial, business, social, financial, and educational institutions. It includes a summary of all statistical sources.

Sweet's Catalog, Sweet's Catalog Service, Division of F. W. Dodge Corp., 330 W. 42nd St., New York, NY 10036. An annual file of manufacturer's catalogs, including names, products, trade names, and market data for the following areas: architectural; light construction; industrial construction; plant engineering; metalworking equipment; and product design.

Thomas Register Of American Manufacturers, Thomas Register Co., 461 Eighth Ave., New York, NY 10001. Lists thousands of manufacturers by product-line, size, and geographical location.

Yellow Pages Classified Telephone Directory, lists local manufacturers and service firms. Available from local telephone companies, or from Leonard Yellow Pages Library, Inc., 207 W. Gregory Blvd., Kansas City, MO 64114. (Latter company furnishes exact photocopies of Yellow Pages in any city for any product or service category.)

Sources of Local and State Information

Directory Of Federal Statistics For States, Government Printing Office, Washington, DC 20402. Describes many sources of statistics for counties, metropolitan areas, cities, and other geographic units; arranged by subject matter.

The Book Of The States, The Council of State Governments, Ironworks Pike, Lexington, KY 40505. Authoritative guide to state government structure and functions, including officials and sources of state statistical data.

Sources Of State Information & State Industrial Directories, Chamber of Commerce of the United States, 1615 H St., N.W., Washington, DC 20006. Lists public and private agencies which supply information about their states; lists manufacturers' directories.

World-Wide Chamber Of Commerce Directory, Johnson Publishing Co., Inc., P.O. Box 455, 8th & Van Buren, Loveland, CO 80537. Lists domestic and foreign chambers of commerce, giving executives, addresses, and phone numbers.

References to Publishers and Magazines

N. W. Ayer & Son's Directory Of Newspapers & Periodicals, N. W. Ayer & Son, Inc., West Washington Square, Philadelphia, PA 19106.

Standard Rate & Data Service: Business Publication Rates And Data, Standard Rate & Data Service, Inc., 5201 Old Orchard Rd., Skokie, IL 60076.

The Standard Periodical Directory, Oxbridge Publishing Co., Inc., 420 Lexington Ave., New York, NY 10017

Ulrich's International Periodicals Directory, R. R. Bowker Co., 1180 Avenue of the Americas, New York, NY 10036.

Indexes to Articles

Applied Sciences & Technology Index, H. W. Wilson Co., 950 University Ave., Bronx, NY 10452 (index to approximately 225 technical publications).

Business Periodicals Index, H. W. Wilson Co., 950 University Avenue, Bronx, NY 10452 (index to contents of over 150 business and financial publications).

F&S Index Of Corporations & Industries, Predicasts, Inc., 200 University Circle, Research Center, 11001 Cedar Ave., Cleveland, OH 44106 (indexes business and financial news from over 1,000 publications).

Reader's Guide To Periodical Literature, H. W. Wilson Co., 950 University Ave., Bronx, NY 10452 (index to contents of over 200 U.S. consumer and non-technical publications, including some business publications).

Wall Street Journal Index, Dow Jones Books, Box 300, Princeton, NJ 08540 (indexes corporate and financial news appearing in the *Wall Street Journal*).

Guides to Trade Associations

Directory Of British Associations, Gale Research Co., 2200 Book Tower, Detroit, MI 48226. Has nearly 8,000 entries on associations in Britain and Ireland.

Directory Of European Associations, Gale Research Co., 2200 Book Tower, Detroit, MI 48226. Lists over 7,000 entries on associations in every nation of eastern and western Europe.

Encyclopedia Of Associations, Gale Research Co., 2200 Book Tower, Detroit, MI 48226. A biannual list of over 16,000 national and regional associations, their addresses, officials, number of members and staff, services, and materials made available.

National Trade And Professional Associations Of The U.S., B. Klein Publications, Inc., Box 8503, Coral Springs, FL 33065. Annual list of about 4,500 national associations, executives, addresses, number of members and staff, and materials made available.

National Trade And Professional Associations Of The U.S., Columbia Books, Inc., Suite 300, 917 15th St., N.W., Washington, DC 20005. Annual list of about 4,300 national associations, addresses, key executives, number of members and staff, and materials made available.

Directories to Directories

American Guide To Business Directories, Public Affairs Press, 419 New Jersey Ave., S.E., Washington, DC 20003.

American Guide To Directories, Prentice-Hall, Inc., Englewood Cliffs, NJ 07632. Contains 2,200 titles in 400 categories.

Bulletin Of The Public Affairs Information Service, Public Affairs Information Service, 11 W. 40th St., New York, NY 10018. Lists all kinds of directories from all over the world giving title, price, publisher, and description of contents.

Guide To American Directories, B. Klein & Co., Box 8503, Coral Springs, FL 33065. Lists virtually every kind of industrial and professional directory in the United States and foreign countries, including 5,000 directories in 300 categories.

Sources Of State Information And State Industrial Directories, State Chamber of Commerce Department, Chamber of Commerce of the United States, 1615 H St., N.W., Washington, DC 20006. Lists information on state and regional directories published by state agencies and private organizations, including title, date of issue, name of sponsoring organization, price, and types of data contained.

Trade Directories Of The World, Croner Publications, 211–03 Jamaica Ave., Queens Village, NY 11429. Lists business directories covering trades in the United States and foreign countries.

Directories to Research Organizations

Advertising Research Foundation Directory Of Members, Advertising Research Foundation, Inc., 3 East 54th St., New York, NY 10022.

Bradford's Directory Of Marketing Research Agencies & Management Consultants In The U.S. & The World, Bradford's Directory of Marketing Research Agencies, P. O. Box 276, Fairfax, VA 22030.

Handbook Of Commercial & Financial Information Services, Special Libraries Assoc., 235 Park Ave., South, New York, NY 10003.

International Directory Of Marketing Research Houses & Services, American Marketing Assoc., Inc., 527 Madison Ave., New York, NY 10022.

Marketing Research Trade Association Directory Of Members, P. O. Box 1415, Grand Central Station, New York, NY 10017.

Selected Reference Sources on Marketing Research

General Information

A Basic Bibliography On Marketing Research, Hugh G. Wales and Robert Ferber. American Marketing Assoc., 222 S. Riverside Plaza, Chicago IL 60606.

A Manager's Guide To Marketing Research, by Paul E. Green and Donald E. Frank, John Wiley & Sons, Inc., 605 Third Ave., New York, NY 10017.

Basic Methods Of Marketing Research, by J. H. Lorie and H. V. Roberts, McGraw-Hill Book Co., Inc., 1221 Avenue of the Americas, New York, NY 10036.

Design Of Research Investigations, American Marketing Assoc., 222 S. Riverside Plaza, Chicago, IL 60606.

Marketing And Business Research, by Myron Heidingsfield, et al, Holt, Rinehart and Winston, Inc., 383 Madison Ave., New York, NY 10017.

Marketing Problem Definition, American Marketing Assoc., 222 S. Riverside Plaza, Chicago, IL 60606.

Marketing Research, by Richard D. Crisp, McGraw-Hill Book Co., Inc., 1221 Avenue of the Americas, New York, NY 10020.

Marketing Research, by Robert Buzzell, Donald Cox, and Rex Brown, McGraw-Hill Book Co., Inc., 1221 Avenue of the Americas, New York, NY 10020.

Marketing Research: A Management Overview, by Evelyn Konrad and Rod Erickson, American Management Assoc., Inc., 135 W. 50th St., New York, NY 10020.

Research For Marketing Decisions, by Paul E. Green and Donald S. Tull, Prentice-Hall, Inc., Englewood Cliffs, NJ 07631.

Research Methods In Economics And Business, by Robert Ferber and P. J. Verdoorn, Macmillan Co., Inc., 60 Fifth Ave., New York, NY 10011.

Research Your Own Industrial Market, Marketing Guidelines, Inc., Park Tower Building, 5200 South Yale, Tulsa, OK 74135.

Analysis, Processing, Tabulation, etc.

Elementary Statistical Methods: As Applied To Business And Economic Data, by William A. Neiswanger, Macmillan Co., Inc., 60 Fifth Ave., New York, NY 10011.

How To Chart, by Walter E. Weld, Codex Book Co., Inc., 74 Broadway, Norwood, MA 02062.

How To Read Statistics, by I. R. Vesselo, D. Van Nostrand Co., Inc., Princeton, NJ 08540.

Quantitative Techniques In Marketing Analysis: Text And Readings, by Ronald E. Frank, et al, Richard D. Irwin, Inc., 1818 Ridge Rd., Homewood, IL 60430.

Statistical Methods, College Outline Series No. 27, by Herbert Arkin and Raymond R. Colton, Barnes and Noble, 105 Fifth Ave., New York, NY 10003.

Tabulation: Elements Of Planning And Techniques, by John A. Coleman, E. Murray and C. H. Hudson, American Marketing Assoc., 222 S. Riverside Plaza, Chicago, IL 60606.

Forecasting and Potentials

Business Forecasting Methods, by Harry D. Wolfe, Holt, Rinehart and Winston, Inc., 383 Madison Ave., New York, NY 10017.

Forecasting Sales, Business Policy Study No. 106, The Conference Board, 845 Third Ave., New York, NY 10022.

Guidelist For Marketing Research And Economic Forecasting, by Robert N. Carpenter, American Management Assoc., Inc., 135 W. 50th St., New York, NY 10020.

Market And Sales Potentials, by Francis E. Hummel, The Ronald Press Co., 15 E. 26th St., New York, NY 10010.

Practical Techniques For Sales Forecasting, by Robert S. Reichard, McGraw-Hill Book Co., Inc., 1221 Avenue of the Americas, New York, NY 10020.

Sales Forecasting: Uses, Techniques And Trends (Special Report No. 16), American Management Assoc., 135 W. 50th St., New York, NY 10020.

Interviewing

Interviewing Costs In Survey Research, by Charles S. Mayer, Bureau of Business Research, Graduate School of Business Administration, University of Michigan, Ann Arbor, MI 48103.

Questionnaires

Professional Mail Surveys, by Paul L. Erdos, McGraw-Hill Book Co., 1221 Avenue of the Americas, New York, NY 10020.

Questionnaire Design And Attitude Measurement, by A. N. Oppenheim, Basic Books, Inc., 10 East 53rd St., New York, NY 10017.

The Art of Asking Questions, by Stanley L. Payne, Princeton University Press, Princeton, NJ 08540.

Report Writing

Business Research And Report Writing, by Robert L. Shurter, 1965, McGraw-Hill Book Co., 1221 Avenue of the Americas, New York, NY 10020.

"For Better Business Writing," by John S. Fielden, *Harvard Business Review*, January–February 1965, pp. 164–72, Harvard Business Review, Boston, MA 02163.

"The Writing Of Readable Research Reports," by Stewart H. Britt, *Journal of Marketing Research*, May 1971, pp. 262–66, American Marketing Assoc., 222 S. Riverside Plaza, Chicago, IL 60606.

"What Do You Mean I Can't Write," by John S. Fielden, *Harvard Business Review*, May–June 1964, pp. 144–56, Harvard Business Review, Boston, MA 02163.

Sampling

Sampling, A Quick Reliable Guide To Practical Statistics, by Morris J. Slonim, Simon & Schuster, 630 Fifth Ave., New York, NY 10022.

Sampling In Marketing Research, American Marketing Assoc., 222 S. Riverside Plaza, Chicago, IL 60606.

Survey Sampling, by Leslie Kish, John Wiley & Sons, Inc., 605 Third Ave., New York, NY 10017.

Selecting and Using Research Firms

Criteria To Assist Users Of Marketing, by Joseph C. Bevis, et al, American Marketing Assoc., 222 S. Riverside Plaza, Chicago, IL 60606.

"Evaluating The Quality Of Marketing Research Contractors," by Charles S. Mayer, *Journal of Marketing*, May 1967, pp. 134–41, American Marketing Assoc., 222 S. Riverside Plaza, Chicago, IL 60606.

Selecting Marketing Research Services, by William C. Gordon, Jr., Small Business Administration, nearest office.

Using Marketing Consultants And Research Agencies, *Studies In Business Policy*, S.B.P. 120, Conference Board, 845 Third Ave., New York, NY 10022.

Standard Industrial Classification System

"Relating Company Markets To SIC," *Journal of Marketing*, April 1963, American Marketing Assoc., 222 S. Riverside Plaza, Chicago, IL 60606.

Standard Industrial Classification For Effective Marketing Analysis, Marketing Science Institute, 14 Story St., Cambridge, MA 02138.

CHAPTER II

Marketing Planning

Introduction

What Is the Marketing Plan?

The marketing plan identifies the most promising business opportunities for the company. It outlines how to successfully penetrate, capture and maintain desired positions in identified markets. Consequently, the marketing plan is the foundation on which the company's other operating plans are built. It defines the goals, principles, procedures, and methods that determine your company's future. It is effective only to the degree that it involves a commitment by all who must contribute to its success, from president to shipping clerk, and to the degree that it is kept abreast of the ever-changing marketing environment. Planning is a continuous process—not a one-shot activity.

The marketing plan is also a communication tool which integrates all elements of the marketing mix—sales, advertising, sales promotion, public relations, trade shows, etc.—into a single comprehensive program for coordinated action at all marketing levels. The plan specifies by product, market and region, who will do what, where, when, and how, to accomplish the company's goals in the most efficient manner.

Benefits of the Plan

In addition, the marketing plan:

Stimulates thinking to make better use of company resources

Assigns responsibilities and schedules work

Coordinates and unifies efforts

Facilitates control and evaluation of results of all activities

Creates awareness of obstacles to overcome

Identifies marketing opportunities

Provides an authentic marketing information source for current and future reference

Facilitates progressive advancement toward a company's goals

Basic Requirements

A marketing plan should be:

Simple—easy to understand
Clear—precise and detailed to avoid confusion
Practical—realistic in application and goals attainment
Flexible—adaptable to change
Complete—covers all significant marketing factors
Workable—identifies responsibilities

Tasks of Marketing Planning

You can develop your marketing plan by accomplishing the tasks shown in the flow chart. These tasks are described in this chapter, together with procedures for developing your own marketing plan tailored to suit your special needs.

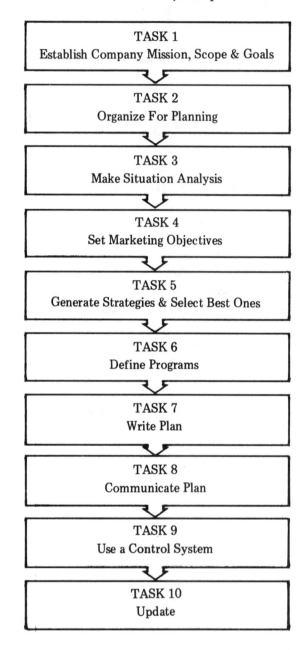

TASK 1
Establish Company Mission, Scope & Goals

TASK 2
Organize For Planning

TASK 3
Make Situation Analysis

TASK 4
Set Marketing Objectives

TASK 5
Generate Strategies & Select Best Ones

TASK 6
Define Programs

TASK 7
Write Plan

TASK 8
Communicate Plan

TASK 9
Use a Control System

TASK 10
Update

Task 1: Establish Company Mission, Scope and Goals

Direction for Marketing Plan

The direction for developing a marketing plan is set by the company's mission, scope and goals. These are established by top man-agement and communicated throughout the company's marketing organization and other organizations that will contribute, support and participate.

Mission and Scope

In essence, mission and scope refer to the nature of the company's product-lines and activities in terms of its ability to serve its markets. This should answer the basic questions: "What business are we in?" and, "What markets should we address?" Also included are future growth and profit opportunities, guidelines and policies for planning, and current and planned levels of resources (e.g., materials, skills, technologies, productivity, and finances).

Goals

Goals are the specific desired results of the company operating plan. The plan is supported by marketing strategies, and by programs, both of which have specific objectives. Reaching your marketing objectives will enable the company to reach its corporate goals. Whenever possible, goals should be defined in quantitative terms, so progress toward them can be measured. Goals should be set high enough to motivate the "doers" to accomplish them successfully. At the same time, the goals must be attainable. There are dollar goals and non-dollar goals.

The only valid dollar goals are those which result in a direct contribution to profit. However, profit can be stated in different ways and depends on the time frame—short, or long-term. Dollar goals are specific short or long-term corporate financial aims (overall, by product-line, or by market), such as profit (dollar earnings), volume and growth of sales, return-on-sales (ROS), return-on-investment (ROI), return-on-assets (ROA), earnings per share of common stock, working capital, inventory turnover, and backlog of orders.

Although many marketeers refer to the following types of statements as goals, they are really strategies which can be employed to reach stated dollar goals.

Develop company image (reputation as a "leader in the field" for "know-how," etc.).
Attain desired standing in specific markets.
Strive for innovation in certain fields.
Support community programs and win public approval.

Task 2: Organize for Planning

Ways to Organize for Planning

There are several ways to organize for marketing planning, depending primarily on company size and capabilities. In large companies, responsibility for planning is often shared among several persons, including the general manager, marketing managers, product managers, marketing planners, regional sales managers, controllers, line managers, and functional staff. In smaller companies, the marketing planning function may be performed by the president, marketing/sales vice-president, controller, sales manager, and a small staff group. Both cases involve coordination with many groups throughout the company and within the marketing department. In any case, the key marketing executive normally is responsible for coordinating and integrating all inputs to the plan. However, as company size increases, the executive may assign this responsibility to a subordinate or to a special planning group.

One approach to planning is through a committee comprised of key corporate and division executives. This assures top management involvement, but may suffer from deficiencies of the committee approach. Another approach is to form a corporate team with the marketing executive, planning director, controller, and individual division managers meeting periodically and dividing up planning activities. A very effective ar-

Responsibilities—Calendar for Marketing Planning

Date Due	Date Completed	Planning Activities	Department Responsible	Person Responsible	Assistance From
		1. Establish company mission, scope, goals and policies.	President - top management		Director of Planning
		2. Establish planning guidelines, corporate plan inputs, and performance standards.	Corporate Director of Planning		Marketing Planning
		3. Perform situation analyses:			
		a. Audit company resources	Marketing Research		Director of Planning, Line & Staff Depts.
		b. Performance history over past 5 years	Marketing Research		Controller
		c. Current position vs. industry	Marketing Research		Director of Planning, Line & Staff Depts.
		d. Current position vs. previous year's objectives	Marketing Research		Director of Planning, Line & Staff Depts.
		e. Current position and forecasts of technology, competition, industry trends, user-industry, market and company ($ and units), and prices	Marketing Research		Sales, Engineering, Controller
		f. Market profile (needs, wants and attitudes)	Marketing Research		Sales, Public Relations
		g. Applicable economic, political and social trends	Marketing Research		Economic Research, Top Management
		h. Overall and detailed forecasts of company sales, expenses, profit, variances and trends (to maintain or increase market share)	Marketing Research		Marketing Administration, Controller, Advertising, Sales
		i. Product and line volume - profit-investment forecasts	Marketing Research		Director of Planning, Product Line Managers, Controller
		4. Combine above situation analysis data from marketing research, product managers, and functional departments to arrive at opportunity-goal-strategy alternatives.	Marketing Director		Marketing Research, Marketing Planning
		5. Select objectives - strategy mix and forward to - product, market and functional managers.	Marketing Director		Marketing Research, Top Management

Task	Responsible	Support
6. Prepare preliminary program plans:		Marketing Planning, Accounting, Marketing Team
a. Sales Plan	Sales V.P./Manager	
b. Service Plan	Service Manager	
c. Promotion/advertising (communications)	Advertising/Promotion Manager	
d. Production	Production Manager	
e. Pricing	Marketing Director	
f. Distribution	Marketing Director	
7. Review plans for adequacy of goals and feasibility.	Marketing Director	Marketing Research
8. Consolidate preliminary plans into a master plan and review with top management.	Marketing Planning, Marketing Director	Director of Planning, Marketing Research
9. Segregate sales plans and send to appropriate field staff for implementation planning (assignment by man, product and so on).	Field Sales	Marketing Planning
10. Develop complementary programs:		Marketing Director
a. Marketing Research	Marketing Research	
b. Training	Training Director	
c. Product Planning & Development	Engineering/Product Development	
d. Acquisitions/mergers	Controller	
e. Plant/facilities expansion	Logistics/Plant Manager	
11. Combine all inputs into a unified plan:	Marketing Planning	Director of Planning
a. Review	Marketing Team	Top Management
b. Update master plan and schedule	Marketing Planning	Marketing Research
c. Prepare sales & expense budgets (by product region)	Sales Manager	Accounting
d. Prepare Proforma P&L's	Controller	
12. Final review, evaluation and adjustment of plan.	Marketing Director / Top Management	Marketing Planning / Marketing Planning
13. Transmit plan to those responsible for implementation.	Marketing Director	Marketing Planning
14. Review and update plan at least quarterly.	All	All

rangement is to have a permanent or ad hoc marketing planning staff reporting to the key marketing executive. This group coordinates the efforts of all departments in developing a fully integrated plan.

Planning Activity Form

The form entitled "Responsibilities-Calendar for Marketing Planning," shows the planning activities to be accomplished, the department and person having primary responsibility for completing each activity, and those departments which support the groups having primary responsibility. If your company does not have departments corresponding to those shown, the responsibility can be given to that person or company group normally performing these activities. For example, if your marketing planner normally performs marketing research, he

could be given the marketing research responsibilities shown on the chart.

Each person assigned to a planning activity should agree on a due date for completing the action for which he is responsible. Write the names of the responsible persons and the due dates in the columns provided on the form. All inputs are submitted to the responsible coordinator for integration. The formal assignments of responsibility should be confirmed by the vice-president, marketing, or the senior marketing individual.

Be sure to coordinate the marketing planning activities with the planning activities of other departments over which you have no control, and with corporate planning. This insures that the interests and limitations of all departments are adequately provided for in the plan, without which the plan cannot succeed. In other words, make sure you keep all participants informed on what's going on and the progress made.

Task 3: Make Situation Analysis

What Does Situation Analysis Tell You?

The situation analysis provides you with the facts needed for planning. It does this by answering some basic questions such as:

Who are your customers (present and prospective), and where are they? What are their problems, needs and wants?

What benefits can your company provide these customers that they can't obtain elsewhere?

Where are you now and where do you want to be "X" years from now?

Why do you want to be there?

What problems must be overcome to get there?

Are your present plans and strategies suitable to get there?

Who are your major competitors? What is your assessment of their apparent goals and strategies relative to their product characteristics? Pricing? Distribution?

Service? Communication with their customers and other publics? Strengths? Weaknesses?

When you have answered these questions, you will be in a better position to set your preliminary marketing objectives—or to revise your present ones.

How to Do It

The situation analysis can be performed by your marketing research staff and/or by reference to Chapter I—Marketing Research, of this book. Forms and guidelines are provided in the marketing research chapter to help you accomplish most of the items listed under "situation analysis" in the "Planning Calendar" (see Task 2). Other situation analysis tasks can be completed by working with departments outside of marketing, as well as with your dealers, distributors, agents, customers, trade press, trade associations, research firms, and advertising agency.

Unless you have a systematic way to accumulate and file all this information, you will drown in details. According to the volume of information you expect to get, you can use a three-ring binder, with index tabs for each category of information, or you can accumulate information in file folders in a filing cabinet. In either case, the key to being able to retrieve information quickly is to use a detailed indexing system.

Task 4: Set Marketing Objectives

What Are Your Objectives?

After senior management has defined corporate goals and a situation analysis has been made, the marketing executive can set his objectives. Objectives provide targets for direction and guidance of marketing strategies. This means: what company profile do you want next year and where do you want to go in terms of all marketing criteria and other considerations? Marketing objectives are actually time-phased sub-goals for achieving overall company goals.

In setting marketing objectives, each must be tested by asking yourself if it will serve the best interests of the company as a whole. This will avoid the pitfall of having an objective that might be ideal from a marketing viewpoint, but which could be contrary to the best interests of one or more other departments. For example, a large, diversified inventory might suit your marketing goals but accomplishing it could create production and financial problems. Each department's objectives should, therefore, be coordinated with the other departments before submitting them for management approval. All objectives should be set within the framework of your situation analysis. Specific emphasis should be given to the marketing environment, company capabilities and market opportunities.

A word of caution—one man's objective is another's strategy, and yet another's program. What you, as marketing manager may consider a *program* may be the *objective* of the sales group. An objective in a given marketing situation may be a strategy in another; e.g., increasing sales penetration may be an objective in one case, but a strategy for accomplishing an objective under different circumstances. To determine whether a concept is a goal, an objective, a strategy, or a program, one must test it in relation to other parts of the overall plan and to the plan as a whole. In any case, all objectives must be consistent with each other and with related strategies. Each objective should be both a catalyst and a compass to continued growth.

Criteria for Objectives

Objectives should be results-oriented, measurable, realistic (attainable), specific (clear), acceptable by all departments, flexible, consistent with each other, and challenging.

Think in Terms of Results

If your objectives satisfy these criteria, you are more likely to think in terms of what, when, who, where, how, and why. This helps make your planning results-oriented. However, don't consider a result, per se, as an objective. For example, you might need more employees and facilities if sales volume requires increased capacity; but increased capacity is not an objective. Feeding a horse more hay won't necessarily make him run faster, and you may make him ill.

Examples of Objectives

Here are a few examples of specific workable marketing objectives for each major marketing criterion. They are not listed in order of importance. Adapt and expand the list to meet your company's particular situation.

Sales Productivity-Volume

Increase the number of customers ___%
by December 31, 19__.

Increase penetration into a specific market with existing products by ___% by
December 31, 19__.

Increase sales volume of product X by
___% in selected regions, districts,
and territories by specific dates.

Attain sales performance goals on calls per
man, orders per call, volume per order,
expense per call, calls per day, etc., by
given amounts by specific dates.

Profitability

Increase overall return on investment by
___% for the next fiscal year.

Increase profit rate for key regions, districts, and territories by ___%, by a
specific date.

Market Share

Increase by ___%, market share in "X"
market by December 31, 19__.

Attain market share sub-goals for regions,
districts, and territories by June 30,
19__.

Distribution

Establish ___ new distributors in specific
geographic regions by December 31,
19__.

Advertising/Promotion

Increase awareness of company products
among key purchase influences in specific new markets by ___% by December 31, 19__.

Develop high quality inquiries at
$___/inquiry for company products.

Product Development

Introduce ___ new products to fill out
product-line offering by specific dates.

Pricing

Prices should be competitive (within 5%
of primary competitors) and yield a
minimum unit contribution to profit of
___%.

Other Objectives

Objectives also must be set for manpower
development and training, margins,
budget adherence, customer relations,
and your service program.

Task 5: Generate Strategies and Select Best One

Marketing Strategies

In its broadest sense, a strategy is a complete plan of exactly how you would make
the best use of your resources to achieve a
goal. In marketing there may be so many
strategies—considering those available to
you as well as to your competitors—that including all of them in your approach would
be impractical. You can, however, narrow
the strategic alternatives by considering only
those that are legal, socially acceptable, and
that offer the greatest probability of success
in achieving a goal. Furthermore, all strategies should be consistent with each other
and with the objectives they are intended to
implement.

Marketing strategy consists of policies,
procedures, and programs relative to product characteristics, pricing, service, and
communication with your customers and
other concerned individuals.

Policies, Procedures and Programs

A policy is a broad statement that defines
a course of action or a principle to use in
choosing a course of action. Policies usually

involve self-imposed restrictions that tend to channel action along certain lines. A *procedure* is a "how-to-do-it" description for accomplishing an action. A *program* is a comprehensive specification of the who, what, where, when, and how elements of the resources needed for achieving a specific goal; because every program has a price tag, it can be listed as a line item of a budget.

Statements of policies, procedures, and programs should be restrictive enough to preclude undesirable consequences, yet flexible enough to allow creative specialists to work effectively.

Generate Strategies

Strategies can originate from many different sources. These sources range from a flash of insight by an experienced marketing executive to complex committees which generate strategies. In any case, don't discourage freedom of intuition in search of an ultra-sophisticated system for generating and selecting ideas. Before conducting an evaluation and selection, generate a list of alternatives, rather than accepting the first "good" idea as the "best" one.

Selecting the Best

After alternative strategies are devised, evaluate them to determine those that can best satisfy your objectives. Also determine which can be implemented efficiently within your company's resources and capabilities, and within the limits imposed by potential problems. Strategies can often be tested in advance through field experimentation, mathematical analysis and/or computer simulation.

The formulation of marketing strategy has traditionally been developed on a function by function basis. Although functional marketing groups will do the work, it is better to think in terms of the objectives to be achieved. Concentrate on what must be done, where it must be done, and when it must be done to reach objectives. Specific

people or departments to do the work can be assigned after strategies are determined.

Examples of Strategies

Examples of specific marketing strategies are given below. Only a few examples are given for each major marketing function. You may wish to adapt some of these strategies to fit your own special situation. Remember that a strategy should be selected for each function in terms of how to reach each market.

Product Planning and Development

Distinguish your product from that of competitors as viewed by your customers.

Offer only one product and try to attract all buyers (i.e., use an "undifferentiated" strategy).

Develop separate products and marketing programs for each market segment (i.e., use a "differentiated" strategy).

Create new uses for existing products (through improved performance and/or exclusive features).

Diversify into new markets with new products, either through acquisition of companies or through internal development of new products.

Establish product leadership through development of quality products.

Develop ____ new products for commercialization consideration each year, beating competition to marketplace and establishing a reputation for innovation.

Sales/Service

Expand geographic area of operations to penetrate high potential regions not currently approached.

Reshape distribution channels (i.e., dealers, distributors, agents and company sales force) to more closely satisfy market buying preferences.

Develop more competent sales force and/or dealer-distributor organization.

Require sales force to improve their

knowledge of customers and their products.

Employ target marketing to identify and reach high-potential customers and prospects.

Maximize reciprocal purchases with suppliers, where prudent.

Increase sales effort on most profitable products and customers.

Advertising/Promotion

Employ "push" strategy to encourage dealers, distributors and company sales force to move your product-lines (good margins, bonuses, services, and advertising and promotion subsidies).

Employ "pull" strategy to stimulate customer demand through increased brand, concept and product acceptance.

Maximize advertising and promotion coverage to increase volume, which will permit mass production and distribution.

Address advertising and promotion to key customers and "best" prospects to maximize the benefits of these expenditures in a limited market segment.

Pricing

Set low price for new products to discourage competitive entry into market.

Set low price for products to encourage high sales volume which permits mass production and low unit cost.

Provide minimum "extra" services in order to permit lower prices.

Price parts, service, and repairs at cost or with slight markup to gain maximum good will.

Price products to obtain principal profit on original sale, rather than on follow-up service and parts.

Offer quantity discounts to encourage larger unit purchases.

Distribution

Warehouse your products at locations that enable quick delivery to each distributor and customer.

Provide additional outlets to reduce distribution costs per sale.

Use only one warehouse to minimize inventory control problems.

Task 6: Formulate Detailed Programs

Procedure

Although a company may concentrate on selected programs, it almost always employs a large number of programs to some extent. For example, low prices in themselves don't do any good unless you tell people about them (e.g., advertise). Decisions can be made to spend more on hiring salesmen, improving product quality or increasing advertising. These elements must not be decided on independently by departments. The primary task of top marketing management is to select the optimum combination of these programs.

The top marketing executive forwards information concerning the approved objective/strategy mix to his product, market and functional managers. These managers, assisted by market planning, develop alternative program plans, evaluate them, assign priorities, and schedule them for implementation. When functions (tasks to be done) are determined, an organization to perform them is created and people are assigned. To facilitate program planning, the executive gives each manager the policies, authority and instructions for coordinating all activities assigned to the manager.

Examples of Programs

The size, purpose and scope of programs can vary widely, depending on whether they are overall programs or sub-programs (also called "derivative" programs). For example, the work of the entire marketing department could be regarded as a single, overall program to achieve the total marketing objectives. At the other end of the scale you could have a derivative program for the training of field salesmen. Program objectives are achieved by performing specific activities in a logically comprehensive sequence, in which each activity has a definite time-phased beginning and end.

Some examples of marketing programs are given below. Not mentioned, but inherent in all programs, are the derivative programs for budgeting and measuring effectiveness of a program.

Sales Programs

Recruit, select, and organize sales force, dealers, distributors, and agents in company product-lines, and train them in selling techniques and the best use of sales aids.

Organize sales, engineering, and service working teams.

Conduct sales contests and offer incentives for motivation.

Follow-through on target market identification and sales calls on key customers and prospects.

Determine quotas for salesmen, territories, products, and markets.

Develop slides, film clips, flip charts, and other sales presentation aids, including photographs showing products in use, scale models of products, and samples.

Develop price lists, product bulletins and technical literature.

Advertising

Determine and select coverage, appeals, media, frequency and timing, copy and layouts.

Plan direct mail campaigns and prepare copy for letters and mailing pieces.

Develop customer education programs.

Implement procedure for rapid inquiry handling and follow-up program.

Promotion Programs

Produce catalogs and promotional literature.

Evaluate and select trade shows and exhibits to announce new products and techniques.

Hold customer contests and sales contests.

Conduct publicity programs and promotional give-aways.

Develop packaging, trademark and branding programs.

Pricing Programs

Determine quantity discounts, corresponding quantity "break points," and other discounts.

Determine competitive price levels in terms of the company's financial objectives and the market's willingness to pay for values offered.

Distribution Programs

Select appropriate transportation means and channels for distributing products, including number and location of inventory centers, and appropriate control and reorder systems.

Coordinate required inventory levels with sales and production forecasts.

Product Planning & Development Programs

Search for, screen, and appraise new product ideas.

Market test, set up pilot production runs for test case, and make new product "go, no-go" decisions.

Develop and implement procedure for obtaining protective patents and licenses.

Service Programs

Establish strategically located maintenance and repair facilities with adequate stocks of spare parts, and trained trouble-shooters and repairmen.

Determine and publicize warranty and guarantee policies.

Develop user's operating and maintenance manuals.

Marketing Research Programs

Evaluate use of in-house and outside marketing research capabilities.

Subscribe to selected publications with market analysis and other secondary literature sources.

Conduct primary market research investigations (customer profiles: requirements, premises, how they buy).

The above examples, which are by no means complete, indicate the variety of programs that may be needed to implement the strategies for accomplishing your marketing objectives. The next step is to integrate your programs into an overall, logically time-phased marketing program, and to determine your manpower requirements.

Estimate Duration of Activities

Break down each of your programs into component activities. For example, producing a brochure involves writing copy, developing illustrations, designing format, preparing camera-ready art, printing, folding, assembling, and so on.

Then estimate the man-hours (days, weeks or months) required for each element. Time estimates should be fairly accurate, not offhand "guesstimates."

If a given activity will take two men for two weeks, that's four man-weeks. If your resources will provide only one man, then you must allow four weeks for the job—unless, of course, your company policy will allow overtime work. At any rate, each work estimate must be translated into a *certain* number of people, working for a *specific* period of time.

Arrange Activities in Chronological Order

On a large sheet of paper, draw a time scale (week numbers or dates) across the top and/or bottom to provide a basis for scheduling activities. Then write the activities on slips of paper, each about half an inch wide, and scaled in length proportional to the time an activity will require.

Develop a Master Program Schedule

For example, if a certain activity will take two weeks, you could make the slip of paper two inches long by using a scale of one inch per week. (You can change the format of these slips to fit your own situation.) Lay the activity slips (call them "Time Bars") out on this chart, where you can shuffle them around until you have arranged them according to the best sequence of accomplishment. If you need more space you could use a wall on which large sheets of chart paper have been tacked. These charts may be detailed to include from sixty to more than a hundred different sub-activities plotted over designated time periods. The important thing is to include all significant activities and allow adequate time for their accomplishment.

After scheduling your activities on a program-by-program basis, you can combine the derivative programs into the larger functional programs (sales, advertising, distribution, etc.). These program schedules can then be developed into an overall schedule that makes the best use of your available resources—a Master Program Schedule—that can be used for controlling the marketing operations.

Get Management Approval

Help management to understand your chart quickly. Explain why you believe the time and cost estimates for the major activities are realistic, and why you believe your sequencing of jobs is logical and feasible. Describe the areas where problems might arise because of uncertainties, and how you propose to deal with the problems if they occur—a sound plan must always anticipate possible contingencies. If you have done your homework thoroughly, you should have little difficulty in getting management's approval of your plan.

After your master program has been reviewed and approved, prepare the official copy. Leave space near the bottom for entering manpower and budget dollar totals (by weeks or another suitable period) on separate lines. You might provide several manpower lines for various groups in your company's functional organization. Thus, on a line for the advertising group, you would enter the number of people whose work will be scheduled in certain weeks (also discussed below). The number of publicity people could similarly be totaled and scheduled by weeks. You can even show budgets by weeks, related to various functional groups.

Put People into the Plan

Now that you have planned, scheduled and priced the activities, you can think in terms of functions and specific people.

For each planned program or activity, you can convert estimated man-hours and man-weeks into the number of people (positions) required to do each job. This figure can be compared with the employees available, less anticipated manpower losses during the coming year. Then develop appropriate recruiting schedules, or plans for transferring, or releasing employees which are surplus to your planned requirements.

In staffing your plan, the important thing is to be sure that each activity in the Master Program Schedule is assigned to an *individual*. Everyone involved in the plan should be instructed in his special role in the program. Finally, create an *organization* of people, with clear lines of control and relationships that are understood by all. Everyone must know who has prime responsibility, who takes directions from whom, and who is supposed to coordinate with whom before acting. All personnel functions, responsibilities, relationships, and controls should be reduced to writing to avoid possible misunderstandings later.

Various Approaches to Marketing Organization

The above suggestions for structuring a marketing organization assume that a formal organization already exists. All that remains is assigning its members specific activities taken from a marketing plan. You might currently use product managers, market managers, or some combination of both methods in which product managers concentrate on selling existing products, while market managers analyze market characteristics and requirements, and then try to meet those requirements. In any case, your organization should be structured around the work to be done.

Task 7: The Written Marketing Plan

Scope

It is impossible to generalize about the scope and length for a written marketing plan. However, to be effective, it should contain the basic data as outlined in this chapter. In practice, plans will vary according to factors such as company size, diversity of products, and number and kind of markets served. One company may be satisfied with a one-page sales forecast. Another may need an extremely detailed plan involving a hundred or more pages. Ideally, the plan should satisfy the basic requirements set forth in the introduction to this chapter. In other words, the plan must be tailored to meet the requirements and objectives of the company.

The "Contents of Marketing Plan" chart shows the suggested content of a fairly comprehensive marketing plan. You can use it as a "shopping list" for developing your own plan, tailored to your company's needs. Most items, except those which are self-explanatory, or which are obtainable from

Contents of Marketing Plan

ITEM	DESCRIPTION
1. Table of Contents	Subjects covered in plan and where to find them.
2. Introduction	Purpose and uses of plan.
3. Executive Digest	Summary of major provisions of plan.
4. Company Mission, Scope and Goals	Nature of business (markets) and product lines; contribution to corporate purpose; company profile; capabilities; where company wants to go.
5. Situation Analysis	Facts and assumptions on which plan is based.
a. Assumptions	Report on economy, environment, politics, social, technological and competitive factors.
b. Company Resources	Key personnel, talents, resources, capabilities and techniques.
c. Market Potentials/ Forecasts/Facts	Quantitative and qualitative information on size (dollars & units) of each market, growth rates, customer profiles, customer wants, needs and attitudes.
d. Market Share	Company share of total industry sales.
e. Sales History	Sales over past 3-5 years in each market; current position vs. previous years' objectives.
f. Sales, Expense and Profit Forecasts	Product line - volume - profit-investment forecasts.
g. Current & New Opportunities	High potential markets and products.
6. Current Marketing Organization	Structure and purpose; lines of authority; responsibilities.
7. Marketing Objectives	Results to be produced and where you want to be next year (and future years).
8. Marketing Strategies, Policies, Procedures	General courses of action to reach objectives.
9. Marketing Programs	Specific courses of action (tactics) with respect to sales, service, promotion, advertising, pricing, distribution, marketing research, and product planning and development.
10. Schedules/Assignments	Who does what, where, how and when (milestones).
11. Personnel Plan	Availability and needs.
12. Budgets	Required resources, costs and risks.
13. Proforma P&L Balance Sheet	Accounting statements from controller.
14. Controls	Procedure for measuring and controlling progress of planned actions.
15. Continuity	Procedures for keeping plan updated.

departments other than marketing, are discussed elsewhere in this chapter.

How Organized?

The plan should be presented in sufficient detail so that everyone knows what is expected of him. Each major subject can be treated in separate sections of the plan. For example, in a function-oriented marketing organization, you could have a separate plan for each of the following major marketing functions: product mix; product planning and development; sales force; advertising and promotion; distribution channels; pricing; marketing research; physical distribution; and marketing organization. In a product-oriented organization, you could have a plan for each product. In a customer-oriented organization, you might have a plan for each market category.

There will always be conflicts between having a plan comprehensive enough to cover every situation, yet simple enough to be workable in practice. If you have standard operating procedures for dealing with normal situations, and if your personnel are well trained, then the amount of detail in your plan can be kept to a minimum. Experience has shown that the most successful plans are often the simplest ones.

Sub-plans

In any case, sub-plans for advertising and sales promotion, and for the sales force should be developed. The advertising and sales promotion plan should include a summarized allocation of funds, by media, objectives and themes; and plans for special campaigns to introduce new products or to penetrate new markets. The sales force plan should include information on hiring, training and assigning personnel, as well as schedules for sales meetings, incentives, quotas, and so on.

Planning Tools

The "Product/Market Information" Form, and the "Marketing Planning Matrix" form can be used to organize your planning job. Use the "Product/Market Information" Form to summarize the basic facts of your marketing operation, as well as your forecasts for the future. You can change the time span to suit your needs. One of these forms might be used for each of your products or for each market served.

Use the "Marketing Planning Matrix" to organize your planning of (1) Company Goals/Objectives (i.e., what the company wants to accomplish); (2) Marketing Objectives (i.e., what marketing will do to help achieve company's objectives); (3) Marketing Strategies (i.e., the specific ways in which marketing proposes to reach its objectives); and (4) Marketing Programs (i.e., the specific what, who, when, where, how, and why for implementing the strategies for accomplishing marketing objectives).

Task 8: Communicate and Implement the Plan

Guidelines

Marketing plans are often published in elaborate binders, distributed widely, and launched with fanfare, only to be filed on a bookshelf and never touched until replaced by next year's edition. The goal of the marketing plan—setting direction—cannot be reached in this manner. The following guidelines help to ensure that the plan is economically and efficiently communicated and employed:

> Contributors of inputs to the plan will be more receptive to implementation requirements if broad two-way communication is used early in the planning process.

Product/Market Information Form

Product _____		Date _____

	Last 3 Years	Forecasts
	19___ 19___ 19___ Actual Actual Actual	19___ 19___ 19___ Est. Est. Est.
A. Market Sales (units)	____ ____ ____	____ ____ ____
B. Market Sales ($)[1]	$____ $____ $____	$____ $____ $____
C. Company Sales (units/yr)	____ ____ ____	____ ____ ____
D. Company Sales ($/yr)[1]	$____ $____ $____	$____ $____ $____
E. Profits per year ($)[1]	$____ $____ $____	$____ $____ $____
F. Profits (% of sales)	____% ____% ____%	____% ____% ____%
G. Market Share	____% ____% ____%	____% ____% ____%
H. Return on Capital Invested	____% ____% ____%	____% ____% ____%
I. Prime Competitors	_____	_____

[1] Current dollars. Do not include price increases unless they will apply in current budget year.

Marketing Planning Matrix

COMPANY GOALS, OBJECTIVES	MARKETING OBJECTIVES	MARKETING STRATEGIES	MARKETING PROGRAMS

Have plan formally approved by senior marketing executive.

Do not distribute a master copy of the plan to all managers. Each member of the organization who has a role in implementation should receive that part needed to perform his duties effectively—what is expected of him and why? Each manager, in turn, gives appropriate plan elements to his subordinates on a "need-to-know" basis.

Schedule sessions to explain provisions of the plan as it pertains to affected managers and salesmen. Invite discussion and questions. Make certain that everyone understands the plan in the same light. A plan that isn't understood is more a liability than an asset.

Keep all participants advised of progress and accomplishments.

Departmental Distribution

Copies of the plan should be distributed to the following departments for associated reasons:

DEPARTMENT	REASON
Marketing	Adherence to sales, advertising and promotion plans
Controller	Capital expenditure plans and budgets
Accounting	Cash flow control
Research	New product expectations and direction
Manufacturing	Production scheduling and control
Purchasing	Procurement and inventory plan
Top executives	Guidance and profit plan

Task 9: Use a Control System

Focus on Controlling People

A suitable control system is needed to measure performance in achieving the objectives of the marketing plan, and to provide for effective action to correct excessive deviations from desired standards of performance. A basic principle of controlling is that you don't control *costs*, or *schedules*, or *standards* of performance; *you control the people who are responsible for costs, schedules, and standards.* You do this by making people responsible for certain results, and then holding them accountable for producing results.

Therefore, your control systems must be people-oriented and should suit the activity being controlled. It should be objective, flexible, economical, and easy to use. In addition to detecting deviations before they can cause major problems, the system should indicate corrective action and provide "work-arounds" (alternatives for working around temporary delays and other problem areas).

The detection and correction of deviations from planned results must be kept within the realm of reason. Extremely precise control systems can also be extremely costly. Overcontrolling can result in unstable swings above and below a desired control point. As in production quality control systems, a management control system should permit performance variations within an acceptable tolerance range.

The control process involves three phases: (1) establish standards; (2) measure performance against standards; and (3) correct deviations from standards and plans.

Establish Standards

The first step in developing a control system is to establish standards—criteria against which results can be measured. Standards may be physical (operating levels), dollars (operating costs or sales), capital (application of dollar measurements to physical items), program budgets and milestones, and other intangibles not capable of specific physical or monetary measurements.

Measure Performance

Performance must be measured and deviations from standards detected and analyzed as early as possible. Regular reports of an accounting and financial nature (sales, revenues, expenses) should be compared with budgets and objectives; and operating results should be compared with schedules to determine if they meet or exceed deadlines and milestones. There are many advanced control techniques suitable for such analysis: direct costing; logistics systems; operations research; and program evaluation and review technique (PERT), to name a few.

Correct Deviations

When deviations are detected, investigate to determine their cause. Don't take corrective action unless you understand the cause/effect relationships involved. Watch the trends, and be prepared to take timely corrective action if deviations threaten to become excessive. If major deviations occur, you may want to modify goals, revise schedules and budgets, schedule overtime work, assign additional personnel, provide additional training, develop "work-arounds," or assign more competent leadership.

Task 10: Update Plans to Keep Abreast of Changing Conditions

Changing Conditions

Planning is a continuous job—unless, of course, your company goes out of business. But it is the business of planning to keep the company in business. Change is the only constant factor in business. Economic conditions change, customers' needs change, people's attitudes change, technology changes, your company's goals and plans change, and—most important—your competitors change.

In fact, all the INPUTS to your original plan represented only a snapshot of conditions THEN. In reality, your plan started to be obsolete the day you started it. To keep abreast of changing conditions, you should review and update the plan at least quarterly, or more frequently, depending on the changing situation.

A realistic soundly-based plan seldom requires major changes. On the other hand, frequent changes in direction may cause confusion, destroy confidence, cost time and money, and more important, could help assure your competitors' success.

Marketing Planning Reference Guide

"A Basic Guide to Planning New Products," by R. G. Murdick, *Industrial Marketing*, August, 1963, pp. 91–95.

"Are You Really Planning Your Marketing?", by Leon Winer, *Journal of Marketing*, January, 1965, pp. 1–8.

Marketing Management Analysis and Planning, by John A. Howard, Richard D. Irwin, Inc., Homewood, IL 60430.

"Marketing Planning for Industrial Products," *Harvard Business Review*, September–October 1968, p. 103.

Planning And Problem Solving In Marketing, by Wroe Alderson and Paul E. Green, Richard D. Irwin, Inc., Homewood, IL 60430.

Plotting Marketing Strategy, by Lee Alder, Simon and Schuster, Inc., 630 Fifth Ave., New York, NY 10020.

The Marketing Mode, by Theodore Levitt, McGraw-Hill Book Co., Inc., 1221 Avenue of the Americas, New York, NY 10020.

"The Strategy Selection Chart," by R. William Kotrba, *Journal of Marketing*, July, 1966, pp. 22–25.

III

Product Planning and Development (PP & D)

Introduction

What Is PP&D?

You can add new products, drop old ones, or make present products more competitive. In each case, the proposed action must be reduced to fundamentals. It can then be evaluated in terms of profitability and return-on-investment. This process is called "Product Planning and Development"—or PP&D for short.

PP&D is needed to help avoid new product failures. Products frequently fail due to:

Inadequate market analysis or marketing
planning
Technical, production, or product problems
Costs higher than anticipated
Poor timing and/or impatience
Competitive strengths and reactions

This chapter stresses the scientific approach to PP&D, reinforced by use of proven methods. But success also depends on three other factors: intelligent timing, dedicated and persistent effort by all concerned, and—LUCK. The total PP&D process involves a judicious blending of all of these factors and the application of critical judgement—especially in assessing the risks (i.e., the effect of chance)—in each of the process steps.

If you build a better mousetrap, will the world beat a path to your door?—not necessarily. According to C. Fitzhugh Grice, president of Grice Engineering, of Houston, Texas, you must be able to answer each of these questions favorably: [1]

1. Are you sure the customer's problem is mice?
2. Are you sure the customer knows he has mice? He may know something is rattling around in the woodwork, but he has not yet defined the problem.
3. If the customer has mice and knows it:
   a. Does he truly want to get rid of them?
   b. Has he decided to live with the problem, or—
   c. Is he perhaps building a better mousetrap himself?
4. Are you sure the customer wants to catch the mice himself, or would he prefer that you do the job for him?

What Can PP&D Do for Your Company?

A PP&D program could benefit a company in a number of ways. For example, you

---

[1] *Industrial Marketing*, December 1971, p. 18.

can develop products matched with customer needs, desires and usage patterns; thereby increasing customer acceptance; overcoming innovation by competitors; and helping increase company's share of market.

A PP&D program also allows a company to counteract technological obsolescence, improve outdated facilities and machinery, and capitalize on government tax laws favoring write-offs of PP&D expenses. Added benefits include the possible offsetting of industry declines, reducing seasonal/cyclical slumps and other economic fluctuations, improving job security and morale, and making use of waste and by-products.

Why Some Companies Don't Use PP&D

PP&D offers many advantages. Then why do some industrial companies ignore or refuse to use it? Here are some criticisms often leveled at PP&D:

- It increases overall expense and cuts short-term profits.
- It often requires expensive new production processes.
- Customers are often slow to accept new industrial products.
- Conflicts often arise between PP&D staff, marketing, production, and financial personnel.
- Executives want new products, but don't know what kind of products to develop.
- R&D people don't know what to invent or develop.
- The company with many past failures may reject future attempts at PP&D.

Chapter Plan

The PP&D process is quite simple when approached step-by-step. It's easiest to follow if you plan around four phases of logically-related steps. Each phase is described in a separate section of this chapter.

- Section A covers organizing, planning and budgeting to perform PP&D.
- Section B includes searching for and screening new product ideas, and appraising them in relation to existing products.
- Section C includes specifying, developing prototypes, establishing product identification, and market testing new product models.
- Section D deals with the moment of truth when management must decide either to launch the product or to write it off as a poor risk.

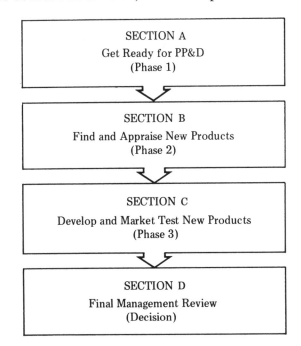

SECTION A
Get Ready for PP&D
(Phase 1)

SECTION B
Find and Appraise New Products
(Phase 2)

SECTION C
Develop and Market Test New Products
(Phase 3)

SECTION D
Final Management Review
(Decision)

Phase 1: Get Ready for PP&D

Purpose of Phase

The purpose of this phase is to set objectives, organize, plan, and establish a budget for product planning and development. These steps help prepare a company for the search, appraisal and development of new and improved products.

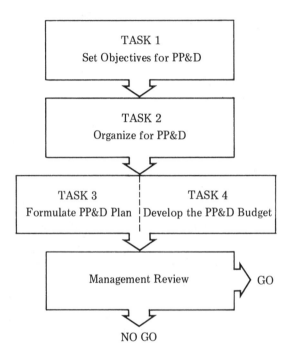

Task 1: Set Objectives for PP&D

Set PP&D Objectives

Once aware of what PP&D can do, decide specifically what it should do for you. Three steps are required: (1) review overall company's objectives; (2) make a list of company's resources (dollars, personnel, facilities, materials, and so on) available for PP&D; and (3) choose PP&D objectives consistent with the company's overall objectives and resources.

Review Overall Company Objectives

PP&D objectives must be consistent with the company's objectives. Otherwise, all subsequent activities will be wasted. For example, if your company wants to become a leading industry innovator it needs a PP&D department more than if it were content to be a "steady grower" through increasing sales of *existing* products year after year.

92

List Company Resources

List and analyze company's resources to determine if they are suitable for supporting an effective PP&D program. Evaluate these resources relative to your competitor's resources and programs. An inventory of your resources and capabilities will help you to set realistic PP&D objectives and to prepare plans that will make the most efficient use of resources in achieving your goals. On the other hand, if your resources are limited in certain fields, you may plan to augment them in order to achieve your objectives.

Set Specific Objectives

When you clearly understand your company's goals, strengths, and weaknesses, define specific objectives for your PP&D pro-gram. For example, create 5 new uses for existing products (through improved performance and/or exclusive features); or develop 3 new products to consider for commercialization this year in order to beat competition to the market, and to establish a reputation for innovation.

All statements of objectives, policies and procedures should be made available in writing to all persons concerned with PP&D. These statements should be reviewed periodically to reflect changing business and company conditions, and to avoid spending valuable time and money investigating ideas that don't fit basic company needs and capabilities.

After your objectives are clearly and precisely defined, you must create an organization to achieve them. This is Task 2 of the PP&D process.

Task 2: Organize for PP&D

Alternatives

PP&D requires a strong management and technical team. For best results, coordinated efforts are needed from most company departments. However, each department wants to control the PP&D function rather than have it control them. Here are six approaches that have been used for organizing PP&D programs:

Corporate Venture Group (CVG)
New Product Department
Vice-President, Marketing
Research & Development Department
Marketing Research Department
New Product Development Committee

Corporate Venture Group (CVG.)

The CVG has a flexible life span. It is actually a small company (profit center) within the larger company. Its highly specialized personnel are hired from outside the company or transferred into the group from other parts of the company. When the group develops a successful product, the group can be "spun off" to operate as a separate division or department for full scale commercialization of the product. Alternatively, the product, with a nucleus of personnel, can be handed over to an established division or department within the company.

Since the CVG manager is accountable for the profitability of his products relative to development costs, he must be respected by all other managers in the company. He should be a good organizer, have uncommon business sense, willingness to take risks, and ability to motivate people. If such a person is going to be effective, he must be given some additional form of incentive/reward to justify his personal risk. In other words, if he fails, the typical result is being fired, mocked or excluded from resuming an upward career. These results are perhaps justifiable; but so then should be the incentive/reward for success.

Here are some of the major pros and cons of the CVG approach to PP&D:

Pros

> Reporting directly to company president assures top management support.
> Has complete control over own funds, personnel, salaries, expenses and overall phases of PP&D from initial screening of new product ideas to ultimate commercialization.
> Authorized to draw support from other functional departments within the company.
> Avoids strangulation by jealousy and fear within the company.

Cons

> In some cases, must pay inflated prices for support provided by the company.
> Is often expensive and time-consuming to organize and operate.
> It is often difficult to find the right personnel willing to accept such responsibilities.
> Not needed for minor modifications of a product.
> Reduced willingness to take risk is a stifling influence on creativity.

New Product Department

An independent group of specialists can be formed into a new product department to provide a focal point for PP&D efforts. This approach is probably the next best choice after the CVG method.

Pros

> Reporting directly to company president assures top management involvement which encourages all line managers to support the group's efforts.
> Enables PP&D decisions to be made and implemented with minimum delays.

Cons

> Might be too specialized to evaluate business risks objectively.
> Might lack financial and functional autonomy.
> Lacks authority commensurate with responsibilities except that which is invoked in the name of the president.
> Not needed for minor modifications of a product.
> Reduced willingness to take risk is a stifling influence.

Vice President—Marketing

Product managers can report to the vice-president, marketing, and have profit responsibility for both new and existing products. In smaller firms, product managers may report directly to senior management.

Pros

> Well-suited to product modifications and slightly differentiated new products.
> Can readily identify market needs and wants.

Cons

> Vice-president, marketing, may lack decisiveness to stake his reputation on the outcome of risks inherent in new product decisions.
> Few managers have the experience in business and financial matters, as well as the knowledge of technical aspects of product development, to evaluate risks objectively.
> Lacks authority over other line departments.

Research & Development Department

R&D can handle the PP&D job, although probably would not have profit responsibility. The R&D head may report directly to senior management.

Pros

> Increases objectivity by removing PP&D responsibility to a position outside normal functional groups.
> Well-suited to product modifications or completely new innovations.

Cons

> Often too technical—more concerned with developing "great," or new products than with producing ones having a sellable price tag and meeting customer needs.
>
> May lack business and financial savvy.
>
> Lacks authority over other line departments.

Marketing Research Department

Marketing research often gets responsibility for PP&D, although probably would not have profit responsibility. The marketing research head normally reports to the vice-president, marketing.

Pros

> Can readily identify market needs, wants and other characteristics.
>
> Can readily oversee minor product modifications and extensions of product-line.

Cons

> May lack financial and technical savvy.
>
> Often demands undue emphasis on statistical reliability of data gathered before being able to make a decision.
>
> Lacks authority over other line departments.

New Product Development Committee

A special "task force" of representatives from appropriate departments is often formed to work on product development projects. This committee meets regularly—at least once a month—to discuss new ideas and review progress on active new product projects. The head of the group generally reports to the vice-president, marketing, to the new products manager, or to the R&D department head. The committee approach is frequently used when efforts by an individual or department have failed to solve a problem.

Pros

> Problems arising in particular functional areas can be referred by the committee to the appropriate department for necessary action.
>
> Adds expertise from all requisite areas: finance, marketing, production, engineering, and so on.

Cons

> Suffers from usual problems of committee approach.
>
> Might reject brilliant, but risky, ideas in favor of safer product ideas.
>
> Usually slows decision-making because final decisions have to be made by the departments represented on the committee.
>
> Because the committee is only temporary, and assignment to it is usually considered an "additional" rather than regular project, the committee often takes a back seat to normal responsibilities.
>
> Rarely results in explicit instructions for action; and when they do, someone else must execute.

Summary

Although each organizational set-up recognizes the need for the PP&D function, all except CVG suffer from four weaknesses:

> It is difficult to credit or blame the right individual because no single person holds total responsibility for results.
>
> Little individual risk or pressure may cause lackadaisical attitudes.
>
> Generally have little or no control over funds.
>
> Shared responsibility often diminishes incentives to excel.

CVG does the best job of overcoming these problems. Whatever approach is used, top management participation and commitment is essential. When everyone knows top management backs a project, things get done faster and with less bickering among department heads. Furthermore, new product efforts will more likely succeed if top management has defined clear corporate objectives for the new product development process.

Whatever form of organization you establish for PP&D, its first job will be to prepare a plan for achieving your objectives. This is the next task.

Task 3: Formulate PP&D Plan

Why a Plan?

A plan of action for achieving the goals of PP&D helps to shorten the PP&D cycle, speed reaction time, and keep the pipeline full of new possibilities.

Document Plan

The plan clearly defines *WHAT* is to be done, by *WHOM, WHEN, WHERE* and *HOW*. Each decision is supported by a clear statement explaining *WHY* the decision was made. A fully-documented plan of action provides all the facts needed for your PP&D operation. The remainder of this chapter provides practical guidance for developing your plan.

The plan should allow for changes to be made as conditions outside of your control alter. These changes should be documented, listing reasons, dates of each change, and who made and approved it. These details will be needed during periodic review of the PP&D process, as well as when documented reports are required.

Outside Help

As you develop particular sections of the plan, you may discover your in-house resources are inadequate for PP&D. You may have to call on an outside consulting firm, such as management consultants, industrial designers, package designers, marketing and research firms, traffic (transportation) consultants, and independent laboratories. Each of these are discussed further in the chapter. Also, the reference guide to this chapter suggests several sources for finding consultants of each type.

When and How to Hire Consultants

Whether to engage an outside consulting firm is a decision that involves balancing various factors. On one side is the extent of your company's need and your limitations to meet it through internal means. On the other side is the cost of employing consultants (in terms of dollars as well as executive hours spent working with the consultant), and the question of professional ability.

Whatever your problem, always investigate several consulting firms before making a final selection. Examine each consultant's client roster and examples of his work. Then request a written proposal delineating services to be provided, names and qualifications of specific individuals to be working on your project, and the associated costs for services rendered.

Management Consulting Firms

Management consulting firms range in size from one-man operations to several hundred persons. They provide the following types of services:

Assist in product planning and development, sales forecasts, competitive evaluations, market and customer analysis, marketing program development, pricing, budgeting, scheduling, and integration of activities.

Conduct executive/employee search and screening.

Make time-and-motion studies of production, handling, and shipping procedures/costs.

Investigate new raw material sources and costs.

Analyze possible mergers, acquisitions, and financial ventures.

Industrial Designers

Industrial designers assist in product and package design and development. They provide the following types of services:

Increase product appeal by suggesting new raw materials and components which reduce costs, improve performance and give product better appearance, increased versatility, and competitive advantages.

Improve product safety, including reductions of noise, vibration, rough edges, emissions, etc.

Develop quicker and less expensive methods for installation and servicing.

Graphic/Package Designers

Graphic/package designers can analyze all related requirements from plant to warehouse to final customer. Such firms generally provide the following types of services:

Test present package for function, economy and convenience.

Ensure that style and appearance of package suits nature and use of product.

Design shipping carton, labels and product closures, including size and shape.

Investigate various packaging material suppliers and cost reduction possibilities.

Suggest appropriate packaging materials providing required protection and desired advertising and identification messages.

Conduct "drop tests" to ensure package's ability to withstand rough shipping and handling.

Design trademarks, logotypes, identification marks, enclosures, and instruction booklets.

Assure that imposed federal, state, and local labeling, packaging, and environmental requirements are satisfied.

Determine whether package is to have re-use value.

Marketing and Research Firms

Marketing and marketing research firms help in all phases from market identification through product development and commercialization. Key services include:

Forecast product, company, and market potentials.

Identify product usage and purchase patterns.

Determine customer preferences for pricing structures.

Determine most effective promotional strategies.

Determine customer preferences as to product attributes and servicing policies.

Perform competitive analyses.

Conduct product and market testing.

Traffic Consultants

Traffic consultants generally perform some or all of the following types of physical distribution management jobs:

Control movement of materials and products.

Recommend protective packaging and shipping crates.

Determine optimal shipping lot quantities.

Recommend warehouse distribution locations, inventory sizes and related costs.

Select and schedule shipments by appropriate mode of transportation and specific carriers.

Develop emergency shipment procedures.

Establish procedures for handling returned products.

Independent Laboratories

There are a number of independent research and consulting laboratories that assist in product design, testing and improvement. Such firms often have staffs of engineers, physicists, chemists, metallurgists, biologists, bacteriologists, industrial safety experts, patent lawyers, as well as complete testing facilities and equipment. Using a combination of debugging and quality control tests, physical and chemical breakdown tests, and other sophisticated laboratory procedures, laboratories will:

Analyze product structure and composition.

Rate your product against various competitors' product.

Design and develop new products based on given specifications.

Suggest product modifications (e.g., fewer, newer, or better components) to increase product life and performance, and/or reduce costs.

Planning and Budgeting are Interdependent

Planning is as indispensable to budgeting as budgeting is to planning. They are mutually supporting activities. Keep this in mind as you consider the next task—budgeting.

Task 4: Develop PP&D Budget

Integrate Plan and Budget

While planning for PP&D, evaluate the financial impact of each action. If this is not done, you might end up with an unrealistic plan you can't afford. If you integrate plan and budget, you can use the budget to control operation of the plan.

How Much?

Each step of your PP&D plan must be accompanied by a "price tag" based on the cost of estimated man-hours of effort by labor categories, the cost of materials and supplies, and the cost of any services that must be procured.

How much to budget is a perplexing question. The amount varies with the industry. In the machinery industry, for example, PP&D budgets have varied from about 2% to 4% of sales. In the electronics and aerospace industries, however, they might range from about 8% to as much as 20%. Information on industry budgets is available through business associates in other companies, trade associations, professional societies, trade journals, and similar sources of industry information.

As a general rule, however, it's unwise to use industry comparisons as a deciding factor to determine the size of your PP&D budget. Instead, use them as a guide. Then plan and price your own program. *Evaluate*

it as a business venture in terms of profitability in relation to costs. Some tools for doing this will include Task 8—Break-even Analysis; Task 9—Calculating the Cash Payback Period; and Task 10—Cash Flow Analysis.

As rough guidelines in planning and budgeting, several consulting firms say that of the time devoted to PP&D, 15% is spent on screening and analyzing new product concepts, while 85% is needed for product development. Also, less than 10% of total expenditures are allocated for screening and analysis, over 30% goes for development, and 60% for testing and commercialization of a new product.

Because the cumulative cost of PP&D increases rapidly from phase to phase, and from task to task within phases, allocate budget funds sparingly in the earlier steps of the process. The procedures in Phase 2 help you apply this principle.

Get Management to Review Your Plans

After completing tasks in Phase 1, submit your plans to senior management for review and approval to begin Phase 2. If your plans are realistic, you should have little difficulty in getting a "go ahead," and funding for the next phase—Finding and Appraising New Products.

Section B
Phase 2: Find and Appraise New Products

Purpose of Phase

The purpose of this phase is to select product ideas which fit your objectives. Any failure to evaluate potential risks may produce drastic results such as project cancellation, or excessive costs and deficits in overall corporate earnings.

The PP&D process is like a poker game in which the ante keeps rising with each round of play. The object is to weed out poor risks as early as possible. As the risks are narrowed, you are compelled to raise the ante to stay in the game. As in poker, it takes a real "gut decision" to get out at the right time, rather than pay to "see" the final hand—which may tell you that you have lost the gamble. To win, the game takes a combination of science, intuition (playing the hunch), hard work, and luck.

A word of warning before you begin: in the new product game, intentionally use every strategem to make your competitors draw the wrong conclusion about the strength of your hand. Keep your plans secret. Cover your true purposes and operations. As in poker—"keep your cards close to your chest."

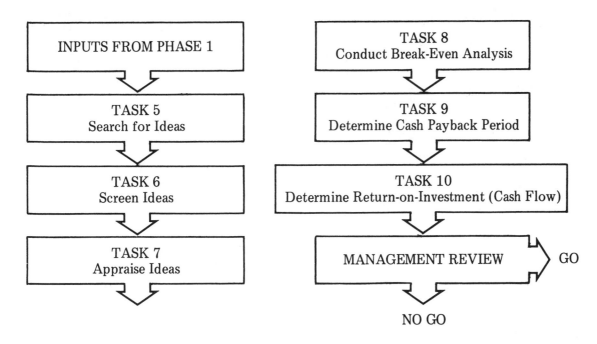

99

Task 5: Search for Distinctive Product Ideas

Guidelines

Every new product starts off as an idea. Since a large number of ideas must be generated in order to find one good one, it is best to organize a systematic search for new ideas, distinctive new products, product improvements, and for ways to differentiate your products from your competitors'. Here are some guidelines to help in your search:

- Get your marketing research staff and sales force to help you gain better understanding of your customers' needs, purchasing habits, motives, product usage patterns, problems encountered, and product characteristics considered desirable. This may suggest new product opportunities or product improvements. You could hire an outside marketing research firm to get this information for you.
- Consider applications of new technologies, traditional technologies, and combinations of both. This may uncover ideas that broaden your scope of business and prevent you from staying with a dying technology.
- Concentrate on specific customer groups and market segments for your search. Don't use a "shotgun" approach. Instead of "tires," concentrate, for example, on "passenger car tires," or "truck tires." Situations in each segment are usually distinct enough to require separate analysis and focus.
- List all product ideas on a "Product Status Chart," such as shown in this task. The chart shows who is responsible and the status of development for each product. It also provides a basis for your business development plan.

Use All Sources of Product Ideas

Use a systematic approach to gather information from internal and external sources. From the user's viewpoint, investigate ideas for making the product do its job better, quicker, more accurately, more economically, and more conveniently. Look for more efficient production, distribution and marketing methods. For example, you could evaluate using less expensive but equally effective materials. The key is to serve the customer in a way that makes him prefer your products and your way of doing business.

The "Idea Generator" chart in this task asks questions that spur ideas for new and improved products. This tool can be used in conjunction with the internal and external sources listed below. Regardless of source, always be receptive to all suggestions.

Internal Sources

- Encourage department heads to suggest ideas for new products, product improvements, or ways to differentiate your products from those of competitors.
- Institute a formal suggestion box system, using a form that makes employees think about the possibilities for new products, product improvements and differentiations. To be effective, this program must be widely advertised in the company, and each employee suggestion must be acknowledged with appreciation within a few days. The employee must also be told that his idea will be evaluated by a given date, and that he will be informed of the results. Prizes or bonuses can be given as awards for ideas that are adopted. Rewarding employees for really profitable suggestions will encourage them to offer other ideas in the future. Winners of "suggestion" awards should be announced in the company newspaper.
- Coax company and distributor salesmen to suggest new product ideas. The sales force has firsthand experience with customers' unsatisfied needs and complaints. Salesmen are often the first to learn of competitive developments.

Provide space on salesmen's call reports to list new ideas and complaints. Discuss these ideas at sales meetings and recognize outstanding contributions with awards or prizes.

Organize "brainstorming" sessions. Encourage freewheeling idea-gathering sessions at which everyone submits ideas on a given problem. Discourage criticism of a new idea until everyone has had time to mull it over. Otherwise, individuals may hesitate to propose ideas that might be considered impractical or absurd. Even absurd ideas can trigger someone's mind to suggest a novel approach to an old problem.

External Sources

Solicit ideas and suggestions from members of your Board of Directors—who often have a broad knowledge of the problems of your industry—and from your more active stockholders.

Ask customers and prospects to suggest ways to improve your products, and for ideas about new products they would like. Never limit your questions to factors that you have already decided are important. Coordinate this with your marketing research department. Specifically:

a. Have your engineers travel with your salesmen as they call on customers. Ask, "What don't you like about this product?" or, "What troubles are you having with it?" Encourage the customer to think about negative aspects of a product, because these are potential sources of customer dissatisfaction. Any dissatisfied customer is a valuable source of a new product and product improvement ideas.

b. Evaluate inquiries from company advertising and publicity for possible ideas. Sometimes a customer reads an ad and inquires as to whether the product does something not specifically mentioned in the ad.

c. Send questionnaires to users of your product to learn how they use it, what they think of it, and if there are any new features they would prefer.

d. Have a panel of customers and prospects discuss products, attributes and benefits. Pick a representative sample from the market you want to reach. Sometimes you can hold such meetings at trade shows; others require special timing. In either case, you should plan on paying each attendee a small fee, or give some gratuity for participation.

Ask suppliers for their ideas. Vendors are always interested in your company's welfare because your business growth contributes to their earnings.

Analyze national economic forecasts and trends in the market to identify potentials for new products that might be needed in a changed environment.

Analyze articles and new product columns in trade journals. Read special studies and reports made by trade associations.

Attend meetings, seminars, and conventions held by professional groups, research groups, and trade associations in your industry.

Watch developments in competitor's product-lines and activities. Obtain their promotional literature and ads. Attend key industry trade shows and exhibits.

Contact inventors (listed as such in the Yellow Pages) to learn if any are interested in your field.

Contact agencies listed in the Yellow Pages under "Product Designers" and "Product Development." At the local telephone office, you can refer to the Yellow Pages books for various cities in the nation.

The "New Patents" column of some trade publications lists abstracts of new patents granted by the U.S. Patent Office. If not already assigned to a firm, these new ideas might be valuable to your company, or they might stimulate your thinking to suggest ideas for new or improved products that are actually quite different than the newly patented inventions.

Serious discussions, or even "bull sessions," with your professional associates might stimulate an idea worthy of further analysis.

Studies and reports by government agencies and commissions may contain clues to unfulfilled needs (Department of Commerce, Small Business Administration, Patent Office, etc.).

Your company's commercial banker may be able to provide leads to new product or product improvement ideas.

There are several publications catering to readers interested in new product developments, and techniques for generating new product ideas. The reference guide to this chapter contains an annotated listing of such publications.

Senior editors of trade publications in your field are often privy to much potentially-valuable patent and product information.

Now reduce the list of ideas to those deserving more thorough evaluation. This is the purpose of Task 6, which we consider next.

New and Improved Products Idea Generator [2]

ALTERNATIVE	QUESTIONS TO ASK
Put to other uses?	New ways to use as is? Other uses if modified?
Adapt?	What else is this like? What other idea does this suggest? Does past offer parallel? What could I copy? Whom could I emulate?
Modify?	New twist? Changing meaning, color, motion, sound, odor, form, shape? Other changes?
Magnify?	What to add? More time? Greater frequency? Stronger? Higher? Longer? Thicker? Extra value? Plus ingredient? Duplicate? Multiply? Exaggerate?
Minify?	What to subtract? Smaller? Condensed? Miniature? Lower? Shorter? Lighter? Omit? Streamline? Split up? Understate?
Substitute?	Who else instead? What else instead? Other ingredient? Other material? Other process? Other power? Other place? Other approach? Other tone of voice?
Rearrange?	Interchange components? Other pattern? Other layout? Other sequence? Transpose cause and effect? Change pace? Change schedule?
Reverse?	Transpose positive and negative? How about opposites? Turn it backward? Turn it upside down? Reverse roles? Change shoes? Turn tables? Turn other cheek?
Combine?	How about a blend, an alloy, an assortment, an ensemble? Combine units? Combine purposes? Combine appeals? Combine ideas?

[2] Source: Alex F. Osborn, *Applied Imagination*, 3rd. rev. ed. (New York: Charles Scribner's Sons, 1963), pp. 286–87.

Product Development Status Chart [3]

STEPS IN PP&D PROCESS		PROJECT NUMBERS					
		PPD-1	PPD-2	PPD-3	PPD-4	PPD-5	PPD-6
Project Title							
Assigned To							
Date Assigned							
Screening	Begun						
	Completed						
Appraisal	Begun						
	Completed						
Management Decision	Proceed						
	Abandon						
	Study Further						
Specifications	Begun						
	Completed						
Prototype	Begun						
	Completed						
Market Testing	Begun						
	Completed						
Management Decision	Proceed						
	Abandon						

[3] Use a chart like this to keep track of the status of each new product under consideration and development. Under the applicable product column, insert the required information and the date of each step of the PP&D process. Modify chart as appropriate to fit the needs of your own PP&D program.

Task 6: Screen New Product Ideas

Purpose

The purpose of screening is to reduce the list of product ideas to those worthy of detailed appraisal in Task 7. This preliminary evaluation is not intended to be either precise or all-inclusive. At this stage, common sense and sound judgment may be more useful than complex formulas in purging the list of all unworthy product concepts. The earlier you eliminate the poor ideas the better, because each step in the PP&D process costs more than the preceding one.

Use All the Help You Can Get

Solicit a diversity of viewpoints to help you with the screening task. The judgment of experienced technical men and chief engineers may help eliminate the technically unsound and impossible ideas. Experienced users, operators, and maintenance men identify ideas that may be impractical from the user's viewpoint. The judgment of experienced financial men can weed out the obviously unprofitable and financially risky ideas. The sales manager can quickly appraise the marketing aspects of the idea with a "gut-feel" approach.

Ask each person interviewed to give reasons for his opinion: ask, "Why do you think that?" This approach is particularly important when you get a rash of negative opinions from people who are opposed to change of any kind, or who want to be able to say, "I told you so," if the product isn't successful. If this type of individual can't support his opinion with facts, perhaps his opinion is invalid or at least suspect. When you contact someone to get his viewpoints, try to arrange a private interview so that the "opinion leaders" won't influence the opinions of others.

Initial Screening

The first step in the screening process is to answer some basic questions about the new product concept:

What will it do for the customer? Does it fill a real need or desire? Specifically, how would it do this?

Will it help the customer save time, labor, materials, facilities, or money? Specifically how?

Will it make the customer's work easier, more convenient, or more pleasurable? In what specific ways?

In each of the above, how does the idea compare with existing products (either yours or those of your competition)? are the differences significant, or only marginal?

Is the product compatible with your company objectives?

Is it an idea whose "time has come"? (A long list of products have died because they were ahead of their time.)

Can you design, test, produce, and get the product to market before there is any significant change in economic, technological or competitive conditions?

Further Screening

The product ideas that survive initial screening may now be evaluated with respect to a more technical set of criteria, including compatibility with company's operations and present product-lines, potential market, marketability, engineering and production capabilities, financial attractiveness, and legal aspects.

Use the "Screening Form for New Product Ideas" to evaluate product ideas relative to each of these criteria (recognizing that no

form will cover every situation). Draw on the experience, judgment, and expertise of persons mentioned in the paragraph above entitled, "Use All The Help You Can Get," to help you rate the product as "good," "average," or "poor," relative to each item on the screening form. Then weight these ratings by assigning them numerical equivalents of 3, 2 or 1, respectively. Write the assigned numerical values in the last column (headed "Total Points"), and write the total of this column on the last line of the form. The maximum possible "score" is 111 points (3 points per item times 37 rated items).

If the total rating of a new product idea isn't at least 78 points (i.e., 70% of 111), the idea may not deserve further consideration. At least, take a hard second look at it before you accept it as a candidate for the more intensive appraisal in Task 7. Set your own minimum acceptable score based on your company's objectives and current situation. Although a product may pass this initial screening, beware of any specific points which raise reasonable doubts.

How to Assign Relative Weights

The criteria listed on the form may not be of equal importance to all companies. To allow for this, you can assign relative weights to each of the criteria. To do this, identify all criteria you consider "most important." Then identify those you consider "least important." You now have two extremes of a weighting scale. Next, decide on the ratio that should exist between these extremes. For example, you might decide that the most important criteria should have a weight of 5, as against a weight of 3 for the least important ones. This leaves a weighting factor of 4 for the remaining criteria (between most important and least important).

Then add 2 columns to the screening form, to the right of the "total points" column. The first new column is labeled "weight," and the second column is labeled "adjusted total points." For each criterion rated "most important," a "5" (or whatever number you choose to represent the weight for "most important") is placed in the "weight" column. For each criterion rated between "most important" and "least important," a "4" is placed in the "weight" column. For each criterion rated "least important," a "3" is placed in the "weight" column. These weights are multiplied by the score shown in the "total points" column for each criterion, with the resulting figure placed in the "adjusted total points" column. Now, add the numbers in the "adjusted total points" column to yield an adjusted score which can be compared against other products or against some absolute standard.[4]

Select Best Ideas for Detailed Appraisal

When you have sifted the best ideas from the original list, you should have only a few really good ideas that merit the more detailed appraisal of Task 7, which comes next.

Task 7: Appraise New Product Ideas

Appraisal Charts

Now we are ready to undertake the critical appraisal and selection of those product ideas that you will develop and test. Because developing and testing involves more extensive analysis and a much greater commitment of company resources than merely screening ideas, the product appraisal process must be far more detailed.

The appraisal is made easier by using the set of "New Product Appraisal" charts which follow. There are 6 charts, one for each of the following broad categories:

Company operations
Potential market
Marketability
Engineering/Production
Finance
Legal aspects

Notice that the headings of these charts coincide with major criteria listed on the screening form used in Task 6, but the appraisal process is now much more thorough. Each chart has seven columns. In the left column, headed "characteristic," are listed aspects that must be rated with respect to the influence they might have on the product idea being evaluated.

The next five columns contain a scale of values ranging from "excellent" (worth 5 points) to "poor" (worth 1 point). The definitions that correspond to these ratings may be altered to fit your own scale of values and to adapt them to your company's particular objectives, type of business, accounting methods, and financial objectives.

In the last column, headed "points," write the number of the rating given to a particular characteristic. For example, on the first chart (headed "company operations"), the first characteristic is "compatibility with current product-line(s)." If the new product idea complements and reinforces an otherwise incomplete line (i.e., "excellent"), write "5" in the right-hand column. Rate the other characteristics on each chart in a similar manner.

Sources of Rating Data

It is often difficult to make precise comparisons of alternative projects and absolute evaluations of individual projects. Generally, limited data are available for predicting the success, total expenditures required, and operating costs for a new project. Nevertheless, you must identify the various monetary and non-monetary factors which can provide a logical basis for abandoning, revising, or proceeding with a product idea before large dollar commitments are made.

---

[4] Although this method of weighting and adding different criteria affords a simple solution, it is analytically incorrect because you are adding different dimensions—like apples and bananas. For an analytically correct, but more complex method of evaluation, see pages 161–165 of *Executive Decisions and Operations Research*, by Miller and Starr (Prentice Hall, Inc., Englewood Cliffs, NJ, 07632, 1960).

Screening Form for New Product Ideas

Product: _____ Date: _____

Description and Use: _____

Major Advantage to User: _____

Major Disadvantage to User: _____

CRITERIA	GOOD (3 points)	AVERAGE (2 points)	POOR (1 point)	TOTAL POINTS
1. Company Operations:				
a. Compatible with company efforts—really our business	___	___	___	___
b. Would not require interruption of present activities	___	___	___	___
c. General know-how available	___	___	___	___
d. Ability to meet customer service requirements	___	___	___	___
2. Potential Market:				
a. Market Size—Volume	___	___	___	___
b. Location	___	___	___	___
c. Market Share (Potential)	___	___	___	___
d. Diversity—needed in several industries	___	___	___	___
e. Industry growth assured	___	___	___	___
f. Stability in recessions	___	___	___	___
g. Foothold in new field	___	___	___	___
3. Marketability:				
a. Estimated price vs. competition	___	___	___	___
b. Have qualified sales personnel	___	___	___	___
c. Ease of Promotability	___	___	___	___
d. Suitability of existing distribution channels	___	___	___	___
e. Originality/differentiation of product	___	___	___	___

f. Degree of Competition
  — Present
  — Potential
g. Life expectancy of demand
h. Customer loyalty
i. No opposition from environmentalists, ecologists, and conservationists.

4. Engineering/Production:
a. Technical feasibility of product
b. Adequacy of technical capability
c. Development cost
d. Adequacy of production capability
e. Materials availability (in both peace and war)
f. Facilities: equipment available
g. Service support available
h. Storage availability
i. Tooling and manufacturing cost

5. Finance:
a. Expected return on investment
b. Capital availability
c. Payback period
d. Break-even point

6. Legal Aspects:
a. Patentable
b. Favorable legislation
c. Product warranty problems

TOTAL POINTS
(111 maximum)

Compare with Existing Products

If the new product is similar to existing products, use the latter's records when making logical estimates.

Conduct Literature Search

A literature search entails contacting all related trade publications and associations to obtain relevant surveys, articles and other

New Product Appraisal—(A) Company Operations

CHARACTERISTIC	EXCELLENT 5	ABOVE AVERAGE 4	AVERAGE 3	BELOW AVERAGE 2	POOR 1	POINTS
1. Compatibility with current product line(s).	Complements and reinforces an otherwise incomplete line.	Easily fits current line, but not necessary.	Fits current line, but may compete with it.	Does not fit well. Competes with and may decrease sales of current line.	Does not fit at all. Endangers or replaces an otherwise successful line.	
2. Ability to produce a safe product. (Also environmental concerns.)	Completely feasible - no functional or environmental hazards to overcome.	Mostly feasible - only slight functional or environmental hazards to overcome.	Possible - several functional or environmental hazards to overcome.	Difficult - many functional or environmental hazards to overcome.	Impossible to overcome all functional or environmental hazards.	
3. Interruption of present activities.	No interruption.	Little interruption but correctable or acceptable.	Little interruption only some of which is correctable or acceptable.	Great interruptions resulting in hard-to-improve economy.	Complete interruption resulting in chaos.	
4. Long-range growth and security of firm.	Definitely helpful.	Somewhat helpful.	Maybe helpful.	Not at all helpful.	Hindrance.	

New Product Appraisal—(B) Potential Market (Feasibility)

CHARACTERISTIC	EXCELLENT 5	ABOVE AVERAGE 4	AVERAGE 3	BELOW AVERAGE 2	POOR 1	POINTS
1. Industry growth & structure.	In growth stage. Increasing sales & profits at an increasing rate. Increasing demand.	Reaching maturity stage. Increasing sales & profits at a decreasing rate.	Turning from maturity to saturation stage. Leveling out of sales & profits.	Sales and profits have begun to decline.	Sales & profits are decreasing at an increasing rate. Decreasing demand.	
2. Market diversity and stability.	Covers many industries. Highly stable.	Covers several industries, with a growing number of uses.	Covers a few industries with a static number of uses.	Covers a limited number of industries, with a decreasing number of uses. Unsteady.	Reaching obsolescent stage.	
3. Dependence on general economy (Recession-proof)	No reliance on economy.	Large degree of resistance to economic change.	Some resistance and some sensitivity to economic change.	Moderately sensitive to economic changes.	Highly sensitive to economic changes.	
4. Seasonal variation of sales.	None.	Minor.	Predictable.	Varying intensity.	Severe fluctuations.	
5. Geographic dispersion of customers.	Easy to reach concentrations.	Slight dispersion, but mostly concentrated.	Some concentrations and some dispersions.	Mostly dispersed.	Very sparse concentration and highly dispersed.	
6. Purchasing patterns across various industries.	Similar purchasing patterns.	Only slight differences in purchasing patterns.	Differences, but easy to adjust.	Somewhat different purchasing patterns.	Completely different purchasing patterns.	

information on trends and factors which may influence the product. A complete discussion of how to do a secondary literature search is presented in Chapter I—Marketing Research.

Company Search

In most cases you can rely on your company's functional departments (e.g., finance, production, purchasing and legal) for an informed evaluation of appropriate characteristics on the appraisal charts. For example, questions related to company policy are directed to top management and public relations personnel for a general impression; while specific questions are directed to departments more qualified to respond (e.g., "ability to produce a safe product" should be directed to engineering and manufacturing personnel). Don't forget to consult with salesmen, sales representatives and sales management in addition to other functional departments.

The marketing and financial departments should cooperate in making the financial analyses of break-even points (Task 8), cash payback period (Task 9), and return-on-investment (Task 10).

Outside Sources

Qualified non-competitive sources outside your company that could benefit from your new products may be eager to contribute opinions about your new product ideas. There sources include suppliers, distributors, prospective users and the user's customers. In the latter case, try to get views from several influences: general management, engineering, production, purchasing, design, marketing, research, transportation and equipment operators as the situation requires.

Your contacts with outside sources will help you to evaluate probable markets, potential users' reaction to the idea, existence of real need, possible applications for the product, desirability of product attributes and relative importance of each, indications of pricing alternatives, probable sales volume potential, and the most suitable marketing channels and promotional tools.

Who Gathers Information and How?

Your marketing research, sales, technical staff, or outside representatives may be in the best position for contacting outside sources. Personal interviews, telephone interviews, mail questionnaires, as well as trial usage can be used individually or in combination to obtain required information. In some cases you go to the respondents; in others they might come to your facility.

Chapter I—Marketing Research, covers complete procedures and suggestions for conducting personal interviews, telephone interviews, and mail questionnaires, plus advantages and disadvantages of each method. Briefly, personal interviews are well suited for complicated product concepts, allowing in-depth analysis of product attributes, benefits and interest levels, as well as encouraging useful unsolicited comments. Telephone interviews are best suited to well-defined, basic product concepts or for specific product features as a supplement to other research results. Mail interviews are most effective for evaluating well-defined product concepts where specific and brief answers are required.

Guidelines

Whichever process is employed, personal, telephone, mail or trial usage, there are several guidelines which make survey testing more productive:

Give clear examples of the use and functions of the new product.

All terminology should be easily understood by respondents.

Attempt to have respondents compare the physical and performance characteristics of your product with those of your competitors.

Determine products currently purchased to perform functions similar to your new product and relate the two.

List and describe expected new product advantages and disadvantages.

New Product Appraisal—(C) Marketability

CHARACTERISTIC	EXCELLENT 5	ABOVE AVERAGE 4	AVERAGE 3	BELOW AVERAGE 2	POOR 1	POINTS
1. Cost/effectiveness and availability of existing or new channels of distribution.	Readily distributable to major markets via present channels.	Can use present channels for majority of major markets; plus some new channels.	Must utilize new and present channels equally.	Requires many new channels to be developed.	Requires all new channels, none of which are compatible with existing channels.	
2. Can be attractively priced/quality with competitive products (initial and maintenance)	Better quality and lower cost than all competitors.	Either lower priced and equal quality, or equal price and better quality than competition.	Equal price — same quality as competition.	Either higher priced or lower quality than competition.	Both higher priced and lower quality than competition.	
3. Suitability and potential of methods and costs of promotional tools.	Selling attributes are superior to competing products; lends to existing promotion and advertising techniques.	Features compare favorably against competition; has demonstrable characteristics. Can utilize some of current promotional techniques.	Equal to competing products' features; slight similarities in promotion required.	Few promotable features; must develop new promotional tools.	Does not compare favorably with competitive products; all new promotion techniques are required.	
4. Possible discount allowances, deals, over and above competition.	Easily accomplished.	Can beat out smaller competitors.	Most firms already offer substantial discounts.	Would make company appear to be discount house.	No increase in sales would result, since products are bought solely on quality.	
5. Executive talent and marketing management.	Complete and qualified staff currently available.	Large part of qualified staff available.	Some adequate staff available.	Need many new staff members.	Need totally new staff.	
6. Replacement market/brand loyalty.	Lends self to repeat purchases.	May repeat if conditions merit.	Equal chance of repeat or switching.	Little chance of repeat purchase.	"One shot" only.	

Criterion					
7. Product differentiation (unique).	Fills a need, not currently satisfied. Is original. Leader.	Improvement over existing competition — an adaptation.	Some individual appeal, but basically a copy of another product with minor differentiation.	Barely distinguished from competitors.	Same as competitor's product. No distinctive or unique advantages.
8. Market life/obsolescence (longevity, durability).	Significantly longer life than competition.	Slightly longer life than competition.	Equal life to competition.	Slightly shorter life span than competition.	Significantly shorter life than competition.
9. Degree of competition — established or potential.	No competitive or substitute products foreseen.	Only slight competition from alternatives.	Several competitors to different extents.	Many competitors.	Would be completely outclassed. Other firms are entrenched.
10. Customer acceptance.	Readily accepted by customers.	Only slight resistance.	Moderate resistance.	Appreciable customer education needed.	Extensive customer education needed.
11. Sales to present customers.	All present customers.	Most of present customers.	Some present customers.	Few present customers.	Entirely different customers.
12. Knowledge of purchase, consumption and use patterns of customers.	Complete knowledge.	Extensive knowledge.	Partial knowledge.	Little knowledge.	No knowledge.
13. Packaging available to provide (a) product protection in shipping, storage and handling, (b) customer convenience, and (c) manageable cost.	Meets all criteria.	Satisfies most criteria.	Satisfies half of criteria.	Satisfies few criteria.	Satisfies none of criteria.

New Product Appraisal—(D) Engineering/Production

CHARACTERISTIC	EXCELLENT 5	ABOVE AVERAGE 4	AVERAGE 3	BELOW AVERAGE 2	POOR 1	POINTS
1. Economical access to resources—raw materials, facilities, personnel, capital, and production know-how.	Adequate amounts are readily available via dependable sources. Present idle plant is usable. Substitutes are available if needed.	Little new equipment and other resource sources are required. Plant may require slight additions.	Some new equipment, personnel, and other resources are needed.	Mostly new equipment, personnel and resources are needed.	Limited supplies. All new plant, personnel and resources needed.	
2. Technical know-how in manufacturing, technical support, process familiarity, etc.	Currently available and qualified.	Most available.	Some available.	Need many additional "know-how's".	Need all new "know-how's".	
3. Can be manufactured at a marketable cost.	All resources are obtainable and can be processed at lower than competitive costs.	Most resources are obtainable and can be processed at a lower than competitive cost.	Some resources are converted into finished product at lower than competitive cost.	Few resources are convertible at competitive costs.	No resources can be processed competitively.	
4. Adequate storage facilities.	Space to spare.	Some available after reorganizing inventories.	Can be obtained after inventory reorganization or space acquisition.	Little space available now or in the future.	No space available.	
5. Industry entry requirements.	Excellent fit available at low cost—through internal development or acquisition. Few other companies can enter.	Good fit available at low cost—through internal development or acquisition.	Partial fit: available, but high cost.	Rarely available at any cost. Many companies can enter.	Poor fit. Can be made by any size firm.	

112

Criterion					
6. After-sale service requirements.	Present service organization adequate in personnel and facilities.	Minor reinforcement in personnel and/or facilities will present no serious problems.	Moderate adjustments needed but can be accommodated.	Major adjustment of service organization needed.	Present service capability totally inadequate.
7. Ability to produce a durable product (temperature, impact, abrasion, tearing, resist deterioration).	Completely feasible to withstand conditions of use and environment.	Mostly feasible to withstand conditions of use and environment.	Somewhat feasible to withstand conditions of use and environment.	Difficult to withstand conditions of use and environment.	Impossible to withstand conditions of use and environment.
8. Dollars and time estimates for research are within budget constraints.	Completely within budget.	Mostly within budget.	Possible and probably within budget.	Difficult to accomplish within budget.	Impossible without major budget increase.
9. By-products.	Can completely utilize by-products which otherwise would have been extremely expensive to purchase.	Partial utilization of by-products at a cost savings.	Some use of by-products at no particular savings.	No use of by-products.	Problem in storage and disposal of by-products.
10. Operating cost.	Significantly less than competing products.	Slightly less than competing products.	About same as competing products.	Slightly more than competing products.	Significantly more than competing products.

Indicate expected price or price range so that respondent can answer all questions more intelligently.

Limitations

Although contacting sources outside your company is useful, it does have several drawbacks which might lead to inconclusive results or those in which the validity is questionable:

You frequently must disclose valuable information which might be useful to competitors.

Testing can be expensive and time consuming.

Your concept may be difficult for respondents to grasp.

Respondents often overstate their desires or tell you what they think you want to hear. In either case, results could be misleading.

New Product Appraisal—(E) Finance

CHARACTERISTIC	EXCELLENT 5	ABOVE AVERAGE 4	AVERAGE 3	BELOW AVERAGE 2	POOR 1	POINTS
1. Profitability— expected return-on-investment (before taxes).	Over 20% per year.	10-19% per year.	6-9% per year.	3-5% per year.	2% and under per year.	
2. Payback period.	Less than 2 years.	2-3 years.	4-5 years.	6-7 years.	8 years or more.	
3. Availability of dollars for capital expenditures and working capital.	Abundant.	Easily obtainable.	Obtainable at high interest rates.	Difficult to obtain at any interest rate.	Impossible to obtain.	
4. Putting capital to best use.	Cannot be invested in a more lucrative investment.	There may be other ventures equally as lucrative.	There are several equally as lucrative investments.	There are many other more lucrative investments.	Can be invested in much more lucrative investments.	

New Product Appraisal—(F) Legal [5]

CHARACTERISTIC	EXCELLENT 5	ABOVE AVERAGE 4	AVERAGE 3	BELOW AVERAGE 2	POOR 1	POINTS
1. Patent Protection.	Impregnable. Exclusive license or rights.	Some resistance to infringement; but not foolproof. Few firms have similar patents.	Probably not patentable; but defies replication. Patent issue is unsettled.	Not patentable; can copy some attributes; open field.	Easy to copy with no problems. Many licenses are outstanding.	
2. Meets legal restrictions applying to product, label, advertising, and shipment.	Meets all.	Meets most.	Meets some.	Meets few.	Meets none.	
3. Trademark/copyright protected.	Impregnable.	Some light copying of mark.	Several infringements may occasionally arise.	Many infringements on mark; or no trademark allowed.	Trademark not allowed; some firm already owns mark.	
4. Claims to royalties or other indemnities.	Completely settled.	Tentative agreement reached.	Still in negotiating stage.	Minor disagreements as to claims.	Major disagreements as to claims.	
5. Labor/Union Relations.	Complete contract settlements are in accord and favorable to company.	Contracts are resolved, but not completely favorable to company.	Still in negotiating stage.	Major negotiating problems.	Complete impasse.	
6. Existing or impending legislation that could affect product.	Completely favorable.	Somewhat favorable.	Hard to determine effect.	Some problems will result.	Completely detrimental.	

[5] See Chapter XII—Legal Aspects of Marketing, for additional guides.

Some respondents may not cooperate, fearing participation in survey may obligate them at a future date.

Combine Ratings

After rating each characteristic, use the "New Product Evaluation Matrix" for combining the ratings to derive an overall index.

The evaluation matrix comprises four columns. Column (1) lists characteristics from the first column of the New Product Appraisal charts. Column (2) contains factors proportional to the relative importance of each characteristic. Although these factors are based on historical averages across many industries, you may wish to adjust the weights to suit your own company's experience or preference. If you change the relative weights, make certain that the total of all weights in column (2) equals 20 (see bottom of evaluation matrix). Column (3) contains spaces in which you can write the ratings given each factor on the New Product Appraisal charts (ranging from 1 to 5).

Column (4) provides spaces to write the weighted value of each characteristic—column (2) times column (3). The values for the six broad characteristics should be totaled. Then the six totals are added to yield a grand total. According to the ratings given on the New Product Appraisal charts, the grand total can range from 20 to 100.

Evaluation and Management Decision

After completing this evaluation, each product idea can be compared by assigning the following ratings:

100 points = Excellent
80 points = Above Average
60 points = Average
40 points = Below Average
20 points = Poor

Management Review

Those products receiving highest ratings should be given a final "gut feeling" scrutiny by the appraisers. This helps ensure that

they are potential winners. As such, they become candidates for a full-scale management review.

During this review, management is brought up to date on the whole story—which should include a thorough briefing on methods and results of each step of Phase 2. It is possible that management may require further analyses to be made—which may indicate that you haven't done as thorough a job as you should have. On the other hand, management may be satisfied that certain products have a satisfactory potential, considering profitability, return-on-investment, producibility, and marketability. These products then become eligible for entry into Phase 3 of the PP&D process.

But what about the rejected product ideas? Here are some suggestions for disposing of them.

What to Do With Rejected Ideas

If some product ideas are rejected during the appraisal and review process, don't simply discard them. Either file them for future investigation or sell the ideas to another firm. Many firms may buy your product or process outright if you decide not to go ahead with it yourself. There are two basic approaches for selling your idea: sell it yourself or go through an intermediate firm.

If your decide to sell it yourself, check with trade associations in fields related to the product. They may have publications which publicize products (patents) for sale.[6]

The second approach to handling rejected ideas is to check the Yellow Pages index under inventors, management consultants, marketing research and analysis, product designers, and product developing. Interspersed with firms listed, there are names of organizations that either will buy your idea or find a firm to buy it and develop it.

---

[6] Two such publications bring buyers and sellers together by publishing information on products, inventions and patents available to make, license or purchase outright; they also list individuals and firms with venture capital to invest in new product ideas. They are: *Technology Mart*, Thomas Publishing Company, 461 Eighth Ave., New York, NY 10007; and *Business Exchange Bulletin*, P.O. Box 2290, Newport Beach, CA 92663.

New Product Evaluation Matrix [7]

(1) CHARACTERISTIC	(2) RELATIVE IMPORTANCE WEIGHT	(3) RATING (1,2,3,4 or 5)	(4) VALUE COL(2) x COL(3)
A. COMPANY OPERATIONS			
1. Compatibility	0.6	————	————
2. Safe Product	0.6	————	————
3. No Interruption	0.4	————	————
4. Long-Range Growth	<u>1.4</u>	————	————
TOTAL (A)	3.0		————
B. POTENTIAL MARKET			
1. Industry Growth	1.2	————	————
2. Market Diversity	0.6	————	————
3. Dependence on Economy	0.4	————	————
4. Seasonal	0.2	————	————
5. Geographic	0.3	————	————
6. Purchasing Patterns	<u>0.3</u>	————	————
TOTAL (B)	3.0		————
C. MARKETABILITY			
1. Channel Cost/Effectiveness	0.4	————	————
2. Price/Quality	0.4	————	————
3. Promotable	0.4	————	————
4. Discounts/Deals	0.2	————	————
5. Marketing Management	0.3	————	————
6. Customer Loyalty	0.3	————	————
7. Product Differentiation	0.3	————	————
8. Market Life	0.2	————	————
9. Competition	0.4	————	————
10. Customer Acceptance	0.4	————	————
11. Sales to Present Customers	0.2	————	————
12. Knowledge of Customers	0.4	————	————
13. Packaging	<u>0.1</u>	————	————
TOTAL (C)	4.0		————

(1) CHARACTERISTIC	(2) RELATIVE IMPORTANCE WEIGHT	(3) RATING (1,2,3,4 or 5)	(4) VALUE COL(2) x COL(3)
D. ENGINEERING/PRODUCTION			
1. Access To Resources	0.4	————	————
2. Manufacturing Expertise	0.5	————	————
3. Marketable Cost	0.4	————	————
4. Storage Requirements	0.2	————	————
5. Entry Requirements	0.4	————	————
6. Serviceability	0.3	————	————
7. Durability	0.2	————	————
8. Research Budget	0.2	————	————
9. By-Products	0.2	————	————
10. Operating Cost	0.2	————	————
TOTAL (D)	3.0		════
E. FINANCE			
1. Profitability	1.6	————	————
2. Payback	0.6	————	————
3. Available Capital	1.0	————	————
4. Best Use of Capital	0.8	————	————
TOTAL (E)	4.0		════
F. LEGAL			
1. Patent Protection	0.8	————	————
2. Meets Product, Label and Advertising Restrictions	0.8	————	————
3. Trademark Protected	0.6	————	————
4. Royalties Settled	0.2	————	————
5. Labor Relations	0.2	————	————
6. Other Legislation	0.4	————	————
TOTAL (F)	3.0		════
GRAND TOTAL:	20.0		════

[7] Instructions: In Column (3), write the numerical ratings of each corresponding characteristic as given on the preceding rating charts. Multiply the numbers in Columns (2) and (3) and write the products in Column (4). Write the total of Column (4) in the place provided above. The total of Column (4) is the weighted rating. A total weighed rating of 80 points corresponds to an "Above Average" rating.

Such intermediate firms are generally identified by the words "developers," "new product marketing," "venture capital," "patent marketing and development," or "product search."

Evaluate Existing Products

The New Product Appraisal charts, and the New Product Evaluation Matrix, can be used for appraising existing products as well as new product ideas. This analysis might take the form of a continuing product audit. Don't wait until a crisis develops to analyze your existing products. When problems arise, they may be solvable only at exorbitant cost in terms of company resources and sacrifice of other program objectives. While deletion or modification of products (based on this evaluation) may be depressing, in a changing market it is almost as vital as adding new products. Just as a crust of barnacles on a ship's bottom retards its movement, so unprofitable products slow a company's progress.

Detect Weaknesses

In addition to using the evaluation matrix for existing products, continuously look for signs of marketing weaknesses, such as:

Financial, production, sales, and marketing resources spread too thin

Excessive management time or capital required

Price and sales forecasting increasingly difficult

Short production runs and expensive setup times; diminishing backlog

Excessive advertising and sales expenditures in proportion to revenues

Customer doubts about company

Decreasing industry sales potential

Changing customer requirements or buying procedures

Many new superior competitive products that cannot be matched profitably

Products become slow movers or obsolete resulting in decreased sales

Decreasing market share; lagging market acceptance

Downward trend in a product's price which is traditionally stable

Declining gross margin; low overhead coverage; decreasing profit contribution

Decreasing sales in relation to total company sales

Return-on-investment below company average

Decreasing sales dollars per order

Little contribution to sales of other products

Phase Out Products

There are several alternatives when phasing out or abandoning a product—drop outright, find another manufacturer to buy and produce the product, license it out, and so on. Once a decision is made to abandon, study the circumstances which caused the decision. You could learn a great deal that may prevent future failures.

Here are some suggestions to consider when phasing out a product:

Time phase-out to cause minimal adverse impact on affected employees.

Announcements should be sent to affected customers well in advance of abandonment to avoid surprising them, and to give them time to make other arrangements.

Plan ways to dispose of inventories and work-in-process, to recover the working capital invested in them.

Consider the salvage value of stock and unneeded capital equipment.

Plans must be made for appeasing distributors who must be discontinued.

Alternative sources of supply should be sought for loyal customers who may continue to want a suitable substitute for the product being phased out.

Changes should be made in promotional material referring to product.

Summary

In this task, the New Product Appraisal charts were used to make an in-depth analysis and evaluation of the new product can-

119

didates. The ratings were weighted and combined using the New Product Evaluation Matrix, and the final results were presented for management review and decision. Further financial analyses can be done in Tasks 8–10. Then, the products which sur-

vive the process of critical analysis and evaluation can become the inputs to Phase 3, in which the products are developed through the prototype stage and subjected to market tests. This phase is discussed in Section C.

Task 8: Conduct Break-Even Analysis

What Is Break-Even Analysis?

Break-even analysis is a method for evaluating relationships among sales revenues, fixed costs and variable costs. Such analysis identifies the point at which total revenue (TR) equals total cost (TC) for a specific product. This break-even point determines the number of units you need to sell to cover all costs in developing, producing and selling a product. Break-even yields satisfactory, quick estimates of how total revenue and total cost vary at different selling prices and levels of expenditures for advertising, promotion, distribution, and production facilities. It also provides quick product mix decisions. In calculating break-even points, you can change any variable (e.g., selling price) and see how many more or less units must be sold to break even.

Limitations

Break-even analysis is a useful tool for quick decision-making, but must be employed in light of its limitations.

- Break-even tends to oversimplify decision-making, especially for multiproduct companies.
- Break-even assumes selling price and variable costs per unit remain constant over specified periods and ranges of production. This does not hold in the "real world," as most relevant variables are dynamic (e.g., prices may change due to market considerations; unit variable cost may decrease because of more efficient operating and production pro-

cedures; learning curve savings may be offset by increased cost of materials and labor).
- Changes in price alter the break-even point, but the new point in no way reflects accepted demand levels.
- Adequate and valid data are rarely available with respect to precise volume and profit relationships, except in a few companies with effective cost and managerial accounting systems.
- Break-even does not consider the opportunity cost of capital, present values, effects of marketing efforts, estimates of risk levels, or data reliability.
- Break-even does not consider social and environmental costs which might arise after sale.

How to Calculate

The following explanation and forms help you to calculate the break-even point for any product. Before performing any calculations, determine the range of production over which costs and revenues are to be estimated. As the range of production increases, cost per unit tends to decrease, thanks to economies of scale (e.g., quantity discounts) and the learning curve (e.g., performing certain operations "smarter"). Once the range of production is determined, break-even calculations may be made.

Determine Number of Mixes

There can be several different break-even (BE) points for a product depending on the number of mixes of revenue and cost functions. To determine the number of possibil-

No. of Possible Unit Selling Prices		No. of Possible Unit Variable Costs		No. of Possible Total Fixed Costs						No. of Possible Mixes or BE Points
				Production & Amortization		Advertising & Promotion		Distribution		
☐	X	☐	X	☐	X	☐	X	☐	=	☐
(1)		(2)		(3)		(4)		(5)		(6)

ities, multiply the number of revenue functions by the number of cost functions. The form immediately above assists in this determination.

The example shown below analyzes two possible selling prices; one possible unit variable cost; one possible production facility, equipment and research cost; two possible advertising and promotion budgets; and two possible distribution budgets. Entering these figures in the form for determining the total number of alternative mixes, the result is eight.

On the "Break-Even Analysis" form, list the 8 alternative mixes in column (1).

On the "Master Mix" form, write mix numbers 1 through 8. Fill in data on unit price, and various marketing expenses as calculated. This form can be referred to during the later calculations rather than recording the mix over and over again.

Estimate Price—Column (2)

"Price" is amount of money (or other exchangeable consideration) charged, or paid for the value, or worth of a product or service. Chapter V—Pricing, will help in determining appropriate prices. For new prod-

ucts as well as price changes for existing products, the following areas can be considered: industry norms, competitive prices, previous marketing inputs, rough approximations of costs and elasticities of demand (change in quantity demanded because price changed), cross-elasticities (change in quantity demanded because a competitor changed his price), sales forecasts (number of units that can be sold at each price), profits desired, as well as additional subjective views held by salesmen and executives. The number of criteria analyzed depends on the degree of reliability required. At this stage, rough estimates should suffice.

Now estimate the price range in which your product should sell. Assume that after narrowing down the initial price range, it is decided to charge either $9.00 or $10.00 per unit. It was previously determined that 8 mixes would be considered. Since there are 2 price alternatives, it is simple to determine that 4 mixes are tested at one price and 4 at the second price (8 mixes divided by 2 prices equals 4 mixes per price). Under column (2) on the Break-Even Analysis form, list the $9.00 price corresponding to mixes 1—4; and the $10.00 price corresponding to mixes 5—8.

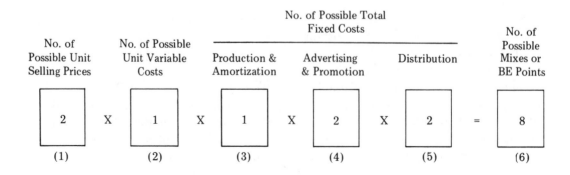

No. of Possible Unit Selling Prices		No. of Possible Unit Variable Costs		No. of Possible Total Fixed Costs						No. of Possible Mixes or BE Points
				Production & Amortization		Advertising & Promotion		Distribution		
2	X	1	X	1	X	2	X	2	=	8
(1)		(2)		(3)		(4)		(5)		(6)

Break-Even Analysis

Product _____ Date _____

(1) MIX NUMBERS	(2) PROPOSED UNIT SELLING PRICE	(3) UNIT VARIABLE COST	(4) UNIT CONTRIBUTION TO PROFIT COL(2)−COL(3)	(5) TOTAL FIXED COSTS	(6) BREAK-EVEN IN UNITS COL(5)÷COL(4)	(7) BREAK-EVEN IN DOLLARS COL(6) X COL(2)
1	$ 9.00	$5.00	$4.00	$190,000	47,500	$427,500
2	9.00	5.00	4.00	240,000	60,000	540,000
3	9.00	5.00	4.00	210,000	52,500	472,500
4	9.00	5.00	4.00	260,000	65,000	585,000
5	10.00	5.00	5.00	190,000	38,000	380,000
6	10.00	5.00	5.00	240,000	48,000	480,000
7	10.00	5.00	5.00	210,000	42,000	420,000
8	10.00	5.00	5.00	260,000	52,000	520,000

Master Mix Form

MIX NUMBERS	UNIT SELLING PRICE	MARKETING FIXED COSTS		
		ADVERTISING & PROMOTION	DISTRIBUTION	TOTAL
1	$ 9.00	$50,000	$100,000	$150,000
2	9.00	50,000	150,000	200,000
3	9.00	70,000	100,000	170,000
4	9.00	70,000	150,000	220,000
5	10.00	50,000	100,000	150,000
6	10.00	50,000	150,000	200,000
7	10.00	70,000	100,000	170,000
8	10.00	70,000	150,000	220,000

Determine Unit Variable Cost—Column (3)

Unit variable costs are those that vary directly with sales volume, production volume, or percent of plant capacity used. The following elements are normally included in unit variable cost:

Supplies, raw materials, and purchased parts

Direct labor and supervision, and chargeable indirect labor

Pro rata part of factory burden (lights, heat, maintenance)

Variable part of general and administrative expense

Packaging, handling and shipping

Sales commissions and margins given to intermediaries (channels of distribution) in payment for services

Royalties and license fees paid on a unit basis

Cost of returned products (estimated percent returned or cancelled times the cost of handling returns and refurbishing the product)

Bad debts (percent expected times selling price)

In a strict accounting sense, costs may be semi-variable or semi-fixed. Since break-even is concerned with the short-run, this differentiation can be ignored. Therefore, we shall classify cost as either variable or fixed.

The unit variable cost remains essentially constant over the range of production being studied. Assume that calculated unit variable cost was $5. If production resulted in 100 units, total variable cost would be $500 ($5 times 100). If production was increased by 1 unit to 101, total variable cost would increase by $5 to $505. This also holds if the increase was from 200 to 201 units; variable cost increases by only $5 from $1,000 to $1,005 ($5 × 201).

Production, engineering, and cost accounting departments provide estimates of individual variable costs. Generally, these costs are estimated for the upcoming period, unless insufficient time compels you to rely on historical data. Projections are partially dictated by market demand and production capacity (figures from marketing research, production, and engineering departments); while historical data are provided in the form of past financial statements from financial and accounting departments.

In the example being presented, it is assumed that one possible unit variable cost is suggested—$5. For each of the eight alternative mixes being analyzed, enter $5 under column (3)—Unit Variable Cost—on the Break-even Analysis form. Other unit variable costs could be considered if higher or lower quality materials and/or workmanship were being evaluated.

Calculate Unit Contribution to Profit—Column (4)

Unit contribution to profit is that portion of unit selling price which, after covering unit variable costs, can be applied against fixed costs. It is calculated by subtracting unit variable cost—column (3) from proposed unit selling price—column (2). In mix 1, for example, $9 less $5 equals $4 unit contribution to profit. $4 is then entered in column (4) under mix 1. This calculation is repeated for each mix and the result is entered in column (4).

Determine Total Fixed Cost—Column (5)

Fixed costs are assumed to remain relatively constant and to occur even in the absence of production. These costs may be divided into two broad categories: (a) planning and production-oriented and (b) marketing-oriented.

Planning and Production

Planning and production costs include direct and indirect expenses such as:

Research and development expenses

Capital expenditures for plant, equipment, machinery, tools, jigs, and fixtures

General administration and management salaries

Depreciation, insurance, interest, property taxes and leases

Finance and production departments are normally responsible for furnishing this data. In the example, it is estimated that planning and production fixed expenditures will be $40,000.

Marketing

Marketing costs include advertising, promotion, sales, and distribution expenses. These costs are often the only elements of fixed costs which vary over a range of production. Such changes depend on the intensity of the marketing effort. Some analysts call marketing expenses "semi-variable," since they tend to fluctuate, but not in direct proportion to sales volume (unless changes are extremely large). Allocations for advertising (including promotion), and distribution (including sales) are normally budgeted at the beginning of a specified period. This commits the firm to these expenditures for that period. Regardless of sales volume achieved, the fixed cost of advertising and distribution is incurred. Changes can be made during the year, but it is difficult to attribute sales levels to any specific campaign or advertising expenditure level. This is the primary reason for listing such marketing expenses as fixed costs.

In the example, it is assumed that both advertising and distribution have 2 alternatives. The advertising and promotion budget can be $50,000 or $70,000, depending on the method employed. The sales and distribution budget can be $100,000 or $150,000, depending on the type of channels employed. This gives 4 (2 × 2) alternatives, each of which is used in 2 mixes—one with each of the prices ($9.00 and $10.00). These alternatives are illustrated in the completed Master Mix Form.

Add Categories

Both of the above major categories must be added to arrive at total fixed cost. In each mix, the planning and production fixed costs are $40,000. Marketing fixed costs range from $150,000 to $220,000. The alternatives for each mix are listed in the next column.

Mix Numbers	Planning & Production	Marketing	Total Fixed Cost
1	$40,000	$150,000	$190,000
2	40,000	200,000	240,000
3	40,000	170,000	210,000
4	40,000	220,000	260,000
5	40,000	150,000	190,000
6	40,000	200,000	240,000
7	40,000	170,000	210,000
8	40,000	220,000	260,000

The total fixed costs for each mix can now be entered in column (5)—total fixed costs—on the Break-Even Analysis Form.

Calculate Break-Even—Columns (6) & (7)

Break-even for each mix of price and cost variables can be calculated by dividing fixed cost, column (5), by the corresponding contribution to profit, column (4). This gives the number of units required to break even. Enter the result in column (6). Then multiply the unit break-even in column (6) by the corresponding unit price in column (2). This yields the break-even point in dollars, which is entered in column (7).

Estimate Profits for Each Mix

Thus far, we have determined the break-even volume of sales needed to support various combinations of price, advertising costs, and distribution costs. But merely breaking even won't produce profits. We must determine the estimated profits that might result from the various "mixes." Then products can be evaluated in terms of company financial goals and policies, and in comparison with other products. The "Break-Even Profit Analysis" form will enable you to do this in an organized manner. It compares estimated total sales volume with break-even volume for each alternative mix.

To illustrate use of the form, the example will be continued here.

Column (1): Write the numbers 1 through 8, each on a separate line. This represents the number of mixes being considered for each product. You can readily refer to the Master Mix Form for the composition of each mix (price, advertising and distribution decisions). Keep a copy of the Master Mix Form with the Break-Even Profit Analysis form for ready reference.

Column (2): Enter the total (fixed cost) dollars allocated for planning and production, advertising and promotion, and distribution. These figures are obtained from column (5) of the Break-Even Analysis form.

Column (3): Enter break-even volume from column (6) of the Break-Even Analysis form.

Column (4): The data for this column are estimates of total units that could be sold in light of the marketing mixes of prices, advertising and distribution alternatives. Thus, for a product price of $9 and advertising and distribution efforts of $50,000 and $100,000 respectively, total sales might be estimated at 44,500 units. These sales estimates can be made by marketing research, salesmen, and executives. (Note that price increases generally cause decreased sales; while increased expenditures for advertising and distribution generally increase sales.)

Column (5): This column is derived by subtracting the data in column (3) from the data in column (4). The result is the sales volume that exceeds the break-even volume (or that falls short of break-even volume, when the figures are in parentheses).

Column (6): In this column, write the figures from column (4) of the Break-Even Analysis chart. This is the profit contribution that results per unit sold.

Column (7): This column shows profit or loss that results from using each marketing mix. Figures are obtained by multiplying corresponding figures in columns (5) and (6).

Column (8): Since different dollar investments are required in different mixes, it is often wise to convert profit to a percentage based on total fixed cost invested. Divide the figure in column (7) by its corresponding figure in column (2). The resulting percentages are then compared. In the example presented, mix 4 results in the greatest percentage return on fixed expenditures.

Break-Even—Profit Analysis

(1) MIX NUMBERS	(2) TOTAL FIXED COST	(3) BREAK-EVEN VOLUME	(4) ESTIMATED TOTAL SALES VOLUME	(5) VOLUME ABOVE BREAK-EVEN COL(4)−COL(3)	(6) UNIT CONTRIBUTION	(7) DOLLAR PROFIT OR LOSS COL(5)xCOL(6)	(8) PERCENT RETURN ON FIXED COSTS COL(7)÷COL(2)
1	$190,000	47,500	44,500	(3,000)[8]	$4.00	($12,000)[8]	(6.32%)[8]
2	240,000	60,000	62,000	2,000	4.00	8,000	3.33
3	210,000	52,500	55,000	2,500	4.00	10,000	4.76
4	260,000	65,000	71,000	6,000	4.00	24,000	9.23
5	190,000	38,000	34,500	(3,500)[8]	5.00	(17,500)[8]	(9.21)[8]
6	240,000	48,000	49,400	1,400	5.00	7,000	2.92
7	210,000	42,000	43,900	1,900	5.00	9,500	4.52
8	260,000	52,000	56,500	4,500	5.00	22,500	8.65

[8] Figures in parentheses are negative results, or loss.

Use Formulas

Some people prefer using the formula approach to solving break-even. This approach symbolically displays the easier "filling-in form" process previously demonstrated.

In the previous discussion, it was noted that break-even is that point where total revenue equals total cost. This can be solved mathematically by setting the equations for these values equal to each other:

(1) Total Revenue (TR) = Units (U) × Price (P)
(2) Total Cost (TC) = Units (U × Variable Cost Per Unit (V) + Fixed Cost (F)

Then,

$$U \times P = (U \times V) + F$$

Solving for U, $U = \dfrac{F}{P - V}$

From the previous example, calculate the break-even for mix 1:

Substituting F = 190,000; P = 9; V = 5

$$U = \frac{190,000}{9 - 5} = \frac{190,000}{4} = 47,500$$

Break-Even Charts

Break-even charts present vivid pictures of the profit and loss possibilities of a business plan or project. They demonstrate the interaction of revenue, expenses, profits, and volume. Charting is helpful in visualizing the effects of changes in sales and distribution programs, products, prices, and advertising and promotion expenditures.

The steps for constructing a break-even chart are described below with the demonstration of mix 1.

Define Axes

Draw a chart with a horizontal and vertical axis. On the horizontal axis, mark off a scale in terms of volume of activity (units sold or produced, dollar sales volume or percent of capacity). On the vertical axis, mark off a scale in terms of dollars to represent expenses and income.

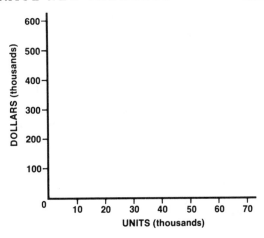

Plot Revenue Line

Plot the sales revenue line (SR), which graphically portrays the relation between sales revenue (dollars plotted on the vertical axis) and sales volume (units plotted on the horizontal axis). This results in a straight line starting at the intersection of both axes and running through a series of points representing total revenue at various price/quantity relationships. For example, from mix 1, the selling price per unit is $9.00. At zero units sold, revenue is zero dollars. At 50,000 units sold, revenue is $450,000 (50,000 units × $9). Connecting these points defines the sales revenue line. Note that revenue is assumed to be directly proportional to the number of units produced and sold.

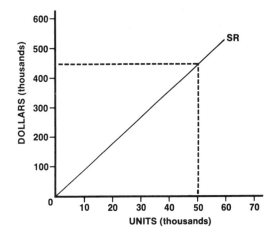

Plot Fixed Cost Line

Draw a fixed cost (FC) line so that it is parallel to the horizontal axis and intersects the vertical axis at a point which equals total fixed costs. This indicates that fixed costs are constant throughout the range of volume (units). The area between the FC line and the horizontal axis represents fixed costs incurred at any level of sales.

From mix 1 again, fixed costs total $190,000. Locate this point on the vertical axis, and draw a horizontal line through it.

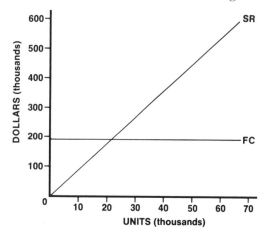

Option

Break-even charts can be constructed with steps in its fixed cost line. These steps reflect changes in fixed cost (added productive capacity) required to reach the next highest level of output.

Plot Total Cost Line

Where the FC line intersects the vertical axis is the starting point of the curve that represents the total cost line (fixed plus variable costs). Plot a point on the chart which represents total fixed and variable costs. Draw a line from the intersection of the vertical axis and the FC line to the point just plotted. This is then the total cost (TC) line. The area between the TC line and the FC line represents the total amount of variable costs at each volume of sales.

The costs between TC line and the horizontal axis represents the total costs incurred at various levels of sales. You can do this by starting at any point on the horizontal scale and measuring up to the TC line and across to the vertical scale.

The variable costs per unit from our example are $5. Using a convenient volume of sales, say 50,000, the total variable cost will

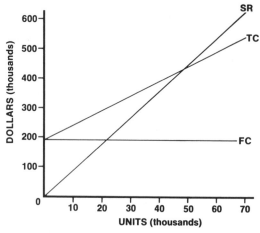

be 50,000 × $5 = $250,000. Add the $250,000 to fixed costs of $190,000 which gives a total cost of $440,000 for 50,000 units sales. Therefore, you plot a point of 50,000 units and $440,000. This point is connected with the intersection of the FC line and the vertical axis to yield a total cost line.

Analyze

The break-even point is at the intersection of TC line and SR line (point B). The amount of sales in dollars needed to break even is read on the vertical axis; the number of units on the horizontal axis.

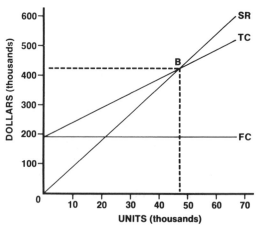

The break-even point for the $9 price example is 47,500 units and $427,500 in sales. The wedge-shaped area to the right and above this point (B) shows how profits increase with increasing unit sales. The wedge-shaped area to the left and below this point represents losses. The vertical distance between the revenue line (SR) and TC line equals the amount of profit to the right of B, and the amount of loss to the left of B.

Task 9: Determine Cash Payback Period

What Is Payback?

The cash payback period (sometimes called the "payout period") is the time required to recover a specific investment; usually indicated in years and fractions of years. Payback is generally used as a measure of liquidity, rather than profitability.

The reciprocal of payback (i.e., 1 ÷ number of years) is supposed to approximate the rate of return on a project. For example, if an investment is recovered in four years, the supposed rate of return is 25% (1 ÷ 4). Unfortunately, the supposed relationship between payback and rate of return on an investment is not logical since a project may end abruptly after six months, or yield additional profits for twenty years.

Some managers prefer the simplicity of payback analysis because early recovery of an investment (i.e., in two or three years) avoids risks inherent in longer term projects. Early recovery of an investment is particularly important to companies needing working capital.

Limitations

Payback analysis is a useful tool for evaluating timing of the return-on-investments, but you should be aware of its limitations:

Short-term investments are inherently considered more desirable than long-term investments, regardless of true rate of return.

Investments in which highest earnings come early are deemed more valuable than investments whose highest earnings come late, regardless of true rate of return.

Capital recovery is often erroneously treated as income.

Variations in year-to-year earnings and earnings produced after the payback period are not considered in payback analysis.

How to Calculate

The "Payback Analysis" form helps calculate payback for individual investments. The form should be completed as follows:

STEP 1—Determine expenditure levels for each element of the capital investment. List these levels on lines 1-A—1-E; then place the sum of these figures on line 1-F—Total Capital Investment.

STEP 2—Estimate the number of units you can sell annually. This annual sales figure is often averaged over a 5 or 10 year life period (or even longer). Record this number on line 2-A.

STEP 3—Obtain unit contribution to profit (unit selling price less unit variable cost from accounting or finance department. If possible, this figure should be calculated on an after-tax basis. Record this number on line 2-B.

STEP 4—Multiply estimated unit sales per year (line 2-A) times unit contribution to profit (line 2-B) to arrive at total annual contribution to profits. Record this number on line 2-C.

STEP 5—Divide total capital investment (line 1-F) by annual contribution to profits (line 2-C) to arrive at payback in years. Record this number on line 3.

STEP 6—Divide annual contribution to profits (line 2-C) by total capital investment (line 1-F) to arrive at approximate annual return-on-investment (in percent). Record this number on line 4.

Example

An example of a completed payback analysis is presented on the next page. Follow the steps listed above to see how the form was completed.

Payback Analysis

PROPOSED PROJECT_____"Widget"_____ DATE 11/1/72

---

1. Total Capital Investment

    A. Research & Development $ 20,000

    B. Production Development $ 30,000

    C. Project Cash Requirements $ 30,000

    D. Market Development $ 25,000

    E. Other $ 15,000

    F. Total (Add lines A,B,C,D and E) $ 120,000

2. Estimated Annual Contributions to Profits

    A. Estimated Sales per year   5,000 units

    B. Unit Contribution to Profit $ 8.00

    C. Total (line A times line B) $ 40,000

3. Payback in years (1-F divided by 2-C)   3 years

4. Approximate Annual Return on Investment (2-C divided by 1-F)[9]   33-1/3 %

---

[9] WARNING: Because capital recovery is NOT the same as income, any resemblance between rate of return determined by this method and the true rate of return is virtually coincidental.

Task 10: Determine Return-on-Investment (Cash Flow)

What Is Cash Flow Analysis?

Cash flow analysis is an accurate tool for determining the realistic return on a capital investment. Cash flow makes allowance for the fact that sums of money returned on an investment may be received at different times in the future. In other words, money has time-value. By converting all future revenues to their present values, cash flow analysis eliminates the time factor. This conversion makes it possible to view future revenues in terms of today's dollars (assuming no inflation). Projects of different life spans and cash flows can be compared using cash flow analysis.

Limitations

Cash flow suffers from several drawbacks.

Traditionally, explanations of the cash flow method have been shrouded in the esoteric language of mathematicians (i.e., "equilibrating rate of return"). Confusion, misuse and limited use of cash flow analysis has resulted. The fact is, if you can add, subtract, multiply and divide, you can make a cash flow analysis. A modern desk calculator reduces the job to simple button-pushing.

Annual earnings are assumed to be received at, or near, the end of each year of the project. In practice, however, earnings may be received at periodic intervals throughout the year and be put to other productive uses upon receipt. This increases the real annual rate of return-on-investment. End-of-year discounting conservatively tends to understate the rate of return when earnings are really received throughout the year. (Interpolations can, however, consider mid-year revenues.)

In spite of its apparent sophistication, cash flow analysis does not consider effects of inflation on the future value of money, or the uncertainty inherent in any estimates of the future. However, the estimates of future after-tax earnings could be multiplied by a "de-rating" factor to allow for these influences before making the cash flow analysis.

How to Calculate Cash Flow

In making a cash flow analysis, both future value (FV) and present value (PV) of money are considered. Future value and present value of money are influenced by time (t), and the "opportunity cost of capital" (c).

Time is usually expressed in whole years, which simplifies calculations. Opportunity cost of capital is simply the average annual rate of return expected from other available sources of investment. This might be the average rate of return from overall business operations. Opportunity cost of capital is always expressed as a decimal fraction (i.e., 15% per year is expressed as 0.15).

Future Value

The future value of money is simply the number of dollars resulting from investment over a given number of years at a specified interest rate. A simple example is the amount of money resulting from investing $1,000 at 5% for one year. This example yields $1,050 at the end of one year.

When the investment runs for several years, the compound interest formula should be used:

$$FV = PV \times (1 + c)^t$$

where: FV = Future Value
PV = Present Value
c = Opportunity Cost of Capital
t = Time (in years)

As an example, what is the future value of $2,500 in 3 years, compounded annually at 12%?

$$FV = PV \times (1 + c)^t$$
$$FV = \$2,500 \times (1 + .12)^3$$
$$FV = \$2,500 \times (1.12)^3$$
$$FV = \$2,500 \times [(1.12) \times (1.12) \times (1.12)]$$
$$FV = \$2,500 \times (1.4049)$$
$$FV = \$3,512 \text{ (to nearest dollar)}$$

Present Value

Although future value is fine for analyzing savings accounts, present value is more useful in marketing analysis. Converting future values back to present values is called discounting. The discounting formula is:

$$PV = FV \times \frac{1}{(1 + c)^t}$$

For example (using the previous future value analysis), assume that $3,512 will be received after 3 years. Discount this future value at 12%, the opportunity cost of capital:

$$PV = FV \times \frac{1}{(1 + c)^t}$$
$$PV = \$3,512 \times \frac{1}{(1 + .12)^3}$$
$$PV = \$3,512 \times \frac{1}{(1.12)^3}$$
$$PV = \$3,512 \times \frac{1}{(1.12) \times (1.12) \times (1.12)}$$
$$PV = \$3,512 \times \frac{1}{1.4049}$$
$$PV = \$3,512 \times 0.7118$$
$$PV = \$2,500 \text{ (to nearest dollar)}$$

In this example, 0.7118 is the discounting factor. It is simply the reciprocal of the compounding factor; but think of it as a present value factor which converts a future sum of money into its present value.

To   simplify   discounting   calculation,

Present Value Factors [10]
(For End-of-Year Discounting)

FUTURE YEAR IN WHICH DOLLAR IS RECEIVED	PRESENT VALUE OF $1.00 WHEN YIELD OR DISCOUNT RATE IS:												
	6%	9%	12%	15%	18%	21%	24%	27%	30%	35%	40%	45%	50%
1	.9434	.9174	.8929	.8696	.8475	.8264	.8065	.7874	.7692	.7407	.7143	.6897	.6667
2	.8900	.8417	.7972	.7561	.7182	.6830	.6504	.6200	.5917	.5487	.5102	.4756	.4444
3	.8396	.7722	.7118	.6575	.6086	.5645	.5245	.4882	.4552	.4064	.3644	.3280	.2963
4	.7921	.7084	.6355	.5718	.5158	.4665	.4230	.3844	.3501	.3011	.2603	.2262	.1975
5	.7473	.6499	.5674	.4972	.4371	.3855	.3411	.3027	.2693	.2230	.1859	.1560	.1317
6	.7050	.5963	.5066	.4323	.3704	.3186	.2751	.2383	.2072	.1652	.1328	.1076	.0878
7	.6651	.5470	.4523	.3759	.3139	.2633	.2218	.1877	.1594	.1224	.0949	.0742	.0585
8	.6274	.5019	.4039	.3269	.2660	.2176	.1789	.1478	.1226	.0906	.0678	.0512	.0390
9	.5919	.4604	.3606	.2843	.2255	.1799	.1443	.1164	.0943	.0671	.0484	.0353	.0260
10	.5584	.4224	.3220	.2472	.1911	.1486	.1164	.0916	.0725	.0497	.0346	.0243	.0173
11	.5268	.3875	.2875	.2149	.1619	.1228	.0938	.0721	.0558	.0368	.0247	.0168	.0116
12	.4970	.3555	.2567	.1869	.1372	.1015	.0757	.0568	.0429	.0273	.0176	.0116	.0077
13	.4688	.3262	.2292	.1625	.1163	.0839	.0610	.0447	.0330	.0202	.0126	.0080	.0051
14	.4423	.2992	.2046	.1413	.0985	.0693	.0492	.0352	.0254	.0150	.0090	.0055	.0034
15	.4173	.2745	.1827	.1229	.0835	.0573	.0397	.0277	.0195	.0111	.0064	.0038	.0023

[10] Computations by Forrest G. Allen 2/18/72

present value factors are listed in the "Present Value Factors" table. For example, under the 12% column, on the 3-year line, the factor 0.7118 (calculated above) is listed.

Project Profitability

Cash flow can be used as a quick check on the profitability of alternative projects or product introductions.

Gather Basic Data

The first step is gathering information on the extent of the capital investment, its expected life span, the opportunity cost of capital and estimated after-tax earnings. As an example, consider a capital investment of $138,000 in a new product project whose estimated life span is three years. The company's average opportunity cost of capital is 12% per year, derived from normal operations. Annual after-tax earnings of this project are estimated as follows:

END OF YEAR	ESTIMATED AFTER-TAX EARNINGS
1	$ 35,000
2	125,000
3	18,000

Convert to Present Values

Convert after-tax earnings to their present values by discounting at 12% per year. The present value factors are found in the table under the 12% column, rows 1, 2 and 3, respectively. Multiply each factor by the estimated after-tax earnings for the corresponding year. Next, add the present value dollars to arrive at the present value of annual earnings.

END OF YEAR	ESTIMATED AFTER-TAX EARNINGS	×	PRESENT VALUE FACTORS	=	PRESENT VALUE OF ANNUAL EARNINGS
1	$ 35,000		0.8929		$ 31,252
2	125,000		0.7972		99,650
3	18,000		0.7118		12,812
			Total Present Value		$143,714

Compare Present Value against Investment

Compare the total present value of annual earnings with the amount of the original investment. If the total present value is greater than the original investment, the rate of return on the proposed new product project exceeds the opportunity cost of capital. This gives a quick "yes" or "no" check on the relative profitability of the project.

From the example, total present value of annual earnings of this project exceeds planned capital investment by $5,714 ($143,714 less $138,000). It is estimated that the project generates earnings at an annual rate which exceeds the cost of capital. The ratio of total present value of annual earnings to planned investment (in this case: $143,714 ÷ $138,000 = 1.0414) can be used as a figure of merit for comparing alternative new product proposals.

Determine Rate of Return

The next step is to determine the "true" rate of return. Rate of return from an investment is defined by economists as the rate at which the sum of the flow of after-tax earnings, discounted yearly to determine their present value, equals the cost of the investment.

This can be explained by reviewing the previous "quick check" of profitability of a new product project. After discounting annual after-tax earnings at 12% per year, the "sum of the flow of discounted after-tax earnings" was $143,714. This was $5,714 more than the $138,000 planned capital investment in the project.

Suppose that, instead of discounting at 12%, we used a heavier rate to reduce overall present value to $138,000. *Whatever discount rate it takes to do this is, by definition, the true rate of return on investment* (subject to any error in your estimates of after-tax earnings).

There is no straightforward way to determine the discount rate that reduces total present value to $138,000. Trial and error must be used. It was already determined that a 12% discount rate is too light. A heavier discount rate is needed. Experimenting at 15% per year yields the followd ing:

END OF YEAR	ESTIMATED AFTER-TAX EARNINGS	×	PRESENT VALUE FACTORS 15%	=	PRESENT VALUE OF ANNUAL EARNINGS
1	$ 35,000		0.8696		$ 30,436
2	125,000		0.7561		94,513
3	18,000		0.6575		11,835
			Total Present Value		$136,784

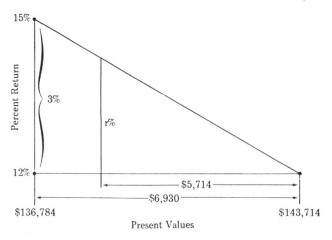

A 15% discount rate is too heavy. Overall present value ($136,784) is less than the planned investment ($138,000). But, through trial and error, the true rate of return has been bracketed between 12% and 15% per year. Most present value tables do not cover all values (i.e., between 12% and 15%). Therefore, the true discount rate must be found by interpolation.

Interpolation

An interpolation diagram shows the geometrical relations between the two present values at the 12% and 15% rates. The diagram shows two similar triangles: a small one whose vertical side is r% (the unknown) and whose horizontal side is $5,714; and a large one whose vertical side is 3% and whose horizontal side is $6,930.

Since the two triangles are geometrically proportional, they can be related algebraically:

$$\frac{r\%}{\$5,714} = \frac{3\%}{\$6,930}$$

$$r\% = \$5,714 \times \frac{3\%}{\$6,930}$$

$$r\% = 2.4736\% \text{ (rounded to 2.47\%)}$$

Because "r" is the increment by which the true discount rate exceeds 12%, the final rate is 14.47% (12% + 2.47%).

Error

If you were to substitute this rate of return in the basic present value formula you would obtain a present value of $137,977. This is $23 less than the assumed investment of $138,000—an error of less than two-hundredths of one percent. There are two reasons for this error:

Calculations are rounded to four decimal places.

A simple linear method of interpolation is used, whereas the relationships are actually non-linear.

Comparison with Cash Payback Method

If in the above example we assume that the $125,000 estimated after-tax earnings in the second year were received in equal monthly increments of $10,417, it could be shown that the $138,000 investment would be recovered in 1.825 years. According to the cash payback method, this would imply an annual rate of return of $1 \div 1.825 = 0.548$, or 54.8%. This rate of return clearly bears no resemblance to the more conservative "true" rate of return yielded by the cash flow analysis method, which turned out to be 14.47%.

Present Value Calculating Aid

The blank "Present Value Calculating Aid" form can be used to calculate the present value of future earnings resulting from individual investments. One form should be completed for each investment.

In column (1), list the number of years the project is expected to run (e.g., for an eight year project, list 1, 2, 3, 4, 5, 6, 7, and 8 on consecutive lines). In column (2), list the estimated annual after-tax earnings attributed to the investment. In column (3), write the present value factors for each year from the Present Value Factors Table (e.g., if discounting at 9% for three years, enter the factors .9174, .8417, and .7722 corresponding to years 1, 2, and 3 respectively). Multiply the estimated after-tax earnings by its corresponding present value factor in each row, and enter the product in column (4)—present value of annual earnings. Add all entries in column (4). This is the result of the first trial and error calculation as described earlier. If it is less than the capital investment, you have discounted too heavily. If it is more than the capital investment, you have not discounted heavily enough. In either case, additional trial calculations will be necessary until you have bracketed the rate of return closely enough to find the true rate of return by interpolation.

Present Value Calculating Aid

PROPOSED PROJECT _____ DATE _____

(1) END OF YEAR	(2) ESTIMATED AFTER-TAX EARNINGS	(3) PRESENT VALUE FACTORS	(4) PRESENT VALUE OF ANNUAL EARNINGS COL (2) x COL (3)
TOTAL			

Section C

Phase 3: Develop and Market Test New Products

Purpose of Phase

The objective of this phase is the development and market testing of a well-tested prototype product that can be put into production. The phase includes Tasks 11 through 15. Product specifications are developed in Task 11. In some cases performance specifications are prepared first; after these have been reviewed and approved, the detailed prototype model specifications are prepared.

In Task 12, the prototype model is developed, proved in laboratory tests, and produced in sufficient numbers for a field market test. While these activities are in progress, a preliminary marketing plan (Task 13) is prepared, parts of which are needed to support the market test operations. The details of the market test program are in Task 14.

Finally, and in parallel with some of the above tasks, a preliminary production plan (Task 15) is prepared, based on product specifications. This production plan is needed to determine tooling, raw material, personnel, and financial requirements, based on various assumed production schedules and volume levels (but the production plan itself is not, of course, a marketing responsibility).

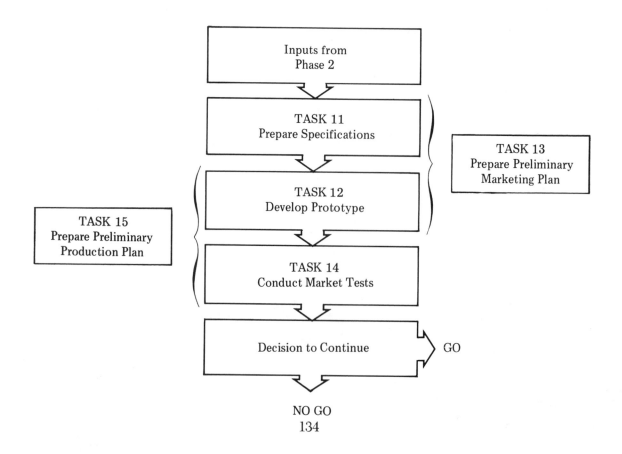

134

Task 11: Prepare Product Specifications

Inputs to Engineering Department

Based on the results of Phase 2, marketing and market research groups provide information needed by the engineering department to develop product specifications. These inputs should include as many of the following items as possible:

Functional description of the product in terms of customer needs and preferences, such as:
  a. Performance requirements
  b. Reliability, durability, and operating life
  c. User convenience features
  d. Acceptable price and quality
  e. Approximate size, weight, color, finish and appearance
  f. Warranty and service requirements

Estimated sales volume, by quarters

Characteristics of the user's operating and maintenance personnel (e.g., education, training, experience)

Safety, anti-pollution, anti-noise, and similar "environmental and social responsibility" requirements

Information about the environments in which the product may be used, such as:
  a. Temperature and humidity ranges
  b. Sand or dust conditions
  c. Atmospheric corrosion (e.g., salt air, smog, acid fumes)
  d. Vibration, shock, and wind resistance
  e. High and low altitude usage
  f. Magnetic fields
  g. Marine surface and underwater conditions

Distribution and shipping requirements

Suggested performance test requirements

Prepare Preliminary Specifications

Draw up preliminary specifications (based on inputs to the engineering department) to define the functional performance and design requirements for guiding final design, development, test and acceptance of the final end product. Also, submit sketches of how the product will look. Include user interfaces, such as "human engineered" controls and instruments, seating arrangements, platforms, oil and grease points, viewing openings, and similar features.

Preliminary specifications should be evaluated by a panel including members from senior management, marketing and market research, production, engineering, legal, and finance. Priority is given to user needs and preferences, and specific user benefits achieved through various product applications. Trade-offs between price, performance, quality and delivery should be evaluated, and all decisions clearly set forth in writing to guide the engineering department.

Preliminary specifications and sketches can be shown to customers of long standing and known loyalty to get a potential user's reaction to the proposed product. Avoid a "selling" approach by having a member of the marketing research department make the contact, rather than having a salesman do so. Emphasis should be on "What don't you like about this product?" Discussion of pricing should be avoided. Information on potential availability of the product should be in the most general terms—"perhaps next Fall."

Prepare Final Specifications

After all reviews and suggestions have been made, engineering prepares final specifications. During this stage, a production engineer should work closely with design engineers to ensure that the product will be easy to produce and will incorporate all reasonable production economies. This enables the product development and production group to plan purchases of needed materials and to make advance preparations for production prototypes needed for laboratory and market testing.

During this task, marketing, engineering, production, and legal departments should be alert for any proprietary features of the product or its promotional materials that may require patent or copyright protection (see Chapter XII—Legal Aspects of Marketing).

Task 12: Develop Product Prototype

Advance Preparations

Advance preparations are needed between preparing specifications and developing the prototype. These preparations (normally a production department responsibility, with support from the engineering and possibly marketing departments) include:

Prepare rough plan and schedule for prototype development. Anticipate requirements for materials, tools and personnel, and make preparations to procure them.

Set aside a secure area in the plant where development work can proceed without interference from, or interfering with, normal production work.

Analyze indicated development steps to anticipate and define potential problems that might arise. Explore possible solutions and prepare contingency plans to be used, if needed.

Design reporting forms for documenting time, costs, problems, solutions, and all decisions made (with names, dates and circumstances). File this information for later engineering, production and management reviews, and to support patent claims.

Assign responsibilities for key steps in the development program, making sure that each person involved understands the importance of such product development to the company, all key steps, and any special security precautions to be enforced.

What Should Marketing Do?

Although this task is not a primary marketing function, there are some things that marketing should do during the prototype development task:

Observe, and stay informed on progress made. Keep informed of accumulated costs and time in relation to scheduled costs and time. Obtain revised estimates from the production department whenever problems may adversely affect product development. Learn of possible impact on the project, including an updated estimate of the time and cost to completion.

If problems pose a serious threat to the development program, marketing should advise management to immediately review the entire project. The purpose of this review is to decide whether to drop the project, or to continue it for the time being, after "calculating" the risks.

Closely follow related economic and marketing events and continue to monitor new product reports and advertisements in the trade press. Instruct the sales force to be alert for news of other companies' developments. Keep mangement informed of any industry developments, news, or rumors, that might bear on the company's plans for the new product.

Preliminary Marketing Plan

Now let's turn our attention to Task 13— Prepare a Preliminary Marketing Plan, which has been in parallel progress with Tasks 11 and 12.

Task 13: Prepare Preliminary New Product Marketing Plan

Purpose

Introducing a new product involves many decisions and preparations to ensure the product has the best chance of acceptance and survival. The purpose of the preliminary marketing plan is to document these decisions and preparations, and to prescribe an orderly procedure for product introduction. This plan is developed simultaneously with Tasks 11 and 12.

Responsibility

Because this step is vitally important, the top marketing executive in a company should direct every detail. Planning activities are coordinated with the corporate director of planning, market planning and marketing research, as well as with other key company departments, to ensure total involvement and commitment to the new product program.

Procedure

There is no such thing as "a" marketing plan. Plans for introducing one product may be vastly different from the plans for an-other. Furthermore, a marketing plan is actually an interlocking set of plans, each of which concerns a particular facet of the new product marketing program. A detailed description of the overall marketing planning function is contained in Chapter II— Marketing Planning. These procedures can be readily tailored to fit the new product situation. Basic approach includes making a situation analysis, setting objectives, generating and selecting strategies, detailing specific programs, writing the plan, communicating the plan, and controlling its activities.

Market Test

The planning process is primarily directed at the first stage of the marketing program. In some cases where there is a high probability that the product will be a success, you might go into full-scale production and marketing. In most cases, however, it is wise to conduct some form of market test prior to incurring the large expenditures of introducing the product on a full-scale basis. Market testing is discussed in Task 14, which follows.

Task 14: Plan and Execute a Market Test

Objectives

The idea of market testing is to conduct a controlled experiment on a small scale to learn what to expect when a new product enters full-scale production and is marketed on a large scale. No market test should be undertaken until you are able to define the exact purposes of the test. The major questions a market test can answer are:

What are users' reactions to the product in general and to such associated characteristics as performance, desired attributes, reliability, design, and so on.

In what applications and usage levels would users employ the product?

Are there any high potential markets where the product fits a real need in the user's operations?

Who are the key purchasing influences in high potential markets?

What volume of sales and profits (and market share) can be expected under full-scale marketing at various price levels?

To what degree will sales resistance probably be experienced in a full-scale program?

What are the preferred delivery schedules and distribution channels to satisfy purchasing patterns and habits?

What are the relative effectiveness of various sales and promotional techniques?

What are users' reactions to various price possibilities?

What are users' reactions to various warranty, maintenance and service programs?

Basic Types of Tests

Industrial products are often more easily market tested than consumer products. Most industrial products have a smaller number of total users than consumer products. The users are generally concentrated in a limited number of industries, and are not so geographically dispersed as are consumer product users.

Basically, there are three types of market tests used for industrial products: product use tests, product displays at trade shows or dealer showrooms, and limited market operations. Each of these methods is briefly described and analyzed in the accompanying chart (Market Test Alternatives), with advantages and limitations of each.

Procedure

Whichever market test procedure is employed, follow these steps:

Compile complete list of all product users
Determine sample size and design
Determine methods and controls
Execute test
Analyze data

Compile List of Product Users

Compile a comprehensive list of all known potential users of the product. In the language of statistical sampling, this is the "universe" from which the market test sample of users will be drawn. Analyze each industry and company in the list to determine how each differs from others relative to gross annual sales, geographical location, possible applications and other appropriate characteristics. This compilation should be done regardless of testing procedure employed.

Determine Sample Size and Design

Determine the size and design of the sample to be drawn at random from the list of users identified above. Procedures for the statistical determination of sample size are presented in Chapter I—Marketing Research.

The design of the sample depends on your choice of test method and individual company circumstances. For example, if you select a product-use test, you might meet with ten of your best current customers to discuss and observe the product in actual use. You could let your key sales representatives select the customers or this can be done at the marketing administration level. If you are going to exhibit the product at a trade show, be sure that the product fits a possible use by show attendees. If you employ a limited marketing test, you must determine the geographical and industrial segments to test.

In any case, the basic problem is to select "members" of the test market sample so they accurately represent characteristics of the universe of potential users identified above. The sample must be designed to include the probable preferences and prejudices, wants and needs, relative largeness and smallness, and problems and resources that characterize the universe of users—and

Market Test Alternatives

	DESCRIPTION	ADVANTAGES	LIMITATIONS
Product-Use Test	Common method of verifying product's performance. Informal method: Company representative can show new product to prospective buyers on sales calls and learn prospective buyer's reactions. When satisfied that enough customers "like" the product, add it to your line. Formal method: Company personnel supervise tests in your shop or the prospective customer's facility, directly observing and handling complications. Prospect gets use of product free, at a low cost, or for a delayed payment after the product is proven.	□ Concerned parties can validate product performance under actual conditions–firsthand reactions □ Can revise product's design or specifications before full-scale marketing or withdraw before anticipated losses or embarrassment □ Excellent source of testimonials	□ Exposure of product to competitors □ Oftentimes consuming and expensive □ Some quantity and quality features cannot be tested □ Products tested may be given stricter quality control than during full-scale production □ Test results may differ from actual full-scale results □ Bias □ Customer misuse during test may cause dissatisfaction
Trade Show/ Dealer Showrooms	New products can be displayed at dealer showrooms or at trade shows. Displays at trade shows can be particularly effective since attendees come primarily to see new products. A complete description of this procedure is in Chapter 8, Trade Shows.	□ Usually incur very little cost over and above normal expenses for a show or dealer display □ Quick evidence of interest levels through inquiries and follow-up interviews □ Provides good monitoring and control	□ Limited applications □ Exposes product to competitors □ Information may be superficial □ Inquiries do not necessarily indicate willingness to buy □ Respondents may not be typical of entire market you are trying to reach
Limited Market Operation	New products are made in a limited or pilot production run, using either the manufacturer's facilities or renting those of another company, or in a job shop. Products are then marketed on a limited scale to selected industries on a controlled basis. Limited market operations are previews of full-scale marketing and can help determine whether to discard the new product or go into full-scale production and marketing when justified. At this point, production and marketing plans are integrated for the first time.	□ Measures general market interest and opportunities via actual sales □ Forecasts probable size and nature of market □ Pinpoints marketing problems and evaluates alternative solutions □ Gives company actual production, selling and promotion experience before full-scale marketing □ Checks on product performance in actual use	□ Exposure of product to competitors □ Oftentimes consuming and expensive □ Might not be able to determine and utilize test areas representative of total market

in approximately the same proportions as in that universe. Otherwise, your sample will be biased, and any conclusions drawn from using it in a market test will not be valid. A random sample of adequate size usually satisfied these requirements.

It would be wise to consult a market test professional to help answer these and other design questions.

Determine Methods and Controls

Determine operational methods and controls to be used for collecting sample data, and for compiling data for analysis. The operating methods, selling techniques, emphasis on product features, direct mail formats, advertising appeals—everything—used in the market testing phase must be as identical as possible to those to be used during full-scale marketing operations. All techniques must be standardized, and all participating personnel trained to use standard procedures.

Special data collection forms, questionnaires, and standard procedures for gathering data are needed. Every detail of experience must be observed and recorded for future analysis. Accuracy and objectivity in observing and recording is essential to eliminate bias in estimates and conclusions. If any changes are made in the methods, the changes should be carefully documented as to reasons for making them, a description of the new methods, who authorized them, and when.

The design of all forms, records, and reports and the method of documenting every essential detail of the experiment should consider the methods to be used in analyzing the data.

Execute Test

Here are some suggestions to help maintain standardization and to reduce bias so that market test results will be more reliable:

Eliminate day-to-day variations in the approaches of company contacts with respondents.

Don't ask leading questions (i.e., which suggest an answer).

Structure questionnaires so they are easy to answer and maintain high interest levels.

Probe to get respondents' specific reasons for liking/disliking product features.

Design test to produce data needed to answer questions posed at outset of program.

Ensure no mistakes are made in entering data on forms.

Prevent personal opinions of company personnel and other subjective influences from coloring the test results.

Analyze Data

The final step in the test should answer specific questions raised in the first step of the process (Objectives). The validity of conclusions drawn depend on the care exercised earlier in the test process. Every conclusion at each stage of analysis must be questioned for statistical validity and analyzed for its marketing implications.

Prepare Report

Prepare a final report to document all aspects of the market. In the final report, unfavorable findings must be given at least as much, if not more prominence as the favorable results. Unfavorable findings must not be "brushed off" with rationalizations. It is better to face bad news now, rather than wait until more money has been poured into the full-scale marketing program.

Keep the final report as short as possible, and design it so management can grasp vital facts quickly and easily. Here is a suggested list of contents:

Part 1—PURPOSE: Briefly describe reasons for the market test program, including questions it was designed to answer.

Part 2—SUMMARY OF CONCLUSIONS AND RECOMMENDATIONS: Describe salient findings and recommendations. Cross-reference each item to specific places where substantiating details are found.

Part 3—OVERVIEW OF TEST: Describe major steps in process, the people and organizational elements that participated (and their roles), and precautions taken to keep bias from invalidating results.

Part 4—TEST RESULTS: Describe how data were collected, methods of analysis, and results of analysis. Don't include lengthy tables of data, or mathematical computations. These should be put in appendices. Cross-reference all details in the body of the report to the *specific* location in the appendices for further details and backup information.

Part 5—DETAILED CONCLUSIONS AND RECOMMENDATIONS: This is similar to part 2, except that it is a completely detailed presentation of *all* conclusions and recommendations derived from the market test program.

Part 6—APPENDICES: Include all tables and mathematical computations, bibliography, and similar data.

Task 15: Prepare Preliminary Production Plan

Marketing and Production Coordination

Although production planning is not a primary marketing function, the marketing department has certain supporting responsibilities. Production plans are based on the marketing department's sales forecasts (and sales orders once commercialization is in full swing) and on product specifications developed during the prototype development task (Task 12) and the market testing task (Task 14). Consequently, these activities must be closely coordinated throughout Phase 3 of the PP&D process.

When the preliminary production plan has been produced, you have completed Phase 3 of the PP&D process and a full-scale management review should be scheduled.

Section D
Final Management Review

To Launch or Not to Launch?

Schedule a management review to answer the crucial question: "Shall we launch full-scale commercialization of the new product?"

If the product is rejected, analyze the circumstances leading to this decision. Such analyses help perfect future PP&D efforts.

If the "go-ahead" is given, proceed with marketing your product. Follow the steps suggested in Chapter II—Marketing Planning. Then proceed with developing functional and overall strategies, setting budgets, and detailing programs at the functional and local levels. The actual commercialization process involves all those marketing activities covered in later chapters of this book: establishing distribution channels; pricing the product; promoting the product; and general management of the many intricate functions of marketing.

Timing

If you want to get attention from top management, particularly around the launching period, you should allow for a reasonable interval between each new product launching—at least several months. This gives adequate time to evaluate market test results and to prepare for the significant changes that must take place.

Legal Concerns

It is also wise before final go-ahead to review legal issues which might affect your product. These include product safety, consumerism, ecology, and other topics covered in Chapter XII—Legal Aspects of Marketing.

Product Planning and Development Reference Guide

Associations of Management Consultants

American Management Assoc. (AMA), 135 West 50th St., New York, NY 10020.
Association of Consulting Management Engineers (ACME), 347 Madison Ave., New York, NY 10017.
Association of Management Consultants (AMC), 811 East Wisconsin Ave., Milwaukee, WI 53202.
National Institute of Management Counsellors (NIMC), Box 193, 45 North Station Plaza, Great Neck, NY 11022.

Associations of Industrial Design Firms

Industrial Designers Society of America (IDSA), 1750 Old Meadow Road, McLean, VA 22101.
International Council of Societies of Industrial Design (ICSID), Rue Paul Lauters 2, 1050 Brussels, Belgium.

Sources of Industrial Laboratories

American Council of Independent Laboratories, Inc. (ACIL), 1725 K Street, N.W., Washington, DC 20036.

American Society for Testing Materials (ASTM), 1916 Race St., Philadelphia, PA 19103.

National Research Council, Director of Industrial Research Laboratories of the United States, 2101 Constitution Ave., N.W., Washington, DC 20418.

Directory of Independent Commercial Laboratories Performing Research and Development, National Science Foundation, 1951 Constitution Ave., N.W., Washington, DC 20050.

Sources of Graphic and Package Design Firms

American Institute of Graphic Arts (AIGA), 1059 Third Ave., New York, NY 10021.

International Council of Graphic Design Associations, 7 Templeton Court, Radnor Walk, Croydon CRD 7N2, England.

Package Designers Council (PDC), P. O. Box 3753, Grand Central Station, New York, NY 10017.

Packaging Institute (PI), 342 Madison Ave., New York, NY 10017.

Sources of Traffic Consultants

American Society of Traffic and Transportation (ASTT), 547 West Jackson Blvd., Chicago, IL 60606.

National Council of Physical Distribution Management (NCPDM), 222 West Adams St., Chicago, IL 60606.

National Industrial Traffic League (NITL), 1909 K Street, N.W., Suite 410, Washington, DC 20006.

New Product Development Publications

Design News, Cahners Publishing Co., Inc., Cahners Bldg., 221 Columbus Ave., Boston, MA 02116. For design engineers and engineering management. Usable and adaptable design ideas in graphic form are presented in the principal areas of OEM design engineer activity: mechanical design; electrical design; and materials selection.

Industrial Design (ID), Design Publications, Inc., 717 Fifth Ave., New York, NY 10022. Published for independent industrial designers, company design management, and other executives responsible for initiation, approval and planning of products, packaging, and displays. It covers creativity, sales and market research, information on the cost and availability of materials, and components and finishes that go into products and packages. ID also explores problems and progress in design,

and investigates both new markets for new materials, and new uses for traditional materials.

Innovation. Innovation, P. O. Box 14147, Cincinnati, OH 45214. Presents proven strategies and tactics on how to look at emerging markets and technologies, and analyzes the path from concepts to fully-developed products.

Innovation World, Innovation World, 230 Park Ave., New York, NY 10017. Offers facts, forecasts, and expert opinions about product creativity. Contains articles on business trends, patent, and trademark news.

Machine Design, Penton Publishing Co., Penton Plaza, 1111 Chester Ave., Cleveland, OH 44114. For design engineers. It provides technical information on (1) design and development, "how-to", in-depth technical articles; (2) current technical news coverage; (3) ideas and examples of how design problems have been solved; (4) personal, professional and management information; and (5) new product announcements and manufacturer's literature listings.

New Equipment Digest, Penton Publishing Co., Penton Plaza, 1111 Chester Ave., Cleveland, OH 44114. Describes new or improved equipment, materials, processes, and literature in the general industrial field, with primary emphasis on plant operation, production, maintenance, engineering, design, and purchasing.

Official Gazette, U.S. Patent Office, Washington, DC 20231. (Weekly) Reviews patents, trademarks, and designs issued each week by the U.S. Patent office.

Product Design & Development, Chilton Company, Chilton Way, Radnor, PA 19089. A product news service for design engineers. Content describes new or improved materials and parts, design and test equipment, and manufacturers' literature listings.

Technology Mart, Thomas Publishing Company, 461 Eighth Ave., New York, NY 10007. (1) Publishes (without charge) descriptions of products and processes available to make on license or to purchase outright. (2) The products search section presents special items representing a need that perhaps you can fill; each is an opportunity for business not now in existence.

Product Planning Books and Articles

"A Basic Guide to Planning New Products," *Industrial Marketing*, August 1963, pp. 91–95.

"Competitive Strategies for New Product Marketing Over the Life Cycle," by Philip Kotler, *Management Science*, December 1965, pp. 104–119.

"Criteria for Evaluating Existing Products and Product Lines," in *Analyzing and Improving Marketing Performance, Management Report No. 32*, American Management Assoc. Inc., 135 W. 50th St., New York, NY 10020.

"Exploit the Product Life Cycle," by Theodore Levitt,

Harvard Business Review, November–December 1965, pp. 81–94.

"Increasing the Success-Odds in Marketing New Products," *Journal of Marketing*, January 1961, pp. 74–75.

Management of New Products, Booz, Allen, & Hamilton, Inc., 245 Park Ave., New York, NY 10017.

New Product Planning and Development, by Dharmendra T. Verma, Utah Manufacturers, Bureau of Economic and Business Research, University of Utah, Salt Lake City, UT.

"Phasing Out Weak Products," *Harvard Business Review*, March–April 1965, pp. 107–118.

Product Strategy and Management, by T. L. Berg and Abraham Schuchman (eds), Holt, Rinehart & Winston, New York, NY 10017.

"Selecting Profitable Products," by John T. O'Meara, Jr., *Harvard Business Review*, January–February 1961, p. 83.

"The Death and Burial of 'Sick' Products," by R. S. Alexander, *Journal of Marketing*, April 1964, p. 1.

"The Strategy of Product Policy," by Charles H. Kline, *Harvard Business Review*, July–August 1955, p. 100.

CHAPTER IV

Distribution Channels

Introduction

Functions of Distribution Channels

Businessmen use the term "distribution channels" to describe the ways by which goods and services reach their final buyers.[1] Some goods are sold directly to their ultimate buyers. Others pass through "middlemen" (i.e., a firm acting as intermediary between manufacturer and buyer) before they reach their final buyers. This chapter explains how to select distribution channels for your products.

Perhaps the most important generalization about selecting a channel is: "Does the channel have good access to the market you want to reach?" This access is important because channels of distribution accomplish two primary functions: (1) they transfer ownership of goods; and (2) they physically move goods from the manufacturer's facility to the purchaser's. Distribution channels also fulfill many other secondary, but important functions.

Examples of Distribution Channel Functions

Warehouse (i.e., store) products
Transport and deliver the products
Share in financial and time investments
Grade or sort products
Combine goods from several sources to fill a buyer's order, thereby making all the goods more useful to the buyer
React to needs of customers and relay this information to the manufacturer
Provide marketing communications and promotional services
Grant credit to buyers

Your Channel Objectives

Probably every company has its own unique set of channel objectives. Some seek maximum coverage of the market(s) they want to reach. Others want good dealer relations and enthusiastic support for their products. Still others believe that profits outweigh all other considerations. Nonetheless, certain channel objectives turn up in company after company. Some of the most frequently named channel objectives include the following:

Minimum distribution for seller
Saturation of market (market coverage)
Provision of whatever services the buyers want
Rapid, accurate feedback of information from buyers

---

[1] In marketing jargon, the word channel is used loosely to refer to the distribution process, as well as to the people who are responsible for the process, such as salesmen, agents, and distributors. It is so used in this chapter. A dis-tribution channel, in the broadest sense, might extend from a firm extracting raw chromium to the man who buys a shiny new bumper for his car.

Chapter Plan

This chapter contains information on how to organize, review, or change a company's channel mix. The established company can use it as a check on previous decisions, as well as use it as a guide for working with its channels. The new company can use this chapter as a guideline to selecting, reviewing, working with, and changing channels.

The flow of the chapter plan is:

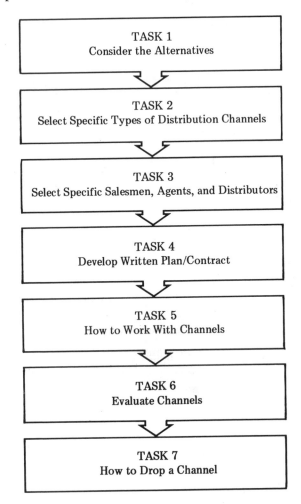

Task 1: Consider the Alternatives

Selection Overview

Most industrial companies have some freedom to choose the kind of channel arrangements they want. Only rarely is a company forced to use a particular kind of channel, like it or not, because "it's the only crap game in town." The basic reason for this freedom of choice is that distributors, manufacturers' reps, wholesalers, etc., deliberately offer different kinds of service to meet the varied needs of many different channel users. Clearly, this differentiation also benefits the various channel types because each has certain unique advantages and profit-making opportunities.

The general approach for your company to follow is to ask what tasks, or functions, you want your channel to do for you. First, list everything necessary to move your product from your shipping dock to your buyer's receiving room. Next, search out the possible channels which you might use, determine what functions each can perform for you, and then determine what tasks will still have to be done by you if you use a certain channel.

Assuming that you are satisfied by your analysis of the functions to be done, complete your study by estimating your sales, your costs, and your profits for each possible channel. Bear in mind, too, that your choice will be a long-run one. Once a choice has been made, it is often difficult to switch to another distribution channel. Accordingly, your sales, cost, and profit estimates should be made for the product's entire life cycle. Then use capital budgeting techniques, if at all possible, to calculate the present net worth of each channel alternative. Also, consult with your accounting department to determine the impact of inventory costs, accounts receivable, credit risk, and freight as a percentage of selling price charged in each channel alternative.

Basic Alternatives

Industrial companies have three basic distribution channels from which to choose: direct sales force, manufacturers' agents (representatives), and distributors. Agents, who tend to specialize in serving a given market, usually supply a variety of products, often unrelated except by application. Distributors usually handle a line of related products.

The direct sales force comprises company employees, while agents and distributors are independent business firms. These independent firms are often called middlemen, or intermediaries, because they transact sales between the company and its ultimate customers. The three basic channels can be used independently or in a variety of combinations, as the following figure shows.

Prevalent Usage Patterns

The most prevalent industrial distribution channel uses a combination of a direct sales

Possible Channels of Distribution

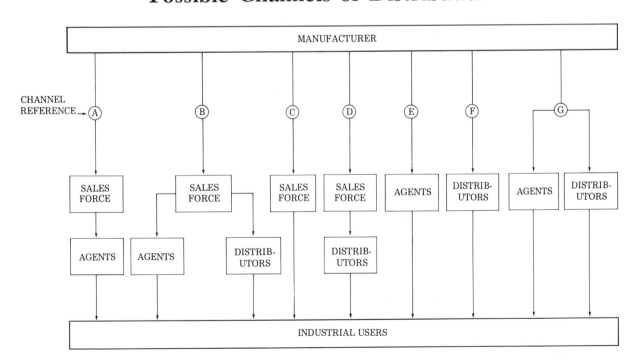

force and agents (channel A in above diagram). The second most common channel uses a direct sales force, agents, and distributors (channel B). Then there is a toss-up between use of a direct sales force (channel C) and a combination of direct salesmen and distributors (channel D). A good number of companies use only agents (channel E). A smaller number employ only distributors (channel F) or some combination of distributors and agents (channel G).

The channel mix used differs significantly depending on the industry, product sophistication, knowledge of market, control required, etc. For example, in SIC 38 (Professional, Scientific and Controlling Instruments; Photographic and Optical Goods, Watches, and Clocks), the use of agents is slightly more prevalent than that of direct salesmen, and double that of distributors. In SIC 33 (Primary Metals), almost all companies employ a direct sales force; about half of them complement the sales force with distributors, and slightly over one-third use agents or representatives.

As a general guideline to the use of channels, there is a tendency to use a direct sales force as companies and product-lines grow, and market potentials and concentrations increase (i.e., in select industries or geographical areas).

Having given these principles of channel selection, the remainder of this task now surveys the activities and functions of the leading types of channels.

Direct Sales Force

Use of a direct sales force entails direct marketing through salesmen operating from company headquarters, sales branches and field offices. The direct sales force calls on wholesale distributors, who in turn call on dealers and end customers, or they themselves may call directly on end customers. The use of a direct sales force requires the company to provide all those functions which a channel must satisfy (e.g., negotiate, storage, transport, finance, etc.)

Conditions Often Conducive to Use of Direct Sales Force [2]

COMPANY
1. Established company with substantial financial, manpower, and facilities resources.
2. Varied, broad, and mature product lines.
3. Routine manufacturing processes allow increased management attention to marketing channels.
4. Good reputation and image in eyes of end customers.
5. Can readily supply total promotional support required.
6. Good market share.
7. Competitors use a direct sales force.

PRODUCT
1. Is well established, perishable, non-graded, stylish, technical, custom-designed or rapidly becomes obsolete (e.g., specialized accessories, certain raw materials, electrical components and parts, capital goods, data processing equipment).
2. Has high price/value per unit or total sales and a wide profit margin.
3. Often sold under long-term agreements in large quantities.
4. Those with volatile prices, making it difficult to maintain fair and equitable compensation levels for middlemen.
5. Consistent with company's primary product-line.
6. High degree of market acceptance.

SERVICE
1. Requires technical sales advice.
2. Requires skilled handling, installation, and maintenance.
3. Need not be stationed close to point-of-purchase and use.

MARKET
1. Composed of a few large, well-defined, and highly concentrated customer groups.

---

[2] Any one of the following ideas may be sufficient to justify direct sales.

2. Customers want quantity or original equipment manufacturer discounts or otherwise prefer direct sale.
3. Market and sales potential can support direct sales force.
4. Customers require applications advice.
5. Considerable negotiations may precede sale.

MIDDLEMEN

1. Limited in availability or adequacy (e.g., can't or won't stock, install, or service products).
2. May sell competitive products.
3. Product requires aggressive sales and promotion efforts not furnished by middlemen.

Types of Direct Sales Forces

The direct sales force can sell the full product line directly to end users or to middlemen. The sales force can work out of company headquarters, from a branch office carrying inventories, or from a sales office which doesn't carry an inventory. They may also furnish repair services. Different types of forces may be used to target on specific market segments, problem areas, or geographic areas. These sales forces may be for OEM, national accounts, products, markets, and/or applications.

Usual Advantages of Direct Selling

Since a company's direct salesmen devote most of their time to selling one company's products, closer customer contacts permit firsthand study of market problems and needs, and generally result in increased sensitivity to customer attitudes and increased customer loyalty. The company can provide increased specialization in product applications; and has better control over price and service. This selling method generally satisfies a customer's desire to buy direct to obtain added discounts, service, and information.

Usual Disadvantages of Direct Selling

Because a sales force requires continuous support, higher fixed costs and increased investment (in offices, salaries, training, paperwork, and inventory storage facilities) tend to raise the break-even point for a company's product-line. Also, it is time-consuming to build, train, and supervise a sales force; and the company must provide an increased number of functions (e.g., credit, delivery, etc.).

Manufacturers' Agents (Representatives)

Thousands of manufacturers' agents daily substitute for direct salesmen at countless companies. Agents, ranging from an independent salesman to an organization of salesmen, are employed in almost every industry. Most agent organizations have less than four employees.

How Agents Work

Agents sell a relatively narrow offering of non-competing, but related product-line(s), with approximately one-third operating within an exclusive territory.

They may be authorized to sell a specified quantity of manufacturer's product.

Agents usually work under a continuing contractual arrangement lasting several years. Normal period for termination notice is 90 days.

They don't take title to the goods they sell. Manufacturer ships and bills the purchaser direct.

They are commonly paid by fixed commission or fee, increasing with number of services rendered (e.g., local advertising, installation, training, maintenance, inventory, etc.). Rates vary inversely with volume; in seven digits, it may be as low as 2% plus allowances for advertising and promotion. On low volume, it may be as high as 20% or more. The rate also depends on the industry and profit margins achieved. Commissions are paid on the net amount of all orders accepted and shipped to assigned territory, after discounts, freight, taxes, returns and allowances, etc. Average commissions for manufacturers' agents are between 5 and 7% for most industries. Commissions are paid only after goods are delivered and in some instances only after goods are paid for. This sales method is somewhere between the cost of direct selling and using distributors.

Agents may or may not carry (take possession of) stock. There is a trend toward some inventorying of emergency stocks and replacement parts. Approximately 15% carry stock.

Over 50% sell direct to industrial buyers, 25% sell to distributors (wholesalers), and approximately 20% sell to retailers (per U.S. Department of Commerce reports).

Agents have limited authority over pricing and terms of sale; these are usually preset by manufacturer.

For the benefit of both parties, a written agreement should always be made.

Conditions Often Conducive to Use of Manufacturers' Agents

COMPANY

1. Smaller or new company or division of larger company not having financial or manpower resources to organize, maintain, and support own sales force in particular lines or geographical areas.
2. Prevalent in companies with single product or limited product-line; or in multi-product companies with one product going to distinct and separate markets.
3. Sales force is already burdened with existing business.
4. Company is not well-known.
5. Seller can provide partial promotional support.

PRODUCT

1. New product in existing or new markets, or one differentiated from primary line.
2. Important in the sale of standard machinery/equipment which is useful across several industries, and

some specialties (e.g., wiring supplies and apparatus, automobile equipment, steel products, plumbing, heating equipment and supplies, hardware, electrical specialties, industrial chemicals).
3. Infrequently purchased product (e.g., seasonal or cyclical) requiring year-round contact where sales volume won't support year-round salesmen.
4. Average market awareness and acceptance.

SERVICE

1. Requires some technical advice, possibly including installation and maintenance, but most often not.
2. Requires the performance of fewer marketing functions than with complex, technical products.

MARKET

1. Market is thin—few customers or it is different from those approached with major product-line.
2. Expanding to new geographic areas or industry segments where sales volume cannot completely support a direct sales force, either because of marginal potential or too distant.
3. Market is spread out geographically.
4. Customers are accustomed to dealing with agents.
5. Some specialized information is required.
6. Some price negotiations may precede sale.

MIDDLEMEN

1. Are more well known in local area than manufacturer.
2. Carries narrow enough line to be knowledgeable on all product aspects, but wide enough to overcome possible infrequent or small sales of a particular line.
3. Need fair amount of aggressive sales and promotional efforts.

Other Types of Agent Middlemen

The manufacturers' agent is one of five basic types of agent middlemen. Each of the other four offer distinct differences in approach. They are brokers, commission merchants, resident buyers, and sales agents.

A broker is usually a person/firm operating on a noncontinuous relationship of bringing buyers and sellers together to negotiate a sale. A broker can, but seldom represents both parties. However, he can represent one or more clients simultaneously in different transactions. The broker usually deals with highly specialized products with sparse demand; but he rarely handles the goods (except possibly samples), and never takes title. The broker cannot usually bind the principal (manufacturer), since every transaction must be approved by the latter. For his service, the broker is usually paid a set commission, or fee, upon exchange of merchandise.

The commission merchant is similar to the broker except that he can bind the client. Commission merchants generally specialize in consumer products, textiles, naval stores, and lumber. They sometimes take physical possession; finance the products; deliver; and often sort, grade and repack.

Resident buyers are generally located in large consumer market areas (e.g., New York City). They supplement retail stores' purchasing staffs by informing manufacturers of market conditions; and actually buy "fill-ins" after principal purchases are made. They are usually paid by commission.

Sales agents are commonly used by small manufacturers selling to distant markets. They are most prevalent in the textile trade, industrial machinery, coal and coke, metals, and chemicals. They act under a continuous relationship in lieu of a company's sales force, with the exception that they may handle more than one non-competing line. The sales agent sells the entire output of a manufacturer, or a specified portion to a usually limited territory. They offer the manufacturer a variety of marketing services (e.g., financing, warehousing), and often can specify prices and terms within a range set by the manufacturer. The sales agent is paid a commission depending on the amount of services provided; possibly based on achieving an agreed-upon quota. After a satisfactory working relationship is developed and the need arises, the sales agent is often integrated into the company.

Advantages of Using Manufacturers' Agents

When using manufacturers' agents, the manufacturer can concentrate its efforts on production and product-line expansion without incurring financial expenses of establishing company sales offices. Salaries, social security contributions, and fringe benefits which employers normally provide are eliminated. This allows predetermined control of selling costs—which will vary with sales volume—but not fixed overhead. The manufacturer also minimizes its costs for sales force recruiting, training, and managing.

The manufacturers' agent generally receives lower percentage commissions than those paid to wholesalers/distributors. The manufacturer lowers its sales-expense ratio through spreading agent's costs over products of several companies. Also, there is little or no selling cost until the sale is consummated, or in some cases, until the end customer has paid the manufacturer.

The manufacturer using agents can sell to small market segments not economically covered by a direct sales force. It is much easier to quickly establish nationwide distribution than by going direct (e.g., accessibility to agents' previously developed contacts and markets).

It is easy to check and control prices, terms, and credit quoted by agents, since the manufacturer bills the purchaser direct. However, the agent can assist in local credit checks.

Agents usually give more attention to a product-line than distributors do. They maintain regular and intensive customer calls on all accounts. This makes it somewhat easier to train agents than a distributor sales force, which handles many products.

The manufacturer can readily reward and promote agents through increased commissions without the associated moving expenses, explanations to customers, and other problems relating to the reshuffling of an in-house sales force.

Another excellent advantage of agents is that they can select a number of good customers to field test a new or changed product and reliably report to the manufacturer information on product qualities and drawbacks.

Disadvantages of Using Manufacturers' Agents

The use of agents often lessens control over the selling operation, since agents may represent many manufacturers and possibly neglect your firm to concentrate on primary accounts. It's common for an agent to have a maximum of 5–6 principals. Control is reduced since some agents may deliberately hold down sales so as not to create a market capable of supporting the manufacturer's direct salesmen. In essence, the company has less direct contact with his customers, causing reduced awareness of end problems.

Most agents dislike report writing—most communications to manufacturers are demands and complaints. Provision of market data is usually sporadic. Customer audits, scheduled routes, daily reports, and campaign programs are difficult to implement, unless clearly agreed to in contract form.

Some agents may take your line simply to prevent other agents from getting it. Others think in terms of immediate sales, with no concern for building long-term business. Selling expense may be excessive on a large sales volume.

Some agents won't, and can't, always carry every manufacturer's samples and sales kits. Some don't follow up on inquiries. Some refuse to provide customer mailing lists and insist that all customer dealings go through them in order to protect their accounts. Some agents do not adequately train and supervise their salesmen.

Distributors/Wholesalers

Distributors are independent firms offering sales and a variety of other services to certain manufacturers. Distributors are located in almost every area of high industrial concentration. They can be vertical (carrying products for only one industry) or horizontal (carrying products used across many industries).

How Distributors Work

Distributors can represent only one manufacturer producing a wide line of products, or many separate manufacturers. In either case, an attempt is made to sell a wide range of related goods, sometimes even competing goods in local areas. The distributor regularly contacts key plants in the territory, with a sales organization of from 1 to 50 or more salesmen.

Take title to goods and carry inventories close to point of use. Some distributors even purchase the products outright and resell them under the distributor's name. They help the manufacturer by eliminating the small order business, cut inventory and storage costs for the manufacturer, and provide quick delivery of goods. The distributor may also break down large shipments and combine products from different manufacturers and reship to ultimate buyers.

Provide local product promotion via direct mail campaigns, catalog distribution, etc.

Grant credit to their purchasers; provide some information/advice of market conditions potential, needs, trends; provide services such as delivery, installation, repair.

Cost of using distributors varies depending largely on unit price and market potential. Usually paid by granting them a discount or margin from list price. For example, a manufacturer may set a price of $100 on a piece of equipment, and allow the distributor a price of $65. The distributor then re-sells the equipment at $100, making a profit margin of $35 per piece sold. Obviously, the bigger the margin, the more distributor interest will be created (assuming that turnover is not strongly affected by selling price).

Some distributors are given exclusive rights to sell certain manufacturers' products in a given territory.

Manufacturers supply the product in desired quality and quantity packages, provide specification and price sheets, catalogs, and other promotional materials, as well as set sales price, terms, etc.

Conditions Often Conducive to Use of Distributors

COMPANY

1. Smaller or new company with single product or narrow product-line which is insufficient to sustain own sales force in field.
2. Company has little or no knowledge of ultimate consumer/user of product or exact use of product-line.
3. Company has limited financial, facility, and manpower resources.
4. Company has small market share.
5. There is little customer awareness of company as a supplier of specific products.

PRODUCT

1. Nontechnical and standard products, requiring little sales engineering support (e.g., small equipment and machinery, tools and supplies, repair and maintenance parts and accessories).
2. New products with small profit margins and/or small unit purchase.
3. Several on-the-spot substitutes necessitate fast delivery.

SERVICE

1. Buyer needs on-the-spot stocking, servicing, and handling of complaints.
2. The product requires some installation and repair work.

MARKET

1. Wide variety of industrial plants. Customers are widely separated geographically, causing prohibitive costs in time, travel, etc., to contact them all.
2. Small orders (in size and/or profits) are prevalent.
3. Customers require little technical information.

MIDDLEMEN AVAILABLE TO MANUFACTURER

1. Need prestige of an established and known firm to help penetration.
2. Little negotiations required.
3. Aggressive sales and promotional efforts desired, but not essential.
4. Widely available.
5. Middlemen customers insist on buying from a distributor.

Types of Distributors

There are four basic types of distributors: full-line, specialized, limited-line, and departmentalized. Each is distinguished by the amount of services or functions performed for the manufacturer, and the extent of product-lines carried.

Full-line distributors, also called general-line or mill supply houses can be used to reach wide horizontal markets (e.g., maintenance supplies, general machinery, cutting tools, fasteners) or narrower vertical markets (e.g., oil wells, foundries, construction). They can stock as many as several hundred product-lines; some stock over 10,000 industrial items, some of which may be competing brands. They cannot give intensive sales promotion to products of all manufacturers represented. They offer a limited amount of technical service; but most do offer credit. Full-line distributors make it possible for a customer to place a single order for his needs. Also, they make it possible for him to get all items on a single delivery.

Specialized distributors usually concentrate on products requiring a high degree of product information, technical service, and applications engineering. They are prevalent in the sale of bearings, cutting tools, abrasives, power transmission, materials handling, portable power tools, air and hydraulic equipment, power plant equipment, welding equipment and supplies, electronics, scientific/medical instruments, etc.

Limited-line distributors are generally smaller distributors specializing in a dozen or more unrelated product-lines requiring salesmanship, technical service, speedy delivery, and on-the-spot stocking. They provide merchandising efforts and close control of costs, margins, and profits on each line carried. They prefer to handle "door-opening," high margin, fast turnover products, providing entrees for specialty sales teams. Limited-line distributors generally specialize in industrial supplies, equipment, or machinery.

Departmentalized distributors carry a full line, grouping product offerings into departments for the sake of better merchandise management. They possess in depth knowledge of products and applications, and sell and service more profitable key product-lines on a competitive basis with specialized and limited-line distributors.

Advantages of Distributors

Distributors are a ready-made sales force, providing manufacturers with quick national entry, expansion, experience, knowledge of local market conditions and demands, and entrance to relatively inaccessible buyers.

There is little or no cost incurred until sales are made. Straight commission allows predetermined selling expense. Distributors eliminate the expense for recruiting, selecting, training and supervising the sales force, as well as warehousing and some servicing. They eliminate small orders and reduce credit problems, inventory, storage, and delivery costs for manufacturers.

Distributors provide local stocking, and local representation for servicing and handling complaints. They can handle broken stocks (i.e., breakdown large shipments and sell "onesies" and "twosies"). They can assemble order requirements (i.e., take one or two units from different manufacturers and combine them for sale to one customer).

Disadvantages of Distributors

Distributors lessen the manufacturer's control over sales activities (e.g., frequency of sales calls), pricing, and marketing planning. The limited manufacturer contact with end customers permits the distributor to readily switch its customers to new suppliers if disagreements arise between the distributor and the manufacturer.

It is often necessary to give special benefits (e.g., discounts, incentives) to obtain favorable or equal service from distributors or they may drop your line. The cost of selling a product in an advanced stage of sales development may be higher with distributors.

Use of distributors often lessens control over the feedback of market information, final product and package condition, local advertising and promotion effort, and how inquiries are followed up.

Task 2: Select Specific Types of Distribution Channels

Preliminary Selection Process

After considering the alternative distribution channels discussed in Task 1, a *new* company can select a channel (or mix of channels) which best provides complete market coverage without gaps or duplication. An established company can analyze its current channels for their suitability. However, most companies in either position still need additional qualitative and quantitative screening techniques for selecting their distribution channels.

Selection Steps

The following steps may be used as a guide to making distribution channel decisions. Although the process is primarily qualitative, some quantitative determinants are suggested. The actual steps described, and their sequence are not mandatory. Use only those steps that best suit your company's situation.

Pinpoint markets to be reached. This is really an objective of the company—which customer groups to approach. Determine whether these groups are concentrated in specific geographic or industry segments or dispersed.

Classify the market segments to be reached by user-industry or customer group. This follows from the previous step.

Determine the market and sales potential for each market segment. How many customers are there? How much will each customer buy on the average? Use government, trade association, and publication research sources, or conduct your own studies to obtain this information. (See Chapter I—Marketing Research).

Determine relative importance of each market, industry, and geographic segment. This can be a mere priority ranking, or a sophisticated approach weighting a variety of factors to determine ranking and how much more important one segment is than another. Include expected market share in the analysis.

Gather insights and opinions on the markets and channels from sales and marketing executives in your company; from noncompetitors in the same industry; from middlemen; and from customers. Ask related trade associations and trade publications for information on channels customarily employed.

Use all secondary and primary research sources at your command to study the industry for possible long-range market changes which affect channel decisions.

Determine which channels your competition is using and why. Use this only as a guideline, not as a sole determiner for your selection.

Estimate sales manpower needs.

List all activities the distribution channel is expected to do (i.e., those they must do, those you would like them to do;

e.g., sell, stock, promote, frequency of calls, number of men needed, etc.).

List those activities which your company can or must do (because some other company or channel won't do them).

Describe your company (in order to get a better feel for what your channel requirements are).

1. How new is it? What is the stage of company development? Reputation in customers' eyes?
2. What are the current market share levels being achieved?
3. What are the company's objectives?
4. Does the company have appropriate selling and promotional capabilities?
5. What is the extent, variety, and breadth of product-line?
6. What stage in life cycle are most of your company's products (e.g., new, mature)?
7. Are special distribution services needed because of technical, customized, or other product characteristics?
8. What is the frequency, size of sale, and margins achieved?
9. What order-filling procedure is currently employed?

List the channel or chain of channels currently used to contact end-user (including alternatives not currently employed) to bridge gap between customer and company. Which are most desirable?

Match the capabilities and resources of each channel against the requirements dictated by overall company and marketing objectives. Compare the cost to set up and operate each. Compare aggressiveness of sales and promotion efforts achievable.

Eliminate channels which cannot or will not fulfill essential activities.

Rank remaining channels according to ability to accomplish assigned tasks and to best satisfy end-users' needs.

Calculate estimated total costs to the company per unit of sales through alternative channels (covering expected volume ranges over a period of at least three years). Include average frequency, size and profit per sales call on end-user. Include all costs: inventory control, shipping, sales expense, supervision, advertising, billing, carrying accounts receivable, etc. Use break-even analysis to evaluate each alternative channel considered.

Eliminate channels the company clearly cannot afford because of imposed return-on-investment standards.

Rank the remaining channels according to:
1. Estimated profitability (sales less expenses) [3]
2. Ability to fulfill essential and desirable activities
3. Effectiveness in reaching marketing goals
4. Advantages and disadvantages

5. An overall comparison of commission methods with the cost of operating your own sales force and providing the associated services required

Analyze the top two channel mixes to determine whether, and to what extent, all desired goals and activities are achieved.

Conduct formal surveys and market tests to obtain indication as to most effective channel. This is an optional task which may be too costly and time-consuming for most small companies to undertake.

Determine how the company can accomplish remaining activities and reach desired goals in the case of direct or indirect channels remaining under consideration.

Select channel offering best balance of serving target markets and returning profits for the company.

Task 3: Select Specific Salesmen, Agents, and Distributors

Selection Steps

After determining the channel mix, you must select specific salesmen, agents, or distributors. The following steps are suggested for this purpose. Although most of the steps refer only to specific middlemen, they are equally applicable to selection of other members of the distribution channel.

Develop job description, including responsibilities, activities, priorities, qualifications required, and relationships with other members of the distribution channels. Include such factors as training, related experience, knowledge of product and so forth.

Review recruiting sources. Analyze past records (if they exist) to determine

sources of most successful salesmen, agents, or distributors.

Discuss your selection problem with (existing and potential) significant key accounts. Ask them if they can offer a recommendation or would prefer dealing with a specific middleman.

Check other recruiting sources for referrals: sales managers of noncompetitors in the same industry; editors of related trade publications; officials of prominent trade associations; employment agencies; business associates; present employees and channels; social contacts; schools and colleges; competitors; suppliers; trade schools.

Determine whether suggested salesmen, agents, or distributors are currently (or have had experience in) calling on the type of customers and territory desired by your company.

---

[3] Channel yielding greatest sales volume is not necessarily the largest profit producer.

Discuss with each applicant middleman your proposed working arrangement. Eliminate all those on which a good rapport between the middleman and the company is questionable.

Have each applicant middleman under consideration complete an application/data form.

Conduct informal sessions with remaining channel possibilities to determine:

1. Technical competence and familiarity with product lines, materials, tooling, concepts, tolerances, applications
2. Knowledge of markets and established contacts with potential buyers
3. General comprehension and ability
4. Degree of concentration or specialization in a few specific related product-lines, so that aggressive representation may be afforded all
5. Sufficient sales personnel and willingness to adequately cover market
6. If any basic conflict exists between middleman's distribution policies and yours (e.g., agreement to call on end users rather than other middlemen)
7. Willingness and capability to carry inventories
8. Commission rates and structure desired
9. Current and previous principals, product-lines, customer types, and actual commissions received from each
10. Service capability
11. Overall interest in your specific products

Discuss specific ideas for merchandising/selling your products in middleman's proposed territory. Carefully evaluate his comments for interest, ingenuity, and enthusiasm.

Get applicant to ask questions about the job and your company.

Have applicant submit references. (Check these out.)

Contact applicant's previous and current customers and principals, as well as other references he may give, to check:

1. Reputation for honesty and good service
2. Sales ability (qualifications and past performance)
3. Sound judgement
4. Reputation for sticking to a few related lines and calling on same trade
5. Personal background of principals
6. Credit rating
7. Validity of other information provided

Determine acceptable commission structure. Weigh what you can pay against what candidate has earned from other principals (employers) and against sales expectations if working relationship is consummated. Make commission high enough to attract and keep high caliber personnel and to promote aggressive representation.

Resolve any conflicts of interest between your product-line and those of other principals. Make sure that middleman offerings are similar in price, quality, and customer coverage.

Negotiate for all other services which you want the middleman to perform.

Select candidate who appears best able to fulfill your requirements within company cost constraints.

Make a 120-day (or longer) probationary appointment or contract to determine actual field performance prior to finalization of working agreement. Good personnel won't complain about this probation period since they are confident they'll pass. Request a specific investment in time and effort.

Conduct special training and plant tour to increase middleman's familiarity with your products, technical and manufacturing process, company policies and marketing programs. Get personnel into field as soon as possible.

Verify potentials and provide list of prospects/accounts on which middleman can call.

Have your sales manager spend time with

the middleman in his territory to provide field training and obtain an on-the-
spot evaluation.

Keep middleman's interest high, especially during the break-in period. Consider these suggestions:

1. Give increased commissions on the
first few orders obtained
2. Pay middlemen advances or re-
tainers against anticipated future
commissions
3. Give praise, use score cards, and

Representatives' Data Form [4]

Name of Organization: _____ Date: _____

Principals: 1 _____ 2 _____

Address: _____
         Street   City   State   Zip

Telephone No.: ___ (___) _____
       Area   Number

1. No. of years in business: _____
2. Territory covered: _____
3. Branch locations: _____
4. No. of salesmen: _____
5. How many sales calls per month can your organization commit to our line? _____
6. Gross sales volume last year: $ _____
7. Do you have your own advertising/promotion program? ☐ Yes ☐ No
8. Do you have stocking facilities? ☐ Yes ☐ No
9. Do you have a service staff? ☐ Yes ☐ No
10. Please list bank references: _____

11.

Manufacturers currently represented (include addresses)	Products	Territory	No. of years representing

12.

Principal customers	Approximate $ volume sold to each last year

[4] This basic form can be used for obtaining data from agents and distributors. Of course, you can add other questions to obtain data relevant to your company's situation.

challenges; set up quotas and objectives (not always dollar ones) with the middlemen
4. Provide continuing education and training to middlemen (e.g., technical manuals, formal classes, field training)
5. Encourage two-way flow of information from company to middleman to market place; and from the market place to middleman to the company
6. Provide merchandising aids and supports

7. Give the middleman every chance for a successful long-term working relationship with your company
8. Provide enough time to adequately evaluate performance

Develop written agreement detailing all responsibilities on the part of channel and company. Suggestions for preparing written agreements and contracts are covered in Task 4, which follows.

Task 4: Develop Written Plan/Contract

Value of a Written Plan

Always prepare a written agreement and distribution plan outlining for each channel (internal or external) its specific responsibilities, authorities, and relationships tying them together. This ensures that no marketing facet is omitted, that there are no breaks in the distribution process from company to end-users, and that all parties know what is expected of them. Sample agreement/contract forms can be obtained from a variety of sources listed in the reference guide to this chapter.

What to Include

The plan, contract, or agreement can be a formalized contract, or a simple signed memorandum, depending on the circumstances and preferences of individuals involved. In any case, the following key elements should be included:

Duration of agreement and definition of relationship between channels and the company, and other channels at all levels of distribution.
Statement of geographical markets, industries, and customer types to which channels will sell, each ranked in order of importance; and whether channel has exclusive rights of coverage in these segments or will share responsibilities.
Specific products or services to be sold.
Kind and amount of marketing effort to be provided by the manufacturer and by each channel. Ideally, these activities should be weighted in terms of importance and time allocated to each. Examples of items to be covered include:
1. Functions to be performed
2. Merchandising aids, product samples
3. Education and training by manufacturer
4. Support to be provided by manufacturer (engineering and sales assistance, identification of prospects, etc.)
5. Sales call planning
6. Two-way communication of market information between channel and manufacturer
7. Services provided by channel
Policy statements regarding conflicts (e.g., handling of competing lines; who receives credit for sales to national accounts residing in middleman's or salesman's territory).
Estimated annual sales volume for next three years.
Incentive, commission, and bonus struc-

ture for moving products to users, and for fulfilling other tasks. How they are derived and paid. Are sales quotas involved?[5] If so, what are they? How are they determined? State as precisely and simply as possible so channels can keep track of their earnings. Be flexible to meet changing conditions. Include windfall and bad time provisions, and an expense plan.

Statement of how the customer benefits by the company using certain specified channels.

Statement of permanence of working relationship to reduce fear by agents or distributors of loss of product-line when market has been fully cultivated.

Sales policies, including prices, terms, discounts, credit, invoices, collections, cancellations, changes, returns, and profit margins (where appropriate).

Product warranties and guarantees, and who will fulfill them.

Any special rights held by each of the agreeing parties.

How either party can terminate the agreement.

General conditions

Task 5: How to Work with Channels

Key Areas of Concern

The key to successful long-range relationships between a company and its channels of distribution (whether in-house salesmen or agents or distributors) is good rapport. (Remember, you are "partners in distribution" with those helping you make sales.) This rapport can be built, enhanced, and developed into a favorable working relationship by means of these policies:

Create mutual confidence and cooperation. Good channels can take the bulk of their clientele with them when switching employers or principals. Always demonstrate and have good intentions.

Maintain open communication lines in both directions between the company and its channels; include agents and distributors as if they were direct salesmen.

Involve the channels in your marketing process. Ask their suggestions on packaging, advertising, pricing, and products.

Provide engineering/technical consulting assistance, conduct technical and sales training courses and conferences. (See "Develop Sales Training Programs".)

Give quick home office handling of orders (e.g., introduce order processing shortcuts).

Conduct sales promotion and incentive programs. (See Chapter X—Other Sales Promotion.)

Give recognition and rewards to all channels for work well done.

Give up-to-date facts on deliveries.

Develop and maintain adequate territorial alignment. (See "Develop Sales Territories".)

Assist in customer cultivation. (See "Assist In Customer Cultivation".)

Assist in sales promotion and advertising. (See "Assist In Sales Promotion And Advertising".)

Provide easy-to-use reports. (See "Provide Sales Reports/Forms".)

Analyze channel performance and tell them how they did. (See Task 6.)

Determine Sales Manpower Needs/Calls Required

To effectively plan your manpower requirements for a sales force or other middlemen, this task will be extremely helpful.

---

[5] Quotas are standards of performance governing sales expected by a specific channel in a specific territory over a given time. Quotas can be based on executive or channel estimates, past performance, market potential, trends, and similar criteria.

Ten-Step Process

The following approach yields a rough approximation of the number of salesmen needed to adequately cover specific markets. This "workload" approach focuses on current activity by looking at each account and what it implies for the company.[6] The steps for this technique are listed below.

1. List all customers and prospects in each territory. Review this list with salesmen and sales managers for completeness. Determine the average number of buying influences per plant requiring regular calls.
2. Rank each customer and prospect by profit contribution potential. Group them by classes according to ranges of profit contribution (e.g., $5,000 to $9,999, $10,000 to $14,999, etc.).
3. Determine the number of customers and prospects in each range (classification) of profit potential.
4. Estimate the number of calls required for each group. This is based on past year's activity adjusted for next year's expectations.
5. Determine the total number of calls needed to cover identified market potential adequately.
6. Determine the average number of calls that can be made by one salesman in one year.
7. Divide the average number of calls that one salesman can make into the number of calls required to adequately cover the market. This tells how many men are ideally needed to cover the market.
8. Determine the current number of salesmen employed.
9. Subtract the number currently employed from the number needed to determine how many new sales personnel are required.
10. Continue to add men until the present value of profits falls below the company's cost of capital (i.e., until it

costs more to put the man in the field than profits generated). On the other hand, it may be desirable to accept higher costs as a temporary measure when penetrating new markets or building up existing markets.

The following example and forms (Call Requirements and Salesmen Required) organize the steps in determining sales manpower needs.

Call Requirements

After listing all customers and prospects in each territory, categories of profit contribution potential should be determined. Categories can be adjusted to suit the size of your company. In the example, categories are broken down as shown in column 1 of the "Call Requirement" form. In the territory shown, there are 6 existing customers whose profit contribution is $100,000 or more, 12 prospects with profit contribution potential over $100,000 and so forth, for a total of 291 existing customers and 514 prospects of assorted profit potentials.

Assume that management, in consultation with local sales managers and channels, wants existing *customers* with profit contribution potential over $100,000 to be called upon 40 times a year, and *prospects* in this category seen 10 times a year. Similarly, frequencies desired for other categories of profit contribution potential are as shown in columns 4 and 5.

By multiplying the number of customers (column 2) and number of prospects (column 3) by the desired call frequency (columns 4 and 5 respectively), the total calls to cover specific profit contribution categories of customers and prospects is determined. These numbers should be entered in column 6 for customers and column 7 for prospects. The example shows 240 calls on customers (6 × 40) and 120 calls on prospects (12 × 10) in the over $100,000 profit potential category.

Total calls in each category (column 8) are then determined by adding columns 6 and 7. In the example, the total number of calls for

[6] An alternative approach, the sales potential method, emphasizes future sales potentials and assigns a certain dollar amount to each man.

Call Requirements

TERRITORY: California

(1) CUSTOMER AND PROSPECT PROFIT CONTRIBUTION POTENTIAL	ACTUAL		PLANNED				
			CALL FREQUENCY		CALLS REQUIRED FOR YEAR		
	(2) NUMBER OF CUSTOMERS	(3) NUMBER OF PROSPECTS	(4) CUSTOMERS	(5) PROSPECTS	(6) ON CUSTOMERS (COLUMNS 2 X 4)	(7) ON PROSPECTS (COLUMNS 3 X 5)	(8) TOTAL (COLUMNS 6 + 7)
Over $100,000	6	12	40	10	240	120	360
$75,000 − $100,000	13	24	25	7	325	168	493
$50,000 − $74,999	22	35	12	5	264	175	439
$25,000 − $49,999	37	78	10	4	370	312	682
$10,000 − $24,999	58	100	8	3	464	300	764
$ 5,000 − $ 9,999	70	125	6	2	420	250	670
Less than $5,000	85	140	4	1	340	140	480
Total	291	514	−	−	2,423	1,465	3,888

over $100,000 profit potential customers and prospects is 360 (240 + 120). Column 8 is then totaled for all categories to determine the total number of calls required for the year in a specific territory. In the example, this total is 3,888.

Salesmen Required

The next step is determination of the number of calls a salesman can make in his territory. This requires consultation with field sales managers and salesmen to determine the territory's characteristics and the problems involved in covering it adequately.

On the "Salesmen Required" form, total calls required for the year (from the Call Requirements form—3,888) is entered on line A.

On line B, the average number of calls per salesman in one year is determined. This is the average number of calls per day times the number of working days in the year. In the example, it is assumed that salesmen will make 4 calls per day. Starting with 52 five-day weeks in the year, subtract vacations, holidays and meetings to determine the number of working days in the field. In the example, two weeks vacation (10 working days) and seven days of holidays and meetings were subtracted, yielding 243 working days. Thus, the average number of calls per salesman in one year is 972 (243 times 4).

To determine the number of salesmen needed to cover the market, divide the total calls required by the number of calls a salesman can make in one year (line A divided by line B). In the example, four salesmen are needed. In the case of the decimal fraction, take the next higher whole number.

Lines D, E, and F provide simple extrapolations of the number of new salesmen needed, and the cost of adding them. Line E, the cost of adding new men, includes salesman's salary, expenses, recruiting, training, and so forth.

Develop Sales Training Programs

A logical approach should include at least the following steps (full-scale training programs are considerably more complex):

Salesmen Required

TERRITORY _____ California _____

A.	Total Calls Required For Year (From Call Requirements form)	3,888
B.	Average Number of Calls Per Salesman in One Year (Average number of calls per day times the number of working days in the year)	972
C.	Number of Salesmen Needed to Cover Market (A ÷ B)	4
D.	Number of New Men Needed (C − present number of salesmen)	2
E.	Cost of Adding New Men (D times cost per salesman)	$70,000
F.	Cost of Entire Sales Force (C times cost of employing one salesman)	$140,000

1. Determine training objectives in terms of results desired (e.g., improved performance, knowledge of new products, new sales techniques, etc.).
2. Determine who is in charge of the training program (e.g., sales or personnel department).
3. Determine what subjects to cover (e.g., see list of subjects to include below).
4. Determine training methods (e.g., on-the-job, formal classroom instruction, etc.).
5. Select training vehicles (e.g., lectures, group discussion seminars, demonstrations, case histories, role playing, etc.).
6. Select training aids to use (e.g., audiovisual aids, instruction manuals, textbooks, working models programmed instruction texts, etc.).
7. Select facilities (e.g., conference room, hotel suite, production floor, customers' offices, etc.).
8. Determine timing (e.g., continuous or one-time, during working hours or after hours, over how many weeks, length of each session, etc.).
9. Select instructor(s) (e.g., personnel manager, training manager, sales manager, outside instructors, etc.).
10. Select participants (e.g. all sales staff and middlemen, new sales personnel, etc.).
11. Compute training program costs

(e.g., materials, equipment, facilities, instructor, administration, etc.).

12. Check results against predetermined objectives (e.g., rate each sales person at the end of course, or periodically, etc.). This is not always determinable for some time.

13. Publicize program (e.g., announce to participants).

14. Give certificates upon completion of formal programs.

Subjects to Include

The list below can be used to develop a systematic sales training program. For best results, your program should be continuous and should cover one or more of the following items:

Overall company history, policies and practices.

Thorough knowledge of products or services offered (e.g., applications, benefits).

Information on customers and their needs, problems, products, etc.

Information on competitive products and strategies.

Knowledge of advertising, publicity, trade show, direct mail, and sales promotion activities employed by the company to assist salesmen.

Knowledge of company policies on credit, collections, terms, etc.

Management of salesman's time.

How to get leads and how company will help.

Review and develop sales techniques.[7]

---

[7] Techniques should include prospecting, pre-approach, approach, presentation, closing, meeting objections, follow-up, etc. Prospecting is obtaining a list of names of persons or companies having a need for your product and the ability to buy it. During the pre-approach, you obtain information about your prospects in order to prepare your presentation. The approach is the initial period of contact with prospect, gaining attention and interest. The presentation is the main body of your sales call, including demonstrations, discussion of benefits, and so forth. A trial close can be used to determine if the prospect is ready to buy. Objections may have to be overcome. Then comes the close, asking for and writing the order. Follow-up procedures are used to reassure buyers that they have made a wise decision, that all questions are answered as to the product, contract and delivery, and that future needs are satisfied.

Developing sales presentation aids.

Oral communication, human relations, work habit formation, behavioral science in selling.

Generating enthusiasm.

Setting up customer and prospect files.

Suggestions concerning outside training courses.

Nonselling tasks (e.g., reports, correspondence, record-keeping, etc.).

Develop Sales Territories

Sales territories comprise a group of existing or potential customers that can readily be called upon by one or more channels of distribution, normally within a prescribed geographical area.

A new company must define territories and an existing company must re-examine territories because:

They provide a systematic approach for complete market coverage, and to facilitate efficient and regular call planning.

They help relate sales efforts to expected profits.

They help avoid duplication of sales efforts.

They permit comparisons and evaluations of territories, channels, and individuals.

They provide channels with more specific areas to cover.

They afford individuals the opportunity to carry out responsibilities and prove their capabilities.

They equalize opportunities among channels and salesmen.

Steps in Establishing Territories

The determination of territory size varies in current practice from simply using state boundaries or groupings of states to sophisticated operations research and econometric techniques based on mathematical theory. The first approach is straightforward; the second is beyond the scope of this book.

There is no one right method for calculating sales territories for a firm. However, the following paragraphs present a general format and some guidelines for their determination. The following steps are discussed:

Calculate market potentials
Develop distribution index
Determine preliminary territories
Modify preliminary territories

Calculate Market Potentials

Market potentials are often useful in defining sales territories. They equalize territories on the basis of potential product sales within an area, regardless of individual company shares. Some companies rely on sales potentials by adjusting market potentials for past conditions, expected competitive behavior, and other influences. A discussion on calculating market and sales potentials is included in Chapter I—Marketing Research.

Develop Distribution Index

Market potentials should then be distributed to various geographical segments of the market by city, county, metropolitan trading area, state, or other basis. As a first cut, it is advisable to make this distribution to the smallest segments of the market on which data are available and relevant to the specific product-line under consideration.

County data are often more prevalent for industrial products. However, if possible, it is suggested that data be obtained on a trading area basis rather than on political boundaries. This may be difficult, but you'll find that business patterns often flow across political boundary lines and are not constrained by them.

Determine Preliminary Territories

Next, use your judgement and experience to combine smaller geographical areas into preliminary territories. It is often helpful to plot these territories on a map,[8] making sure

---

[8] Some major map suppliers include: Cunes Press, Inc., 2242 S. Grove, Chicago, IL 60616; A. J. Nystrom & Co., 3333 N. Elston Ave., Chicago, IL 60618; Rand McNally & Co., Inc., P.O. Box 7600, Chicago, IL 60680; American Map Co., Inc., 3 W. 61st St., New York, NY 10023; Hamond, Inc., 515 Valley St., Maplewood, NJ 07040. Also helpful is the county outline map available from the Superintendent of Documents, U.S. Government Printing Office, Washington, DC 20402.

that all desired markets are covered and that there are no duplications of effort.

Theoretically, each territory should be made up of approximately equal market potential for a given product-line. In practice, however, this is a difficult task because of differing workloads, traveling conditions, profit structures, buying customs, and other factors.

As a rough rule of thumb, during the development of preliminary territories, make certain no territory has more than two and one-half times the market potential of any other territory. A primary reason for this is to facilitate fair and equitable workloads, quota plans, and compensation schedules. If territories are established with significantly different potentials, compensation schedules should consider these differences.

Modify Preliminary Territories

Now modify preliminary territories to take account of the company's policies regarding distribution and market penetration, and other factors which influence market potential. The "Guideline to Territorial Size" table lists various criteria and conditions that tend to suggest larger or smaller territories.

Above all, compare workloads with profit potentials to ensure adequate return-on-investment. Of course, exceptions can be made when entering nonprofitable areas with the expectation that rapid penetration will result eventually in a profitable selling position.

Assist in Customer Cultivation

One of the most valuable services a manufacturer can provide for his channels is assistance in customer cultivation. Customer cultivation includes identification of industries, markets and companies offering greatest potential in each territory, as well as assistance in developing prospects into customers.

Customer cultivation procedures include:

Help in analyzing prospects and customers in a channel's territory, clas-

Guideline to Territorial Size

CRITERIA	EFFECT ON TERRITORY SIZE	
	SMALLER	LARGER
Nature/Type of product	Supply item	Capital good
Inventory turnover rate	High	Low
Number of prospects	Many	Few
Repeat sales	Frequent	Few
Customer class	General	Technical
Market density	High	Low
Sales call frequency	Frequent	Infrequent
Service/nonselling activities	Many	Few
Product's stage of development	New	Mature
Competition	Vigorous	Limited
Size of a distributor's or agent's selling organization	Small	Large
Geographic, transportation limitations	Many	Few

sified by industry priority, market potential, and buying influences.

Assistance in sales call planning. Help relate frequency of calls to account potential to keep channels from overextending themselves where potential is limited.

Providing contact men to work with channels in their territory to develop more effective sales presentations.

Helping channels penetrate prospect and customer engineering departments because, unless customer's specifications are written to include a particular supplier's products, the latter may not even

be given consideration when the customer's purchasing agent asks for bids or places an order (especially true for original equipment manufacturer sales).

Study end customer production methods and products; suggest improvements to end products or cuts in production costs through better application and utilization of product or service bought by the end customers.

Acting as a liaison between channels and company executives and research and development staff to relay new product applications information.

Sending sales bulletins to channels noting

who is buying, which items are going best, current applications, benefits, and performance data.

There are numerous sources of information that provide names and addresses of key buying influences and prospects in specific industries. Many of the sources are listed in the reference guide to this chapter.

Assist in Sales Promotion and Advertising

Manufacturers provide a valuable service to their channels by assisting in sales promotion and advertising activities. Key areas of assistance include:

Support channels with a long-range communications program to create awareness about your company as a source for particular products and to stimulate inquiries to be qualified and forwarded to channels for follow-up. (See related chapters on advertising, public relations, trade shows, direct mail, sales promotion, and inquiry handling.)

Provide point of purchase displays where necessary.

Make sales tools easy to use and complementary to other aids being employed. Fit catalog and brochure handouts to needs of channels employed (e.g., for distributors, prepare lightweight materials which take up little room, are virtually self-explanatory, and can readily be added to their existing catalogs, ring or post binders).

List location of all channels on promotional materials (e.g., back cover of catalog or brochure).

Conduct sales contests. (See Chapter X— Other Sales Promotion, Task 5.)

Provide gratuities and specialty handouts where appropriate. (See Chapter X— Other Sales Promotion, Task 7.)

Provide audiovisual (and step-by-step) presentation devices where feasible. (See Chapter X—Other Sales Promotion, Task 8.)

Assist channels (agents and distributors) in developing cooperative advertising programs.

Provide Sales Reports/Forms

Several of the primary reasons for using sales reports and forms include:

Provide marketing managers with essential information needed to control and coordinate marketing operations.

Provide liaison between channels and the home office.

Increase awareness levels of controller, production staff, and in-house marketing personnel of field conditions, customer buying habits, competitive behavior, potentials, etc.

Get channels to plan and review their work regularly.

Provide ready analysis of activities and territorial and channel performance.

Types of Reports/Forms

The principal types of reports and forms in prevalent use in distribution channel activities and management include:

Reports on new customers and prospects (related data)

Planning and route reports

Call reports and daily summaries

Total calls made per day, week, month, etc.

Sales reports, order summaries

Expense reports

Shipping authorizations (e.g., bill of lading)

Inventory sheets

Sales invoices

Credit sheets

Adjustment sheets

Commission sheets

Where to Obtain Reports/Forms

You can design your own forms and have them printed locally, or you can buy ready-made standard forms from a variety of major office equipment manufacturers, form printers, business form suppliers, and printing companies. Suppliers may be located by referring to your local Yellow Pages under the titles mentioned above.

Checklist for Effective Reports/Forms

Good sales reports and forms should adhere to as many of the following essentials as possible. In summary, they boil down to getting the maximum information from a minimum of paperwork.

Reports should have a specific purpose that relates to the control and coordination of specific marketing management function. Ask, "Why is the report needed? What will it be used for?"

Eliminate all reports whose utility is not worth their cost.

Schedule reports only on a when-needed basis and ensure that due dates are adhered to. Time reports to pattern of information analyses.

Forms should be easy to use (e.g., convenient size, easy to write on, easy to read, easy to file, etc.).

Make forms easy to read and understand in terms of the mechanics, the purpose, and information presented. Include instructions on the form.

Clearly state who is to fill in what information and who is to get copies.

Make it easy for person completing form to clearly communicate information required.

Never duplicate information available from more accessible sources.

Use alphabetic, numeric or other coding devices to help where repetitive entries are required.

Provide check spaces for recurring activities not needing comment.

Condense and combine with other forms wherever possible.

Periodically review forms to make sure all are up-to-date. Consult department heads, field managers, and channels to obtain their opinions on forms.

Discourage wordy comments about unimportant happenings.

Expenses should always be recorded on separate reports as they are generally approved at local management levels.

Destroy all reports when outdated.

Controlling Reports

A single central point in the marketing organization should be designated to coordinate and control the requirement for all reports. Formal procedures should be prescribed to prevent requiring reports that duplicate information in other reports, and reports whose purpose cannot be justified as to a specific marketing management use.

Task 6: Evaluate Channels

What to Measure

Although this appendix does not provide complete analytical tools for evaluating the performance of channels of distribution, it lists some key areas which you should analyze. A simple form is also provided to use as a tool in analyzing the performance of distribution channels.

For each of the items listed below, set standards of performance and measure actual performance against these standards for possible reward or correction. The list is representative of the types of performance criteria you should analyze on a continuing schedule. Better visibility will result if the data are plotted graphically.

Number of new and lost accounts per year

Number of sales calls or presentations made over a specified period

Number of orders per man-day

Orders per call ratio

Number of days on the road

Average time spent per call

Dollar and unit sales volume, average order size, expenses, profits

Completeness, accuracy and punctuality

of sales reports, orders, and other written materials

Performance Analysis

The Performance Analysis form uses market potentials and actual sales to evaluate territorial performance relative to its own potential and also relative to other territories.

In column 1, list the territories (if comparing territories) or salesmen (if comparing performance within one territory). In column 2, enter the dollar market potential for each territory and total them. (See Chapter I—Marketing Research, for a discussion of determining market potential.) In the example, territory (A) has $100,000 market potential, territory (B) has $250,000, and so forth.

Calculate and enter in column 3 the percent of total potential which each territory's potential represents. For example, territory

(A) represents 5% of the total market potential ($100,000 divided by $2,000,000). Column 3 should total 100%.

Enter in column 4 actual sales achieved over the same time period represented by potentials entered in column 2. In the example, actual sales totaled $730,000.

Calculate and enter in column 5 the percent of total company sales actually made in each territory. This is determined by dividing territorial sales by total actual sales and multiplying by 100%. For territory (A), the $25,000 sales achieved represents 3.4% of the company's total sales.

Then calculate and enter in column 6 the penetration of potential achieved by each territory. This is calculated by dividing column 4 by column 2. For territory (A), the result is 25.5% ($25,000 divided by $100,000 multiplied by 100%).

The relative performance of each territory (or salesman) can then be determined by dividing column 5 by column 3 and multi-

Performance Analysis

(1) TERRITORY OR SALESMAN	MARKET POTENTIAL		ACTUAL SALES		PERFORMANCE INDICES[9]	
	(2) DOLLARS	(3) PERCENT OF TOTAL	(4) DOLLARS	(5) PERCENT OF TOTAL	(6) PENETRATION OF POTENTIAL (COLUMN 4 ÷ 2)	(7) RELATIVE TO OTHER TERRITORIES (COLUMN 5 ÷ 3)
A	$100,000	5.0%	$ 25,000	3.4%	25.0%	68.0%
B	250,000	12.5	75,000	10.3	30.0	82.4
C	200,000	10.0	100,000	13.7	50.0	137.0
D	600,000	30.0	200,000	27.4	33.3	91.3
E	50,000	2.5	40,000	5.5	80.0	220.0
F	150,000	7.5	100,000	13.7	66.7	182.7
G	350,000	17.5	70,000	9.6	20.0	54.9
H	300,000	15.0	120,000	16.4	40.0	109.3
Totals	$2,000,000	100.0%	$730,000	100.0%	36.5%	

[9] Multiply all ratios by 100 to convert from decimal to percentage basis.

plying by 100%, and writing the result in column 7. For territory (A), 68% means that this territory performed only 68% as well as the average company territory. On the other hand, territory (E) performed 220% better than the company territory average.

When analyzing data derived in this manner, don't make the following mistake: many people might compare territories (E) and (G) and state that (E) performed four times as well as (G)—220% vs. 54.9%. It is true that (E) achieved a higher percentage of territorial potential; but it should be noted that territory (G) outproduced (E) in total sales by $70,000 to $40,000. To reduce chance of such mistakes, look at all elements simultaneously. Also, one must consider the profit picture of each territory. The same analysis can be done from a profit standpoint if your accounting data is so refined.

Task 7: How to Drop a Channel

The Need to Drop a Channel

Inevitably, there will come a time when changes in your objectives, the performance of your channel, or the nature of your market signals a need to change channels. This can be done best by realizing that a channel is usually, at best, a fragile alliance of partners.

To some extent, all partners have the same interest: profits from the sale of your products. In other respects, however, each member of a channel has different objectives. For example, manufacturers usually want to maximize sales volume for the sake of production efficiencies; while distributors often seek better customer service, and are frequently hesitant to increase their overhead by hiring additional salesmen to attempt to achieve the manufacturer's sales goal.

Frequently there are tremendous booms that lead to record sales and profits for distributors. During these periods, manufacturers are often hard pressed to meet demands. They have little time to evaluate the performance of the middleman. Distributors, during these boom times, have little time or inclination to complain about poor marketing support provided by the manufacturer.

In more lean times, manufacturers tend to screen their middlemen more carefully, and vice-versa. Tougher policies go into effect. Distribution definitely becomes a prime cost-cutting target on the part of the manufacturer. In some industries, manufacturers bypass the middlemen and sell direct to retailers. In other cases, the manufacturers may drop their own sales force and rely on manufacturer reps, finding the latter more efficient and more motivated.

How to Tell the Channel

In any case, a manufacturer must be prepared to make a change if the middleman performance decreases, or if economic conditions change. If a change is needed, perhaps the most helpful suggestion is to point out that channel members are accustomed to channel changes, even though they may try to prevent it. The fairest way to handle change is to be frank; to let a channel know that it will be used as long as it continues to do what you expect of it.

Distribution Channels Reference Guide

Sources of Information on Manufacturers' Agents and Distributors

Books and Reports

Building Sound Distributor Organization, Experiences in Marketing Management No. 6, The Conference Board, Inc., 845 Third Ave., New York, NY 10022.

Distribution Channels For Industrial Goods by William M. Diamond, 1963, Bureau of Business Research, Ohio State University, 1659 N. High, Columbus, OH 43210.

Marketing Through the Wholesaler-Distributor Channel, Marketing for Executives Series No. 11, by John M. Brion, 1966, American Marketing Association, Suite 606, 222 S. Riverside Plaza, Chicago, IL 60606.

Some Observations On 'Structural' Formation and Growth of Marketing Channels, Theory In Marketing, 2nd Series, by Reavis Cox, Wroe Alderson, and Stanley Shapiro, 1964, (pp. 163–175), Richard D. Irwin, Inc., Homewood, IL 60430.

Magazines

Agency Sales Magazine, Manufacturers' Agents National Assoc., P.O. Box 16878, Irvine, CA 92713.

Industrial Distribution, Morgan-Grampian Publishing Co., 205 E. 42nd St., New York, NY 10017.

Industrial Distributor News, Ames Publishing Co., One West Olney Ave., Philadelphia, PA 19120.

The Representator, Electronic Representatives Assoc., 600 S. Michigan Ave., Chicago, IL 60605.

General Associations and Directories

Encyclopedia of Associations, Gale Research Co., 700 Book Tower, 1249 Washington Blvd., Detroit, MI 48226.

Manufacturers' Agents National Association, P.O. Box 16878, Irvine, CA 92713.

National Association of Wholesalers-Distributors, 1725 K St., N.W., Washington, DC 20006.

Society of Manufacturers' Agents, 7053 Cathedral St., Birmingham, MI 48010.

Verified Directory of Manufacturers' Representatives, Manufacturers' Agents Publishing Co., 550 Fifth Ave., New York, NY 10036.

Sources of Information on Sales Management

Magazines

Industrial Marketing, Crain Communications, Inc., 740 Rush St., Chicago, IL 60611.

Journal of Marketing, American Marketing Assoc., Suite 606, 222 S. Riverside Plaza, Chicago, IL 60606.

Marketing Times, Sales & Marketing Executives International, 630 Third Ave., New York, N.Y. 10017.

Sales & Marketing Management, Bill Communications, Inc., 633 Third Ave., New York, NY 10017.

Books and Reports

A Sales/Management Handbook for the Electronics Industry, Schoonmaker Associates, P.O. Box 35, Larchmont, NY 10538 (Series of articles on marketing technical products).

Allocating Field Sales Resources, The Conference Board, Inc., 845 Third Ave., New York, NY 10022 (Covers organization, matching field effort and sales potential, distribution, and control).

Brass Tacks Sales Management, The Dartnell Corp., 4660 Ravenswood Ave., Chicago, IL 60640 (How to recruit, train, supervise, and motivate the sales force).

Dartnell Sales and Marketing Service, The Dartnell Corp., 4660 Ravenswood Ave., Chicago, IL 60640 (Monthly reports and case histories on methods, plans, and techniques of sales management).

Developing the Field Sales Manager, Sales Executives Club of New York, Hotel Roosevelt, 45th Street & Madison Ave., New York, NY 10017.

Field Sales Management, Experiences in Marketing Management No. 1, The Conference Board, Inc., 845 Third Ave., New York, NY 10022.

Goal Setting and Planning at the District Sales Level, Research Study 61, American Management Assoc., Inc., 135 West 50th St., New York, NY 10020.

How Sales Managers Get Things Done (how to overcome inertia), Prentice-Hall, Inc., Englewood Cliffs, NJ 07632.

How To Tailor Your Sales Organization To Your Markets, by Merrill DeVoe, Prentice-Hall, Inc., Englewood Cliffs, NJ 07632.

Management of the Sales Force, by William J. Stanton and Richard H. Buskirk, Richard D. Irwin, Inc., 1818 Ridge Rd., Homewood, IL 60430.

Marketing for Sales Executives, The Research Institute of America, Inc., 589 Fifth Ave., New York, NY 10017 (monthly report on sales management methods).

Readings In Sales Management, by Thomas R. Wotruba and Robert M. Olsen (eds), Holt, Rinehart, & Winston, Inc., 383 Madison Ave., New York, NY 10017.

Sales Force Management, by Kenneth R. Davis and Frederick E. Webster, Jr., Ronald Press Co., 15 E. 26th St., New York, NY 10010.

Sales Management: Decisions, Policies, and Cases, by R. R. Still and E. W. Cundiff, Prentice-Hall, Inc., Englewood Cliffs, NJ 07632.

Sales Manager's Handbook, The Dartnell Corp., 4660 Ravenswood Ave., Chicago, IL 60640.

Setting the Size for the Sales Force, by Zarrel V. Lambert, Center for Research of the College of Business Administration, Pennsylvania State University, University Park, PA 16802.

Supervising Salesmen In A Competitive Market, The Dartnell Corp., 4660 Ravenswood Ave., Chicago, IL 60640.

The Field Sales Manager: A Manual of Practice, American Management Assoc., Inc., 1515 Broadway, New York, NY 10036.

Time & Territorial Management for the Salesman, Sales Executives Club of New York, Hotel Roosevelt, 45th Street & Madison Ave., New York, NY 10017 (methods, check lists, working forms).

Articles

"General Electric's Scientific Method for Helping Salesmen Generate More Sales," by Robert W. Baeder, *Business Management*, November 1968, pp. 30–33, Business Management, 22 West Putnam Ave., Greenwich, CT 06830.

"How Many Salesmen Do You Need?" by Walter J. Semlow, *Harvard Business Review, Vol. 37*, May–June 1959, pp. 126–132, Harvard University, Graduate School of Business Administration, Soldiers Field, Boston, MA 02163.

"How To Design Sales Territories," by Walter J. Talley, Jr., *Journal of Marketing, Vol. 25*, January 1961, pp. 7–13, American Marketing Assoc., Suite 606, 222 S. Riverside Plaza, Chicago, IL 60606.

"How To Help Your Salesmen Plan Their Travels Better," by A. R. Barrington, *Sales Management*, August 5, 1960, pp. 40–42, Sales Management, Inc., 630 Third Ave., New York, NY 10017.

"How To Set Quotas and Sell Them To Salesmen," *Industrial Marketing*, July 1962, pp. 92–94 and August 1962, p. 158, Crain Communications, Inc., 740 Rush St., Chicago, IL 60611.

Associations

National Council of Salesmens' Organizations, 347 Fifth Ave., Room 1004, New York, NY 10016 (federation of sales organizations representing 40,000 wholly commissioned salesmen in all industries).

Sales & Marketing Executives-International, 630 Third Ave., New York, NY 10017 (studies sales and sales management).

Sales Manpower Foundation, c/o Sales Executives Club of New York, Hotel Roosevelt, 45th Street & Madison Ave., New York, NY 10017.

Sources of Information on Selling Techniques

Books and Reports

Improving Salesmen's Use of Time, Sales Executives Club of New York, Hotel Roosevelt, 45th Street & Madison Ave., New York, NY 10017.

Miracle Sales Guide, Prentice-Hall, Inc., Englewood Cliffs, NJ 07632 (basic binder, plus monthly updates covering key sales tasks).

Profile Your Customers To Expand Industrial Sales, Management Aids No. 192, Small Business Administration, Washington, DC 20416 (or from the nearest SBA office).

Quintessential Salesmanship by Charles B. Roth, Quintessential Sales Course, P. O. Box 8746, Kansas City, MO 64114 (programmed course of 25 lesson booklets, textbook, study guide, and progress quizzes to improve salesmanship).

Salesmens' Call Reports, The Conference Board, Inc., 845 Third Ave., New York, NY 10022.

Textbook of Salesmanship, by Frederic A. Russell, Frank H. Beach, and Richard H. Buskirk, McGraw-Hill Book Company, Inc., 1221 Avenue of the Americas, New York, NY 10020.

The Grid for Sales Excellence, by Robert R. Blake and Jane S. Mouton, McGraw-Hill Book Co., Inc., 1221 Avenue of the Americas, New York, NY 10020 (covers entire selling process).

The Professional Approach To Modern Salesmanship, by Bert H. Schlain, McGraw-Hill Book Co., Inc., 1221 Avenue of the Americas, New York, NY 10020.

The Salesman's Almanac by Charles B. Roth, Funk & Wagnalls Co., 380 Madison Ave., New York, NY 10017 (covers planning and closing).

Articles

"Closing the Sale," *Sales Management*, June 1, 1971 (entire issue), Sales Management, Inc., 630 Third Ave., New York, NY 10017.

"How Many Calls Is Any Given Account Worth?", by R. O. Loen, *Industrial Marketing*, January 1962, pp. 96–98, Crain Communications, Inc., 740 Rush St., Chicago, IL 60611.

"How To Create A Presentation That Sells," by A. R. Forest, *Business Management*, November 1962, pp. 45–47, Business Management, 22 W. Putnam Ave., Greenwich, CT 06830.

"Opening the Sale," *Sales Management*, October 30, 1972 (entire issue), Sales Management, Inc., 630 Third Ave., New York, NY 10017.

"Salesmen Can Help Keep Your Mailing List Alive," by John M. Trytten, *Sales Management*, October 2, 1972, Sales Management, Inc., 630 Third Ave., New York, NY 10017.

Sources of Information on Channel and Salesmen Selection

Books and Reports

"Finding and Hiring the Superior Salesman," *Research Institute Management Reports, Inc.*, Research Institute Bldg., 589 Fifth Ave., New York, NY 10017.

How To Write A Job Description, Management Aids No. 13, Small Business Administration, Washington, DC 20416 (or from nearest SBA office).

The Selection Interview: Essentials for Management,

by Benjamin Balinsky, Martin M. Bruce, Publisher, 340 Oxford Rd., New Rochelle, NY 10804.

Tips On Selecting Salesmen, Management Aids No. 196, Small Business Administration, Washington, DC 20416 (or from nearest SBA office).

"*Tools of Personnel Selection*," by J. J. E. Crissy and Harold C. Cash, Personnel Development Associates, 4133 170th St., Flushing, NY 11358.

Articles

"An Analysis of the Salesman Selection Process," by Thomas R. Wotruba, *Southern Journal of Business*, Vol. 5, January 1970, pp. 41–51, University of Georgia, Graduate School of Business Administration, Athens, GA 30601.

"How To Keep Misfits Out of Your Sales Staff," by C. V. D. Rousseau, *Industrial Marketing*, September 1961, pp. 131–134, Crain Communications, 740 Rush St., Chicago, IL 60611.

"How To Recruit Good Salesmen," by Henry R. Bernstein, *Industrial Marketing*, October 1965, pp. 70–77, Crain Communications, 740 Rush St., Chicago, IL 60611.

"What Makes A Best Salesman?", *Sales Management*, September 15, 1961, p. 94, Sales Management, Inc., 630 Third Ave., New York, NY 10017.

Sources of Information on Compensation, Motivation, Incentives

Books and Reports

Changing Patterns In Salesmen's Compensation, The Conference Board, Inc., 845 Third Ave., New York, NY 10022.

Compensating Salesmen and Sales Executives, by David A. Weeks, The Conference Board, Inc., 845 Third Ave., New York, NY 10022 (reports/trends in compensation packages among manufacturing sales forces).

Compensation of Salesmen, The Dartnell Corp., 4660 Ravenswood Ave., Chicago, IL 60640 (survey of 580 company compensation, expense, incentive programs).

How To Plan and Conduct Profitable Sales Incentive Programs, The Dartnell Corp., 4660 Ravenswood Ave., Chicago, IL 60640 (includes case studies, check lists, and procedures).

How To Stimulate Salesmen To Better Selling, Experiences in Marketing Management No. 4, The Conference Board, Inc., 845 Third Ave., New York, NY 10022.

Incentive Plans for Salesmen, The Conference Board, Inc., 845 Third Ave., New York, NY 10022 (examines 100 incentive plans and establishment procedures).

Incentives for Salesmen, Experiences in Marketing Management No. 14, The Conference Board, Inc., 845 Third Ave., New York, NY 10022.

Motivating the Older Salesman, Experiences in Marketing Management No. 5, The Conference

Board, Inc., 845 Third Ave., New York, NY 10022.

Salesmen's Compensation: Plans, Policies and Trends, Sales Success Unlimited, 717 N. Glenhurst Dr., Birmingham, MI 48009 (reference on how to organize and lead salesmen).

Articles

"How Can Commissions Be Split Among Territorial Salesmen?" *Industrial Marketing*, August 1962, p. 46, Crain Communications, Inc., 740 Rush St., Chicago, IL 60611.

"How Should Salesmen In Weak Territories Be Paid?" *Industrial Marketing*, September 1961, pp. 128–130, Crain Communications, Inc., 740 Rush St., Chicago, IL 60611.

"More Salesmen Compensation (Trends)," by Dr. Jack R. Dauner, *Sales Management*, December 13, 1971, p. 27, Sales Management, Inc., 630 Third Ave., New York, NY 10017.

"New Ways To Pay Salesmen," by W. C. Caswell, *Sales Management*, March 15, 1963, pp. 33–37, Sales Management, Inc., 630 Third Ave., New York, NY 10017.

"Seven Bedrock Rules for Incentive Programs," *Sales Management*, November 2, 1962, pp. 74–76, Sales Management, Inc., 630 Third Ave., New York, NY 10017.

"Should Salesmen's Compensation Be Geared To Profits?", by Ralph L. Day and Peter B. Bennett, *Journal of Marketing*, October 1962, p. 609, American Marketing Assoc., Suite 606, 222 S. Riverside Plaza, Chicago, IL 60606.

"Tips On Better Sales Incentive Programs," *Management Review*, September 1965, American Management Assoc., Inc., 135 W. 50th St., New York, NY 10020.

Sources of Information on Training

Books and Reports

Cup's Show On Salesmanship, The Dartnell Corp., 4660 Ravenswood Ave., Chicago, IL 60640 (16 mm color training film).

Professional Salesmanship, The Dartnell Corp., 4660 Ravenswood Ave., Chicago, IL 60640 (mail training program on selling and techniques).

Salesmanship, The Dartnell Corp., 4660 Ravenswood Ave., Chicago, IL 60640 (semi-monthly bulletin to motivate and teach salesmen various selling techniques).

The Dartnell 10-Point Sales Training Program, by Charles Schlom, The Dartnell Corp., 4660 Ravenswood Ave., Chicago, IL 60640 (step-by-step approach to salesman development).

Training And Developing The Field Sales Manager, by Robert F. Vizza, Sales Executives Club of New York, Inc., Hotel Roosevelt, 45th Street & Madison Ave., New York, NY 10017.

Training And Supervising Salesmen, by Charles L. Lapp, Prentice-Hall, Englewood Cliffs, NJ 07632.

Training Company Salesmen, by Morgan B. Mac-Donald, Jr., and Earl L. Bailey, The Conference Board, Inc., 845 Third Ave., New York, NY 10022.

Articles

"Eighteen Checkpoints For Sales Trainers," by G. Macksoud, *Sales Management*, October 20, 1961, p. 58, Sales Management, Inc., 630 Third Ave., New York, NY 10017.

"The Need For Training New And Old Salesmen," by H. H. Horton, *Industrial Marketing*, July 1959, pp. 52–54, Crain Communications, Inc., 740 Rush St., Chicago, IL 60611.

"Training And Retraining," *Sales Management*, May 1, 1972, entire issue, Sales Management, Inc., 630 Third Ave., New York, NY 10017.

Sources of Information on Sales Meetings

Business Meeting Selector, Crain Communications, Inc., 740 Rush St., Chicago, IL 60611 (reference on ideas and techniques; site and service suppliers).

Business Meetings That Make Business, by John Lobinger, Jr., Collier Books, 866 Third Ave., New York, NY 10022.

How To Plan And Conduct Successful Sales Meetings, The Dartnell Corp., 4660 Ravenswood Ave., Chicago, IL 60640 (includes case histories, techniques, and illustrative materials).

Sources of Information on Channel Evaluation

Measuring Salesmen's Performance, Studies in Business Policy No. 114, The Conference Board, Inc., 845 Third Ave., New York, NY 10022.

Measuring The Performance Of Salesmen, Management Aid No. 190, Small Business Administration, Washington, DC 20416 (or from nearest SBA office).

Sales Planning And Control, by Richard D. Crisp, McGraw-Hill Book Co., Inc., 1221 Avenue of the Americas, New York, NY 10020.

The Arithmetic Of Sales Management, by Fred M. Truett, American Management Assoc., 135 W. 50th St., New York, NY 10020.

Sources of Information on Physical Distribution

Books, Reports, and Directories

ABC World Airways Guide (Airports), Thomas Skinner & Co., Ltd., 111 Broadway, New York, NY 10006.

Air Shippers' Manual, Reuben H. Donnelley Corp., 211 East 43rd St., New York, NY 10017.

Business Logistics: Management Of Physical Supply And Distribution, by J. L. Heskett, R. M. Ivie, and N. A. Glaskowsky, Jr., Ronald Press Co., 15 E. 26th St., New York, NY 10010.

Directory Of American Ship Services, National Association of Marine Services, Inc., 11501 Georgia Ave., Silver Springs, MD 20902.

Directory Of Foreign Freight Forwarders, Budd Publications, Inc., 107 South Tyson Ave., Floral Park, NY 11001.

Distribution Cost Analysis, Small Business Bibliography No. 34, Small Business Administration, Washington, D.C. 20416 (or from nearest SBA office).

Dun & Bradstreet Reference Book Of Transportation, Dun & Bradstreet, Inc., 99 Church St., New York, NY 10007.

Industrial Logistics: Analysis And Management Of Physical Supply And Distribution System, by John F. Magee, McGraw-Hill Book Co., Inc., 1221 Avenue of the Americas, New York, NY 10020.

Inventory Control, Small Business Bibliography, Small Business Administration, Washington, DC 20416 (or from nearest SBA office).

Management Of Traffic And Physical Distribution, by Charles A. Taff, Richard D. Irwin, Inc., 1818 Ridge Rd., Homewood, IL 60430.

Motor Freight Directory, G. R. Leonard & Co., 2121 Shermer Rd., Northbrook, IL 60062.

National Distribution Directory, Local and Short Haul Carriers National Conference, 1621 O St., N.W., Washington, DC 20036.

National Highway & Airway Carriers & Routes, National Highway Carriers Directory, 925 W. Jackson Blvd., Chicago, IL 60607.

Official Airline Guide, Reuben H. Donnelley Publications, 2000 Clearwater Dr., Oak Brook, IL 60521.

Official Guide Of The Railways, National Railway Publication Co., 424 W. 33rd St., New York, NY 10001.

Official Motor Carrier Directory, Official Motor Carrier Directory, Inc., 1130 S. Canal St., Chicago, IL 60607.

Official Motor Freight Guide, Official Motor Freight Guide, Inc., 1130 S. Canal St., Chicago, IL 60607.

Physical Distribution And Marketing Logistics: An Annotated Bibliography, American Marketing Assoc., Suite 606, 222 S. Riverside Plaza, Chicago, IL 60606 (listing of information sources on service, facility location, information flow, inventory management, handling, storage, and warehousing).

Physical Distribution Management, By Donald J. Bowersox, Edward W. Smykay, and Bernard J. LaLonde, Macmillan Publishing Co., Inc., 60 Fifth Ave., New York, NY 10011.

Principles Of Logistics Management, by James A. Constantin, Appleton-Century Crofts, 440 Park Ave., South, New York, NY 10016.

Scientific Inventory Management, by Joseph Buchan and Ernest Koenigsberg, Prentice-Hall, Inc., Englewood Cliffs, NJ 07632.

Site Selection Handbook, Conway Research, Inc.,

2600 Apple Valley Rd., N.E., Atlanta, GA 30319.
Warehousing, Small Business Bulletin, Small Business Administration, Washington, DC 20416 (or from nearest SBA office).

Magazines

Air Cargo Guide, Travel & Transportation Services Division, Reuben H. Donnelley Corp., 2000 Clearwater Dr., Oak Brook, IL 60521.

Air Forwarder, Travel & Transportation Services Division, Reuben H. Donnelley Corp., 2000 Clearwater Dr., Oak Brook, IL 60521.

American Import and Export Bulletin, North American Publishing Co., 401 N. Broad St., Philadelphia, PA 19108.

American Motor Carrier Directory, American Trucking Associations, Inc., Box 13446, 351 Monroe Pl., N.E., Atlanta, GA 30324.

Brandon's Shipper & Forwarder, Brandon's Shipper & Forwarder, Inc., One World Trade Center, Suite 1927, New York, NY 10048.

Cargo Airlift, Reuben H. Donnelly Corp., 2000 Clearwater Dr., Oak Brook, IL 60521.

Custom House Guide, North American Publishing Co., 401 N. Broad St., Philadelphia, PA 19108.

Distribution Worldwide, Chilton Company, Chilton Way, Radnor, PA 19089.

Exporters' Encyclopedia, Dun & Bradstreet, International Div., Dun & Bradstreet, Inc., 99 Church St., New York, NY 10007.

Handling & Shipping, Industrial Publishing Co., 614 Superior Ave., West, Cleveland, OH 44113.

Material Handling Engineering, Industrial Publishing Co., 614 Superior Ave., West, Cleveland, OH 44113.

Modern Materials Handling, Cahners Publishing Co., Inc., 221 Columbus Ave., Boston, MA 02116.

Shipping Digest, Shipping Digest, Inc., Room 551, Cunard Building, 25 Broadway, New York, NY 10004.

Traffic Management, Cahners Publishing Co., Inc., 221 Columbus Ave., Boston, MA 02116.

Transportation And Distribution Management, Traffic Service Corp., 815 Washington Blvd., Washington, DC 20005.

Associations

Air Traffic Conference of America, 1000 Connecticut Ave., N.W., Washington, DC 20036

Air Transport Association of America, 1000 Connecticut Ave., N.W., Washington, DC 20036.

American Chain of Warehouses, 250 Park Ave., New York, NY 10017.

American Society of Traffic & Transportation, 547 W. Jackson Blvd., Chicago, IL 60606.

American Warehousemen's Assoc., 222 W. Adams St., Chicago, IL 60606.

National Association of Shippers Advisory Boards, % American Association of Railroads, 1920 L St., N.W., Room 320, Washington, D.C. 20036.

National Council of Physical Distribution Management, 222 W. Adams St., Chicago, IL 60606.

National Export Traffic League, 507 Fifth Ave., New York, NY 10017.

National Freight Traffic Assoc., 808 Bethlehem Pike, Philadelphia, PA 19118.

National Industrial Traffic League, 425 13th St., N.W., Suite 712, Washington, DC 20004.

National Motor Freight Traffic Assoc., 1616 P St., N.W., Washington, DC 20036.

Where to Get Sample Plan/Contract Forms

Dartnell Sales Manager's Handbook, The Dartnell Corp., 4660 Ravenswood Ave., Chicago, IL 60640 (shows sample agent agreements, distributor contacts, and salesmen's agreements).

Building a Sound Distributor Organization, Experiences in Marketing Management No. 6, provides an example distributor sales agreement. The Conference Board, 845 Third Avenue, New York, NY 10022.

The Society of Manufacturers' Agents, can provide a model agent agreement form. 7053 Cathedral, Birmingham, MI 48010.

The Manufacturers' Agents National Association, Suite 503, 3130 Wilshire Blvd., Los Angeles, CA 90005. Provides standard form agreements in either a short version or a 12-page version, including paragraphs from which you may select to make up a contract to fit your particular needs.

Sources of Data on Identification of Prospects

Company records of past sales.

Trade and professional association membership lists (see Chapter I—Marketing Research, under secondary research sources).

Trade publication circulation lists (see Standard Rate & Data Service, 5201 Old Orchard Rd., Skokie, IL 60076).

Trade show registration of attendees.

Inquiries generated from advertising and publicity.

Market surveys (see Chapter I—Marketing Research).

Industrial, corporate directories (see Chapter I—Marketing Research, under secondary research sources).

Government sources at federal, state, and local levels (see Chapter I—Marketing Research, under secondary research sources).

Chambers of Commerce (see Chapter I—Marketing Research, under secondary research sources).

Mailing list houses (see Chapter IX—Direct Mail).

Credit service (e.g., Dun & Bradstreet, 99 Church St., New York, NY 10017).

Syndicated data services (e.g., Economic Information Systems, 21 W. 38th St., New York, NY 10018).

CHAPTER

V

Pricing

Introduction

Nature of Industrial Prices

"Price" is the amount of money, or its equivalent, asked or paid for a product or service. The "rational buying behavior" of industrial companies makes price an important component of the marketing mix. Every successful manager knows that pricing decisions are crucial to company profitability and survival.

Pricing is a "numbers game"; finding the best or right price if none exists and managing price if one has been estalished. Generally, cost determines the floor on price, while demand and competition determine a flexible ceiling on price.

The pricing function is not an automatic or impersonal process. It is one of the more complicated marketing functions—an elusive art, flavored with a dash of theory and assisted by crossed-fingers.

Pricing Theory

Although an understanding of factors influencing pricing is vitally important to a company, the relationship of all variables can rarely be reduced to a neat mathematical formula yielding the right price. There are simply too many nonmeasurable variables.

However, there is an elaborate body of theory explaining how prices are determined. This theory includes supply and demand schedules, average and marginal costs

and revenues, diminished returns, utility, elasticity of price, demand and supply, and so on. This complex theory describes the abstract forces and tendencies at work, rather than providing a precise price-determining tool. Even if you wanted to apply the theory, a shortage of usable data generally discourages such an approach. Therefore, simply use the theory as a framework for guiding your thinking.

Basic Pricing Law

The basic pricing law states there is an inverse demand pattern associated with pricing strategy: "The higher the price of a product or service, the fewer total units will be purchased; the lower the price, the more units will be purchased."

Additionally, the theory states that price increases of competing products and your increased merchandising activities tend to increase your unit sales.

Cost-Oriented Pricing Techniques

In the past, most firms relied on cost-based pricing techniques.[1] This concept has become somewhat outdated as a sole price determinant, since it completely ignores de-

---

[1] Determine what total costs are and add a certain percentage for profit.

mand (buyers' value levels). Although pricing based solely on cost is considered most naive, cost analysis remains an important determinant of the minimum price to charge. Obviously, no product should be sold below cost unless this is done temporarily for new market penetration, image building, as a loss-leader or for some other strategic reason.

Your marketing staff should work closely with accounting, financial, and production personnel to analyze the firm's economic environment and to determine the exact role which cost should play in price-setting. Then price according to market and competitive conditions, provided that price covers both total costs and planned profit per unit.

How Pricing is Done in Practice (Trends)

Many companies use either tradition or some form of analysis to determine prices for their products and services. In the past, these prices would be put into effect and undergo few changes over time periods as long as two-to-three years. However, recently this procedure is considerably changed.

The ways of setting and maintaining prices in the past may have been successful, but they probably won't be so in the future. Shorter product life cycles, spiraling costs of materials, and new pricing methods will give a new look to traditional pricing theory.

Shorter product life cycles require that pricing structure be more flexible. The time spent on research and development must be faster than that of ten years ago. Your products must be on the market before some other company beats you to the punch. This requires quick pricing decisions.

The spiraling cost of raw materials and the high inflation rate can no longer allow companies to set a price and let it go. To meet inflation and the rapidly increasing costs of materials, a company must continually review prices. No longer will you see a price sheet be in effect for two years without revisions. The trend is to making these changes on a yearly basis at the latest, and more likely on a semi-annual or more frequent basis.

For new products and for existing products, you must continually survey competitive goods of like quality and determine where your products fit. Are there any voids in what is being offered? If so, do you want to fill this void? If not, can you profitably take the competition straight on? Is price or quality the key issue?

The simplest and most effective way to answer these questions is through sampling or testing. Testing can be a formal procedure or the simple asking of questions to current customers, prospects, salesmen, middlemen, and other industry experts. Find out what's happening in the market. Find out how you fit into the total picture. And answer all of these questions as frequently as possible.

Chapter Plan

This chapter gives a detailed description of many possible steps in determining overall price strategies. The details of each step do not need to be followed precisely, and the tasks themselves do not need to be conducted in the order of presentation. Rather, the information is given to stimulate your thinking about areas which are not currently considered, and to give you more insight to those areas which are currently reviewed.

The chapter discussion includes:

Assigning responsibility
Setting objectives
Selecting appropriate strategy
Employing several useful demand-oriented, price-determining tools

Demand orientation [2] is stressed because of the importance of the marketing concept. Cost-oriented areas of pricing are also discussed. Additional counsel by your account-

---

[2] Looking at marketing from the standpoint of what customers want and demand, rather than from the standpoint of what you are able to produce.

ing department can be most helpful in making break-even and profit analyses.

Also included are check lists and discussions of some unique aspects of pricing (e.g.,

licensing, leasing, discounts, pricing new products, and competitive bidding).

The logical flow of the chapter's discussion is shown in the following chart.

Pricing Chapter Plan

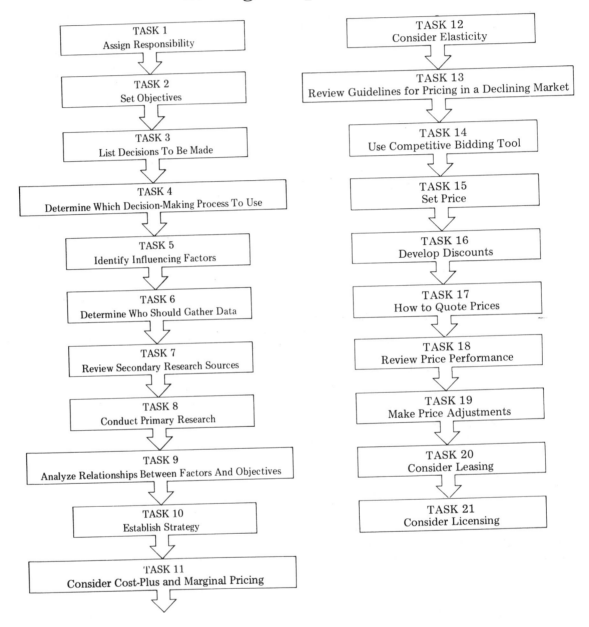

TASK 1
Assign Responsibility

TASK 2
Set Objectives

TASK 3
List Decisions To Be Made

TASK 4
Determine Which Decision-Making Process To Use

TASK 5
Identify Influencing Factors

TASK 6
Determine Who Should Gather Data

TASK 7
Review Secondary Research Sources

TASK 8
Conduct Primary Research

TASK 9
Analyze Relationships Between Factors And Objectives

TASK 10
Establish Strategy

TASK 11
Consider Cost-Plus and Marginal Pricing

TASK 12
Consider Elasticity

TASK 13
Review Guidelines for Pricing in a Declining Market

TASK 14
Use Competitive Bidding Tool

TASK 15
Set Price

TASK 16
Develop Discounts

TASK 17
How to Quote Prices

TASK 18
Review Price Performance

TASK 19
Make Price Adjustments

TASK 20
Consider Leasing

TASK 21
Consider Licensing

Task 1: Assign Responsibility

Current Practice

Although pricing is one of the most complex marketing functions, it is still not regarded as a specialized field, as are advertising and sales force management. These factors, plus those listed below, are the most frequent reasons for poor pricing.

Since most top management personnel have little understanding of the subject, those responsible for pricing are often understaffed, not adequately financed, or not suited for the task by training, experience, temperament, and interest.

Persons responsible for pricing rarely get the assistance of others on whom they must depend to do their job properly.

Prices are rarely given regular reviews to avoid perpetuation of mistakes and/or compensate for changes in demand, competitive prices, etc.

Many companies ignore major market forces (e.g., demand), competitive situations, cost factors, and other economic criteria in pricing analysis. Little reliable, relevant information is available regarding demand, market conditions, etc., for rational price-setting.

Many companies use inconsistent pricing strategies.

Too much reliance is placed on salesmen-originated comments.

A Rational Approach

Top management should delegate to a person or department responsibility for the effective determination and administration of all pricing functions. This responsibility requires more than just clerical skills.

The pricing program will vary from firm to firm, making it difficult to generalize here about the identity, functions, and motivations of people involved. Although pricing should be a staff function backed by top management support, it can be located in various places in the firm, and have numerous reporting structures, none of which will always be ideal. In any case, pricing decisions affect many persons who may be expected to try to influence these decisions (e.g., salesmen quoting prices or price changes to customers).

Many persons are (or should be) involved in routine pricing decisions. For example, some persons must synthesize field sales reports on competition and what customers want, etc. These are commonly sales analysts, plus persons in the advertising, cost accounting, and marketing research departments.

Others should be called upon to make pricing recommendations (product specialists, engineering representatives, purchasing, manufacturing, public relations officials). Finally, responsible decision-makers should review the assembled data and make final price decisions (marketing vice-president, controller, and president).

Committee or Individual Responsibility

Ultimate responsibility for coordinating and overseeing pricing can be assigned to one person or to a committee headed by one person.

Committees comprised of key department heads are ideal for discussion and advisory purposes, but not for making final decisions. It is better practice to make one person responsible for pricing a given item or line of products. Thus, everyone knows who to turn to and who to hold accountable for pricing decisions.

This one person could be the chief marketing executive, controller, or a specialist rather than a top executive. Many companies currently rely on their marketing or merchandising managers for pricing responsibility. Daily contacts with product-line customers often sharpen the marketing merchandising manager's ability to make practical price decisions.

In any case, choose a person with suitable qualifications, rather than the right job title.

Qualifications of Person Assigned Responsibility

Although personal qualities required for pricing differ from industry to industry, the person assigned this responsibility should have sound marketing judgement, an intuitive grasp of the interaction of marketing and economic forces, and should possess a working knowledge of standard and distribution cost accounting, sales analysis and forecasting tools, marketing surveys, economics, supply and demand for his company's products, federal and state price controls (if any), trade, tariff, import/export regulations (if company engages in foreign trade), legal aspects of pricing, and competitive analysis.

Factors Dictating Size and Type of Pricing Organization

The factors listed below dictate the size and type of organization a company needs to perform pricing functions:

> Range of pricing discretion possessed by firm
> Speed of decision needed
> Number of products
> Number of markets or geographic regions
> Qualified personnel available
> Scope and complexity of pricing information available
> Authority needed for making decisions and for requesting information required from others

Whatever medium is established for making and implementing pricing policy, this function must be guided by proper objectives. This subject is covered in the next task.

Task 2: Set Objectives

Objectives Will Guide Your Strategy

After specific target markets are identified, you must decide whether price should be set at, above, or below some average to appeal to selected buyers. This pricing strategy cannot be determined until all factors influencing price are analyzed (see Task 5 for list of factors); but objectives should be established early in the pricing process.

Examples

The proper price is normally one which maximizes long-run company profit. For an individual product, price may be set low and losses deliberately accepted. However, if this low price encourages the purchase of other more profitable products in the line, overall profits may be increased.

In addition to setting a desired and reasonable long-run profit goal for the company (or for key products or markets) you should also select a balanced blend of other complementary short-run objectives. These complementary objectives are really sub-objectives for which priorities need not be established. Examples of both short and long-run objectives are given below. (Note: The examples are cited only as possibilities, and are not intended to be complete or to serve all situations. Matter of fact, it is rarely possible to have all of them at the same time.)

Short-Run Objectives

> Meet existing or discourage new competition
> Stimulate immediate demand
> Recover cash quickly (when capital is needed or you are uncertain of market)

Drive out lower-cost competitors who otherwise could operate successfully under an "umbrella" price set by the leader

Attract new distributors or agents

Long-Run Objectives

Long-run profitability (e.g., return-on-investment, return-on-sales, return-on-assets)

Stabilize price and profit margin relationship

Realize target market share

Reach desired unit volume

Minimize risk of excessive loss

Conform to community or industry standards

Avoid legal prosecution and government investigation

Allow marketing of a product necessary to complete the line, even though it cannot be competitively priced

Maintain price-leadership arrangements in the industry (e.g., you set prices or follow another leader)

Task 3: List Decisions to be Made

Many Decisions Must be Made

There are many pricing decisions to be made. From the list below, select and answer those questions which apply to your company.

How should original prices be set for new or different products and services?

Shall we offer different prices to different types of customers (e.g., volume buyers versus 2-3 unit buyers)?

Shall we offer different prices to different types of distributors?

Shall we offer special deals to certain customers?

How shall prices be changed over time (e.g., high initial price on a new product, then reduce it)?

What discounts shall we offer: quantity, cash, functional? When? How quickly must the customer pay? How much? What are the break-points?

Shall we implement price maintenance policies?

Shall we have individual product or product-line pricing?

How shall we price our products relative to competitive prices?

Should there be a relationship among product prices? If so, what?

How shall we change price to meet technology changes?

How shall we change price to meet changing customer opinions?

Shall we have a uniform national price or vary price regionally?

Shall we advertise price or not?

What about pricing of foreign sales?

What effect does packaging/shipping have on average national price?

When you have compiled your own list of pricing decisions to be made, the next job is to use a logical process to arrive at your pricing decisions.

Task 4: Determine Which Decision-Making Process to Use

Two Alternative Approaches

Two approaches are currently employed in making pricing decisions. Decisions are based either on inductive or deductive reasoning.

The inductive approach calls for arbitrary initial price selection, with profit measured after the product has been pushed through the distribution system. This approach is used frequently by manufacturing-oriented firms, those more concerned with their products than with market demands. This trial and error approach can be successful, but chances of success are enhanced by using a deductive approach.

The far superior deductive technique requires time in identifying a wide range of possible prices, reviewing factors influencing each of them, and ultimately deciding on one price. It is rarely possible initially to pinpoint a specific correct price. But the deductive approach reduces the wide range of considerations to a few which can undergo further analysis, which in turn generally yields a more market-oriented price and greater profits.

Use Intuition and Judgement

Intuition plays an important role in pricing. This is because most product or marketing managers feel: "I have a real grasp of the market situation, and therefore I can set price without analysis of costs, profits, competitors' prices, potential demand and so on. And, if the price is unsatisfactory, I'll try again."

This simple approach may yield satisfactory results if the manager is indeed truly knowledgeable about the market and has the experience and intuition to anticipate customer and competitive reactions. Unfortunately, this is rarely the case. That's why bad pricing decisions are made more often than not. Because of its simplicity, the inductive approach is unfortunately very popular. On the other hand, firms that use the more sophisticated deductive approach to pricing generally make fewer pricing mistakes and benefit from better profits.

However, good judgement, common sense, objective use of information gathering and statistical procedures, and knowing when to take a chance are characteristics of the exceptional pricing manager.

Procedure Guidelines

There is no one best way—no single mechanistic formulation—for setting prices. The approach must be individualized and modified with time and for different products.

The remainder of this chapter contains a logical series of sequential pricing steps. However, in practice, you may find that some steps may be eliminated based on your firm's operation. Also, you may have to backtrack to certain steps along the way. Use the following tasks as a guide, not as a rigid handbook approach to solve your pricing problems one by one.

Task 5: Identify Influencing Factors

Identify Factors

The factors that can influence your pricing decisions may be collected under the six categories listed below. To help you identify relevant factors, the remainder of this task lists, under each category, various questions to ask yourself. Your answers will lead you to identify specific factors that bear on making objective pricing decisions. Many of the questions may not apply to your operation, or they may lead to factors that are trivial.

Therefore, list only those factors which, in your judgement and experience, could have an important bearing on a pricing decision.

Use a loose-leaf binder with dividers for each category to organize the factors as you identify them. Or, in a larger operation, separate binders might be needed for each category of pricing factors. The six categories are as follows:

Company Factors—Your company's market position and internal operation

Competition Factors—Competition facing you

Customer Factors—Customer potential, attitudes, and habits

Market Factors—Markets you select

Middleman Factors—Middlemen you rely upon

General and Government Factors—General/government conditions and regulations

Company Factors

Company factors require analysis of six major areas: (1) channels of distribution/sales policies, (2) prices, (3) products, (4) profitability, (5) promotion, and (6) sales pattern.

Channels of Distribution/Sales Policies

What channels of distribution are currently employed for each product-line? Selling methods?

What are your sales policies and terms (e.g., is freight prepaid)?

Are different costs incurred in serving different classes of customers (i.e., size, type, location)?

Prices

What is the current price range of your products?

Are you a price leader or a follower?

Is there price stability in your industry?

What, in your judgement, are the risk levels at each alternative price?

Products

In what stage of the product life cycle is each full or partial product-line?

What are the comparative product benefits or features in terms of utility, applications, premiums received by buyers, economics, quality, service, and other comparable factors?

Do you have adequate patent controls?

Are any economies of scale possible (i.e., mass production)?

Is a logical allocation of overhead costs used over many products (instead of judgement alone)?

How important is product to buyer? [3]

Profitability

What are current profit levels of each product in your line? Contribution to overhead? Break-even points?

What are the costs for production, development, sales, promotion, distribution, and administration? What is the minimum you can afford to charge at each sales volume level?

Are supplier charges for components, materials, and so on, expected to change in the coming year?

Promotion

What promotional inducements and special offers do you use?

What are your current advertising levels—image and prestige?

Sales Pattern

What is your share of market? Changes in recent years?

Were there any changes in sales of products by region or salesmen over time and compared to industry averages?

What types of customers were won or lost in recent months (in relation to previous price decisions)?

Competition Factors

Consider all items listed above under "Company Factors" as they may apply to a competitor's company.

What is the availability (actual or potential) of competing and substitute prod-

---

[3] Industrial products help produce or become part of other products. If the price of your component product (input) to original equipment manufacturer buyers is reduced by you, the buyer in turn can reduce the price of his end product. If his price cut is proportionally greater than your price cut, he may realize greater sales due to more attractive pricing to his customers, and you may realize greater profits based on your increased sales volume (output). This is especially true if your product represents a large percentage of the end product.

ucts? How similar? How quick to react to your actions?

Have your competitors' pricing strategies significantly affected your sales volume?

Customer Factors

How many customers need the product? In what quantities?

How much are customers willing and able to pay?

What is the degree of price sensitivity (impact of price on sales volume) and awareness?

What are the buying habits and motives?

What most appeals to these customers (e.g., price, quality, service)?

What might customers *think* when prices are reduced (e.g., item is about to be superseded by a later model; item is relatively unwanted—excessive inventories; firm is in financial difficulty and is forced to raise cash)?

What might customers *think* when prices are raised (e.g., items are in short supply—buy before unobtainable; item is in most desirable style; item offers unusually good value; seller could not make a profit at old price)?

What are customers' feelings about fairness of prices?

Where are most potential and actual customers located?

In which SIC are they concentrated?

How are prices charged by your industrial customers influenced by what you charge them (e.g., minor or major part of their total costs)?

Market Factors

Are there any current or forecasted substitutes for your product?

What are your targets (share, volume, market segment)?

Are there any developments affecting sales (e.g., shifting end-user needs or special delivery requirements)?

What are your projections of market size and expected growth at different prices?

Middlemen Factors

Are channels available to put your desired strategy into practice (e.g., penetration pricing requires channels which can make product widely and promptly available)?

Are middlemen offered adequate profit margins?

What are existing behavior and attitudes toward yours and competitive products, costs, and profit margins? Can these be changed by your action?

Would price changes be passed along to middlemen?

What is the size of inventories held?

Will they handle only your products?

Do you reimburse them for inventories not sold?

How much sales support is required?

General and Government Factors

What regulations and legislation can affect your pricing strategy?

Can you easily avoid discriminatory treatment of different customer types?

Are you avoiding "tie-in clauses" requiring buyers to purchase other products to earn right to a new or desired item?

What are the current and projected economic conditions, inflation, interest rates, credit, etc.?

Do trade, tariff, and import/export regulations affect your decisions? If so, how?

Summary of Influencing Factors

After you have identified and classified the major factors that bear importantly on your pricing decisions, you will have made significant progress in understanding some of the complexities of pricing. Next comes the collection of information about your industry and the marketing environment in which it functions. To do this properly, you will need the help of various specialists and departments in your company. The task which follows enables you to pick the right people for each required piece of information.

Task 6: Determine Who Should Gather Data

Who's Responsible?

It is essential that senior marketing personnel have a responsible role in pricing. Because the pricing function is only a part-time job, the tools which these managers can use on a day-to-day basis are rudimentary and few. Specialists should be called upon for technical assistance. Advice from various departments within the company is essential, especially where department heads are involved in preparing product plans and sales programs.

In smaller companies, pricing-oriented activities may be part-time responsibilities of one or more departments. In any case, pricing responsibilities should be clearly defined for all persons assigned direct or indirect responsibilities. This ensures that pricing becomes an integral and formal part of their jobs. The "Participants in Pricing Process" chart lists company functions and the reasons why each individual should participate in the pricing process.

Groundwork is Completed

Up to this point, you have been laying the groundwork for putting into practice the pricing process. You have set your objectives, decided on a process, identified the factors that bear on pricing decisions, and identified sources of assistance in your company's departments. Now you are ready to gather the information you will need to make rational pricing decisions. The next two tasks describe the secondary and primary sources of this information.

Task 7: Review Secondary Research Sources

Tap All Sources of Information

Much information used in making pricing decisions is available through secondary research sources. Knowing what sources exist, and how to use them efficiently are keys to logical pricing. Since no single source of data exists, you'll have to gather fragments and integrate them. Departments listed under the previous task are used in this gathering process. Your job is to organize, plan, direct, and control the information-gathering process.

Specific Sources

Secondary research is covered in Chapter I—Marketing Research. Several frequently used pricing sources include:

Competitive price lists (use as reference points against which you compare your prices)

Competitive advertising, catalogs, and promotional materials

Customer reports about competition and requirements

Sales force, supplier, and distributor data on a regular feedback system

Trade journal announcements of price changes and articles about competitors

Trade associations

Annual and financial reports of competitors

U.S. Department of Commerce for industry price averages

Dun & Bradstreet reports on companies and industries

Department of Labor, Bureau of Labor Statistics: "Monthly Labor Review," "Handbook of Labor Statistics," "Wholesale (Primary Market) Price Index" (monthly), and "Wholesale Prices and Price Indexes" (annual)

Participants in Pricing Process

FUNCTION	WHY HELPFUL
MARKETING (research, sales, advertising, product manager, middlemen)	1. Has primary responsibility for initiating price changes and administering prices. 2. Has knowledge of buyers' needs, attitudes toward company and competitors, and buying behavior. 3. Provides data on company, distribution channels, markets, industry and economic situation. 4. Provides data on competitive prices, reactions, products, strategies, and capabilities. 5. Tracks sales trends and measures market acceptance and reactions to different prices. 6. Conducts pricing experiments and makes field forecasts. 7. Makes estimates of probable volume. 8. Programs marketing costs for existing and new products. 9. Separates truth from fiction, excuses, ignorance and rumors.
CONTROLLER/ FINANCE (accounting)	1. Determines effects required investments will have on working capital. 2. Calculates pricing formulas to net a desirable profit and return-on-investment. 3. Periodically checks validity of and yield from current prices. 4. Sets standards and estimates costs of direct labor, materials, supplies, components, special equipment, overhead. 5. Makes cost, payback, break-even, and performance analyses for each product. 6. Makes risk analyses. 7. Reports findings regularly to product and sales managers.
PRODUCTION/ ENGINEERING	1. Assists in establishing standard costs as a basis for establishing other pricing levels. 2. Anticipates and analyzes production difficulties that may affect prices. 3. Suggests contingency budget for unexpected costs. 4. Compares product benefits, applications, premiums received by buying, utility, production economics, quality, and service with competitive products. 5. Analyzes and suggests potential economies of scale.
LEGAL COUNSEL	1. Assures compliance with pricing and antitrust legislation. 2. Assures proper trademark and patent control.
PUBLIC RELATIONS	1. Measures or estimates effects of price changes and policies on attitudes of customers, distributors, and government. 2. Measures or estimates image and prestige levels of company and competition.
ECONOMIST	1. Determines probable sensitivity of demand to price levels under consideration. 2. Monitors state of general economy and its probable effect on current and future prices.
PRICING SPECIALIST	1. Involved in all of the above. 2. Coordinates and integrates inputs from above functions.

Task 8: Conduct Primary Research

Pricing Research Tools

The most valuable (and difficult) pricing research involves determining customer reactions to alternative prices under consideration. This tells you quantities which current and potential new customers say they would purchase at alternative price levels.

It's hard to predict how much customers will pay for a product by simply asking them. The customer probably doesn't really know, especially for new products. Remember, price is what customers are willing to pay for what they expect the product will do for them (i.e., benefits); not for the product itself. These benefits may be intangible or buried in the customer's subconscious mind. Therefore, in determining price, it helps to know current and potential customers' views of the product (e.g., relative to other products, other uses of their money, and the value they place on money).

There are several ways to estimate customer attitudes, behavior, and relative evaluations of products. Four easy-to-use tools which may be used separately or in combination are discussed below:

    Market trial
    Questionnaire
    Barter experiment
    Statistical analysis of past price vs. sales
        volume relationships

Market Trial

Market trials are similar to test marketing, although on a smaller scale. Although used more often in consumer research, field testing is currently receiving moderate to wide use in industrial marketing, especially for new products.

Market trials involve trying one or more different prices in different geographical areas. Sales and profit results in each market are compared, and the most effective pricing structure is then used on a full-scale basis. A

form for comparing price performance is shown below.

MARKET TRIAL — PRICE COMPARISONS

MARKET	PRICE CHARGED	TOTAL SALES

If the test is to be a fair one, the markets must offer comparable sales potential. With essentially equal levels of advertising, sales efforts, and all other activities in each market, significant differences in sales can be more accurately related to price differences.[4] If the markets vary significantly in sales potential, evaluation of total sales generated must be weighed to avoid giving full credit to the price offered in the higher yielding market. Market trials are like any other form of scientific testing. Test conditions must be stable, comparable, and measurable, or results will be biased.

Limitations

Market trials are subject to several limitations. They are often difficult to conduct and interpret results. They risk exposing new products. They are expensive in time and dollars. They require much consultation with legal experts to avoid prosecution for price discrimination (even though it's only a test). It may be difficult to isolate part of your market for trial.

Competitors may react differently in test market situations than they would under real market conditions; sometimes done deliberately to discredit test results or because the isolated nature of your action may spur a

---

[4] The areas chosen should have comparable economic conditions and the problems of distribution, especially transportation, should be similar.

different reaction than would a national program.

Questionnaires

Testing market reaction to price can be accomplished by personal, telephone, or mail questionnaire surveys. Each of these tools is discussed in Chapter I—Marketing Research.

Briefly, these tools involve analysis of valuations, opinions, preferences, and purchase intentions of potential and current customers, as well as the opinions of other experts (e.g., suppliers and distributors). An attempt should be made to interview persons in appropriate departments of both small and large customer firms (e.g., query engineering, production, and technical people about cost and time savings; the purchasing agent about cost and specifications; and marketing division personnel about product resale).

Questionnaire Development

After you have developed a preliminary questionnaire, have someone in your company serve as a "devil's advocate," ruthlessly ferreting out moot or questionable points requiring further analysis. These potentially critical points can be further evaluated by phrasing them as questions and polling opinions of current and potential customers.

Most questions designed to measure attitudes should be related to pricing. The questionnaire should not be diluted with too many unrelated subjects. The purpose is to determine whether or not there is a large number of customers having sufficient interest in the product to be willing to pay the proposed price.

One key to good question development is using an oblique, nonpersonal question: "Do you think *other firms* in your industry would be interested in . . . . ?" Never ask, "Would *you* be interested in . . . . ?" This latter approach automatically puts respondents on defense possibly causing biased answers, and perhaps lost rapport.

Examples would include: (1) In your opinion, would cost-conscious firms with moderate quality standards be willing to pay a premium price for this product? (2) Do you feel that most firms in your industry are more price-conscious than quality-conscious when buying this type of product? (3) Several potential customers noted a possible weakness in this product. Do you see the weakness they mentioned?

Limitations

Although a questionnaire is a useful, quick, and normally low-cost tool supplementing other research tools, it suffers from several pitfalls. These pitfalls can be partially overcome by using other research techniques to confirm questionnaire findings.

Questionnaires often lack complete accuracy, and may result in little or no useful data. They require selection of a statistically representative sample, which is not always possible. They also require use of sophisticated projective techniques for best results, and persons with these skills are not generally found in smaller companies.

Barter Experiments

Barter experiments are most commonly used in consumer marketing, but might be useful in industrial marketing. They involve asking a series of questions about unrelated subjects, and then, as a reward for cooperation offering a gift that the respondent can select from several items. The gift items must require a distinct choice in the minds of most respondents. It is assumed that a respondent will select the items he values most highly (barring present ownership of some of the items). Then you can ask why the person selected that item.

The major drawback to this tool is that many industrial products would be too expensive to offer as gifts. You can overcome this drawback by offering a discount on one of two fine items, offering a free additional attachment if the main product is purchased, or some other extra which is valuable to the respondent, yet within your budget.

Statistical Analyses of Past Price vs. Sales Volume Relationships

If the product you're asking about has been on the market for a long time, you can compare quantities purchased at different prices over time by using multiple correlation techniques. This comparison provides a tool for predicting future quantities purchased at different prices.[5] This subject requires sophisticated mathematical analysis beyond the scope of this book.[6]

Briefly, however, analysis can be based on historical sales records, or on a cross-sectional analysis between markets, products, companies, advertising budgets, sales force expenditures, cost, and demand functions. Although complicated to the layman, most persons with computer programming and/or mathematical backgrounds can readily develop such simulation models for you.

The mathematical approach has not yet sufficiently proved itself to merit wide usage. However, studying relationships among key factors can help narrow uncertainty over the price range.

Task 9: Analyze Relationships Between Factors and Objectives

Analyze Influencing Factors

Now analyze the relationship between the previously listed factors and your objectives.

Some factors will be within your control; others not. In addition to the statistical techniques, other more practical approaches are readily usable.

[5] It is dangerous to use correlation analysis for prediction if the projected value falls considerably outside the range of past experience.

[6] For a succinct explanation of correlation analysis, with worked out examples, see *Statistical Methods*, by Arkin and Colton, No. 27, in the Barnes and Noble College Outline Series, Chapters IX and X. These paper-cover texts can be found in most stationery and book stores. In some cases, a graphical plot, or "scatter diagram," can be plotted on cross-section paper, and a freehand best representative line drawn through the center of gravity of the plot. The line can be projected for a short distance beyond the plot to predict quantities versus prices.

Analysis of Relationships Between Factors and Objectives

FACTORS	DOES FACTOR INCREASE OR DECREASE THE PAYOFF?	WHY?	HOW MUCH? (in percent)

Pricing Strategy Chart

OBJECTIVE	STRATEGY	WHEN GENERALLY USED	PROCEDURE	ADVANTAGES	DISADVANTAGES
High short-term profit (without regard for long-term)	Skim-the-cream of the market	☐ No comparable competitive products ☐ Drastically improved product or new product innovation ☐ Large number of buyers ☐ Little danger of competitor entry due to high price, patent control, high R&D costs, high promotion costs, and/or raw material control ☐ Uncertain costs ☐ Short life cycle ☐ Inelastic demand	Determine preliminary customer reaction. Charge premium price for product distinctiveness in short-run, without considering long-run position. Some buyers will pay more because of higher present value to them. Then, gradually reduce price to tap successive market levels - (i.e., skimming-the-cream of a market that is relatively insensitive to price. Finally, tap more sensitive segments).	☐ Cushions against cost overruns ☐ Requires smaller investment ☐ Provides funds quickly to cover new product promotions and initial development costs ☐ Limits demand until production is ready ☐ Suggests higher value in buyer's mind ☐ Emphasizes value rather than cost as a guide to pricing ☐ Allows initial feeling-out of demand before full-scale production	☐ Assumes that a market exists at high price ☐ Results in ill-will by early buyers when price is reduced ☐ Attracts competition ☐ Likely to underestimate ability of competitors to copy product ☐ Discourages some buyers from trying the product (connotes high profits) ☐ May cause long run inefficiencies
Become established as efficient manufacturer at optimum volume before competitors get entrenched, without sacrificing long-term objectives (e.g., obtain satisfactory share of market)	Slide-down demand curve (version of skimming, without sacrificing long-term objectives)	☐ By established companies launching innovations ☐ Durable goods ☐ Slight barriers to entry by competition ☐ Medium life span	Taps successive layers of demand at highest prices possible. Then slides down demand curve faster and further than forced to in view of potential competition. Rate of price change is slow enough to add significant volume at each successive price level, but fast enough to prevent large competitor from becoming established on a low-cost volume basis.	☐ Emphasizes value rather than cost as a guide to pricing ☐ Provides rapid return on investment ☐ Provides slight cushion against cost overruns	☐ Requires broad knowledge of competitive product developments ☐ Requires much documented experience ☐ Results in ill will by early buyers when price is reduced ☐ Discourages some buyers from buying at initial high price

190

Objective	Strategy	Conditions	Implementation	Advantages	Disadvantages
Encourage others to produce and promote the product to stimulate primary demand	Competitive-at-the-market price	☐ Several comparable products ☐ Growing market ☐ Medium-to-long product life span ☐ Known costs	Start with final price and work back to cost. Use customer surveys and studies of competitors' prices to approximate final price; deduct selling margins; adjust product and production and selling methods to sell at this price and still make necessary profit margins.	☐ Requires less analysis and research ☐ Existing market requires less promotion efforts ☐ Causes no ill will by early buyers since price will not be lowered soon	☐ Limited flexibility ☐ Limited cushion for error ☐ Slower recovery of investment ☐ Must rely on other differentiating tools
Stimulate market growth and capture and hold a satisfactory market share at a profit through low prices. Become strongly entrenched to generate profits over a long period.	Market penetration	☐ Long product life span ☐ Mass market ☐ Easy market entry ☐ Demand is highly sensitive to price ☐ Unit costs of production and distribution decrease rapidly as quantity of output increases ☐ Newer product ☐ No "elite" market willing to pay premium for newest and best	Charge low prices to create a mass market resulting in cost advantages derived from larger volume. Look at lower end of demand curve to set price low enough to attract a large customer base. Also review past and competitor prices.	☐ Discourages actual and potential competitor inroads because of apparent low profit margins ☐ Emphasizes value more than cost in pricing ☐ Allows maximum exposure and penetration in minimum time ☐ May maximize long-term profits if competition is minimized	☐ Assumes volume is always responsive to price reductions, which isn't always true ☐ Relies somewhat on glamour and psychological pricing which doesn't always work ☐ May create more business than production capacity available ☐ Requires significant investment ☐ Small errors often result in large losses
Keep competitors out of market or eliminate existing ones	Pre-emptive/extinction	☐ Used more often in consumer markets ☐ Manufacturers may use this approach on one or two products, with other prices meeting or higher than those of competitors.	Price at low levels so that market is unattractive to possible competitors. Set price as close as possible to total unit cost. As increased volume allows lower cost, pass advantage to buyers via lower prices. If costs decline rapidly with increases in volume, can start price below cost. (Can use price approaching variable costs.)	☐ Discourages potential competitors because of apparent low profit margins ☐ Limits competitive activity and expensive requirements to meet them	☐ Must offer other policies which permit lower price (limited credit, delivery, or promotions) ☐ Small errors can result in large losses ☐ Long-term payback period

One practical approach is to list all factors, state whether they increase or decrease the payoff, and your evaluation of why and how much.

The comparison of factors and payoffs ordinarily can be done only when pricing is a daily job, given high priority by top management. Smaller companies with fewer products obviously require less analyses, but the problem is proportionately the same. Even if the comparison is made "off-the-cuff," it is better than no comparison at all. At least the comparing process makes you think about the interplay of all factors.

Task 10: Establish Strategy

Relate Pricing Strategy to Objectives

Pricing strategy cannot logically be determined until you have completed the research and evaluation steps described in Tasks 5 through 9. After these tasks are completed, relate the data to your pricing objectives and overall marketing objectives and strategies. (See Pricing Strategy Chart.) It is important to know which overall objectives (company, product-line, product, market, etc.) and strategies are being pursued, since one pricing strategy may be highly appropriate in reaching one objective, yet may inhibit reaching another.

For example, a new product added to the line to fill available production capacity may require a selling price high enough to cover only the variable costs. But this low price strategy may be detrimental to the sale of other products in the line if the new product was added to fill a gap or to broaden a line of products currently selling at the market or at premium price levels. In this case, customers may associate the new, lower-priced product with a lowering in quality of the entire line.

Pricing Strategy Chart

The accompanying pricing strategy chart lists various objectives, associated strategies, when each strategy is used, implementation procedures, and advantages and disadvantages of each strategy. Select from the chart the strategy which best fits your company's operation. You can tailor each strategy to fit your situation.

The column, "When Generally Used," lists situations where strategies are often used. This column is not exhaustive, mutually exclusive, nor do all listed situations need to exist for you to use a particular strategy.

Task 11: Consider Cost-plus and Marginal Pricing Approaches

Introduction

There are two extreme approaches to pricing: cost-plus and marginal pricing. These approaches are discussed below, including the advantages and disadvantages of each.

Cost-plus

Many methods of cost-plus pricing are currently used by manufacturers. The following commonly-used approach is easy, simple, and consistent:

STEP 1—Set up a system of "standard" costs based on an assumed "normal" rate of output over a number of years (i.e., what it would cost to produce and sell "X" units, an arbitrary % of capacity; e.g., 70% expected at the beginning of the year, regardless whether 60, 80, or 90% of capacity was sold). All fixed and variable costs should be added, and the total divided by the number of units to be produced. This gives you the average cost per unit.

The following costs should be included: (1) cost to design (include building and testing pre-product prototype, if appropriate); (2) production (labor and materials); (3) amortized research and development and plant investments; (4) overhead; (5) rent; (6) insurance; (7) handling and packaging; (8) storage; (9) cost of carrying inventories; (10) advertising (assuming you use a percent of sales for determining budget); (11) transportation; (12) record keeping; (13) installation; (14) warranty service costs; (15) patent royalty.

STEP 2—To total cost add a set percent of cost (based on experience) to cover selling, merchandising, and administration costs, plus a "normal" profit to arrive at preliminary price.

STEP 3—Compare preliminary price with the going market price for a similar product, and adjust slightly if needed.

Flexible Variation

A flexible variation on cost-plus pricing uses a variable mark-up in lieu of a constant margin. The margin can vary depending on demand, competition, technology, and so forth. For example, competition and demand may impose low percent markups in some markets and permit higher ones in others. Markups may also be varied across the product-line, depending on competitive analysis, with the proper average margin being the overall object.

Drawbacks of Cost-plus Pricing

There are a number of drawbacks to the cost-plus pricing method. It is difficult in advance to determine such costs as construction, material price changes, and similar costs. It is difficult to allocate joint costs to specific products. Many costs vary with volume, and volume depends on price charged. Cost-plus is not based on realistic profit goals or market share objectives. It doesn't distinguish between out-of-pocket and "sunk" costs. It ignores capital requirements, return-on-investment, elasticity of demand, and the competition. And most important, the buyer is more concerned about the cost and value of product to him than about production and selling costs to supplier.

Marginal Pricing

The objective of marginal pricing is to find price and production levels at which a firm should produce in order to optimize its profit position. The application of marginal pricing by a layman is difficult; however, understanding this theory is important.

Theory

The basic theory of marginal pricing is that price is set at a point where marginal cost equals marginal revenue.

Marginal *cost* is the increase in total cost as a result of producing and selling one more unit of a product. On the diagram below, you can see that from zero production up to a volume of Q_1, marginal cost decreases; then begins to increase. Q_1 represents the point where economies of scale [7] have been exceeded. After this point, marginal costs tend to increase.

---

[7] Economies of scale refer to the fact that if products are mass produced, they normally cost less than if they are custom-made. Quantity discounts on materials and specialization of production processes contribute to the economies. However, these economies eventually level out, and become uneconomical when a company becomes too large, having complicated working procedures, as well as having exceeded break points for quantity discounts.

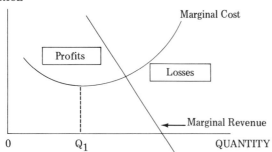

PRICE

Marginal Cost

Profits

Losses

Marginal Revenue

0   Q_1 QUANTITY

Marginal *revenue* is the additional amount received as a result of selling one more unit of a product. Note on the diagram that marginal revenue decreases as quantity increases. This is because of the supply and demand phenomenon, whereby people will buy greater quantities of a product at lower prices.

The reason for producing and pricing at the point where marginal cost equals marginal revenue is as follows: If marginal cost exceeds marginal revenue, the firm incurs a loss on each unit produced and sold beyond the point of the intersection of marginal cost and marginal revenue. If production and sales stop before marginal cost equals marginal revenue, the firm will not realize its full profit potential. Therefore, as long as marginal revenue exceeds marginal cost, it is advantageous to expand production and sales. Conversely, when marginal cost exceeds marginal revenue, business should be contracted.

Marginal pricing involves preparation and comparison of cost and demand schedules. These tasks are described below.

Prepare Cost Schedule

At each level of production capacity, derive cost estimates. The cost schedule presented in this task illustrates how this is done.

The example shows an analysis of an output range from zero to ten units. The analysis can be done for 100, 1,000, or 1,000,000 more units of cost and revenue, but discontinuities should be avoided as much as pos-

sible.[8] Enter the production levels in column 1.

In column 2, enter total fixed cost. Fixed cost is that which does not vary with production output. It must be expended at zero output or at any other output. Examples of fixed costs are rent and plant equipment. In the example, $40 is the fixed cost.

In column 3, enter total variable costs—those which vary with volume of output (e.g., raw materials, direct labor). For example, if zero units are produced, there will be $0 of variable cost; if one unit is produced, there will be $60 of variable cost; and so on.

In column 4, enter the total of fixed and variable costs—column 2 plus column 3. In the example, total cost ranges from $40 for zero units to $460 for ten units.

Compute and enter in column 5 the marginal cost for each level of output. Marginal cost is the addition to total cost associated with an increase in output of one more unit (change in total cost divided by change in quantity). For example, increasing production from zero to one unit has a marginal cost of $60 ($100 less $40, from column 4, rows 1 and 0). Increasing production from one to two units has a marginal cost of $52 ($152 less $100, from column 4, rows 1 and 2).[9]

Prepare Revenue Schedule

At each alternative price level, estimate the number of units expected to be sold and the associated total and marginal revenue levels. The Demand/Revenue Schedule illustrates how this is done.

The example shows in column 1 a price range from $85 to $40. The range can be ex-

---

[8] In the example, there are no discontinuities, because every production level between one and ten is analyzed. If you were to analyze 100, 1,000, 10,000, 100,000, and 1,000,000 units, many discontinuities would result. The ranges between alternative unit levels should be small enough to facilitate interpolation.

[9] Note that since unit volume increased by only one unit, there is no need to divide "change in total cost" by "change in total quantity." However, if multiples of 10 were being analyzed, the "change in total cost" of going up 10 units must be divided by 10 to determine marginal cost.

Cost Schedule

(1) PRODUCTION LEVEL	(2) TOTAL FIXED COST	(3) TOTAL VARIABLE COST	(4) TOTAL COST (COLUMN 2 - COLUMN 3)	(5) MARGINAL COST
0	40	0	40	—
1	40	60	100	60
2	40	112	152	52
3	40	155	195	43
4	40	189	229	34
5	40	205	245	25
6	40	220	260	15
7	40	240	285	25
8	40	280	320	35
9	40	340	380	60
10	40	420	460	80

Demand/Revenue Schedules

DEMAND		REVENUE		
(1) PRICE	(2) NUMBER DEMANDED	(3) NUMBER SOLD	(4) TOTAL REVENUE	(5) MARGINAL REVENUE
85	1	1	85	85
80	2	2	160	75
75	3	3	225	65
70	4	4	280	55
65	5	5	325	45
60	6	6	360	35
55	7	7	385	25
50	8	8	400	15
45	9	9	405	5
40	10	10	400	-5

tended in either direction, but should never exceed production capacity or go below a point where one unit is demanded. These latter calculations would be a waste of time since these production levels are normally not experienced in practice.

In column 2, enter the number of units expected to be demanded by the market at each price level. Fewer units will be purchased at higher prices, since more of the same units add successively less satisfactions to the buyer. In the example, demand ranges from one unit at $85 per unit to ten units at $40 per unit. Columns 1 and 2 comprise what is generally called a demand schedule.

From the demand schedule, a revenue schedule can be derived.

In column 3, enter the number of units expected to be sold at each price. This is equivalent to the number demanded.

Calculate and enter in column 4 the total revenue expected. This is determined by multiplying columns 1 and 3 (price times quantity). In the example, total revenue ranges from $85 for one unit to $400 for ten units sold.

Compute and enter in column 5 the marginal revenue for each level of sales. Marginal revenue is the addition to total revenue associated with an increase in sales of one more unit (change in total revenue divided by change in quantity). For example, increasing sales from one to two units has a marginal revenue of $75 ($160 less $85, from column 4, rows 2 and 1).

Compare Marginal Cost and Marginal Revenue Schedules

Now compare the marginal cost column (column 5) of the cost schedule with the marginal revenue column (column 5) of the revenue schedule. This can be done by transferring those columns to the comparison sheet (at the end of this task), listing number of units in column 1, marginal cost in column 2, and marginal revenue in column 3. Compute and enter in column 4, the difference between column 3 and column 2.

In the example, the differences start at $25 for one unit, decrease to $0 for seven units, and eventually yield a minus $85 for producing and selling the tenth unit.

Note the price associated with the level of production and output at which marginal cost equals marginal revenue. At this one level, theoretically, profits are at a maximum. In the example, this point is seven units.

To check whether this level truly yields maximum profits, calculate and enter cumulative revenue difference in column 5. In the example, the cumulative revenue difference for two units is $48 ($25 + $23 for units 1 and 2 in column 4).

This analysis tells you to produce seven units and sell them at $55 per unit to maximize total profit. The maximum profit is $131 achieved at seven units.

Limitations

In theory, marginal pricing produces the best price-volume relationship to yield maximum profits, and also raises some pertinent questions. Unfortunately, in the "real world," this tool is somewhat impotent even in the simplest case because of several limitations:

Marginal costs and marginal revenues are difficult to identify, except in a broad range. The range of intersections yields only a *range* of prices, not the exact one.

Cost schedules are difficult to prepare; revenue schedules are almost impossible to prepare with sufficient accuracy for price planning.

Businessmen don't think in terms of a single unit; they think in terms of volume.

Errs in assumption that the only right price point between cost and value is the one which maximizes short-run profit.

Compare Marginal Cost with Marginal Revenue

(1) NUMBER UNITS	(2) MARGINAL COST	(3) MARGINAL REVENUE	(4) REVENUE DIFFERENCE	(5) CUMULATIVE REVENUE DIFFERENCE
0	–	–	0	0
1	60	85	25	25
2	52	75	23	48
3	43	65	22	70
4	34	55	21	91
5	25	45	20	111
6	15	35	20	131
7	25	25	0	131
8	35	15	-20	111
9	60	5	-55	56
10	80	-5	-85	-29

Task 12: Consider Elasticity

What is Elasticity?

Elasticity refers to the responsiveness of "quantity purchased" to "price charged." In theory, elasticity tells where total receipts will be the greatest.

The two accompanying charts help explain how elasticity works. The first chart presents several determinants of demand and analyzes each to determine whether demand is elastic or inelastic. The second chart shows the effect of price changes on sales, depending on whether demand is elastic, unitary elastic, or inelastic.

How is Elasticity Calculated?

Elasticity is calculated by the following formula:

$$\text{ELASTICITY} = \frac{\% \text{ Change in Quantity Demanded}}{\% \text{ Change in Price}}$$

where:

$$\substack{\% \text{ Change in} \\ \text{Quantity} \\ \text{Demanded}} = \frac{\text{Change in Quantity Demanded}}{\text{Original Quantity Demanded}}$$

and,

$$\substack{\% \text{ Change} \\ \text{in Price}} = \frac{\text{Change in Price}}{\text{Original Price}}$$

It is difficult to calculate elasticity accurately in the "real world" because an organization cannot hold constant those items an economist holds constant for analytical purposes (e.g., advertising, product differentiation). Elasticity erroneously assumes that a firm knows the shape of its demand curve (i.e., how much will be bought at each price). Also, elasticity does not apply with heterogeneous products and where any buyer or seller is large enough to influence demand.

However, some companies do attempt to calculate elasticity through trial and error or by approximation. The trial and error method requires relating quantity purchased to changes in price over time. Also, one can approximate a few points on the demand schedule for a given product. Unfortunately, it is difficult to determine the shape of the curve between these points and beyond them.

Several tools for measuring (approximating) elasticity of demand are:

Industry trade association reports comparing competitive products
Plot responses to past price changes
Test marketing

Determinants of Demand—Whether Elastic or Inelastic

DETERMINANT	ELASTIC	INELASTIC
☐ Availability of Substitutes	Many	None
☐ Price Relative to Buyers' Budgets	Large part of budget (e.g., $10,000 budget, with $5,000 item)	Small part of budget (e.g., $10,000 budget, with $1 item)
☐ Need	Luxury	Necessary
☐ Price Change	Buyers purchase infinite amount with no change in price	Buyers purchase same amount with any change in price
☐ Ease of Want Satisfaction	Difficult	Easy
☐ Durability	High	Low
☐ Urgency of Need	Can be postponed	Need now
☐ Shifts in Supply	Big shift won't change price	Big shift will change price

Effect of Price Change on Sales

	DEMAND IS[10]		
	(>1) ELASTIC	(=1) UNITARY ELASTIC	(<1) INELASTIC
If Price Is Decreased And Sales increase >% decrease in price	X		
Sales increase proportionately to % decrease in price		X	
Sales increase <% decrease in price			X
If Price Is Raised And Sales decrease >% increase in price	X		
Sales decrease proportionately to % increase in price		X	
Sales decrease <% increase in price			X

---

[10] > = More Than
< = Less Than

Knowledge of competitive production capability vs. total demand (i.e., can they respond?)
Simulation
Executive estimates based on intuition and experience

Dealer and sales staff reactions (often biased)
Customer questionnaires (often biased)
Customer value estimates (hard to get valid ones)
Multiple correlation analysis

Task 13: Review Guidelines for Pricing in a Declining Market

Determine Cause of Decline

If a declining market is affecting your sales, review the situation and diagnose the reasons for the decline before selecting a new price strategy. This is important because a sales decline in an entire industry calls for a different pricing strategy than if only your firm's sales declined. For example, if your product suffers from style or design deficiencies, you'll rarely resolve the problem with price changes alone. Several reasons for decline include:

Economic conditions allowing less money to be spent

Recent purchase of products placing customers in over-stocked condition

Total market deterioration because of new substitute products entering the market, accompanied by shifts in customer preference

Slump in sales of related products or in those in which your product is a component or complement (derived demand declines)

Market saturation

Cultural and social attitudes about an industry (e.g., oil) or product (e.g., microfilm)

Things to Do

Listed below are some of the most successful pricing actions to take during a declining market:

Consider the long-run implications of actions planned to help in the short-run (e.g., will price change do more than riding out the storm?).

Determine benefits to your customer and the end consumer if price is reduced.

Inform all distributors of your intentions

to match all competitive price reductions by a reasonable amount.

Meet competitive price reductions to distributors, original equipment manufacturers or other key accounts.

Be prepared to encounter possible loss in market share when sales are affected by distress selling. (Sales by failing firms cannot be prevented.)

Things Not to Do

Listed below are some of the don'ts in a declining market.

Don't think you currently offer the "right" price for all time.

Don't be "trigger-happy" by reducing price before it's necessary.

Don't confuse rumors with reality (e.g., a customer telling you that your competitor lowered prices might be a ploy to get you to lower yours).

Don't confuse sales decreases with market share decreases.

Don't blame price alone for sales decline (although salesmen frequently blame sales decreases on high prices).

Don't concentrate on prices of individual items to the exclusion of those of the entire line.

Don't wait for a crisis to resolve itself.

Don't pass the blame or responsibility for a problem to subordinates.

Task 14: Use Competitive Bidding Tool as Needed

What is Competitive Bidding?

Competitive bidding results when a customer requests two or more firms to submit proposals detailing the products and/or services to be provided, along with associated costs. This bidding technique is generally employed when several firms offer similar products or services, and price is a primary distinguishing factor.

Put Facts in Order

Although no one can tell you exactly what to bid on every job, there are some guidelines to follow for putting each job in better perspective. The accompanying chart is useful for gathering relevant facts.

In column 1, enter all allowable bids within an acceptable range, using intervals as small as time permits for analysis. In the

Competitive Bidding Tool

(1) ALLOWABLE BIDS	(2) ESTIMATED COST	(3) NET PROFIT (1) − (2)	(4) PROBABILITY	(5) EXPECTED PROFIT (3) X (4)
$ 8,000	$8,200	($ 200)	1.00	($200)
$ 8,200	$8,200	0	.95	0
$ 8,400	$8,200	$ 200	.90	$180
$ 8,600	$8,200	$ 400	.85	$340
$ 8,800	$8,200	$ 600	.80	$480
$ 9,000	$8,200	$ 800	.70	$560
$ 9,200	$8,200	$1,000	.60	$600
$ 9,400	$8,200	$1,200	.45	$540
$ 9,600	$8,200	$1,400	.30	$420
$ 9,800	$8,200	$1,600	.15	$240
$10,000	$8,200	$1,800	.00	0

example shown, allowable bids range from $8,000 to $10,000 with $200 intervals.

In column 2, enter your best estimate of the cost of doing the job, whether it be supplying a product or service. This cost should be the same regardless of the bids. In the example, estimated costs are $8,200.

In column 3, enter the difference between columns 1 and 2. This is the net profit (or loss) expected for each combination of bid and cost.

In column 4, enter the expected probability of a particular bid being accepted by the customer.[11] Generally, the higher the bid, the lower the probability of a bidder being awarded the contract. Probabilities range from a sure thing (100%) to "no way" (0%).

Excluding ties, you can now calculate the expected profit at each bid—cost combination—by multiplying column 3 by column 4. Enter the result in column 5. In theory, you would submit that bid resulting in the highest expected profit. In the example, the bid would be $9,200.

In practice, other factors affect the decision. This competitive bidding tool should only be used as a guide to putting different bids in their proper perspective.

[11] Probability is the relative frequency—or average—expected in the long-run. For example, if you toss a coin 100 times, you would expect 50 heads and 50 tails, with a fair coin.

Task 15: Set Price

Use Instinct

When all information is gathered and analyzed, and strategy selected, the price-setting executive is ready to close in on a price. After reviewing all information and relationships among factors, it is time to use a good instinctive feel for the market and its environment. This feel should be based on a combination of experience, professional judgement, and detailed knowledge of the market. All the previously-derived data does is narrow the range. Cost data sets the floor on price; while demand and competition sets a flexible ceiling on price.

Unfortunately, no sophisticated approach exists whereby you input all these variables and out pops the correct price. Rather, the pricing executive must sift through all data and say, "This price looks about right." [12] Whatever the price decision, always record who made it and why, as well as the date of the decision and the manner in which it was derived.

Relate Price to Company Offer and Background

In narrowing the price range, one must relate price to company offer and background. The chart (Relate Price to Company Offer and Environment) lists elements of the company offer and background, and the state of each in terms of whether a low price or high price should be charged. This chart should be used as a guideline rather than as a final answer to all pricing problems.

How to Price New Products

Different price-setting approaches are used with different levels of newness. Three distinct levels are discussed below:

Identical products
Similar products
Unique products

Identical Products

Products identical to those already marketed may be offered by a new company (e.g., new electric typewriter). Prices will approximate those of functionally identical rival products, unless very specialized market segments are being approached.

Similar Products

Other products may be new to a company or to a market, yet directly competitive with functionally similar products on the market (e.g., electric automobile). Prices will consider those of functionally similar products, with adjustments made for buyer-perceived differences in function or utility. Market studies can help determine how much of a price differential buyers would accept for new features. As in normal pricing, costs should be used as a price floor.

Unique Products

Products truly unique or functionally different from anything on the market cause the most difficult pricing decisions. This uncommon pricing decision is complex because:

No comparative prices exist for competitive or similar products.
Primary data is lacking on production costs, market size, competitive ability to enter the market, and customer expectations on services and conditions of sale.
Initial doubt prevails as to which distribution channels and promotional tools are most effective.

Many pricing experts suggest setting price as high as possible for unique product introductions. This allows broad margins for initial advertising and promotional campaigns. If prices are rejected by buyers, they

---

[12] Sophisticated mathematical formulations may replace this approach, but to date, no proven system exists for all applications.

Relate Price to Company Offer and Environment

ELEMENT TO BE RELATED	LOW PRICE	HIGH PRICE
1. Product class	Commodity with wide availability	Custom, unique, or proprietary
2. Production orientation	Capital — intensive: prices ease as wages outrun productivity	Labor — intensive: prices increase as wages outrun productivity
3. Production method	Mass-produced, yielding economies of scale	Custom, requiring special expertise
4. Product obsolescence	Extended usefulness	Quickly outmoded
5. Product life due to wear and tear in use	Short-life	Long-life
6. Product versatility	One use	Many uses
7. Speed of technological changes in production and distribution	Slow	Rapid
8. Distribution channel complexity	Simple (possibly only one middleman)	Complex (many middlemen each receiving a share)
9. Market coverage	Intensive — many industries in depth	Selective — few industries in depth or several barely covered
10. Market share desired	Large	Small
11. Market development	Mature, with heavy competition	New or declining, prior to and after economies of scale are realized
12. Specialized ancillary services	None or few	Many (e.g., installation, training)
13. Promotion, advertising, and sales expense	Little	Much
14. Promotional contribution to product-line	Rounds out line and helps sell other more profitable products	Little, or product stands on its own
15. Turnover	Fast	Slow
16. Profit potential	Long-run	Short-run

can be lowered quickly to meet realistic demand levels.

Others indicate that in a cluttered market, it is sometimes necessary initially, to come in low, accept a loss (or break even) and recoup on higher pricing once desired level of market share has been achieved.

Pricing Don'ts

Don't ignore demand and depend solely on cost to determine price.

Don't assume that cost data compiled for control and tax return purposes are satisfactory for pricing.

Don't rely solely on some mechanical formula to determine the "right" price.

Don't ignore advertising and promotion expenditures, middlemen costs, research and development expenses, sales force expenses, and so on, in setting prices.

Don't force every product's price to yield

a predetermined, satisfactory profit in the short-run.

Don't ignore competitive pricing actions.

Don't assume that a price cut automatically enables you to win customers away from rivals. It may simply force rivals to match your cuts.

Don't charge different prices to customers who cost about the same to serve.

Don't lower price just because of declining sales.

Don't assume that a price increase will automatically cause loss of your customers to rivals. It may provide a long awaited opportunity for them to match your increase.

Don't change prices upward or downward, and consider the job done. Close monitoring of the effect on overall sales trends within key accounts is essential. Have contingency plans.

Task 16: Develop Discounts

Many Kinds of Discounts?

Discounts and other concessions are granted to customers as an inducement in the pricing offer. Most firms extend some form of discount based on price differentiation. The differentials are based on the assumption that customers can be segregated into classes, and that the cost of serving each class differs. The costs differ because the buyer either foregoes some marketing function or provides it for himself.

Differentials may be included in the price structure of a firm through discounts for order size, delivery method, timing of sales, speed of payment, or distance from shipping point. Other non-price differentials include cooperative advertising allowances, installation, repair, trade-in, rebates, and so forth.

How to Establish Discounts

Discounts and associated differentials are generally based on industry practices. In such cases, your firm has little discretion regarding their establishment, unless you are a price leader and policy setter. However, some companies can establish price differentials independently through use of cost analysis by segregating relevant costs, and by demonstrating a cost savings to the selling company which justifies the discount differential.

Types

The most commonly used discounts include cash (based on timely payment), quantity (based on volume purchased), trade or functional (based on services customer gives you), and promotional (based on your customer's overt promotion of your company's name or products according to your specifications).

Cash Discounts

Cash discounts are frequently given to buyers who pay within a specified time period. Buyers in a liquid cash position cannot afford to pass up cash discounts. The discount should be high enough to yield a greater return than that obtained by the buyer retaining funds in his business. If buyers generally ignore the discount, it is probably improperly set to serve its purpose—that of getting customers to pay quickly.

Terms are generally written in the following form: "2/10, net 30." This means that a 2% discount from the invoice price is offered to those paying within 10 days of invoice date. The full amount is due at the end of 30 days if the discount is not taken. The percent discount, and both discount pay and net pay time periods, can be altered to fit your situation.

Make sure that all details are worked out

in consultation with your accounting staff, because severe cash flow problems can result if cash discounts are illogically set. The importance of this is exemplified by further analysis of "2/10, net 30." These terms mean, in effect, that the manufacturer is willing to pay 2% if the buyer will allow him use of due funds 20 days sooner. This is equivalent to 36.69% annual rate of interest.[13]

Quantity Discounts

Quantity discounts are price reductions based on amounts purchased. They are generally granted to encourage large purchases. Discounts can be noncumulative (on one shipment at a given time) or cumulative (over a specified time period).

Several reasons for offering quantity discounts include:

Encourages larger orders which reduce your costs of selling, packing, shipping, and so forth

Facilitates sale of weak products by applying discount to entire line; reduces stock of slow-moving items

Rewards customers for continued patronage and exclusive dealing

Spurs lagging sales

Quantity discounts have two major drawbacks: (1) Toward the end of a specified discount period, buyers may place larger orders to qualify for discounts. This may disrupt the production process unless floating time periods are employed (i.e., different periods for different customers). (2) There will be many requests for discounts from customers buying just short of the break-even point. For example, if the quantity over which a discount is given is 1,000, and a company bought 975, they may ask for the discount.

Trade or Functional Discounts

Trade discounts are price reductions given to certain buyer groups to compensate them for performing certain middleman marketing functions. Although primarily a consumer product pricing tool (for retailers and wholesalers), trade discounts are employed for industrial distributors, dealers, brokers, and wholesalers.

In many cases discounts do not really reflect differences in the manufacturer's marketing costs. Rather, such discounts are often extended to secure increased distribution. If discounts are larger than your competitors, more middlemen will be inclined to carry your line. Of course, under antitrust laws, such an arrangement is legal only if offered equally to all buyers in the same category. (See Chapter XII—Legal Aspects of Marketing.)

Promotional Discounts

Promotional discounts or allowances constitute a reduction in price granted the buyer as compensation for specific and direct forms of sales promotion (e.g., cooperative advertising programs run in cooperation with dealers).

Task 17: How to Quote Prices

Quotations Include Things Other than Price

Whether prices are negotiated, estimated, or contracted for, they generally include specific provisions for the following:

Relation to List Prices

Net price quotations to distributor
Less discount to distributor

---

[13] $\dfrac{2\% \div 98\%}{20 \text{ Days} \div 360 \text{ Days}} = \dfrac{.0204}{.0555} = 36.69\%$

Provision for Resale Prices

Suggested prices
Maintained prices (e.g., fair trade pricing)
Advertised resale prices

Pricing Extras, Replacement Parts and Repairs

Separate charges, or
Included with original purchase or with main product

Discount Structure

Cash (for quick payment of invoices)
Quantity (for large purchases)
Trade (for being at certain level in distribution process)
Promotional (e.g., co-op advertising)

Delivery/Transportation

Prepaid or C.O.D.
Basing point (i.e., prices are calculated from a specified point, regardless of where shipment originated)
Cost of insurance and freight (C.I.F.)
F.O.B. Factory (Free On Board)—buyer pays cost of transportation to his location, plus the same base price paid by all other buyers
F.O.B. Destination—seller pays cost of transportation to buyer's location
Freight equalization—distant buyer is quoted a delivered price consisting of the F.O.B. factory price, plus delivery charges from competitive location closest to customer; may lower net, but adds business volume
Freight allowed (postage stamp pricing)—seller quotes price F.O.B. to customer's place of business, regardless of location
Zone pricing—divide market for bulky products into zones; delivered prices may vary from zone to zone, but within a zone, all customers pay the same price (see your cost accounting department)
Basing-Point—To the F.O.B., factory price, add the transportation cost from a selected point to the customer's location, regardless of actual point from which shipment was made; for bulky and/or standard products

Other Items Affecting Price Quoting

Guarantee and warranty service
Installation charges
Service/maintenance charges
Allowances (e.g., promotional co-op advertising)

Task 18: Review Price Performance

Is There a Right Price?

Even after you consider all pertinent theories and circumstantial factors and you are satisfied that the price is right, there still is no guarantee you are right. Actually, several prices may be equally good. For many customers, the price will never be right; for others, they'll always want slight modifications or deals. Therefore, price is always on trial, and requires constant review. In theory, however, we can point to times when price is either too low or too high.

When Is Price Too Low?

When one's customers would pay more—the fact that you're easily selling your entire output is a good clue that price is too low.
When price is below cost (except on loss leaders,[14] which are infrequently used for industrial products).

[14] Loss leaders are used when you are willing to take a loss on a particular item to get people interested in the rest of your line.

When Is Price Too High?

- When very little can be sold because of price, or if slight price reduction would greatly increase sales. (But, if substantial price reduction is needed to increase sales slightly, price is almost certainly *not* too high.)
- When you are "out priced" compared with competition for comparable goods, based on an objective judgment of competitive offers.

Frequency of Price Review

The frequency of price reviews depends on company objectives, market, and competitive changes. All prices should be challenged at regular, preestablished intervals to determine if original decisions still apply. Review reasons why prices were set as they were or changed. See if those conditions surrounding original decisions still prevail. At the time of major price changes, consideration should be given to increasing the review frequency. Responsibilities and reporting structure for this review should be clearly defined and understood.

Look for clear signals following price-setting or changing, but be wary of possible "false" signals. For example, salesmen often complain that prices are too high, and that sales are lost to competitors because of failure to cut list price. If price setters acted on each of these complaints, every firm in the country would appear to be continually suffering from a price problem of charging too much.

Be careful not to act hastily. Consider all ramifications prior to making a change. Competitors can use price changes against you, so be certain you can support your actions. Constantly analyze competitors' pricing strategy. A new "deal" gone unnoticed can spell trouble for you in given markets.

Task 19: Make Price Adjustments

Areas to Consider

When price changes are being considered, two areas are of prime concern: new break-even point, and how to announce new price.

Price Changes in Relation to Break-even

Break-even analysis considers the interaction of fixed costs, variable costs, and the extent to which volume and profits change with price changes. By understanding the demand-oriented pricing fundamentals discussed in this chapter and gaining an appreciation of break-even relationships, you can better grasp the decision-making aspects of pricing.

Break-even analysis has been covered in Chapter III—Product Planning and Development. Although break-even analysis does not yield a final "correct" price, it helps put pricing problems in proper perspective. For example, if you plan to cut price by a certain percent, and you know what your current gross profit is, you can use break-even analysis to determine the increase in unit sales needed to earn the same gross profits previously achieved at the higher price.

The "Sales Increase" chart does this for you. To find the percentage of increase in unit sales needed to earn the same gross profits at a lower price, find where the row listing expected price cut intersects with the column listing current gross profit. For example, if you plan to cut selling price by 5% and current gross margin is 20%, you'll need to sell 33.3% more units to earn the same amount of gross profits earned before the price cut.

Announcing Price Changes

Price change announcements are routinely made as news items in business publications, by news releases, by distribution of new pricing sheets, and by oral announcements from sales personnel. Some guidelines for price change announcements include:

Before a price increase, use advance announcements (2 weeks to 45 days) to give customers time to adjust their own plans and perhaps an incentive to stock up on the product before prices go up. Advance announcements connote openness and fairness. On the other hand, price cuts are seldom announced in advance because customers may stop all buying and wait for the lower price. Announcements can take the form of a forecast, rather than statement of fact; or they can detail exact changes. Either approach is acceptable.

If a price increase is small, use sales personnel to relay changes, rather than risking it becoming a major issue if widely publicized.

Justify all price increases. Price increases are less conspicuous and more readily accepted when new, improved models are introduced.

Price reductions are most effective at the time a new model is introduced; however, the reduction may be postponed until newness has worn off and a sales booster is needed.

Sales Increase Needed to Earn Same Gross Profit as Before Price Cut [15]

EXPECTED PRICE CUT	CURRENT GROSS PROFIT									
	5%	10%	15%	20%	25%	30%	35%	40%	45%	50%
1%	25.0%	11.1%	7.1%	5.3%	4.2%	3.4%	2.9%	2.6%	2.3%	2.0%
2	66.6	25.0	15.4	11.1	8.7	7.1	6.1	5.3	4.7	4.2
3	150.0	42.8	25.0	17.6	13.6	11.1	9.4	8.1	7.1	6.4
4	400.0	66.6	36.4	25.0	19.0	15.4	12.9	11.1	9.8	8.7
5	–	100.0	50.0	33.3	25.0	20.0	16.7	14.3	12.5	11.1
6	–	150.0	66.7	42.9	31.6	25.0	20.7	17.6	15.4	13.6
7	–	233.3	87.5	53.8	38.9	30.4	25.0	21.2	18.5	16.3
8	–	400.0	114.3	66.7	47.1	36.4	29.6	25.0	21.6	19.0
9	–	1000.0	150.0	81.8	56.3	42.9	34.6	29.0	25.0	22.0
10	–	–	200.0	100.0	66.7	50.0	40.0	33.3	28.6	25.0
11	–	–	275.0	122.2	78.6	57.9	45.8	37.9	32.4	28.2
12	–	–	400.0	150.0	92.3	66.7	52.2	42.9	36.4	31.6
13	–	–	650.0	185.7	108.3	76.5	59.1	48.1	40.7	35.1
14	–	–	1400.0	233.3	127.3	87.5	66.7	53.8	45.2	38.9
15	–	–	–	300.0	150.0	100.0	75.0	60.0	50.0	42.9
16	–	–	–	400.0	177.8	114.3	84.2	66.7	55.2	47.1
17	–	–	–	566.7	212.5	130.8	94.4	73.9	60.7	52.6
18	–	–	–	900.0	257.1	150.0	105.9	81.8	66.7	56.3
19	–	–	–	1900.0	316.7	172.7	118.8	90.5	70.1	61.3
20	–	–	–	–	400.0	200.0	133.3	100.0	80.0	66.7
21	–	–	–	–	525.0	233.3	150.0	110.5	87.7	72.5
22	–	–	–	–	733.3	275.0	169.2	122.2	95.7	78.7
23	–	–	–	–	1115.0	328.6	191.7	135.3	104.6	85.5
24	–	–	–	–	2400.0	400.0	218.2	150.0	114.3	92.6
25	–	–	–	–	–	500.0	250.0	166.7	125.0	100.0

[15] At intersection of price cut row and current gross profit column find percent increase in unit sales required to maintain the same absolute gross profit as before the price cut.

Task 20: Consider Leasing Equipment/Products

Definition

A lease is a contractual agreement whereby use of an asset is transferred by its owner to another party for a certain time period and for a consideration.

Lease Types

There are three basic types of lease arrangements: flat rate, variable (per unit), and combination.

The flat rate lease is exemplified by the computer industry, where lessors charge a flat monthly rate to the lessee regardless of time the machine is employed.

This arrangement provides the lessor with a certain income, resulting in less fluctuations during depressions. The flat rate appeals to major users of leased equipment, but may discourage usage by firms trying the product for the first time or uncertain of the merits of leasing.

The variable approach depends solely on unit output. This arrangement may cause uncertainties and fluctuations of revenues for the lessor, unless some minimum base fee is charged in the case of small accounts. The per unit approach may not appeal to large volume users, although trial customers or those new to leasing may find the approach appealing.

The combination approach is exemplified by the automobile renting industry, whereby automobiles are rented/leased at a daily, weekly, or monthly rate, plus so much per mile (unit) driven. This approach offers widest appeal to all parties.

When to Lease?

When there is a large number of small potential "buyers" with limited financial resources

When lessee can direct available funds to investments yielding higher returns than through equipment purchase

When there is a high chance of rapid obsolescence

When manufacturer desires control of usage, timing, and distribution of equipment

When supplies and services related to equipment are extremely important to buyer's profitablility

Advantages to Seller (Lessor)

Can produce current revenues and possible later sale

Often maximizes total revenues by obtaining more dollars for the product over lease period than if selling it for a lump sum

Can tie product to purchase of supplies and auxiliary equipment (in cases where legal) and service contract

Lowers sales resistance when buyers have limited funds (i.e., lowers their initial outlays)

Seller controls timing of new models introductions and product improvements

Disadvantages to Seller

Troublesome paperwork and billing

Requires considerable resources to buy or produce equipment

Risk that machine or other leased asset can be returned at any time

Servicing and repair costs may be higher than if products were sold outright, since lessee has less incentive to care for equipment.

Competitive innovations may render seller's equipment worthless as current lease expires; whereas if equipment was sold, the problem becomes that of the user.

Advantages to Buyer (Lessee)

Converts fixed costs into variable costs which reduces liability unless product is used.

Reduces capital expenditures required to be able to benefit from product usage.

Allows usage of latest technological innovations at minimal capital investment.

Leases are completely deductible for tax purposes in the year incurred, where depreciation on an owned machine may not be as great due to amortization over many years.

Disadvantages to Buyer (Lessee)

Payments are normally proportionally higher over a period than if equipment is owned

Some leases have "no break" clauses, causing temporary lock-ins to possibly obsolete equipment

Tying servicing or purchase of supplies to lessor may require payment of premium price

How Much Rent to Charge?

Leasing poses the unique problem of defining a pricing basis. Generally, this basis is ownership cost, adjusted upward to compensate for elimination of high initial ownership downpayments, potential technological obsolescence, interest charges, insurance, and the other disadvantages previously discussed. How much extra to charge depends on your desired profit rate and the risk of the particular situation, as well as recovery of the cost price of the asset within a specific time period.

Task 21: Consider Licensing

Definition

A license is legal permission by a developer or patent holder of a product or process to allow someone else to produce, operate, and/or distribute the end-product in return for an agreed-upon consideration or fee. Some advantages and disadvantages of licensing are:

Licensing is advantageous since it reduces owner's capital investment in plant, equipment, training, etc. It reduces consequences in high risk situations. It can readily be used if product or process is non-complementary to a firm's existing line(s). It provides source of income with minimal investment. It can test market potential, costs, and investment requirements for later entry when start-up problems are ironed out.

Licensing is disadvantageous since there is little direct control over management or operations of licensee. Also, you may be contributing to growth of a later competitor or putting one in business from scratch.

Contractual Arrangements

In addition to receiving a fee, the owner of the equipment, process, or product may require that he be given representation on the licensee's board of directors, as well as an agreed number of shares of the licensee company's stock.

Cost Considerations If You License Your Product/Process

First, estimate the profits for the licensee. Then work back to what he should pay you. There is no tested guideline for determining the share, but licensing agreements normally include an initial payment, royalties, payment for special services, and rentals of your equipment.

INITIAL PAYMENT: This payment is made to recover out-of-pocket costs in negotiating and in maintaining the agreement. This maintenance may include training, loan of key personnel, share in research and development expenditures, attorney's fees, and a performance bond.

ROYALTIES: Royalties are usually the principal source of income from licensing agreements. They include pro-rata cost of continued research and development, plus a share of generated profits. The average usually doesn't exceed 5–6% of sales. Never accept a percent of profits since the licensee can alter the books by bleeding off various expenses. Request a minimum royalty total as a stimulus to licensee to develop the market (e.g., ½–1% of the estimated annual sales through the third year). This minimum can be reduced later if found to be excessive. It is often wise to include a maximum royalty as an incentive to licensee to achieve greater sales and production.

Pricing Reference Guide

And The Price Is Right, by Margaret C. Harriman, U.S. & World Publishing Co., Inc., 225 Lafayette, New York, NY 10012.

Managerial Economics (chapters 7–9), by Joel Dean, Prentice-Hall, Inc., Englewood Cliffs, NJ 07632.

Price And Price Policies, by Walton Hamilton, McGraw-Hill Book Co., 1221 Avenue of the Americas, New York, NY 10020.

Price Policies And Marketing Management, by Robert A. Lynn, Richard D. Irwin, Inc., 1818 Ridge Road, Homewood, IL 60430.

Price Policies And Practices; A Source Book In Readings, by Donald F. Mulvihill and S. Paranka, John Wiley & Sons, Inc., 605 Third Ave., New York, NY 10016.

Price Policy And Procedure, by Donald V. Harper, Harcourt, Brace and World, Inc., 757 Third Ave., New York, NY 10017.

Prices And Markets, by Robert Dorfman, Prentice-Hall, Inc., Englewood Cliffs, NJ 07632.

Pricing Decisions In Small Business, by W. Warren Haynes, University of Kentucky Press, Lexington, KY 40506.

Pricing For Higher Profit; Criteria, Methods, Applications, by Spencer A. Tucker, McGraw-Hill Book Co., Inc., 1221 Avenue of the Americas, New York, NY 10020.

Pricing For Marketing Executives, by Alfred R. Oxenfeldt, Wadsworth Publishing Co., Inc., No. 10 Davis Drive, Belmont, CA 94002.

Pricing For Profit And Growth, by Albert U. Bergfeld, James S. Earley, and William R. Knobloch, McGraw-Hill Book Co., Inc., 1221 Avenue of the Americas, New York, NY 10020.

Pricing In Big Business, by A. D. H. Kaplan, Joel B. Darlan, and Robert F. Lanzillotti, The Brookings Institution, Washington, DC 20000.

Pricing: The Critical Decision, AMA Management Report No. 66, American Management Assoc., 135 W. 50th St. New York, NY 10020.

CHAPTER VI

Advertising

Introduction

What is Advertising?

Advertising is the communication of a message through selected media (e.g., magazines, radio, television, direct mail, etc.) with the intent to influence people to purchase a product or service or otherwise react in a desired manner.

Advertising and the Industrial Manufacturer

Ideally, advertising helps create a better atmosphere in which sales can be made.[1] While direct sales contact is the *best* means of reaching prospects and customers, it's seldom the most cost-effective. Today a call by an industrial salesman costs as much as $80. And he can reach only several hundred potential buyers a year. Advertising helps you be more confident that when your salesman makes his $80 call, he's contacting either an already interested buyer or one who is at least familiar with your products.

Advertising makes the salesman's job easier. It "sets up" prospective buyers. It answers the questions asked by the man in McGraw-Hill's powerful ad stating why you should advertise: a grumpy-looking, hard-boiled buyer leans forward and asks the unfortunate salesman:

> "I don't know who you are.
> I don't know your company.
> I don't know your company's product.
> I don't know what your company stands for.
> I don't know your company's customers.
> I don't know your company's record.
> I don't know your company's reputation.
> Now what was it you wanted to sell me?"

Advertising helps preclude having a buyer ask your salesman such embarrassing questions. Then your salesman can immediately get to his main purpose—to *sell* himself, his company, the company's product-line, and the advertised product.

When to Use Advertising

Maybe you don't need to advertise at all. Maybe your market is so extremely vertical, so easy to reach, and competition is so minimal that your present method of selling will yield an excellent profit year after year. If you're absolutely convinced that every potential buyer knows of your product, then don't advertise. But, if you make an honest appraisal of your market, you may conclude that sales could be higher than the current

---

[1] Advertising itself is not normally designed to actually make the sale, except in the obvious case of direct mail order businesses.

level. In that case, you should consider advertising and the ways it can help your company to sell more effectively.

How Effective is Advertising? [2]

Many studies on advertising effectiveness have been made by advertisers and by outside service organizations such as advertising agencies and research firms. In general, these studies show that money invested in advertising should be regarded as any other investment a company makes in people, salaries, research, plant, and equipment. Specifically, these studies show that:

Greater sales are achieved when advertising is combined with personal selling, than when personal selling alone is used.

Companies maintaining former advertis-

---

[2] In May 1971, Arthur D. Little submitted "An Evaluation of 1100 Research Studies on the Effectiveness of Industrial Advertising" to the American Business Press, Inc. This report summarized the extensive research on advertising effectiveness, and reviewed in detail the most frequently quoted studies on the subject: Buchen Advertising, Inc., U.S. Steel/Harnischfeger, Morrill, Modern Medicine, Allis-Chalmers, American Metal Market, Production Magazine, and Syracuse. A copy of this report as well as others on the effectiveness of advertising are available from American Business Press, 205 E. 42nd St., New York, NY 10017.

ing levels during recession years have better sales and profits than those that cut or eliminate their budgets. Reduced advertising results in less product and brand awareness, and risks a drop in sales activity.

Advertising extends the salesman's reach by locating key buying influences.

Advertising increases reader familiarity with products and helps increase sales.

Advertising influences buyer attitudes.

Products not directly associated with a company's line are more quickly accepted by potential buyers when they see your advertising.

Chapter Plan

This chapter comprises four sections. The basic preparations necessary to organize for advertising are described in Section A (Tasks 1–5). Section B covers the step-by-step procedures for developing a complete advertising program/plan (Tasks 6–10). Section C tells how to implement an advertising program (Tasks 11–12). Section D explains how to evaluate the effectiveness of advertising programs (Task 13). The chapter concludes with a reference guide, containing a list of advertising-related associations and sources of information on advertising.

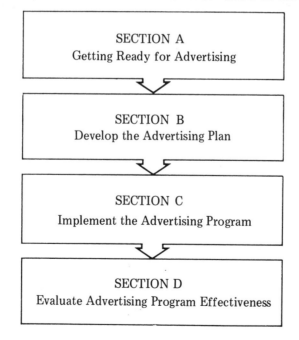

SECTION A
Getting Ready for Advertising

SECTION B
Develop the Advertising Plan

SECTION C
Implement the Advertising Program

SECTION D
Evaluate Advertising Program Effectiveness

Section A

Getting Ready for Advertising

Purpose of Section

The purpose of this section is to define how to organize and staff the advertising department, select an advertising agency, establish the methods to use in working with the agency, evaluate the advertisability of your products, and gather related information on your company and its markets. Completion of these tasks sets the stage for developing the advertising plan (Section B).

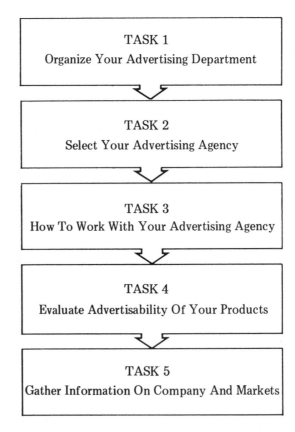

TASK 1
Organize Your Advertising Department

TASK 2
Select Your Advertising Agency

TASK 3
How To Work With Your Advertising Agency

TASK 4
Evaluate Advertisability Of Your Products

TASK 5
Gather Information On Company And Markets

Task 1: Organize Your Advertising Department

Functions of an Advertising Department

Depending on the department's size, number of products it must promote, budget, objectives, and amount of responsibility placed with the advertising agency, the advertising department may perform any or all of the functions below.

214

Consider overall marketing and sales objectives as a guide to advertising planning.

Select and work with advertising agency.

Gather related information on the company, its products, and competitive programs.

Determine advertising objectives and budgets.

Develop program plan with the advertising agency (e.g., publication advertising, direct mail, collateral materials, audio-visuals, and other promotion tools).

Measure program effectiveness (e.g., analyze inquiries, conduct recognition studies, etc.).

Make periodic reviews of market conditions, needs, trends, competitive activity, and other factors influencing your advertising program.

Handle inquiries.

How Large Should Your Department Be?

As the functions of an advertising department vary greatly, so do its staff requirements. Most industrial companies have advertising departments staffed by up to five people. Less than ten percent of industrial companies have advertising departments with more than ten people. Larger departments are generally found in larger companies and in companies where a broad range of functions is assigned to the advertising department. As department size increases, so do expenses; but as size decreases your program becomes vulnerable to setbacks because the risk of one person leaving may disrupt an entire campaign.

Small firms or multi-division companies generally have small (one or two-man) departments, and in some cases advertising responsibility may be one of the many functions handled directly by the marketing manager. As departments grow, a wider variety of specialists is generally employed. Some large advertising departments include copywriters, production artists, photog-

raphers, and so forth. In some cases, the department may assume the role of an in-house agency, if desired by top management.[3] This in-house group can prepare selected advertising campaigns or promotional materials, or develop entire programs in lieu of an advertising agency. Although many companies have attempted the use of in-house agencies, their achievements have been less than universally successful.

Required Personnel

The department needs a strong advertising manager and talented supporting personnel.

In recent years, the competent advertising manager has grown in stature and responsibility within companies. He is a valuable member of the management team, and in many small to medium-sized companies he is highly valued as part of the marketing function, reporting to the senior marketing executive.

Responsibilities of today's advertising manager are concerned more with managing than in *creating* advertising. He is the chief liaison between his company and the advertising agency. To be effective, he must thoroughly understand his company's sales goals and overall objectives and be able to relate them accurately to the agency. It isn't necessary for him to possess creative advertising skills. But he should have innate ability to evaluate work performed by others and to inspire co-workers and suppliers to seek new levels of achievement. And he should, of course, be able to organize, plan, and supervise the work of others.

The office of a competent advertising manager is the control center of all advertising functions. Every task flowing through his department and through the agency is logged somewhere in a readily accessible file.

---

[3] Some companies choose to establish an in-house agency to collect media commissions themselves (usually 15% of media costs). This may result in less objectivity, and the higher operating costs may readily offset any savings in the media "kickbacks."

The advertising manager should have most or all of these qualities:

Work harmoniously with people on all levels.

Communicate clearly and accurately.

Motivate his people to produce outstanding results.

Exercise good judgment.

Possess a sound working knowledge of all marketing functions.

Make creative contributions to the advertising function.

Approach problems with a positive and objective attitude.

Be a strong business manager in his own right.

Be aware of outside sources of creative talent.

Task 2: Select Your Advertising Agency

Why Use an Agency?

Advertisers prefer to use agencies because:

Agencies are specifically staffed to perform a variety of communication functions.

Agencies can draw on broad marketing exposure based on experiences in many different fields.

Being outsiders, they frequently bring a more objective approach to marketing problems than an internal staff beholden to its management.

Charges to their clients are usually more economical than the internal cost of most company-sponsored groups if all costs are realistically evaluated.

They have a strong financial incentive to perform well because if they don't they won't retain the account.

Primary Functions Performed by an Agency

The trend today is for most agencies to offer their industrial clients a broad range of marketing services, including the following basic ones:

Analyze market conditions, conduct situation analyses, and review company sales objectives.

Recommend advertising budgets and programs, including types of media and schedules.

Create and produce communications materials (i.e., for insertion in trade magazines, collateral pieces, etc.).

Purchase advertising space in appropriate media.

Coordinate program execution.

Evaluate results of communication programs.

Evaluate Your Needs

Selecting an advertising agency for your company is one of the most important decisions any marketing man can make. Whatever your particular reasons for changing agencies or selecting your first one, start the process correctly. Begin with self evaluation. What are your company's specific needs?

To understand your company's needs, and to provide an objective basis for selection of an agency, ask yourself these questions (not necessarily in order of importance):

What do we expect advertising to do for us?

What specific problems do we face (e.g., sales, image, etc.) and what are their causes?

What are the long-term and short-term objectives of our company?

What is our planned growth for the coming year? The next two years? The next five years?

How large an advertising appropriation (estimate) will we have to work with?

Which of our advertising needs could be handled internally? Do we really have the capabilities to satisfy these needs ourselves?

Establish Selection Criteria

With your company's needs and problems in mind, list the criteria you want to use for evaluating advertising agencies. Some typical questions which need answering are:

Is the agency involved in any way with competitors that could involve a conflict of interest?

What is the agency's history and growth record? Annual billings? Number of employees?

What is the agency's credit rating? This is important to evaluate periodically, even after you choose an agency. Cases have been recorded where companies have been embarrassed to discover that although they have paid the agency for services rendered, the agency has not paid other suppliers, such as media.

How many accounts are handled by the agency? It is not so important to know the total number of accounts as it is the size and activity level of the accounts. An agency can adequately service only so many continuously active clients. On the other hand, they can service a larger number of small, but relatively inactive accounts.

What percent of the agency's clients are consumer-oriented and industrial-oriented? If your company produces highly technical products, it might be risky to select an agency that specializes in retail clothing advertisements. However, do not insist on an agency having previous experience in your specific product areas. If an agency has a successful record of work in the industrial marketplace and happy clients, then this agency can in most instances learn the unique characteristics of your business.

What percentage of the agency's growth is from new clients? From growth of present client budgets? If an agency is truly successful in performing for its clients, there should be some evidence of internal budget growth from existing clients. This illustrates the success of a communications plan in meeting objectives and the subsequent growth of a client.

Where would your company rank in budget size in relation to other clients the agency handles? Normally, you don't have to be the biggest client. But, it is often foolish for a very small client to select a very large agency. You will have trouble getting the attention of the top agency talent unless special arrangements are agreed upon in advance.

What is the agency's record for retaining accounts? (This is a real clue. Some agencies are good at selling their services initially, but they don't follow through. If an agency has a high turnover of accounts, be cautious. You may be next.)

What is the agency's reputation among media representatives, its clients, and its competitors? A few phone calls will answer this question.

What services does the agency offer? Probe this in depth. Ask for examples, specific case histories of how they have handled certain assignments. Many people promise the sky in a sales presentation, but really have severely limited skills, depth, or experience.

How creative are they? Awards won? Copy excellence? Art excellence? Awards can be valuable to an agency in terms of creating a "hot" reputation. And they are recognition of achievement within an industry. But be careful. One must evaluate just what the awards truly represent—the level of competition involved, etc. Better yet, what did the agency's creative efforts truly accomplish for the client? Ask their client for that answer. The "creative" award-winning industrial advertising ad may or may not have seemed creative to the potential customer.

Agency location. This may or may not be important depending upon your needs and how often you require personal contact. If there is a high level of weekly activity requiring personal contact, your agency should be fairly close in proximity. In one way or another, you will pay for travel time to and from the agency.

What method of compensation does the agency offer? Spell this out in written detail if you are seriously considering an agency . . . and especially before you begin any work assignments.

Who will be assigned to your account? (This is important because an agency is only as good as its people.)

Do you feel comfortable with these people? (Human chemistry is vital in any such relationship.)

Who are the other key people in the agency? What functions do they perform? What effect would their leaving have on the agency? (Analyze the whole structure and working nature of the agency.) What is the turnover ratio of its people?

Develop Your Own Criteria

From the preceding list of questions, select those that are relevant to your particular marketing problems. Add any of your own that may be important because of special circumstances or personal preferences.

Select Agencies for Consideration

Then comes the next major question: which agencies should you consider to handle your account?

Many advertising and marketing managers read regularly the local and national advertising publications to keep abreast of agency news (e.g., which agencies are expanding, what type of clients they handle, etc.).

Another method for finding a list of agen-

cies is to contact several publishers' representatives and editors in your field for their advice. Usually they will recommend two or three agencies that would be appropriate to your needs.

Attendance at meetings of such organizations as the Business/Professional Advertising Association, local advertising clubs, etc., is another way to gain exposure to people in the industry. In addition, you can refer to the *Agency List of Standard Advertising Register*, which lists all U.S. agencies. The register is available from the National Register Publishing Co., 147 W. 42nd St., New York, NY 10036.

Draw up a list of potential agencies. If this list is not too long, visit each agency personally and talk with the key personnel.

If your list is lengthy, or if you need to take a shortcut due to shortage of time, then develop an agency questionnaire. Don't make it too long. Don't demand or expect overly profound answers either. This is a mistake many companies make. It only wastes everybody's time.

Based on the answers to questionnaires, select the most promising agencies and visit them personally. Talk with key people, review work performance for other clients, and briefly discuss your company, its plans, objectives, products, your specific problems and needs, and what you are looking for in an advertising agency. This meeting will give both you and the agency a better understanding of the situation and, if enough interest exists, to continue discussions.

Invite Presentations

After narrowing down the list of possible agencies, select at least three you feel are outstanding and invite them to make presentations to you and your management. Less than three cannot provide a good comparative mix of services, talent, personnel, etc. Don't make the list too long. This may be a waste of your company's executive time and also for the participating agencies. More than six agencies and the situation often gets out of hand. Never invite an agency to present unless they will be given serious consideration.

The agencies selected for the formal presentation should not be asked to do speculative ads or marketing plans unless you mutually agree beforehand on specific compensation for their efforts. It takes a certain amount of time for an agency to truly understand your company's needs. Therefore, most "free" speculative presentations are an economic waste from the agency's viewpoint, and rarely result in successful program recommendations for the client.

Furthermore, the agency's current clients are in reality paying for such speculation. Your company may pay for the next such situation if you encourage agencies to engage in this practice.

Request that the account executive to be assigned to your account attend all pre-selection meetings. Give the identical information about your company and its needs to each presenting agency. Tell each presenting agency which of your company's representatives will be present, what is expected in time and content of the presentation, when the final decision will be made, and the basis on which final selection will be made.

Make Final Selection

To make the final selection, follow basically the same criteria previously used to narrow down the list of agencies. The "Advertising Agency Selection Chart" will help you in scoring each agency.

Each member of management involved in the selection should independently score presentations (using the evaluation chart). Scores should not be disclosed until the final presentation is over and all scores are turned in to the advertising or marketing manager. Then scores can be tabulated and recorded on a summary chart similar to the one used in individual evaluations.

If the agency selection process was a precise mathematical equation, the agency with the largest point total would be automatically selected. However, the numbers on the chart are not the only criteria. They should be used only as aids in making the final judgement.

In addition to the numerical scores, consideration should be given to the personal "chemistry" that is vital to a strong client/agency relationship. You may want to have a final meeting of the management team to discuss any subjective points still questionable. Combine the numbers with your "gut feel" and make a decision.

After a selection is made, separate letters to each agency should cover the following points:

Identify the agency finally selected.
Inform each "loser" why it was not selected.
Express appreciation for the time and effort each agency devoted to its presentation.

Task 3: How to Work With Your Agency

Establish Good Working Relationships

When you have selected an agency, immediately view them as an extension of your company's marketing organization. Let them know you feel this way. Some clients select an agency to handle their communications programs, turn over large

budget appropriations to them, and then foolishly become secretive about corporate plans and competitive data that would be extremely useful to the agency in preparing programs for you.

A successful relationship is based on (1) freedom for agency to perform without undue hindrance with regard to creative solutions from company/client management;

Advertising Agency Selection Chart

CRITERIA

WEIGHTS   TOTAL SCORE   COMMENTS

NAMES OF AGENCIES

EVALUATOR'S NAME & TITLE: _____

DIRECTIONS:
1. List most important criteria based on your company's needs.
2. Choose the advertising agencies to make presentations.
3. Assign weighted value to criteria (one to ten points each; the higher score indicates greater value).
4. Score each agency presentation based on criteria.
5. Tabulate scores of each member of review team.
6. Analyze and discuss the agency(s) with the highest point totals.
7. Arrive at decision by mutual agreement.

(2) mutual honesty, respect, and teamwork; (3) no conflict of interest; (4) a clear understanding of both client and agency responsibilities to each other; (5) a thorough knowledge of client's marketing problems; (6) methods for measuring client and agency performance; (7) a profitable pre-arranged compensation plan; and (8) a written contract.

How Work Flows Through the Agency

The following is a step-by-step flow of a typical advertising program moving through the advertising agency.

1. The account executive (AE) works with the client representative (usually

the advertising and/or marketing manager) to develop advertising objectives.

2. The AE gathers information relating to the client's products, markets, target audience, competition, timing, and objectives (based on research and the client's knowledge and experience).

3. The AE relates the client's input to agency creative/management personnel involved with the account.

4. The creative team (copywriter and art director), media department, marketing department, public relations department and the AE, after becoming familiar with the client dossier and marketing problems, develop a conceptual advertising plan. This plan would include:

    a. Markets/audience to be reached
    b. Media channels to be employed
    c. Message regarding products, pricing, company policy and services offered
    d. How messages should be presented
    e. Cost to develop and execute the complete program

5. After being convinced the plan is on target, the agency presents the plan to the client for approval.

6. Following client approval, the entire agency immediately goes to work.

    a. Creative team develops concepts.
    b. Media department contracts for the best possible communications mix to reach the targeted audiences.
    c. Production department produces finished art, makes all necessary outside purchases (buyouts) such as photography, typesetting, paper, special art effects, plus numerous other materials.
    d. Marketing department develops research and evaluation programs.
    e. Public relations department (if

the agency has one) develops its phase of the total program and coordinates it with the advertising and sales functions.

    f. The traffic department controls the flow of all agency projects, thereby ensuring publication and broadcast deadlines are met.

7. After an advertising message has appeared before its intended audience, the various media involved furnish the agency proof verifying that the advertising did appear.

8. The agency than checks media schedules and appearances against media billings to be sure that the client has received what he pays for.

9. The agency bills the client for work performed, material buyouts, and media. In many cases, all items with the exception of commissionable media (depending on pre-arranged compensation), are marked up to include an agency commission. (Media already includes a commission available only to recognized advertising agencies.)

10. The agency then analyzes the results of the advertising program and makes recommendations to add, modify, drop, or stay with suggested formats.

Tools for Working with the Agency

There are two extremely useful tools which improve any client/agency working relationship: client contact reports and client progress reports.

Client Contact Reports

The client contact report is extremely useful for confirming details of each client/agency meeting. Immediately following each meeting, your agency should prepare a brief summary of all topics discussed and all decisions reached or postponed. Copies should go to all parties involved in the meeting and to any other control points on either the client or agency sides.

Typical Progression of a Client's Program Through the Agency

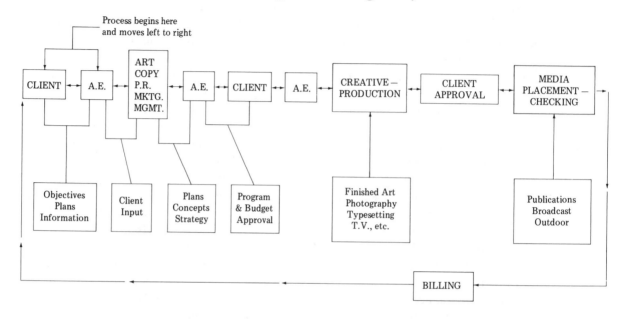

Client Contact Report

CLIENT: _____   DATE: _____

CONTACT: _____   ☐ VISIT   ☐ PHONE

NO.	SUBJECT

BY: _____

Client Progress Report

CLIENT: _____   REPORT DATE: _____

JOB #	DATE ENTERED	DESCRIPTION	DUE DATE	PROGRESS REPORT	EST. COST	DATE COMPLETED	ACTUAL COST

Client Progress Reports

The client progress report can be prepared either by the client, or the agency to keep track by division or product group, of all projects underway. In the column, "Progress Report," fill in who is responsible for the action required. Also, list the status of each job and estimated percent completion.

How to Compensate Your Agency

There are three main sources of income available to an agency:

Media Commissions—Historically, media (i.e., publications, radio, or TV stations) will invoice the purchaser for gross costs of the media used. If the purchaser is a recognized advertising agency, the agency is permitted to deduct 15% of the invoice and remit the net amount to the media while legally charging the client for the gross cost.

Charges for Time Invested by Agency Personnel on Behalf of the Client—Most agencies have established hourly rates to charge for functions and/or skill levels of every person they employ. This rate incorporates the individual's actual salary, plus overhead costs, and an adequate profit.

Mark-ups on Outside Purchases Made by the Agency for the Client—Since agencies act as purchasers for the client for many items such as photography, printing, engravings, etc., it is customary to charge a handling fee on such outside buyouts. This fee will range from 17.65% to 20% depending upon terms agreed between the client and the agency.

From these three income sources numerous types of compensation plans have evolved. There is no one "right" method. Generally, however, industrial media budgets are not sufficient to generate adequate commissions to compensate an agency for its time and buyouts. Therefore, some additional compensation arrangements must be made. Each agency has its preferences based on its own experience. Usually, compensation plans mutually satisfactory to both parties can be negotiated.

Practical Guidelines

Three guidelines are highly recommended for compensation/billing procedures:

If you want an agency to produce good results, it must make an adequate profit.

Require your agency to maintain itemized cost records for their time and for all buyouts. Many clients also ask for the right to examine these records should any questions arise.

If a project takes more than 30 days to complete, or if production on projects overlap monthly pay periods, charges accumulated should be billed at the end of the 30 day period or end of the month cycle. This gives you a more even cash flow and does not burden the agency with large operating expenses and accumulated buyout charges. Thus, cash flow is more predictable for both parties.

Prepare Written Contract

Every client/agency agreement should be formalized in a written contract or letter of agreement. This is necessary for the protection of both parties. The written contract records the ground rules and establishes a basis for doing business without undue confusion or misunderstanding.

Important items to be included in the contract are:

When the contract takes effect

How can termination occur: (e.g., on 30, 60, or 90 days written notice by either party)

Services that will be performed by the agency

How special projects and services not defined in the contract are to be handled and how compensation will be made

Client responsibilities relative to agency

What materials become property of the client

What happens to work-in-progress if the account is terminated

Method of agency compensation

Billing procedures

Cash discounts

Right of client to audit the agency's financial records relating to the client's account

How financial adjustments are to be made

Client personnel responsible for approval of work performed by agency

How agency will be evaluated

Policy against agency acting in similar capacity for client's competitors

The above can be used as a guide in developing your own written agreement based on your company's needs. In addition, consult with your legal department when formalizing the contract. Many agencies have standard contract forms or can prepare a letter of agreement. This may suffice if it is acceptable to you, your company, and your legal counsel.

Evaluate Agency Performance

After working with your advertising agency for about six months, an evaluation will point to strengths and weaknesses in agency services or in agency/client working relationship. Discuss the evaluation with agency management so they are aware of your specific concerns. This gives them opportunity to correct any weaknesses and to be aware of your assessment of their strong points.

Inform the agency that a regular evaluation (every 6 months, or at least yearly) will be made for the benefit of both parties.[4] This

---

[4] Details of method and frequency of agency evaluation should be included in the written client/agency agreement.

policy provides an excellent basis for maintaining an honest and candid atmosphere that will lead to a lasting relationship. The "Agency Evaluation Form" can be used for agency evaluations.

Also, invite the agency to evaluate you as a client. Find out what you can do to make the programs more effective and to maintain a smooth flow of work through all phases of development.

Agency Evaluation Form

NAME OF AGENCY_____ PERIOD COVERED: From_____to_____

EVALUATION MADE BY:_____ Date _____ 19_____

PERFORMANCE STANDARDS	RATING NO.
1. Advertising programs and special projects are produced and submitted for client approval well in advance of publication dates	_____
2. Views of client management are accurately interpreted and presented in agency programs	_____
3. Individual advertisements reflect creativity in:	
(a) Conceptual approaches	_____
(b) Layout and format	_____
(c) Style and presentation of messages	_____
(d) Art and photography	_____
4. Media selections (or recommendations) demonstrate a clear understanding of client's objectives and strategy, and are effective in reaching selected target readership in efficient and economical way	_____
5. Client's publics have reacted favorably to individual advertisements produced by agency	_____
6. Agency demonstrates clear understanding of client's marketing and communication programs, and coordinates its (the agency's) communications to contribute to the client's total communication programs	_____
7. Agency is successful in:	
(a) Planning, organizing, and scheduling projects	_____
(b) Staying within budget goals	_____
(c) Operating within established schedules and deadlines	_____
(d) Assembling and interpreting data for special projects	_____
8. Relations between agency personnel and client personnel are:	
(a) Harmonious and based on mutual respect	_____
(b) Honest and candid	_____
(c) Conducive to pleasant and efficient working conditions	_____

RATING SCALE: Performance relative to standard is:

OUTSTANDING	5
EXCELLENT	4
SATISFACTORY	3
BARELY ACCEPTABLE	2
UNSATISFACTORY	0

Task 4: Evaluate Advertisability of Your Products

Should You Advertise?

In some situations, advertising should not be included in the marketing strategy. Appraising the advertising opportunity before investing could save unnecessary expense and make your products more profitable.

Evaluate the advertisability of your products from the following standpoints:

STAGE IN LIFE CYCLE—If your products are in a growth stage of their life cycles, they are far more advertisable than those in a declining stage.

PRODUCTION CAPABILITY—If your production capacity is extremely limited and you are now selling all you can produce, then advertising expenditures may be wasted if you seek to stimulate more sales and can't deliver.

GEOGRAPHIC—If you can service only a limited geographic area (i.e., have distribution only in New England), it is wasteful to advertise nationally.

KNOWLEDGE OF MARKET—If you have a limited market for your products, personally know all potential customers and all buying influences in each company, then advertising may be wasteful. Be careful, however. Many companies have deluded themselves into thinking they know all buying influences, only to discover how wrong they were.

BUYING MOTIVES—Can your advertising serve an informative role of explaining price, durability, reliability, cost in use, etc.? Advertising's usefulness increases when product benefits are apparent. Where products are nondifferentiated (i.e., commodity items like certain types of metals), the creative advertising assignment becomes more difficult. But, brand preference can be created due to exposure and acceptance of the company or product name.

Task 5: Gather Information on Company and Markets

Work with Other Company Departments and the Agency

Work with your advertising agency and key company departments to obtain information relevant to defining target markets, audience, competition, and other factors. Your marketing research and sales departments should provide primary assistance. The research department probably already has a file of required background information, as well as information on overall company plans. And since advertising should provide maximum help to accomplish sales objectives, a clear understanding of the sales department's objectives, problems, and plans is essential.

Three primary methods of obtaining required data include:

Hold meetings with the agency and key company departments to discuss broad subjects under consideration.

Request that the agency and key departments complete a questionnaire to stimulate their thinking and make available to others all possible thoughts on the program.

Travel with sales personnel on calls to get a general feeling for problems and possible solutions.

Required Data

Information required at this stage includes:

What existing and new products/services are to be sold (i.e., design, sizes, contents, applications, competitive advantages, prices, etc.)?

What are the company goals?

What are forecasted sales volume and goals by product, market segment, and geographic region?

What is forecasted share of market by product, market segment, and geographic region?

Market data

    a. What is current company status in each market?

    b. What is current and projected number of actual and potential customers in each market? Who are the key customers?

    c. Which markets are increasing/declining?

    d. What are the buying habits, needs, preferences, sales resistances in each market?

    e. What are the characteristics of buyers in each market (e.g., job function)? Who are the key buying influences?

    f. What appeals to customers in this market? What are the most important factors considered in making a purchasing decision?

    g. Why do customers buy your products rather than competitive goods?

Industry conditions

    a. Is the industry expanding or declining?

    b. What are current inventory levels at distributors, jobbers, users, etc.?

    c. What are the price trends, terms, etc.?

    d. What are competitive strengths, weaknesses, and trends?

Distribution

    a. What are the current channels and sales tools employed?

    b. How is the sales department organized? How effective is the sales organization (e.g., ability to follow up on inquiries)?

    c. How many salesmen are needed to cover the market? Frequency of calls to average customer? Cost per sales call?

Promotion program

    a. What is the relative copy and media emphasis desired by product and market?

    b. How effective were various tools used in the past?

    c. Any ideas on how to help salesmen and make advertising more effective?

    d. How well does the inquiry handling system work?

Record Data for Planning Reference

Developing an advertising program is no different than developing a sound business operation. It requires an honest analysis of facts and a creatively written action plan. To aid gathering key data and setting objectives, seven forms are provided on the following pages. It is here that all the information from marketing research, planning, sales, and your agency impinge on your communication objectives. The seven forms include:

    Competitor—Space Unit Analysis
    Competitor—Frequency Analysis
    Competitor/Market Share Analysis
    Product Analysis
    Specifying Influence Analysis
    Communication Method Analysis
    Summary: Marketing Communications Program

Competitor—Space Unit Analysis

A copy of The Competitor—Space Unit Analysis form is used in determining the type of advertising your competitors are using in their current campaigns. It also can be used in your annual budget presentations.

There are several useful informational sources for completing this form. In addition to local clipping bureaus and research firms, two are particularly helpful:

(1) ADVERTISING CHECKING BUREAU, Inc., 353 Park Ave. South, New York, NY 10010. Checks advertising insertions for one brand, a company,

or a product classification. Clippings are furnished for each ad. Reports are available showing space, pages, and dollar value of space.

(2) ROME REPORT OF BUSINESS PUBLICATION ADVERTISING, 1960 Broadway, New York, NY 10023. Compiles advertising appearing in approximately 700 business publications representing over 90 publishing classifications. Provides a standard source of competitive media information by company division placing advertisements, address of advertiser's headquarters, publications scheduled, number of insertions, total space purchased, and dollar expenditure in each publication.

Competitor—Frequency Analysis

The Competitor—Frequency Analysis form is used in comparing where your competitors are investing their advertising dollar and how much they are spending. Information such as this can be obtained from the sources listed under Competitor—Space Unit Analysis (see previous section).

Competitor/Market Share Analysis

The Competitor/Market Share Analysis form is intended to become an exhibit of material collected for the marketing plan. The growth of a particular market should be considered, especially as it relates to other markets. Comparisons of competitor shares of market, strengths and weaknesses, and strategies or trends are part of knowing the "adversary." Also, space is provided for plotting three year trends in share of market and market growth. The marketing plan is based mainly on these elements.

Product Analysis Form

The Product Analysis form is a function of competitor/market share analysis in that one ingredient of competitive strengths and

Competitor Analysis

SPACE UNIT ANALYSIS	DESCRIPTIVE CODE	B/W — BLACK & WHITE 2C — TWO COLOR	4C — 4 COLOR SP — SPECIAL POSITION		TIME PERIOD		
PRODUCT / DIVISION / COMPANY	INSERTS	SPREADS	FP	2/3RDS	1/2	1/3	1/4 OR 1/9

weaknesses is an advantage or disadvantage in products or services. The key is to boil descriptions down to the competitive advantage, if any.

A product is a combination of features, each of which has a function, which in turn provides a benefit. This evaluation must be critically objective to get at the salient facts.

Specifying Influence Analysis

The Specifying Influence Analysis form summarizes the relative importance of a given audience in the buying decision cycle. Your product or service must offer a solution to a potential buyer's particular problem, or he is not a valid object of concern. If you can offer a solution, how can you best present your solution to him; what will interest *him* in the most appealing way? Decisions regarding media selection will be based, in part, on the information contained on this form.

Having recorded information on the market, the product or service, and the audience, it is now possible to make decisions (determine strategy) about the results the advertising program should achieve (objectives).

Communication Methods Analysis

The Communication Methods Analysis form is used to record your channel of communication methods (i.e., ad vs. direct mail vs. trade show, etc.). That method is described by a methodology, or how, when, and where you'll do it, and a rationale, or why (explanation and objective) you've chosen the particular method. By including an estimated budget, this table provides a convenient summary of the main elements of your communications methods.

Competitor Analysis

FREQUENCY ANALYSIS			TIME PERIOD _____							
MAGAZINE	COMPANY		COMPANY		COMPANY		COMPANY		COMPANY	
	SPACE	$	SPACE	$	SPACE	$	SPACE	$	SPACE	$
TOTALS										

Competitor/Market Share Analysis

_____
(Market Name & SIC)

MARKET SIZE $_____ (19___ last yr.) $_____ (19___ this yr.) $_____ (19___ next yr.)
MARKET GROWTH ____% (19___ last yr.) ____% (19___ this yr.) ____% (19___ next yr.)

COMPANY	MARKET SHARE %			STRENGTHS	WEAKNESSES	TRENDS	COMMENTS
	19___ (last yr.)	19___ (this yr.)	19___ (next yr.)				

Product Analysis

(Product Name)

PRODUCT FUNCTIONAL DESCRIPTION

FEATURE	FUNCTION	BENEFIT	COMPETITIVE VALUE

Specifying Influence Analysis

(Product Group)

JOB FUNCTION	WEIGHT %	SPECIFYING OR APPROVAL	PROSPECT'S PROBLEMS	SOLUTION OFFERED	POSSIBLE APPEALS	COMMENTS

Communication Methods

PRODUCT GROUP	METHODS (Media)	METHODOLOGY (How, When, Where)	RATIONALE (Why)	BUDGET

Summary: Marketing Communications Program

PRODUCT GROUP	MARKET NAME	MARKET SIC □ OEM □ USER □ TRADE	NO. OF UNITS IN SIC	POTENTIAL SALES WEIGHT BY SIC (%)	TOTAL MARKET SIZE IN DOLLARS	EXPECTED SALES FOR PERIOD ($)	DESIRE % MARKET SHARE	PRIME COMPETITION AND MARKET SHARE %	BUYING INFLUENCES AND WEIGHT (%)	OEM vs. USER vs. TRADE WEIGHT (%)	COMMUNI-CATION OBJECTIVE	COMMUNI-CATION METHOD	ESTIMATED BUDGET	PRODUCT(S) FEATURED

Summary: Marketing Communications Program

The next form presented is used for summarizing your marketing communication program. This form combines the previous ones into a synopsis of key information on which the advertising plan can be based, including supporting documentation, objectives, methods, and budgets.

Summarize Information

Now you can digest, evaluate, and weigh all the facts and trends. Discuss the information summary with the sales department, senior marketing officer, and your agency. Once direction is agreed upon, the information gathered in this task forms the basis for the advertising plan, which is discussed in the following section.

Section B
Develop the Advertising Plan

Purpose of Section

This section helps you develop the advertising plan: set advertising objectives, determine strategy, determine the message, select proper publications and develop the budget. These tasks, in some cases, are interrelated and not necessarily performed in the indicated order.

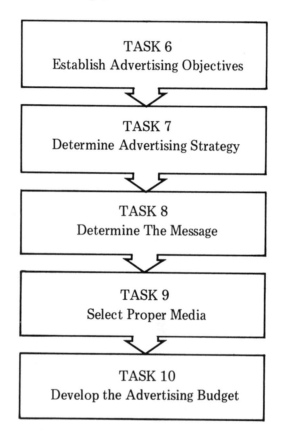

TASK 6
Establish Advertising Objectives

TASK 7
Determine Advertising Strategy

TASK 8
Determine The Message

TASK 9
Select Proper Media

TASK 10
Develop the Advertising Budget

Task 6: Establish Advertising Objectives

Procedures for Establishing Objectives

Advertising is an action tool used to help accomplish a company's goals, plus reach marketing and sales objectives. To develop your objectives, meet with your advertising department, key sales/marketing personnel, and your agency. Conduct this meeting with prime emphasis on how advertising helps accomplish marketing and sales objectives by increasing awareness, acceptance, preference, and insistence.

The combination of advertising and personal selling is a most effective, versatile, efficient, and economical approach to marketing. However, be careful not to confuse advertising objectives with sales objectives. The objective of advertising is to communicate. The objective of the sales effort is to write the order. You can develop a great industrial advertising campaign, generate thousands of sales leads, develop a credibility posture, presell the marketplace, but if the sales force fails to take advantage of these efforts, the disappointing results should not be attributed to the advertising program.

Specific Guidelines

In setting your company's advertising objectives, one should be written for each product-line and market segment. Objectives must be clearly defined (i.e., what action or reaction is desired in what time period in each target market), measurable, realistic, and related to the market/sales objectives. Of course, you should obtain top marketing management approval of objectives before beginning development of programs.

General Examples

Advertising objectives may be company-oriented, or marketing and sales-oriented. The diversity of advertising objectives under each of these types is illustrated below. In practice, however, general statements like these examples must be translated into specific terms that can be measured. Define your own advertising objectives in accordance with the guidelines given above, and to relate to your company's specific requirements.

For example: instead of a general objective such as "Increase inquiries"—which would be impossible to measure objectively—restate it in specific terms: "Develop _____ inquires at $_____ per inquiry from the _____ market for _____ product by _____ date." With a specific objective like this you can count the responses, measure the dollar cost, identify the market and product, and see exactly where you stand by the target date specified. The degree to which your objectives have been attained can then readily be determined.

Examples of Company Objectives (in general form)

Identify company with product (especially if the product is well known but the manufacturing company isn't) or most successful divisions.

Position company in the marketplace vis-a-vis its competition.

Position your company as a product innovator.

Show that your company is "growth-oriented."

If publicly held, gain the attention of the financial community.

Create brand loyalty and identification.

Attract and maintain good personnel.

Examples of Marketing/Sales Objectives (in general form)

Develop an awareness and demand for your company and products.

Introduce a new product or applications to established buying influences.

Maintain market awareness of and credibility for your established successful products.

Expand into new demographic or geographic markets.

Maintain good will and assist distributors or manufacturers' representatives.

Provide market with helpful information about product availability.

Reinforce decision of sold customers.

Secure sales leads and qualify prospects.

Boost sales morale; provide recognition for and give credit to leading sales personnel.

Reach target markets economically; reduce selling and operating expense.

Sell products in areas where it is uneconomical to use salesmen.

Task 7: Determine Advertising Strategy

What is a Strategy?

An advertising strategy is the course of action, expressed in a plan to accomplish your company's advertising objectives. This plan includes the policies, procedures, and programs that relate to your company, its products, markets, and customers.

Select Strategies

Select a strategy or combination of strategies that:

Will best achieve your objectives
Is within your capabilities
Stays within your proposed budget range
Is based on your market and audience analysis

At this point, refer back to the forms completed under Task 5. These forms display information in an easy-to-use format which facilitates strategy selection.

Strategies are not always generated exclusively by analyzing a compilation of facts. Don't underestimate the power of a "gut feel" by a seasoned marketing man. His experience in working with a particular set of problems on a daily basis sometimes produces a "sixth sense" that defies explanation, yet produces results.

Examples of Strategies

Examples of advertising strategies are given below as a guide.

Use a sustained trade advertising program to introduce new product-lines in known markets.
Employ cooperative advertising to increase dealer sales volume.
Use advertising to develop a demand for your products by stressing their benefits to the end-user.
Use test series of advertising in horizontal markets to determine interest in company's products from other vertical marketing areas.
Use direct mail advertising to reach key buying influences.
Use tabloid publications to increase volume of inquiries.

Whatever strategy you choose, it must be elaborated and formulated into a message that will favorably impress the potential buyers of your product, and those who can influence the buying. This is the subject of the next task.

Task 8: Determine the Message

Make Your Message Meaningful

Now decide on the content of your message—the specific points you need to make and the overall feeling you want to convey. Your agency will create the exact wording.

Before you decide hastily on the message content, consider these facts: Few businessmen have much free time. In addition to their daily activities, they are bombarded by countless advertising messages. Why should they read yours? This is the single most important question you can ask yourself.

You know a great deal about your product but, unfortunately, you can become enamored with some of the intricate details or specifications. These details may not be relevant to the end-user, and his only question is—"Will this widget solve my problem?"

Therefore, your advertising message should address itself to that one factor—the specific problems your product will solve, and how. For example, will your product or service:

Increase production?
Decrease manufacturing costs?
Improve the saleability of his products?

Increase profits?

Eliminate or minimize production bottlenecks?

Reduce manufacturing downtime?

Minimize scrap loss?

Increase the life and dependability of his end product?

Simplify maintenance and repair of a product?

Select Appropriate Appeals

Here is a check list of things to consider when selecting potential appeals:

Determine the message of a specific advertisement; i.e., what is it you're trying to convey. A good agency will greatly assist in this area.

The agency provides the creative solution; i.e., the headline, visual elements, and copy. Don't make the mistake of dictating these to the agency. You may be wrong in your approach. If you don't like the agency's solution, ask for a new direction or answer.

Don't fall for old cliches! For example, the beautiful model in an abbreviated bathing suit. This may pull inquiries but mostly for the girl's phone number.

Avoid other cliches, such as, "Think Production, Think XYZ Manufacturing Company." Be specific as to how you can help a potential customer.

It's not as bad as some people think to attack competition head-on and name names. But be certain your facts are completely accurate, and that you don't have any skeletons in the closet which your competitor could throw back at you. Some of the most effective advertising provides competitive comparisons.

Every ad doesn't have to have a photograph of your product. Certainly, it is the most beautiful thing in the world to you, but to the rest of the population it may look just like another black box. Remember, the customer is more interested in what you're going to do for him than what your product looks like.

Your logo! This is another sacred cow that causes problems. A logo is the name of your company done in a special type face, a slogan, or a symbol. A great deal can be said for following a consistent pattern in logo usage, i.e., don't keep changing slogans, type faces or symbols. If you're a multi-divisional company, a manual on corporate identification usage is very important. But in ads, don't insist that the logo be the most prominent item. The headline, the illustration and the basic message are of prime importance. The logo should act as a signature just as your individual name does when you sign a letter.

Don't forget some old basics when you prepare an ad. The words "new," "free," and "how to" have been used for years. Yet they are still extremely effective. Buyers read trade publications for news. If you have some—say so!

If you're advertising a product, ask for action. Tell the reader to contact you for additional information, or that you offer a free brochure. A good salesman always asks for the order. The function of an ad in industrial marketing is to create interest or awareness. Hopefully, it will also lead to buyer interest in gaining more information—the next step in the selling process.

Task 9: Select Proper Media

Assign Responsibilities

Media selection is often considered one of the most important decisions in the advertising planning process. This is because media costs probably represent the largest single expenditure in the advertising budget. This where-to-advertise decision is a critical one.

Thus, it's often wise to combine suggestions of both your company *and* advertising agency.

Some companies feel that "these are our bucks, so we'll make the decisions." Other companies prefer to turn the entire job over to the agency. Realistically, however, working as a team generally produces best results because both parties bring unique capabilities to the decision.

What the Client Contributes

The client contributes:

A good analysis of the editorial coverage and content of various publications, since he understands the publication's terminology and interests, and probably reads them regularly.

An in-depth knowledge of the industry, products, and markets.

A personal interest in doing a job well.

What the Agency Contributes

The agency contributes:

Experience in evaluating media for many different industries and types of marketing problems.

Ability to organize and present only the important information.

Objectivity required to make sound choices, i.e., doesn't let client personnel's personal reading preferences affect decisions.

Evaluation Procedures

There are several thousand business and trade publications from which to choose. Your product-line obviously limits the number of publications to consider. However, there are still far too many publications in a particular field (e.g., 25 publications of major interest in the metal-working field) to say "let's use them all." Therefore, a procedure is needed to narrow the choice. Some key steps in this evaluation process are discussed in this task. They are:

Determine Information Required
Obtain Publication Information
Obtain Readership Information
Make Relative Evaluations
Complete Media Schedule

Determine Information Required

As a first step in the evaluation, list those facts about each publication which will be used as selection criteria. These facts should stress the interests of the publication's audience, the publication's performance, and other related characteristics. Select a mix of criteria which fit your company's situation. Never rely on just one criterion. Frequently used criteria are listed below.

What field does the publication serve?
What is the circulation, broken down by SIC,[5] job title and function, geography, etc.?
Is the circulation paid or nonpaid? Many media analysts feel that paid circulations indicate greater interest on the part of readers, simply because the reader is willing to pay for the publication. This is not always true in practice.
Is the editorial content of value to the type of person you want to reach? Are the articles written by the publications staff, are they contributed by outside practitioners or regular columnists, or are reprints from other publications used?
Is the publication a weekly or a monthly? "Monthly" publishers argue that issues are kept longer and are thereby more valuable. Weekly publishers note their timeliness is important to keep readers abreast of latest industry news. Although both are partially correct, media decisions should be based on editorial content, circulation, rates, and not on the frequency of issue. If the publication truly serves its readers, it will be read regardless of its publishing schedule.

[5] SIC is the U.S. Government's system for numerically classifying the entire U.S. economy.

How often are the readers of a publication qualified; i.e., how frequently does the publication update its circulation list to weed out individuals that have moved, left the business, etc.? If it's every three years, the list will be badly outdated.

What organization makes qualification surveys of publication's readers?

Are they accredited by major advertising associations?

What is the ratio of advertising pages to editorial pages? If there are too many advertisements, your ad may get lost and readers may lose interest.

Are there any buying influence studies which demonstrate that the readers are truly a target for your message?

What is the general reputation of the publication in the eyes of the industry?

What is the inquiry average? Quality? Quantity? Publications can show you many such studies; or you can keep track of your past experience with each.

What is the cost per page for black and white, color, bleeds, special positions, inserts, etc. Compare costs for each publication, and make sure you are comparing "apples to apples."

What is the opportunity for editorial coverage (publication's readers have high interest in your products)? Check with publishers' representatives and editors; but never request free editorial on your company in return for advertising. Most editors of trade publications resent being pressured into editorial coverage.

Is the publication's audience interested in your company's product-lines?

What extra merchandising services and studies are provided to the advertiser by the publication? Such services can be extremely valuable.

What are the readership results (see "Obtain Readership Information")?

Does the publication have good reproduction quality (paper, color)?

Is the publication horizontal (reaches a broad cross-section of audiences) or vertical (aimed at specific market segments)?

Obtain Publication Information

At this point you should obtain detailed information on the characteristics and audience of each publication under consideration. This includes all those factors listed under "Determine Information Required." Three main sources of such information include:

> Published directories
> Audited statements
> Publishers' representatives (media reps)

Published Directories

Several sources of published information are extremely useful in media planning/selection. These directories contain information on each publication's circulation, costs, editorial philosophy, and so forth. The most familiar and widely used directory is Standard Rate and Data Service. The three primary directories and their sources are listed below.

STANDARD RATE AND DATA SERVICE, Business Publication Rates And Data Service, Inc., 5201 Old Orchard Rd., Skokie, IL 60076.

N.W. AYER DIRECTORY OF NEWSPAPERS, MAGAZINES, AND TRADE PUBLICATIONS, N. W. Ayer & Son, W. Washington Square, Philadelphia, PA 19106.

ULRICH'S INTERNATIONAL PERIODICAL DIRECTORY, R. R. Bowker Co., 1180 Avenue of the Americas, New York, NY 10036.

Audited Statements

Most business and trade publications are audited in one way or another to verify their claimed circulation and other related data (e.g., editorial content, inquiry analysis, readership, etc.). These audits are provided upon request by most publishers. The reports (which should be prepared at least annually) conform to procedures established by independent organizations. These organizations are generally run by agencies, advertisers, and publishers. The audits present data in a uniform manner to make it easier to compare publication values.

Major publication auditors include:

> Audit Bureau of Circulation (ABC)
> 123 N. Wacker Dr.
> Chicago, IL 60606
> Business Publications Audit of Circulation, Inc. (BPA)
> 420 Lexington Ave.
> New York, NY 10017

Two additional organizations provide unaudited information on specific publications and advertising in general. American Business Press (ABP), 205 E. 42nd St., New York, NY 10017, is the trade association of audited published-for-profit (as opposed to association-owned) trade journal publishers. The Business/Professional Advertisers Association, 41 E. 42nd St., New York, NY 10017, is an association made up of industrial advertisers, agencies, and trade journals, and issues the "Media Data Form"—which contains a lot of unaudited information on publications.

Within narrow vertical markets, you will sometimes find certain trade magazines that will not provide information regarding their circulation. Thus, they cannot qualify for one or more of the above types of audits. If this reluctance continues over a period of time, then any figures published by that particular magazine regarding its supposed audience coverage would be open to serious question.

Media Representatives

Good media decisions, whether made by the client or the agency, can be made more precise by gaining the help of media representatives. Getting to know publishers' representatives serving your markets is probably one of the smartest things any marketing man can do. Not only does the representative know all the services provided by his company's publication, he also knows the markets and readership it serves.

The media rep is usually one of the first to be aware of significant market shifts or changes, large contracts let or about to be awarded, the reputation of your company and of your competitors in the marketplace, and other current information, all of which is useful. This information, while not confidential, would be difficult and costly to obtain without the help of these representatives who see so many people in your market in the course of conducting their daily business.

Let the media rep know exactly what you hope to accomplish by advertising, how you view your potential markets, and ask him to show you how his publication's editorial and readership profile matches with your profile of markets and prospects. He can interpret in detail what is being said in the publisher's statement and provide other data to use in evaluating and comparing his publication with other advertising vehicles. The good media rep can also interpret audit forms.

After evaluating the publication's primary functions, ask the media rep to explain other services offered by the publisher (e.g., direct mail, market research, reprints, etc.).

Let the rep know who has responsibility for selecting your media (advertiser? agency? agency's media buyer?). This will save his time and yours in making needless sales calls. Be sure when working with a media rep to be totally honest. If, after evaluating the publications serving your market, you decide you prefer certain ones over others, don't hesitate to explain to appropriate reps the reasons you are not choosing their books. Don't evade the issue with the old stand-bys: "we still haven't made a decision," or "the agency will have the final say-so." The media rep is a businessman and can accept a decision that is based on sound judgement supported by facts.

Obtain Readership Information

Readership studies are often made available by publishers. However, you should be wary of any publisher enthusiasm shown because his publication won a readership contest when the survey list was a sample drawn from that publication's own circulation list. Give the most serious consideration to those studies conducted by an independent organization across a list other than from merely one publication.

If, after analyzing the information provided by the publishers and audit services, you still haven't made a media selection, make your own survey using a sample of readers drawn from your customer and prospect list. Determine their reading habits and preferences. After all, these are the people you must reach with your advertising and sales message. If your customer and prospect list is not readily accessible, consult a direct mail list specialist (see Chapter IX—Direct Mail). In most cases, a suitable list will be available. Also, publisher circulation lists can be used as long as you realize that the source will bias any response. In this latter case, you could reduce bias by using several different publishers lists. Publishers are usually glad to cooperate in such requests.

Survey Format

Chapter I—Marketing Research, discusses the best approach to conducting surveys. However, some specific comments on readership studies may be helpful.

The study can be done by mail, over the telephone, or by personal interview. The most common approach is to use mail surveys either designed specifically to answer the readership questions or with readership questions as tag-ons to other studies. Here are some examples of questions to ask in making readership studies:

Which publication do you read regularly?
Specifically, why do you read it?
How does it help you in your job?
How often do you refer to it?
Do you subscribe or receive it "passed-along" from someone else?
How many people in your company share your copy?
Which publication has the best (a) editorial content, (b) reference materials, (c) new product coverage, and (d) design ideas?

After you've narrowed the choice of questions to two or three (more than this number could lower the response rate), design a

brief cover letter and questionnaire format. The letter should come from your department or your agency. There is no need to conceal who is doing the study. But, if you feel that respondents may be influenced by your company's name, then of course use a pseudonym and have responses mailed to a post office box number in your name.

The questionnaire can use aided or unaided recall, meaning, you can provide a list of selected publications or you can leave blanks to be filled in by the respondent. The latter method relies heavily on respondent memory, which may reduce response rate. Therefore, the aided recall method is suggested.[6]

An example cover letter and questionnaire is shown below.

Make Relative Evaluations

Now put all data into a useful format for evaluation. In this section, two forms are presented for your use: (1) Trade Publications Evaluation Form, and (2) Publication's Circulation Coverage Chart.

Trade Publications Evaluation Form

The Trade Publications Evaluation Form helps organize publication evaluation, by pinpointing ten key areas for comparison.

PUBLICATION—In column 1, list the publications serving your markets. For comparison purposes, all should fall within the same general classification; i.e., metal fabrication, product design, etc.

TOTAL CIRCULATION—In column 2, enter the publication's circulation figures. If the publication's circulation is paid (subscription), indicate this with the letter "P" after the circulation figure. If the circulation is controlled (i.e., free to those qualifying by job

---

[6] An effective variation of the aided recall approach includes showing a picture of each magazine cover or logo. This avoides confusion since many magazine names are so much alike.

function, etc.), use the letter "C" after the circulation figure.

CIRCULATION BY JOB FUNCTION— In column 3, enter circulation figures broken down by job functions that influence the purchasing decision for your product. For example, if top management, design engineers, and production management are key buying influences, you should favor those publications with the heaviest circulation in these categories.

CHASE RESEARCH COMPANY, 1400 NORTH HARBOR BOULEVARD, FULLERTON, CALIF. 92635 (714) 526-6623

Dear Sir:

One of our clients in the packaging business needs your help. This firm wants to better communicate important developments to you. Thus, it would like to know which publications you read regularly and which one is most helpful to you in your job.

Will you please take a minute to check the names of the magazines you read regularly in column 1 and then check the one which is most helpful in your job in column 2. Please note that blank spaces are provided in case you wish to add a publication which was inadvertently not included.

Then slip this letter into the enclosed postage paid envelope and drop it in the mail. Your help will be much appreciated since it will enable our client to keep you informed of new products and developments through those publications which you prefer to read. Thanks for your cooperation.

Sincerely yours,

Ken Barasch

Ken Barasch
President

Publication	(1) Which of these publications do you read regularly?	(2) Which ONE publication is most helpful in your job?
Boxboard Containers		
Food And Drug Packaging		
Modern Plastics		
Modern Packaging		
Paperboard Packaging		
Package Development		
Package Engineering		
Packaging Design		
Packaging Digest		
Packaging Review		

What is your job title: _____

COST PER PAGE—In column 4, indicate the total cost per page. Always compare the same page elements: color or black and white, bleed or non-bleed, etc.

COST PER THOUSAND—In column 5, enter the cost per thousand (i.e., cost of reaching each thousand subscribers). This figure is determined by dividing the total page cost by the number of thousands in circulation. For example, if the publication has a circulation of 25,000 and their page cost is $1,000, the cost per thousand is $40.[7]

FREQUENCY OF ISSUE—In column 6, indicate whether the publication is a weekly, biweekly, monthly, or quarterly. Also, note whether there are special issues (e.g., for trade shows).

TYPE OF AUDIT—In column 7, enter the audit system used and what organization is responsible; i.e., BPA, ABC. These are discussed in detail under "Obtain Publication Information."

QUALIFICATION FREQUENCY—In column 8, indicate how often the publication reviews its circulation list and checks to ensure that it is current and accurate.

NUMBER OF EDITORIAL PAGES DEVOTED TO YOUR PRODUCTS—In column 9, enter the number of editorial pages related to your products. Your media representative should be able to provide this information. This is a primary indicator of the publication's interest in your field.

INQUIRY AVERAGE—In column 10, enter each publication's inquiry publishing average. Media reps can provide an average inquiry response per ad to determine the publication's ability to generate leads. Keep in mind that this is not always a true picture of what you can expect with your ads.

Publications' Circulation Coverage Chart

The Publications' Circulation Coverage Chart gives an additional evaluation of publications in terms of reaching certain SICs.

PUBLICATIONS—In column 1 list publications serving your markets. These publications should be in the same general field or discipline.

CIRCULATION—In column 2, enter total circulation.

PRIMARY SICs—In column 3 enter the most important SIC categories in your market. They can be either 2, 3, or 4-digit SICs. The example shows 2-digit analysis. List each publication's circulation coverage of that category. In the example, SICs 34, 35, and 36 are given primary emphasis. Under each SIC, breakdowns are given (i.e., for publication A, there are 15,250 subscribers in classification 34).

SECONDARY/TERTIARY SICs—In columns 4 and 5, enter the SIC numbers and circulation coverage by each publication for industries of secondary and tertiary importance.

RATE PUBLICATION COVERAGE OF SICS—In columns 6 through 8, repeat the SIC headings from columns 3 through 5. Then assign a score to the magazine with the largest coverage in each SIC, second largest coverage, and so forth, using the rating index in the lower right-hand corner of the chart.

Complete Media Schedule

Now make the final evaluation of raw data, select specific publications, and decide how many times to use each one. After a careful review, you should be able to choose those publications best fitting your market profile. This data can then be entered on a media schedule.

A sample media schedule is presented. The example shown is for Hardware Products, Inc. The schedule uses four publications at various times throughout the year,

[7] Another beneficial analysis is determining the cost per thousand of effective circulation, i.e., in particular job categories.

Publication Evaluation Form

(1) PUBLICATION	(2) TOTAL CIRCULATION	(3) CIRCULATION BY JOB FUNCTION					(4) COST PER PAGE	(5) COST PER THOUS.	(6) FRE-QUENCY OF ISSUE	(7) TYPE OF AUDIT	(8) QUALIFICATION FREQUENCY	(9) NO. OF EDITORIAL PAGES DEVOTED TO YOUR TYPE OF PRODUCTS	(10) INQUIRY AVERAGE	COMMENTS
		MGMT.	DESIGN	ENGRG.	QLTY. CONTROL									
A	45,111-C	5,957	22,841	12,852	3,461		$1,250	27.9	Weekly	BPA	Semi-annual	26	15	Not enough inquiries
B	60,820-P	8,800	39,860	7,032	5,128		1,500	24.5	Weekly	ABC	Annual	14	26	
C	22,420-P	1,040	7,580	8,056	5,744		1,800	81.8	Monthly	BPA	Semi-annual	18	33	
D	6,800-P	256	4,300	1,608	636		900	128.5	Weekly	BPA	Quarterly	32	55	May be too technical
E	18,200-C	3,250	11,756	980	2,214		1,000	55.5	Monthly	ABC	Annual	28	30	
F	36,818-P	6,406	18,250	6,365	5,797		2,000	54.0	Quarterly	ABC	Semi-annual	53	82	High inquiry return

Publication's Circulation Coverage Chart

(1) PUBLICATION	(2) TOTAL CIRCULATION	(3) PRIMARY SIC'S			(4) SECONDARY SIC'S			(5) TERTIARY SIC'S			(6) PRIMARY SIC'S RATING			(7) SECONDARY SIC'S RATING			(8) TERTIARY SIC'S RATING			(9) TOTAL SCORE
		34	35	36	37	38	30	29	28	26	34	35	36	37	38	30	29	28	26	
A	45,111	15,250	6,200	3,001	4,150	2,200	4,530	4,600	3,805	1,375	12	8	8	8	4	8	6	6	4	64
B	60,820	12,600	8,635	4,755	6,275	3,895	8,690	7,342	6,850	1,778	10	12	10	10	10	10	8	8	8	86
C	22,420	6,050	2,105	1,672	2,208	2,653	1,708	2,300	1,865	859	6	4	6	4	8	2	2	4	2	38
D	6,800	2,100	1,450	680	1,042	390	865	132	115	26	0	0	0	0	0	0	0	0	0	0
E	18,200	4,365	2,750	1,205	1,400	2,300	3,607	1,825	350	398	4	6	4	2	6	6	0	0	0	28
F	36,818	8,650	8,300	6,300	4,100	2,165	1,894	3,042	865	1,502	8	10	12	6	2	4	4	2	6	54

Header groups (3), (4), (5) fall under: PORTION OF PUBLICATION'S CIRCULATION COVERING SELECTED SIC CATEGORIES
Header groups (6), (7), (8) fall under: RATING OF PUBLICATION'S COVERAGE OF SELECTED SIC CATEGORIES

RATING INDEX

Place	Primary	Secondary	Tertiary
1st	12 pts.	10 pts.	8 pts.
2nd	10 pts.	8 pts.	6 pts.
3rd	8 pts.	6 pts.	4 pts.
4th	6 pts.	4 pts.	2 pts.
5th	4 pts.	2 pts.	0 pts.

Media Schedule [8]

CLIENT HARDWARE PRODUCTS, INC. DIVISION CONSTRUCTION MARKET DATE October 13, 1972 PERIOD Jan. 1973 TO Dec. 1973 PAGE 1 OF 1

HARDWARE AGE
Circulation 49,695 · Published Monthly · Closing Date As stated. · 6 X Rate $1100. · Contract Period 1/73 to 12/73

	JAN.	FEB.	MAR.	APR.	MAY	JUNE	JULY	AUG.	SEPT.	OCT.	NOV.	DEC.	COST
A	1 page			1 page			1 page				1 page		
B	B/W Bld.			B/W Bld.			B/W Bld.				B/W Bld.		
C	#1			#2			#2				#3		
D	1488			1743			1909				2065		
E	Closes 12/4			Closes 2/28			Closes 5/27				Closes 9/30		
F	$1100.			$1100.			$1100.				$1100.		
G	New Prods. Issue			Show Issue			Show Issue						$ 4,400.

APARTMENT CONSTRUCTION NEWS
Circulation 25,960 · Published Monthly · Closing Date 1st prec. mo. · 3 X Rate $495. · Contract Period 1/73 to 12/73 (Tabloid)

	JAN.	FEB.	MAR.	APR.	MAY	JUNE	JULY	AUG.	SEPT.	OCT.	NOV.	DEC.	COST
A			1/3 page		1/3 page					1/3 page			
B			B/W		B/W					B/W			
C			#1		#2					#3			
D			1655		1887					1887			
E			Closes 2/1		Closes 4/1					Closes 9/1			
F			$495.		$495.					$495.			
G										Readex Issue			$ 1,485.

CONTRACTOR
Circulation 36,094 · Published 1st & 15th mo. · Closing Date 5th & 18th prec. mo. · 6 X Rate $1075. · Contract Period 1/73 to 12/73 (Tabloid)

	JAN.	FEB.	MAR.	APR.	MAY	JUNE	JULY	AUG.	SEPT.	OCT.	NOV.	DEC.	COST
A		1 page		1 page		1 page		1 page		1 page		1 page	
B		B/W Bld.		B/W Bld.		B/W Bld.		B/W Bld.		B/W Bld.		B/W Bld.	
C		#1		#1		#2		#2		#3		#3	
D		1574		1746		1911		1911		1941		1941	
E		Closes 1/5		Closes 3/5		Closes 5/18		Closes 7/18		Closes 9/18		Closes 11/5	
F		$1075.		$1075.		$1075.		$1075.		$1075.		$1075.	
G						N.A.P.H.C. Show Issue				A.S.A. Conv.			$ 6,450.

DE/JOURNAL
Circulation 21,032 · Published Monthly · Closing Date 10th prec. mo. · 6 X Rate $525. · Contract Period 1/73 to 12/73

	JAN.	FEB.	MAR.	APR.	MAY	JUNE	JULY	AUG.	SEPT.	OCT.	NOV.	DEC.	COST
A		1/2 page	1/2 page		1/2 page		1/2 page		1/2 page		1/2 page		
B		B/W	B/W		B/W		B/W		B/W		B/W		
C		#1	#1		#2		#2		#3		#3		
D		1575	1656		1845		1912		1912		1912		
E		Closes 1/10	Closes 2/10		Closes 4/10		Closes 6/10		Closes 8/10		Closes 10/10		
F		$525.	$525.		$525.		$525.		$525.		$525.		
G		Readership Study											$ 3,150.

TOTALS $15,485.

KEY NUMBERS #1 – New product introduction ad #2 – Inquiry-oriented ad #3 – Service-oriented ad

CODE A Size B Colors C Key No. D I.O. No. E Misc. F Cost

248

8 Media costs are based on current publication prices. Subject to change without notice.

for a total cost of $15,485 (not counting costs of producing the ads).

To complete your own form, start by listing the following information under the publication heading:

Name of each publication.

Circulation of each publication (i.e., the number of people who receive the publication in their own name, the number of publications received by individual companies, and the copies that are received by educational and research institutions; does not include pass-along readership).

Frequency of publication (i.e., monthly, bimonthly, weekly, etc.).

Closing date (i.e., final date set by publication for receiving your space contracts and materials necessary for publication of your ad).

Frequency rate (i.e., predetermined cost per page of advertising purchased; usually decreases as total number of pages purchased by advertiser increases; 1-time rate might be $1,000, the 3-time rate $800, and the 10-time rate $600).

Contract period (i.e., time period for which you are protected by contract for given rates; you must actually run your agreed-upon number of times within this contract period or pay a short rate; drop back to costs for running less frequently).

Then fill in the date that each ad is to run in a certain publication. Also include the information requested under the codes A through F (given at bottom left side of page): [9]

(A) Size (i.e., half page, full page, 2-page spread, etc.)

(B) Color (i.e., black and white, 2 color, 4 color)

(C) Key number (i.e., refers to the number assigned to each ad

scheduled for insertion and its title or description).

(D) I.O. number (i.e., Insertion Order number issued for a particular publication)

(E) Miscellaneous comments as to bleed, special issue, etc.

(F) Cost refers to the total cost of the advertisement for a particular publication and month at a given size, color, special position, bleed, and any other special requirements.

Evaluate Other Media

A variety of alternative media can be used, including tabloids, directories, prefiled catalogs, hybrids, newspapers, and Yellow Pages. Each of these are discussed below.

Tabloids

The tabloid-type publication is half the size of a standard newspaper page. Its contents are devoted to timely new product and new literature information for the industries it serves.

The tabloid is one of the prime exponents of the "bingo" card—a postage paid detachable service card that enables the reader to request specific data from a manufacturer by using the publication as the intermediary.

If companies make any strategic errors, it is often to ignore the power and effectiveness of the tabloid. "But they're cluttered." Or, "Who reads them?" Or, "I don't want my ad to be lost in that sea of fractional page ads." These are the comments so often heard. These people have much to learn.

Ask yourself this question: "Does our company want and need inquiries to aid our sales force?" If, so then don't overlook the tabloid. In many instances, it is historically among the best inquiry pullers in terms of sheer numbers.

Other considerations include:

The fractional page format allows for use of small page, low cost ads without necessarily being buried in the back of the

---

[9] Codes can be added for other factors such as premium positions.

book as are most fractional ads in standard-sized magazines.

Products can be tested for their interest level. Use of horizontal-type tabloids permits testing of response from industries not normally thought of as key markets.

Tabloids are not the ideal place for corporate image type ads.

Ads about your service capability will not draw heavy inquiry response either.

Emphasize new products and new literature. Don't get cute in your headlines or visuals. Tell it straight, fast, and offer a strong benefit, i.e., "Free Grinding Mill Catalog. . . ."

Directories

Industrial directories list supply sources for a particular industry or a series of industries. Such directories fill a vital need in business publication advertising. And millions of sales dollars result each year from directory advertising. When the potential buyer is stimulated to act after reading business publication ads, he frequently turns to a directory for more in-depth product information or for the name of a local manufacturers' representative or outlet.

Purchasing agents are heavy users of directories, often buying directly from such sources. Engineers and product design people also find directories invaluable in their daily efforts to solve problems or to evaluate products currently available.

Directory ads should include:

As much product/services information as possible.

Top quality photos, drawings, or schematics of your products.

Sales and service outlets, including phone numbers.

A "keyed" address to determine source of inquiry. It is often difficult to measure the total effectiveness of directory advertising. To obtain a better record, some companies will use a special address in their directory ad. For example, your company's correct address is 6300 Main Street. Yet your plant actually covers from 6300 to 6315 Main. In the directory, you could list 6310 Main Street; then you would know that any inquiry received with that address was a result of the directory ad. Different P.O. Box numbers, and fictitious department numbers are also used as keyed addresses.

Referral statements to other directory sections for secondary products.

Pre-filed Catalogs

Pre-filed catalogs differ from industrial directories in that they are bound volumes of manufacturers' catalogs arranged in order by the publisher. These catalogs may be furnished to the publisher for binding by the advertiser, or the publisher may request camera-ready artwork, negatives or plates and the publisher does the printing.

Hybrids

These are directories that include a section for pre-filed catalogs. This section is cross referenced with the company name and product-volumes. The Thomas Register is a good example of the hybrid directory.

Newspapers

In discussing the potential of an industrial business using newspapers for advertising, an immediate decision must be made. You must differentiate between the daily newspaper with general news; i.e., *The Chicago Tribune*, the *Los Angeles Times*, etc., and a business paper like the *Wall Street Journal*.

The former is not normally a good medium for the usual product type of advertising done by most manufacturers. The reason is obvious. . . . waste circulation. Housewives and most of the readers are not buyers of costly electronic gear, brake shears, or whatever.

There are times when the financial pages of the daily paper can be used to achieve special objectives such as corporate awareness or to portray some special achievement that will materially benefit the community or the nation; e.g., the construction of a new facility that will provide employment for people in the area; or development of an instrument which detects prenatal birth defects.

Business papers such as the *Wall Street Journal* are extremely effective for specific advertising purposes. They reach the financial community and business leaders (opinion makers).

Corporate image advertising often appears in this media. But don't overlook certain types of product advertising either. Business machines, aircraft, computers, all types of products which affect and/or are utilized by the higher levels of management can benefit from exposure in such media.

When preparing your newspaper advertising, keep the following in mind.

> Be extremely careful of photographs. Newspapers are printed on very thin, porous paper. And photographs are screened with larger dot patterns than are used by magazines. Thus, gray tones turn darker; black in some instances. Don't, for example, use a picture of a person in a dark suit standing in front of a dark background. All you will see is his face.
>
> Line art (drawings made without extensive shading) are effective.
>
> Use big enough type that is easily read.
>
> If you plan to use long copy, it must be good. People don't normally dwell when reading a newspaper. Copy must, therefore, tell an exciting story to hold reader interest.

Yellow Pages

The telephone company's Yellow Pages is considered a valued tool by thousands of small, medium, and large businesses. A study in 1966 [10] conducted by Audits and Surveys on the "industrial usage of Yellow Pages" showed that buyers in manufacturing firms over a 12-month period used the Yellow Pages as follows:

> 412,000 industrial buyers turned to the Yellow Pages to locate business-related products or services. Their usage resulted in 35.4 million references to the Yellow Pages—or an average of 85 times per user.

Industrial advertisers can benefit from Yellow Pages because:

> Yellow Pages are referred to by people *after* they have made decisions to buy.
>
> They are as available as the telephone. Virtually every household and business has Yellow Pages (over 150,000,000 distributed).
>
> A variety of advertising is available (from a line-item listing to a full-page display ad).
>
> Guidelines are set for ad content, format, and size limitation. Thus the Yellow Pages makes an effective medium for small firms by allowing them to compete on a more equal basis with larger companies.
>
> They offer broad market coverage plus vertical market segmentation.
>
> They afford a simple means for information retrieval.
>
> They supplement other advertising media.

Task 10: Develop the Advertising Budget

Alternative Methods

Five methods for developing the advertising budget are described below. Although the first three approaches are often used, the latter two generally yield more effective results. The format varies from company to company. Work with your company's ac-

---

[10] Copies of studies may be obtained through nearest Bell Telephone Co. regional office.

countants and agency to develop the best approach. The basic alternatives include:

> Matching competition
> Management edict
> Percent of sales
> Task method
> Task method plus percent of forecasted sales

Matching Competition

The matching competition method boils down to "My competitors are spending $ _____ advertising so I'd better do the same." Essentially, this is an attempt to remain even or guard against losing business. However, trying to match competitor expenditures doesn't make sense when you consider that your company has its own set of marketing problems, objectives, product features, size of sales force, number of dealers/distributors, and so forth.

Some companies use an industry average figure for setting their advertising budgets. This approach is as erroneous as matching your competitors' budgets.

Management Edict

The management edict method occurs when a top executive in the company sets the advertising budget at a figure he thinks the firm can afford. It usually approximates what the competitors are spending, what was spent last year or the last few years, or what he feels can be spent without causing financial risk or embarrassment to his company.

Sometimes the edict approach is used by management which lacks in-depth understanding of various communications disciplines and what those disciplines can accomplish. Management too blind to understand or believe in advertising's value generally views it as an expense, not as a means to help make profits. It is quite possible that this attitude results from experiences with poorly conceived or amateurish advertising programs.

Percent of Sales

Setting advertising budgets based on a percent of sales is the most common method used in industrial advertising. A predetermined percentage (e.g., 2–5%) can be multiplied by past sales, forecasted sales, or an average of both to determine the advertising budget. This percentage can be based either on your experience or on industry averages.

The percent-of-sales method automatically arrives at a set dollar figure without regard to what must be done to accomplish the objectives. The budget may or may not be adequate. It implies that advertising is the result of sales rather than sales the result of advertising. The probable reason this method is so popular is because of its simplicity, and because in most cases, advertising is part of the selling expense included in the price of the product.

The advertising budget form can be used for determining the advertising budget by percent of forecasted sales. List each product to be considered in column 1. In column 2, list forecasted sales for each product. In column 3, enter the desired percent of forecasted sales to be allocated to advertising. Then multiply column 2 by column 3 for each product and enter the result in column 4. The total of column 4 is the total advertising budget. Then enter in columns 5 through 7, alternative advertising methods, and the pros and cons of each. Estimate the costs of each method and enter in column 8. The total of column 8 for any individual product must not exceed the budget level established in column 4. Then in column 9, enter your decision as to which alternative methods to use.

Task Method

The task method is based on company, marketing, and sales objectives (i.e., what needs to be accomplished). The advertising appropriation is made only after determining the reasonable means (tasks) of attaining these objectives. This approach can be used only when you know nearly everything about your market conditions, audiences, company and products, current advertising costs, sales problems, and any other factors potentially influencing your advertising budget.

The task method, as sound as it is, still has its drawbacks since it can fall victim to human error. Successful advertising attempts to *achieve objectives*. Yet the program selected may or may not be the best or most reasonable. An advertising manager could go overboard in estimating the extent of work and costs needed to achieve advertising objectives.

To help you in the task method of budgeting, a sample form is provided. List objectives, alternative tasks, associated pros and cons, make a decision, and price each element.

Advertising Budget— Percent of Forecasted Sales Method

(1) PRODUCT OR PRODUCT LINE	(2) 19___ FORECASTED SALES	(3) % OF FORECASTED SALES	(4) ADVERTISING BUDGET (COL. 2 x COL. 3)	(5) ALTERNATIVE ADVERTISING METHODS	(6) PROS	(7) CONS	(8) COST ($)	(9) DECISION
TOTAL								
TOTAL								
TOTAL								
TOTAL								

Task Method Budget Form

(1) OBJECTIVES	(2) ALTERNATIVE TASKS	(3) PROS	(4) CONS	(5) DECISION	(6) HOW MUCH
1.	a. b. c. d. e. f.				
2.	a. b. c. d. e. f.				
3.	a. b. c. d. e. f.				
4.	a. b. c. d. e. f.				
TOTAL					

Task and Percentage of Sales Method

This approach is similar to the task approach in that you first determine what you need to accomplish, the tasks for doing this, and how much the tasks will cost. But no matter how financially sound your company is and how large your current budget, there will never be enough dollars to do all that you want to accomplish. Therefore, priorities must be assigned to the tasks. Compare the tasks and associated costs with what can reasonably be expected to be approved by company's management (possibly based on some historical pattern).

Then set your objectives and define the required tasks in order of importance based on accomplishing sales objectives. If it is not possible to provide the money needed to support all sales objectives, concentrate on the most important ones.

There are times and circumstances when you should let the task, not the percentage of sales or other historical method, be the predominant factor. A new product introduction that will significantly affect the company's long-term growth or the need to combat a particular competitive situation may call for scrapping all previous budgeting calculations.

What Should Be Charged to the Advertising Budget?

There are certain obvious items that should be charged to the advertising budget. These include:

Paid advertising in all recognized mediums
Brochures, catalogs, direct mail
All art work and preparation charges
Agency fees and costs
All administrative costs for the advertising department
Contingency budget for special unforeseen projects

In addition to these, there are numerous grey areas that some companies charge to the advertising budget and others don't. The list is almost endless (e.g., public relations, special promotions, events, trade shows, etc.). It is the duty of the advertising manager to carefully review every item of his budget with the accounting department to be certain that items truly belong or don't belong in his budget. If the ad manager neglects this, he will find himself burdened with endless hidden costs and his budget will become the dumping ground for virtually every miscellaneous company expense.

Many problems arise regarding relationships between what is a sales expense and what is truly an advertising expense. For example, trade show costs. The advertising budget may be charged for the booth space and display costs in some companies. But it would be grossly unfair to charge advertising for the salesmen's expenses while attending the trade show. This should be a sales department expense. Baseball or football tickets for entertaining customers is another example of sales, not advertising expense.

Presenting the Budget

The more you can make top management understand what advertising is, what it can do for the company, and how it fits into the marketing/sales picture, the more they will believe in its benefits. And the easier your job will be selling the program to them.

Before presenting an advertising budget (program) to top management, prepare yourself to defend it by answering all objections. Management will be more receptive to your proposals if you:

Can prove exactly how your advertising program directly contributes to solving company marketing/sales problems.
Have set measurable advertising objectives and ways to compare results to objectives (produce 1,500 inquiries from potential buyers of X product in Y market).
Can show how advertising helps reduce selling costs; reaches buying influences

unreachable by direct selling methods; reinforces market position; builds product acceptance; and generates greater profits by making sales calls more worthwhile.

Enlist Support Before Presenting

It is difficult for anyone to reject an idea they've helped develop. Thus, during program and budget development, a smart advertising manager involves the marketing or sales manager and all necessary product or division managers in planning. This is not only a political move to gain their support during the critical presentation to top management; these executives should be experienced and extremely knowledgeable when it comes to their company's marketing problems. Therefore, you'll find their input most valuable in ensuring that your advertising goals dovetail with sales goals.

The Form of Presentation

Presentation format usually depends on complexity and size of the proposed plan and appropriation. In some companies the presentation is simply a discussion between the president and ad manager; in others, a management team may make a full scale conference room presentation. Some ways to present budgets to management include:

Written proposal
Flip charts
Slide presentation
Films
Combination of the above

Your budget presentation is very similar to a product sales presentation, and your prospects (top management) can be influenced and sold on how well you deliver your "pitch." In some cases, ideas for proposed ads, storyboards, literature, P.O.P., and other media can be created to lend support to your programs. Good prior planning generally results in having requested budgets *approved.* And plan your presentation to deal with both specific needs and potential results. If you do your homework well, there

is a good chance that your advertising budget will be approved.

What to Include

Top management wants to know how the company's money will be spent. Therefore, your budget should be broken down by product-line, markets, tasks, and media. It should be allocated on a monthly cash-flow basis so company financial executives experience no "surprises" during the program. Dollars must be equated to projects. If cuts are made, it must be clear to those involved that they are cutting actual programs, not just dollar amounts. Monthly planning also shows management that advertising is flexible for meeting changes in market conditions, supporting introduction of new products, and adapting quickly to shifts in direction.

In order to substantiate every item in your suggested program, present the program and budget as a total entity, not piecemeal. The following five-part presentation has proven effective for both oral and written presentations:

1. Results of past year's advertising program
   a. Appeals, media, and promotions used
   b. Evaluation of program effectiveness
   c. Relation of program to company posture
2. Current product/market status
   a. National/regional trends in sales and consumption
   b. Changes in distribution, pricing, promotions, competition, marketing activities, etc.
3. Marketing objectives/requirements
   a. Areas of opportunity
   b. Problem areas
   c. Proposed advertising targets
   d. How advertising helps sales effort
   e. What will be accomplished in each market, for each product, in each territory
4. Recommendations/tasks
   a. Copy approach—appeals

b. Media and schedules, and reasons for selection
c. Other promotions by type and cost
d. Special operations
e. How to measure program effectiveness
5. Budget
a. Total amount and method of determination
b. Comparison with objectives and expected returns
c. Contingency funds for unforeseen market opportunities

Guidelines for the Presentation

Be honest. Don't go in high expecting anything you propose to be cut. Tell management that the budget is not padded. Rather, it is a realistic estimate of what it's going to take to accomplish the objectives.

Take a firm stand. Strongly defend your programs.

Make a written outline of what is to be covered.

Present facts, not generalities.

Offer realistic solutions to problems.

Use some showmanship, be dramatic, use props. But use each with a purpose and objective in mind.

Make Revisions as Required

Sometimes the budget may have to be revised to bring total costs within limits dictated by management. This level may be restricted because of other more urgent needs (i.e., new production equipment) to carry out the overall company plan.

If revisions are required, it's usually better to eliminate an entire lower priority program, rather than to "water down" across the board. It is better to have a few, successful programs than for all to fail due to spreading resources too thin.

Budget Controls

After the advertising budget is approved, the advertising manager must set up controls to make sure advertising dollars are ef-

ficiently spent, and that costs remain within amounts specified. Good accounting practices are essential. The details of such programs are beyond the scope of this book. However, some suggestions are given below.

The control system should be divided into three phases:

Expenditure control
Commitment control
Management control

Expenditure Control

This phase covers day-to-day costs for advertising materials and services. The advertising manager controls all funds used by the advertising department and the advertising agency. The following items should be considered in this phase:

System to ensure receipt of all cash, frequency and/or quantity discounts from sources such as publications.

System to ensure that all goods and services received by the advertising department are of the quality and quantity specified.

System to control inventories (literature, P.O.P., displays, photos, etc.) used for advertising purposes.

System to approve and pay invoices only after they have been compared against commitments and estimates.

Notify all vendors that all invoices submitted must include itemized documentation.

Use a cash flow billing basis (i.e., after one month, roughly one-twelfth of the year's budget should be expended).

This avoids cases where an ad manager might be asked to explain why underruns have occurred or face budget cuts to an amount for the year which is based on the rate of spending to date. Also, such a system helps prevent criticism of overspending.

Commitment Control

Commitment control covers media schedules and media contracts for advertising time and space. It also covers cost estimates and anticipated expenditures for all materials and services (photography, typesetting, research, etc.) performed on request by the advertising manager. The management control phase should include:

A checking system to ensure that all budget items are subject to purchase orders, authorization forms, and approved estimates or schedules.

Establish (with accounting department) a coding system to identify all advertising jobs.

Record all commitments when they are made and record changes when they occur to keep accurate accounts.

Your agency can assist you in organizing commitment and expenditure controls. It's to your advantage to get them involved in the budget control system.

Management Control

This phase of the control system is used as an audit and review of advertising expenditures to keep top management aware of what is taking place and the results that can be related to objectives. It includes:

A reporting system for each product category showing the amount budgeted, amount committed, actual expenditures, and the difference between amounts committed and spent.

A system for comparing expenditures against charges to your department by the accounting department.

Budget Forms

The two forms presented can be used for your own budget controls. The Total Advertising Expenditures Versus Budget form should be filled in monthly. In column 1, list the amount budgeted for each month of the year. As the year progresses, enter in column 2 the actual expenditures for each month. Enter in column 3 the difference between columns 1 and 2. This is the variance (i.e., either overrun or underrun). In columns 4 through 6, the same analysis can be made on a year-to-date (YTD) basis.

The Specific Project Expenditure form can be used to evaluate whether suppliers' costs are actually within the estimates given before the job was undertaken. If suppliers are consistently overrunning their estimates, either change suppliers or find out why the overruns are occurring.

Total Company Advertising Expenditures
Versus Budget 19___.[11]

MONTH	(1) BUDGET	(2) ACTUAL	(3) VARIANCE[11]	(4) YTD BUDGET	(5) YTD ACTUAL	(6) YTD VARIANCE[11]
JANUARY						
FEBRUARY						
MARCH						
APRIL						
MAY						
JUNE						
JULY						
AUGUST						
SEPTEMBER						
OCTOBER						
NOVEMBER						
DECEMBER						
TOTAL						

[11] Enclose overuns in parentheses.

Specific Project

Project _____

_____

Date Started: _____ Date Completed: _____

SUPPLIER	DATE OF INVOICE	ITEM	ESTIMATED COST	ACTUAL COST	DIFFER- ENCE
		TOTALS			

Remarks: _____

_____

Date: _____ Submitted by: _____

Section C
Implement the Advertising Program

Purpose of Section

This section tells you how to implement the programs developed in previous sections. The section covers two major tasks, as shown below.

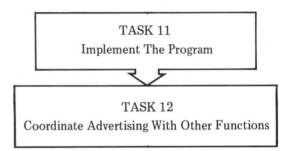

Task 11: Implement the Program

Employ the Four Ps

The "four Ps" in advertising are Preparation, Pretest, Production, and Placement. Since your advertising agency is responsible for these functions, it's not within the scope of this book to discuss these phases in depth. However, brief comments on each area are presented below to increase your familiarity with the subject.

Preparation

Preparing advertising begins with developing campaign themes and ideas. There so-called "concepts" are based almost totally on your knowledge of the company, its products, markets, market conditions, and objectives.

Then the agency creates the ads. Actually, the creation is a joint effort of the agency's copywriter and art director, and the client's ad manager. The ad manager should stress the product benefits and selling points, and the agency will translate these factors into the ad's copy and graphic elements. In some cases, copywriters do more than write text and headlines. They frequently are called on to help plan layouts, illustrations, and overall concepts. Similarly, the role of the art director often crosses over into that of the copywriter, suggesting headlines and so forth.

It is vitally important that you double-check the accuracy of all advertising or promotional copy of any sort. Be truthful. Don't alter the facts. There is a growing body of legislation today that provides stiff penalties for violations. Check with your legal counsel if you have doubts about any wording.

Pretest Advertisements

The agency should be able to pretest advertisements at the client's request. In some cases this is done automatically by the agency (an increasing trend).

The main objectives of pretests are to measure the ad's attention-getting power, clarity, and impact, as well as reader attitudes. In its simplest form, a sample of persons can be chosen from the target audience and tested via personal interviews. An attempt should be made to present the ad in a normal setting (i.e., to a representative group of readers in its actual final format). Reader reactions are solicited relative to:

ATTENTION-GETTING/INTEREST— Question and observe respondents' reactions to an ad or portfolio of ads (e.g., note time spent reading each ad).

CLARITY—Question respondents as to what message an ad conveys.

IMPACT—Question respondents as to significance and believability of ideas presented.

ATTITUDES—Ask questions about respondents' opinions and feelings regarding the company and its products, both before and after ad is shown; ask overall feeling about ad.

Production

Briefly, this includes all physical developments of advertising (i.e., art and copy preparation, printing, hiring and supervising talent for radio and television, developing scripts, purchasing type, photography, directing vendors and film makers, and performing other necessary tasks).

As part of the production process, a traffic control system is set up to ensure meeting publication deadlines for insertion. This system ensures that copy, art, type, printing, and all production needs are coordinated and sent to the selected publications.

Three forms may be used in the production process: the Cost Estimator; the Printing Purchase Order; and the Advertising Production Schedule. The Cost Estimator allows you to keep track of all cost elements and to obtain total cost estimates for any job. The Advertising Production Schedule is the agency's production manager's responsibility. The Printing Purchase Order form facilitates orderly use of outside suppliers, keeping track of project status.

Placement

Placement involves choosing media, developing schedules, purchasing space (print) and time (broadcast), mailing direct mail pieces, shipping printing plates, tapes, ad inserts, film, negatives or camera-ready art to proper media with instructions on position/timing and checking the publications and broadcasters to ensure the advertisements were properly executed.

Agencies are normally responsible for paying media. If an advertiser fails to pay the agency, it's the agency's loss not the medium's. If advertisers fail to pay the agency on time, the agency still must pay the medium. In this situation, the agency cannot assume this "finance company" role for extended time periods. If a client forces this situation to occur, business-minded agencies will resign the account. So if your agency does good work for you, pay them on time.

When placing an order with various media, use an insertion order. Most of the advertising-related associations in the reference guide can provide such forms. A sample Insertion Order form is presented further in this task.

Inventory Control

Companies with relatively diverse product-lines often have problems in controlling inventories of catalogs and sales literature. Making sure that there is always an adequate supply is a primary goal. To satisfy this objective, the Inventory Control form may be used. The form provides a list of all materials, quantity held by the supplier, quantity you have in stock, total available supply, and minimum required stock levels. If this sheet is updated frequently, one can be alerted when additional materials need to be ordered.

Cost Estimator [12]

JOB TITLE:_____

JOB NUMBER:_____

DATE: _____

APPROVED BY:_____

DATE: _____

JOB DESCRIPTION	
SIZE	
COLOR	
STOCK	
PAGES	
BINDING	
QUANTITY	
ENVELOPES	

ESTIMATED COSTS (ART AND COPY DEPARTMENTS)	
COPY	
ART LAYOUT	
COMPREHENSIVE	
MECHANICAL ART	
FINISHED ART	
RETOUCHING	
STORY BOARDS	
STATS/COPIES	
PHOTOGRAPHY	
MODEL/TALENT	
PHOTO/HAND LETTERING	
PHOTO DIRECTION	
TYPOGRAPHY	
SUBTOTAL	

PRODUCTION DEPARTMENT	
ENGRAVING(S)	
OFFSET POSITIVES OR NEG(S)	
REPRINT(S)	
MAT(S)	
ELECTRO(S)	
PRINTING/BINDING	
ENVELOPES	
POSTAGE/SHIPPING	
MISCELLANEOUS	
SUBTOTAL	

ESTIMATED ART—COPY COST	
ESTIMATED PRODUCTION COST	
TAX	
TOTAL:	

[12] Estimate given on a plus or minus 10% basis. Estimate subject to change as specifications change.

262

Advertising Production Schedule

DATE: _____

JOB NO.	DATE OPENED	DESCRIPTION	DATE REQ.	DATE DEL.	APPROX. BUDGET	ACTUAL BUDGET	LAYOUT	COPY WRITING	PHOTO COPIES	ILLUS TRATIONS	COPY TYPING	TYPO- GRAPHY	FINISHED ART	COMPANY APPROVAL	PRINT (COPIES)	MEDIA	MAIL (QUANTITY)	COMMENTS

Printing Purchase Order

TITLE OF JOB _____ JOB NO. _____

QUANTITY _____

NO. OF PAGES _____ PAGE SIZE _____

_____

STOCK
- COVER _____
- BODY _____
- OTHER _____

INK
- COVER _____
- BODY _____
- OTHER _____

_____

BINDING _____

_____

PACKAGE _____

_____

ADDITIONAL INFORMATION _____

_____

_____

_____

ESTIMATED DELIVERY (in working days) _____

ESTIMATED PRICE _____

To Printer	Brownline Due/Color Key Due				Final Proof O.K.	Wkg. Days After Final Proof O.K.

Insertion Order

NUMBER

DATE

TO

ACCOUNT

TITLE

AD SIZE

POSITION

DATE

ADD. INSTRUCTIONS

ENGRAVINGS

RATE

TEAR SHEETS

REP

BY: _____

Be governed by the terms of the contract and insert this advertising as instructed.

Compare printing material with proof and advise of any discrepancy before insertion.

Send invoices and proof of insertion to this office and also furnish checking copies to the advertiser.

The above procedure is important and your compliance will insure prompt settlement of bills.

Inventory Control Form

(date) _____

ITEM NO.	DESCRIPTION	QUANTITY			REORDER LEVEL	SOURCE OF SUPPLY
		AT SUPPLIER	IN COMPANY STOCK	TOTAL		

Task 12: Coordinate Advertising with Other Functions

Coordinate Advertising with Product Distribution

Advertising should be coordinated with product availability. Don't advertise a product until you are physically able to meet the demand that will be created. Have enough product in inventory. Premature promotion causes prospects to become excited, then highly disappointed with your nondelivery. They may even buy your competitor's product.

Long before the advertising campaign begins, presell your proposed advertising to your salesmen, distributors, agents, jobbers, and others involved with product distribution. Understanding the advertising campaign and its timing will aid them in coordinating distribution at each level and help you build staunch supporters for the product being advertised.

Coordinate Advertising with Personal Selling

Advertising should dovetail with the company's personal selling efforts. The sales department should be informed of every advertisement and campaign that is planned, and the timing of each. The sales department should be apprised of the following:

Media—In what publications will the ads appear?

When? How will this choice *help* the salesman?

Appeals—The theme and appeals of each ad; special offers such as quantity discounts, special pricing, etc.

Sales Aids—Furnish the sales force with complementary sales aids such as advertisement and editorial reprints, catalogs, brochures, samples, etc.

Coordinate Advertising with Sales Promotion Activities

Coordinate your advertising with sales promotion activities such as:

Collateral—Through distribution of catalogs, brochures, and data sheets, you can substantiate claims made in publication advertising with more in-depth factual materials.

Direct Mail—Coordinate with mailings related to shows, product sales, con-

tests, etc., enhancing overall program.
Trade Shows—Advertise to make audience aware of company's participation, products highlighted, and other incentives to build traffic for company exhibit.

Coordinate Advertising with Publicity

The combination of advertising and publicity can provide maximum impact on your target audience. Publicity can focus attention on a particular product-line or service with news and product releases, featured editorials in trade and consumer publications, radio and television coverage, grand openings, press conferences, and other vehicles. Publicity lends validity to your advertising because it is a form of nonpaid communication, and people are more inclined to believe what they read in an editorial feature than a paid advertisement. For in-depth information on publicity and public relations, see Chapter VII—Public Relations.

Product features and company services can be covered in greater detail if advertising is supplemented with publicity. Publicity extends coverage of message over broader range at far less cost than paid advertising. It lends validity to advertising. It provides up-to-date "news" information. It creates awareness within primary, secondary, and fringe markets.

Coordinate Advertising with Cooperative Advertising Programs

National advertising programs can be greatly enhanced at the local level by co-op advertising programs. They can be included (when applicable) early in your planning effort so a budget can be established for them.

In cooperative advertising, the manufacturer shares advertising costs with his dealers or distributors to support the sale of products on a local basis. The manufacturer benefits from this arrangement because he supplements his national advertising program on the local level at half the cost of the local rates or whatever cost ratio is established. The dealer also gains spin-off recognition from the national program and thus is able to deliver his sales message to potential buyers in his market place at half the cost.

Cost Sharing

There are countless numbers and types of co-op programs, but all are variations of this theme. The usual ratio of sharing advertising costs is 50-50. The manufacturer reserves a portion of his total advertising budget and allocates these funds according to a set percentage or amount per unit of advertising space purchased by the dealer.

Cooperative programs are usually planned within a set time period (e.g., quarterly or yearly). Time limits help to restrict your company's dollar exposure and provide time periods for review of the program's success. The manufacturer may occasionally allow charges to be made to dealer funds in anticipation of future purchases. This is allowed in order to start dealer advertising programs early in the year.

How Co-op Advertising Works

The dealer runs an advertisement in selected media and pays for the total cost. He then furnishes the manufacturer with proof of payment in the form of an invoice and requests reimbursement. The manufacturer will reimburse either by cash or credit memo. For example, if the dealer purchases $5,000 worth of merchandise from the manufacturer who is reserving 2% of purchases for advertising and sharing costs on a 50-50 ratio, the dealer's account would be credited with $100 (ratio can be 40-60, etc.). Suppose the dealer ran an ad on the manufacturer's product in the local newspaper at a cost of $80 and paid the media in full. He would then furnish proof of payment to the manufacturer and receive 50% reimbursement ($40) and still retain $60 in his account for future advertising.

Co-op Advertising Services

The manufacturer in most cases will provide advertising material to aid the dealer in his advertising program. These materials may include:

> Ad mats and slides
> Photographs and screened slicks
> Radio and television scripts, films and tapes
> Zincs (printing plates)

Requirements

The manufacturer will require tearsheets (newspaper clippings) or an affidavit from the radio or television station for broadcast media before reimbursement is made. He will also require the dealer to include in the ads company identification, product illustrations, brand names, or logotypes. Manufacturers have the right to review dealer ads prior to publication if they are sponsoring the advertisement on a cooperative basis.

Regulations

Co-op advertising is covered in the Robinson-Patman Act and regulated by the Federal Trade Commission. For your own protection and for a better understanding of the legal problems involved with co-op advertising allowances, write to the Division of Legal and Public Records, Federal Trade Commission, Washington, DC 20580, for a copy of "Advertising Allowances and Other Merchandising Payments and Services."

Some Precautions

Co-op advertising should not be undertaken blindly. First, review all of the legal ramifications noted above.

Secondly, it is not easy to budget for co-op advertising, particularly in the first year, as you have no history of the degree to which your dealers or distribution sources will use the program.

Thirdly, you will have to assign adequate staff personnel to check every item, invoice, etc., to be certain it is accurate. If not, you can be subject to the many abuses that can arise from co-op advertising. Some companies don't want the headaches of such verification and subsequent negotiations with their dealers, so they use an impartial outside source, such as the Advertising Checking Bureau (353 Park Ave. South, New York, NY 10010) to handle such details.

Above all, don't rush headlong into a co-op program. Analyze every facet before you begin. Enter with your eyes wide open and an adequately funded pocketbook.

Section D
Evaluation of Advertising Program Effectiveness

Purpose of Section

Now that you have planned and implemented your advertising program, you need to determine whether it was a success. Allocate approximately 5% of your total budget for this evaluation. And be ready to accept the results—they may surprise you. One manufacturer recently thought about cutting his ad budget believing all potential clients knew about his firm and products. One quick recognition study showed that less than 20% of the key buying influences in his markets actually had heard of the company! Program evaluation will allow you to capitalize upon current successes, select the best communications alternatives, and justify future directions.

Task 13: Measure Advertising Results

Alternative Measurement Techniques

Management spends sizeable sums of money on advertising and expects accountability as to the effectiveness of the programs. When a company buys a new piece of equipment they can soon determine the return-on-investment. Unfortunately, advertising is one area where such precise measures simply don't exist. However, there are some tools which should be used at every opportunity. Such tools will materially affect funding and direction of future campaigns. Some of the more common tools include:

Letters and Comments
Inquiry Reports
Publisher Studies
Readership Studies
Awareness/Preference Studies
Recall Tests
Market Tests

Letters and Comments

Don't overlook letters, comments, and correspondence from your customers, sales group, and general public. These people took time to communicate because they reacted positively or negatively to what you have done. A file of such comments can be used to substantiate field reaction to a campaign. It can also pinpoint weak areas of your program that should be strengthened.

Inquiry Reports

If your company uses inquiries in conjunction with its selling efforts (and most industrial companies do), carefully compile an inquiry report containing:

Number of inquiries generated
Source of these inquiries (e.g., trade show, advertisement, publicity)
Action generated from inquiries (see

269

Chapter XI—Inquiry Handling for follow-up procedures). Wherever possible, you should set up a system to trace inquiries to sales or to situations of negotiation (i.e., actual quotations or sales presentations). These relationship figures are extremely valuable and meaningful to top management.

Be certain to evaluate total inquiry numbers relating to your specific markets. For example, some groups such as the oil, food, and paper industries historically are not high inquiry pulling areas. This is in contrast to the electronics and instrumentation markets that generate many requests for information and literature.

Maybe your goal is not a high volume of inquiries but rather a smaller number of extremely good prospects. Your inquiry report should state this explicitly and provide some substantiation of this in terms of specific companies or markets reached and the results achieved.

Publisher Studies

Many trade publications give advertisers tools for measuring the results of advertising campaigns. These methods range in level of effectiveness and value. But you are seeking every possible means of documenting advertising effectiveness, so don't ignore these tools.

Inquiry follow-up studies—Publications often make a free follow-up study over a limited number of respondents to your ads to determine if the prospect received the literature you offered, if a salesman called, and if the prospect ultimately bought. Check with your media representative. He can aid you in constructing an appropriate questionnaire and handling the details of the study (if his publication offers this service).

Telephone follow-up studies—Some publications offer telephone survey services to follow up on inquiries. These studies

can provide in-depth answers to a predetermined series of questions. Usually, publications will have some charges for this service.

Readership Studies

Many firms offer one or more services such as Ad Chart, Starch Readership Reports, Harvey Readership Studies, etc., to measure such items as how many people saw your ad in a specific issue and the degree to which they had read, remembered, and comprehended your information. Obviously, this type of research can be conducted by your own group or by an outside research service.

Awareness Preference Studies

Some of the leading publications spend thousands of dollars to conduct surveys of how various manufacturers rate in the eyes of their readers in terms of awareness and preference. These studies can be used to measure the accumulated results of advertising efforts over a period of years.

Awareness/preference studies are easy to make and tabulate quickly and at low cost, and can be made by mail or telephone. For best results, such a study should be done at the beginning and at the end of the program.

There are four methods for measuring awareness/preference data:

Use yes-no questions (e.g., Have you heard of Jonathan Tool Co.? Yes ____No ____).

Open-end questions (e.g., Name three companies that make optical lenses).

Check list questions (e.g., Which of the following products does Jonathan Tool Co. make? Heavy duty machinery——Tools and Dies——Hand tools——).

Rating scales (e.g., How would you compare Shafer hand tools with other brands of hand tools? Better ____About the same ____Not as good ____).

Recall Tests

Recall tests help determine the extent to which advertising themes or messages have been remembered by readers. The depth of inquiry may range from asking the reader if he remembers a slogan or logo, to a deeper study of the meaning of a particular ad.

Recall studies suffer from several disadvantages:

What is recalled may not influence reader at time of purchase.

Ease of recall is not the same as conviction.

Respondents can't always remember required date.

Types of Recall Tests

There are two basic types of recall tests: unaided and aided. In unaided recall, you simply ask individuals to indicate the brand names which occur to them when specific product categories are mentioned. For example, "Can you recall any new brands of fasteners being advertised in the last few months?" There is little chance of leading the respondent with this method. However, it is often difficult to obtain sufficient answers from all respondents.

Using aided recall, you can give to the respondent a list of brand names in a product category and ask him which he knows of, uses, or once used. It is advisable to include a fictitious brand name to test for lying. Always list all brands available on the market. This latter aspect tends to bias answers towards some of the lesser known brands, but the alternative of deciding which brands to omit makes it advisable to accept this limitation. Too much aid may cause respondents to exaggerate findings or guess. However, people do need to have their memories stimulated, and aided recall does focus attention on the ad being studied.

Market Tests

Select two comparable geographical sales regions. Measure sales in these areas over a specified time period. Then conduct some form of promotional activity such as regional publication advertising or a direct mail program in only one of the areas. Now measure sales in each area to determine whether the campaign significantly affected sales.

Present Results to Management

Finally, summarize all results of your measurement efforts in a report to management. Monthly or periodic memos are valuable during the course of the year. And, obviously, these should be incorporated in your annual budget presentation to show management the results of the current program.

Advertising Reference Guide

Advertising Associations

Advertising Council, 825 Third Ave., New York, NY 10022.

Advertising Research Foundation, Inc., 3 E. 54th St., New York, NY 10022.

Affiliated Advertising Agencies Intl., 516 Fifth Ave., New York, NY 10036.

American Advertising Federation, 1225 Connecticut Ave., N.W., Washington, DC 20036.

American Association of Advertising Agencies, 200 Park Ave., New York, NY 10017.

American Business Press, 205 E. 42nd St., New York, NY 10017.

American Management Assoc., Marketing Division, 135 W. 50th St., New York, NY 10020.

American Marketing Assoc., Industrial Marketing Division, 222 S. Riverside Plaza, Chicago, IL 60606.

American Newspaper Publishers Assoc., 11600 Sunrise Valley Drive, Reston, VA 22091.

Association of National Advertisers, 155 East 44th St., New York, NY 10017.

Association of Publishers Representatives, 850 Third Ave., New York, NY 10022.

Business/Professional Advertising Assoc., 205 E. 42nd St., New York, NY 10017.

Direct Mail Advertising Assoc., 6 East 43rd St., New York, NY 10017.

First Advertising Agency Network, 411 North 10th St., St. Louis, MO 63101.

International Advertising Assoc., 475 Fifth Ave., New York, NY 10017.

League of Advertising Agencies, 205 West 89th St., New York, NY 10024.

Magazine Publishers Assoc., 575 Lexington Ave., New York, NY 10022.

Center for Marketing Communications, P.O. Box 411, 575 Ewing St., Princeton, NJ 08540.

Mutual Advertising Agency Network, 5001 W. 80th St., Suite 399, Minneapolis, MN 55437.

National Advertising Agency Network, 420 Lexington Ave., New York, NY 10017.

National Federation of Advertising Agencies, Sarasota Bank Bldg., Sarasota, FL 33577.

Print Advertising Assoc., 211 East 43rd St., New York, NY 10017.

Publimondial, U.S.A., 20521 Chagrin Blvd., Cleveland, OH 44122.

Transamerica Advertising Agency Network, 304 Ivy St., San Diego, CA 92101.

Sources of Information on Advertising

General Sources

Dictionary Of Terms Useful To Buyers Of Advertising, Standard Rate and Data Service, 5201 Old Orchard Rd., Skokie, IL 60076.

Encyclopedia Of Advertising, Fairchild Publications, Inc., 7 E. 12th St., New York, NY 10003.

Industrial Advertising And Sales Promotion, by W. H. Grosse, Amacom, American Management Assoc., 135 W. 50th St., New York, NY 10020.

International Handbook Of Advertising, McGraw-Hill Book Co., 1221 Avenue of the Americas, New York, NY 10020.

Marketing And Communications Media Dictionary, NBS Co., Publishing Services, Box 246, Norfolk, MA 02056.

1973 Handbook Of Independent Advertising And Marketing Services, Executive Communications, Inc., 54 Park Ave., New York, NY 10016.

Tables Of Contents Of Selected Advertising And Marketing Publications, Center for Marketing Communications, P.O. Box 411, 575 Ewing St., Princeton, NJ 08540.

Magazines/Newsletters

Advertising Age, Crain Communications, Inc., 740 N. Rush St., Chicago, IL 60611.

Editor And Publisher, 575 Lexington Ave., New York, NY 10022.

Gallagher Report (The), 230 Park Ave., New York, NY 10017.

\A *World Directory Of Marketing Communications Periodicals*, International Advertising Assoc., 475 Fifth Ave., New York, NY 10017.

Industrial Marketing, Crain Communications, Inc., 740 N. Rush St., Chicago, IL 60611.

Journal Of Advertising Research, Advertising Research Foundation, Inc., 3 East 54th St., New York, NY 10022.

Journal Of Marketing, American Marketing Assoc., 222 Riverside Plaza, Chicago, IL 60606.

Marketing/Advertising Research Newsletter, Business/Professional Advertising Association, 205 East 42nd St., New York, NY 10017.

Media Decisions, Decisions Publications, Inc., 342 Madison Ave., New York, NY 10017.

Sales and Marketing Management, Bill Publications, 633 Third Ave., New York, NY 10017.

Advertising Agency Relations

A Handbook For The Advertising Agency Account Executive, Addison-Wesley Publishing Co., Inc., Reading, MA 01867.

Fee Methods Of Agency Compensation, Association of National Advertisers, 155 E. 44th St., New York, NY 10017.

Management And Advertising Problems In The Advertiser-Agency Relationship, by Booz, Allen and Hamilton, Association of National Advertisers, 155 E. 44th St., New York, NY 10017.

Provisions In Advertiser-Agency Agreements, Association of National Advertisers, 155 E. 44th St., New York, NY 10017.

Standard Directory Of Advertising Agencies, National Register Publishing Co., Inc., 5201 Old Orchard Rd., Skokie, IL 60076.

"The Advantages Of Ignorance: How Not To Pick An Agency," by Walter Weir, *Advertising Age*, December 11, 1972, Crain Communications, 740 N. Rush St., Chicago, IL 60611.

The Development And Approval Of Creative Work, Association of National Advertisers, 155 E. 44th St., New York, NY 10017.

Advertising Budget

An Analytical Approach To Advertising Expenditure Strategy, by Robert S. Weinberg, Association of National Advertisers, Inc., 155 E. 44th St., New York, NY 10017.

How Much To Spend For Advertising, by Dr. Malcolm McNiven, Association of National Advertisers, Inc., 155 E. 44th St., New York, NY 10017.

The Advertising Budget—Preparation, Administration And Control, Association of National Advertisers, Inc., 155 E. 44th St., New York, NY 10017.

Advertising Management

Advertising Manager's Handbook, Dartnell Corp., 4660 Ravenswood Ave., Chicago, IL 60640.

Handbook Of Advertising Management, McGraw-Hill Book Co., 1221 Avenue of the Americas, New York, NY 10020.

McMahan's New Dynamics Of Advertising, Crain Communications, Inc., Book Dept., 740 Rush St., Chicago, IL 60611.

What Management Should Know About Industrial Advertising, Gulf Publishing Co., Book Division, P.O. Box 2608, Houston, TX 77001.

Advertising Objectives

Defining Advertising Goals For Measured Advertising Results, Association of National Advertisers, Inc., 155 East 44th St., New York, NY 10017.

Setting Advertising Objectives, Studies in Business Policy No. 118, The Conference Board, 845 Third Ave., New York, NY 10022.

Advertising Research (Effectiveness)

Advertising Measurement And Decision Making, Marketing Science Institute, Allyn & Bacon, Inc., 470 Atlantic Ave., Boston, MA 02210.

"Can Sales Measure Ad Effectiveness? 'Yes,' Says Collins; 'No,' Says Britton," *Advertising Age,* November 30, 1964, Crain Communications, Inc., 740 N. Rush St., Chicago, IL 60611.

"Evaluating Advertising Effectiveness," *Practical Guides and Modern Practices for Better Advertising Management, Volume VII,* Association of National Advertisers, Inc., 155 E. 44th St., New York, NY 10017.

Guide To Advertising Research Services, Advertising Research Foundation, Inc., 3 E. 54th St., New York, NY 10022.

Journal Of Advertising Research, Advertising Research Foundation, Inc., 3 E. 54th St., New York, NY 10022.

Measuring Advertising Effectiveness, by Darrell Lucas and Stewart Britt, McGraw-Hill Book Co., Inc., 1221 Avenue of the America, New York, NY 10020.

Measuring Advertising Readership And Results, by Daniel Starch, McGraw-Hill Book Co., Inc., 1221 Avenue of the Americas, New York, NY 10020.

Measuring The Sales And Profit Results Of Advertising: A Managerial Approach, Association of National Advertisers, Inc., 155 East 44th St., New York, NY 10017.

Reality In Advertising, by Rosser Reeves and Alfred Knopf, Random House, Inc., 201 E. 50th St., New York, NY 10022.

Sources Of Publishers Advertising Research, Advertising Research Foundation, Inc., 3 E. 54th St., New York, NY 10022.

Cooperative Advertising

A Management Guide To Cooperative Advertising, Association of National Advertisers, Inc., 155 E. 44th St., New York, NY 10017.

Prevailing Cooperative Advertising Practices And Trends, Association of National Advertisers, Inc., 155 E. 44th St., New York, NY 10017.

Media Evaluation/Selection

"A Probabilistic Approach To Industrial Media Selection," by D. A. Aaker, *Journal of Advertising Research,* September 1968, pp. 46–54; 3 East 54th St., New York, NY 10022.

Advertising Media: Creative Planning In Media Selection, by Lyndon D. Brown, et al, The Ronald Press Co., New York, NY 10010.

Bibliography On Computer Use In Media Selection, Business/Professional Advertising Association, 205 E. 42nd St., New York, NY 10017.

Evaluating Media, by H. D. Wolfe, et al, The Conference Board, 845 Third Ave., New York, NY 10022.

"How To Evaluate And Select Business Media For More Effective Advertising," by Henry D. Gudrian, *Industrial Marketing,* November 1972, Crain Communications, 740 N. Rush St., Chicago, IL 60611.

Media In Advertising, by Roger Barton, McGraw-Hill Book Co., Inc., 1221 Avenue of the Americas, New York, NY 10020.

CHAPTER VII

Public Relations

Introduction

Public Relations—a Valuable and Inexpensive Tool

Public relations (PR) is one of the most inexpensive communication tools your company can use. Understand that it is not synonymous with publicity. The latter is only one aspect of the former. Briefly stated: PR is "good performance publicly appreciated." Obviously, performance must precede PR efforts. Then the PR man can focus attention on company accomplishments in ways that earn public appreciation.

The total audience you want to reach comprises numerous special "publics": customers, employees, shareholders, suppliers, creditors, distributors, dealers, bankers, credit rating agencies, and the community at large.

Each "public" sees your company from a different viewpoint. Therefore, communications about your company should originated from one coordinating source, with consideration given for the special needs of each particular "public." Other-

wise, a newsworthy event or achievement could be misunderstood, causing credibility gaps that can hurt your public image.

To better understand PR's value to some companies, browse through *Business Week*, *Forbes* or *Fortune*. If articles in these magazines seem unattainable to you, then look through trade magazines in your field. You'll find many articles describing people, products, processes and companies, including companies like yours. Properly handled, PR will benefit your company in ways that could never be achieved by advertising.

Principal PR Activities

This chapter comprises two sections. The basic preparations necessary to perform PR are described in Section A (Tasks 1–3). These tasks should be conducted sequentially. Examples of more well-known PR activities are discussed in Section B (Tasks 4–8). These latter five activities can be performed simultaneously or one at a time, not necessarily in order of presentation.

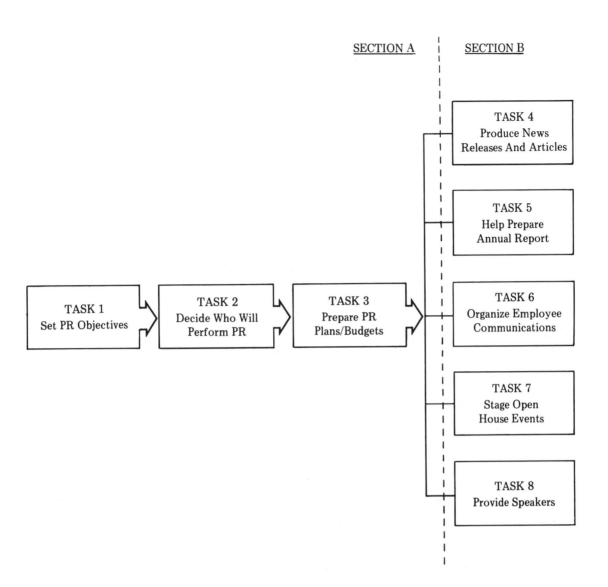

Section A
Getting Ready for PR

Task 1: Set PR Objectives and Select Ways to Meet Them

Focus on Your Publics

You can best define PR objectives by stating the *results* you want. These results, of course, must be compatible with your company's overall objectives.

Your publics are the logical targets of your PR activities. Who are they? What do they expect from you (i.e., why are they interested in your firm)? How would you like them to react (i.e., why are you interested in them)? How can you communicate with them?

PR Action to Take with Respect to: [1]

YOUR "PUBLICS"	WHY INTERESTED IN YOUR FIRM	WHY FIRM INTERESTED IN PUBLIC	WAYS TO COMMUNICATE WITH SPECIFIC PUBLICS[2]
Employees	Personal recognition Pleasant working conditions Approval of company social and economic policies Salary and fringe benefits Support of local industry Opportunity for career growth	Employee relations Increased productivity Stable labor force Support of company policies and actions Relations with ethnic groups	Employee communication program Local publicity (articles and releases) Open house Closed circuit TV Informal "get-togethers"
Investment bankers, trust and fund managers Brokerage and insurance firms Stockholders Prospective investors Security analysts Financial press Venture capital suppliers	Dividends Stock growth & appreciation Speculation Economic well-being of industry Potential merger or acquisition	Venture capital source New operating capital source Support of policies and actions Favorable press coverage Fair market appraisal of company's stock	Annual & quarterly reports Publicity in financial media Meetings with security analysts and financial groups Press conferences with financial media Stockholder meetings Financial news releases and "fact sheets"
Customers/Suppliers	Quality products Sufficient volume Fair prices Excellent service	Increased sales Improved service from suppliers Support of policies and actions Potential for expansion	Publicity in trade publications Company speakers at strategic conventions Open house Customer & supplier trade conventions
Public leaders and other opinion makers (government, media, law, business, bankers, students, teachers, community, etc.)	Economic development Local purchasers & civic growth Plant appearance Personal gain (employment, standard of living, payroll, tax bite, product usage, education)	Favorable legislation Favorable civic relations Product purchase and use Personnel recruitment Support of policies and actions	Annual report Publicity Open house Meetings with political & community representatives Address meetings of local public groups Support local charities and community programs

---

[1] Use this chart to analyze your various "Publics". The third column, in particular, will help you to frame your PR objectives in specific terms.

[2] These are often useful for publics other than shown.

276

Check List of Public Relations Potential Benefits [3]

CATEGORIES OF PR ACTIVITIES	POTENTIAL BENEFITS		
	HIGH	MEDIUM	LOW
A. PRODUCT PUBLICITY[4] (Usually for applicable trade publications)			
1. New products			
2. New literature announcements			
3. New uses for existing products			
4. How the product is manufactured/engineered			
5. Price changes			
6. Product applications			
7. Product technical data			
B. EMPLOYEE PUBLICITY (Usually for local media and trade publications)			
1. Promotions, elections			
2. Retirements/deaths of key employees			
3. Awards (professional, suggestion system)			
4. Participation in community events and speeches			
5. Employee sports, hobbies and unusual jobs			
6. Attendance at national meetings			
7. New appointments			
8. Management changes			
C. COMPANY ACTIVITIES/PUBLICITY (Usually for local, national and trade press, depending on firm's size in industry)			
1. Customer relations programs			
2. Dealer/distributor relations programs			
3. Opinions of company top management on pertinent subjects (growth and trends of your industry, etc.)			
4. Speeches at local and national meetings			
5. Community relations/civic projects			
6. Fairs, exhibits and shows			
7. Industry betterment programs			
8. Quarterly and annual reports			
9. Open-house events, picnics and outings			
10. Policy statements			
11. Government relations programs			
12. Labor relations programs			
13. Major contracts received			
14. Plant visits by well-known people			
15. Mergers and acquisitions			

[3] Rate each PR activity as High, Medium or Low, in terms of its value in reaching your PR goals. Then select the most fruitful activities to include in your PR plans.

[4] Can also be adapted for firms whose "product" is a service.

The "PR Action To Take With Respect To" chart will help you find answers to these questions. The third column will help you frame your PR objectives in concrete terms.

Choose the Most Fruitful Activities

Next, use the "Checklist of Public Relations Potential Benefits" chart to evaluate the potential benefits from engaging in diverse categories of PR activities. Consider carefully the value of each category, and rate them as high, medium, or low, according to your estimate of their potential in achieving your goals.

Finally, select the best mix of categories and, within each, develop a list of specific PR projects that will help accomplish your objectives.

Task 2: Decide Who Will Perform the Public Relations Job

Alternatives

Now that you have decided WHAT needs to be done, the next question is WHO shall do it? There are three choices: conduct your own in-house PR program, employ a professional PR firm, or combine both approaches.

Qualifications Required

Whatever the approach taken, persons doing the work should have most, if not all, of these qualifications:

Education normally should include liberal arts subjects, such as public relations, sociology, English, business administration, journalism, marketing, advertising, and psychology.
Flair for detail, without being picayune
"Can-do" attitude and congeniality
Creativity
Proven writing and speaking abilities
Good judgment and orderly thinking
Working knowledge of sales and distribution methods
Ability to work under heavy pressure and to control many diverse tasks simultaneously
Ability to inspire others to work in a "team" effort

Pros & Cons of Retaining a PR Firm

Listed below are some pros and cons of hiring a public relations firm.

Pros

Your company may have no working knowledge of PR.
PR done "outside" appears unbiased and gives you a professional appearance.
PR firms often have access to the financial and communications centers of the nation.
The professionals may already know key influential contacts in your industry.
You get professional results from practitioners whose salaries could not otherwise be afforded by a single firm.
PR firms offer increased objectivity, scope and flexibility.

Cons

Members of your firm may be antagonistic toward outsiders, especially regarding PR counsel to top management.
The outside counselor may have only a superficial grasp of your company's unique problems and mix of products, procedures, and personnel.
If you are one of the PR firm's smaller clients, you may not get full attention, or access to the most creative minds.

Using an Outside PR Firm

If you do hire an outside PR firm, choose on the basis of its experience and demonstrated ability to get results. Investigate claims about qualifications and experience. But don't rule out a small company or a new one with performance yet to be proven; such firms might have skilled, creative personnel who could serve you very well.

A PR firm's output can be no better than your input; be patient with your PR firm. Help it to understand your products and business philosophy. Then you will be justified in demanding effective performance. Anyone can offer PR services, but not everyone can do a results-oriented professional job. Before engaging a PR firm, talk with principal or senior members to find out how they would handle specific problems. Also ask about the background and qualifications of the agency people who would be assigned to your accounts. Meet them, if possible.

Finding a Firm

The Public Relations Society of America (845 Third Avenue, New York, NY 10022) can provide a list of reputable local PR firms. Accreditation by the Public Relations Society of America (PRSA) is tantamount to a lawyer passing his bar exam. It means the accredited member qualified in PRSA's eyes, as a competent, professional public relations counselor. Also, see Richard Weiner's *Professional Guide to Public Relations Services* (Prentice-Hall, Inc., Englewood Cliffs, NJ 07632). It reports on 600 PR firms and services, including key members of each company, fees, costs, and other information. Local firms are listed in the Yellow Pages of the telephone directory.

Billing Methods of PR Firms

Several methods are used:

- Monthly fee, plus buyouts (outside purchases) at cost.
- Minimum retainer, plus cost of time (hourly or per day).
- Lump sum (monthly), including time and buyouts (with buyouts, either at cost or marked up a certain agreed percentage).
- Special assignment charges, usually hourly, for organizing national sales meetings, grand openings, groundbreakings, etc. This may be in addition to the firm's regular monthly fee.
- Project-by-project billing, where the firm submits an invoice for each news release mailed, each article written and placed, etc., at a prearranged price or price range.

Most Workable Method

The most workable method is the monthly fee for PR services rendered, plus all out-of-pocket expenses (printing, postage, photography, etc.) billed at cost to the client, or marked up by an agreed percentage to cover overhead.

If the PR firm's rate is $25 an hour and it spends an average of 50 hours a month on your account, the fee is $1250, with out-of-pocket expenses (buyouts) extra. You should be allowed access anytime to the firm's hourly records for your account, so you can verify charges.

But mere man-hours spent is not enough—you are entitled to expect tangible results for that time. If results are only fair, negotiate for a reduction of the fee and demand results. If results are outstanding, you might increase the fee, thereby keeping the firm interested in working for you.

Using an In-house PR Staff

If you should decide on an in-house PR staff, there are three points to consider:

How many people?
Full or part-time?
Profit center?

How Many People?

It is difficult to set guidelines determining how many persons suffice for an internal PR staff. PR activities must be based on the number of markets a firm serves and the span of publics it desires to reach. A medium-sized firm with diverse product-lines in multiple markets may need more PR people than a giant firm that builds only sewer pipes for cities.

Full or Part-time

Small firms often find full-time PR functions too costly. In this case, work is assigned to someone from a staff department, such as personnel or industrial relations. This solution, however, frequently causes confused loyalties and interdepartmental conflicts. Nonetheless, if fiscal reality dictates part-time PR efforts, here are some suggestions:

> Top management must assign PR responsibility to one person, and demand full cooperation from all employees. To ensure this cooperation, the PR man must be given authority equal to his responsibility.
>
> Management and the PR man must allocate the days or hours per week for PR work.
>
> The individual must be trained, either by a hired professional, or through college PR extension classes.

PR Department as a Profit Center

An internal staff might operate as a profit center, with its own monthly overhead. A dollar value could be given each job done on behalf of the company—either at an hourly rate, or a "piece rate." For example, a news release to 100 publications might be given a dollar value of $150, minus buyouts, to arrive at a gross profit figure. Articles might receive a dollar value, say between $350 to $600 for most trade stories, and twice that amount for long features stories. If the department's overhead were set at $2,700, then any gross profit above that amount could be considered a "working" net profit. Such a plan provides adequate cost controls, and permits options for incentive programs based on a percentage of the net. There have been cases where PR became a true profit center through the sale of films and books originally prepared as part of the PR effort.

Locating the PR Function in a Company

In many firms, a PR director reports directly to the president or to a vice president of communications. This usually indicates that top management is alert to the many benefits possible from a well-run PR campaign. Small firms using part-time internal PR help often assign those duties to persons in advertising or in other staff departments. Whether your operation favors a full time executive or a part-time PR representative, you must give your PR man sufficient authority to get his job done efficiently.

You've now determined your basic PR needs. You know your objectives, what must be done to achieve them, and who will do the job. Next, define your specific PR operating plan.

Task 3: Formulate Your PR Operational Plan

Specific Objectives

The PR operational plan defines specific objectives to be met, or results desired, such as:

> Win public acceptance of a new plant at (location).

Overcome bottlenecks slowing sales of product "X."
Publicize company growth and stability.
Win employee acceptance of proposed new work rules.
Solve major marketing problems faced (i.e., combating competitor price-cut-

ting, or rumors being spread about your firm).

Other areas in which PR will help your firm's growth and sales effort. (These must be specifically defined or top management should not buy your plan.)

Content of Plan

Questions to be answered when preparing the detailed plan are:

WHAT must be done to achieve objectives?

WHO shall control each element of the work?

WHEN are work elements scheduled for completion?

WHERE will work be done (e.g., if plans involve coordinated actions at different locations)?

HOW will work be accomplished?

WHAT is management's policy on requesting PR inputs from various company departments and key personnel?

WHAT methods would best measure the effectiveness of PR in reaching stated goals?

Getting the Plan Approved

Success of your plan depends, to a great degree, on its acceptance by other departments. (Department heads will be more likely to accept your plan if they've taken part in developing it.) When you get each department head to contribute ideas and sign his approval of the plan's provisions that affect him, top management approval should be relatively easy to obtain.

Develop the PR Budget

The budget is the financial expression of your PR plans. The budget summary sheet shows, in the left column, the individual items of direct expense, and the overhead expense allocations to finance the PR activity categories under colums A, B, C, and D. Except for column D (special projects, including contingencies), columns A, B, and C correspond to the activity categories listed in Task 1, on the Check List of Public Relations Potential Benefits—and those contained in your PR operational plan.

The budget summary sheet should be supported by detailed budget sheets for each specific activity you plan to pursue during the year. A detailed budget sheet is shown following the budget summary sheet.

The aggregate budget estimates from the detailed budget sheets in the categories under columns A, B, C, etc., are entered on the budget summary sheet, and totalled across and by columns.

Column D, "Special Projects," is for allocating funds reserved for unforeseen events, new promotions, and other contingencies that cannot be planned when you are preparing the budget estimates.

If you operate the PR function as a profit center, then the items of overhead expense (see bottom portion of budget sheets) should be allocated to the various PR categories and activity budgets. The formula for such allocation should be obtained from your company controller, or from the chief accountant.

Budget Summary for Public Relations [5]

DIRECT EXPENSES	PUBLIC RELATIONS ACTIVITIES				
	A. PRODUCT PUBLICITY	B. EMPLOYEE PUBLICITY	C. COMPANY ACTIVITIES	D. SPECIAL PROJECTS	TOTAL
Salaries	$_____	$_____	$_____	$_____	$_____
Artwork	_____	_____	_____	_____	_____
Photography/Retouching	_____	_____	_____	_____	_____
Films/Visual Aids	_____	_____	_____	_____	_____
Reproduction Service	_____	_____	_____	_____	_____
Printing	_____	_____	_____	_____	_____
Clipping Service	_____	_____	_____	_____	_____
Travel	_____	_____	_____	_____	_____
Entertainment	_____	_____	_____	_____	_____
Postage	_____	_____	_____	_____	_____
Other Misc. Expenses	_____	_____	_____	_____	_____
TOTAL DIRECT EXPENSE	$_____	$_____	$_____	$_____	$_____
OVERHEAD ALLOCATION					
Office Space	$_____	$_____	$_____	$_____	$_____
Office Supplies	_____	_____	_____	_____	_____
Telephone	_____	_____	_____	_____	_____
Utilities	_____	_____	_____	_____	_____
Maintenance	_____	_____	_____	_____	_____
Other Misc. Expenses	_____	_____	_____	_____	_____
TOTAL OVERHEAD EXPENSE	$_____	$_____	$_____	$_____	$_____
TOTAL PR BUDGET	$_____	$_____	$_____	$_____	$_____

[5] Use this form to summarize the detailed budget allocations for direct and indirect expenses (taken from the detailed budget sheets for each PR activity).

Detailed Budget for a Specific PR Activity [6]

BUDGET CATEGORY: _____ (A) Product Publicity _____

PR ACTIVITY: _____ New Product Releases _____

BASIS: _____ per month @ $_____ each = $_____ per year _____

PREPARED BY: _____ DATE: _____

Direct Expenses

Salaries (man-hours times hourly rate)	$_____
Artwork	$_____
Photography/Retouching	$_____
Films/Visual Aids	$_____
Reproduction Service	$_____
Printing	$_____
Clipping Service	$_____
Travel	$_____
Entertainment	$_____
Postage	$_____
Other misc. expenses	$_____

TOTAL DIRECT EXPENSE: $_____

Allocation of Overhead Expense

Office Space	$_____
Office Supplies	$_____
Telephone	$_____
Utilities	$_____
Maintenance	$_____
Other misc. expenses	$_____

TOTAL OVERHEAD EXPENSE: $_____

TOTAL ACTIVITY BUDGET $_____

---

[6] A detailed budget must be prepared for each specific activity in your PR plan. The aggregate of the expense items from the detailed budget sheets are summarized on the budget summary sheet. Modify the budget line items and column headings to suit your particular PR plan.

Section B

PR Activities

Task 4: Produce News Releases and Articles

Publicity

Publicity is the planning, creation and placement of favorable news into the editorial channels of local, national, or international media. Its objective may be oriented toward the stimulation of demand for a product or service, or toward the development of a favorable image, or public understanding of an industry problem.

Product publicity usually takes the form of free editorial space in trade and consumer media. Non-product publicity is either the reporting to the media of an institution's or industry's activities deemed newsworthy, or the staging and reporting of "newsworthy" events, such as ground breakings, dedications, etc.

Task Sub-headings

Now let's examine ways of getting publicity—one of the chief roles of the industrial PR man. This function is described under seven task headings:

Establish harmonious relations with key media personnel
Develop mailing lists
Establish files for releases and articles
Gather information for news releases and articles
Prepare news releases and articles
Distribute news releases and articles
Measure and report on publicity effectiveness

Establish Harmonious Relations with Key Media Personnel

Your PR staff should contact selected trade, business and newspaper publishers and editors, and television and radio station owners and managers. Knowing the "right man"; reading his publication or monitoring his show, and working with him, helps you better understand his editorial preference and needs. Then, offer the most interesting material available about your company's people, products, policies, and activities.

How to Work with Key Media Personnel

Build mutual confidence (i.e., never "make-up" news).

Be cooperative and honest; don't try to "buy" favors.

Give service. Provide newsworthy, interesting, and timely information in a readily usable form requiring minimal, if any, rewriting.

Never beg attention or find fault if you don't get it. Media's job is satisfying broad reader and audience interests.

Never request "kills" on unfavorable stories. Instead, stress preventing unfavorable situations that might result in such stories.

Avoid favoring one editor or station manager over another. Don't offer "exclusive" news releases, if they are actually nonexclusive.

Don't exaggerate. "Tell it like it is" in a way that your audience will understand.

Don't harass an editor by asking when he will run your story, or why it hasn't run. Printing, delaying, or rejecting a story is editorial prerogative—you can only damage relationships by pestering.

Obtain clippings and page proofs from a clipping service. Editors resent providing this service, and you may lose their goodwill if you demand it.

Never pressure editors or station managers through a mutual friend in the publishing company or on the television or radio station.

Never deceive the media or a civic leader. This could destroy your credibility forever. Always consider the potential consequences of your actions.

How to Contact Media Representatives

There are five basic ways to contact key personnel of the press and broadcast media:

Telephone
Visits to you by media representatives
Your visits to media offices
Mail
Press conferences

Steps for each method are presented below.

Telephone

1. Before phoning an editor (or any key media personnel), write down reasons your story idea might interest his readers.
2. Introduce yourself, your firm, and as briefly as possible, explain your concept. Perhaps you've learned one of your customers slashed production costs 25% by using one of your products or systems; the editor will want to know how this was achieved. To tell him, you will need all the *facts*. Do your homework before calling; otherwise, you'll sound foolish when you're unable to answer questions.
3. If the editor turns down your idea, don't argue. Ask him if there's anything special he's seeking editorially. If he needs something your firm can pro-

vide, tell him you think you can help and you'll find out for sure; then contact him later. Follow-up with a letter to alert him. Get the story and send it to him—with photos if possible.

4. Remember—you're just another voice on the phone to that editor. You have about 30 seconds to get his attention. You do that by offering a story that will *interest his readers*.

Visits to Your Facility by Media Representative

1. Define purpose of the visit in advance (e.g., general orientation, specific new product or system).
   a. Gather all *facts* related to the purpose.
   b. Suggest presence of a photographer during visit (offer company's photographer).
   c. Provide previsit briefings and literature to orient the editor, and to excite his interest.
   d. Fix date and time for visit.
2. Set up a tentative schedule.
   a. Who to see, at what time, about which topic.
   b. Check with your people to assure their availability.
3. Confirm arrangements by letter or telephone call to the editor.
   a. Tell him whom he will see, by name, title, and responsibility.
   b. If by phone, send confirming note with carbon copy to all concerned.
4. The day before the meeting, remind secretaries of people concerned. Take nothing for granted: a "no show" could be embarrassing.
5. Act as company host.
   a. Remain with editor during meetings.
   b. Introduce him to all parties.
6. Have a portable tape recorder available.
7. Provide all requested information as soon as possible, during or after visit.

a. Be sure you understand all requests.
b. If you can't answer a question, don't make one up. Say that you'll get facts by a certain time—and don't miss.

Your Visits to Media Offices

Visit media offices only when you have newsworthy information to offer. For example:

1. Delivering an important release or story requiring:
   a. Immediate attention by the editor
   b. Interpretation of data by PR man
2. Developing a lead into a full-blown story that may require lengthy discussion.
3. Providing background information for articles or TV and radio spots, in cases where a key representative from the media specifically requests that you work with him in his office.

Mail (*Also see* Develop Mailing Lists)

There are three approaches, depending on the newsworthiness of your material:

1. Send the editor a query letter (or telephone him) asking if he is interested in your story idea. Give a brief description of the idea. Be sure to include interesting facts from the viewpoint of his readers.
2. If your material is fairly short—a thousand words or less—send it with your covering letter. Your letter should give a concise reason why you think his readers would be interested. It should not summarize or "sell" the story. The article you mail will be judged on its own merit.
3. If you believe your story is worthy of a feature article—several thousand words—outline the story theme and how you think it could be developed. Offer to send a comprehensive packet of facts and photographs for the editor's feature writer to use.

Press Conference

To hold a press conference, invite interested media personnel (editors, reporters and/or station managers) as a group. The conference subject must always warrant taking the time of media personnel, as well as that of your own company personnel. Some justifiable reasons for calling a press conference are:

Announcing (and perhaps demonstrating) a major new scientific discovery or "breakthrough."
Announcing important new products that have significant implications for the nation, industry, or community.
Showing an important new manufacturing or engineering facility.
Making an important statement of company policy (only when company is large enough so that the statement affects many publics, an entire industry, or community).

If what your company has to disclose, announce, or demonstrate justifies a press conference, here are the basic steps to take:

1. *Prepare/Coordinate Plans.* Have all concerned company personnel agree on purpose, goals, date, time, and place for the conference. Line up company speakers and others who should participate. Get agreement on the method of presentation, and on media representatives to be invited. Select a date and time not conflicting with other events—particularly ones having news value (so your event won't share the limelight with equally important news). Avoid scheduling Mondays and Fridays, and just before and after important holidays.
2. *Brief Top Management and Get all Details Approved.* Leave a fact sheet with the president and any concerned vice-presidents. Offer to prepare remarks for them to make at the press conference.
3. *Invite Media.* Select media having audiences most interested in what will be

disclosed at the press conference. Invitations should include the purpose, date, time, place, and reasons why the conference will benefit the media's readers. Include several of the most interesting facts about the product, development, or process to be disclosed. Request that you be informed whether a press representative will attend, and his name. Give your telephone number for telephone replies and include a self-addressed, stamped card for mail replies.

4. *Prepare Press Kits.* Assemble fact sheets, photographs, a formal press release, background information, and biographies of company personnel whose works are the main reason for calling the conference (e.g., the inventor, key engineering and technical contributors, etc.). Distribute a press kit to each attendee. Later, distribute press kits to any media representatives unable to attend the press conference, and to other media whose readers and audiences would be interested in the subject.

5. *Rehearse.* Schedule a "dry-run" rehearsal to iron out any rough spots or gaps in presentations. Encourage critical comments and suggestions from an audience of "devil's advocates" and revise the presentation as indicated. Time permitting, hold several rehearsals until every detail runs smoothly. Anticipate possible questions from media representatives, and have answers prepared in advance. Have one person designated to "field" any questions, and to refer them to the person best qualified to answer. Don't fabricate if an answer is not immediately available. Tell press members that an answer will be provided as soon after the conference as possible (and by a given deadline).

6. *Before the Press Conference Check all Details One Last Time.* Remind all company participants of the schedule (or changes in plans, if any). Ensure

conference room availability and readiness for the meeting. Make sure press kits are on hand, and someone is appointed to distribute them. Have a check list for all "props" (chalk board, chalk, eraser, easel, charts, projectors, someone to operate projector, to dim and raise lights, pointers, lectern, lighting for lectern when house lights are dimmed, etc.—including any product to be "unveiled"). A successful press conference must be "staged," directed, and managed down to the last detail. Good planning makes good conferences.

7. *Always make a tape recording* of the entire conference proceedings. Have stenographers transcribe the proceedings to provide a written record.

8. Just before the conference, *distribute copies of speeches* to all attendees. This enables them to follow talks and to mark subjects for later questions. Reading, as well as hearing a talk, strengthens and reinforces the communication. Unfortunately, rattling of papers and more penetrating questions may result.

9. *Follow-up.* List and analyze all questions asked. This may provide material useful in preparing later articles. Make note of "boners" and "foul-ups" so they can be avoided in future conferences.

Develop Mailing Lists

This section covers approaches for reaching various audiences under the following headings:

Trade Press
General Business Community
Financial Community
General Public
Community Leaders and Government Officials
Miscellaneous Sources of Mailing Lists

The Trade Press

Because your firm's primary interest is to sell industrial products, initial communication should be with trade publications rather than business and financial ones. Although there are over 6,000 trade publications in the United States, you need reach only those whose readers are interested in your products.

First, list the markets in which your products are to be sold (e.g., agricultural equipment and supplies, autos and trucks, electronics, power plants, shipbuilding, etc.).

Then, refer to one of several directories that list various trade publications in the United States. The reference guide lists several of these directories. Under your category of business, you will find trade publications you might use in your publicity campaign. From these, compile your own list of publications with names and addresses of editors. If a national publication has an office in your area, find out where it is and the name of its local editor; a copy of any release to that publication's headquarters should also *always* be sent to the local editor.

General Business Community

Over 20 national magazines and publications serve the business community. Regarding local press, the telephone Yellow Pages can be used to expand your mailing list; see directory headings for Publishers—Directory and Guide, Publishers—Periodical, and Publisher's—Representatives. Local chambers of commerce may also provide lists of local business publications. (See reference guide.)

Financial Community

Approximately 20 national financial and business magazines serve the financial community. Detailed information is available in Standard Rate & Data Service's listing of business publications. (See reference guide.)

In addition, local newspapers, as well as local business magazines in your city, county, and state usually print financial columns. Editors of these papers want news about local businesses. Your chamber of commerce may provide useful leads. In addition, commercial banks can often suggest

media interested in news about local businesses.

Releases to these publications should emphasize financial aspects of your company, including comparative details about past and present sales, earnings, potential earnings outlook, net working capital, current ratio, inventory turnover, capitalization ratios, dividends, earnings per common share, and other key financial statistics. Brief biographical information about the company's chief financial and/or operating executives, and their plans for the future interests financial readership. *However, do not make any fiscal predictions* without guidance from your legal, accounting, and PR professionals.

General Public

Companies that make capital goods, services for industry and raw materials (as contrasted with consumer goods, such as footballs, motor cars, and detergents), don't often have occasion to release news items of interest to the general public. But such developments as new methods for pollution control, machinery that reduces the price of consumer goods, or new scientific discoveries benefiting everyone should be brought to the public's attention.

National press and electronic media are prime outlets for such publicity, but don't fail to consider also your local newspapers, radio, and television outlets. If your company uses a professional advertising or public relations agency, reaching these media presents no problem. When you contact the media directly, always address your queries to an editor or station manager by name and not merely by his title.

Community Leaders and Government Officials

Your firm is an integral part of the social and economic structure of your community. You should have readily at hand the names of community leaders, officials, heads of public services, and key politicians. Officials serving in elective and appointive positions, and in voluntary public service capacities, are understandably ready to "point with pride" to accomplishments of local firms such as yours. If you can involve them in your accomplishments, and give them appropriate credit, they may be eager to promote your firm in the press and broadcast media.

Successful firms are able to win the admiration and goodwill of the community by participating in, and keeping abreast of community activities. Your top officers—including the PR representative—should seek opportunities to join with leading citizens in various community efforts. For example: your company could become an active member of the chamber of commerce; key officers could speak at service club meetings (Kiwanis, Rotary, Lions, etc.); and they and their wives could volunteer to head community funding drives. But in your involvement in community affairs, be careful to avoid associating the company with purely "political" issues. Politics can turn the public against you.

In developing an index of leading citizens, you should have their names, titles (in public life or business capacity), addresses, telephone numbers, and perhaps, information on their accomplishments. Keep this information filed on $3'' \times 5''$ cards by their community titles, or by last names, or both. Information on the following positions should be kept on file:

Mayor
Members of City Council (especially the member who represents your area)
City Manager
City Clerk
County Administrative Officer
County Assessor
County Supervisors (especially the one who represents your area)
City Police Chief and Fire Chief
County Sheriff and Fire Chief
Congressman from your company's district
State Assemblyman from the company's district
The local representatives of your Congressman and State Assemblyman

The president of the local chamber of commerce
Publishers and Editors of local papers
Managers of local television and radio stations
Leaders of local service clubs and civic organizations

Miscellaneous Sources of Mailing Lists

Numerous other sources of mailing lists are presented below. Most are self-explanatory. Others are discussed in related sections of this book.

Brokers who sell mailing lists
Sales records
Shipping records
Telephone inquiries
Salesman's call reports
Service staff recommendations
Advertising inquiries
Prior lead-producing publicity
Trade show registrants
Current customer recommendations
Product warranty registrations
Yellow Pages
Business and industrial directories
Thomas Register of Manufacturers
Standard Advertising Register
Poor's Register/Moody's Industrial Manual
Association membership rosters
Stockholders
Dealers/distributors
Subscriber lists (purchased from magazines)
Special mailing lists (e.g., "all barley farmers in Michigan") obtained on request from government agencies

Establish Files for Releases and Articles

Log books and job envelopes are essential tools for keeping your articles and releases organized. Both of these subjects are discussed below.

The Log Book

The log book is a serially numbered listing of each article or press release or project you prepare. Treat each of these as separate "jobs." When you begin a new job, give it a serial number and title. Start a new series of log numbers each year (e.g., PR77-1, PR77-2, etc.). Write the serial number on all materials and correspondence concerning a particular release or article.

Every time you make a log book entry for an article (but not for press releases) prepare a 3″ × 5″ index card, similar to those used in libraries. Near the top of the card write the subject category which the article concerns. Then write the title of the article, followed by its serial number and data. Use additional cross-indexing cards (by target publication) if you think they will help you to locate entries in the log book (which eventually will have hundreds of entries). Here is a sample format for a subject category index card.

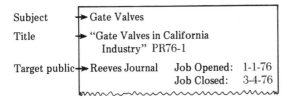

When a job is finished, make an entry on the card showing date of completion.

The Job Envelope

A job envelope (or folder) should be used for storing all materials relating to a given job, such as roughs, originals, photographs, release forms, and other working materials. A convenient envelope size is 11″ × 17″. The job serial number, followed by its title, should be written near the top left-hand edge so it will be visible when the envelope is filed. Here is a sample format for a job envelope.

```
←-------------- 17" --------------→

      ┌─────────────────────────────
      │ PR73-1
 ↑    │ Gate Valves
 │    │ Article – "Gate Valves in Calif. Industry"
11"   │ REEVES JOURNAL
 │    │ Job Opened:  1-1-76
 ↓    └
```

Place envelopes by number and subject in an "open" file on a shelf while work is in progress. When work is completed (i.e., been published or broadcast), transfer the job to a "dead" file shelf (called a "morgue"). In both cases, keep the file in numerical order under each subject matter so that you can quickly find all that's been written previously on a given topic.

Gather Information for Releases and Articles

In addition to being out-of-the-ordinary, news must be interesting to the reader, timely, informative, accurate, and unbiased. In his search for material having these qualities, the PR man is similar to a newspaper reporter with a "nose for news."

A PR man normally gathers news in three ways: (1) be where the action is—at important meetings held by company personnel; (2) screen company reports and memoranda about current sales and operations; and (3) interview people who have information about what's happening.

News Sources

Here are some good news sources:

Key personnel within your company (department heads, top management).
Product design engineers (new product releases).
Customers (product application stories). Your customers will often welcome chances to have their names in print with your firm's product because they're getting free publicity.
Company salesmen/distributors/reps (application stories). Follow-up sales, gather data on performance, then write case history stories.
Vendors (they may welcome publicity on how your company uses *their* products and services).

The Interview

Interviews with the right people are an effective way to get "leads." But before contacting anyone, have a definite purpose in mind—a reason to make the person feel he is helping do something important to him and to the company. Organize your interview; busy people don't like rambling. Be tactful. Be courteous, respectful, and appreciative of any information you get—and, when appropriate, express sincere admiration. During each contact make the person aware of the value of publicity in furthering the company's (and the person's) well being, *but don't make outlandish claims or promise anyone anything.* Remember, in PR you cannot "guarantee" publication dates as you can when buying a page of advertising.

As you gain experience in interviewing, you will find that most people like to be interviewed—perhaps because they enjoy expressing their opinions and offering their knowledge. If you have a "game plan" for getting the facts you need by asking the right questions, you should have little difficulty. But some people will be ultra-cautious in their replies to questions; others will give snap answers rather than taking time to check their facts. It is best to allow both groups more time to think things through by themselves.

Whenever you sense it would be better to let a person "think it out," you can tell him that you know he is a very busy man, and leave one or more of the three questionnaire forms found further in this task. Explain the organization of the form, and tell the person that it will help him provide the needed information in a minimum of time.

In some interviews, you may feel you have uncovered something of major significance which may require detailed documentation. Leaving one or more of the questionnaires can be of major assistance.

When you close the interview, allow the respondent more time to compose his thoughts (or to record them on the forms), thank him for his time, and arrange a date and time for another meeting (at the respondent's convenience, if possible).

If you leave one of the questionnaires with a respondent, assure him that all you need are the facts—and that you will have someone organize them into a suitable article or news release.

Occasionally, you will encounter a procrastinator who will keep putting you off with excuses. Exasperating as this may be, you can't afford to show impatience. Instead, offer a little subtle praise, a reminder about how important the information is to the company, assurances that he need not worry about preparing finished copy (all you need are the facts), and help in explaining each section of the information forms. A gentle reminder that the material has a "deadline" to meet may spur some action.

If you leave a form with someone, write the title of the subject near the top of the form, together with your name, telephone number, and desired completion date. Indicate that if the respondent will telephone, you will personally pick up the form.

Prepare News Releases and Articles

Now we come to the payoff task—writing the news release or article. You don't have to be a seasoned journalist to handle this publicity job. Just express yourself simply, factually, clearly and according to a logical plan. What we cover here will not make you a professional journalist. But you'll learn some basics of communicating facts about your company.

Remember the Audience

Your job is to communicate. Communication involves a sender and a receiver. You can talk, you can write, but if the receiver—the listener or reader—doesn't understand, you might as well talk to yourself. You must tailor your message so it matches the reader's experience. If your reader is an engineer or scientist, you can use technical terminology. But if your reader is Mr. Average Citizen, give him examples that an intelligent layman can understand.

And don't forget that an intelligent layman instinctively knows when you overstate your case, oversimplify it, exaggerate beyond the realm of ordinary credibility, or reason in a

Case History Report [7]

Information from this form helps us prepare accurate case histories and magazine articles for media use. When you've answered all questions please return this sheet to _____ (your address).

The details you provide will answer the five journalistic "W"'s: who, what, where, when, why, plus how. PLEASE PRINT OR TYPE. DO NOT WRITE.

Fill in each blank. Use "N/A" (not applicable) only if logical comment is impossible. Please provide as much information as you can. Elaborate. Give specific sizes, weights, lengths, etc. As you fill this out, think, "What would a reader be most interested in knowing about this application." Thank you for your help.

WHO?

Your company: _____

Division or branch office: _____ Main product/service: _____

Your name: _____ Phone number: _____

Title: _____

Name of company you served in this application: _____

Address: _____

Person there you worked with: _____ His title: _____

Mailing address: _____ Phone number: _____

List companies, individuals, etc. who must approve a completed case history or feature article prior to publication: _____

WHAT?

In simple, declarative sentences state briefly what product/service you provided. Be specific: _____

What exact customer need did you fill? This information is essential. Pinpoint your answer: _____

Describe the way the customer's product/system operated prior to this application: _____

How did you improve this condition? Elaborate: _____

WHERE?

Name specific city, location, address, proximity to well-known landmarks, etc., relevant to this application: _____

Give name of particular unit or system in which your product/service was applied (i.e. valve, boiler, electronic or fluid-handling system, pier, etc): _____

Describe your product's exact location in the unit or system. Use specifics: _____

Define the main function(s) of the customer's unit and/or entire system. Give a complete narrative description: _____

Give a summary of what your product/service contributed to the unit or system's end result. This is vital information. Answer fully: _____

[7] Useful in gathering data from salesmen, dealers, reps, customers, etc., on how your product/service proved successful for a firm. A good structure for such a story is "Problem/Solution/Results."

292

Now, describe this whole case history completely, in the simplest and easiest-to-understand way you can:

_____
_____
_____
_____
_____
_____
_____
_____
_____
_____
_____
_____

Draw your own diagram of the completed installation. Attach the drawing to this sheet. Be sure to show your product/service's relationship to other parts of the system. Display it in a way that clearly illustrates its value to the customer. Do not merely attach a blueprint, unless you can provide explicit collateral explanation.

Attach pertinent photographs, diagrams, additional explanations, descriptions, etc., so that a detailed article, ready for publication, could be developed directly from the information provided here.

Please carefully review your finished report.

Thank you for taking the extra care to write a good case history.

Your signature_____

WHEN?

(1) Give the date this application of your product/service was completed: _____ (4) How long before it becomes obsolete?_____ (2) Is it still in operation?_____ (3) How long will it last?_____ (5) Give any significant or interesting details regarding the above:_____

WHY?

(1) What caused the consumer to choose your product/services? Was it price? Availability? What, then? Be frank in your answer. (2) Was it uniquely suited to his needs? (3) Could he have used a competitor's product as well? If not, why? Please number and answer each of these questions here:_____
_____
_____
_____
_____
_____
_____

Approximately how many firms could have provided similar products/services? Name all that you know of:_____
_____
_____

Name your direct competitors:_____
_____

HOW?

(1) In this application, did designing, production, installation, etc., pose any unique problems to you that might be of interest to designers, engineers, your other customers, or the general public? (2) Was a custom design necessary? If so, discuss it. (3) If this product/service application was part of a larger project, explain its function as a component of the end result. (4) Was this a new market for your company? Number and answer each of these questions in detail:_____
_____
_____
_____
_____
_____
_____
_____

293

New Product Information Sheet [8]

Your firm:

Proprietary name of new product:

Generic name:

Its uses: (1) Primary:

           (2) Secondary:

           (3) Others:

Who would use it?

Industries   Applications

_____   _____

_____   _____

_____   _____

_____   _____

List job title(s) held by persons we want to influence (i.e. design engineer, lab technician, housewife, etc.):

_____

_____

What need does the product fill:

_____

_____

Give a narrative description of all its key features IN ORDER OF PRIORITY:

_____

_____

List those features which are unique when compared with conventional products:

_____

_____

How does each of the above features help a customer do a job faster, at less cost, more accurately, or efficiently, etc.?:

_____

_____

List specifications which you feel would interest buyers:

_____

_____

What is the price?

_____

What is delivery time in days?

_____

Add any other details you feel are important:

_____

_____

Give name of person to contact for more information:

_____

[8] Use when preparing new product news releases. The "Who Would Use It?" section helps you pinpoint markets, thereby choosing a better mailing list.

Biographical Data Sheet [9]

Information from this form helps us prepare accurate news releases for media use. When you've filled out the form, please return it to the above address.

Company: _____

Division or branch office: _____

Main product or service: _____

Name: _____ Age: _____

Title: _____

Responsibilities: _____

_____

_____

Date assumed new position: _____

Previous positions, titles, dates with current employer: _____

Previous two employers, titles, and dates (For all employers, briefly describe their business i.e. "Major Appliance Manufacturer"): _____

_____

_____

Other employment history, include firms, titles, responsibilities, and dates: _____

_____

_____

_____

_____

_____

Education. Include dates, degrees, school names: _____

_____

_____

Military experience, rank: _____

_____

Home address, phone and city: _____

_____

Spouse's name: _____

Additional Information. Social, civic, fraternal, professional participation, awards which might be of interest to readers: __

_____

_____

_____

_____

_____

_____

_____

_____

Signature _____

---

[9] Use when preparing releases on new manufacturers representatives and company promotions or new hires.

roundabout manner to cover up something (the technical "snowjob"). All you are expected to do is to "tell it like it is."

Most of your publicity will be either in news releases, or article format. In either case, select media whose audience is interested in your subject.

News Releases

News releases normally go to trade publications. But don't send out news releases until you see the *kind* of releases that get published. Get a half dozen trade magazines that serve your market and study their releases. Try to get a feel for the audience's interests so you can tailor your stories to tap that interest. You may send news releases to editors of every publication reaching your market. A news release is an economical "broadside" attempt to reach many people, simultaneously, with the *same* story. Never send a news release out unless your message is really *news*. Be careful to avoid giving technical aspects of a product/process helpful to competitors.

Articles

Articles are another thing. Usually, they are authored by experts on a particular subject. Before sending an article to an editor, you should "query" him by letter or telephone, to learn if the subject interests him. The letter or call should summarize what the article is about, and explain why it would interest the editor's readers. Unlike releases, these queries are not broadside to numerous editors—instead, one editor is given exclusive rights to an article. If he turns it down, the query can be sent to another editor, and so on.

Kinds of News Releases

The following kinds of news releases are most frequently printed in trade publications and in special interest newspaper sections:

A. Product Stories
   New product announcements
   New literature announcements

   Announcements of major price changes, with reasons
B. Employee Publicity
   New employees; new assignments
   Promotions
   Retirements
   Deaths
   Awards
   Participation in community activities
C. Company activities
   Labor agreements
   Earnings statements
   Acquisitions and mergers
   Industry forecasts
   New contracts
   New construction/equipment

You'll find advice on writing news releases later in this section. But first, let's consider practices professionals use in preparing news releases.

The Professional Way to Prepare Releases

"Professional looking" news releases have a better chance of being used. Here are some rules for giving news releases a professional appearance. The rules conform to customs of the publishing industry.

News Release Format

Following is a list of news release format guidelines. They are not necessarily presented in order of importance.

Use only one side of standard 8½" × 11" white paper. Include company name, address, etc., plus name, address, and telephone number of the person to contact for more data.

Avoid phrases such as "News," and "Important." Simply use "News Release."

The words "FOR IMMEDIATE RELEASE" should be shown in the top right-hand corner of the release.

Leave the equivalent of ten lines of white space in the area between "FOR IMMEDIATE RELEASE" and the start of the release. This makes room for the editor to make notes.

Write a headline—in capital letters, centered atop the first page of the release. This is not necessarily the headline the editor will use, but it should tell him at a glance what the release is about.

Double space all copy. This makes reading easier and gives the editor room for making changes.

The word "more" should appear at the bottom of each page when another page follows. "End" or "—30—" should appear at the conclusion of the release, centered below the last line of type.

Mimeograph releases if you must, but offset printing looks better, is quite inexpensive, and its appearance helps "sell" the release.

Use a dateline as shown on the examples later in this section. This lets an editor know the timeliness of the release.

Do not split paragraphs when you approach the bottom of a page. News copy is often sent to linotypers a page at a time and splitting would cause confusion.

Writing Techniques

Following is a list of writing techniques to make your releases and articles more readable, understandable, and acceptable.

Begin with a headline that tells what the story is all about. A good "head" lures the editor to read more.

Next comes the lead paragraph—the story introduction. The "lead" summarizes *who, what, when,* and *where,* sometimes even telling *why* and *how.* A snappy lead should stand alone and still have meaning. It should make one want to read further for more details. Writing a good lead often takes more thought, time, and revision than all other paragraphs of the story.

After the lead, additional paragraphs (called the body) fill out the story with more and more details. Especially in news releases, use the "inverted pyramid" format, in which each paragraph gives less important facts than the preceding one. This enables editors to trim the piece from the bottom up when space is limited.

Gain reader involvement by showing how one might personally benefit from what you've written.

Use simple words and "subject—verb—object" sentence construction whenever possible. After finishing a paragraph, circle all the repeated words. Then select alternates. Scratch excessive articles and conjunctions such as "the," "then," and "and." This "dead wood" slows reading and is usually unnecessary.

Get to the main point quickly—then add details. Help your reader get the information with a minimum of concentration and effort.

Use concrete words that picture ideas relating directly to your reader's experience. Don't say ". . . a wood beam," when you mean ". . . an 8″ x 12″ x 4″ kiln-dried white oak beam." On the other hand, don't elaborate unnecessarily.

Make sentences "live" by using active verbs, and a structure conveying rapid movement of ideas. For example: don't say "Give consideration to . . ." when the action verb "consider" is faster and shorter.

Use the reader's language, nomenclature, and trade terms. Use them consistently to avoid semantic confusion. Don't call the same thing by possibly-misunderstood different names.

When you finish writing the first draft of your release, go back over it until it reads well *aloud.* Cross out all words which do not add something to the thought at hand. Rearrange words and phrases to improve meaning. Check facts for accuracy. Rewrite all ambiguous statements—words that could be misinterpreted. Replace with words having only *one* logical interpretation in the context used.

Check all adjectives, ensuring none "editorialize," or overstate a quality or feature.

Suggestions on Writing

Two additional suggestions on writing are presented below:

PR writing is a "selling" kind of writing. Along with telling what a product is, you must tell *what it can do for the user*. In PR writing, you sell *benefits* first. The product described is only a thing the reader buys to gain these benefits. That's why good "selling" releases often begin: "A new (product name) providing/enabling (benefit), (benefit) and (benefit) is now available from (your firm)." Here, the product is generically named, not described. That's so the release can move quickly into the "selling" part—the benefits. A good second sentence might be: "Primary applications are (use), (use) and (use) in the (type), (type) and (type) industries." With this, the reader knows what the product is, how it can be used, and where. Hopefully, you've named an area in which he's involved—you've identified with the reader, and he's interested enough to read succeeding details. The point? Sell the sizzle, not the steak.

Good writing gets harder, not easier, because it is mostly sweat and not talent or experience. Those who know this find writing more a labor as it's being done and more a joy when finished. You try to reach a level where you've thought of every objection anyone could possibly make to the way you've said something. Then, when they object, it's not because you said it badly; it's because you didn't have all the facts. The two items—good writing and sufficient facts—are always interdependent. Together, both produce good communication.

Some DO's and DON'Ts About Using Photographs

DO—

Furnish well-composed, professionally-taken, high quality glossy prints, preferably 8″ x 10″ or 5″ x 7″.

Show product to best advantage—ideally with people using it.

Show people in action—not standing in static "say cheese" poses. Exception: mug shots.

When more than one person appears in a scene, provide identifying captions lightly taped to the back of the photo so they can be removed easily.

Always use a professional photographer.

Use imaginative, believable photos; they can be retouched or airbrushed to eliminate needless detail, or to emphasize important parts—but NEVER to convey a false impression.

Leave a white border on all four sides for the editor to write instructions to the engraver.

Write "TOP" in the top margin if this is not obvious.

Use chipboard stiffeners to protect photos in mailing.

Order prints as close as possible to desired size, plus 50% larger if they will need retouching. It is difficult for an engraver to enlarge a print more than twice the size, or to reduce it to less than one-sixth original size.

Use a professional service specializing in making "multi-photos" at a cost far less than individual prints.

Use on-the-job photos showing employees using safety equipment required by the Occupational Safety and Health Act.

DO NOT—

Use paper clips or staples on photos.

Request that photos be returned (unless the editor has asked for photos and promised to return them).

Tell the editor you can furnish photos "if he wants them." If photos are needed for illustrating a release, furnish them with the release.

Send group photos of everyone looking at the camera, unless the editor asks for them. (Instead, show people in action.)

Use, show, or refer to brand names without prior written approval.

Overprint identifying data on photos, unless in an obviously "croppable" area.

Furnish product data on reverse side unless the same data has been included in an accompanying release.

Send photos separately from releases to which they pertain.

Send matte finish prints, unless glossy prints are unobtainable.

Use a photo for releases if the same photo will be used in ads.

Use photos in which retouching will be obvious when published (there may be exceptions to this).

Use "cheesecake" photos, unless specified by the editor—the product should be the main attraction.

Use gray-on-gray or black-on-dark backgrounds, or monotones.

Finding Photographers

The "Directory of Professional Photography" lists commercial photographers in the United States, Canada and England for industrial advertisers, agencies, and other buyers. Contact the Professional Photographers of America, Inc., 1090 Executive Way, Des Plaines, IL 60018 (free).

Also, UPI/COMPIX, located in major cities throughout the United States, provides world-wide photographic capabilities. Their local offices can be found in your city's Yellow Pages.

Keys to Writing Specific Types of Releases

Each type release has key elements to be stressed. These elements are discussed under the following headings:

New Products
New Literature
Promotions
Retirements/Deaths
Awards
Participation in Community Activities
Labor Agreements
Earnings Statements
Acquisitions and Mergers
Industry Forecasts
Price Changes

New Product Releases

Do not editorialize, or make your release read like an advertisement. Just inform! Editors want to know:

What is the product?
What will it do for the user?
What is its field of application? Where and how can it be used?
What makes it better than existing products?
What is really new about the product?
What is the price? Where is it sold?
Are there any major time or cost savings?

If possible, send a photo showing the product operating in "real world" surroundings. Do not photograph the product out of context (e.g., with a girl in a bikini). When you publicize a product, be sure your sales department can deliver it within a reasonable time—otherwise, you may find you are selling your competitor's *similar* product. Also, be sure collateral product information materials are on hand to satisfy requests for additional information.

New Literature Releases

Many trade publications have a section or column reserved for information on new literature available from manufacturers. New literature releases should not exceed three-quarters of a page in length and should cover:

The topic of the literature, in content very similar to a new product release
Its cost, if any
How to obtain it

Promotion of Employees

News about promotions, new employees or employee reassignments, is often carried in local newspapers and, if the situation involves a key position, by trade journals. Information required for these releases includes:

The employee's name
Address (for local newspapers only)
New title and responsibilities
Former title
Former employers, titles, responsibilities
Educational experience (if significant and relevant)
Social/civic/trade affiliations

Any other significant biographical information

A recent photograph ("mug shot")

Do not "plug" another company official in these releases. Too many firms have made this mistake. The news concerns the promoted employee, not an official making the announcement. Mention of another name only distracts a reader from the subject.

Retirement or Death of Employee

These releases are generally reserved for employees having long service, key positions, or community stature. They should include:

Name and address of employee
A straightforward (non-flowery) statement of his company history and important achievements. Extra details may be included for key officials, or community figures.
Employee's future plans (if retiring).
Names of immediate surviving family (if a death).
Photograph of employee. For retiring employee, send a picture taken at retirement ceremony or similar event.

Awards

Awards make outstanding releases (especially if interesting to a large segment of industry).

Send photographs of the individual or group that received the award.
If for a "suggestion" award, emphasize the process—not the individual.
Include appropriate remarks by key officials.

Participation in Community Activities

It is good publicity to recognize employees as good community citizens. But news about company or employee participation in community activities may smack of "tooting one's own horn." It's best for community leaders and heads of community committees and organizations to take the initiative in announcing a company's contribution of products, money, time, or special skills to a community program.

There may be occasions which justify a company-oriented news announcement, as when the company appoints a member to a community board or agency. But in every case, the company's PR man should first discuss with community representatives any plan for a news release.

Labor Agreements

List all major agreements and provisions. To avoid charges of bias, make a *joint release* with the union.

Earnings Statements

If the company publishes an annual report, key financial information should be released to the press. Avoid making predictions (they usually come back to haunt you). Send releases to financial editors. Before making any release, check with persons familiar with Securities and Exchange Commission (SEC) regulations regarding financial public relations (e.g., financial PR firms, or your lawyers, accountants, and stockbroker).[10] Treat Quarterly Report releases in the same manner. (Refer to Task 5—"Help Prepare the Annual Report.")

Acquisitions and Mergers

If your company acquires or merges with another firm, information should be released to the press. Stress why the merger took place; discuss both firms, the new officers, and how the action benefits customers of both firms. If either company is publicly held, tell how the action will affect earnings.

Industry Forecasts

News releases containing industry forecasts are appropriate only if your company is a leader or qualified spokesman for your industry.

---

[10] For publicly-held companies, SEC law requires that any news—good or bad—which may materially affect the market valuation of the stock be released promptly. Check with financial PR counsel.

NEWS RELEASE

COCHRANE CHASE & COMPANY, INC. 1400 NORTH HARBOR BOULEVARD, FULLERTON, CALIF. 92635 (714) 526-6623

FOR FURTHER INFORMATION CONTACT:

Person who can direct an editor
to the proper source

Title

Phone Number

FOR IMMEDIATE RELEASE

↑
¦
¦
¦

10 lines

¦
¦
¦
↓

HEADLINE HERE; ONE OR TWO LINES

Dateline here . . . . (Copy)

At bottom of page write "more" or "–30–" — as appropriate

Price Changes

Price changes are normally announced in "price change letters," mailed direct to customers, rather than in normal news releases. Price change news releases are appropriate only when revised pricing affects the national interest (e.g., a major price change in the steel industry).

If you decide a price change news release is necessary, make the announcement read as simply as possible. Identify the product affected, and whether the stated new price represents an increase or a decrease, and—if appropriate—give reasons for the change.

A timely news release on price increases may be especially important because competitors always like to be first in telling the news to your customers. If this happens, your customers may wonder why *you* didn't tell them first.

Writing Articles for Publicity

Most editors prefer an exclusive article to a news release. But, few editors will print your story merely because your firm buys advertising in his magazine. Most editors resent being approached on this point—*never* mention advertising when discussing editorial matter. The first requirement of an article is that *it fills the editor's needs—as he sees them*. It's his job to know what his readers want. If your story doesn't fit, he won't publish it, no matter how many ads you buy.

As mentioned earlier, take time to read about six copies of a publication in which you'd like a story. Study kinds of articles published, their average *length* (usually ranging from about 1,000 words to 5,000, depending on the publication), the accepted writing styles, and the "slant" (editorial approach) used by the publication.

If you have a really good idea for an article that appears to "fit" the publication, see subtask entitled, "Gather Information for your Articles and Releases." Next, get it written! There are two approaches:

Gather factual material, photographs and sketches for later artwork and illustra-

tions. Then discuss the idea with the editor. An inexpensive way is to write a letter to the editor (called a "query" in the trade), explaining the gist of the idea, describing the factual material and photographs available, and telling why the story might interest his readers. Ask him if he would rather have one of his staff writers handle the job.

Alternatively, you could submit a story written by someone in the company. Before you spend a lot of time having the article written, telephone, or send a query letter to the editor to find out if the article would interest him. Ask whether he wants biographical information on the author. Sometimes a "byline" detracts from an article's objectivity; sometimes it helps establish a company or individual as an authority on a subject.

Query letters should be single-spaced and not over a page in length. If the article is technical, briefly outline the writer's qualifications. In reply, the editor may turn you down, or he may simply agree to read the article on speculation (he will rarely commit to run a story until he has read it).

The format for articles is different from news releases. Margins are always wider—about one and a half inches on all sides. Copy is always typewritten (not multiprinted) and double-spaced on 8½" x 11" white bond paper.

The headline should be centered about halfway down the first page. Four spaces down from the heading, begin the first paragraph. Indent the first line of each paragraph at least five spaces.

Editors call the lead paragraph a "hook" because it either captures the reader's attention, or loses it. The lead must also tell the reader what the article is about, suggest the author's viewpoint, and suggest (or imply tacitly) what the reader's reaction should be, that is, what the author wants the reader to do.

After hooking the reader's interest, let him know you have an important message for him or are offering a "benefit" if he will read the article; be sure to keep this promise.

The hook and promise of a benefit or message comprise the beginning of an article; the middle contains the main story. The writing techniques are the same as for a news release, except that the "inverted pyramid" format does not necessarily hold. Instead, the author develops his thesis along those lines which most logically fit his story material, and organizes it to convey main points in the way easiest for the reader to digest. Use photographs and line art to illustrate the story whenever possible.

To close the article, the author may state his conclusions, or he may summarize—by paraphrasing—the main points covered in the body of the article. If he wants the reader to act in some way, his final words call for, or imply, the action wanted.

Distribute News Releases and Articles

Primary considerations in distributing publicity releases and articles are *timing* of the distribution and physical mailing of releases.

Coordination and Timing—Key Elements

Coordination and timing are key elements in the successful distribution of articles and releases. You should adhere to the following suggestions:

Be sure the release is suited to the medium.

Time release mailing carefully:
  a. Mail releases to newspapers three to seven days before desired publication date.
  b. Releases to monthly periodicals may be mailed from 30 to 90 days prior to publication.

Do not make follow-up calls unless offering valuable additional information to the editor.

Case histories of product applications which are suitable for use both in pub-

licity and in advertising should always be used first as publicity. This helps eliminate the possibility of diluting or entirely killing the news content of the case history insofar as trade press editors are concerned.

Addressing and Mailing

There are two primary considerations when addressing and mailing releases:

Releases must be mailed as quickly and efficiently as possible. There is a wide choice of methods—from manual through complete automation, including folding, gathering, addressing, and postage metering. A list of suppliers of equipment for such activities may be found in your local Yellow Pages or in the Thomas Register.

Generally, however, even the largest industrial plants would not operate their own mailing service. Most would hire an outside mailing house to do this. These are listed in your Yellow Pages under "Direct Mailing Houses." One firm of specific interest is Media Distribution Services, Inc., a public relations media and mailing specialist. Their system includes 70,000 editors, broadcasters and syndicated columnists by name, all trade, technical and professional journals, daily and weekly newspapers, wire services, syndicates and syndicated writers, consumer magazines, and radio and television stations in the United States and Canada. Tailor-made access is provided, along with complete lettershop facilities to select media, print material, have photos reproduced, and mail or messenger all releases. Address: 260 West 41st Street, New York, NY 10036. Bacon's Publicity Checker is another service of similar nature.

Measure and Report on Publicity Effectiveness

Measuring and reporting effectiveness of your publicity efforts should be done regularly and systematically. Various ways are discussed under these headings:

The Column Inch Report
Competition Reports
Clip Books
Publicity vs. Advertising
Publicity and Sales Objectives
Publicity and Merchandising
Opinion Studies
Inquiry Studies

The Column Inch Report

One commonly used measure of publicity effectiveness is the column inch report. Some public relations specialists consider it a waste of time. In spite of this, it continues to be widely used. Often it serves only as an "ego builder."

It is simply a monthly, yearly, etc., tabulation showing total column inches of publication space mentioning a company or its products. The report may be broken down by type of publication (consumer, business, newspapers), or by product, with subclasses. An example of a typical column inch chart is shown below.

Column inch reports must be made continually so you can compare the trend of results and past performance with your goals. The report shows where publicity efforts have been most successful and which publications have given you the least publicity. If too many releases are in the latter category, perhaps something is wrong with the releases themselves.

The number of column inches can be charted, and trends studied. Then, you can analyze peaks and valleys to determine their causes and possible meaning. Preparing column inch reports is not difficult if a reputable clipping service [11] is hired to gather clippings from publications in which your publicity is likely to appear. Charges for this service are nominal.

A handy form for keeping tallies by product-line for various publications is presented on the opposite page.

Competition Reports

Clipping services are also used to check effectiveness of your competitors' publicity operations.

Clip Books

"Clips" of your company's releases and articles should be kept in a large scrapbook that can be shown to management and other interested parties. File the releases by date of release or product-line with the corresponding clips immediately behind each release.

Publicity vs. Advertising

No attempt should be made to compare the column inches of publicity received with

_____
[11] See your Yellow Pages under "Clipping Bureaus." Clipping services are also available from Bacon's Clipping Bureau, 14 East Jackson Blvd., Chicago, IL 60604, and from Luce Press Clippings, Inc., Graybar Building, 420 Lexington Ave., New York, NY 10017.

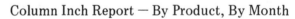

Column Inch Report — By Product, By Month

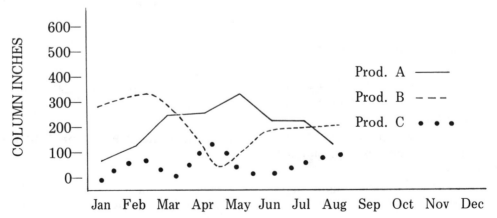

your advertising costs since they are intended for different purposes. There is no connection between them, because advertising is space that you pay for, whereas column inches of publicity clips results from your mailings of news releases and articles. You can, however, compare column inches of publicity with the total cost of your news release operations. The number of column inches of publicity per dollar of news release cost can be a useful index of the growing efficiency of your news release operations.

The cost of publicity is generally a mere fraction of advertising costs, yet if properly handled can have much more impact. Nonetheless, advertising is still necessary to direct reader attention to a specific message the company wants to deliver. Also, advertising is not subject to editing by publishers, and it will appear on a date chosen by the company, not the editor. Advertising can be more consistent, thus quickly building a corporate image. Publicity and advertising must complement one another for each to be most effective.

Publicity and Sales Objectives

Although it is difficult to quantify, comparing publicity results with sales results is a better tool than column inch reports and most other publicity measures. Essentially, you look at a product-line to see what has happened to sales in that area. The question is: "Has publicity timing coincided with sales volume of the company?" If it has, then perhaps the publicity was part of the reason those additional sales (or reduced sales) occurred.

Publicity and Merchandising

Check the possibility of tying-in publicity with merchandising activities. Can reprints of your published stories be used with direct mail letters, or by salesmen as handouts? Publicity and advertising moves the buyer

The Column Inch Report [12]

PERIOD COVERED _____ TO _____

PRODUCT(S)	PUBLICATIONS SERVING EACH PRODUCT	COLUMN INCHES PER PUBLICATION	TOTAL COLUMN IN. PER PRODUCT

GRAND TOTAL . . . .

[12] Indicate product in the first column, then group the publications serving that product in the second column. Record column inches received for each publication in the third column; total column inches received for each product in the last column.

toward the product—merchandising moves the product toward the buyer.

Opinion Polls

Opinion polls can determine how well publicity builds the company's name, its products, and its relations with the community and your employees. These polls demand close coordination with the marketing research department. If this is not possible, the methods described in Chapter I—Marketing Research, will help you sample

and question selected publics. A "benchmark" opinion study before and after a specific campaign can tell you how much you have changed public attitudes, or helped to open doors for your salesmen.

Inquiry Studies

Inquiry and analyses should also be made. A comprehensive description of these tools is presented in Chapter XI—Inquiry Handling.

Task 5: Help Prepare the Annual Report

Objectives of the Annual Report

"All annual reports bring their readers written messages whose rhetoric ranges from stodgy to mod, from murky to clear. . . . The purpose of these messages . . . is to put the best face possible on whatever has happened to the corporation during the year. There is nothing wrong in this, for optimism is no less a virtue in corporate executives than in generals."

This somewhat cynical view of annual reports was taken from the third edition of "How to Read a Financial Report," published by Merrill Lynch, Pierce, Fenner and Smith, Inc.

The annual report is one of the most important communications of a publicly held company. It must influence attitudes your various publics have formed, or will form, about your company. Therefore, regardless of who in the company is responsible for preparing and publishing the report, you—the company's PR representative—should help prepare its messages.

Major purposes of the annual report are to:

Inform stockholders and other interested publics [13] about financial facts of the

company's business operations during the past year.

Describe what the company accomplished in its several operating fields and what it hopes to accomplish in the future (sometimes supported by the company's assessment of economic trends that influence its fortunes).

Encourage stockholders and others interested in the company to have confidence in the company's future and to promote company products and services. It builds this confidence on the competency and progressive attitudes of its management.

Key Things to Consider

Research studies reveal that stockholders hold many false beliefs about their company and the way it is managed. This is partially due to some stockholders regarding with suspicion anything that management says about the company and to a failure in communication between the company's management and its stockholders.

A recent study by a national publication

---

[13] For an annual report, these "publics" include newspaper editors, financial writers, investment analysts, bankers, business school libraries, employees, customers, dealers and distributors, vendors who supply the company, major stock brokerage houses, credit rating firms, stock exchanges, investment statistical services, and prospective investors.

listed some specifics about which stock-holders are most likely to complain:

High executive salaries
Pension and option plan for executives
Ownership of stock by management, and
    possible conflicts of interest
Cumulative voting
Need for women directors
Selection of public accountants
Size of dividends
Discounts on products

All such problems should be recognized by the president and his PR man in planning the company's stockholder-relations campaign. The annual report is the principal instrument of that campaign.

Ways to Say it

Many companies have "humanized" annual reports by using "plain talk" most stockholders understand. This annual report opens with a letter from the president summarizing salient aspects of company operations, its hopes, and an explanation of why profits declined in some areas (if they did). Then the report has several picture pages showing the firm's diverse operations, with accompanying explanatory text. These pictures often include action shots of managers, supervisors and workers. In other cases, they show how the company's products benefit people. The final pages contain financial statements, analyses of sales trends, earnings and dividends, plus any technical information needed to support accounting or performance statements.

Some companies also publish specialized sections for key audiences:

For sophisticated investors, analysts, bankers, and similarly informed experts, a comprehensive compilation of financial statistics is published.
For the employees, a highly simplified summary of what the company's last year means to them. This version is sent to the union and to workers, along with a copy of the regular annual report.

Tasks in Preparing the Annual Report

Every president manages his firm differently. Your president may or may not expect you to play major roles in preparing an annual report. But if he does, these suggestions may help you do a better job.

Structuring the Schedule

The "Annual Report Schedule" form found in this task offers a guideline for speedier preparation of your company's annual report. You should fill in your own specific dates for each operation. Functions are not necessarily sequentially dependent; they can be accomplished over the indicated span of time, coincidental with other chronological stages. Be sure that those responsible for each task participate in determining the schedule.

Theme and Layout

Advise on concept, theme, organization, and design layout of the report. While art aspects require professional talent, you can ensure that the report's appearance, organization, tone of messages, and method of presenting facts convey the most favorable impression to readers.

The Text

Prepare or help prepare and edit "messages" requiring a PR "touch." For example:

The president's letter to stockholders
Condensed highlights
Description of company products and services
Corporate objectives and policies
A brief history of the corporation and its development
Any "bad news" contained in the report, and its interpretation
Explain new competitive challenges
Describe new improvements that will increase efficiency and future earnings
Explain past or possible problems, their impact, and what management's reaction is, or will be (strikes, natural catas-

trophes, R&D cutbacks, corporate divestments, management reorganizations, etc.)

Plans for company growth

Additional Information

For additional information, see *Annual Reports*, Richard A. Lewis, Hastings House Publishers, Inc.[14] ($25). This 204-page volume, containing more than 400 illustrations, gives you a look at dozens of top-flight annual reports, plus step-by-step instruction in preparing attractive, informative pieces.

Things to Cover

The annual report should include, but not be limited to the following items:

Cover

The cover should capture stockholder attention, and invite readership. The company name or logo should be prominent. The words "ANNUAL REPORT," and the period covered should appear.

Introductory Page

The introductory page is for ease of reading and reference. It includes corporate name, address, and table of contents. This is not mandatory.

President's Letter to Stockholders

The president's letter should be both brief (about one page) and frank. It should answer main questions a stockholder (or the public) might ask. Use subheads and paragraphs to break up blocks of type. Do not make precise predictions of future earnings. Do review previous year's sales, earnings, financial position, acquisitions, new products/services, and short general statement of outlook. This may be written by the PR man or by the president himself. Should include: informal photo, signature, and date. Address stockholders as "you" and "your" in speaking of their company. Avoid using "I" and "We." Never begin a president's letter with "I" or "We."

---

[14] 10 East 40th St., New York, NY 10016.

Financial Highlights

The financial highlights should be an easy-to-read summary, one page or less on the inside of the front cover page or on the first inside page. Always remember to tell what the company is and what it does. Compare two or more year's figures and percentages (e.g., net sales, earnings before taxes, taxes, earnings after taxes, net earnings per common share, dividends, stockholders' equity per share, net working capital, ratios, number of common shares outstanding, and number of employees).

Financial Statements

Financial statements should be prepared by the vice-president, finance, treasurer, and/or C.P.A. firm. They include an auditor's report, balance sheet, and income statement.

Previous 5-10 Year's Financial Summary

Previous 5-10 year's financial summary shows essentially the same information as presented on financial statements, plus cash-flow tabulations, and analysis of funded debt.

Products and Services

A list of products and services can be shown to demonstrate increasing diversification and innovative philosophies.

Names of Officers

The names of officers, their titles, affiliates, and outside directors can go on the inside front cover or the inside back cover.

Miscellaneous Information

A variety of other informational items could be included, when appropriate:

Charts, graphs and photographs of product being manufactured or in use; buildings, plants, materials, people.

General history; corporate objectives and policies; map or list of offices.

Divisions or departments in company.

Narrative on any of the above, plus sales trend, earnings trend, dividend policy; stockholders (number), trend, class,

Annual Report Schedule

OPERATION	RESPONSIBILITY	START DATE	FINISH DATE	WORKING DAYS ALLOWED	CUMULATIVE WORKING DAYS
Planning meeting to discuss budget, schedule, format & organization					
Develop general theme and content presentation					
Preliminary format in rough outline form					
Management review of preliminary outline					
Select printing paper — size, color, weight					
Specifications to printer for pricing					
Weigh blank dummy and envelope to establish estimated postage costs					
Expand outline, gather all photos and information, draft president's letter					
Select printer; enlist his aid; order paper					
Finalize photos, data, and all revised text material					
Select typeface					
Comprehensive layout					
Presentation of final copy & layout to management					
Final alteration of copy & layout and circulation for approvals					
Final copy and photos to artist for preparation					
Develop mailing list					
Proofread type prior to paste-up					
Final artwork from artist; stats of assembled book with photo indications in place					
Review and approval of final artwork and copy					
Last minute alterations made					
All artwork to printer					
Pre-address mailing envelopes					
Brownlines for approval					
Press proofs for approval					
Check job on press and in bindery					
Insert and mail					

geographic distribution, sex, and average holdings) or employees, length of service, worker productivity, pensions, and management changes.

Efficiency indexes such as turnover of fixed capital, turnover of inventories, turnover of accounts receivable, or average collection period for receivables.

Map, or list of plants and offices.

Task 6: Organize Employees' Communication Program

Responsibility

If your company has a formalized industrial relations or personnel program, this task may not fall under the PR function. However, you might be asked to help the industrial relations director improve employee communications.

Information to Convey

Employees want information about the company they work for. High interest subjects include:

Employee benefits
Expansion and construction plans
Advancement opportunities
News about employees
Wages and working conditions
Management attitudes toward employees
Safety programs
New equipment and how it helps them and the company
Company products and how used
Company prospects for the future
Economics of the company and how this affects employees
Developments in the industry.

To learn other subjects that may interest your firm's employees, use the survey techniques described in Chapter I—Marketing Research.

Ways to Communicate with Employees

A company's employees are its most important asset. This principle should be totally accepted at all management levels. Management is often quick to admit that "we must communicate with our employees," but what they are really thinking of is one-way talk—"down" to the employees. In practice, management *should* have a "down" channel for informing employees about subjects that interest them. But, equally, management *should* provide ways for its employees to respond "upward." Lacking two-way communication, there is really *no* communication.

The ubiquitous suggestion box—which may or may not be taken seriously by management—is one overt way to let employees be heard. But they have more *questions* than suggestions. Therefore, the following list of various employee communication devices includes a "Question Box" to help develop two-way communication with employees.

Newsletter or Memo

Many decisions must be made about a newsletter or employee memo. How often should it be published? How many pages? Budget? Which employees should receive it? Should it be delivered in-plant or to the employee's home? Basically, the larger the company, the more frequent the issues should be, and the more information presented.

Suggestion Box

This is a useful tool for incentive purposes. It creates a good atmosphere for creativity and competitiveness. However, problems sometimes arise when employees spend too much time trying to earn a suggestion award.

Bulletin Boards

Bulletin boards help alert employees to events of daily interest. Timeliness of notices should be watched carefully. All out-dated notices should be removed immediately. One way to assure each visitor to your plant receives red carpet treatment is to post greetings each day on a simple bulletin board in the reception area. Not only will customers, guests, and salesmen be flattered, everyone in your plant will know who is coming. This makes employees feel more a "part of the action."

Closed Circuit Television (CCTV)

Employees must be frankly informed why CCTV is being installed. They must realize they are not being spied upon; there are no cameras—only monitors. Although a CCTV system is expensive, many experiments have shown increased employee motivation in large plants with CCTV "broadcasts" talks by executives.

Employee Recreation and Assistance

Picnics, annual company outings, discount tickets, literature on legal and educational aid, etc., should all be be coordinated and expanded upon by the PR department.

Employee Question Box

The question box gives employees an open channel to communicate "upward" to management. Any questions that an employee wants answered can be submitted. The employee should not have to sign his name. Anonymity may be the secret to success of a question box program. But, if the program is to become a believable instrument of employee communication, the questions must be answered frankly and within some preset time limit, say, within one or two weeks. If a "tough" question requires more time, it should at least be *acknowledged* within the time limit, and a promise made as to when an answer will be given. In a large plant, question boxes should be located in convenient areas where employees will see them—usually near cafeterias, restrooms, or food machines. Questions and answers can be printed in the company newspaper or posted on bulletin boards.

Task 7: Stage "Open House" Events

Steps for Staging an Open House

Here are some key steps to follow in staging open houses:

Set Objectives
Appoint Someone to be in Charge
Compile Guest List
Set Date and Time
Determine Budget Needs
Distribute Publicity About Open
    House
Ensure Facilities Are in Proper Order
Conduct Plant Tours
Serve Refreshments
Provide Printed Material
Follow-up

Set Objectives

Do you need an open house? Do you have legitimate news? Would having an open house meet at least one objective listed below? If not, forget the open house. A few open house objectives are:

Improve community relations (e.g., tell about new jobs)
Increase employee loyalty, morale, and family support
Explain company policies and benefits
Show a new plant, office, product, or line
Demonstrate how products are manufactured
Attract prospective employees
Entertain visiting VIPs

Appoint Someone to Be in Charge

One individual must be appointed to "run the show." Generally, the individual is from the PR department. He should enlist the support of all supervisors and foremen, and contact all unions for cooperation. If the responsible person decides a committee is necessary, each department should be equally represented.

Compile Guest List

The key to a good open house is tailoring the number of guests to your budget and available facilities. Obtain recommendations of company executives on whom to invite. Check and double-check your invitation lists. Depending on the objectives, consider inviting these individuals as guests:

Employees and families
Customers
Community leaders and opinion makers
Stockholders
Teachers, administrators, educators
Suppliers
Manufacturers
Dealers
Other industry and trade leaders
Retired employees
Special guests suggested by executives
Media representatives

Set Date and Time

If possible, coordinate the date with your company's anniversary, or some other appropriate occasion.
Avoid conflict with other simultaneous local events
Choose the least busy day of the week. This varies, but basically, Monday and Friday should be your last choices.
Consider a school holiday so entire families may attend.
Allow ample time for registration, tours, and refreshments.
Always set an alternate date in case of bad weather or emergency.

Determine Budget Needs

Money required for your open house generally is nominal. The time expended, however, is tremendous. Open houses involve monumental detail, requiring many weeks of planning and preparation. Once you know how many guests are to be invited and have estimated how many may attend, you can estimate costs for:

Refreshments, catering service, decorations.
Printing of invitations, displays, signs.
Identification ribbons, cards, or pins.
Souvenirs.
Mailing expense, postage.
Payroll for overtime, preparations, extra help.
Special security arrangements.
Traffic control and parking arrangements.

Distribute Publicity about Open House

See Task 6—Employee Communication, of this chapter for communicating facts about the open house to employees. Use the techniques described in Task 4 of this chapter to publicize the open house in the local press and other media. Always send a R.S.V.P. card with invitations to determine the expected number of attendees.

Ensure Facilities are in Proper Order

Be sure preparations include:

Convenient, large reception area and registration arrangements (if any).
Parking spaces with attendant or easy-to-follow signs.
Checkroom as required.
Nursery, if children will attend (or means for getting "lost children" back to their parents).
Clean facilities (especially restrooms).
Plant in excellent working condition.
Safety precautions.
Informative in-plant signs and direction arrows (e.g., "Restrooms").
Facilities for serving refreshments.
Public address system for announcements.
Exhibits dramatizing company products and growth.
Badges or nameplates for executives, guides.
First aid and emergency arrangements.

Conduct Plant Tours

After a brief welcome speech by a company representative, the plant tour can include:

Films on company products and history.

Proof of quality being built into products.

Proof of rigid inspection standards.

Safety and health precaution demonstration.

Equipment and displays for guests to operate (check with legal department regarding company liability).

Display of modern office equipment, and plant tools.

A walk through the recreation area, lounge, library, cafeteria, main plant, and executive offices.

Guidelines for Plant Tours

Select a large entrance area for guests to wait in before tours begin.

Limit size of groups for easier handling.

Coordinate routing of tours to save time and steps and to avoid conflicts between different tour groups.

Brief the guides. Make dry runs to time tours and schedule them accordingly.

Arrange for tour guides to give identical explanations about machines, processes and plant features.

Phrase lectures in simple, nontechnical language.

Schedule a question and answer period at points of major interest during the tours.

Serve Refreshments

Use quick service items that can be eaten while standing.

Use cafeteria or lunchroom.

Employ a catering service if cafeteria is not handy or suitable.

Make sure you have enough refreshments, paper supplies, plastic implements, and large waste containers in strategic locations.

Keep refreshment areas neat and clean.

Provide Printed Materials

Invitations

Return, postage-paid postcards to accept or decline invitations

Mimeographed instructions for guides

Company history booklets to save tour time

Programs noting points of interest

Identification cards or badges

Maps of building layout

Registration forms

Follow-up

Mail guests a copy of the company publication carrying article on the open house.

Recognize, by letter or luncheon, those who worked on open house.

Get visitors' comments and suggestions—in writing if possible.

Hold critique of the event soon afterward.

Keep, for future use, committee chairmen's files and reports.

Keep employment applications on hand, if appropriate.

Task 8: Place Company Speakers

Value

You may be asked to furnish a speaker for a convention, seminar, trade show, or community event. Even if you're not asked, it is easy to arrange to be invited to supply a speaker. Speaking engagements are valuable in getting your company, through its speakers, recognized as an industry leader.

Finding Platforms

Lists of potential speaking engagements are available from: (1) local chambers of commerce; (2) *Directory Of Conventions* ($20 per year), 144 E. 44th Street, New York, NY 10017; and (3) *Exhibits Schedule* ($35 per year), 144 E. 44th Street, New York, NY 10017.

Assisting the Speaker

You shouldn't have to coach key speakers. If, however, there are many calls for speakers, you might suggest that they join an organization such as Toastmasters International to improve their speaking abilities.

You can also refer to a book called *The Public Speakers' Treasure Chest* which presents thousands of ideas to make a speech sparkle on any subject: jokes and jests, similes, applications, amusing definitions, classical and Biblical quotations, 174 colorful phrases, witticisms and epigrams, selected quotations, proverbs, interesting facts, biographies—over 4400 items. The book gives "do's" and "don'ts" of public speaking in 14 major points and fifty enlightening subpoints. The book is available from Harper & Row, 51 East 33rd Street, New York, NY 10016.

Coordinate between the inviting organization and the speaker. For him, find out:

Who is the audience? What subject will interest the audience?

How much time will be allotted for the talk?

If a brief biography of the speaker is desired.

The speaker's time of arrival, escort, and at what point in the program he is to deliver his talk.

Who will chair the program? If the speaker will meet the chairman before, or during the meeting.

If an advance copy of the program agenda is available.

If press will be present.

If there will be a question and answer period.

If it will be all right to send advance copies of the talk to the wire services and local papers.

Public Relations Reference Guide

Public Relations Associations

Industrial Publicity Association, % Vincent J. Biunno, Manager, News Bureau, Worthington Corp., 401 Worthington Ave., Harrison, NJ 07029.

International Public Relations Association (IPRA), 110 William St., New York, NY 10038.

Public Relations Society of America (PRSA), 845 Third Avenue, New York, NY 10022.

Sources of Information on Public Relations

Handbook Of Practical Public Relations, by Alexander B. Adams, Thomas Y. Crowell Co., 201 Park Ave., New York, NY 10003.

Handbook Of Public Relations, by Howard Stephenson, McGraw-Hill Book Co., Inc., 1221 Avenue of the Americas, New York, NY 10020.

PR Reporter, PR Publishing Co., Inc., Meriden, NH 03770.

Practical Public Relations, by W. H. Depperman, 24 Old Mill Road, Choppoqua, NY 10514.

Practical Publicity: A Handbook For Public And Private Workers, by Herbert A. Jacobs, McGraw-Hill Book Co., Inc., 1221 Avenue of the Americas, New York, NY 10020.

Public Relations Handbook, by R. W. Darrow et al, Dartnell Corp., 4660 North Ravenswood Ave., Chicago, IL 60640.

Public Relations Handbook, Third Edition, Philip Lesly, Editor, Prentice-Hall, Inc., Englewood Cliffs, NJ 07632.

Public Relations Journal, Public Relations Society of America, 845 Third Ave., New York, NY 10022.

Public Relations News, Denny Griswold, Editor and Publisher, 127 East 80th St., New York, NY 10021.

Public Relations Quarterly, Public Relations Aids, Inc., 205 East 45th St., New York, NY 10017.

Publicity Record, Television Index, Inc., 150 Fifth Ave., New York, NY 10011.

How to Reach Your Publics

N. W. Ayer & Son's Directory Of Newspapers And Periodicals, N. W. Ayer & Son, Inc., West Washington Square, Philadelphia, PA 19106. A yearly publication providing pertinent facts on newspapers and periodicals, and information concerning the states, cities, towns, and marketing areas in which these publications are issued and circulated. Cross-indexed by state and area of interest.

Bacon's Publicity Checker, Bacon's Clipping Bureau, 14 East Jackson Blvd., Chicago, IL 60604. Annual publication analyzes publicity requirements of almost 4,000 business, trade, farm, and consumer magazines published in the United States and Canada; lists over 600 daily newspapers covering the industrial and marketing areas of the United States and Canada; names of over 30 wire services and feature syndicates and their business/financial new product columnists.

Broadcasting Yearbook, Broadcasting Publishing Co., 1735 DeSales St., N.W., Washington, DC 20036. A special issue giving information about television and radio stations in the United States and Canada; includes news and program directors, network affiliation, and color facilities.

Business Media Guide International, Directories, 1718 Sherman Ave., Evanston, IL 60201. Annual publication in six parts. Presents rates, requirements, circulation figures, and key personnel for business management, industrial, technical, professional, scientific, and trade publications on an international basis. Broken down by market classification.

Chamber Of Commerce Business Directories, U.S. Department of Commerce, Washington, DC 20230. Directories of local chambers of commerce.

Editor & Publisher International Yearbook, published by *Editor & Publisher* magazine, The Editor & Publisher Co., Inc., 850 Third Ave., New York, NY 10022. This yearbook contains a state-by-state and city-by-city listing of daily newspapers in the United States and Canada with information on their circulation and names of executive personnel.

Editorial Offices In The West, Simon Public Relations, 12011 San Vincente Blvd., Suite 603, Los Angeles, CA 90049. Lists magazines having editorial offices in California, Oregon and Washington; gives names, addresses, and phone numbers of editors; lists types and sizes of photographs used; shows which magazine uses bingo cards; frequency of publication; circulation field offices; description of audience; name of publishing company, etc., all by industry (subject).

Gebbie Press All-In-One Directory, Gebbie Press, Box 1000, New Paltz, NY 12561. Includes information on 1,790 daily newspapers, 360 farm publications, 8,450 weekly newspapers, 898 television stations, 210 general consumer magazines, 7,062 AM-FM radio stations, 430 business papers, and 2,900 trade papers. Covers editor names and positions, publication titles and frequencies of all print media, special audiences and circulation figures, call letters and studio locations for radio and TV, addresses, and affiliations.

Luce Press Clippings, Inc., Luce Press Clippings, Inc., Graybar Building, 420 Lexington Ave., New York, NY 10017. A complete directory of 1,900 daily newspapers, 8,200 weekly newspapers, and 3,000 trade and consumer magazines, all listed alphabetically by state.

Standard Rate & Data Service—Business Publications, Standard Rate & Data Service, Inc., 5201 Old Orchard Road, Skokie, IL 60076. Presents rates, requirements, circulation figures, editors, key personnel, and defines readership in detail for the leading business and trade publications in the United States. Other directories cover newspapers, television, radio, and consumer-oriented areas.

State Directories Of Manufacturers, American Marketing Association, 202 South Riverside Plaza, Chicago, IL 60606. The American Marketing Association publishes a booklet—*Industrial Directories*—containing a list and description of state industrial directories.

The Working Press Of The Nation, The National Research Bureau, Inc., 424 N. Third St., Burlington, IA 52601. This publication is a reference to basic communication media in the United States. It has four volumes: *Newspaper Directory; Magazine Directory; Radio & TV Directory;* and *Feature Writer and Syndicate Directory*. Presents names and addresses of over 100,000 publishers, management executives, key media personnel, editors, freelance writers, photographers, financial press, press, newsreel, news service, feature syndicate, subjects covered, titles, and phone numbers.

Ulrich's International Periodicals Directory, R. R. Bowker Co. P. O. Box 1807, Ann Arbor, MI 48106. Information on 50,000 periodicals from all over the world. Two volumes cover almost all major language publications—2,000 pages—indexed under 223 subject areas covering almost every human endeavor: science, technology, business, humanities, sports; tells whether advertising, book reviews, illustrations, etc., are carried; name and address of publisher; circulation figures; full title; former title (if changed); editor's name; subscription rates; frequency of issue; year first published; languages used in text; where indexed or abstracted; foreign money exchange tables with conversion rates and formulas.

Writer's Market, Writer's Market, 22 East 12th St., Cincinnati, OH 45210. Annual directory for freelance writers, listing over 4,000 publications, including a section on trade, technical, and professional journals. Lists name of editor, address, and type of articles preferred by each publication.

How to Reach Financial Community

Editor & Publisher Annual Syndicate Dictionary, *Editor & Publisher*, 850 Third Ave., New York, NY 10022 (March, 1975 issue). Lists more than 70 nationally syndicated business and financial page features.

Financial Analysis Federation—Membership Direc-

tory, Financial Analysts Federation, Tower Suite, 219 East 42nd St. New York, NY 10017. Lists over 13,000 analysts in the United States and Canada by industry and functional specialty.

Financial Publicists Directory, Investment Dealers' Digest, 150 Broadway, New York, NY 10038. A listing of financial public relations firms, classified according to the publicly owned corporation they serve, whose job it is to answer questions from, and provide data to, the investment fraternity. Issued semi-annually, the survey includes a list of corporations which do not employ "outside" public relations counsel, but which have supplied the name and title of the officer who will answer inquiries.

Investment Companies, Arthur Wiesenberger & Co., 61 Broadway, New York, NY 10006. Annual volume on over 150 open-end and approximately 50 closed-end funds. The book gives the address, background, management objectives, performance data, and holdings of each fund listed, as well as names of top officers.

Register Of Directors & Executives, Standard & Poor's Corp., 345 Hudson St., New York, NY 10014. A Standard & Poor's listing which gives pertinent information on over 216,000 individual officers and directors of corporations.

Security Dealers Of North America, Standard & Poor's Corporation, 345 Hudson St., New York, NY 10014. List, with addresses, description of business and the names of key personnel covering more than 10,000 brokerage, investment, and commercial banking firms in the United States and Canada.

CHAPTER VIII

Trade Shows

Introduction

Unique Promotional Tool

Trade shows are a mass collection of exhibits or booths, each representing a different company. Trade shows are a unique promotional tool because they can expose your firm to thousands of potential customers in a short time. In fact, they are an extension of the oldest method of marketing, or selling, which was based on bartering in the village marketplace. They enable your sales, advertising, promotion, and technical personnel to meet prospective buyers face-to-face. Trade shows will likely be the only time during the year when potential customers come to you. Such a reversal of roles offers unique selling opportunities. But a decision to enter a trade show must be weighed carefully because it involves a commitment to precision planning, hard work, many man-hours, and considerable expense to ensure success.

Trade Shows on the Increase

The number of shows, cost of participation, and gross dollars spent on trade show exhibits increases every year. Annually, there are approximately 5,000 major shows world-wide, plus hundreds at local, county and state levels. The number varies according to the economy and trends in market preferences. For example, several years ago, numerous shows emphasized environmental protection through technology. A few years later, the number of such shows was greatly reduced.

Expenditures on Shows

Company trade show expenditures range from several thousand to fifty thousand dollars or more. This money buys equipment, promotion, attendants, displays, public relations, entertainment, travel, hotels, and other items discussed later under Task 4 (Budgeting). Estimated annual trade show expenditure in the United States is from one to two billion dollars. Exhibitors continually spend such sums because the exposure they gain influences immediate and long-term sales and, ultimately, profits.

Chapter Plan

The thirteen tasks of this chapter are related as shown in the flow chart on page 318 The process begins with an evaluation of trade shows as a marketing tool. Because there is an increasing economy in hiring outside specialists to design, build and deliver exhibits and accessories to a hall, we have emphasized this "vendor" approach. We also cover each planning step involved so you can use your own company's resources if they are suitable. The final tasks, evaluation of results and follow-up of sales leads are especially emphasized to help you benefit most from show participation.

Trade Shows—Chapter VIII Plan

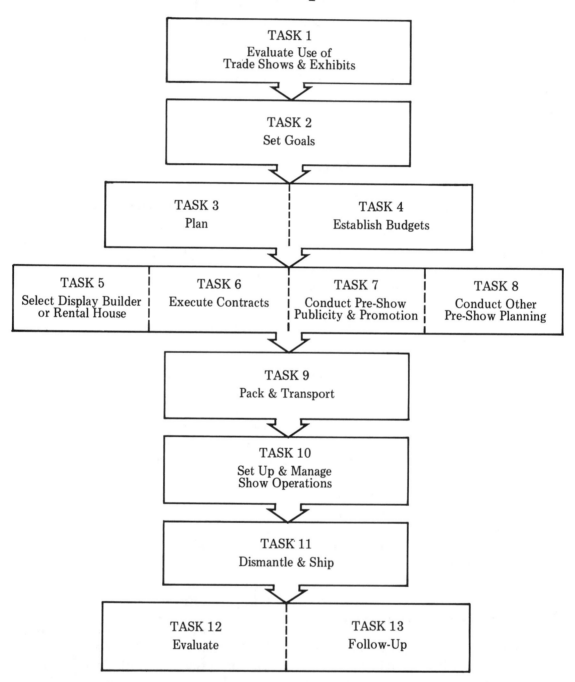

TASK 1
Evaluate Use of
Trade Shows & Exhibits

TASK 2
Set Goals

TASK 3
Plan

TASK 4
Establish Budgets

TASK 5
Select Display Builder
or Rental House

TASK 6
Execute Contracts

TASK 7
Conduct Pre-Show
Publicity & Promotion

TASK 8
Conduct Other
Pre-Show Planning

TASK 9
Pack & Transport

TASK 10
Set Up & Manage
Show Operations

TASK 11
Dismantle & Ship

TASK 12
Evaluate

TASK 13
Follow-Up

Task 1: Evaluate Use of Trade Shows and Exhibits

To Show or Not to Show

This task should help you decide whether to use trade shows as a marketing tool. Start by listing results you hope to achieve by participating in a trade show. But don't expect miracles. For example, simply exhibiting won't solve marketing problems stemming from inadequate, or poorly trained salesmen.

Some Pros and Cons of Trade Shows

Listed here are frequently mentioned pros and cons concerning the use of trade shows as a communications tool.

Pros

Lets you show your company's entry into, or leadership in a market. Reinforces company's image.

Complements activities of regular sales force.

Allows appeals to all senses (sight, sound, touch, taste, smell), thus increasing audience involvement.

Provides opportunity to demonstrate benefits, applications, and competitive advantages. Especially important for products which cannot be easily demonstrated by salesmen.

Directs precise in depth information to interested, qualified buyers, potential buyers and decision-makers.

Generates inquiries and leads for expanding mailing lists and expanding market penetration.

Provides a catalyst for focusing advertising, promotion, and sales staffs on the prime goal of selling products.

Minimizes the cost per sale ($5.00 to $20.00 per sale for trade shows vs. $80 or more for personal sales call).

Enables sales force to make hundreds of contacts in a few days.

Offers unique chance to study industry interest in new or old products by tallying and qualifying names and titles of persons registering in your booth.

Enables your most successful salesmen to work on sales to key firms outside their usual area. (Always staff your booth with top salesmen.)

Cons

Requires time that salesmen, dealers, and distributors would ordinarily spend in the field; extremely time-consuming for advertising, promotion, and key technical personnel.

Produces few new buyers in some cases; often promotes greater familiarity with existing customers who are already "sold."

Increases cost of overall effort (more money might be spent on one show than adding 3–4 salesmen for an entire year) which may be difficult to justify, although cost per sale is lower than personal selling.

Booth attendants must work quickly to make their points with selected visitors.

Often too much time is spent with the competition and the curious, rather than with bonafide buyers (especially when the booth manager is inexperienced or inept).

Sources of Information about Trade Shows

We recommend you review the reference guide to this chapter. Start with *Trade Shows and Exhibits*, by Donald G. Stewart (available from Association of National Advertisers, 115 East 44th Street, New York, NY 10017). This is a handbook on creating, executing and evaluating trade shows and exhibits. It tells you the best way to use shows as a marketing tool. Also, write for a free copy of *Great Show*, containing valuable information on the better use of shows (available from Exhibit Designers and Producers Association, 521 Fifth Avenue, New York, NY 10017). Information on trade shows is also available from various associations and publications.

Task 2: Set Goals

What Can You Accomplish?

Accomplishing specific goals depends on your company's sales-production-distribution mix. Trade show goals are almost self-setting, based on the company's overall goals—such as "maintain or increase market awareness." The prime goal, of course, is to SELL MORE PRODUCTS. Here are some examples of specific trade show goals (i.e., RESULTS to accomplish):

Introduce and demonstrate new products, product-lines, technical services, marketing policies.

Build or expand list of prospective customers.

Enter new sales territories or establish new distribution channels.

Market-test new products for customer acceptance, and desired design changes to improve performance, appearance, and convenience in use.

Stimulate sales, advertising, promotion, and technical personnel to work together more closely.

Bring together key executives, sales personnel, dealers and distributors, for training and promotion conferences in addition to the usual purposes of the show.

Enhance company's image as a viable, participating industry force.

Attract new distributors, representatives, licensees, etc.

After Goal-Setting

When you have clearly defined results you expect your trade show to produce, you are ready to prepare a detailed plan for achieving these results. This is covered in the next task.

Task 3: Planning for Trade Show Participation

Begin Early

Choosing the right show and meticulous planning are the two most important keys to getting what you want from a show. Begin your preparations early—as much as a year ahead for a major exhibition. Many decisions must be made, including booth space assignment, administrative details, assignment of responsibilities, developing a show schedule, developing exhibit concepts, determining work to be done in-house and by outside vendors, advertising and publicity considerations, and making accommodation and transportation arrangements.

Assign Responsibilities

One person should have overall responsibility and authority for planning, coordinating, and implementing the exhibit. This person normally should be a marketing man, preferably from advertising, promotion, or sales departments.

Notify All Persons Concerned

As early as possible, the person in charge should notify all who will participate, either physically or indirectly, regarding planning, preparation, and conduct of the show. Contacts include: marketing managers, product managers, salesmen, public relations staff, advertising and sales executives, key corporate executives, regional managers, engineering and technical personnel, etc.

Each participant should be given a *written* directive outlining his specific responsibilities, with whom he should coordinate, and a schedule of dates by which specific results are desired.

Develop Annual Show Schedule

As early as possible, develop an annual schedule of shows at which you will exhibit. This permits assignment of adequate budgets. Evaluate all major shows so you can exhibit in the right ones, at the right time, and under the most favorable circumstances to support your marketing goals.

Factors to Consider

Choosing the right show is akin to selecting the right media in which to advertise. Here are some major considerations, each of which should be evaluated in relation to your goals:

Markets reached
Attendance
Distribution of visitors by industry
Geographical distribution of visitors
Concurrent competitive shows
Sponsor of show
Technical papers to be presented
Topics of speeches, seminars, workshops
Physical location of exhibit booth relative to auditoriums, entrances, traffic loading docks (not too close—too much traffic; not too far—time and cost), and other key elements.
Ventilation, lighting, utilities, services provided by show sponsors, etc.
Job classifications of attendees

This information can be obtained from the exhibit sponsors who also can provide a show prospectus giving data on cost schedules for various booths, plots showing booth layouts, union labor considerations, setup/teardown times, utility costs, and other pertinent information. Most of the projections about audience makeup are derived from previous show results.

Directories of Shows & Exhibits

The directories in the reference guide to this chapter contain "shopping lists" and demographics of annual exhibits, conventions, and trade shows, from which you can select shows best suited to your goals.

Compile a Trade Show Worksheet and Schedule

After you have assembled and digested all the available information and made a selection of shows best suiting your purposes, list all shows selected on the trade show work sheet provided in this task. Alongside them, add key information corresponding to your needs.

Request a workbook from the management of each show on your list describing services available, restrictions, and additional information valuable in planning your booth.

Develop Rough Concepts of Exhibits and Displays

Next, determine the best mix of products, demonstrations, sales techniques, and sales/technical staff to use at the show. All determinations should focus on the desired objectives, with a tie-in theme related to other advertising, promotions, and to requirements of the overall corporate marketing plan. Specifically, concentrate on achieving maximum impact on attendees while maintaining your company's image. Also, consider the after-show value of your exhibit (e.g., display in dealer showroom, lobby exhibit, etc.).

What Captures Visitor Interest?

Booth visitors prefer seeing an overall layout which:

Is orderly, attractive and meaningful
Conveys a unified concept
Is easily absorbed and understood

Trade Show Worksheet and Schedule

DATES OF SHOWS (Chronologically)	SHOW AND SPONSOR	LOCATION	BOOTH NUMBER	EXPECTED ATTENDANCE	COST BOOTH SPACE	TOTAL BUDGET	Select Builder	Reserve & Pay For Booth	Conduct Pre-Show Promotions	Conduct Other Pre-Show Planning	Pack and Ship Exhibit	Set Up and Manage Show Operation	Dismantle– Ship Exhibit & Equipment	Evaluate Show	Follow-Up Leads

KEY DEADLINES

Is arranged to allow two-way communication with visitors

Visitors expect booth attendants will be:

Interested in being there

Qualified to answer technical and application questions

Familiar with price, delivery, discounts, and service information

Alert, neat, courteous, and well-trained personnel, there for a specific purpose (not merely pretty girls used only to attract attention, unless your product is used by pretty girls)

Visitors like seeing products, live demonstrations, displays and models which:

Are distinct from your prior years' exhibits

Demonstrate benefits, applications flexibility, end results, ease of operation, and performance advantages (concentrate on facts—not abstract superlatives)

Run continuously (to avoid long waits)

Allow attendees to participate, rather than observe static presentations

Cannot normally be shown by field salesmen

Visitors expect you to offer literature which:

Combines technical (i.e., engineering data) and price information (including trade discounts)

Analysis of Alternative Exhibit Styles

EXHIBIT TYPE	ADVANTAGES	LIMITATIONS	DESIGN FLEXIBILITY	EXHIBIT COST	FIELD[1] COST
Self-Contained	□ Packing case unfolds into exhibit. □ Easy to set up, dismantle and pack. □ Few packages to keep track of. □ Minimum space needed.	□ Design is restricted by container configuration. □ Restricted presentation capabilities. □ Damage to packing case damages exhibit itself.	Low to Medium	High	Low
Performance (live talent or demonstration)	□ Increases interest. □ Allows detailed answers to inquiries.	□ Large response at exhibit sometimes reduces ability to identify key buying influences.	High	Low to High	High
Modular	□ Permits interchangeability of elements. □ Allows flexibility in arrangement and size.	□ Many packages to keep track of.	Medium to High	Medium	Medium
Cubic Content	□ Utilizes three dimensions, having properties in the air space over entire area to height of 8' or more. □ Practically eliminates competitive booths from view.	□ High cost	High	High	High
Rental	□ Useful during interim periods of promotion & one-shot shows. □ No storage or expenses between shows. □ Tailor to application.	□ Somewhat inflexible. □ Look-alike exhibit. □ Limited approach.	Medium to High	Medium	Medium
System	□ Series of professionally finished parts. □ Looks customized	□ Other advertisers may use same parts.	Low to Medium	Low to Medium	Medium
Single Use	□ Useful for unique presentations & short campaigns.	□ Ends in scrap. □ Limited budgets.	Low to Medium	Low to High	Low to High
Table Top	□ Ideal for local shows. □ Easy set up □ Simple shipping	□ Not applicable for larger, national shows	Low	Low	Low
Mobile	□ Flexible in pinpointing markets. □ High audience reception. □ Avoids repetitive take downs and set ups.	□ Continuous traveling costs.	Medium	High	High

[1] Freight, drayage, erection, rentals, maintenance, dismantling.

Provides interesting, informative reading

Can be sent to them after the show, reducing the number of items they need to carry around. At the booth, you can show examples of additional literature that can be obtained by filling out an inquiry/request card; this provides sales leads and avoids literature throwaways at the show.

Size and Style

The exhibit size and style should suit your objectives, the type of show, your budget, hall layout, services available, and requirements of products to be displayed. A reputable exhibit design firm or systems rental group will be able to help you make a suitable choice. The Analysis of Alternative Exhibit Styles helps you determine the type of exhibit best for your needs and limitations.

Whatever your decision, you should acquire the artist's pictorial concepts of the booth, and its elements, or scale models of them, to help you visualize how the finished item will look and function.

Task 4: Prepare Budgets

Price the Plan

If your planning has been realistic and complete, you should have little difficulty in pricing each plan element. Be prepared to justify each proposed expenditure with sound reasons, backed by written-out facts, to get management's approval. In practice, parts of this task, and the preceding task, may be accomplished simultaneously; pricing and planning often go hand-in-hand.

Rough Estimates

For planning purposes, you can estimate space rental for your booth at $5 to $25 per square foot—depending on whether the booth is strategically located on main traffic aisles or remote from them. Ultimate costs for a trade show appearance (other than rent) normally range from five to six times space rental charges. For total budget estimates, some firms simply add 5% to last year's budget. A good 8-foot high display likely costs from $150 to $500 per running foot.

Sample Budget Form

A sample budget form for accumulating estimated show expenses is shown here.

Meet with your company's accounting department to ensure your budget form is compatible with the company's chart of accounts (they will assign individual account numbers against which various expenses may be charged).

How to Keep Costs Down

Use simple, clean exhibit designs.

Demonstrate only the most dramatic aspects of your products. Make sales appointments to elaborate upon finer details.

If possible, make modular displays which save time in unpacking and setting up at show sites and save on labor costs.

Use functional and protective crate designs providing versatility and longer exhibit life.

Read carefully the fine print on your service contracts. This may save money and avoid last minute problems.

Avoid overtime charges for construction, assembly, and shipping, through early planning and early submission of service orders.

Reduce last minute, at-the-show exhibit alterations by carefully inspecting its condition before shipment.

Ship your exhibit early enough so it arrives at the show on time.

Use land transportation wherever possible.

Trade Show Budget Form [2]

SHOW:_____

DATE:_____ LOCATION (CITY):_____

SIZE, BOOTH NUMBER & DESCRIPTION OF SPACE:_____

_____

_____

COSTS:

1. Advance Planning
   (rough concepts, schedules) $_____

2. Administrative Assistance (typing, etc.) $_____

3. Exhibit Design (including copy, artists) $_____

4. Exhibit Construction $_____

5. Peripheral Supplies, Badges, Materials & Literature $_____

6. Advertising and Public Relations $_____

7. Packing & Shipping Exhibit:

       a. To Show $_____

       b. From Show $_____ $_____

8. Personnel Transportation, Lodging and Meals $_____

9. Cost of Products to be Displayed $_____

10. Insurance $_____

11. Installation (set up) $_____

12. Booth Space Rental $_____

13. Staff Time (manning, by sales, advertising, and
    technical personnel) $_____

14. Entertaining Guests (exclusive of hospitality room) $_____

15. Services and Rentals:

        a. Furniture $_____

        b. Electric $_____

        c. Telephone $_____

        d. Miscellaneous $_____ $_____

16. Hospitality Room & Related Expenses $_____

17. Dismantling and Refurbishing Exhibit $_____

18. Post-Show Evaluation $_____

                                        TOTAL $_____

---

[2] Using a form such as this helps you develop your trade show budget. Initial estimates may be used for planning purposes, but fairly accurate figures should be obtained for final management approval. A budget form should be prepared for each show that you plan to attend as exhibitor.

If your exhibit arrives too early, show management will help prepare for possible storage by display builder, shipper, drayage house, or at the convention center.

Carry your own tools and supplies. Tool rental is a hassle and building supplies are generally more expensive in show cities. Be careful of union regulations.

If your exhibits are reusable, their costs can be prorated over several shows. Also, consider the cost of storing them between shows.

Before shipping displays, literature, and supplies back to your plant, consider transferring them to local dealers for their use, or to the next show to avoid double shipping costs. If the exhibit goes into storage, keep track of where it is, its condition, and where it can be used in the near future. Shipping and storage schedules should also allow time for booth repairs before the next show.

Task 5: Select and Work with Display Builder or Exhibit Rental Service

In-house vs. Outside Builder

Some exhibits are designed and constructed in-house. However, more effective exhibits usually result when outside experts are used.

Once you establish trade show goals, many firms can assist you in the concept, design, and construction of customized exhibits. They'll also help you with graphics, props, animations, photographs, transparencies, sound equipment, projectors, artwork, and other details. These firms either sell exhibits for permanent use, rent them for one-time use, or lease exhibits for a specified period. Some even install and dismantle booths; set up telephones; provide furniture; consolidate charges for freight, crating, storage, refurbishing, and insurance costs; ensure that you meet city building codes; and provide appropriate electrical outlets that match the hall's voltage level. Many also provide assistance in showroom design, mobile exhibiting, private show planning, dealer displays, sales meetings, and point-of-purchase displays. Allow these firms anywhere from 60—90 days for construction of your exhibit.

In contrast with early trade show days, today most booth rental and design firms offer a wide selection of booths from which to choose. If you are willing to sacrifice in-detail styling and a little flexibility, an exhibit rental/design firm may prove to be an economical choice. Many will tailor a booth to fit your specific product/space requirements for each show. New modular construction techniques make this possible. Most rental firms transport, setup and dismantle your booth, saving you time, money, shipping, and handling costs. All show billing is consolidated in one invoice. Renting can be advantageous in that you are not faced with storage or restoration expenses between shows.

How to Choose

It is important to choose the right exhibit builder—one with talent, experience, and facilities for putting your basic concepts into an effective three-dimensional display suitable to your goals.

First obtain a list of exhibit builders. You can obtain a recommendation from any of the exhibit trade associations. Then carefully study the promotional materials supplied by each company to understand their capabilities. Specifically, you can evaluate exhibit builders by answering the following questions:

What is their estimate of design and construction costs?

Do the majority of the builder's previous clients believe their work is satisfactory? Do all exhibit elements in their samples contribute to telling the desired story?

Is their staff experienced with type of exhibit desired?

Does their work demonstrate knowledge of current state-of-the-art materials, methods, techniques and improvisations, and familiarity with convention hall rules and regulations?

Do they have access to, and arrangements with, vendors in show cities?

You can either prepare drawings and specifications in advance and submit them to several bidders, or you can choose one firm specializing in the type of exhibit you want and have them handle all details.

Work with Builder

Become intimately familiar with the capabilities of the selected firm. Visit their facilities. Show that you are interested. Be humble—not a "know-it-all." Better working relationships often yield better final results. Work closely with the builder. Don't leave the selected firm in the dark. Tell your contacts the precise purpose of the exhibit, products to be emphasized, whether actual products or samples will be shown, and as much precise direction as you can supply.

Listen to the exhibit firm's advice. An experienced builder should easily advise you on layout, electrical and fire codes, labor contracts and what can and cannot be displayed at every major exhibit hall in the United States.

To reduce labor disputes and other problems often arising at shows, consider having the builder handle all details of design, parts assembly, and installation of complete electrical systems, either at the exhibit hall or at the builder's plant. Your electrical engineer should work with the builder to ensure all electrical requirements for your exhibits are satisfied (e.g., sufficient load capacity, outlets).

Miscellaneous Reminders

Design exhibits to convey a single message. In effect, your exhibit is like a magazine advertisement, only three-dimensional.

Order all services and supplies in advance to ensure availability and to avoid overtime charges.

Provide sufficient compressed air and other special supplies, if required.

Design identification signs to be visible at a distance and make sure corporate logo is prominently displayed.

Anticipate need for tools and equipment required for unpacking and setting up exhibit (e.g., hammers, saws, power tools, extension cords, etc.), as well as for product maintenance. Consider union regulations.

Obtain and comply with the list of exhibit hall regulations.

Display only the most interesting items in your product-line, but include enough products to demonstrate the scope of your capabilities. Plan to have a main focal point of interest, with two or more subordinate satellite points complementing the main point.

Task 6: Execute Show Space Contracts

Reservation Form

Have the show sponsor give you a booth space reservation form. This form is designed to guarantee a specific booth location and size. However, executing space contracts involves more than filling in a form. The size and location of the booth are prime considerations. Reservations should be made early to assure space size to accommodate the planned booth. If reservations are made late, you may have to take whatever size is left.

Booth Location

The main consideration in selecting a location is proximity to exhibit hall entrances, exits, and probable traffic flow pattern. Locations near entrances and main traffic arteries will get maximum "exposure," but will cost more. Many companies believe the best bet is in the "main hall" or central area. A smaller booth on a good traffic artery is more valuable from a sales standpoint than a large booth in a relatively obscure location.

Avoid booth locations isolated from main traffic aisles, and avoid "dead ends," congested areas, and bottlenecks. Don't pass up a good location merely to stay away from your competitors' booths. If you do locate near a competitor, your best strategy is to make sure you have a more interesting display and sales story than his.

The best booth locations are normally given to past exhibitors based on the number of years they have exhibited. Aside from this criterion, *the earlier you submit an application, the better your chance of obtaining a prime location.*

Try to select your location a year in advance whenever you plan to exhibit at the same show again. For example, while at a show, its management generally makes available a blueprint of the layout for next year's show. After reviewing the proposed layout, walk the floors and survey all locations which might fit your needs. This on-the-spot evaluation often yields a better site than if the selection was made in your office later.

Task 7: Conduct Pre-Show Promotion

Create Awareness

Pre-show promotion makes your "publics" aware of your participation in a trade show (location of your booth, show dates, etc.). The objectives of these efforts should be to increase: (1) number of visitors to your booth; (2) interest of visitors; and (3) non-visitor interest in your products.

Suggestions

Here are some promotion ideas to help make your show a success:

Prepare for your sales force a printed fact sheet about your company's exhibit and any other participation in show activities. Stimulate salesmen, dealers and distributors with letters and other periodicals telling why the show will help increase sales of the products being shown. Encourage them to "pass the word" to current and potential customers.

Conduct in-house show campaign, displaying notices wherever employee, customer and prospect traffic is greatest.

Promote show in routine correspondence to customers and prospects.

Remind customers and prospects to make early reservations.

Mail show-supplied or custom invitations imprinted with your company's name and booth number to customers and prospects. They should be distributed through general sales and district offices with a cover letter signed by appropriate managers or contacts. Other theme materials, tie-ins and promotional giveaways can motivate customers and prospects to visit your booth.

Include a note about the show and your booth number in trade magazine advertisements appearing a few months before the event. Be aware of all "show" issues which highlight products being introduced.

Send interesting news releases about your company's participation in the show to appropriate trade and industry publications. Emphasize new or improved products and applications to be unveiled at show.

Try to place articles in key trade publications on some unusually interesting aspects of your company's participation in the show. Send color transparencies of your show products to tabloid magazines serving your market. If you've mailed these photos 2–3 months early, they may appear on the tabloid's color

cover the same month the event takes place.

Prepare press kits to leave at show. Dozens of kits are left for members of the press at shows. Some editors take one of everything for later study, while most pick up only those kits offering the best stories. Your kit should gain attention with solid news value, not simply color and design. The headline or lead should be clearly visible at a glance, and the kit easy to open (i.e., not sealed). Inside, place important releases, properly captioned photographs, fact sheets, and if related to the show, data on key executives. Do not include copies of ads and your routine personnel and literature releases.

Task 8: Conduct Other Pre-Show Preparations

Check Lists

Most trade show managements will send you a complete workbook, with step-by-step check lists for pre-show preparations and planning. Some additional suggestions merit mention.

Suggestions

Reserve hotel and hospitality rooms as early as possible. Be specific as to singles and doubles required. Ask for confirmation in writing on space and rates.

Personally visit hall months ahead to check booth area for possible obstructions, beams, pillars, etc. Check storage facilities.

Prepare three-dimensional "elevation" view drawings of equipment and display, including furnishings to help plan and set up the booth. This ensures visibility and "walk-around" space for booth visitors.

Have adequate supplies of product data sheets and literature. Design forms which visitors can use in your booth to

request further data on your products shown.

Prepare information and instruction sheets for all company personnel involved in the show (hall layout and facilities, maps, transportation, telephones, etc.).

Check out all equipment to be used in the show. Have spare supplies on hand, such as bulbs for panel lights, fuses, replacement parts, and demonstration materials.

Inquire of show management how to obtain operating and emergency supplies and services (e.g., electricians and carpenters). Prepare and submit all service orders early in the planning process.

Buy insurance on items not covered by show management (personal liability, theft, property damage, workmen's liability, fire, acts of God).

Be sure to comply with required space prepayment methods to avoid last minute delays. Show managers may prevent you from erecting your booth if proper payment has not been made.

Arrange for ashtrays, wastebaskets, trash disposal, and floor coverings.

Arrange I.D. badges for all booth attendants, key visitors, and determine how, when, and where they'll be distributed.

Have a label imprint machine and marking pens in booth to label company tools, crates, etc.

Prepare emergency plan to use if booth is delayed or lost in shipment.

Prepare "tool kit" with items for emergency repairs, clerical equipment, pads, pencils, extra sales manuals, and housekeeping equipment.

Task 9: Packing and Transport

Who is Responsible?

Your company's exhibit manager is responsible for transporting the booth and related supplies to the hall on schedule. He can make these arrangements through the company's traffic department, or assign this task to the exhibit builder.

Packing/Shipping Pointers

List all booth contents down to the smallest tools. Use this list when dismantling and repacking at end of show.

Make sure crating is adequately strong. A broken or smashed display costs more than the dollars spent in professional packaging.

Minimize the number of crates. It's harder to lose one large case than two or three small ones.

Provide all packing crates and large pieces with means for easy handling (e.g., attachments for slings, eye bolts, and cutouts for handholds), and stamp crates "use no hooks," "this side up," when appropriate.

Make sure that shipping crates will fit through doors, elevators and aisles at the show.

Make certain there is only one shipping label per case, and that all labels are correct. Carefully follow the show-provided directions for addressing shipments. Mark all labels: "Show Material—Do Not Delay." (Remove all old labels.)

Listing true contents may invite pilferage. Instead, use a coding system for packing and marking crates.

Paint crates and boxes with a distinctive color or symbol for quick identification.

Pasting packing instructions inside the lid of each crate saves valuable time later in repacking.

Too many locks may suggest valuable contents—another invitation to theft.

Ship all items at one time to benefit from bulk shipping discounts.

Always plan for a few extra days in transit to protect against unusual carrier delays and ensure meeting "target date" arrival often required at major shows.

Prepay the shipping charges (outgoing and incoming). If you send the shipment collect, chances are the carrier won't put it in the booth until someone pays the charges.

Immediately after you ship the exhibit, send shipping data to the show's receiving agent, to the installer, and to your setup man at the show site. Make sure your setup man has carrier's name, bill of lading number, number of crates, weight of each, etc.

Have someone report to you the minute your exhibit arrives at the show site (or doesn't arrive on time). This may save you time and allow you the time to find your display if it is lost during transit.

At exhibit hall, use security rooms provided by the show management for storing high value items.

Your company representative should arrive at the show prior to arrival of the exhibit shipment. He should supervise setup and other work so as to reduce outside supplier assembly costs. To facilitate locating your shipment, he should have the information listed on the tracing form.

Selecting a Transportation Method

If you build and ship your own exhibits, the transportation chart lists alternatives helpful in determining the best type of carrier. In choosing, consider the nature of

items to be shipped (weight, bulk, fragility), available shipping time, and handling facilities available. To avoid overtime charges, have the carrier deliver the shipment to the hall early in the day on a given date. An early check-in time by the truck driver is the key to "on time" delivery.

Insurance Tracing

Always insure your shipment against possible loss or damage. Record all transporting information so you can trace the shipment in case it's lost. The form on page 332 helps you trace a lost shipment.

Task 10: Set Up and Manage Show Operations

Services Offered by Show Management

Predetermine what kinds of services and suppliers will be available at the show site. The exhibitors' manual provided by show management usually includes order forms for most services. Make all requests weeks in advance. In many cases, shows require you to use their services and none from outside suppliers. The services offered by most show sites are:

Official handler (unloading, receiving, shipping, storing, etc.)—drayage
Decorator (drapery, carpets, furniture, florist, signs)
Photographer
Electrical
Plumbing
Cleaning and waste removal
Telephone

Charges

When ordering labor, remember that a minimum charge of one hour is customary, and double time is charged for all overtime. Overtime is determined by the hour of the day, not by how long someone actually works for you. If any labor disputes arise, go

directly to the show's management. Don't get into an argument on the spot.

Set Up

Designate one person to supervise setting up and dismantling your exhibit. There are several ways to do this:

Have the official contractor and his crew setup and dismantle the exhibit according to your instructions. Because this approach often saves time, as well as overtime for personal supervision, it is widely used.
You, or one of your staff, or a salesman could have these duties. This is a preferred method when your exhibit is extremely complex or technical.
Arrange for your display builder or rental firm to provide a supervisor, hire local labor, or to use a local display builder's services.
Hire an exhibit setup specialist.

Whichever method you employ, provide floor diagrams and color pictures of how the booth is supposed to look when set up. These aids save workers' time and assure proper erection. Make sure all parts are re-

Tracing Form

SHOW: _____ LOCATION _____

A. Carrier	B. Place of Pick Up	C. Date of Pick Up	D. Destination	E. Date of Delivery	F. Freight or Shipment No.	G. Waybill, Airbill, or Bill Of Lading No.
_____	_____	_____	_____	_____	_____	_____
_____	_____	_____	_____	_____	_____	_____
_____	_____	_____	_____	_____	_____	_____
_____	_____	_____	_____	_____	_____	_____
_____	_____	_____	_____	_____	_____	_____

H.   Number of pieces _____ I.   Total weight _____

J.   Number, weight, and description of cases:

Number _____ Weight _____ Description _____

Number _____ Weight _____ Description _____

Number _____ Weight _____ Description _____

Number _____ Weight _____ Description _____

K.   Name and title of person who signed shipping order _____

Transportation Alternatives [3]

METHOD	REQUIRED PACKING	COST	COMMENTS [4]
RAIL	Extensive	Most economical for large shipments over long hauls — lowest average unit costs.	Can be carload or less than carload. Reliable, even in bad weather. Can use cars as warehouses. Damage-reducing packing, bracing, loading and unloading systems are being introduced.
PIGGYBACK	Medium to Extensive	Low fixed tariff by commodity rating. Marked economies for distances of 200 to 500 miles. Save on intervehicle handling. Over 500 miles, boxcar is as economical as piggyback.	Combines rail and overland truck. Can provide pickup and delivery. May be exclusive or mixed load. Might need redistribution in transit. High loss possibilities. Damages are less likely than in boxcars. There is a trend toward container standardization.
RAIL EXPRESS	Medium	Medium	Truck-rail-truck door-to-door service for lighter, smaller items.
HIGHWAY	Medium to Extensive	Medium to expensive	Shorter transit time and flexibility: truck can start when loaded. Low damage rate. "Beck and call" pickup and delivery service.
AIR CARGO	Medium to Extensive	Expensive	Fast. Only light cargo.
AIR EXPRESS	Medium	Very expensive	Some provide door-to-door service. Flexible — many flights. Five times faster than other services. Reduced damage and theft.
DEFERRED AIR FREIGHT	Medium to Extensive	Medium to expensive	Long haul air freight waits available cargo space, usually 1 to 2 days at a reduced rate.
AIR FREIGHT FORWARDERS	Medium to Extensive	Expensive	Pool shipments at a lower rate than normal air express.

[3] This chart helps you evaluate and select a method of transporting your exhibit to the trade show.
[4] Remember, the more people that handle your crates, the greater the chance of late delivery.

moved from crates before they're sent to the storage area.

After the booth is set up, place catalogs and sales literature where they will be accessible to visitors. If the catalogs are bulky and expensive, provide samples in plastic covers for display. Ask interested visitors to fill out a request card if they'd like material sent to them after the show. This procedure prevents waste of promotional literature and also provides you with a prospect list. This is the key to getting sales leads at a show. Handing out literature at the show usually means sales leads are lost forever, or at least they cannot be followed-up immediately by salesmen. Soon after the show closes, send a thank-you note to all inquirers and ask on a reply card if they would like a company representative to call.

Before the show opens, and before each day's operations, all displays should be checked to ensure they are in perfect working order, and that there are adequate quantities of all supplies.

If demonstrations are given, but are not continuous, post a time schedule in a conspicuous spot. Exhibitors often use a simulated clock with movable hands pointing to the time of the next presentation.

Safety Precautions

Adherence to the following safety precautions helps reduce major complications at a show.

Don't leave operating equipment unattended (provide protective devices at all times).

Don't leave "hot" exhibits; even warning signs don't always work.

Don't use demonstrations which cause sparks or flying materials unless properly shielded.

Don't place moving equipment close to aisle—most shows specify all operating equipment must be one foot from aisle.

Don't wait for union man to wipe up a spill. At least throw a rug or paper on it to avoid accidents from slipping.

Don't use electrical cords unless they are taped down full length or run beneath carpets.

Manning the Booth

Anything you can do to make the floor-hours of your staff more productive is to your company's advantage.

Have enough staff—but not too many. This includes thoroughly trained sales personnel to sell, and technical personnel to solve customers' problems and to make effective technical demonstrations. All staff should be selected for their knowledge and ability. Put your best people in the booth; don't rely on trainees. Appoint one man (booth captain) to be *in charge* of each shift during show hours.

Develop and distribute firm written schedules; allow plenty of rest time so that booth personnel are continuously alert. Two to four hour shifts are usually best. Make sure schedules are followed. Know where all personnel are at all times. Have a method for locating anyone, anytime, day or night. Assign specific responsibilities to all staff; one to give demonstrations; another to check literature supplies, etc.

Present favorable impression by not sitting down in the booth (avoids lazy impression); have staff dress conservatively; do not eat in booth; keep booth clean; if you need to smoke a cigarette, take a break.

Listen to staff contacts with visitors to ensure proper presentation, and that leads are written up accurately. Attempt on-the-spot qualification of purchasing potential and record such data on card.

Avoid idle conversation in the booth while potential customers are waiting; don't allow families to use your exhibit as a meeting place; never hold a staff meeting in the booth during show.

Don't corner customers for personal talks in the booth.

If your booth or product-line warrants it, arrange for security guards if not provided by show management. Lock your booth telephone with a dial lock at night to prevent unauthorized long distance calls.

Have each booth attendant see the entire show as soon as possible—especially your competitors' exhibits.

Editors visiting your booth should be given "extra" information in addition to press kits, plus immediate access to available top management, product managers, etc.

Hospitality Rooms

Some firms provide a hospitality room to meet with customers away from the show floor. Improved hospitality can greatly build the image of your company if handled correctly. If possible, establish a theme which relates to the show or your current advertising and promotional campaigns. However, don't plan a suite your company cannot staff or afford.

When you have hospitality rooms, it might be appropriate to instruct your company personnel to use them instead of—or in addition to—other forms of entertainment.

Reservations

If you decide that hospitality rooms will be advantageous, reserve them well in advance. The hotel location should be easily accessible to visitors. The room should be comfortable, well-decorated, and large enough to accommodate all invited guests. If possible, ask for a room into which soft background music can be piped. Always request reservations from the hotel in writing. If the suite is away from hotel headquarters, plan to provide guests transportation to the suite.

Invitations

Announcements, maps, and direction signs must be prepared well in advance of the show. Guests may be invited to hospitality suite events by advance mailings or by personal invitation. Do your best to qualify invitees. The offer of free drinks can attract many individuals who are not bonafide prospects.

The invitation should explain the why, when, and where of the hospitality room. Follow-up your invitations to your best prospects with a letter or phone call a day or so before the trade show.

Supplies

Plan the supply of food, liquid refreshments, and bartenders to meet your expected needs. Always use high-quality, name brands of liquor and other beverages. Always have a more than adequate backup supply. It is better to have some left over than to have to make frantic calls and sit and wait for refills. The hotel can provide the food, liquor, and help (i.e., bartender); or you can provide these yourself. In either case, be prepared to pay a "corkage" charge based on the number of bottles used on the premises. For larger affairs, always employ professional help and get cost/labor agreements in writing. Employment of professional help frees your people for hosting chores. Make sure there are sufficient chairs available.

Personnel

Always staff the hospitality suite with sufficient personnel to handle an expected crowd. If your budget can stand it, assign personnel to the suite other than those working in your booth. One or more of your executives or representatives should act as "official greeter" at the door at all times. The greeter gives attendees his name, asks theirs, and introduces them to someone inside the room. The host should be easily identifiable as such (e.g., with a name tag). Other company personnel should circulate among guests, not slighting any visitors.

Closing Up

Don't keep the suite open for extended hours. Have prearranged signals or a time set so bartenders know when to close the bar. Give everyone a chance at last call, rather then quietly closing the bar and sneaking out. Be as gracious a host as you would be in your own home.

Additional Information

For additional information write "Hospitality Managers," Brown-Foreman Distillers Corp., Box 1080, Louisville, KY 40201, for their brochure and check lists on hospitality rooms (suites).

Task 11: Dismantle and Ship Exhibit and Products

Disposition

The disposition of your exhibit, products, and materials after the show deserves careful thought and attention to avoid damage and loss of valuable articles. As in the setup phase, a supervisor should be in charge of the dismantling and shipment of all articles.

Consult Show Schedule

If your overall planning for exhibiting in several shows during the year has been thorough, you will know exactly how to dispose of your exhibit. To be safe, however, check your show schedule to determine if the exhibit is needed for another show, and when. If the next show is soon, your plans for refurbishing and shipping the exhibit will have to be made accordingly.

Dismantle—Refurbish—Ship

Assign an individual to supervise the dismantling and shipping of your exhibit. A careful count of exhibited products should be made at key stages of the dismantling and packing process to make sure that none are stolen. If refurbishing is needed, the work can be done by a local exhibit builder on contract, or it can be deferred until the exhibit has been returned to your plant. The key criterion governing refurbishing and shipment is whether or not the exhibit will be needed soon for another show.

If another show is scheduled in the near future, you can avoid double shipping charges (i.e., to your plant and back to the next show) by arranging for temporary local storage, either at the shipping or receiving end (depending on availability of facilities). In either case, part of the "slack time" can be used to have refurbishing done.

Some companies try to sell equipment or products directly from the show booth. This process normally occurs on the last day of the show. Such a procedure eliminates shipping equipment and products back to the plant and then to customers.

Cooperate with Union Demands

In cities where there is a strong union, be sure to comply with union demands, regardless of any apparent logical inconsistency. There have been cases where "unfortunate accidents" have occurred where this advice was disregarded. In event of any problems with the union, report all details to the show management as soon as possible.

Task 12: Evaluate Results of Show Participation

Document Your Experience

Regardless of whether your participation in the show was successful or disappointing, document the salient features of your experience for future use.

Post-Show Evaluation [5]

Name of Show _____

Dates _____

Location _____

CRITERIA	ANALYSIS

1. TOTAL SHOW

		Good	Average	Poor	Comments
A.	Attendance				_____
B.	Cooperation of Show Management	☐	☐	☐	_____
C.	Adequate Utilities	☐	☐	☐	_____
D.	Contractors' attitudes, cost and effectiveness	☐	☐	☐	_____
E.	Adequate Storage	☐	☐	☐	_____
F.	Handling of properties between dock and booth.	☐	☐	☐	_____
G.	Adequate Publicity by Show Management	☐	☐	☐	_____

2. YOUR BOOTH

A.	Sales orders	$ _____ Units
B.	Number of valid inquiries	_____
C.	Cost of your booth	$ _____
D.	Number of visitors to booth	_____
E.	Cost per visitor	$ _____ /visitor
F.	Percent of show attendees visiting your booth	_____ %

		Good	Average	Poor	Comments
G.	Content	☐	☐	☐	_____
H.	Use of Space	☐	☐	☐	_____
I.	Image	☐	☐	☐	_____
J.	New and improved products displayed	☐	☐	☐	_____
K.	Competent staff	☐	☐	☐	_____
L.	Location	☐	☐	☐	_____
M.	Sales appeal	☐	☐	☐	_____
N.	Interest created	☐	☐	☐	_____
O.	General booth design	☐	☐	☐	_____
P.	Audience involvement	☐	☐	☐	_____
Q.	Adequate demonstrations	☐	☐	☐	_____
R.	Adequate handouts	☐	☐	☐	_____

[5] Use this (or a similar) form to evaluate your company's participation in a particular trade show or exhibit. Save the form for reference when planning your participation in future shows.

Meet Objectives

You entered the show with certain expectations and goals. The extent to which your goals were fulfilled is the best measure of whether your participation was worthwhile.

Failure to fulfill any goal should be analyzed to determine the reason why. Was it because of inadequate planning? Was it because of disappointing attendance at the show (both in number and in quality)?

At this point ask yourself the questions below. Specifically, what were your tangible marketing accomplishments?

Did you write any new sales orders? Were they from new customers?

Did you meet any new buyers? How would you qualify them as prospects for potential sales in the year ahead?

Approximately how many buyers, possible buyers, and total visitors did your booth attract?

How many product literature request forms were submitted? Were they from new prospects? To what degree did you enlarge your mailing list?

Did your exhibit receive any worthwhile post-show publicity in the trade press (i.e., other than being mentioned in a list of exhibitors)?

If you market-tested any products, were the results encouraging?

What mistakes did you make and how can they be corrected?

Detailed Evaluation

The Post-Show Evaluation form may be used as a check list for documenting your detailed reactions to the show. This will be useful for determining the value of the show in relation to future show programs.

The form lets you evaluate the overall show plus your own booth. It compares and evaluates merits of trade shows as compared with other means of communication.

Show management tabulates total attendance with breakdowns by industry or business, job titles, and geographical location.

Be sure to request such audited accounting of attendance. Counting of wives, exhibitors themselves, and multiple counts for the same attendee (due to leaving the show and then returning) should be eliminated from the totals. Show management can often give you a roster of attendees.

Other evaluations and comments can be added by booth staff, visitors and show management. After the show, get detailed written reports from each person having anything to do with your participation in the show. Allow respondents complete freedom to criticize and make suggestions.

Additional data can be gathered through personal interviews at the show or follow-up mail questionnaires. You must have show management approval to do at-show interviewing. If permission is granted, it is preferable to interview at an exit, out-of-sight of your booth. Always use a trained person to conduct such research.

One approach is to ask a random sample of attendees as they leave: "In your job, are you directly involved in selecting or recommending of suppliers of _____ products? If so, in what way are you involved?" This method tells you what percent of attendees are important to your company.

Another valuable piece of information is booth attendance. You can ask leaving attendees which booths they specifically remember visiting for more than a few minutes. If your booth wasn't mentioned, hand them a card with the names of several exhibitors from your same aisle. Ask the attendee to check those he remembers. As a control, add a company to the list which might logically display at this show, but didn't. This added factor helps separate "guessers" from honest respondents. Studying these research totals gives you a relative measure of how much impact your booth had compared to competitors'.

Other types of analyses and questions may be asked at the show or through a mail survey after the show.

Mail questionnaires can be sent to a random sample of attendees, selecting every "*nth*" name from those registering at the show. This roster is available from show management. If you use a mail questionnaire, send it out soon after the show while memories are fresh. As in personal interviews at the show, limit your questions to those yielding measurable data (i.e., the number of attendees who recall seeing your booth).

Task 13: Post-Show Follow-up

Lead Generation

One key benefit of trade show participation is the number of inquiries, or leads received, in addition to sales. If these leads are not followed up, you're wasting a large part of your trade show dollar.

During the show you should have a supply of multiple part fanfold forms (3-part minimum) for visitors to use in requesting literature, or to have their names put on your mailing list.

Inquiry Handling

After the show, you should immediately fill each request for literature. If you delay too long, your competitor may get his literature to a prospect who visited both company's booths—and you may lose a prospect. Each mailing of literature should be accompanied by a *personal* letter (rather than a form letter); if the number of requests should make this impractical, at least send personal letters to the most interesting prospects.

Send "hot leads" to appropriate sales representative for immediate follow-up calls. A complete description of the inquiry handling process is contained in Chapter XI—Inquiry Handling.

Trade Shows Reference Guide

Guides to Associations

Business/Professional Advertising Association, 205 East 42nd St., New York, NY 10017. Upgrades the exhibit medium as a marketing tool, including sponsorship of an exhibits awards program.

Association Of National Advertisers, ANA Shows and Exhibits Committee, 155 East 44th St., New York, NY 10017. Seeks to improve working relationships between show managers, exhibitors and suppliers of products and services for exhibiting.

Exhibit Designers And Producers Association, 521 Fifth Ave., New York, NY 10017. Sets standards of business opportunities for its members and promotes education in the exhibit medium; provides glossary of exhibit terminology.

Exposition And Conference Council, % IEEE, 155 E. 47th St., New York, NY 10017. Publishes guidelines for audio-visual systems, floor plans, display heights, deposits and refunds for space, security, registration and reporting.

National Association Of Exposition Managers, 1301 Waukegan Road, Suite 204, Glenview, IL 60025. Founded to improve exhibitions and expositions.

National Trade Show Exhibitors Association, 4902 Tollview Dr., Rolling Meadows, IL 60008. Promotes trade show exhibiting by offering study and survey data, and by fostering good relations via interindustry communication.

Directories of Shows and Exhibits

Directory Of Conventions, Bill Communications, Inc., 633 Third Ave., New York, NY 10017. Annual directory of names, dates, scope, number of exhibits, estimated attendance, headquarters, title of event, executive in charge for each convention; classified by industry, geographically, and chronologically.

Exhibit Surveys, Exhibit Surveys, Box 327, Middletown, NJ 07748. Conducts exhibit and audience evaluation surveys on 60 industrial trade shows in the United States, England, France and Germany. A data book—*Show Facts & Trends*—is published which includes demographic data on 50 major trade shows.

Exhibits Schedule, Bill Communications, Inc., 633 Third Ave., New York, NY 10017. Annual directory of names, sites, dates, number of exhibits, sponsoring association, estimated attendance, and trade show manager for virtually every major national and regional trade and industrial show; classified by industry's geographical location, and chronologically.

National Trade Show Exhibitor's Association, 4902 Tollview Dr., Rolling Meadows, IL 60008. Can provide attendance data and show audits on most national trade shows. Facts come direct from exhibiting companies.

Tradeshow, Budd Publications, Inc., 107 S. Tyson Ave., Floral Park, NY 11001. Annual (November) 650-page directory of over 6,500 domestic and international trade shows, fairs, exhibits, expositions; cross-referenced by city and commodity, location, audience analysis, booth sizes and costs, site information. Also includes directory of facilities and services. Purchase includes supplement and subscription to *Exhibit* magazine.

Magazines/Guides

Meetings & Conventions, Ziff-Davis Publishing Co., 1 Park Ave., New York, NY 10016. Monthly publication covers meetings, seminars, conferences, exhibits and conventions. Provides material on techniques of planning and executing meetings and conventions of different types and sizes. The annual January edition—*Gavel*—lists hotels, convention bureaus and halls, hotel and motel chains, show managements, roster of speakers, airlines, associations, audio-visual services, cruise lines, hotel representatives, exhibit builders and show suppliers, and group travel services.

Meetings & Expositions, M-E Communications Corp., 22 Pine St., Morristown, NJ 07690. Published monthly, serves an audience whose job responsibilities include trade shows, expositions, conventions, corporate meetings and incentive travel. Articles cover planning, executions, logistics, and economics of those kind of meetings.

Meeting News, Gralla Publication, 1515 Broadway, New York, NY 10036. Published monthly. Reports the news, trends, ideas, methods and specific locations that affect the work of the meeting planner/director. Main emphasis is on corporate and association meetings & conventions, with substantial coverage also given to trade shows and exposition, privately sponsored educational seminars & incentive travel programs.

Official Meeting Facility Guide, Ziff-Davis Publishing Co., 1 Park Ave., New York, NY 10016. Published semiannually. For corporation, association, & travel agency executives responsible for business meeting, convention and/or incentive travel site selection and transportation planning. Some 50 cities listed with maps and points of interest plus other pertinent facility information.

Tradeshow/Convention Guide, Budd Publications, Inc., P.O. Box 7, New York, NY 10004. Annual publication. For association executives, exposition managers, meeting planners, and exhibitors. Data on facilities available for conventions and trade shows. Also covers information on World-wide and seven-year future period conventions.

Trade Show Exhibit Planning Guide, Guideline Publishing Co., 5 Holmes Rd., Lexington, MA 02173. Guide combines ideas, check lists and step-by-step procedures to help organize the job of exhibit planning.

Direct Mail

Introduction

What is Direct Mail?

Direct mail is a communications tool used to transmit messages (letters, circulars, cards, etc.) via mail to carefully selected individuals. It can be used exclusively, or in harmony with other communications tools, to help reach desired corporate objectives.

Advantages of Direct Mail

Direct mail offers many advantages. For example:

Pinpoints specific market or industry target publics most likely to be interested in the products or services you offer. Segmentation of these groups can be established by industry (SIC), job title, function, ZIP code, size of plant, purchase influence, those who have bought or inquired before, or any other definitive criteria.

Is economical in that your communications dollar becomes highly cost effective because you're reaching only those persons you want to reach. Conversely, when you buy advertising in magazines, charges are based on the publication's total circulation—much of which consists of persons you are not specifically interested in reaching.

Provides flexible timing not available with other media.

Is personalized and confidential.

Communicates complicated and detailed messages in a controlled and explicit manner.

Often reaches more qualified prospects at a lower cost-per-thousand than possible through other media.

Captures readers' attention better because it does not compete with other media (except other companies' direct mail).

Permits flexible and unlimited creative alternatives in terms of production, techniques, copy, novelty, and so on, within the constraints of budget, talent, and U.S. postal regulations.

Permits fast, simple response by recipient via return of enclosed business reply cards or envelopes.

Can provide research data valuable in measuring effectiveness of advertising ideas, regional interest, list selection, interest in offers, etc., before full-scale mailings are made.

Chapter Plan

This chapter describes seven interdependent tasks and various related sub-tasks. You should grasp the overall *concept* of direct mail before jumping into a full-scale campaign. Read the entire chapter quickly to get oriented; then start at the beginning and study each task carefully.

Bear in mind at all times that Task 7, in which you test your mailing list and approach, is the key to a successful direct mail campaign. If the results of the test mailing aren't up to your expectations, it's "back to the drawing board." Are your objectives specific enough? Is your mailing list too broad? Have you aimed at the most likely segment of your market? Is your printed message sufficiently interesting, clear and concise?

A full scale mailing should never be made until your test mailing produces successful results. The test results then can influence other steps in preparing the campaign.

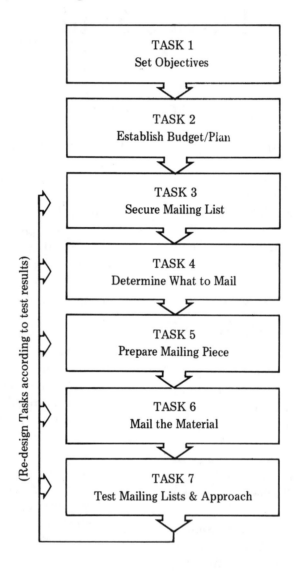

Task 1: Set Objectives

Evaluate Situation

To set proper objectives, first evaluate your company's:

Products (e.g., features, benefits, applications, advantages, disadvantages, acceptance levels)
Pricing structure (e.g., discounts, deals)
Distribution and selling channels
Promotion package (e.g., advertising theme, media, copy)
Policies and reputation
Market (e.g., influences, trends, appeals, buying patterns)
Past experiences
Competitive environment

Select Audience

Direct mail can convey messages to virtually any audience. It can reach your own organization's personnel, the trade, marketplace, or any combination of these. The marketplace audience consists of suspects (potential customers), prospects (those declaring interest), and customers (those who've already bought). First decide which audience you want to reach, then define who constitutes each of these audiences.

Examples of Objectives

Shown below are some typical direct mail objectives.

Supplement selling activities by gaining orders via mail without a sales call.
Obtain a high volume of fresh, qualified sales leads (inquiries) for follow-up by the sales force.
Make customers, suspects and prospects more receptive to sales personnel through preselling and delivery of background materials.
Encourage prospects to visit an exhibit, demonstration, or discussion.
Reach customers and prospects in marginal territories not covered by salesmen or representatives, in areas where customers are difficult to contact on a regular basis.
Welcome new customers, acknowledge orders and payments, and thank customers for their business.
Obtain research data from employees, dealers, and the market for product or market testing.
Inform, teach, and motivate salesmen, dealers, and distributors to greater efforts.
Secure and educate new dealers or distributors and help them promote your products to their prospects and customers.
Inform various publics of any company changes affecting them (e.g., announce new or improved products, key "hidden" qualities of existing products, new policies, or price changes to existing or new markets).
Build employee morale.
Stimulate interest in upcoming events.

Be Specific

Specific, measurable goals must be set before you can determine direct mail program effectiveness. Study the sample objectives above. Then state your objectives in explicit, written form. Suppose you decide more orders is your goal. Then you must compute how many dollars or units of sales are desired. Such steps guide you in planning and budgeting the entire program.

Many variables can influence your specific dollar or unit objectives. Although a 20% desirable result achieved in one year may mean untold profits, in another period it could cause serious cash flow or production problems. If you're not virtually certain of the effect good results will bring, you should at once consult a direct mail specialist. (Contact Direct Mail Advertising Association, or other sources listed in the reference guide to this chapter.)

Task 2: Establish Budget/Plan

Procedure

Before reading further, you already should have pinpointed customers, prospects, buying influences, and specific additional audiences to be reached by your mail campaign. If this has not been done, do it before proceeding further. The next step is to budget your campaign. This requires evaluation of alternative formats, production processes, mailing lists, mail houses, and other elements.

During initial budgeting planning stages, consult with your in-house group or agency public relations, advertising, or marketing specialists. Also, get quotes based on proposed quantities from your printer, engraver, typographer, photographer, paper, binder and envelope supplier, mail house, lettershop, list supplier, and local post office. After rough creative approaches are determined, based on objectives of the individual direct mail item, experts can suggest paper stock, design, trimming, binding, and so on. These last items are usually selected after considering the probable attitudes of persons you want to reach.

Costs largely depend upon how many pieces you're mailing. For example, if you want to achieve total awareness of your company by the 500 key buying influences, you'll need 500 pieces for a single mailing. If you sell a low cost, high volume item via mail, the situation changes somewhat. For example, say you want 100 direct product orders from your mailing, and you guess (from experience) that 1% of all recipients will buy. With this logic then, you must produce and mail 10,000 pieces for the estimated result. Knowing this, ask your printer and mail house to supply cost estimates based on the 10,000 unit amount.

Detailed budgets must accompany each direct mail canpaign. You summarize these individual plans to determine your annual direct mail budget. An example of budget preparation steps for one direct mail campaign is shown on pages 346–347. All items should be estimated regardless of whether tasks are to be done in-house or by a printer, mail house, or lettershop. Review the form, get rough cost estimates from suppliers, then go back and complete the form.

Estimate Effectiveness of Campaign

An important element of any direct mail campaign is judging program effectiveness. In industrial direct mail, effectiveness can be measured by number of responses. Responses can be "requests for more literature," "accepting an invitation to attend a technical seminar," "dollars of sales and profitability," and so on. To further illustrate measurement of campaign effectiveness, let's analyze the profitability factor.

When selling through the mail, you can estimate the total cost of a mailing campaign and compare it with the expected revenue from the sale of goods or services, or with other anticipated returns, and thus estimate whether the operation will be profitable. Better yet, a break-even analysis could be made to get a clearer picture of the profit and loss factors in the campaign.

In the example previously presented, suppose a 10,000 piece mailing campaign costs $5,000. If the expected return is 100 orders (a 1% return), and the sales revenue per order is $80, the total revenue from the campaign would be $8,000—or a gain of $3,000.

On the other hand, if your product sold for only $40 per unit, 100 orders would yield a return of $4,000—resulting in a loss of $1,000. Thus, you can see that a low percentage return on a mailing could be acceptable only if the price of your product is high enough to pay the cost of the mailing, plus the cost of the product, plus the cost of delivering the product, and still yield a suitable profit.

The goal, of course, is to get a higher percentage of orders. A difference of a few percent return one way or the other can mean the difference between profit and loss. For this reason, every reasonable inducement must be used to garner more orders per thousand mailings. To get an order you must *ask for it*, and you must *make it easy* for the prospect to write the order.

After you have developed your direct mail campaign budget(s), the next step is to get a mailing list. This is the subject of the next task.

Task 3: Secure Mailing List

Mailing Lists: a Valuable Asset

A mailing list is a compilation of names and addresses of persons, firms, etc., the selection of which is based on a variety of specific criteria (e.g., industry, job function, location).

Selection is made by concentrating on segments whose subjects possess the greatest number of *concrete* characteristics directly related to your purpose. From a general class of targets you must select those *specific segments* that most likely contain a particular class of people or businesses having certain desirable characteristics relating directly to your product, service, or purpose.

Direct mail success depends on having mailing lists whose targets have been defined as specifically and as concretely as possible. If your offer is mailed to companies which don't or can't use your product, an entire mail campaign will fail.

Once a suitable list has been compiled, it must be continuously updated to keep abreast of the changing addresses and qualities of the target population.

There are various ways to obtain a mailing list. You can compile your own list, trade lists, or parts of lists with others, or rent, or buy a list from a broker, compiler, or publishing house.

Build Your Own List

First, define your target audience (i.e., who has both need and use for your product/service). Then compile a list of the persons in that audience you would like to reach. This may be difficult, but names, etc., can be gleaned from any of the following sources:

Sales, credit, shipping, and warranty card records (for current and former customers)

General correspondence, telephone inquiries, previously received "bingo" or reply cards, inquiries from advertising, publicity, trade shows, contests, premium or sample offers, plus earlier direct mail campaigns

Sales force, dealer, distributor, and service organization reports, recommendations, prospect lists, and invoice records

Employee, stockholder, supplier, and customer recommendations

House organ distribution lists, especially those who have requested they be added as recipients

Directories: telephone, industry, chamber of commerce, financial, and association membership directories (see Chapter I—Marketing Research)

Trade and business publication circulation lists

Government sources

Collection of company and individual names in specific fields appearing in magazines and newspapers. Clipping services can supply these names.

Lists exchanged with other owners

Rent or Buy a List

Virtually every type of business or industry has been segmented into mailing lists

Direct Mail Campaign Budget for One Mailing

NAME OF MAIL PIECE: _____

OBJECTIVE: _____

DATE: _____

PREPARED BY: _____

A. DIRECT EXPENSES

1. Planning/Administrative/Operating
   Salaries (Man-Hours times Hourly Rate) $ _____

2. Creative Costs/Preparations

   a. Copy $ _____

   b. Layout $ _____

   c. Artwork $ _____

   d. Photography/Retouching $ _____

   e. Printing Preparation $ _____

3. Printing/Paper/Materials $ _____

4. Other Enclosures $ _____

5. Envelopes $ _____

6. Mailing List Rental/Purchase $ _____

7. Mailing List Maintenance $ _____

8. Mailing Piece Preparation (folding, collating, inserting,
   labeling, addressing, metering, sorting, tying, etc.) $ _____

9. Postage

   a. Outgoing $ _____

   b. Return $ _____

10. If Selling Merchandise

   a. Cost of Merchandise $ _____

b. Packaging $_____

c. Handling $_____

d. Postage/Shipping $_____

e. Royalties $_____

f. Refunds/Cancellations $_____

g. Refurbish Returns $_____

h. Bad Debts $_____

i. Storage $_____

11. Other $_____

TOTAL DIRECT EXPENSES $_____

B. ALLOCATION OF OVERHEAD EXPENSE

1. Office Space $_____

2. Office Supplies $_____

3. Utilities $_____

4. Maintenance $_____

5. Salaries $_____

6. Travel $_____

7. Accounting $_____

8. Taxes, Licenses $_____

9. Other $_____

TOTAL OVERHEAD EXPENSES $_____

C. TOTAL CAMPAIGN BUDGET (A + B) $_____

D. PLUS 5 - 15% FOR TESTING $_____

E. ADJUSTED TOTAL CAMPAIGN BUDGET (C + D) $_____

347

by someone. It's often easier to rent or buy one of these lists instead of compiling a new one.[1] They are sold or rented by direct mail specialists and priced per name or per thousand names. Charges vary widely depending on selectivity required and difficulty of compilation.

Types of List Suppliers

There are several ways to purchase or rent a mailing list. You can go through a compiler, list house, broker, various publications, or even go "piggyback."

Mailing list firms tailor lists to your specifications, then store them for future use. The compiler uses his company's records, external printed sources, and original research to find desired names and addresses—essentially the same sources used by a company compiling its own list. Although compilers normally sell their lists, some also rent. Be sure to distinguish in your contract between *buy* or *rent* so you'll avoid later disagreements over possible charges for reusing the list.

A *list broker* generally rents lists on a one-time use basis. He is often an agent or middleman between the list owner or compiler and the company seeking mailing lists. The broker normally receives a standard 20% commission from the list owner. Brokers constantly seek new lists to provide list users with updated alternatives.

More and more business publications rent circulation lists for use in direct mail campaigns, broken down by geographical location, job function, SIC, or industry. Several of these publications also provide addressing, labeling, folding, metering, and other mailing services. Some publications offer prescreened lists (e.g., those readers who have

requested copies of specific editorial articles and thereby demonstrated an interest in a particular product category).

Cooperative and "piggyback" mailings offer another less expensive approach. (1) Piggyback mailers can be sent along with your billing statements, with another company's statements, or with a other company's direct mail program. (2) Cooperative mailings are those in which several advertisers mail their messages together to the same logical market or industry. Your appeal, or offer, must be similar in nature to others in the co-op, but not directly competitive. But if companies with questionable reputations use the service, decline its use. It is best to test the co-op before a full-scale mailing (see Task 7). One major drawback to co-op mailings is that you are restricted to a standard size and format. List brokers and compilers can assist you with a co-op mailing.

Procedures

Outline your specific requirements to a broker or compiler and let him do your research and legwork. You should contact the broker or compiler early during planning stages, not at the last minute when you're ready to mail. Give him all information on the product, function, type of user, quantity purchased, price, etc. Specialists can determine which specific list will, or will not, be suitable.

Once your list is compiled and the mailing piece prepared, arrange to ship pieces to the compiler or broker for addressing and mailing. Conversely, pieces may go to the compiler or broker, who then ships the mailing list to a local mail house for processing. The mailer is billed for the list, handling and postage. Be sure to write all instructions and agreements in explicit terms to avoid later disagreements. Receipt of your list, once requested, takes from five days up to three weeks, depending on whether it is a stock or customized list.

---

[1] This statement applies to single or limited mailings. With continuous mail campaigns it it is often less expensive to compile your own list.

Formats

Generally, it's best to address direct mail to an individual, giving his full name, title, company, address, and ZIP code. Names are supplied in a number of formats:

3 x 5, or 4 x 6 index cards—filed by state, city, and name for permanent visual record and distribution to field offices, dealers, or distributors. Additional marketing information can be added to the back of each card. Each card should be dated to show the most recent revision.

Sheet listing for file—similar to cards.

4-across Cheshire labels—heat transfer for direct addressing to envelop or mailing piece; or ungummed for machine affixing; or gummed perforated labels for machine or hand affixing.

4-across pressure-sensitive labels on a sheet for removal and hand affixing.

Computer magnetic tape or punched cards for use on your own computer if frequent mailings are required.

Address plates for machine addressing.

Other Services Offered by Direct Mail Specialists

Many direct mail specialists help in record keeping, computer applications, testing, evaluation, plus various lettershop and mail handling services. Most provide advice on postal service regulations, the use of premiums and incentives or gimmicks to increase the number of responses, and proper timing of mailings. Many guarantee their lists to within 99% accuracy, giving you double postage credit for returns of incorrect addresses.

Source Selection

Source selection is normally based on past experience. If you've never conducted a mail campaign, you can find the names, addresses, and telephone numbers of direct mail list compilers, brokers, and mailing houses in the classified section of most local telephone directories under "Mailing Lists," and "Addressing and Lettershop Services."

Also, the reference guide provides sources of listings of mailing services, brokers, compilers, lettershops, and available lists.

Criteria for Selecting a List

With thousands of lists owned by hundreds of different organizations, naming millions of people, how do you choose among lists that look alike? Generally, a list broker or compiler helps you decide. However, you must ask these questions:

Will the list be customized for your mailing (e.g., prime prospects), or is it a stock list?

Is a complete description of where the list came from available?

Are lists guaranteed available for future follow-up mailings? Are there guaranteed delivery dates and refunds for undeliverables?

Are names provided in convenient form for mailing (e.g., computer letters, pressure-sensitive labels)?

Will test mailing list be representative of full-scale mailing list? Is nth name selection possible (e.g., every 10th name on the list for random sampling)?

Can "dummy" names be used to check deliverability?

Is there legal protection against competitive mailings, and use of the list by compiler for same purpose as this mailing?

Is the list maintained, updated and free of duplicates? When was the list last "cleaned"?

What is the cost per thousand possible contacts? Is a minimum quantity order required?

Maintain the List

Inaccurate and out-of-date lists can ruin an otherwise excellent direct mail campaign. No one likes his or her name or title to be wrong, or for a Miss to be called Mr. People change jobs, titles, responsibilities, locations, companies, retire, quit, or die, while many companies move to another location, merge, or go out of business. The high cost of postage today dramatically reinforces the need to reach the right people at the right place with the right message on the first mailing.

Mailing lists must be systematically reviewed and updated at regular intervals. This can be done by asking salesmen, dealers, and distributors to review lists, or by you comparing them with new directories, phone books, and trade publications. Also, the U.S. Postal Service has several low-cost ways to keep mailing lists current. Reliable list houses, compilers, or brokers can handle list maintenance.

Task 4: Determine What to Mail

What Makes a Good Mailing Package?

What should a good mailing package contain? The correct answer depends on the objective of your program. First of all, you must determine the desired quantity and quality of sales leads. For example, if you want only highly-qualified inquiries, you can eliminate the reply card. This leaves the reader no choice but to write or call you, indicating greater interest. If, in answering the inquiry with a card, you include the alternatives, "Please call me," or "Have a salesman contact me," and the person checks either box, there's little point in continuing to reach this party with direct mail. Instead, do what he asks.

Usual elements in a print-oriented mailing package are outside envelope, letter, enclosures, self-mailer, reply device, and follow-up mail piece. Each of these elements is discussed below. Although these elements are stressed in this section, use your imagination to come up with other unique mailers (e.g., a miniature of your product). Whatever this other element is, make it relevant.

Outside Envelope

Don't neglect the envelope in a direct mail campaign. It makes an initial impression on the secretary who opens the mail. If she has been instructed to discard certain types of direct mail, the recipient may never see your mailing. If he does receive the envelope, it must appear to contain a message worthy of his time. Some mail experts suggest the following for industrial mail program envelopes:

> Use standard size white business envelopes, large enough to contain all enclosures without bulging the envelope. The most commonly used sizes for letters are the No. 10 (4-1/8″ x 9-1/2″) and the No. 6¾ (3-5/8″ x 6-1/2″).
>
> Don't print teasers, illustrations, or offers on the envelope.
>
> Make sure postage is sufficient and properly affixed or metered to avoid embarrassing "postage due" notices annoying to recipients.

Letter

Many experts recommend including a personalized (or computer addressed) letter to take full advantage of the direct mail medium. The letter can be used alone or with other pieces. The letter must offer the recipient a solution to a specific marketing problem he's probably facing. Or, it should satisfy an economic and/or psychological buying need on his part. Such a direct mail letter must be carefully prepared with maximum attention to tone, subject matter, and mechanics.

Contents

Listed below are suggestions mail experts often give for producing strong direct mail letters. In about one minute's reading time, these items should be covered. If not, your mailing piece will likely end up in the waste-basket because you lost the reader's interest.

Always address the piece to the individual by name or title, not "to all customers." (Some situations where names are not available may prevent this.)

Remember, people don't buy products, they buy what the product does for them. So, get to the point. Grab the reader's attention with a benefit-filled opening, or newsy, timely item directly related to *his* job.

Don't simply list features. Instead, immediately stress how the product saves him money, time or effort. Be specific in how he can benefit.

When appropriate, ask a question that provokes the reader to agree with you. Get him on your team (i.e., show thinking similar to his).

Command his attention. Inform him. Show or describe your product or service in use, with believable, truthful, confidence-inspiring *testimonials* and guarantees. Build conviction and desire. Give him specifications and features but "specs" should come last.

Give him a reason to act today. Restate your offer. The offer can be for a salesman to call, for a free estimate, a free sample, a demonstration, a free trial, a discount, a conditional sale, a free gift, guaranteed buy-back, or further printed information. Although such offers generally come near the end of the letter, it is one of the first details to be worked out before any copy is written. In any case, the offer should be clearly stated.

Close by asking for the reader's order or action. The potential for hastening action is one of direct mail's primary advantages over other media. Tell him point-blank what to do (e.g., "send the enclosed reply card for offer"). You might promise a premium or price cut for acting now; or set a time limit on the offer; or note that "supply is limited." Stress time and price.

The call for action should be the last point in the letter.

Tone

Simple, personal, low pressure, sincere, and informal letters generally work best. Pretend you are talking to the reader, rather than sending him a letter. Make the reader feel you have *his* needs in mind. Don't pretend to be more of an expert than the reader in his own business. Be fresh and original.

You can increase the chance of having your mailing piece read if you:

Use personal, friendly and pictorial words.

Use "you," and "your," but don't use "I," "we," and "us" too often. Sentences that begin with "you," and "your," are particularly appealing.

Use vocabulary familiar to the reader's experience.

Use action verbs in present tense and descriptive adjectives and adverbs, but not words like "very," "exceptionally," "extremely," etc.

Avoid abstract words and ideas.

Avoid extravagant clauses, trite sayings and qualifying phrases.

Mechanics

Proper mechanics can increase readership. Good format gains and holds the reader's attention. The following suggestions are helpful:

Personalize each letter with a dateline.

Use short, simple sentences, rather than long, complex ones.

Use impeccable grammar, punctuation, and spelling.

Use a distinctive type face that is legible and easy to read.

Start with a short attention-getting sentence or paragraph; then vary the length of subsequent paragraphs.

Use smooth and logical transitions between paragraphs and ideas expressed.

Use sub-heads, underlining and indentions for emphasis at key points.

Use liberal spacing and margins.

Don't overwrite (e.g., too many words).

Use a second color (e.g., red) sparingly and where it does not tend to cheapen the mailing piece. Some experts claim that the cost of printing the second color cannot be justified on a results-basis; others insist it can be. Good judgment and good taste should be your guide.

Print writer's signature in blue or with bold face to personalize it from a black text.

Appraisal

Letters often need dozens of revisions before being sent. If you answer "no" to any of the questions below, revise your letter, reorganize it, polish it, and revise it over and over until it is as close to perfection as you can make it.

Does the letter give the reader enough information to provoke the desired response? Does it answer all potential questions?

Are only essential facts included?

Have all unnecessary words been eliminated?

Is language clear and easy to understand on the first reading?

Has all factual information been double-checked for accuracy?

Has the letter been proofread by a qualified person for grammatical, spelling and punctuation errors?

Is the letter clean (e.g., no typing errors) and formatted for pleasing appearance?

Have all "ten-dollar" words been replaced by shorter words having the same meaning?

Enclosures

Supplementary enclosures may be used to tell the entire story. The right kind of enclosure can be a great stimulant to response. These may include circulars, folders, brochures, pamphlets, booklets, price lists, advertisement or article reprints, bulletins, catalogs,[2] house organs, and annual reports.

Enclosures should provide the answers to frequently asked questions about product benefits, uses, prices, guarantees, and so on. The story can be further illuminated with photographs, drawings, charts, graphs, and schematics. Sometimes product samples or other unique premiums can be included to excite interest.

Stimulate Enclosure Ideas

The type of enclosure used is limited only by the degree of ingenuity employed by the creator. The alternatives run the gamut from printed novelties (e.g., blotters and calendars) to die-cuts, pop-ups, gadgets, unusual art, containers, and so forth.

You may want to present your message on some unusual stock, or in some unusual shape, size, layout, or design. For example, a firm selling electronic plotting equipment may use graph paper. A firm selling lumber products may use wood veneer. A firm selling electronic data processing equipment may use simulated IBM cards.

There are many other unique approaches. For example, if your product has a relatively low price tag (e.g., under $10), a mail campaign offering a free sample to *key* prospects may increase market penetration. If the product's price prohibits giving samples (e.g., heavy capital equipment), many novel alternatives are available. Perhaps you can develop and offer in your direct mail, a slide calculator that helps the user compute and compare a variety of factors related to his job.

Sweepstakes and prize offers also often motivate recipients to respond. On the other hand, the use of sweepstakes has been criticized as self-defeating, since many respondents may be interested only in winning a prize and not in the product itself. However, many firms using sweepstakes can directly

---

[2] Enclosures such as catalogs and other items are discussed in Chapter X—Other Sales Promotion. See Task 3 for a listing of alternative tools.

relate significant sales increases to use of such programs.

Self-Mailer

Most printed matter can be folded, stapled and mailed without use of an envelope. This approach is used in lieu of letters and enclosures. A sturdy stock is needed to survive the stress of folding and mailing. Adequate space must be allowed for the address, indicia or stamp, and postmark. Check with the local post office for regulations concerning the sizes and thickness of post cards.

Reply Device

A reply device (not necessarily an order form) should normally be included in a mail package. This makes it easy for the reader to act. It should look important. A restatement of the offer and the guarantee should appear on the card. Tests have shown that two-color reply post cards are effective in developing inquiries. Colors should be different from those chosen for the letter and other enclosures. Reply cards which are part of the letter or folder are sometimes less effective than totally separate cards. This is because a hurried reader may say, "it's too much bother," or, "I'll cut it out later." Your job is to make it easy for him to respond, not add to his daily burden. Postage should always be prepaid.

The card should ask the reader only for information you truly need. Some tests show response rates increase dramatically when the self-mailer already includes the reader's name and address, so he does not have to write it out. Reduced effort for the reader often overcomes his inertia not to act.

The use of self-addressed, postage-paid reply envelopes rather than cards sometimes increases the rate of cash orders when *selling* via mail. Do not require prepayment, but ask the prospect to sign the order and say that you will invoice him later. However, on a small unit of sale, prepayment may be advisable. In some cases, you might offer to prepay shipping charges if the customer sends payment in full with his order.

Follow-up Mail Pieces

Multiple or follow-up mailers often increase response rates, but direct mail program costs also increase. People soon forget prior mailings. Successive mailings can refer to previous ones. However, this is not always advisable. Referring to a previous mailing may cause the reader to think, "Why read this one? I read the previous one and rejected the idea." Also, you can't always expect perfect recall on the part of the reader. If the second mailing takes up where the first one left off, be sure that the first one was memorable and the transition apparent. Also, stressing a different appeal and repeating good appeals in a new format with different colors helps increase response rates.

There is no sure-fire formula for determining timing and quantity of follow-up mailings for a specific promotion. For the most part, you'll have to rely on trial and error. One piece of advice can be given for sure: "Don't overmail." The number of mailings generally considered sufficient to convey maximum impact is subject to considerable debate. In some cases, three mailings provide maximum impact. In other cases, up to the fifth and sixth mailings continue to provide additional impact above costs incurred. A recent campaign yielded only 5% return on the first mailing. The second mailing yielded 10%. By the fifth mailing, cumulative returns were close to 50%, with each preceding mailing building a story which eventually resulted in reader action. The number of mailings used in a multiple program always depends on the situation, the story required, and the audience receptivity.

Task 5: Prepare Mailing Piece

In-House or Outside Service

Either your company's graphics/art department or an outside service can prepare your direct mail piece. Outside services include direct mail specialists, art studios, printers, advertising agencies, free lancers, and sales promotion agencies.

The decision to do the job in-house or to go outside depends on the amount and complexity of the job, plus the size and capabilities of the in-house staff, and budget available. If you completely understand your in-house capabilities, limitations, and projected cost levels, the decision is somewhat easier. In many cases, since outside sources specialize in such programs, they can save you time and money. They also can offer a fresh objective view, although you may have to educate them about your company and its products.

If the decision is made to go outside, interview several suppliers. Review samples of their work. Even more important, discuss your problem with the specialist assigned to your account to determine his apparent ability to understand your problem in the context of your company's marketing environment.

After narrowing the field of outside suppliers to two or three, request preliminary estimates for the job, broken down by each stage of work: planning, copy, layout, mechanicals, etc. Usually allow plus or minus 10% for *your* budget.

Production Suggestions

When choosing a production house, consider price, reputation, quality, and reliability. If a direct mail specialist is engaged, he generally selects the production source. But you can offer several suggestions.

Never pit suppliers against each other in the same meeting.

What out for the "low-ball" price from printers or other sources. Although initial cost savings may be substantial, the results can be less than adequate. In general, you get what you pay for.

Consider consolidation of artists, engravers, printers, and paper purchase by using a single source. This saves time, but may cost a slight premium.

Select paper stock to fit the job (e.g., color, weight, coating, texture), and use standard sizes of paper and envelopes for economy.

If the piece to be produced is extremely simple, have a small lettershop prepare it rather than pay higher-cost printers. But remember, quality work must first be proven by the lettershop.

If you have the space and resources to store supplies, buy your paper stock and other major items of material direct from manufacturers in order to avoid printer's markups.

Task 6: Mail the Material

The Alternatives

After the material has been prepared, it can be mailed through your own in-house facilities, or by a commercial lettershop, direct mail house, or mailing service. In this section both methods are described, in addition to pertinent postal regulations and services.

Although mailing is one of the last activities in a direct mail campaign, during initial planning stages, decisions must be made to avoid the later comment from the post office—"Sorry, that can't go through the mail."

Normally at least two mailings will be

required. The first is a test mailing sent to a sample drawn from the entire mailing list (see Task 7). After the results of sample testing are in, a full-scale mailing is made to the remainder of the list. In either case, the mailing techniques described here can be used.

Internal vs. Outside Mailings

Some companies handle their own mailings in-house, but most use a commercial lettershop for folding, collating, inserting, sealing, addressing, metering, and so on. The choice depends on whether the quantity of mailings justifies the purchase and maintenance of required equipment, assignment of personnel to the operation on a full-time basis, and the cost of overhead elements. It can be expensive to do your own mailing if it is a small one with a small possibility of returns. Figure your own costs on a per thousand basis and compare them with those quoted by a lettershop. You may find that unless you mail at least one thousand pieces per week, it will be more economical to use a lettershop.

Internal Equipment Requirements

Considerable equipment will be needed to establish an internal mailing capability. At a bare minimum, you'll need an electric typewriter; duplicator (mimeograph, multigraph, ditto, or offset lithograph); file cabinets; work surface for assembling, wrapping and labeling; postage meter; and a truck or station wagon for transporting mail to the post office.

Advanced mailing facilities also have equipment for folding, inserting, sealing, collating, addressing, labeling, binding, computer robotyping letters, and other equipment.

Suppliers are listed in the Yellow Pages or can be found by referring to associations and directories listed in the reference guide at the end of this chapter.

Lettershops/Mail Houses/Mail Services

Many mail programs are coordinated by mail houses, services, or lettershops. Such firms should be consulted at the very beginning of your planning cycle. They are direct mail consultants familiar with postal rates and regulations, schedules, duplicating, printing, folding, scoring, inserting, sealing, collating, addressing, labeling, stamping, metering, binding, and robotyping (computer) letters. Their suggestions, based on experience, often greatly improve a mail program.

Postal Regulations/Services

Before proceeding with any direct mail campaign, you should familiarize yourself with applicable federal, state and local laws, regulations and services. Such factors constantly change.

Sources of Information

A mailing list broker, compiler, envelope manufacturer, direct mail house, lettershop, local libraries, and most important, your local post office, should be consulted for information and advice on the latest rates, regulations and availability of special services. The following booklets are also helpful. They're available from the U.S. Government Printing Office, Washington, DC 20402.

Combination Mailings (letters and packages)
Directory of International Mail—services & rates to other countries
Directory of Post Offices—lists all post offices, branches and stations in the United States
Domestic Postage Rates and Fees
How to Address Mail
How to Pack and Wrap Parcels for Mailing
How to Prepare Second and Third Class Mailings
Instructions for Mailers—lists regulations, procedures, and rates for mailing service

International Mail
Mailing Permits
National Zip Code Directory—ZIP codes
for each mailing address in the United
States and its possessions
Postal Bulletin—weekly report covering
new regulations and developments in
postal service and mail handling
Postal Laws
Postal Manual—services, rates, fees, pro-
cedures, personnel

Classes of Mail [3]

First class includes wholly or partly written matter, invoices, statements, bills, statements of accounts, letters, postal or private
mailing cards, price lists with written
changes of prices or terms, business reply
mail, printed or duplicated forms with
blanks to be filled in, cancelled or uncan-
celled checks, imitations, reproductions of
handwritten or typewritten matter, and all
other sealed matter. Does not have to be
sealed. Can include airmail up to seven
ounces; also books, periodicals, music manuscript copy accompanying proofsheets or
corrected proofsheets, and drop letters de-
posited for local delivery at an office without
letter carrier service. Rural route carrier collection may be accepted and sent at other
than first class rates. Such mailings are given
priority attention and speedier delivery.
Generally reserved for prestige mailings or
those requiring fast delivery. Higher cost
than other classes.

Second class includes newspapers, magazines, and periodicals issued on a regular
basis from a known office at stated intervals
of at least four times per year. All second
class mail must be marked as such. Special
rates are offered for publications, newspapers, and bulk mailers.

The bulk of direct mail advertising is sent
third class and includes *single mailings* of unsealed greeting cards, printed matter, booklets, catalogs, and books; bulk material of
identical pieces of same type as in single
mailings, plus certain products and mer-

[3] Consult local post office for current rates.

chandise up to 50 pounds or 200 pieces
mailed at one time—textual matter can vary,
but the physical makeup in size and weight
cannot vary; *other matter* such as newslet-
ters, guides, advertising circulars, and self-
mailers which are readily inspectable without unfolding, unstapling, or unwrapping.
Personalized, multigraphed, or otherwise
copied letters with the name of addressee,
handsigned with sender's signature, may be
mailed third class in a minimum quantity of
20 identical copies in unsealed envelopes
which must be presented at the local post office for approval before mailing. Individual
pieces may be up to, but not including, 16
ounces; other than that which is mailable
through first and second classes. Such mail
can be sent unbundled, but may require
separation by post office, state and city. Bulk
postage must be prepaid by precancelled
stamps, permit imprint, meter stamp or in
precancelled government-stamped envelopes.

Fourth class includes parcel post, books,
merchandise, printed matter, 16 ounces or
more but not exceeding 70 pounds. Consult
postmaster for weight and size limits, for exceptions, and for fourth class rates on catalogs and similar advertising matter.

List Maintenance/Checking/Updating

The post office provides several services
helpful in improving deliverability and accuracy of your mailing list.

FIRST CLASS AUTOMATIC FOR-
WARDING: All the first class mail is
forwarded to a new address if one has
been given to the post office by prospective recipients of your mailing
piece. All undeliverable mail is returned to you if you have furnished a
return address on the package. The returned package will show the reason for
nondelivery.
RETURN REQUESTED SERVICE: On
the mailing envelope you can print "Return Requested," "Return Postage
Guaranteed," or "Forwarding and Return Postage Guaranteed," below your

name and address in the upper left-hand corner to specify what you want done with undeliverable mail. All undeliverable third and fourth class mail returned to you is marked "Undeliverable as Addressed" without an explanation of why. Postage at applicable rate is charged and collected upon return to sender. Additional forwarding postage is then collected from the addressee if the mail is forwarded from one post office to another.

ADDRESS CORRECTION SERVICE: The sender can obtain a new address or the reason for undeliverability of a mailing piece by printing "Address Correction Requested" beneath the return address. The post office gives you all available data on the status of the name and address. This service is available for first, third, and fourth class mail at a uniform charge of 10 cents for each notice furnished or piece returned. The service won't correct spelling and title changes.

MAILING LIST CORRECTION SERVICE: The post office corrects mailing lists if individual names and old addresses are submitted on post card size cards—one to a card. Charges are 5 cents per card, with a minimum of $1. The sender's name must appear in the upper left-hand corner of each card. Spelling and title changes are not corrected. Postage is paid at first class rates for handwritten or typed cards, or at third or fourth class rates if names are imprinted by stencils or other mechanical means.

Tips for Mailing

Check your postage scales for accuracy; even small errors can double the cost of postage.

If your mailing piece weighs slightly more than it needs to be, consider trimming to decrease mailing rate per piece.

Don't use the next higher class of mail if a lower one will do.

Attach metered postage tapes or stamps securely to preclude them falling off and causing annoying postage due charges to recipients.

Always use registered mail when the item being mailed has insurable value.

Certified mail with return receipt provides proof of delivery.

ZIP code all mail for better service and faster delivery without any extra cost.

Use metered mail if mailing twelve or more pieces per day. This avoids extra handling and cancelling of stamps at the post office before being sorted.

Save all unused metered postage (e.g., spoiled tapes and envelopes with metered postage) for redemption at 90% of face value at the local post office.

Notify the lost post office before executing large or special mailings. They can make suggestions to speed and improve your mailing and also make appropriate handling preparations.

Save money by weighing bulk postage by the pound, not the piece. Contact your local post office for information on bulk mailing.

Mail early to meet dispatching schedules set by the local post office.

Mail from the main branch within your city to avoid intra-city post office transfers before shipment to destination.

Avoid fraudulent use of the mails (e.g., misleading claims) which may lead to prosecution and loss of mailing privileges.

If products are sold through the mail, obtain information about the Federal Food, Drug & Cosmetics Act provisions pertaining to standards for products (FDA, Washington, DC 20250); and additional information from your state Tax Commission to see if sales or use taxes need to be added to retail price of merchandise.

Use "business reply mail" when requesting recipient to inquire or take other action. Obtain Form 3614 from the local post office—"Application to Distribute

Business Reply Cards, Envelopes and Labels." After being granted such a permit, you can print envelopes, cards and labels with a "postage to be paid by" above your name. Postage need not be prepaid—it is collected on each piece of business reply mail at the time it is delivered, with a postage due bill or Form 3582-A affixed.

Task 7: Test Mailing Lists and Approach

Why Test?

Before committing yourself to the expense of a full-scale mailing to your entire mailing list, it is advisable to make a sample mailing to test the drawing power of the list itself, as well as other aspects of the mailing. By following certain rules based on the science of statistical sampling, tests can yield reliable data to use in predicting the probable results to expect from the larger mailing. Direct mail specialists suggest that 5% to 15% of your direct mail budget may be allocated to finance the tests.

What Elements to Test

The effectiveness of the mailing list should always be pretested before making a full-scale mailing. In addition, other elements of the entire mailing package that might be appropriate for testing are listed below. Many of these elements could be tested in small scale pilot tests before testing the mailing list itself.

Mailing list
Offer (price, terms of payment, product, premiums offered)
Copy (headlines, appeals, themes)
Layout (format, colors, artwork)
Timing (date and season of offer)
Enclosures
Envelopes
Reply devices
Type of postage employed
Complete package

How to Test

Know exactly what you want each test to accomplish. Then develop your own test or have a direct mail house or specialist assist you.

Keep all factors the same except the one being tested, or test the entire package. For example, the same offer, copy, layout, and timing can be used to test which of two mailing lists works best. The same layout and timing can be used with one list to test which of two copy offers works best.

Some mailers test two or more complete packages—each package having some element that differs from a corresponding element in the other packages. Although such tests can indicate which package yielded the best results, they can't isolate the reasons for the better performance.

How Large a Sample Should be Tested?

The statistical reliability of the test results depends on the size of the sample test mailing—not on the size of the whole list being tested. Sampling errors are more frequent in small test mailings than for large ones.

The size of the test sample depends on the expected response percentage of the whole mailing. For example, a small rate of return can be acceptable if the price of the product offered is sufficiently high.

According to one authority, the minimum number of responses needed to evaluate a sample test mailing is about 40. Thus, if you expect a return of only 1% (based on prior experience or on an educated guess), you would need a test sample containing 4,000 names (40 divided by 0.01) to get 40 responses. On the other hand, if you expected a return of 4%, your test sample would need only 1,000 names (40 responses divided by 0.04). In each case, the indicated test samples would be adequate regardless of the size of the whole list of names, which could range anywhere from 10,000 names to hundreds of thousands of names. This is one of the most astonishing facts of sampling theory—a fact which many laymen find almost impossible to believe.

Choosing the Best Mailing List

Suppose you have a choice between two different mailing lists, each offered by a different broker to accomplish a common purpose. To determine which list would be most productive, test each and choose the best one. Because the two lists might contain a number of duplicate names, ask one broker to provide you with a random selection of 4,000 names (based on the first example in the preceding paragraph) taken from the first half of the alphabet—A through M. Have the other broker provide a similar sample of 4,000 names taken from the remaining half of the alphabet. The statistical assumption here is that each sample will be representative of the total population of names in the whole mailing list offered by each broker.

Now, make *identical* test mailings to each of the two sample lists. When the results are in, you can select the list that produced the best results. Or can you?

What if one list yielded a return of 45 responses (1.13% of 4,000), and the other list produced 52 responses (1.30% of 4,000)? A quick calculation will show that 1.3% is over 15% greater than 1.13%, which would naturally lead one to conclude that the second list was more effective. Is it really?

In this instance, the difference is really significant, and the list that yielded 52 responses is actually a more effective list than the first. But you can't always assume that the list which yields a higher percentage of responses is really the better of the two. Bear in mind that both lists were samples drawn from larger lists. And whenever you deal with samples, you always encounter sampling errors.

To compare two sample percentages—as in the preceding example—requires statistical processes for the "testing of hypotheses," and these processes are beyond the scope of this book. But the processes are important because the sample which yields a higher percentage of responses under certain conditions may not necessarily be superior to a competing sample. The samples may be equally effective, and the differences resulting from tests could have resulted only from sampling errors.

So what can you do under these circumstances? For one thing, you could take the problem to your marketing research department if your company has one, and if it has the services of a mathematician who knows how to test statistical hypotheses. Or you could engage the services of a consultant who is experienced in such matters. Finally, if your own background includes a course in statistics, you could consult a book on statistical method and brush up enough to make your own tests of statistical significance. One excellent book on the subject is *Statistical Techniques in Market Research*, by Robert Ferber, McGraw-Hill (1949), Chapter V.

Drawing a Random Sample for Test Mailing

Suppose you had to draw a random sample of 4,000 names from a mailing list that contained 80,000 names. How can this be done in a simple, direct, and inexpensive way? A true random sample is one in which every name has an equal chance of being selected. This requirement can be met by selecting every "nth" name from the list. In the present case, it would be every 20th name (80,000 divided by 4,000). This is called "systematic sampling."

To use the nth name method, a random starting point is needed. A simple way to achieve this is to write the numbers from one to ten on equal sized slips of paper, put them in a container, shake them, and draw a slip.

If the names on the list are uniformly spaced, instead of counting off every 20 names, you could make two marks 20 names apart on a card, and use it for measuring 20 names at a time. If the list is on index cards, select a starting point by drawing a number at random. Then make two marks on a card to use in measuring every 20 cards in the stack or file drawer. Using this method you won't always select the exact 20th card, but the results will be acceptable for all practical purposes.

For other methods of drawing a random sample from a larger population, refer to a textbook on statistical methods.

Keep Records

Keep records to show which of the elements listed at the beginning of this task performed best when tested. A form similar to the one presented below can be used for this purpose. It can be modified to fit your special needs if it is not suitable in its present form.

Column (1) is simply a number system for identifying different tests. For example, test number 1 may be a check of price; test number 2 may be a check of lists; test number 3 may be a test of copy; and so on, with each test being conducted independently and preferably over different time periods.

Column (2) is used to record how the test elements were varied. Although only two spaces are provided for alternatives in each test, the number may be increased if desired. For example, test 1, which may be a check of price, might be $39.50 or $49.50 or $59.50. In this case, space for three alternatives is required in column (2), rather than the two spaces shown. In any case, some record must be kept to distinguish which variable (e.g., price) produced the best results. If reply cards are to be returned by the recipient of your mailing piece, different color ink or paper stock can be used to code the elements being tested.

In column (3), write the number of pieces mailed, in thousands, for each test element. In column (4), write the cost per thousand pieces for each test element. Unless the list price or creative approach and production costs vary, the figures in both columns (3) and (4) will always remain the same (e.g., if price is being tested, all other costs remain constant). In column (5) write the product of columns (3) and (4).

In column (6), record the number of re-

Test Mail Campaign Record Keeper

(1) TEST NUMBER	(2) TEST ELEMENT	(3) NUMBER OF PIECES MAILED (Thousands)	(4) COST PER THOUSAND (Cost of List, Postage, Mailing Piece)	(5) TOTAL COST: COLUMN (3) x COLUMN (4)	(6) RESPONSES (Inquiries, Sales, Visits)	(7) COST PER RESPONSE COLUMN (5) ÷ COLUMN (6)	(8) COMMENTS
1	#1						
	#2						
2	#1						
	#2						
3	#1						
	#2						
4	#1						
	#2						
5	#1						
	#2						
6	#1						
	#2						
7	#1						
	#2						
8	#1						
	#2						
9	#1						
	#2						
10	#1						
	#2						

sponses produced by each alternative test element listed in column (2). Then determine the cost per response [column (5) divided by (6)], and enter the result in column (7) for analysis.

Column (8) is for brief comments or for your evaluations of the test results for alternative test elements.

Project Test Results to the Full-scale Mailing

When the results of the test mailing have been derived, they can be projected to estimate the results you will probably get from the full-scale mailing. The table on the following page is used for this purpose. It is based on statistical theory for a 95% confidence level. This means that 95 times out of 100 the true results of the full-scale mailing will lie within the percentage ranges given in the table (provided that the test mailing was a random sample truly representative of the whole mailing list).

To use the table, in the left column find the size of the test mailing. On this line, under the column for percent return on the test mailing, find the percentage range within which the results of the whole mailing will lie.

For example: if you test-mailed 3,000 pieces, received a return of 2%, and your whole list includes 20,000 names, the return from the whole mailing will lie somewhere between 1.50% and 2.50% of 20,000—or between 300 and 500 responses.

When you make the full-scale mailing to the remainder of the mailing list (i.e., less the test mail addresses), be sure that every detail of this mailing is "identical" to the methods used in the test mailing. Otherwise, the projection made using the table will not be valid.

Conduct Readership Tests

Readership of your mailing piece is generally not quite as important as achieving sales or other desired actions. However, many mailers conduct follow-up readership tests to ask recipients whether they have read the material, what they did with it, why they didn't respond, and to explore recipients' attitudes toward the company and its products.

A complete discussion of these techniques is contained in Chapter I—Marketing Research, and Chapter VI—Advertising. Some brief comments may be appropriate at this point. Industrial direct mail readership tests are most often conducted by mail, and sometimes by telephone. These tests should be scheduled between three and five weeks after initial mailings. Before three weeks, the recipient may still intend to act, but has not yet been able to do so. After five weeks, there is a good chance that the recipient has completely forgotten about your mailing piece.

If a mail readership test is used, you can select a random sample of names from the original mailing, and mail them a small reproduction of the original mailing. One frequently used approach is to note, "The attached letter was recently mailed to you. To help us provide more useful data in the future, we would appreciate it if you would do us a favor and answer the following questions."

1. Do you remember receiving the attached mailing piece?
   ☐ Yes   ☐ No
2. If yes, did you:
   ☐ Read most of it?
   ☐ Read some of it?
   ☐ Read none of it?
3. Did you:
   ☐ Throw it away?
   ☐ Save it for reference?
   ☐ Route to others?
   ☐ Buy this product?
   ☐ Buy from a competitor?

Future Mailings

Current mailings often build the groundwork for future mailings (i.e., those who purchase this time can be added to future mailing lists). Those who bought your prod-

Projecting the Results of Test Mailings with the Aid of Probability Theory [4]

IF THE PERCENT RETURN ON THE TEST MAILING IS:

THEN 95 TIMES OUT OF 100, THE PERCENT RETURN ON AN IDENTICAL MAILING TO THE WHOLE MAILING LIST WILL BE BETWEEN:

SIZE OF TEST MAILING	1%	2%	3%	4%	5%	6%	7%	8%	9%	10%	15%	20%
100	0-2.95	0-4.74	0-6.34	0.16-7.84	0.73-9.27	1.35-10.65	2.00-12.00	2.68-13.32	3.39-14.61	4.12-15.88	8.00-22.00	12.16-27.84
250	0-2.23	0.26-3.74	0.89-5.11	1.57-6.43	2.30-7.70	3.06-8.94	3.84-10.16	4.64-11.36	5.45-12.55	6.28-13.72	10.57-19.43	15.04-24.96
500	0.13-1.87	0.77-3.23	1.50-4.50	2.28-5.72	3.09-6.91	3.92-8.08	4.76-9.24	5.62-10.38	6.49-11.51	7.37-12.63	11.87-18.13	16.49-23.51
1,000	0.38-1.62	1.13-2.87	1.94-4.06	2.79-5.21	3.65-6.35	4.53-7.47	5.42-8.58	6.32-9.68	7.23-10.77	8.14-11.86	12.79-17.21	17.52-22.48
2,000	0.56-1.44	1.39-2.61	2.25-3.75	3.14-4.86	4.04-5.96	4.96-7.04	5.88-8.12	6.81-9.19	7.75-10.25	8.69-11.31	13.44-16.56	18.25-21.75
3,000	0.64-1.36	1.50-2.50	2.39-3.61	3.30-4.70	4.22-5.78	5.15-6.85	6.09-7.91	7.03-8.97	7.98-10.02	8.93-11.07	13.72-16.28	18.57-21.43
4,000	0.69-1.31	1.57-2.43	2.47-3.53	3.39-4.61	4.32-5.68	5.26-6.74	6.21-7.79	7.16-8.84	8.11-9.89	9.07-10.93	13.89-16.11	18.76-21.24
5,000	0.72-1.28	1.61-2.39	2.53-3.47	3.46-4.54	4.40-5.60	5.34-6.66	6.29-7.71	7.25-8.75	8.21-9.79	9.17-10.83	14.01-15.99	18.89-21.11
6,000	0.75-1.25	1.65-2.35	2.57-3.43	3.50-4.50	4.45-5.55	5.40-6.60	6.35-7.65	7.31-8.69	8.28-9.72	9.24-10.76	14.10-15.90	18.99-21.01
7,000	0.77-1.23	1.67-2.33	2.60-3.40	3.54-4.46	4.49-5.51	5.44-6.56	6.40-7.60	7.36-8.64	8.33-9.67	9.30-10.70	14.16-15.84	19.06-20.94
8,000	0.78-1.22	1.69-2.31	2.63-3.37	3.57-4.43	4.52-5.48	5.48-6.52	6.44-7.56	7.41-8.59	8.37-9.63	9.34-10.66	14.22-15.78	19.12-20.88
9,000	0.79-1.21	1.71-2.29	2.65-3.35	3.60-4.40	4.55-5.45	5.51-6.49	6.47-7.53	7.44-8.56	8.41-9.59	9.38-10.62	14.26-15.74	19.17-20.83
10,000	0.81-1.20	1.73-2.27	2.67-3.33	3.62-4.38	4.57-5.43	5.53-6.47	6.50-7.50	7.47-8.53	8.44-9.56	9.41-10.59	14.30-15.70	19.22-20.78

[4] Tabular computations by Forrest C. Allen

uct when you offered a free gift as an incentive may not buy again unless you continue to offer gifts. Those who bought your product when you allowed liberal credit terms may not buy again if you offer only cash deals. Remember, given offers attract different types of customers.

Direct Mail in a Nutshell

Know exactly what you want each direct mail program to accomplish. Then develop realistic, profit-oriented plans and budgets to achieve your goals.

Divide and conquer. Define the exact market segments you must reach in terms of specific needs, interest, and concrete characteristics. Develop or procure mailing lists tailored to these specifications.

Industries are composed of people. Direct your sales appeal to them. Keep it interesting, simple, and to the point. Sell the benefits of your product or service. Ask for the order and make it easy to order.

Use sampling test techniques to evaluate mailing lists and the key elements of your total approach. When you find a combination of elements that produces successful results, stay with it—don't change one iota of a proven success pattern.

In testing, never lose sight of your basic goals. Keep records of methods, results, and costs. Don't over-test—each test should be worth its cost.

Direct Mail Reference Guide

Direct Mail Associations

Associated Third Class Mail Users, 1725 K St. N.W., Washington, DC 20006.

Business/Professional Advertising Association, 205 E. 42nd St., New York, NY 10017.

Direct Mail Marketing Association, 6 E. 43rd St., New York, NY 10017.

Mail Advertising Service Association International, 7315 Wisconsin Ave., Suite 818E, Washington, DC 20014.

Mailing List Brokers Professional Association, 541 Lexington Ave., New York, NY 10022.

Books and Reports

Building And Maintaining Industrial Direct Mail Lists, Report #10, Center for Marketing Communications, P.O. Box 411, 575 Ewing St., Princeton, NJ 08540.

Direct Mail And Mail Order Handbook, R. Hodgson, Dartnell Corporation, 4660 Ravenswood Ave., Chicago, IL 60640.

Direct Mail Design International, Raymond A. Ballinger, Reinhold Publishing Corp., 430 Park Ave., New York, NY 10022.

Direct Mail Idea Library, National Research Bureau, Inc., 424 N. 3rd St., Burlington, IA 52601

Handbook Of Industrial Direct Mail Advertising, Business/Professional Advertising Association, 205 E. 42nd St., New York, NY 10017.

How To Produce Successful Direct Mail Campaigns, Peter L. Shugart, Box 566, South Pasadena, CA 91030.

How To Start And Operate A Mail-order Business, J. Simon, McGraw-Hill Book Co., Inc., 1221 Avenue of the Americas, New York, NY 10020.

How To Think About Industrial Direct Mail, Hoke Publishing Co., 224 Seventh St., Garden City, NY 11530.

How To Win Success In The Mail Order Business, Arco Publishing Co., Inc., 219 Park Ave. South, New York, NY 10003.

144 Ways To Sell Printing By Mail, C. Owen Brantly, North American Publishing Co., 134 N. 13th St., Philadelphia, PA 19107.

Planning And Creating Better Direct Mail, J. Yeck and J. Maguire, McGraw-Hill Book Co., Inc., 1221 Avenue of the Americas, New York, NY 10020.

Printing And Promotion Handbook, D. Melcher & N. Larrick, McGraw-Hill Book Co., Inc., 1221 Avenue of the Americas, New York, NY 10020.

Successful Direct Mail Advertising And Selling, R. Stone, Prentice-Hall, Inc., 70 Fifth Ave., New York, NY 10011 (out of print).

Directories

Directory Of Mailing List Houses, B. Klein & Co., 27 East 22nd St., New York, NY 10010.

National Mailing List Houses, Small Business Bibliography No. 29, U.S. Small Business Administration, Washington, DC 20416, or local field office (see telephone directory).

Purchasing Guide To Direct Mail Advertising, Mail Advertising Service Association International, 7315 Wisconsin Ave., Suite 818E, Washington, DC 20014.

Standard Rate & Data Service—Direct Mail List Rates And Data, 5201 Old Orchard Rd., Skokie, IL 60076.

Magazines

Advertising Age, Crain Communications, Inc., 740 N. Rush St., Chicago, IL 60611.

Direct Marketing (formerly *Reporter Of Direct Mail Advertising*), Hoke Publishing Co., 224 Seventh St., Garden City, NY 11530.

CHAPTER
X

Other Sales Promotion

Introduction

What is Sales Promotion? [1]

In many marketing textbooks, the term "sales promotion" includes advertising, personal selling, product publicity, and trade shows. In this book, however, each of these subjects is covered in individual chapters. We do this to parallel the way many of today's firms set up separate departments to handle advertising, trade shows, public relations, and sales, with a separate group established to administer sales promotion. This group assists the other departments in achieving their objectives.

The distinction between the various tools is adroitly explained by Stanley L. Goodman, of EGR Communications, Inc.—a leading sales promotion agency in New York:

> In advertising, you use the existing media as a channel of communication to carry your message. In public relations, you use the news segment of those same media. In sales promotion, you create the appropriate media. [2]

Thus, sales promotion includes specifically designed, paid forms of communication such as direct mail, literature (manuals, catalogs, product flyers, price sheets, and brochures), incentives, special events, sales contests, audio-visual presentations, sales aids, plus many other tools. All of these tools are designed to stimulate audience interest and acceptance of a product or service.

Billions of dollars are spent annually on tools used to stimulate purchases of a company's products. These tools are most frequently used to motivate customers and prospects. They can also be used to motivate or assist sales management, salesmen, and/or middlemen to push products and services through the distribution process. In some cases sales promotion tools are used to influence public officials and other non-buying publics.

Chapter Plan

This chapter describes the tasks involved in the sales promotion process. The planning task, which describes a general procedure for developing any promotional program, also includes a list of twenty-nine ideas (i.e., tools) that can help you develop your own campaign.

Although each of these tools could be regarded as a "task" in the sales promotion process, the use of most is so obvious that any instructions would be superfluous. However, the four most widely used

[1] John C. Aspley, *Sales Promotion Handbook*, Dartnell Corporation, 4660 Ravenswood Ave., Chicago, IL 60640.
[2] Martin Everett, "From Brass to Class," *Sales Management* (November 1, 1971), p. 21, Sales Management, 633 Third Ave., New York, NY 10017.

items—sales contests, catalog preparation, advertising specialties, and audio-visual aids—involve some difficulties if not properly developed. Consequently, these four tools are discussed in some detail in Tasks 5 through 8 of this chapter.

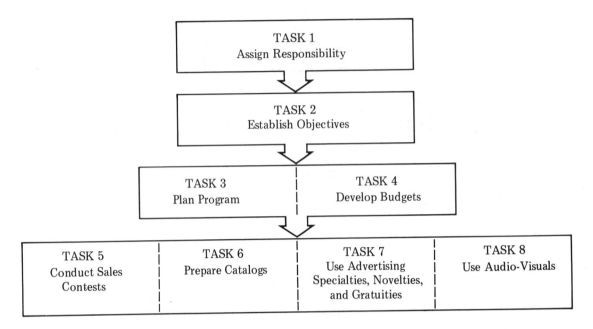

Task 1: Assign Responsibility

Who is Responsible?

In small or new companies, economics generally require responsibility for all advertising, public relations, trade shows, and sales promotion to fall to one person or department. As companies grow, specialized departments are usually established. In some cases, sales promotion becomes a subdepartment within the advertising department, although separation of the functions is more common.

Whatever the organization, be sure that the assignment of responsibility is accurately defined, the degree of responsibility is established (i.e., planning, recommending, executing, budgeting, etc.), the approval cycle agreed upon, and access to sources of information and guidance provided.

Task 2: Establish Objectives

Set Clear Supportive Objectives

Sales promotion is a supplement to the traditional marketing communications tools of advertising, sales, public relations, trade shows, etc. Hence, sales promotion objectives—which normally may be established for an entire year—must be designed to support, coordinate, and assist these functions in achieving their respective objectives. Because of the supporting nature of sales promotion objectives, they must be developed in close coordination with members of other departments and the marketing team.

Examples

Sales promotion objectives can be quantitative or qualitative. They can be directed toward a company's own sales force and management, its industry and trade channels, or to purchasers and end-users of a product. In any case, sales promotion should support key marketing objectives. Some examples of sales promotion objectives are:

Increase distribution of a product, line, or model.

Dispose of inventories currently held by the company's distribution channels in order to make room for new products.

Broaden customer base through initial customer usage of a product, leading to repurchase based on satisfaction.

Introduce a new image, logo, or product; major improvement in established product; or new uses for existing products.

Improve competitive standing of an already accepted product.

Encourage existing trade channels to speedily accept new product.

Amplify results of concurrent advertising campaign.

Increase customer and trade channel awareness of product's existence, characteristics, prices, and availability.

Create favorable psychological attitudes toward product.

Add value to the product by expanding utility or improving image.

Supplement and/or counteract price competition (e.g., through offer of a premium).

Increase trade channel and customer goodwill toward company.

Provide promotional tools to increase salesmen's effectiveness.

When Not to Use Sales Promotion

There are times when sales promotion does not work effectively. For example, sales promotions:

Rarely work more than once for inadequate or overpriced products.

Rarely help a product with poor distribution channels.

Are not always effective in selling products out-of-season.

Rarely work overnight.

May so increase the cost of the product that investment might better be spent on improving service, lowering prices or increasing quality.

May be too costly when attempting to reach a large multi-public audience.

Generally are not very effective on established brands with declining market share.

Are generally not very effective on established brands unless new product changes are introduced.

Rarely succeed without the support of other marketing functions.

Are not effective against competitive promotions which are comparatively more elaborate, frequent or intensive.

Task 3: Plan Program

Team Effort

Planning sales promotions requires a team effort. Managers from advertising, public relations, trade shows, and sales departments should be consulted, as well as any product or brand managers. The team approach ensures that sales promotion programs are consistent and integrated with other marketing efforts. Plans should include year-long campaigns, special target programs, and anticipated opportunities, as well as possible contingency programs to counteract potential competitive developments.

If a sales promotion agency is to be used, contact them early in the planning cycle. Their suggestions may improve the entire development of your program.

Planning Steps

A sales promotion manager has considerable direct control over his programs. To benefit from this control, he should follow the planning steps listed below, each step being consistent with objectives established in Task 2:

STEP 1—Identify and describe select market segments to become targets of the sales promotion campaign. Include information about target market habits, characteristics, wants and needs. Also identify specific appeals potentially effective in dealing with each market segment selected.

STEP 2—Review nature of product, sales history, stage in life cycle, nature of buying process, and competitive strategies. These factors determine the optimum promotion mix. For example, you should never use a promotion to accomplish a task that really requires complete restructure or modification of the product itself or revision of the entire marketing plan.

STEP 3—Learn the comparative costs and capabilities of promotion tools. Keep a record of each time a tool was employed, the circumstances surrounding its use, and the results. File articles about other companies' promotions. The record and file make an excellent reference source when selecting specific tools.

STEP 4—Choose a promotional tool or combination of tools best suited to reach target market segment and accomplish desired results. Try to select unusual tools related to product, in good supply, advertisable, and offering utility (usefulness) to audience.

STEP 5—Relate the theme and message of the promotion to the real or imagined needs of your target audience. Tie these needs to your product.

STEP 6—When feasible, test the effectiveness of chosen tools, theme, and message, using a sample chosen from target market. This is an optional, but highly desirable, step.

STEP 7—Write a plan for each promotion. The plan should include a statement of the objectives, key audience, appeals and tools to be used and why, when the promotion will occur, and how its effectiveness will be measured. Circulate plans to marketing management (advertising, public relations, trade shows, product managers, etc.) for coordination.

Twenty-Nine Specific Tools to Use

Sales promotion includes a wide variety of tools relating to sales, advertising, public relations, or other marketing departments. The list below demonstrates the wide choice of alternatives. It is not all-inclusive; rather an "idea generator" to stimulate your imagination. The key to a successful sales promotion program is imagination,[3] homework, and facts.

Most of the tools listed are self-explanatory. For those which are not widely known, brief explanations and references are provided.

Audio-visual aids for sales force to use in introducing new products, demonstrate product uses, display complete product-lines, and augment infrequent sales calls (see Task 8)

Booklets, brochures, and catalogs about the company, its products, prices, and services (see Task 6)

Bulletins and circulars about company or product development progress, prices, and services

Business cards and specially designed letterheads

Calculator slide rules, charts, and dials—useful tool providing quick answers involving relationships among several variables by turning a dial or pulling a slide

---

[3] See *Idea Source Guide*, Idea Source Guide, P. O. Box 66, Fairless Hills, PA 19030. A bi-weekly report on sales promotion ideas.

Calendars or other useful objects imprinted with company's name

Canned advertising (seal a jingly device—e.g., pennies, plus advertising message—inside tin can)

Contests and incentives to motivate salesmen, middlemen, and/or customers and prospects (see Task 5)

Correspondence to dealers, customers, and other key publics

Dealer assistance (point-of-purchase displays and identification signs)

Demonstration materials, samples, equipment, and models

Direct mail programs (see Chapter IX)

Displays and signs for company lobby or showroom

House organs (newspaper distributed to company employees) are helpful in motivating order desk, customer service, product service personnel, etc.

Manuals (sales, training)

Match books imprinted with company's name

Meetings for sales force [4]

Notification to sales force of upcoming advertising or public relations campaigns, new products, new catalogs, literature or reprints

Novelties and gadgets (e.g., pencils, scratch pads, etc.) for salesmen to give away (see Task 7)

Packaging designs

Posters of products and applications

Price lists

Product photographs (see Chapter VII, Task 4)

Promotion kits

Sales rooms and displays

Telegram advertising to prospects and customers

Testimonial letters

Trade show assistance—special effects (see Chapter VIII)

Vehicle signs

Sources of More Information

In addition to coordinating with many company departments, whoever is responsible for sales promotion must rely quite heavily on outside suppliers for the actual production of promotion tools. Local suppliers of such tools can be suggested by your advertising agency or found in the Yellow Pages under "Sales Promotion," or the specific tool desired. References to specific sources of sales promotion tools are listed in the reference guide of this chapter.

Task 4: Develop Budgets

What Other Companies Do

Some industrial companies allocate a specified percent of the total marketing or advertising budget for sales promotion (from 2 to 35%). This is not always effective because sales promotion requirements differ depending on newness of product, life cycle of product, competition, pricing, changes in distribution, etc. Also, this approach is not always successful since some companies use promotions less effectively than others.

Don't establish a hard and fast percentage. Changing marketing conditions require complete flexiblity, rather than a fixed percent approach.

What You Should Do

The budget should be adequate to accomplish tasks assigned to it. This may be difficult to do since data is often unavailable on the effectiveness of various promotion tools. Ideally, you should allocate funds to specific product campaigns on the basis of territorial or market potentials and past sales performance.

[4] See "Planning & Staging Company Meetings," $5, from SM/Sales Meetings, 144 E. 44th St., New York, NY 10017.

In the real world, the theory presented in the preceeding two paragraphs is difficult to apply. All you can really do is list every program planned for the year, obtain an idea of the costs of each program before development, and add in a certain percent or dollar amount for a contingency fund. You must assume that competition, the economy, and other factors will force you to modify your plans.

Proceed with Tool Development

After your plans and budget have been developed and approved, proceed with the various sales promotion tasks. Four of these tasks are sufficiently involved to require detailed instructions, and are covered in the following sections:

TASK 5 — Sales   Contests/Incentive Programs
TASK 6 — Catalog Preparation
TASK 7 — Advertising   Specialties, Novelties, and Gratuities
TASK 8 — Audio-Visuals

Task 5: Conduct Sales Contests/Incentive Programs

What are Sales Contests?

Sales contests are used to motivate a company's sales force, dealers, distributors, representatives, or other middlemen to greater performance and profits. Prizes or other incentives are offered to those individuals exceeding specified performance goals.

Procedures for Contest Planning [5]

Procedures for conducting a sales contest are presented in this task. Whoever is in charge should coordinate contest planning with the sales department. The following steps are discussed below:

Set objectives.
Prepare plan, assign responsibility (e.g., using outside specialists), determine who will participate, determine budget size, select theme, establish contest rules, and select prizes.
Inform participants about the contest.
Distribute periodic progress reports.
Announce winners to participants and when feasible, to customers and in-

dustry through news releases to appropriate trade publications.
Send follow-up notification to all participants.
Evaluate contest results (i.e., does it appear the incentives offered actually increased sales?).

Set Objectives

Sales contests are often used by sales managers wanting a quick and simple way to increase dollar sales and/or unit volume. Unfortunately, sales contests are not so simple. They require considerable detailed planning and should never be used as a substitute for effective sales management.

Examples

Before detailed planning, you must know exactly what you want the sales contest to accomplish. As a first step, the contest planner must answer this key question: "Is the contest intended to create lasting new volume, add new regular customers, or will results end with the contest?" Note that whatever the objectives are, a contest should show a little more sales effort from everyone involved, not just a major push from a few top

---

[5] Also, see *How To Plan and Conduct Profitable Sales Incentive Programs*, Dartnell Corp., 4660 Ravenswood Ave., Chicago, IL 60640.

producers. Several examples of sales contest objectives are presented below. Some are unique to special situations, while others are universal.

- Reduce salesman, dealer, distributor, or representative boredom, and increase excitement and enthusiasm.
- Introduce new products or models, or move slow-selling, seasonal, or weak items.
- Stimulate existing sales channels, enter new territories, and increase sales calls and demonstrations.
- Offset competitive promotions.
- Add new customers and reactivate former customers.
- Recognize achievement via tangible reward for a job well done.
- Measure sales performance relative to objectives.

Prepare Plan

Planning for a sales contest should begin at least two to three months before the contest is to begin. Responsibility should be assigned to one person, whose first job is to interest top management in the contest. Participants need to know that top management is backing the contest and is concerned with its outcome.

Consider Using an Outside Specialist

Consider hiring a firm specializing in sales contests and incentive programs. These firms provide counsel and handle a great number of tasks:

- Plan and execute program.
- Purchase, inventory, ship, and award nationally advertised merchandise.
- Coordinate travel awards, trophies, and certificate programs.
- Conduct contest promotions.
- Keep accurate records of sales goals and overall sales force performance.

These services may cost you as little as $1, or more than $100 per participant, depending on contest complexity, number of participants, and value of prizes.

Always request proposals from at least two incentive specialists before selecting one. A list of such firms in your area can be found in the local Yellow Pages under "Sales Contest Organizers." Many firms supplying premium/incentive merchandise also provide sales contest consulting services (e.g., appliance manufacturers, airlines).

Who Will Participate?

Sales management must determine who will participate in the contest. It is generally best to include all channels of distribution employed by the company (i.e., salesmen, dealers, distributors, and sales representatives). Also, some incentives for "support" departments (e.g., credit) can motivate them to help the sales department. In any case, clearly state who is eligible and who is not.

If wives are in some way included in the prizes (e.g., an all expense paid vacation for two), they will provide added motivation to the salesmen.

Budget

The key questions when establishing the budget for a contest are: "Will the contest pay for itself with a new volume of business?" and, "If the previously set goal is reached, how much profit can be expected?"

The exact budget size depends on the duration and objectives of the contest. A minimum allowance of ½—1% of sales (forecasted for the contest duration) should be allocated for prizes. Some industries (i.e., those with high profit margins) allow as much as 10% or more of sales for prizes. Promotion costs for the contest can range from 5¢ to $50 per participant. You should budget for the contest according to what you think the objectives are worth.

Select Theme

A contest theme which is exciting, dramatic, and interesting to all participants is a strong motivator. The theme or purpose should build and sustain enthusiasm. The theme should relate to an emotional need of the participants and also tie in with the goals of the company—for this builds esprit de corps and profits.

Establish Rules

Clear and concise rules should be established and written in straightforward language allowing only one interpretation. The following points must be covered:

TIMING—Depends on how long interest can be maintained, and how long it takes for all salesmen to cover all key accounts. The length of a sales contest may range from 30–90 days, and seldom runs more than that. If you plan a longer contest, be sure to offer a major, dramatic prize at the end of the campaign (e.g., trip to Hawaii, a car, etc.). Be sure not to lock yourself into an extremely long contest. If one or two top salesmen jump off to a big lead, it could cause the other salesmen to lose interest and stop trying—the contest could work against you for the remainder of the contest period.

JUDGING—Specify how the contest will be judged and who will judge it, and that "decision of the judges will be final." The judges should be chosen for their impartiality.

STANDARDS—Be reasonable in establishing fair quotas to measure each salesman's performance. Quotas should be based on past performance, and adjusted for current sales region potential. Be sure that each participant can reach his quota and earn a prize with a reasonable amount of extra sales effort. In short, make the challenge realistic and state terms in concise language so salesmen know and understand the goals for which they are shooting. Make it possible to have many winners. Motivate both high and low achievers to excel. Having sales personnel competing against their last performance and territorial conditions is better than having them compete against each other. Competition between members of the sales force can undermine cooperation, expose latent grievances, and encour-

age personality cults. In any case, provide all contestants a copy of the contest rules.

CREDIT PROVISIONS—Be realistic about credit requirements if the contest loads dealers with merchandise. Plan to take back merchandise if the contest fails.

Prizes/Recognition

The overriding key to a sales contest is what motivates its participants. Prizes make the contest worthwhile to win and, therefore, important to each participant. Always use top quality, brand name incentives justifying the efforts expected of participants. And, of course, prizes should be those which appeal to the majority of contestants.

In several cases, companies offer winners options of different prizes. Frequently-used prizes include:

> Cash
> Trips (vacations)
> Merchandise
> Automobiles
> Household appliances (small and large)
> Radios, color televisions, stereos
> Jewelry, watches, clocks, cameras
> Sporting goods
> A night on the town for two

Some experts suggest not giving cash, especially where commission systems have already proven to be poor sales stimulants. Furthermore, cash prizes don't always satisfy the many psychological aspects involved in motivating people: recognition, excitement, competition, and so forth. Conversely, many companies have found cash to be the most coveted prize.

Always avoid prizes with questionable delivery dates, quality, and re-order potential (e.g., some imported products). Work closely with prize suppliers. Request complete written specifications, including description, value/price, and delivery plans.

Use Interest Builders

Keep interest high with periodic incentives during the contest (small prizes for the man of the week, biggest sale, biggest increase, etc.). Other interest builders include duplicate prizes for all ties, and consolation prizes for all participants who almost reach their quotas. This latter group probably worked as hard as the winners and deserve something for their extra effort. Acknowledgement of these efforts builds team spirit and encourages enthusiastic efforts for future contests.

Trips

Since general affluence has put a color television in 50% of American homes, many salesmen, dealers, and distributors want more than merchandise. Trips can provide a novel incentive. The broad choice of destinations and price ranges, and the increasing sophistication of the travel industry (e.g., jumbo jets, group travel rates) have made trips a most desirable incentive. Trips often meet the essential requirements of a good incentive (i.e., exciting and motivating with outstanding remembrance value).

Trips are not low priced. If a trip is given as a prize, consider the tax outlay by the recipient, plus the time away from his job.

Plan trips carefully.[6] Here are some guidelines:

Look at proposals from at least two incentive companies, airlines, shiplines, hotels, travel agencies, and so forth, for each prospective site.

Let an expert travel agent handle all extended and foreign trips. Make all reservations as far in advance as possible.

Tailor trip length, destination, and itinerary to ages and interests of participants.

Provide a choice of sites, each of which would motivate the average man in the sales force.

Check for adequate insurance coverage (liability and transportation).

Investigate transportation alternative, frequency of schedules, how tickets are made available, when, baggage handling procedures, and costs.

Go first class, even on short trips (transportation and accommodations).

Stay away from low-cost charters where your participants represent a small part of the charter group; if other group doesn't get enough sign-ups, the trip may be cancelled for all.

Schedule very few activities on the first day so participants can adjust to the new time zone.

After the first day, keep participants busy through planned activities and scheduled relaxation.

Personally investigate facilities at site (hotels, sightseeing, etc.) for highest possible luxury, quality, and accommodations.

Tell winners what is paid for, and what is not, dates, times, expected weather conditions, special affairs, local customs, tipping practices, how to be reached by relatives in case of an emergency, required documents (e.g., passport), immunizations and how to get them, how much personal funds in local currency will be required, shopping guides (e.g., duty free), list of other trip winners, available extras, and activities.

Be prepared to award alternate prizes if some winners can't go on the trip.

Arrange publicity on winner during trip (i.e., photographs of places visited, parties, hotel, etc.). This goes a long way in stimulating salesmen in future contests, and also provides good local news.

Make contingency plans for servicing salesman's customers while he is away.

Inform salesman's customers that he has won a trip through their orders. This is a nice way to thank them for the business and helps raise the salesman's esteem in their eyes.

Study Legal Ramifications

Remember that all prizes are subject to federal, state, and local regulations. Prizes are taxable at list price. Provide income tax regulation data to all prize recipients. Your

[6] It is often advisable to utilize the services of a group travel supplier. They are listed in your local telephone Yellow Pages. Some of the most well-known services include: American Express Co., 65 Broadway, New York, NY 10006; Ask Mr. Foster Travel Service, One Park Ave., New York, NY 10016; and Thomas Cook & Sons, Inc., 587 Fifth Ave., New York, NY 10017.

accountant can provide assistance in this area. Also, consult your lawyer on federal legislation (e.g., Robinson-Patman Act) and the myriad of state and local laws affecting contests.

Recognition

Recognition for outstanding achievement is as important to salesmen, if not more so, than the contest prize. It singles him out as being the best among his peers, adds pride to his position, and motivates other participants, as well as the winner, to greater achievement in the future. Examples of how salesmen are recognized:

Presenting plaques, or trophies, or quality pins distinguishing them as top producers.

Job promotions.

Publicity in company newsletter, trade publications, and local newspaper.

Inform Participants about the Contest

The next step is to tell participants about the contest and its rules. It is advisable to have a kick-off meeting in addition to any promotional materials which are distributed. Require all participants to attend this meeting unless geographical constraints prevent this. In such cases, make sure adequate promotional materials are available. If cost is a major constraint, regional kick-off meetings considerably reduce travel expense. In some cases, wives are invited to kick-off meetings to get them interested and involved. In a dramatic and enthusiastic manner, tell the participants about the contest's objectives, theme, prizes, rules, how the contest will be judged, and ideas and tools to help participants reach their goals.

Although "volume" might be the contest's goal, caution participants against overselling customers to unnecessary high stock levels which might make customers feel abused and cause sales following the contest to decline due to overstocked accounts. Also, never use "increased sales calls" as an objec-

tive, since this may encourage participants to use poor planning and call on marginal accounts.

Distribute Periodic Progress Reports

During the contest, issue periodic progress reports and additional promotional materials to all participants. This helps keep the contest rolling and interest levels high.

To avoid chaos, keep accurate sales records throughout the contest. You'll find that record keeping takes time and competence, but will be well worth the effort in settling conflicting claims or charges of unfair conduct.

Announce Winners

The announcement of winners should be made shortly after the close of the contest. For this event, the key questions to be answered are:

Who should make the announcement?

Who should present the prizes?

Who should attend the presentation ceremony?

What sort of occasion should provide the background for the presentation (formal, informal, at a luncheon, at a dinner, at a general meeting, program of events)?

Whatever the occasion, it should be planned to have maximum impact and to bestow appropriate honors and recognition on all winners. The presentation of awards should be made by a company officer whose standing in the company reflects the importance of the contest. In addition to any material prizes, a certificate suitable for framing might also be awarded to each winner.

Names of winners and details of the presentation ceremony should be announced in the house organ, as well as in news releases to the trade media and local papers. Copies of all releases and extra photos should be given to the winners. Also, ask them where they'd like the news releases sent (i.e., alumni publication, home town newspaper, etc.).

Send Follow-up Note to Participants

After the contest, a letter of appreciation signed by an appropriate top company officer should be sent to each participant. The letter should thank the participant for his efforts during the contest and express admiration for his accomplishments—even though he was not among the winners. Everyone should be made to feel that his efforts were a double benefit because what benefits the company benefits the company's employees. If the budget permits, a token gift might be made to the non-winners as an expression of appreciation for their work. The surest way to win employee loyalty is to show sincere appreciation for their efforts on behalf of the company.

Evaluate Contest

Soon after its close, review and evaluate all details of the contest and document the lessons learned for use in future contest planning. Both statistical and qualitative results help improve planning for the next contest. Did sales increase? How much? Did the higher level continue after the contest? What was the basic reaction of participants? What situations should be avoided next time? What elements were especially successful and worthy of repeating in future contests? All things considered, was the contest really worthwhile?

Be sure that sales management is aware of your evaluation. This will help ensure their support of subsequent programs.

Task 6: Prepare Catalogs/Literature

Sales Literature Preparation

Companies require a variety of printed sales promotion materials about their products and services. These materials may include catalogs, brochures, flyers, data sheets, capability brochures, and so forth. Data sheets and flyers are generally one to two pages in length, while brochures and catalogs are longer. The shorter pieces concentrate on specific subjects (e.g., price, specifications, applications, etc.), while the longer pieces can cover a greater number of subjects as the number of pages increase.

The procedure for preparing each piece of literature is very similar, differing primarily in magnitude rather than in the types of things done. Therefore, only the preparation of catalogs is discussed in this chapter. Other pieces follow similar steps on a smaller scale.

In-House or Outside Supplier?

Many industrial companies prepare their own catalogs and promotional materials.

Therefore, the preparation steps discussed in this chapter should be used as a guideline in catalog preparation.

Other companies rely quite heavily on their advertising agency or other outside services. In this latter case, the following discussion serves primarily as a guideline for working with your outside services.

Catalogs

Catalogs contain comprehensive printed matter about a company's products and services. They are used to inform, explain, persuade and assist the prospect in purchasing.

Catalogs reinforce claims made in personal sales presentations and other mass media. They often become the company's only representative when your salesmen can't personally show actual samples of all items or visit all buying influences.

It is most important to distribute catalogs to potential buyers, current customers and those influences who rarely see a salesman (e.g., committee buyers of capital equipment). Remember that you do not produce catalogs to sit on a shelf. A catalog only works when it's in the hands of potential buyers. So plan ample funds to provide for proper distribution.

Catalogs vs. Other Communications

Generally, the more your sales communications are individualized to match the prospect's particular interests, the more they cost.

The chart which follows compares four communication tools. It shows that sales catalogs are exceeded in cost and message completeness only by the personal sales call.

METHOD	COST PER COMMUNICATION	MESSAGE COMPLETENESS
Publication Advertising	Lowest	Brief — shotgun (same message to all)
Direct Mail	Low	Brief — rifle shot
Catalogs	Medium	Complete — rifle shot [7] (standard content)
Personal Sales Call	High	Complete — rifle shot (individualized appeal)

[7] Can also be shotgun depending on use.

Types of Catalogs

There are two basic types of industrial catalogs: general and specialized. In companies with one major product-line, a general catalog is usually recommended. Companies with numerous product-lines reaching many diverse markets often need specialized catalogs.

General Catalogs

Many companies produce catalogs describing the complete product-line and often include individual applications for various primary markets. For increased flexibility, loose-leaf formats are frequently used to reduce the cost of revisions when the product-line changes. Such a format permits economical distribution of applicable pieces. General catalogs have relatively long lives, serving as buyer's references in the absence of a salesman or technical expert. They are commonly used for selling standard type products whose characteristics are not subject to rapid change.

Specialized Promotional Pieces

Although not a true catalog, many specialized promotional pieces, brochures, specification/data sheets and booklets are considered catalogs by many industrial marketers. These pieces normally describe individual products or show company capabilities in various markets. While giving limited technical data, they emphasize product introductions or broad utilization within one or several vertical markets. The brief brochure should emphasize what the product is and what its benefits are to the buyer. Graphics should be simple, with the initial purpose of gaining readership and the secondary purpose of moving the prospect from *interest* to *preference*. To enhance readership, use inherently intriguing pictures on the cover rather than simple product photographs.

Small literature pieces are easier to revise, file, or carry around, and are less expensive to mail than general catalogs. They can either supplement or be part of a general catalog. These specialized pieces direct customer interest to an item otherwise presented only as "another" catalog entry.

Schedule Catalog Preparation Steps

After you determine that a particular catalog format will best satisfy your communications requirements, detailed production scheduling can begin. For efficient catalog preparation, write down all steps and deadlines in the process, assign responsibilities, and carefully monitor progress. This section provides directions for accomplishing each step required.

Establish catalog objectives and plan
Prepare rough budget ceiling and timetable
Collect and organize data
Establish theme and format
Prepare roughs and first copy drafts
Finalize budget

Get preliminary approvals
Produce catalog
Proofread
Get final approvals
Print catalogs
Distribute catalogs

Establish Catalog Objectives and Plan

Marketing, product, and sales managers should be first to recognize need for sales aids describing new products, modifications to products, or changing customer needs requiring new printed material. These managers must request to the advertising/sales promotion manager that a catalog be prepared, specify when they need it, tell quantity required, and set any general guidelines regarding elaborateness, art work, and photographs. Customer benefits, product points, and appeals should be indicated during this planning stage.

A new catalog, however, should never be produced to satisfy only one man's personal request. He *could* be dead-wrong, even if he's company president. Before seeking senior marketing management's approval for a new catalog, get agreement from all sales, market, and product managers on the need to be satisfied by the literature. Have these persons complete the literature request form on page 378.

Establish Precise Objectives

Precise objectives for a new catalog depend on the kind of product. Examples are:

TYPE OF PRODUCT	CATALOG OBJECTIVE
High-priced, infrequently purchased	Get reader interest and answer frequently-asked questions
Standard, off-the-shelf supplies, replacement equipment (low cost, highly competitive, local suppliers)	Enable readers to make buying decision quickly relating to quality, dependability, reliability of service, accessibility of replacements, standardization, etc.
Highly competitive, standard, outlet sales type goods (chemicals, metals, tubing, etc.)	Convince reader your prices are competitive, and you offer much more back-up service

Who Should Prepare Catalog?

Should your catalog be created by a company department, by your advertising agency, or by an art service? The key question is: "Who can do it best?" (i.e., on time, within budget, and with professional quality).

Whether your literature is to be produced in-house or by outside services, be professional. The additional time and money spent on improving literature from mediocre to excellent will be paid back in profits many times over.

For in-house production, you'll need good technical writers, creative artists, and *plenty* of their man-hours to direct photography, specify type, select paper stock, get departmental approvals, select a printer, proofread galleys, layout, paste-up, and so on. Consider going outside for catalog preparation even though it may increase your out-of-pocket cost. It will usually pay for itself by decreasing excess time required of your internal staff, and will almost always result in a better catalog.

In-house production is sometimes justified from an economic standpoint if you have multitudes of brochures to create, especially highly technical ones, requiring close work with an engineering staff. Even so, if your outside production source is competent, it can still save you both time and money while producing superior material. Remember, a poorly-produced, cheap-looking catalog can lose sales for you if your competitors' literature is comparatively more sophisticated and persuasive.

Sources of Information on Catalog Preparation

Besides advice provided by your advertising agency, information on creating and producing literature is available from major paper companies and prefiled catalog publishers (e.g., Thomas Register of Manufacturers). A list of these sources is presented in the reference guide.

Prepare Rough Budget Ceiling and Timetable

Many companies regularly allocate a percentage of the advertising budget for catalog preparation. Other firms simply budget based on "what we spent last year." Avoid these approaches because they are arbitrary and fail to consider the changes that occur in the present marketplace.

Catalog budgeting is best when it seeks to satisfy a distinct objective. First, find out how many brochures/catalogs are needed. Then ask product, marketing, and sales managers, and others requesting literature

Literature Request Form

Your Name: _____   Return to: _____

Your Title: _____   Department: _____

Your Department: _____

Today's Date: _____

----

1.   What sales literature do you need (e.g., catalog, data sheet, etc.)?

2.   Why do you need it (i.e., what is its major objective)?

3.   In descending order of importance, what product/service benefits should the piece provide?

4.   If there is existing literature, what are its shortcomings?

5.   How many do you need for the next year? When do you need them? Is this to be a stock item or a temporary item?

6.   Describe why you feel a particular quantity is required.

7.   Please provide specific suggestions for degree of refinement, art work, and photographs to be included.

8.   What product benefits do you want to emphasize?

9.   We welcome your use of extra, attached sheets or notes on the reverse side if you feel sufficient comment is not possible in the space provided.

for an estimate of the quantity they'll need for next year.

Quantity is only one consideration in budget preparation. In talking with managers, stress "how important is the product in the total line?" "Is it significant enough to warrant 4-color treatment?" "Does it require 8 pages or 90 pages to tell the story?" However, do not be surprised to discover that management often doesn't know the answer to these questions. In the final analysis, the sales promotion manager must solidify the vague recommendations of management into a concrete proposal that is realistic, economical and effective.

Also, useful life and appearance of the catalog are most important. For example, if the catalog is frequently used but not changed over an extended period of time, high-quality, long-lasting paper should be used. Also, the sooner you need the finished catalogs, the more they will cost. Suppliers (e.g., printers) charge more for rush service. You can always exchange time for money. You must determine if such an exchange is worthwhile.

Next, inform vendors about all your art, paper, quantity, catalog-life needs, etc., so they can give you more accurate price quotes. You should obtain estimates from several sources for each item listed in the catalog budget form. And each source should be given an identical description of what is to be done. Make a standard form listing the number of pages, total quality, color, etc. At this point, the budget form is only a preliminary guideline. Later the form becomes a firm budget ceiling.

Collect and Organize Data

To enable you to establish a theme and rough layout, first collect data. The quality and quantity of data collected affects the theme and layout.

Any catalog must have sufficient descriptive information to permit objective product comparisons and selection. Examples of such information can be found in previous catalogs, bulletins, literature, preliminary engineering documents, and other sources noted below. This information may include:

Generic name of the product
Trade, manufacturer, or brand names authorized for use
User-oriented advantages and benefits (e.g., durability, performance data or "what need does the product fill?")
Primary applications and users
Company background
Distribution (i.e., do you need to consider imprinting by dealers, inclusion in dealer catalogs, etc.?)
Photographs and illustrations
Testimonials
Service, distribution, maintenance, and installation facilities
Features, standards, design, components, sizes, attachments, accessories, structure, properties, and specifications
How to purchase or get more information (e.g., availability, specifying, locations of representatives or outlets, ordering, delivery data, rates)

It also helps to review competitive literature which may suggest ideas for contents, layout, and overall approach to design (i.e., what to do or not to do).

You may encounter departmental pressures for inclusion of certain elements (e.g., engineers want to include detailed specifications, marketing people want to include many sub-benefits, etc.). Satisfying all such requests may produce a boring and hard-to-read catalog.

Nevertheless, much can be gained by soliciting the opinions of these various influences through discussions and use of an easy-to-answer written questionnaire. This step must be completed for either in-house or outside literature preparation. The assembled and summarized data is turned over to the appropriate in-house department or outside agency for final production of the piece. By this stage in development, key managers will know you're preparing a new catalog, and it's up to you to get their advice on what to include. Consult your product managers, marketing people, and field sales groups, dealers, distributors, represen-

Catalog/Literature Budget Form

Catalog/Literature Title: _____

Catalog Number or Year: _____

Date of Estimate: _____

Budget Approved By: _____
                              (name)

Title: _____

- -

1. Planning and administration $_____

2. Data gathering $_____

3. Creative work $_____
   A. Artwork $_____
   B. Layouts $_____
   C. Photography $_____
   D. Copy $_____
   E. Illustrations $_____
   F. Paste-up $_____
   G. Legal fees $_____

4. Printing preparation $_____
   A. Typesetting $_____
   B. Engraving $_____
   C. Readying Press (make ready) $_____

5. Production $_____
   A. Paper $_____
   B. Printing $_____
   C. Binding $_____
   D. Envelopes/Imprinting $_____

6. Distribution $_____
   A. Addressing $_____
   B. Inserting/handling $_____
   C. Postage $_____
   D. Mailing list rental/maintenance $_____
   E. Mailing carton/envelopes $_____

TOTAL $_____

tatives and jobbers; prospects and customers; and your marketing research department. Ask such "open-ended" questions as:

What do customers and prospects want to know about applications, performance, specifications, economy, ease of operation?

How will this information support a buying decision?

How are products purchased?

How are products used and in what environment?

How should catalog be presented to best inform readers (e.g., with pictures, technical drawings, graphs, etc.)?

What products should be included and why?

What other product applications may interest readers?

What specifications must be met by each market segment?

Should prices be included with product descriptions or should they be on a separate price list?

Put Data into Folders

Divide data into clearly defined, logical sections and visual units and put the materials (copy, illustrations, data) into separate labeled folders. It may be advisable to group products by specific uses or functions. This gives a broad view of the material and facilitates review for completeness and filling of gaps.

Establish Theme and Format

Now that you've gathered data, a theme or overall approach can be created. Outline in writing the contents of the catalog. This outline organizer will later help you decide on the basic design.

Prepare Roughs and First Copy Drafts

Arrange the labeled folders in order of importance to the user, relative newness, oldness, etc. Then condense data as much as possible to stay within the number of pages allowed by the budget. Refine and compose the data into a graphic rough, including desired format, color stock and ink, binding, etc. This is where individual pages are designed. Sometimes the layout is done following the copy. Sometimes the copy is written to the layout. Either way, each aspect is created with the other in mind. It is often best to write a rough draft and from it develop a rough graphic layout. Then go to finished copy and art.

General Format/Layout Guidelines

Make your catalog easy to use by following these general guidelines:

Select page size which is easy to handle, mail, store, etc. (e.g., 8½ by 11 inches).

Allocate page space according to priorities, allowing enough space to tell the whole story.

Prepare "thumbnail" (i.e., rough sketches) layouts for review by staff and management before final approvals.

Select a simple, legible typeface for the body copy.

Use inherently intriguing cover, rather than simple product photographs.

Combine a logical visual flow with white space and color, to lead the reader's eye from section to section thereby holding his attention.

If information in a section requires two pages, avoid confusion and possible loss of attention by using a two-page spread (i.e., facing pages), rather than the front and back of the same page.

Use uncluttered drawings, pictures, charts, diagrams, photographs, and illustrations to make a point wherever possible rather than wordy text.

Use generous white space in margins or borders to increase readability and direct the reader's eye.

Use short lines of text for easy readability. Body copy should not exceed twice the length of the alphabet set in the specified type.

Prominent and strategically-placed headlines, subheads, and indentations often get attention for key points, make text easier to read, and alert readers to new sections.

Don't distract reader through unnecessary ornamentation and irrelevant displays.

General Copy Guidelines

Make your catalog easy to use by following these general copy guidelines:

The tone of all catalog copy should be factual, relevant, persuasive, informative, and interesting; not boring or bragging; avoid exaggerated claims, overuse of adjectives and adverbs.

What the product will do for the reader is usually more important than how it does it. People buy what products do, not how they do it. Remember that people do not buy ¼″ drills, they buy ¼″ holes.

The catalog's cover, including company name, product name and illustration, trademark, or other distinctive device, should present the desired company image and enable readers to identify the issuing company or product class at a glance. In many cases, however, a good reader-oriented, intriguing headline is usually better than a product-name headline.

Always use an index, table of contents, and/or cross-reference guide of generic names if the catalog is extensive and covers various products. Tell the reader how the catalog is organized so he can use it efficiently.

Relate paragraphs and captions to graphic elements.

Give dimensions on all important drawings.

Give information tailored to reader's needs––benefits and features, descriptions, capabilities, applications, and specifications.

Provide enough specifying information to enable reader to make the proper selection for his application. Perhaps you should include an order form.

On the inside or outside back cover, list the main plants, branches, sales offices, dealers, and representatives—making it easy for the reader to act. Facilitate the next buying step by providing telephone numbers and addresses. Do you need to leave space for imprinting of dealer name and address?

Specific Guidelines

For high-priced, infrequently purchased products, always:

Provide complete technical data.
Describe product makeup (i.e., contents) and sales features.
List uses and applications, including relevant pictures, diagrams, graphs and tables. Make sure all important drawings have dimensions and captions.

For standard, shelf-type supplies and replacement equipment, which are normally presold by advertising media other than catalogs/brochures:

List all company products and relative information.
Tell in simple steps how to get the products (e.g., order from literature).
Use concise, easy-to-understand terminology.
Include prices if not frequently changed.
Discuss delivery and back-up services available for this type of product.

For highly competitive, outlet-sales type goods, where cost is a major criteria:

After featuring price information, list physical features, delivery capability, availability (time and quantities), dependability of source, comparative quality.
Show some primary applications.

Finalize Budget

At this point you can get tight estimates on printing, photography, illustration and other costs. The form previously presented is useful for this purpose. If, in order to accomplish your goals, you have to go over the rough budget ceiling, go back to management now and ask for more money, or change the objectives.

It is often helpful to separate fixed and variable costs. Fixed costs are those needed to get the catalog ready for the press regardless of how many copies are printed. Then show the costs of printing different quantities. As quantity increases, average cost per catalog generally decreases.

Get Preliminary Approvals

Approvals by all interested and concerned managers often take a long time but are necessary to ensure accuracy, completeness, and relevance of data. Since catalogs are considerably more complex than one-page advertisements, allow each approver adequate time to study the subject matter. However, specify a positive deadline. Make sure that market managers, research managers, engineering, sales, and senior marketing executives agree with the manner and content of presentation. Also check with legal counsel to avoid possible legal pitfalls.

The approval form presented on page 384 helps you obtain approvals of catalogs, as well as other communication tools.

Produce Catalog

Production is a considerable task requiring sufficient lead time. It requires coordination of photography, illustrations, typesetting, retouching, paper and envelope selection, finished art, plate making, proofing, and so on. Closely follow schedules established in the catalog planning stages for best results. Note: the key to producing a quality catalog is good, reliable suppliers.

Proofread

Any errors in typesetting made by the printer are reset without charge. But "author's alterations"—not the fault of the printer—are legitimate reasons for extra charges by the printer. Author's alterations are caused by last minute changes or over-

sights. Printer's charges for corrections can cause severe budget overruns. It is, therefore, extremely important that the final manuscript be meticulously proofread several times.

It's best to use a professional proofreader for catalog copy—not the person who wrote the copy. It is also advisable to have two people do the job: a proofreader reading the copy out loud—including all punctuation—and a copy holder checking against the original. They should also check for grammar and context; use a dictionary to check spelling and word usage, and be critical of bad spacing of letters, lines, words, or paragraphs, typographical errors, broken type, poor punctuation, omissions, and hanging "widows" (printer's term for the last word or few words, or single line of a paragraph, carried over as the first line of a column or page).

To avoid misunderstandings or arguments, keep a copy (by office copying machine) of the approved proofread and corrected text that you return to the printer for production.

Get Final Approvals

Use the same procedure and form presented for getting preliminary approvals to obtain final approvals.

Print Catalogs

After obtaining final approvals, printing and binding can take place. Your printer should have been involved by this stage, so only a simple "go-ahead" is required once proofing is finished.

Distribute Catalogs

The catalog has no sales value until in a prospect's hands. There are two extremes to catalog distribution. One makes catalogs available to all prospects at all times. The other makes catalogs available only to intensively cultivated markets; and to lesser cultivated markets should the budget allow it.

Determine the best distribution method(s) prior to producing a new catalog. There are five basic methods for distributing catalogs:

Direct mail campaign
Requests from advertising/public relations
Sales calls

Prefiled catalog (multiple manufacturer catalogs)
Trade show handout

Mail Campaign

Catalogs can be mailed to customers and prospects without their specific request.

Approval Form

Please review the attached material entitled:_____

This piece is to be used for:_____

_____

When you are satisfied that it is <u>technically</u> correct and complete, place your initials and the date in the blank by your name. Could you please accomplish this by the date and time shown next to your name? Then pass the material to the next person on the list, or call me and I'll pick it up. Thank you.

Name	Title	Due Date	Initials	Date
_____	_____	_____	_____	_____
_____	_____	_____	_____	_____
_____	_____	_____	_____	_____
_____	_____	_____	_____	_____
_____	_____	_____	_____	_____
_____	_____	_____	_____	_____
_____	_____	_____	_____	_____

Date Issued:_____

Date Completed:_____

_____
Signature

_____
Name Typed

Title:_____

Telephone:_____

Office Location:_____

Names can be accumulated from current company records, supplemented with purchased mailing lists pinpointing specific SICs, titles, company size, and location. Catalogs can also be mailed to respondents to company advertising, public relations campaigns and visitors to trade show booths.

Advertising/Public Relations Requests

You can encourage catalog requests via advertising and publicity programs. Since this distribution is difficult to control, you may realize an increased distribution budget. However, satisfying advertising and public relations responses is more precise than arbitrarily mailing to certain industry direct mail lists because interest is already established.

Sales Calls

When catalogs are distributed by salesmen calling on customers and prospects, the catalog can be a "door opener" or leave-behind item providing salesmen a chance to show prospects the company's entire product-line. With the cost of the average sales call over $80, care must be exercised not to make delivery of literature the sole purpose of the call. Conversely, when making a sales call, it's no time to be tight in handing out catalogs. All potential buying influences in a firm should get a copy if possible.

Prefiled Catalog

Prefiled catalogs are catalogs of numerous manufacturers bound together in alphabetical order by manufacturer name. Such catalogs are typical in mining, food, oil and gas, textile, electrical, chemical, power, and architectural industries as well as general purpose prefiles (e.g., Thomas Register, Sweet's Catalogs) which reach readers in many industries. Catalogs may be pre-printed and then sent to a prefile catalog

maker for binding, or the publisher will print material from your camera-ready copy and bind it together with catalog data from other manufacturers.

"Prefiles" are advantageous because they are:

Kept up-to-date via loose-leaf format for periodic publication

Rarely lost because they usually are highly valued references

Systematized and indexed for easy usage

Lower in cost of postage, printing, binding, and distribution

Usually property of a group or department, not an individual—permitting increased access per copy to buying influences

A quick reference to buyers making comparisons

Trade Show Handouts

Catalogs are frequently distributed at trade shows. See Chapter VIII, Task 10, for a further description of how this distribution system works.

Task Summary

After developing a catalog, it is wise to evaluate its effectiveness. Note positive and negative reactions of salesmen, distributors, customers, and prospects. Is the catalog generating interest? Is it being used frequently as a reference source for purchasing?

All reactions should be recorded in a log book, analyzed, and taken into consideration when preparing your next catalog. It is useful to maintain a catalog correction file to incorporate all the minor changes or inaccuracies discovered during the life of the catalog. When the catalog is revised, this correction file will be a time-saving source of information.

Task 7: Use Advertising Specialties, Novelties, and Gratuities

When to Use?

Advertising specialties include novelties, gimmicks, giveaways, and gratuities, such as many of those items listed under Task 3 (e.g., pencils, pens, ashtrays, slide calculators, etc.).

Specialties should be used with caution. They are popular with salesmen who like to give away anything. However, this is not enough reason for using them. Careful evaluation should be made of actual usefulness. The specialty item must *not* be looked upon as *just* something to give away or a scheme to keep a company's name before the public, or as a door opener for salesmen. It must be considered as an integral part of the total sales promotion program.

In most industries, certain specialties can be worthwhile (e.g., scratch pads, telephone message pads, etc.). Unfortunately, some salesmen tend to rely on them as a crutch. The best usage of specialties occurs in industries where salesmen make repetitive calls on the same accounts and need such items as conversation pieces. Specialty items are not as effective in industries where sales calls are infrequent and highly customized presentations prevail.

Selection Requirements

When selecting a specialty item for your sales promotion program, several criteria should be considered. The specialty item should:

Enjoy frequent use of many people (e.g., used as reference source)—the more often used, the more often your name, logo, or trademark are seen

Permit appealing display of advertiser's name in quality vs. gimmick form, and always in good taste

Permit wide circulation and viewing (i.e., placed on a desk rather than in a drawer)

Be of value; something wanted for its utility or appearance

Be a familiar, tasteful, and accepted item, preferably a brand name

Allow personalization (e.g., engraving)

Be easy to mail or ship (low postage, plus speed in delivery)

Be nonbreakable and durable, and if requires service or repairs on moving parts, be simple, quick and inexpensive to fix

Have a long life (i.e., if item is consumed immediately, loses potential effectiveness over time)

Have tie-in possibilities with product-line or other promotions

Where to Buy?

There are hundreds of firms in the United States supplying millions of advertising specialty items. Magazines and trade associations which can provide directories and lists of such firms are listed in the reference guide.

Also, sources can be found in your local telephone Yellow Pages directory under "novelties," "advertising specialties," "gadgets," or the desired product type.

Gift-giving

Gift-giving on holidays and special occasions often helps develop a friendly and favorable attitude toward your company on the part of recipients—employees, customers, and suppliers. This show of consideration, appreciation, and goodwill can make gift-giving an effective public relations tool.

Who Should Receive Business Gifts?

Employees, customers, and suppliers are all good prospects for receiving business gifts. Employees appreciate small remembrances on occasions such as birthdays, anniversary with the company, holidays (e.g., Christmas), or even more important, when an extra effort is given to increase productivity or get out a special job quickly.

Customers like to know you appreciate their business, so remember them on special occasions such as new plant openings, extraordinary orders, holidays, etc.

Token gifts to suppliers also help since no business is better than the quality of its suppliers. Remember suppliers for their fast delivery, special services, leads which bring you new customers, etc.

Business Gifts Compared to Incentives

Business gifts differ from incentives or premiums. Incentives have more than nominal value and are used to motivate recipients to efforts over and above normal output. Tasteful business gifts are simply tokens of appreciation thanking a recipient for his order, business over the years, good work above and beyond the call of duty, etc.

Basic Rules for Business Gifts

Be in good taste to ensure no misunderstanding.

Give nominal gifts.

Be personalized and appropriate (e.g., don't give golfballs to a nongolfer).

Give proportionately large gifts for larger accomplishments, business orders, etc.

Personally sign card sent with gift, and include a small note of thanks.

Gift-wrap to remove commercial appearance.

Choose your supplier carefully—send the best quality available of the item selected.

Choose gifts not commonly available on local store shelves.

Gifts for an individual should be sent to his home. Gifts for an individual and his staff should be sent to the office.

Establish a tickler file, arranged by date of occasion to be remembered, with name of employee, customer, or supplier. Have responsible person check all cards which will come up over the next two weeks to give suppliers time to deliver. Verify addresses, job changes, etc.

A popular gift price range is $5 to $10, with an approximate ceiling of $25 because of Internal Revenue Service provisions limiting deductions over this amount. Exceptions to this statement and complete regulations on business gifts are contained in IRS Publication 463—*Travel, Entertainment, and Gift Expenses*, available from Internal Revenue Service, 1111 Constitution Ave., N.W., Washington, D.C.20037.

Pitfalls of Gift-Giving

Several pitfalls of gift-giving have caused many firms to completely ignore it as a sales promotion tool. Some dangers include:

Can be expensive.

Tough to compete if other suppliers give away better gifts.

Hard to stop once started—expectations on the part of the recipient grow each year.

Some companies discourage employees from accepting gifts (i.e., to prevent allegations of bribes and favoritism to certain suppliers).

Task 8: Use Audio-Visuals

Alternatives

A wide variety of audio-visual tools are available for use in advertising, public relations, training, sales, merchandising, and other presentation forums. Such tools increase the sender's control over his message, producing greater impact and specific results.

Some presentations use only visual techniques (e.g., slides, silent movies, film strips, overhead projectors, etc.); some use only audio formats (e.g., tapes, disc recordings, etc.) allowing the audience to imagine its own pictures. However, in most cases, greater effectiveness is achieved combining audio and visual techniques.

Most A/V tools are self-explanatory, but a brief listing of some of the more commonly used tools might be of help at this point.

Blackboard—One of the most basic and frequently used A/V mediums. Not effective if audience is larger than 50 people.

Flannelboard—A flannel-covered board to which other flannel pieces (letters, numbers, shapes, etc.) adhere simply by contact. Ideal for presentations requiring building-block approaches.

Magnetic Board—A metal board to which magnetic pieces (e.g., letters, numbers, shapes, etc.) simply adhere by contact. Excellent for status keeping (production plans, schedules, traffic control, etc.).

Hookboards—A board of any substance with hooks on which objects can be hung. Best for displaying diagrams, blueprints, charts, etc.

Easels—A stand for displaying prepared messages on flip cards or flip charts. Also used to hold paper pads on which ideas can be written.

Overhead Projectors—Used to project 8″ x 10″ acetate sheets (e.g., prepared pictures, copy, statistics, designs, etc.) onto a screen or light surface. Also accommodates blank sheets for writing on during presentation. A good medium for detailed presentations.

Tape Recorder—One of the most useful A/V tools available. Newer models feature electro/mechanical synchronization units for tying-in audio (from the recorder) to external video sources. Applications are limited only by imagination.

Film Strips—A series of pictures on film (16mm, 35mm) which are edited together to convey a message. Some units are available with sound sync systems for adaptation of tapes. Frequently used to illustrate step-by-step or sequential messages. Sometimes used where slow-moving motion is required.

Slides—A name which has become generic for 35mm transparencies mounted in plastic or paper holders, capable of having its images projected onto a screen or light surface. Other types of slides (such as glass-mounted lantern slides) are also used for A/V presentations. However, the 35mm transparency (slide) is without question the most used audio-visual tool on the market today. Newer slide projectors featuring rotary trays or multiple position casings have added greatly to the versatility and practicality of this medium. Computerized control of sound synchronization and multiple dissolve units will provide even more flexibility to slide projection systems. Applications are varied, for slides can be used whenever words are not enough and actual motion is not needed. Suffice to say, slide projection systems will continue to be *the* basic A/V tool for years to come.

Motion Pictures—Motion pictures are produced in various formats: 70mm (wide screen), 35mm (standard for professional motion pictures), 16mm (formerly the only truly economic, quality format available to industry), and super 8mm—the emerging giant of industrial motion pictures.

Owing to super 8's quality and greatly increased color balance over standard 8mm film, it has become one of the fastest growing, most used A/V tools. The fact that super 8 film adapts itself to cartridging is greatly responsible for its popularity. These instant-loading cartridges have helped eliminate the one big obstacle formerly encountered with 16mm systems: you don't take 10 minutes setting up a 5-minute film. Just slip in the cartridge and show the film. With these new continuous-loop cartridges, no threading or rewinding is needed. Look for Super 8 films (especially cartridges) to become as popular as the slide projector in years to come.

Closed Circuit TV—A system of televising events by transmission over a wire telephone line or cable to receivers (TV sets) stationed at key locations. Useful for simultaneous transmission of information especially by an authoritative and recognizable spokesman.

Video Tape—An electromagnetic tape on which electronic impulses produced by video and audio portions of a presentation are recorded by special equipment.

Which Tools to Use?

The requirements of the presentation will dictate which audio-visual technique to employ. Often, a combination of techniques is warranted. First, answer the following questions.

Who is the audience?

What is the audience's background, related experience, problem, prejudices, vocabulary, knowledge level, awareness of symbols, abbreviations, and acronyms? (i.e., how sophisticated is the audience in reception and utilization of information?)

What is your objective? What message are you trying to relay to the audience? What degree of understanding is required? Is your objective to influence action, create awareness, explain, etc.?

How large is the audience? Can they all be gathered together in one room? (i.e., will they come to the presentation or will the presentation have to go to them?)

Where will the presentation be given? Are there any peculiar room characteristics?

How many times will the presentation be repeated?

What treatment will best relay your message (e.g., photographic, cartoon)?

How much time do you have? To show it?

To prepare it? Between presentations? What is your budget?

For further information on each A/V method, review the Evaluation of Audio-Visual Presentation Methods presented on the next page.

Develop Tools

After answering these questions and evaluating alternative techniques, seek advice from professional audio-visual experts. Since modern audio-visual techniques are extremely flexible, experts can tailor specific tools to fit your needs and budget.

Audio-visual suppliers can be found by contacting the sources listed in the Reference Guide.

Some tools (e.g, flannel board, blackboard, overhead projectors, flip charts) are relatively easy to create. Other techniques (e.g., motion pictures, video tape, closed circuit television) require extensive facilities and coordination with a variety of suppliers, such as producers, writers, graphic artists, design studios, narrators, sound studios, film laboratories, and talent. Slide presentations are one of the most effective and popular A/V tools that can often be prepared by a company's own staff. For these reasons, slide preparation is discussed below in more detail.

Prepare Slide Presentations

A good slide presentation complements, clarifies, or otherwise amplifies the verbal message, but never repeats it. The presentation helps command audience attention, stimulate interest, and keep the speaker on the track.

Use Story Cards/Boards

After you've:

Determined the broad message;
Considered audience desires;
Gathered related data;
Organized and categorized the data;

Evaluation of Audio-Visual Presentation Methods

METHOD	IMPACT (ATTENTION-GETTING/ MEMORABLE)	FLEXIBILITY OF USE	ADAPTABILITY (APPLICATIONS)	CHANCE OF ERROR		COST	
				HUMAN	MECHAN-ICAL	ORIGINAL	DUPLICATES
Blackboard	Low	Low	High	Little	None	Low	Low
Flannelboard } Magnetic Board Hookboard }	Low-Medium	Low-Medium	High	Little	Little	Low	Low-Medium
Written Handouts	Low-Medium	Low-Medium	High	None	None	Low-Medium	Low
Flip Cards Charts Easels	Low-Medium	Low-Medium	Medium	Some	None	Low-Medium	Low-Medium
Overhead, Vu-graph, Transparency Projectors	Low-Medium	Low-Medium	Medium	Some	Little	Low-Medium	Low-Medium
Phonograph Recording	Low-Medium	Low-Medium	Medium	None	Little	Low-Medium	Low-Medium
Tape Recorder	Low-Medium	Low-Medium	High	None	Little	Low-Medium	Low-Medium
Filmstrip	Medium	Medium	Low-Medium	Little	Some	Medium	Low-Medium
Slides	Medium	Medium	High	Little	Some	Medium	Low-Medium
Motion Picture (8 and 16mm)	High	High	Medium-High	Little	Some	High	Medium-High
Super-8 Continuous Cartridge	High	High	High	None	Little	High	Medium-High
Closed Circuit Television	Medium-High	Medium-High	Low-Medium	Great	Some	High	High
Video Tape	Medium-High	High	Low	Some	Some	High	Medium-High

Checked the subject matter with an authority;

it's time to organize your presentation. First put the data on 4″ x 6″ story cards. Make only one point per card. Each card should contain room for the visual and a written summary of the idea or what will be said. An example card is shown below.

At this point it's advisable to consult a communications specialist or audio-visual production expert. He will help translate

Example Story Card

Visual

Job No. _____

Illus. No. _____

Production Notes _____

_____

_____

_____

_____

_____

Commentary/Summary: _____

_____

_____

your roughs into an effective visual form. Your advertising agency can assist at this time or recommend an appropriate source.

Now take the rough story cards and put them into desired sequence of presentation on a storyboard. After much shifting of cards and revising of contents and visuals, an illustrated rough script can be prepared (see following example). This script is useful for both the lecturer and the projectionist. After slides and text have been finished, a final operating script should be prepared.

Tips for Preparation of Slides

Include only one point or idea per slide. Two or more simple slides are more effective than one complicated slide.

Delete extraneous and nonessential information.

Show close-ups, important details, and overviews, but do not include total surroundings unless relevant.

Make detailed slides legible to ensure that people in rear seats can readily see them on the screen.

Rough Script

DATE:_____   TITLE:_____

Due	Video	Audio
1) When to go to next slide	1) Description	1) Description

Use simple graphs with few captions, rather than tables, for quick comparisons.

Have all slides respect limitations of human eye.

Use lower case type for easier reading. Upper case can be used where necessary to avoid confusion between such things as proper and improper nouns.

When projecting letters, words, etc., use light and/or bright colors against dark colored backgrounds.

Use white (or light) type on black (or dark) background for better viewing. It is easier on the eyes in a darkened room.

Use series of slides for progressive disclosure, pointing up minor copy or art changes from one frame to the next.

Mix visuals with type, if possible, to achieve greater audience involvement.

Vary size, type and perspective of visuals (e.g., angles, long-shots, close-ups).

Limit slide content to those items to be discussed (no more than 30–40 words of copy per slide).

Avoid imperfections and smudges on original art, since these are magnified when projected.

Leave a space at least the height of a capital letter between lines of copy.

Leave visuals on screen for enough time to eliminate confusions, but not too long to cause boredom.

Don't leave slide on screen after discussing its subject.

Use duplicate slides if needed later in the presentation, rather than "flipping back."

Put sequence number on each slide corner.

Store slides in cartridge or magazine for ready ordering.

Maintain a set of duplicate slides in case the originals are lost or damaged in transit. Duplicate sets also allow you to be in two places at one time.

Use blank slides (i.e., opaque film or paper in a slide mount) when you want no image on the screen. Always make the last slide in the tray blank to avoid ending your presentation with a glaring, harsh, empty projection screen.

Lettering should be large enough to be read from the slide without magnification.

Tips for Actual Slide Presentation

Visit room before presentation to make sure equipment is in proper working order.

Rehearse to improve timing and sequence.

Discuss presentation with projectionist.

Reserve the proper projector and have it on hand well before needed. Projector should have sufficient wattage to produce a bright image. Have a spare projector bulb for emergency use.

Match screen size to audience requirements. No viewer should be farther away than six times the width of the screen. (See Screen Size—Seating Capacity Chart.)

Avoid placing seats behind posts or other obstructions.

Use remote control to operate projector from lectern or develop a signal device to alert projectionist.

Lower lights enough for required contrast, but not darker than necessary for your purposes.

Place projector on a four-legged stand for maximum stability during your presentation.

Task Summary

Although this task dealt primarily with slide presentations, other audio-visual devices should be considered and discussed with experts. You'll need to rely quite heavily on these suppliers when using most of the sophisticated audio-visual devices such as closed circuit TV and films.

Screen Size—Seating Capacity Chart

APPROXIMATE SCREEN SIZE (in feet)	FURTHEST VIEWER FROM SCREEN (in feet)	CLOSEST VIEWER TO SCREEN (in feet)	MAXIMUM AUDIENCE SIZE	SEATING SPACE (in square feet)
3½ x 5	30	5	88	531
4½ x 6	36	6	125	755
5 x 7	42	7	169	1018
6 x 8	48	8	224	1345
7½ x 10	60	10	350	2100
9 x 12	72	12	502	3010
10½ x 14	84	14	684	4110
13½ x 18	108	18	1175	7050
15 x 20	120	20	1400	8400

Other Sales Promotion Reference Guide

Guide to Associations

Council of Sales Promotion Agencies, 2130 Delancey Pl., Philadelphia, PA 19103.

Marketing Communications Executives International, 2130 Delancey Pl., Philadelphia, PA 19103.

Point-of-Purchase Advertising Institute, 60 East 42nd St., New York, NY 10017.

Sources of Information on Catalog Preparation

Crown Zellerbach Corp., One Bush St., San Francisco, CA 94104.

Effective Catalogs, John Wiley & Sons, Inc., 605 Third Ave., New York, NY 10016.

Hammermill Paper Co., 1453 East Lake Rd., Erie, PA 16507.

International Paper Co., 220 East 42nd St., New York, NY 10017.

Kimberly-Clark Corp., North Lake St., Neenah, WI 54965.

Mead Corporation, 118 West First St., Dayton, OH 45402.

Mohawk Paper Mills, Inc., 465 Saratoga St., Cohoes, NY 12047.

Nekoosa-Edwards Paper Co., 100 Wisconsin River Dr., Port Edwards, WI 54469.

Sweet's Catalog Services, McGraw-Hill Publishing Co., 1221 Avenue of the Americas, New York, NY 10020.

Thomas Register Catalog File, Thomas Publishing Co., 461 Eighth Ave., New York, NY 10001.

S. D. Warren Co., 89 Broad St., Boston, MA 02101.

Directories to Audio-Visual Suppliers

Audio-Visual Communication Equipment Directory, United Business Publications, Inc., 750 Third Ave., New York, NY 10017.

The Audio-Visual Equipment Directory, National Audio-Visual Assoc., Inc., 3150 Spring St., Fairfax, VA 22030.

Audio-Visual Marketplace, R. R. Bowker & Co., 1180 Avenue of the Americas, New York, NY 10036.

Audio-Visual Source Directory, Motion Picture Enterprises, Inc., Tarrytown, NY 10591.

Blue Book of Audio-Visual Materials, Educational Screen & Audio-Visual Guide, 434 S. Wabash Ave., Chicago, IL 60605.

Books/Magazines on Sales Promotion

Industrial Marketing, Crain Communications, Inc., 740 Rush St., Chicago, IL 60611.

Potentials In Marketing, Lakewood Publications, Inc. 731 Hennepin Ave., Minneapolis, MN 55403.

Sales and Marketing Management, Bill Communications, 633 Third Ave., New York, NY 10017.

Sales Promotion Handbook, Fifth Edition, John C. Aspley and Ovid Riso, Dartnell Corp., 4660 Ravenswood Ave., Chicago, IL 60640.

Directories to Premium/Incentive Sources

Gift & Decorative Accessory Buyers Directory, Geyer-McAllister Publications, Inc., 51 Madison Ave., New York, NY 10010.

Incentive Marketing/Incorporating Premium Practice, Bill Communications, Inc., 633 Third Ave., New York, NY 10017.

National Premium Manufacturers Representatives (NPMR), P.O. Box 1295, Danbury, CT 06810.

National Premium Sales Executives (NPSE), 1600 Route 22, Union, NJ 07083.

Premium Advertising Association of America, 420 Lexington Ave., New York, NY 10017.

Premium & Incentive Product News, Gellert Publishing Corp., 33 W. 60th St., New York, NY 10023.

Premium/Incentive Business, Gralla Publications, 1515 Broadway, New York, NY 10036.

Premium Industry Club (PIC), 307 North Michigan Ave., Suite 720, Chicago, IL 60601.

The Premium Buyer, The Premium Buyer Publishing Co., 100 Mercer St., Hightstown, NJ 08520.

CHAPTER XI

Inquiry Handling (Sales Lead Control)

Introduction

Why an Inquiry Handling System?

Your company communicates with potential customers in many ways, viz., advertising, publicity, trade shows, direct mail, etc. These communicative efforts cost money, and are most worthwhile when they bring maximum desired results at minimum cost. One desired result is to develop inquiries from potential customers.

An inquiry is both a positive show of interest in your products and a request for more information about them. Inquiries are made for reasons ranging from "collecting literature," to "being better able to make a buying decision."

A large percentage of inquiries results from readers returning a "bingo card," "reader service card," "reader inquiry card," or "business reply card." Most trade publications today key their advertisements and editorial items with a number on the bingo card. When the reader finds an interesting item described, he simply circles the "keyed" number on the preaddressed, postage-paid card, and mails it to the magazine, which then generally sends the particular manufacturer a computer-printed list of all those who made an inquiry. The question is,

"What should the manufacturer do in response to these inquiries?"

An inquiry should indicate buying interest on the part of a person who may ultimately buy your product. But *realistically*, only a portion of inquiries result in direct sales; the trick is knowing which portion.

Although you can't always be sure why inquiries are made, you should build an efficient system for handling and evaluating them. This system is valuable because it can lead to sales and provide valuable marketing data that make your communication efforts more worthwhile—more cost effective. Chances are your competitors may have also received an inquiry from the same individual. So by having a better inquiry handling system you could get your message to the inquirer first.

Where to Start?

What to do? To help you prove to disbelievers why a good inquiry handling system enhances the sales effort, you should develop a system giving the most promising ("hot") inquiries top priority, and the less promising a *careful* evaluation.

The system is valuable to sales personnel only if they can be sure leads are hot—

meaning "qualified" (i.e., somebody is *truly* interested in evaluating and ultimately buying your product). Historically, giving all inquiries to salesmen tends to discourage them. Sales managers, too, are sometimes tough to sell on the value of inquiry systems. Why? Because they've learned that only a small percentage of the total number of inquiries are hot leads. How different they might feel if even one in five of the leads you gave them brought a sale! The research and analysis forms shown in Task 8 of this chapter help document the value of inquiry systems, both to the salesmen and to sales managers.

A sound inquiry handling system should answer basic business questions such as:

How well are we telling our sales story? (i.e., how many leads did we get?)

Of the total leads, how many were "hot?" (i.e., did we reach the right people?)

How many sales resulted from the "hot" leads? (i.e., how is our sales force doing?)

Objectives

At the very least, your inquiry handling system should do the following:

Respond quickly to inquirers' requests

Qualify "hot" prospects

Reduce selling cost by helping concentrate your sales efforts on most promising prospects

Assure timely personal meeting between salesmen and "hot" prospects

Evaluate and increase effectiveness of communication program

Serve as a marketing research and planning tool

Provide valuable information on prospects, product applications, and ideas for potential new products

Criteria of a Good System

To attain the above objectives, the system must be:

QUICK—provides requested materials while inquirer interest is still high; forwards qualified leads to sales force without delay.

EFFICIENT—doesn't become a self-defeating, paper-monster.

ACCURATE—records all data correctly.

MEASURABLE—includes information for evaluation of communications and the system itself.

QUALIFICATION-ORIENTED—automatically determines best candidates for sales force follow-through.

FOLLOW-UP ORIENTED—automatically determines whether follow-through has been made by salesmen.

FLEXIBLE—can handle a hundred or thousands of inquiries per month.

SUPPORTABLE—easily understood and accepted by staff, sales force, and top management to assure compliance.

The Difficulties

Establishing an effective inquiry handling system, especially where no system has existed before, is not easy for several reasons:

TIME INVOLVED—in both installation and operation

COSTS—in manpower, paperwork, and postage

FOLLOW-THROUGH—sales force staff and management often are initially skeptical and may downgrade the system.

However, if operated properly, the system pays for itself many times over. It's amazing how quickly salesmen begin cooperating once you've built a strong system capable of bringing them more sales volume. Sales managers and top management react the same way. But your system has to be good!

You Need an Inquiry Handling Center

Set up a central point for receiving, handling and recording inquiries and for forwarding literature and notices. This focal point can be in your advertising department, sales department, public relations department, or whichever department in your company seems best suited to the task. The advertising department is usually ideal for the job because it sees the results of its campaigns (in terms of inquiries received) and can, thereby, improve its messages or better select its audiences when the ads are not "pulling" sufficient inquiries.

If in-house capabilities are not available, a

Inquiry Handling System

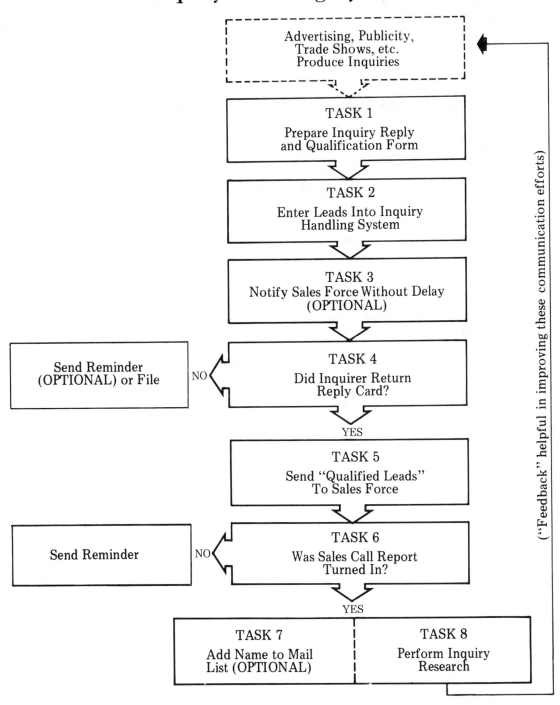

number of excellent outside services are available. (See your Yellow Pages.) Many of these services process materials and reply cards more efficiently and at a lower cost than could a company-run facility.

Chapter Plan

It's generally agreed that effective marketing communications bring in inquiries which help bring sales. An efficient "closed-loop" inquiry handling system is needed to speed this "communications to sales" cycle. Without it, many communication and sales call dollars will be wasted. Worst of all, your firm misses many valuable inquiry-stimulated sales possibilities.

The chart on the previous page shows the main steps of an integrated, closed-loop process for handling, evaluating, and following-up inquiries. The chart can be adapted to suit the size of your company and method of doing business.

Task 1: Prepare Inquiry Reply and Qualification Form

Several Systems are Available

An "inquiry handling system" (called "IHS" in this chapter) can range from a highly sophisticated computerized one, to intermediate level systems using address plates, to the simple multi-part forms that require only a "one time" typing operation.

The system you choose should be based on several factors:

The volume of inquiries you now generate or expect to in the near future. If the total number is relatively small, then you may want to process them in-house using the part-time services of a secretary. Some companies process as many as ten to sixteen thousand inquiries per year in-house with one girl handling all of the mechanics of the system. Usually, however, this process does not include sufficient analysis of each inquiry.

The type of data you expect from your system. If your annual volume is significant (i.e., more than five or ten thousand inquiries) and/or if you wish to do extensive market analysis of these leads, you should investigate the use of a computer service (one you set up internally or buy from an outside source). This is no doubt the easiest way to develop and process data. Surprisingly, it can also be your cheapest solution in the long run.

The bulk of this chapter centers around some of the more elementary systems. The discussion in no way represents an endorsement of a specific system as a cure-all; rather it is a basis for understanding inquiry handling fundamentals.

Address Plates

Address plate systems handle up to several thousand inquiries per month. They enable you to use one plate per prospect (or customer) for more than one reason, such as forwarding requested literature, generating mailing lists, and for addressing invoices and other communications. Suppliers of mechanical systems include Elliott, Cheshire, Scriptomatic, Addressograph-Multigraph, Pitney Bowers, and Xerox. See your Yellow Pages under the heading "Addressing Machines and Supplies."

Snapout Multi-Forms

The simplest and least expensive IHS uses multi-part "snapout" forms, designed so that a single typing imprints an address on all copies.[1] In responding to inquiries, four snapout parts are common:

Mailing label
Inquiry reply and qualification card

---

[1] A standard form used by many companies is supplied by Sales Essentials, 10555 Lunt St., Rosemont, IL 60018. Also, see your Yellow Pages under "Business Forms and Systems."

Second notice followup card
File copy

Prepare Form

One version of a simple four-part snapout form is illustrated on the next page. The four basic parts are discussed below.

1. Gummed Mailing Label

This is simply a gummed mailing label for the envelope containing literature sent to a prospect. As the address is typed on the label, it is simultaneously imprinted on the other three parts by carbon paper inserts or by a special chemically-treated paper which eliminates carbon paper inserts.

2. Reply to Inquiry and Qualification

A business reply postcard thanks the inquirer for his interest, directs his attention to enclosed literature, and elicits marketing information for qualifying him. Ideally, the card is already filled in with the recipient's name. It is self-addressed and prestamped so it is easy to mail. The purpose of preaddressing is to reduce the inquirer's work to a minimum.

3. Second Notice for Follow-Up

Another business reply postcard; this can be used to follow-up a prospect who has failed to return the above business reply postcard. In addition to repeating the qualifying questions, the message on this part opens with a suitable greeting and a reference to the product literature previously mailed.

4. Master File Copy

This part, identical to number 2, is retained in your master inquiry file. It could contain handwritten notes of dates on which initial and follow-up cards were mailed to the prospect. Such data helps if a third follow-up is desirable later.

Note: Log Numbers for Quick Retrieval

A sequential log number on each part (except address label) can be used for matching each reply with the proper inquiry, and for tracking progress of the qualification/sales process. When salesmen make a sale, they can include this number on the order. Then research can be done to determine which source of qualified leads produced the most sales.

Task 2: Enter Leads into Inquiry Handling System

Send Materials Right Away

Enter the sales leads into the IHS and forward requested materials as soon as possible—within 48 hours. Interested prospects want information fast—possibly to make an immediate buying decision. Long delays in replying are worse than sending no reply at all. Inquirers often resent tardy replies; they may forget about the request, withdraw from the market, or buy from another company. Obviously, you should never try to generate inquiries if you have no material to send. But logistical problems occasionally occur. If requested material is not immediately available, send a brief note or postcard to the inquirer telling him:

His inquiry has been received
Why reply can't be made immediately
When reply will be made

It's embarrassing being unable to send product literature because your supply is depleted. This could also result in loss of a sale. Therefore, you should have an effective inventory control system ensuring that adequate stocks of literature are always on hand.

Send Optional Material

Depending on circumstances, there are several optional items that may be included in the material sent to an inquirer:

Inquiry Reply/Qualification Form

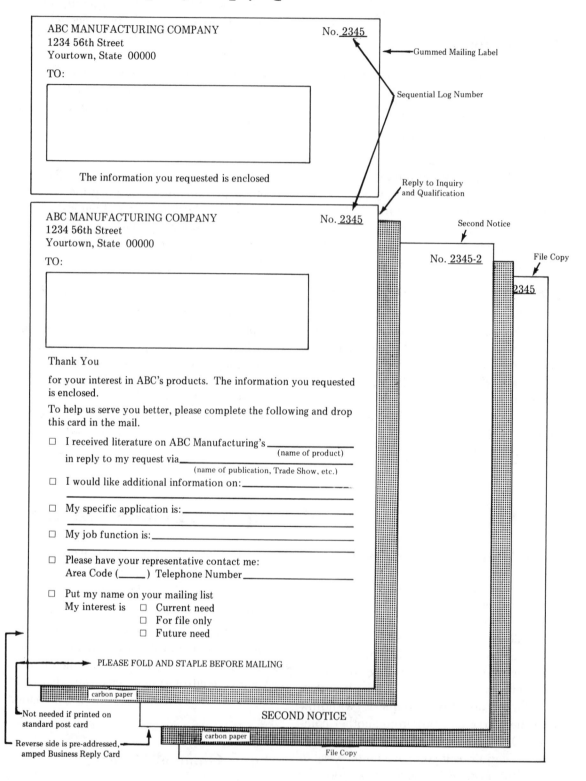

ABC MANUFACTURING COMPANY
1234 56th Street
Yourtown, State 00000
No. 2345

TO:

The information you requested is enclosed

Gummed Mailing Label

Sequential Log Number

Reply to Inquiry and Qualification

Second Notice

File Copy

No. 2345-2

No. 2345

ABC MANUFACTURING COMPANY
1234 56th Street
Yourtown, State 00000
No. 2345

TO:

Thank You

for your interest in ABC's products. The information you requested is enclosed.

To help us serve you better, please complete the following and drop this card in the mail.

☐ I received literature on ABC Manufacturing's _____
   (name of product)
   in reply to my request via_____
   (name of publication, Trade Show, etc.)

☐ I would like additional information on:_____

☐ My specific application is:_____

☐ My job function is:_____

☐ Please have your representative contact me:
   Area Code (____) Telephone Number_____

☐ Put my name on your mailing list
   My interest is   ☐ Current need
                     ☐ For file only
                     ☐ Future need

PLEASE FOLD AND STAPLE BEFORE MAILING

carbon paper

Not needed if printed on
standard post card

Reverse side is pre-addressed,
amped Business Reply Card

SECOND NOTICE

carbon paper

File Copy

Instead of the standard inquiry form (prepared in Task 1), a special forwarding business letter may be more appropriate. This can be a prepared form letter, or a specially composed letter. In either case, the letter might point out some special features of the product that would be of interest to the inquirer. Organize the letter to include these points:

1. Thank inquirer for interest in your company's products.
2. Invite his attention to enclosed material satisfying his request.
3. Point out product features and benefits that may be of particular interest to inquirer.
4. Provide name, address, and telephone number of your company representative in inquirer's area.
5. Suggest the next step for inquirer to take (if appropriate), or tell him to feel free to contact your local office for further information.

A list describing literature available on other products, and an offer to send them on inquirer's request.

A list of your sales offices, dealers, or distributors. Alternatively, the address of representative closest to inquirer's area could be stamped on the standard inquiry/qualification form. The way you handle this is immaterial—the main idea is to tell the inquirer where to find the closest representative.

Depending on the situation, you might include a company brochure describing your facilities and capabilities, or other literature of interest to your inquirer.

Mailing Options

Choosing the best way to send information to an inquirer depends on several factors, the most important of which is the urgency of the situation. Don't economize on postage when a potential big sale is at stake.

Here are some suggestions for handling your mailing problems:

Try to keep package weight within first class limits; you'll get quicker delivery.

If literature packages are too heavy for first class rates (without paying priority mail heavy pieces rates), consider using third class. Be sure to print under your return address the words "Address Correction Requested." [2] That way, the post office will inform you of material not delivered, and the new address (if known).

Large companies having mail rooms may refuse to deliver third class mail internally because it may overload their facilities. In that case, the "Address Correction Notice" will cause the post office to notify you of non-delivery. Future mailings to that company should be via first class mail.

If you have a large volume of inquiries, and there is no urgency, try using "Bulk" mail if your mailing pieces weigh more than three or four ounces. You'll save money and the address correction line will eventually let you know whether or not your material is getting through. Spot checks by telephone can also be used to determine this.

Whether or not you make high volume mailings, familiarize yourself with postal regulations governing mail. Your local post office offers a folder, "Domestic Postage Rates, Fees and Information." Another postal service publication covers international postage rates and fees. In certain cases, you may wish to use services such as special handling, special delivery, [3] insured mail, registered or certified mail with return receipts, or C.O.D. mail.

Business Reply Cards and Envelopes

To use business reply cards, envelopes and mailing labels, you must obtain a permit

---

[2] See Chapter IX—Direct Mail (Task 6) for complete description of "Address Correction Requested" and other mailing procedures.

[3] In large metropolitan areas "Special Delivery" may actually delay receipt of your materials. For example, if your "special" package is undelivered because a firm is not operating on Saturday, the piece may become misfiled and the misfiling not discovered for several days.

from the postmaster of the office to which they will be returned. Make application on a form supplied by the postmaster. The design of card, envelope, or mailing label used must conform to those prescribed by the postal service.

Although you pay two cents more per card or envelope returned to you, you don't have to pay for any business reply mail *not* returned. Contact your local postmaster for full information on obtaining and using business reply mail.

Metered Mail

A postage meter located in your offices may be used for printing and recording postage when you have a moderate to high volume of mailings. Various types of meters are available (see your Yellow Pages under "Mailing Machines and Equipment"). Your postmaster can also provide information on their use.

Master Control File

Copies of your replies to inquiries should be filed for easy retrieval and reference at every step of the inquiry handling process described in this chapter. Organize the file to best meet your own particular needs. You can use the sequential log numbers (see Task 1), or file the copies by product category, alphabetically by inquirers, geographically, or by catalog, or model number. The method should fit your way of doing business, and should enable you to retrieve a particular file quickly.

Task 3: Notify Sales Force Without Delay (Optional)

Send Inquiries Before Qualification

Some companies may choose to notify the sales force *before* the inquirer has been qualified as "hot" by his return of the qualifying (questionnaire) card. Field salesmen can review these advance notices for information on activity in their sales area and may choose to follow up on selected inquirers. No attempt should be made to track these advance notices. On the other hand, don't be surprised if you find that your field salesmen are less than enthusiastic when you send them large numbers of unqualified inquiries.

Send Prequalified Inquiries

Generally, the field sales force prefers to receive only highly qualified leads. In some cases, original inquiries meeting predetermined standards may be considered qualified leads and entered into the system as such.

However, most companies have neither time nor money to prequalify all inquiries. The extent of prequalification depends on the volume of inquiries expected and the resources available for prequalification. Some companies make special studies to evaluate the relative pay-off resulting from extensive prequalification versus minimal prequalification.

Some companies use the telephone to contact a prospect immediately upon receipt of an inquiry.[4] This has the advantage of speed in reaching a possible hot prospect to get answers to questions like those on the qualifying card and to discuss the prospect's specific interests and applications. If appropriate, you could then have your local sales representative follow-up with a sales call. In this way, you might cut as much as two to four weeks off the qualification cycle. These face-to-face contacts should be made from six to ten days after literature has been mailed to an inquirer.

---

[4] If your prospects are widely dispersed, and if the volume of your business by telephone warrants, you might consider subscribing to the WATS service (Wide Area Telephone Service). Contact your telephone company for rates.

Prequalification Criteria

Criteria used to prequalify inquiries could include:

Personal letter requests

Trade show inquiries
Direct mail replies
Telephone calls
Existing prospects

Task 4: Did Inquirer Return Reply Card?

Process Returned Cards

This is a critical action point in the inquiry handling system. If the inquirer returns the reply card, stating a current interest (or meets prequalification standards), he is considered a qualified "hot lead." You should immediately notify the appropriate field sales office or representative and request follow-up. Information provided by the inquirer that may help the salesman should (1) be added to the master control card, and (2) be forwarded to appropriate field sales personnel.

Send Reminders (Optional)

Set a "suspense" limit for the return of reply cards (e.g., 30–45 days). When the card is received, send the lead to the sales force (see Task 5). If the inquirer has not replied within the set time limit, you can send a second request for information (see Task 1, Second Notice for Follow-up). This second request is an optional step. In some cases it will "flush out" interested parties who have been forgetful, or tardy, or who were not yet ready to talk business. The reminders can be duplicates of the originals with a polite "reminder" notice on the form.

Evaluate the Cost per Inquiry

Task 8 describes some methods for evaluating cost per inquiry. By keeping accurate records of results you can determine cost per inquiry, and the total cost of sending follow-up reminders. One agency offering an IHS reports that you should try to get *some* response from 25% to 40% of the inquirers to whom you sent literature; and about one out of four of these might be "qualified." But if you try to get responses *above* the 40% level, your cost per qualified lead tends to reach the point of diminishing returns.

Task 5: Send "Qualified Leads" to Sales Force

Qualified Leads Preferred

In Task 3 it was noted that a company could send all inquiries to appropriate salesmen before any qualification. The salesman is then responsible for his own sorting and qualifying, or he can wait for later qualification. When using dealers or representatives, a company must provide only the "best" leads, since it only gets a portion of the middleman's time. Also, many salesmen prefer not to be bothered with the task of qualifying inquiries, and frown on receiving a stack of inquiries which may or may not contain "hot leads." On the other hand, in small companies the salesmen may *have* to do their own qualifying.

Notice to Sales Force

Notice of qualified sales leads should be sent to the appropriate field office as soon as possible.[5] This notice should include space for a salesman to report results of his follow-up, as well as information provided by the inquirer which may lead to a later, more productive sales call. In addition, computer systems facilitate development of a summary listing of all verified leads for sales force review.

A sample Field Sales Notice form is shown on page 405. The three-part snapout design can be used to save typing prospect identifying/qualifying information on the upper half of the form more than once. These notations, derived from inquirer replies to the form prepared under Task 1, are made by the office responsible for operating the inquiry handling system. The lower half of the form contains boxes for the salesman to check after he has followed-up the lead, either by telephone or by a sales call. Note the log number in upper right-hand corner, which is keyed to the identical log number on the inquiry reply and qualification form (see Task 1).

The first and second parts of this form can be printed on light card stock that can be folded, stapled, and returned to the inquiry handling office as a business reply card. The third part is retained in the master file.

Action by Salesman

The salesman's action depends on the type of product and respondent. Sometimes a telephone call by the salesman or his secretary can evaluate the lead and save time. The following paragraphs suggest best ways for the home office and the salesmen to handle inquiries from various sources.

Purchasing Agents

Never side-step a purchasing agent who requests information. He holds a strategic position to help or hinder you. Send him everything he requests. If the qualifying card is returned, have your sales representative call on the purchasing agent to update his files on your company's products and techniques, and to provide any additional information that may be helpful.

The salesman should ask the purchasing agent for suggestions and comments after the sales presentation. The purchasing agent can tell you who are the key buying influences in his company, major upcoming projects, what competitive products are being considered, key specifications (price, delivery, and so on), and other valuable information.

Presidents/Top Executives

Top executives are the busiest and most influential men in a company. Always send them facts they want as completely, accurately, and quickly as possible, with a personal letter (never a form). After a qualifying card is returned, have your salesman call the executive's secretary to verify if the materials have been received. The salesman should also ask to speak briefly with the executive or his representative so he can request an appointment to provide additional information in person.

Company Librarians

Some companies maintain technical libraries including files of catalogs, data sheets, and other information on various companies' products—including those of your competitors. Consequently, never ignore a company librarian's request for product information. Librarians often give your salesmen names of personnel responsible for product selection, or they may make recommendations directly to those persons.

Important Job Title, Known Company, Known Product

This could be a "hot lead." It should be handled fast, but judiciously. Send requested literature and notify a salesman immediately. Make an appointment to bring additional information, samples, quotes, etc.

---

[5] If you sell technical products you may wish to have a product engineer immediately contact the prospect by telephone to discuss the engineering problems involved. The product engineer can sense the prospect's interest and, if appropriate, arrange for a sales representative to call on the prospect. The engineer might even accompany the salesman on such calls.

Field Sales Notice

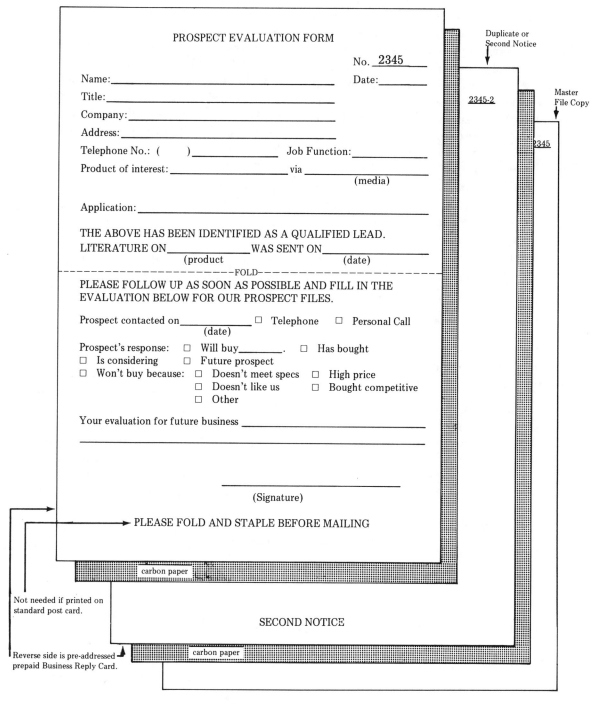

PROSPECT EVALUATION FORM

No. 2345

Name:_____ Date:_____

Title:_____

Company:_____

Address:_____

Telephone No.: (   )_____ Job Function:_____

Product of interest:_____ via _____
                                      (media)

Application: _____

THE ABOVE HAS BEEN IDENTIFIED AS A QUALIFIED LEAD.
LITERATURE ON_____WAS SENT ON_____
                (product)   (date)

-----------------------------FOLD-----------------------------

PLEASE FOLLOW UP AS SOON AS POSSIBLE AND FILL IN THE
EVALUATION BELOW FOR OUR PROSPECT FILES.

Prospect contacted on_____ ☐ Telephone ☐ Personal Call
                 (date)

Prospect's response: ☐ Will buy_____. ☐ Has bought
☐ Is considering ☐ Future prospect
☐ Won't buy because: ☐ Doesn't meet specs ☐ High price
                          ☐ Doesn't like us ☐ Bought competitive
                          ☐ Other

Your evaluation for future business _____

_____

_____
                 (Signature)

➤ PLEASE FOLD AND STAPLE BEFORE MAILING

carbon paper

SECOND NOTICE

carbon paper

Duplicate or Second Notice

2345-2

Master File Copy

2345

Not needed if printed on standard post card.

Reverse side is pre-addressed prepaid Business Reply Card.

Important Job Title From Unknown Company and End Product

Notify the appropriate salesman about the inquiry and qualification. Assist the sales force by getting them information about the company from *Thomas Register, Dun & Bradstreet, Standard & Poor's Register*, etc., and other references named in Chapter I— Marketing Research. The more information you provide the salesman, the better prepared he will be, thus improving his chances of making a sale—or paving the way to a future sale.

No Title, No Company, Unfamiliar Address

Notify the appropriate salesman. This can be considered a low priority inquiry, but if the volume of your inquiries is also low, have a secretary make a follow-up call to find out if material was received and if it was adequate. Ask the name of the company and position of the requester. Forward this information to the salesman and enter it in the inquiry handling system.

"Corporate" Inquiries

Notify the appropriate salesman about the inquiry and qualification. Have salesman call inquirer and ask for an appointment. If an appointment is granted, in addition to discussing product-lines the salesman should try to find out:

Relationship between central office and plants
Where specifying is done
If there was a particular application in mind when inquiry was made
Which field representatives should be contacted

The salesman should also try to obtain a company telephone or personnel directory, as well as product or capabilities literature which might be useful in better serving this customer's needs.

Direct Competitor

The direct competitor is merely trying to get more information about his industry and his competition. It's a policy of some companies to send their competitors no more information than requested. Others may ignore the request to save postage and to make it more difficult for a competitor to get more information. However, they will eventually get the literature through the help of a friendly customer, or by using a pseudonym, or by using the home address of one of their salesmen. There obviously is no need for a follow-up.

Inquirer Using Home Address

Inquiries often come from students, from people working out of their homes, or from persons who—for whatever reason—choose to use their home address. Notify the sales representative of qualification, unless it is obviously a nonprospect.

Students

Students inquire for various reasons. Eventually, some may be in a position to specify or buy your company's products. Forward all requested information as an investment in future good will and thank the student for his interest in your company. There is a documented case history in which a student inquiry led to a $220,000 order within three years. Some companies have special direct mail programs for students as part of their long-range programs. It's quite likely that today's student inquirer will be tomorrow's businessman.

Task 6: Was Sales Call Report Turned In?

What to Do when Reports are Received

When a sales report is returned, the information provided by the salesman should be entered on the file copy of the master inquiry form. All information pertinent to that inquiry will then be available in one place, thus simplifying filing and retrieval for evaluation procedures. These evaluation procedures help determine which communications and media approaches were most effective producers of inquiries and sales.

Sent Reminder

If the sales force has not replied within 30 to 45 days, send a reminder to the salesman requesting a report of action he has taken.

This can be a duplicate of the original with a "reminder" notation on it (see "second notice" business reply card described in Task 5).

Sometimes salesmen don't respond even after the reminder has been sent. In this case, a telephone call is more effective than further written reminders. Another approach to ensure follow-through is to send a list to the appropriate sales office of all qualified leads which have not been reported on, with a copy to the sales manager. A cover letter should stress the necessity for follow-up, a reminder that these were qualified leads, and some recent examples of sales resulting from leads.

Task 7: Add Inquirer's Name to Mail List (Optional)

Add Names

If a salesman's call report indicates a lead is a good prospect, or if an inquirer requests, his name should be added to your regular mailing lists (viz., to announce new product bulletins, extend trade show invitations, provide application stories, or to introduce new sales representatives or dealers).

Although adding inquirers' names to mailing lists is frequently done, it may not be effective since it is difficult to know when to remove their names, or when they have changed jobs or companies. Several key points to help "clean" lists include removing names when material is not deliverable, and also including space on your reply cards which allows prospect to request his name be deleted.

Task 8: Perform Inquiry Research

Types of Research

Many types of research and analyses can be performed on your inquiry handling system. For example, you can evaluate inquiries received, sales call reports, and actual sales made as a result of inquiries. In fact, the sale is the ultimate pay-off of the inquiry system, and all inquiry-stimulated sales should be fed into the inquiry handling system for evaluation. Or to be even more precise, measure inquiries to "negotiations" (i.e., how many inquiries reached the stage where meaningful sales-oriented discussions took place with inquirers; quotes, bids, or estimates submitted). Then it becomes the sales department's responsibility to measure how many of these negotiations resulted in sales. All such evaluations help determine return-on-investment of your various communication programs.

However, the method used in researching sales information depends on the type of product and customer. Some products lend themselves to first call sales. Other products, such as those for original equipment manufacturers, may take 6–12 months to sell, or longer. In any case, remember that producing qualified sales leads is a *communication's* goal; producing sales is a *sales force* goal.

The basic types of research discussed here include:

Measuring effectiveness of alternative media and techniques
Developing market profiles
Conducting territorial, product, and salesman analysis

For each of these purposes, inquiries generated by your communications program should be tallied on receipt (in an inquiry log.) Forms for recording and analyzing data are presented at the end of this task.

Measure Effectiveness

The purpose of the first analysis is to measure the effectiveness (power to pull inquiries) of such factors as:

Alternative media
Alternative ad styles
Specific ads
Copy approaches in both ads and publicity items
Location in a publication
Four-color vs. black and white
Action vs. static illustrations
Repeat vs. first-run ads
Other techniques

Two key measures of effectiveness are cost per inquiry (C.P.I.) and cost per qualified lead (C.P.Q.L.). The seven forms at the end of the chapter are useful in making such analyses.

Advertising Inquiry Analysis

The Advertisement Inquiry Analysis form is used for analyzing individual ads, news releases, or trade shows. Although the word "advertisement" is used, it can be interchanged with "news release," "article," or "show," etc.

After you run a new product release, advertisement, or exhibit at a trade show, record the date and number of inquiries received in columns (2) and (3). A running (cumulative) total should be kept in column (4). Then divide column (4)—the total number of inquiries—by the total cost of the ad, show, or release, and write the resulting dollar figure in column (5). In column (6) enter the number of qualified leads (qualified leads are valid sales prospects as determined by the inquirer's return of a reply card or a sales representative's call report noting level of inquirer interest). Column (6B)—cumulative number of qualified leads—should be divided by the cost of the ad, release, or show, and the resulting dollar figure entered in column (7).

Column (8)—total dollar sales directly related to an inquiry—is often difficult to obtain without a precise inquiry tracking system. One tactic is to send a questionnaire to the inquirer approximately 2–6 months after the initial inquiry to find out if he bought the product he inquired about *from anyone.* Also, you can monitor sales call reports or sales invoices to help in relating inquiries to sales. In any case, when this figure (column 8B) is determined, divide it by the total cost of the ad, show, or release to determine the sales per dollar of media investment. Enter this figure in column (9).

Magazine Inquiry Analysis

The Magazine Inquiry Analysis form is similar in design to the advertisement form. At year-end, it accumulates all data from the individual ad sheets and records all ads which appeared in one magazine, or all inquiries from one show. This permits an overview of the effectiveness of *specific* magazines or shows.

Comparative Media Analysis

The Comparative Media Analysis form compares *all* magazines, shows, and other media. This and the two previous forms can be slightly modified to compare the effectiveness of different techniques (e.g., black and white vs. color).

Sales Action Measurement

If inquiries are closely monitored and a follow-up questionnaire is mailed to inquirers, an additional analysis can be made using the Sales Action Measurement form. This form compares all ads in terms of type of sales response obtained. It also can be used to measure effectiveness of literature mailed and of various alternative promotional techniques employed.

Develop Market Profiles

Another type of analysis (Inquiries/Market Profile form) is based on a simple tally as inquiries are received, broken down by job titles, functions, industry class, and product interest. This tally can be compared with sales force activities to determine if efforts are being directed toward the prime interest groups. The form should be filled-in for each ad or media employed. As inquiries are received, two tallies should be made in appropriate rows—one by job function and one by SIC. Some magazines provide this service free of charge.

Conduct Territorial/Salesmen Analysis

Of the several types of territorial/salesmen analyses, two are most useful (see following forms).

Inquiry Coverage Ratio

The Inquiry Coverage Ratio form is used to keep track of the cumulative number of leads sent to a salesman or territory versus the cumulative number followed-up. Areas where salesmen are not following up sufficiently are readily pinpointed. In the left-hand column on the form, list the salesman, territory, or dealer. Under each month, record the cumulative number of leads sent to the dealer or representative (column 1), and the cumulative number of call reports returned as evidence of follow-up contact by the sales representative (column 2). Divide column 2 by column 1 and write resulting percentage in column 3. This figure represents the cumulative percentage of leads sent out which were actually contacted by your sales representative. In this way you can evaluate his cumulative performance over a period of time.

Advertisement Inquiry Analysis [6]

PUBLICATION OR MEDIA _____ COST $ _____

LOCATION _____ SIZE _____ SPECIAL CHARACTERISTICS _____

THEME _____ DATE _____ PRODUCT _____

(1) NUMBER OF WEEKS AFTER APPEARANCE OF AD (lease, show, etc.)	(2) DATE (week) INQUIRIES RECEIVED	(3) NUMBER RECEIVED THIS WEEK	(4) RUNNING TOTAL OF INQUIRIES (cumulative)	(5) COST PER INQUIRY: COST OF AD ÷COLUMN (4)	(6) NUMBER QUALIFIED LEADS		COMPUTE EVERY 4 to 6 WEEKS			(9) SALES PER $ OF MEDIA INVESTMENT: COLUMN (8B) ÷COST OF AD
					(A) THIS WEEK	(B) RUNNING TOTAL	(7) COST PER QUALIFIED LEAD: COST OF AD÷ COLUMN (6B)	(8)[7] SALES TRACEABLE TO INQUIRY (A) THIS WEEK	(B) RUNNING TOTAL	
1										
2										
3										
4										
5										
6										
7										
8										
9										
10										
11										
12										
13										
14										
15										
16										
17										
18										
19										
20										
21										
22										
23										
24										
25										
26										

[6] This form analyzes effectiveness of advertisements in terms of the number of inquiries "pulled," and sales stimulated. Form headings can be modified to make it suitable for analyzing effectiveness of news releases, articles, and trade shows. See Task 8.
[7] Time period is dependent on selling cycle of product.

Sales vs. Inquiries

A similar analysis (Sales vs. Inquiries form) measures cumulative sales (dollars) versus cumulative inquiries in a territory, or for salesmen, or dealers. Write the absolute cumulative number of inquiries received from a territory in column 1 under each month. Add all inquiries for year to date (on a monthly basis) and determine the percentage of the total that the territorial figure represents. Record this figure in column 2. Record the cumulative amount of sales from a territory in column 3. Add all sales for year to date and determine what percentage of the total the territorial figure represents. Then compare columns 2 and 4.

If more inquiries than sales are received, there may be some untapped potential in that territory. The cumulative nature of this analysis offsets the time lapse between inquiry and order.

Inquiry Handling in a Nutshell

Now that research is completed, study the results. Determine where problem areas exist. Most important, check results against objectives set for the IHS (e.g., were "hot" prospects really qualified?). Remember, this process should be completed frequently and results incorporated into communications and sales programs.

Magazine Inquiry Analysis [8]

PUBLICATION _____

(1) DATE OF ISSUE/ PAGE NO.	(2) SIZE OF AD/COLOR OR B&W	(3) NUMBER OF INQUIRIES RECEIVED	(4) COST OF MEDIA EMPLOYED	(5) COST PER INQUIRY: COLUMN (4)÷ COLUMN (3)	(6) NUMBER OF QUALIFIED LEADS	(7) COST PER QUALIFIED LEAD: COLUMN (4) ÷ COLUMN (6)	(8)[9] $ SALES TRACEABLE TO INQUIRY	(9) SALES PER $ OF MEDIA INVESTMENT: COLUMN (8) ÷ COLUMN (4)

[8] This form evaluates inquiry response resulting from ads appearing in a single magazine, or responses from a single trade show. See Task 8.
[9] Time period is dependent on selling cycle of product.

Comparative Media Analysis [10]

(1) SOURCE OF INQUIRIES (magazines)	(2) NUMBER OF INQUIRIES RECEIVED	(3) COST OF MEDIA EMPLOYED	(4) COST PER INQUIRY: COLUMN (3) ÷ COLUMN (2)	(5) NUMBER OF QUALIFIED LEADS	(6) COST PER QUALIFIED LEAD: COLUMN (3) ÷ COLUMN (5)	(7)[11] $ SALES TRACEABLE TO INQUIRY	(8) SALES PER $ OF MEDIA INVESTMENT: COLUMN (7) ÷ COLUMN (3)

[10] This form compares results—in terms of inquiries received—from all media (magazines, shows, etc.). It helps determine return-on-investment in specific media and compares their relative cost/effectiveness. See Task 8.

[11] Time period is dependent on selling cycle of product.

Sales Action Measurement Analysis [12]

(1) MEDIA SOURCE (date)	(2) NUMBER OF INQUIRIES	(3) NUMBER OF QUALIFIED LEADS	(4) % RESPONSE: COLUMN (3) ÷ COLUMN (2)	(5) NUMBER RECEIVING LITERATURE	(6) NUMBER SPECIFYING PRODUCT	(7) NUMBER RECOMMEND-ING PRODUCT	(8) NUMBER APPROVING PRODUCT	(9) NUMBER PURCHASING PRODUCT	(10) NUMBER INVESTIGATING PRODUCT	(11) TOTAL SALES ACTIONS: COLUMNS (6+7+8+9+10)	(12) ACTIONS AS % OF THOSE RECEIVING LITERATURE: COLUMN (11) ÷ COLUMN (5)

[12] This form compares all ads in terms of the type of sales response obtained. It can also measure effectiveness of literature mailings and various other promotional attempts. It is based on follow-up surveys of inquirers, and sales reports. See Task 8.

412

Inquiries/Market Profile [13]

PUBLICATION _____ ISSUE _____

PAGE _____ SIZE OF ADVERTISEMENT _____

B&W OR COLOR _____ HEADLINE _____

PRODUCT _____

BY JOB FUNCTION,	TALLIES	TOTALS
Administrative		
Engineering		
Design		
Plant Operations		
Production		
Purchasing		
Marketing		
Other		
GRAND TOTAL:		

BY SIC NO.[14]	TALLIES	TOTALS
No.		
No.		
No.		
No.		
No.		
GRAND TOTAL:		

_____

[13] This form tallies inquiries resulting from a single advertisement in terms of the inquirer's job title (function, industry class, and product interest—by minor alteration of the form), as well as by SIC number. See Task 8.

[14] Standard Industrial Classification Code (SIC).

413

Inquiry Coverage Ratio [15]

SALESMAN OR TERRITORY	JANUARY			FEBRUARY			MARCH			APRIL			MAY			JUNE			JULY			AUGUST			SEPTEMBER			OCTOBER			NOVEMBER			DECEMBER			TOTALS		
	1	2	3	1	2	3	1	2	3	1	2	3	1	2	3	1	2	3	1	2	3	1	2	3	1	2	3	1	2	3	1	2	3	1	2	3	1	2	3

Column 1 = Cumulative number of leads sent to dealer or representative
Column 2 = Cumulative number of follow-up calls
Column 3 = % of leads followed-up (Column 2 ÷ Column 1)

[15] See Task 8.

414

Sales Versus Inquiries [16]

SALESMAN OR TERRITORY	THROUGH JANUARY				THROUGH FEBRUARY				THROUGH MARCH				THROUGH APRIL				THROUGH MAY				THROUGH JUNE				THROUGH JULY				THROUGH AUGUST				THROUGH SEPTEMBER				THROUGH OCTOBER				THROUGH NOVEMBER				THROUGH DECEMBER				TOTALS			
	INQUIRIES		SALES		INQUIRIES		SALES		INQUIRIES		SALES		INQUIRIES		SALES		INQUIRIES		SALES		INQUIRIES		SALES		INQUIRIES		SALES		INQUIRIES		SALES		INQUIRIES		SALES		INQUIRIES		SALES		INQUIRIES		SALES		INQUIRIES		SALES		INQUIRIES		SALES	
	1	2	3	4	1	2	3	4	1	2	3	4	1	2	3	4	1	2	3	4	1	2	3	4	1	2	3	4	1	2	3	4	1	2	3	4	1	2	3	4	1	2	3	4	1	2	3	4	1	2	3	4

COLUMN 1. Number of Inquiries to Date
COLUMN 2. Percent of Total Inquiries to Date
COLUMN 3. Dollar Sales to Date
COLUMN 4. Percent of Total Dollar Sales to Date

[16] See Task 8.

415

CHAPTER
XII

Legal Aspects of Marketing[1]

Introduction

Legal Aspects of Marketing are Important

Marketing decisions are always subject to complex legislative considerations. Both civil and criminal penalties face those who try to "beat the system." For example, violation of the Sherman Act—a misdemeanor—may be punishable by fine not exceeding $50,000, and imprisonment for one year, or both. Civil penalties may include triple damages, plus attorney fees.

You may encounter legal questions such as these:

Do federal, state, or local government laws/regulations in any way restrict, or significantly raise costs of production, distribution, sale, or use of a product? (These laws and regulations cover labeling, advertising, pricing policies, trade practices, and distribution systems for the product itself, as well as any materials, parts, or subassemblies needed.)

Do industry agreements or labor union regulations affect the production, sale, shipment, installation, servicing, or use of a product?

Is maximum patent and trademark protection held for products?

If not, are all outstanding claims to royalties or other indemnities settled to permit making the product(s)?

Do federal, state, or local licensing or tax requirements affect producing and marketing certain products?

Do clear contractual understandings govern each link in distribution channels?

Are promotional and protective warranties adequate?

Chapter Plan

This chapter should help you understand the more important legal aspects of marketing. It begins with a brief list of the types of legal questions you may encounter. There follows a general discussion of the historical development of marketing legislation to make you more aware of legal questions which may be raised about your company's actions (Task 1). Procedures for obtaining patents (Task 2), trademarks (Task 3), and copyrights (Task 4) are described. Contractual arrangements (Task 5), consumerism, ecology, product safety, warranties (Task 6), and fair trade laws (Task 7) are also covered. The chapter concludes with suggestions concerning additional sources of legal information in the reference guide.

---

[1] This chapter in no way replaces your need for legal counsel. It merely points out situations where legal advice often applies. If questions arise in areas covered by this chapter, you should seek competent legal counsel. You won't find qualified answers to your particular problems in this chapter. Moreover, this chapter pertains to federal laws only.

Task 1: Review of Marketing Legislation

Degree of Legislation

Laws and public policy influence most major marketing decisions. Many legislative and regulatory devices maintain the free enterprise system—make it work more effectively. This mountain of laws includes several major acts and amendments, many minor acts, and thousands of federal and state court decisions. Numerous government agencies are empowered to enforce the laws, and each state contributes its own unique interpretations of federal acts, as well as designing its own regulatory laws.

Types of Legislation

There are two broad categories of marketing legislation: monopoly and unfair competition. The former is mainly a corporate problem, while the latter is primarily a marketing issue. Both areas are discussed in this section.

Monopoly legislation aims to maintain free competition by preventing persons from gaining exclusive control of the means of producing and selling a commodity or service. It also strives to prevent "price fixing."

Unfair competition legislation attempts to control false and misleading advertising, misbranding, "under-the-table" deals with buyers, industrial espionage, false and disparaging statements about competitors or their products, pirating employees away from competitors, selling "seconds" as high quality "firsts," and various types of "tying"

clauses (in which patented articles are sold on condition that all accessories be purchased from the seller).

Purpose of Discussion

The descriptions of marketing legislation in this section are intended to make you aware of the basis for legal questions possibly raised about your company's actions. Whenever a doubt arises as to the legality of these actions, you should consult counsel skilled in the practice of business law.[2] Even then, it is often difficult to obtain precise interpretations of marketing legislation due to (a) the changing business climate, (b) the legal reasoning and interpretations by certain judges, and (c) the confusion caused by a large "gray area" inherent in many laws. However, your legal counsel is always your most knowledgeable advisor and is your ultimate authority in all matters of the law.

Specific Legislation

The chart on pages 418–419 summarizes selected acts (exclusive of agricultural and consumer-oriented legislation) affecting various areas of marketing strategy. To highlight their historical development, the acts are listed in chronological order.

The legal environment affecting marketing constantly changes. This is due to pending legislation and daily court decisions. Therefore, the chart given here cannot represent the latest situation.[3]

Task 2: Patent Protection

What are Patents?

Patents protect innovators from competitors imitating the product, sharing in profits,

yet avoiding research and development costs. The first U.S. patent laws were passed in 1790. They were aimed at providing monetary incentive for inventors by granting

---

[2] If you lack corporate legal counsel, see your local Bar Association for a number to call when you need specialized legal advice.

[3] "On the Road to Regulation," by Theodore F. Craver, *Conference Board Record*, October 1975, pp. 20–26, presents a summary of recent legislation.

Acts Affecting Each Area of Marketing Strategy

	NAME AND BRIEF DESCRIPTION OF ACT	AREAS OF MARKETING STRATEGY			
		PRICING	CHANNELS	PROMOTION	PRODUCT
1887	INTERSTATE COMMERCE ACT: Controls rates of interstate passenger and freight carriers, and eliminates rebates to large-scale users of their service.	●	●		
1890	SHERMAN ANTITRUST ACT: Prohibits contracts, combinations, trusts, or conspiracies in restraint of trade, and prohibits monopoly or attempts to monopolize interstate commerce. Some actions which are not "unduly" restrictive or "unduly or improperly exercised" are legal although they may constitute relatively minor restraints of trade. Condemns price-fixing agreements between competing firms. In most cases agreements on common trade-in allowances, price differentials, profit markups, adoption of single or multiple basing point system, and collusive bidding practices are restrained. Resale price maintenance agreements are, in general, illegal[4]. Exclusive dealing requirements contracts may violate the Sherman Act. Condemns firms using predatory tactics against competitors (i.e., cutting off competitor's source of supply, disparaging a competitor's products or ability, threatening or using actual intimidation). Amended by Clayton Act (1914) and Miller-Tydings Act (1937).	●	●	●	●
1906	FOOD AND DRUG ACT: Created the Food & Drug Administration to prohibit sale or shipment in interstate commerce of any food or drug that is adulterated or fraudulently misbranded, or which contains decomposed, putrid or filthy materials. Supplanted by Food, Drug & Cosmetic Act (1938); amended by Food Additives Act (1958).			●	●
1914	CLAYTON ACT: Supplements Sherman Act by prohibiting price discrimination between purchasers when such discrimination is not justified on the basis of cost differences; forbids exclusive and tying contracts whereby a producer sells a product only on condition that the buyer acquires other products from the same seller and not from competitors; and prohibits interlocking directorates and intercorporate stockholdings "where the effect . . . may be to substantially lessen competition or tend to be contributory to monopolistic discounts or allowances, except for actual brokerage functions or other legitimate services performed." Amended by Robinson-Patman Act (1936) and Celler-Kefauver Act (1950).	●	●		
1914	FEDERAL TRADE COMMISSION ACT (FTC): Created the Federal Trade Commission, a body of specialists with powers to investigate and issue cease and desist orders and remedial orders to correct actions deemed to be unfair competition, cartels organized for price fixing or discrimination, false and misleading advertising, labeling and misbranding. The FTC is currently one of the most important administrative agencies with which business must deal. The FTC works closely with the Federal Communications Commission, the Food & Drug Administration, Post Office Department, Department of Justice, The Securities and Exchange Commission and Internal Revenue Service. Amended by Wheeler-Lea Act (1938) and McGuire-Keogh Act (1952).	●	●	●	
1915	STANDARD BARREL ACT: Standardizes barrel sizes and bans use of false bottoms, odd sizes and questionable practices.				●
1916	SMALL CONTAINERS ACT: Reduces number of container sizes for handling produce.				●
1916	UNITED STATES WAREHOUSE ACT: Federally licenses approved commodity warehouses and issues negotiable warehouse receipts.		●		

418

				Year	Act
●				1918	**WEBB-POMERENE ACT:** Exempts American Exporters from the antitrust laws by permitting them to form export trade associations.
	●	●	●	1936	**ROBINSON-PATMAN ACT:** Amends Clayton Act by explicitly prohibiting a number of discriminatory pricing practices (fictitious brokerage, disproportional supplementary services and allowances, indefensible quantity discounts when such discounts are not justified on the basis of actual cost economies arising from mass buying, and the knowing inducement of discriminatory prices by buyers). Added phrase, "to injure, destroy or prevent competition."
●	●		●	1937	**MILLER-TYDINGS ACT:** Amends Sherman Act to permit resale price maintenance in interstate commerce within limitations set by states. Exempts from antitrust legislation, resale price maintenance contracts for branded and trademarked goods when such contracts are permitted by state legislation. (The McGuire-Keogh Act, 1952, reinstated the legality of the nonsigner clause.)
●	●			1938	**WHEELER-LEA ACT:** Amended Section 5 of FTC Act by outlawing unfair business practices, with emphasis on elimination of fraudulent advertising in interstate commerce. Added phrase, "unfair or deceptive acts or practices." Includes unfair pricing and misrepresentation of products.
	●			1938	**FOOD, DRUG AND COSMETIC ACT:** Amends FDA Act (1906) to include any food, drug, cosmetic or therapeutic device which is adulterated or misbranded. Requires listing weight and ingredients on labels.
●		●		1946	**LANHAM TRADEMARK ACT:** Stipulates that properly registered trademark becomes user's property after five years unless its use is contested within that time.
		●	●	1950	**CELLER-KEFAUVER ANTIMERGER ACT:** Amended Section 7 of Clayton Act to provide that acquisition of assets or stock where the effect "may be substantially to lessen competition or create a monopoly" is illegal. Bans acquisition of some distributors and some products if such action threatens to lessen competition.
●	●			1952	**McGUIRE-KEOGH ACT:** Amended Section 5 of the Federal Trade Commission Act to bind all dealers in a state to resale-price maintenance contracts if any one dealer in that state authorizing resale-price maintenance signed such a contract.
●	●			1960	**HAZARDOUS SUBSTANCES LABELING ACT:** Gives FDA power to adjudge specified household products hazardous and to require prescribed warnings on these products.[4]
●				1966	**FAIR PACKAGING AND LABELING ACT:** Provides for regulation of industry's packaging and labeling practices by FTC and The Secretary of Health, Education & Welfare. Ensures truthful disclosure of product identity, producer identity, quantity of contents of product, and other relevant packaging practices.[5]
				1970	**OCCUPATIONAL SAFETY AND HEALTH ACT (OSHA):** Created the Occupational Safety and Health Commission, ten regional offices and fifty area offices throughout the U.S. to be responsible for administration of the act. Investigates "places of employment" to ensure that they are "free from recognized hazards that are causing or are likely to cause death or serious physical harm." Standards are amended and expanded periodically.
●				1970	**WILLIAMS-STEIGER SAFETY & HEALTH ACT:** Extends scope and coverage of safety and health standards to any business with one or more employees affecting interstate commerce whether by trade, traffic, commerce, transportation or communication.

[4] However, see Miller-Tydings Act

[5] There are numerous federal statutes and regulations pertaining to the labeling of other non-hazardous products, such as wool, fur, textiles, and flammable fabrics

them exclusive rights to produce, use, or sell a new product for a period of 17 years in the United States and its territories and possessions. Patents are issued by the Commissioner of Patents, U.S. Department of Commerce. They are not renewable, except by act of Congress.

What is Patentable?

To obtain a patent you must have a product or process that is both novel and workable. Here is a partial list of various types of patentable items:

A new, useful industrial or technical process.

A machine, manufacture, or composition of matter (generally chemical compounds, formulas, and the like), or new and useful improvement thereof.

A new, original, and ornamental design for an article of manufacture (non-operating, non-functional device, such as a new auto body design).

A distinct and new variety of plant, other than tuber-propagated, which is asexually reproduced.

What is Not Patentable?

There are many new items which are not patentable. For example:

An idea or concept, as opposed to a workable mechanical device.

A material handling method (such as assembly lines) other than structural or mechanical innovations.

Printed matter already covered by copyright laws.

"Computer programs" which the U. S. Supreme Court recently rejected as unpatentable.

An inoperable device.

Improved operation of a device resulting from improved mechanical skill, unless it is a novel approach.

You also must consider the matter of *statutory bar* to patentability. For example,

under U.S. patent law, an idea patentable *per se*, may lose that status if, prior to filing of an appropriate application, the applicant has sold the product or published a description of the idea. As to what constitutes "selling" or "publishing," judicial precedent is not quite clear-cut. This is a situation where patent counsel should be consulted.

Legal Counsel

Any company having the potential of developing a patentable item should establish contact with reputable patent counsel on a retainer, or at least on a periodic review and consultation basis.

It is essential that you consult legal counsel in these four areas of patent concern: interference, infringement, foreign patents, and selling part interest.

Interference

Make certain your product design does not infringe on any previously patented products. If several individuals claim to have invented a product, a patent is issued to the person presenting proof of the earliest date of invention. In some cases, a workable model must be submitted, while in others the application of earliest date is granted the patent.

Infringements

To protect your product from possible infringements, you can file suit in a federal court for damages, or seek an injunction against anyone who, without your authority, manufactures, uses, or sells your patented product. There are no established ways to discover infringements of your patent. Your best bet is to hire a clipping service and have them review related trade publications for references to specific words (nouns) normally associated with your products use or function.

If you suspect infringement, consult your legal counsel immediately. Do not handle it yourself. The recent tendency of defendants in patent infringement suits to defend or cross-complain on the basis of antitrust violations and the friendly hearing such actions are receiving in the federal courts can make suits to defend patents risky and expensive business.

Foreign Patents

Anytime you wish to manufacture, use or sell your patented product in a foreign country, you must obtain a patent from that country if you expect continued protection from international competitors. If you plan to do business in another country at a later date, don't wait to file until just before beginning foreign business operations.

Under applicable international conventions, a U.S. citizen (including corporate citizen) must file for a U.S. patent first (or else lose, by law, any right to U.S. patent protection regardless of any foreign patents that may be issued). After a U.S. application, the applicant has a grace period of one year (less one day) to file in any foreign country. It is advisable to file during the grace period because the priority of the foreign patent automatically (under international convention) dates back to the filing date in the United States. The disadvantage of overrunning the grace period is that a foreign patent may no longer be obtainable, because a statutory bar to issuance may now exist.

Depending on the patent laws of a country, the time required to obtain a patent may be relatively long (accompanied by better protection), or relatively short (with risky protection). In some countries (such as the industrialized members of the British Commonwealth, Germany, and France), the patenting procedure is similar to that in the United States. Prior to issuance, the patent office conducts a lengthy examination of prior patent files to determine whether the claimed invention is truly novel. In this case it may take years to get a patent (as in the United States), but there is a comparatively good chance that the patent can be successfully defended against competitors and infringers.

In other countries (for example, Belgium), patents are issued in a matter of months. In this case, granting a patent simply means

that you have complied with all formal procedures. It is then up to you to establish and defend your patent against infringement, because it was granted without thorough examination of the prior art. Whereas any patent issued anywhere is, in rather cynical terms, merely a "license to sue," this is more truth than cynicism in the "fast-issue" countries.

When seeking a foreign patent, obtain a patent counsel fully knowledgeable of the laws of the country in which you seek a patent.

For further information on foreign patents, order the *Summary of Patent Laws in 125 Countries*, from J. J. Berliner & Staff, Berliner Research Bldg., Danbury, CT 06810.

Selling Part Interest

You can sell or license your patent to others, permitting them to manufacture and sell the product. Complex legal problems arise in this situation because part owners can freely use the patent as if they owned it outright. Always seek legal counsel to establish a sales/licensing agreement.

Procedure to Obtain Patent

To obtain a patent:

(1) Obtain proof of origin
(2) Conduct search
(3) Submit application
(4) Await Patent Office review (be prepared to defend by documentation, challenges by Patent Office examiner).

Step (1): Obtain Proof of Origin

Reduce your idea to writing in order to define it and establish legal proof of origin. This protects you at a later date. Have witnesses sign your disclosure document to verify the date you first thought of the idea.

An effective and legal way to establish the date of conception of a patentable idea is to use the Disclosure Document Program

(DDP) provided by the U.S. Patent Office. This program accepts and preserves "Disclosure Documents" as evidence of the dates of conception of inventions. This procedure should be used in addition to the conventionally-accepted method of having evidence of conception of your invention witnessed and notarized. The program is an economical shortcut to establishing a date of conception in circumstances where early in an R&D program you don't know whether you'll really care subsequently to spend, not $10 (the required fee for DDP), but more like $2,000–$10,000 to obtain a legal patent.

The DDP document is not a patent application and its receipt by the Patent Office does not become the effective filing date of any subsequently filed application. The document is kept in confidence by the Patent Office for two years and is then destroyed unless it is referred to in a related patent application. The document should always be referred to in new patent applications.

The DDP document should contain a clear and comprehensive explanation as to how to make and use the invention. This explanation should be sufficiently detailed to enable an individual familiar with the field of the invention to make and use it. Drawings, photographs and descriptions of all possible known applications of the invention should also be included. The document must be accompanied by a stamped, self-addressed envelope and a separate forwarding letter in duplicate, signed by the inventor, requesting that material be processed under the DDP. The request may take the following form:

> The undersigned inventor of the disclosed invention, requests the U.S. Patent Office to accept and preserve for a period of two years, the enclosed papers under the Disclosure Document Program.

Precise details for format of the document are available from the U.S. Patent Office. A fee of $10 is charged for this service. Payment should be sent to the Commissioner of Patents, Washington, DC 20231.

Step (2): Conduct Search

The next step is to have your patent attorney conduct a search of existing patents and applications. He can do this faster, more accurately, and more thoroughly than you. This search is to ensure that other firms do not hold prior rights to similar products. Existing patents may be reviewed in the "search room" of the U.S. Patent Office, Washington, DC 20231. Pending patents, however, are not listed for public perusal. Several million domestic patent records are maintained, as well as millions of foreign patents. If your invention appears to be patentable (i.e., no one else has been granted patent on a similar invention) and marketable (you are convinced that you can produce and sell it), submit a patent application. You don't have to prove marketability to apply, but it is helpful to know before spending any resources.

Step (3): Submit Application

Applications are filed with the Commissioner of Patents, Washington, DC 20231. Only attorneys and agents registered with the U.S. Patent Office may file an application. The Patent Office in Washington, DC, or the local field office (generally in the U.S. Department of Commerce field office) can provide a geographical and alphabetical listing of more than 5,000 registered "practitioners." This *Directory of Attorneys and Agents Registered to Practice Before the U.S. Patent Office*, is also available for $1 from the Superintendent of Documents, U.S. Government Printing Office, Washington, DC 20402.

The Patent Office cannot, however, recommend a particular attorney or agent, nor assume responsibility for your selection. But professional and trade associations can help you make a suitable choice. Patent attorneys and agents are also listed in telephone directories of most major cities.

Your lawyer or agent will submit the application in your name or assign it to another individual or company designated by you. The application must include:

Specification and disclosure of invention
Drawings
Applicant's oath that he believes himself the first and original inventor
Applicant's full signature, nationality, and address
Fee of $30 by certified check or money order via registered mail made out to the Commissioner of Patents

After submitting your application, mark your product "Patent Pending." This provides no "real" legal protection, but tends to discourage potential infringers.

Step (4): Await Patent Office Review

The complicated Patent Office processing can take from one to four years. First your application is examined to make sure it is correctly prepared. If it isn't, it is immediately returned to you. If it is, the Patent Office assigns it a serial number and filing date.

The application is then turned over to an examiner to ensure that your patent is truly distinctive from existing patents. When any objections are raised by the examiner, you are given an opportunity to counter them. If rejected again, you can appeal the decision to the Patent Office Board of Appeals for a $25 fee.

When finally granted, a brief description of your patent will be published in the Official Gazette of the U.S. Patent Office with all others granted that same week. You will be formally notified and provided with documentary evidence that you have been granted a patent.

Use and Defense of Patents

Courts have consistently held that patents, representing in essence, legal monopolies, must be used and defended with reasonable diligence and vigor. Courts have invalidated patents if the holder failed to "reduce the invention to practice." In other words, if a company simply owns patents neither used in marketing, nor made available for licensing to a degree acceptable to the courts, those patents can be judged "sleeper" patents, and in essence be taken away from their original holder.

Other Information Sources

The U.S. Patent Office has several publications which describe the patenting process in more detail. Two of these are *Rules of Practice of the U.S. Patent Office*, and *General Information Concerning Patents*.

Another excellent reference is *Drafting Patent License Agreements*, by Harry R. Mayers (Bureau of National Affairs Books, 1231 25th Street, N.W., Washington, DC 20037; 288 pp., $25). This book explores the licensing of patent and know-how arrangements and provides a clause-by-clause examination of every significant element of the patent licensing agreement. Appendices include a summary of U.S. patent law and practice, and examples of simple and complex license agreements.

The key to correctly obtaining and maintaining in force a sound patent is to retain the services of an authorized patent attorney at the outset. All too often, patentable ideas are lost or stolen due to premature disclosure or improper administration. Good patent attorneys can save you time and money if their advice is sought at the birth of an idea.

Task 3: Trademark Protection

What are Trademarks?

A trademark identifies a product with its particular maker or seller. Properly selected and protected trademarks become the exclusive, proprietary marketing symbol of their owners and may become a valuable asset. They enable a purchaser to distinguish one product from a competitor's, either due to previous satisfactory use, or on the basis of a conviction or persuasion to purchase inspired by advertising and promotion or corporate identity. The mark also serves as a guarantee of consistent quality.

Trademarks include brand names, logos, product marks, monograms, and similar identifying marks found on the signs of company buildings, letterheads, envelopes, calling cards, trucks, advertisements, catalogs, brochures, packaging, and most other visual representations of the company.

Legal ownership and exclusive right to use a trademark on a product protects your position. The Lanham Act of 1947 allows owners to protect trademarks in the United States by recording them on the Patent Office's principal register. Similar protection may also be obtained if use is only intrastate in scope, under state law.

Form of Trademark

The trademark can be a letter of the alphabet, a coined or ordinary word, a word suggesting some characteristic of product function of quality, a name, initials, numerals, a symbol, design or device, or any combination of these. The name of the manufacturer is a common type of trademark for industrial goods, particularly when employed as a brand name.

Examples of the trademark forms mentioned above include XEROX reproduction machines, RCA appliances, Chevron gasoline, NL Industries' "Dutch Boy" paint, Mack Truck's "Bulldog" trucks.

Guidelines for Selection

The mark can be arbitrary, suggestive, or descriptive. Here are some guidelines for selecting a trademark:

- Use short, simple, and distinct trademarks (brand names) which are easy to spell, recognize, pronounce and remember.
- Use marks conveying appropriate connotation to buyer (image).

- Use only legally protectable trademarks. (See Usage Guidelines, page 426.)
- Use marks having graphic adaptability.
- Don't use personal names unless applicable and necessary.
- Don't use a generic term or common descriptive name.
- Don't use product family trademarks for association if products differ greatly in quality.
- Don't use offensive, obscene or negative trademarks.
- For international marketing use brand names that are pronounceable in foreign languages (Xerox, Kodak, Coca Cola).
- Use a mark which can be extended to include new goods.

Success May Destroy Protection

The great success of trademarks may destroy their protection. This paradox arises when a brand name or trademark is identified so completely with a product that it becomes the common or generic name for the product itself. The classic example for industrial products is the "escalator." Otis Elevator Company lost the right to object to the use of the word "escalator" by other manufacturers of competitive products, simply because they continued to use the term "generically" in their advertising. Similarly, DuPont still hurts from the nylon case in which "nylon" was declared generic.

Outside Design Firm

It is advisable to engage an outside design firm to develop new trademarks. Company employees tend to develop loyalties to old marks and to have prejudices based on various points of view. To locate a suitable outside design firm, see your telephone Yellow Pages under "Trademark Consultants," and "Trademark Designers." Once you have engaged a designer, give him your objectives and image desires and then allow him full freedom to develop your trademark design without interference by you or members of your company. Do not become emotionally involved. Try to remain objective.

Avoid Infringement

When you begin using a trademark, you automatically acquire certain rights which protect you as long as you continue to use the mark, but be sure to document the date of first use. To acquire federal, as opposed to state protection, at least one interstate use is required. However, to avoid infringement suits against you by other firms using similar marks on related products you should, early in the mark selection process, have a search made of the files of registered and unregistered trademarks. It is best to have a patent attorney do this whether or not you intend to register your mark (see Yellow Pages under "Trademark Registering").

Some authorities point out that searches are not always foolproof because they may not cover all marks. For this reason, it might be advisable to have two independent searches made by different organizations.

Search Sources

Several private organizations, as well as the U.S. Patent Office, maintain extensive files of registered and unregistered trademarks. They will supply search reports for a modest fee or, in the case of the Patent Office, let the public search their files. These reports include such information as: pending applications, registrations, abandonments, oppositions, cancellations, owners, date of filing, date of first use in commerce, publication data, serial number, Patent Office classification, and description of goods and services covered.

In addition to trade associations, which often maintain records of trademarks on products in their industries, additional sources are listed in the reference guide. These sources distribute information on the use, regulation, and protection of trademarks.

Procedure for Registering

The first step is to hire an attorney knowledgeable in trademark matters. Also, obtain from the Superintendent of Documents, Government Printing Office, Washington, DC 20402, or direct from the U.S. Patent Office, all information available on trademark procedures. Particularly useful are *General Information Concerning Trademarks,* and *Rules of Practice in Trademark Cases.* Your attorney can also provide similar information.

Rights

As previously noted, trademark rights depend on actual usage. Even an unregistered trademark is enforced by the courts if its use has been established. However, your legal right to the trademark is strengthened by registering it with the Commissioner of Patents, U.S. Patent Office, Washington, DC 20231.

The registration makes your mark a matter of public record and establishes a legal notice of your rights. Before application for federal registration, however, the mark must have been in use in interstate commerce (affixed to products themselves). After a registered mark has been used continuously for 5 years, it can be made incontestable. Bear in mind, if your use does not qualify for federal protection, you may still qualify for state registration and state common law protection.

Application for Trademark Registration

The actual application is a simple process. Submit a formal document with:

Company name
A drawing of the mark
Date of the first interstate usage
List of goods and services on which the mark is used
The state and date of first usage
Manner of usage
Sworn statement by an authorized company officer declaring that the company is owner of the mark, and to his best

knowledge no other company has the right to use the mark.

Five specimens of facsimiles showing the mark in use

Registration fee

When the Patent Office receives the application, your request is assigned a serial number. The Patent Office examiner then checks all records for prior claims. He can send you a written rejection if your request conflicts with prior applications or existing marks, or if the mark is deceptive, scandalous, descriptive, or geographical in nature. If your mark is rejected, you can submit through your attorney, a legal argument to defend your use of the mark. This argument is directed to the examiner, and if rejected again may be submitted to the Trademark Trial & Appeal Board for final ruling.

If your mark is approved, notification will be published in the weekly Patent Office bulletin, "Official Gazette." Other possible claimants to the mark may contest your claim up to 30 days from the date of publication. If there is no opposition, the Commissioner of Patents will issue a certificate of registration giving you sole rights to use the mark for 20 years. The mark is renewable indefinitely.

Usage Guidelines

You must ensure that your trademark is always identified as such wherever it appears. There are several ways to educate your organization, distributors, dealers, and customers to use your trademark as a trademark, rather than as a generic term:

Use and defend your trademark with reasonable diligence and vigor. For example, DuPont automatically sends a complaint letter to any medium that fails to indicate "TM" (or some equivalent statement) in conjunction with a DuPont product that does enjoy trademark and trade name protection.

Use a distinctive style to set off your trademark from nontrademark language (i.e., capital letters, quotation marks, a different type face, script, italics, bold face, underscored, different type size, framed, or a different color).

For unregistered trademarks, place the word "trademark" or the abbreviation TM directly following or beneath the mark.

For registered trademarks, place the letter R enclosed in a circle, or "Reg. U.S. Pat. Off.," or "Registered in U.S. Patent Office," on the shoulder of the trademark.

Use a verbal trademark in correct grammatical form—as an adjective. Never use the mark as a noun, in the plural, as a verb, or in the possessive, which in each case might suggest that the mark is actually the generic name of a product.

Use the generic term for the product immediately following a verbal trademark.

Do not detract from the mark by additions or abbreviations.

Use the mark for a line of products rather than a single product.

Task 4: Copyright Protection

What is a Copyright?

A copyright is a legal right granted for a limited period to an author, composer, playwright, publisher, or distributor, to the exclusive publication, production, sale, or distribution of a literary, musical, dramatic or artistic work. It is advisable to get copyrights on all your company literature. Before publication, you can rely on common law copyrights and the use of secret disclosure agreements. However, the date or origin is often difficult to prove. Therefore, a common law copyright is not as effective as the actual application.

Copyright Notice

Before applying for a copyright, the material must be published and contain an appropriate copyright notice. For a book, the copyright notice must appear on the title page or page immediately following. For a periodical, the copyright notice must appear on the title page, upon the first page of the text, or under the title heading. For a musical work, the copyright notice must appear either on the title page or first page of music.

The copyright notice can take several forms, but must include three key elements:

Word "Copyright," abbreviation "Copr.," or symbol "©"
Year of publication
Name of copyright owner
For example: © 1973 John Smith

Procedure to Register Copyright

Promptly after you have published your work with the copyright notice in the correct position, you can register the copyright. Application forms are available by mail request from the Copyright Office, Library of Congress, Washington, DC 20540, or you can obtain them in person at Room 101 of Building No. 2, Crystal City Mall, 1921 Jefferson Davis Highway, Arlington, Va. There are no branch offices.

Who Can File?

You need not hire an attorney to file your copyright application. However, if you do, you still must personally sign the application. The following persons are legally entitled to submit an application:

Author of work
Person given right to secure copyright from author
Authorized representative of agent of author

Step (1): Select Correct Form

On request, the Copyright Office will send you a copy of circular 5—"Copyright Application Forms." This circular lists 20 different forms for different purposes. You can choose the appropriate forms from the circular or from the list which follows. The Register of Copyrights will issue the application forms free.

Form A—Books manufactured in the United States
Form A-B Foreign—Foreign books, periodicals and contributions to periodicals
Form A-B Ad Interim—Certain books, periodicals, and contributions to periodicals
Form B—Periodicals manufactured in the United States
Form BB—Contributions to periodicals manufactured in the United States
Form C—Lectures, sermons or addresses prepared for oral delivery
Form D—Dramatic and Dramatic-Musical compositions
Form E—U.S. musical compositions
Form E Foreign—Foreign musical compositions
Form F—Maps
Forg G—Works of art, or models or designs for works of art
Form H—Reproductions of works of art
Form I—Drawings or sculptural works of a scientific or technical nature
Form J—Photographs
Form K—Prints and pictorial illustrations
Form KK—Commercial prints and labels
Form L-M—Motion Pictures
Form N—Sound recordings
Form R—Renewal copyright
Form U—Notice of use of copyright and music on mechanical instruments

Step (2): Mail to Register of Copyrights

Promptly after publication, mail to the Register of Copyrights, Library of Congress, Washington, DC 20540:

Two copies of the best edition of the published work
Notarized application form
Fee of $6.00 payable to Register of Copyrights

Step (3): Approval

After it has been reviewed and approved, your copyright is good for 28 years, and is renewable once for a like period.

Task 5: Distribution Channel Contracts

What are Contracts?

Contracts are legal vehicles for the transaction of business. Specifically, a contract is a mutually agreed statement of rights, duties and privileges, whereby legal controls govern the relationship between two parties. Primary elements of an enforceable contract, whether written or unwritten, include:

> Mutual agreement as to a definite offer, certain terms, and an acceptance
> Negotiated price consideration paid for a promise to act
> Legal capacity of parties (in view of laws about minors, mental incompetents, and corporations)
> Subject matter not voided by statute or common law

When Do You Need Contracts?

Whenever you have an arrangement with a distribution channel, you need written contracts to avoid later misunderstandings and friction. This includes the use of company salesmen, sales agencies, manufacturers' representatives, distributors or dealers. Each of these distribution channels represent a company or companies before other third parties (e.g., buyers). These representations often include making collections, disbursing company funds to cover expenses, and taking responsibility for company property, all while working with little or no direct supervision. The length and details of formal contracts depend on the particular conditions within individual companies. In all cases, however, there is a definite need to establish the rights, duties and privileges of both parties.

Contract Provisions

Contracts should contain suitable clauses, provisions and conditions to protect each party from arbitrary actions by the other. The contracts can be in the form of a series of letters or a single formal document. It is generally wise to have contracts with your own salesmen; dealers, agents, distributors and representatives; and with original equipment manufacturers that you supply direct, and vendors who directly supply you.

Salesmen

Contracts with salesmen should have the following information and provisions (as well as any other specific requirements and agreements):

> Identification of parties concerned
> Beginning and ending dates of contract period
> General statement of obligations and duties of salesman and employer
> Nature of employment (products to be sold, sizes, territory assigned to salesman, and kinds of customers to be cultivated)
> Specific compensation arrangements (methods, rates, and dates of payment)
> Scope and limits of authority given to salesmen governing acceptance of orders, price quotations, answering complaints, verbal warranties on contents and quality of products, collecting debts, and signature of company's name on contracts
> Frequency and scope of reports to be submitted by salesmen
> Quotas assigned to salesmen
> Procedure for termination or cancellation of contract, extent and form of notice required
> Provision covering travel, entertainment, and other expenses
> Clause covering salesman's financial responsibility for his samples and other company property (vehicles, promotional materials, etc.)
> Clause preventing salesman from "pirating" current customers or revealing company secrets if he leaves the company subsequent to termination of employment

Remedies for breach of contract or damages

Procedures for handling orders

Protection of company through surety bond

Requirement of salesman to devote entire time exclusively to the company and not take concurrent employment to sell another company's products

Signatures of both parties and dates of signatures

Provisions for attendance at training or sales meetings

Exceptions to any of the above

Dealers, Agents, Distributors, and Representatives

As with your own salesmen, you should have comprehensive written contracts with your dealers, agents, distributors, or representatives. These contracts should have the same type of information and provisions as for salesman contracts. In addition, they should include:

Nature of territorial delineation (i.e., exclusive representation of company products while agreeing not to sell competitive items) bearing in mind antitrust restrictions

Requirements to refrain from (or provision for) representing or selling competing lines

Clause stating that all orders are subject to manufacturer's approval. This reduces manufacturer's liability for agent errors or unallowable considerations

Description and extent of advertising and promotion allowances and merchandising supports to be provided by company and agent

Provision for manufacturer to retain and service "house," or "national" accounts, even in an agent's given territory

Provision for shipping costs to be paid by buyer or seller

Requirements for inventory stocking (minimum levels, provision for handling slow-moving items, and return of unsold inventory upon termination of contract)

Whether or not goods will be taken on consignment

Provision for purchase orders (made out to company or agent) and responsibility for paying cost of errors

Definition of who is responsible for checking credit ratings of all customers

Whether company name can be used by agent on local office buildings, directories and doors

Provision for payment by company of agent's operating expense

Provision for allocating interterritory commissions where two or more territories share in a user order

Original Equipment Manufacturers

Special contractual arrangements must be established for original equipment manufacturers (OEM) who regularly purchase your products direct in large quantities. These situations often involve special discounts or commission rates which normally would accrue to middlemen. In most cases, the OEMs are actually large dealers who handle only their own purchases.

Model Contracts

The contractual arrangements discussed above all have similar contents, with few exceptions. To obtain copies of model (standard form) contracts, contact the Manufacturers' Agents National Association, Suite 503, 3130 Wilshire Blvd., Los Angeles, CA 90005. This organization can provide a model contract form having selectable paragraphs for developing dealer, agent, and distributor agreements.

Additional Information

For further information, a copy of *Summary of Agreement Termination Laws in 30 Countries* is available from J. J. Berliner & Staff, Berliner Research Bldg., Danbury, CT 06810. This report covers legislation and practices on termination requirements, procedures, and obligations.

Task 6: Review of Consumerism and Ecology Laws

Introduction

Some of the most significant legal developments in the history of the United States are now at hand. It is ironic that most of the developments are extremes on both sides of the spectrum, rather than a middle-of-the-road course. With cries from the public that government control has become too great, the current administration is seeking to reduce federal government's control by guiding funds back to state and local governments, and to deregulate many heavily regulated businesses, such as the airlines, rails, and trucking industries. At the same time, cries from consumer activists and corporations alike are causing the government to strengthen environmental restrictions, product safety standards, and a multitude of additional consumer legislation. More legislation is now being passed into law than in any other time in our country's history.

The following areas are covered under Task 6:

Product Safety (to the user)
Guarantees and Warranties
Advertising Claims
Product Safety (to the environment)

Product Safety (to the User)

Failure to ensure product safety has resulted in some costly legal settlements. An airplane manufacturer had to pay over $20 million in a legal settlement because he failed to provide baffles in a wing tank. Another court case resulted in a nearly $2 million verdict against a manufacturer and a distributor of a bottle whose contents became contaminated because of a crack in the glass not detected during an inspection step. Also, there was a stiff judgement against a punch press manufacturer because of a negligently miswired switch.

The following checks are important when considering whether products are safe to use:

Consider safety features in design specifications.
Conduct product safety tests.
Consider possible misuse of product.
Include conspicuous safety warnings on labels, nameplates, instructions and maintenance manuals.

Liability

Prior to 1966, virtually all jurisdictions held that liability terminated at the doors of the immediate vendor (i.e., manufacturer's representatives, wholesalers, dealers, and so forth), and extended only to the purchaser who bought from the immediate vendor.

However, legal doctrine today permits liability claims to affect the OEM, the OEM's component suppliers, and so forth. Consequently, legal claim recovery rights may now extend to the family and associates of the buyer. This is an area where competent legal counsel (plus, possibly, consideration of product liability insurance) is particularly essential.

Guarantees and Warranties?

"Warranty" and "guarantee" are used interchangeably in most business and legal references, although they have quite different legal origins. A minor difference has been to regard guarantees as "oral" and warranties as "written." This distinction is not necessarily valid. In this chapter, the term "warranties" is used to cover both cases.

A warranty is part of the sales offer which pertains to a product being sold. It assures a buyer that he will receive good performance after purchase. This assurance might be for repair of all imperfections or replacement of materials which deteriorate over time, even though they are not in use, making amends for faulty installations, or for fixing components which are not inspectable before sale. This assurance may be provided by the company's reputation, its publicity, labeling and packaging, sales messages, and knowledge that manufacturer must abide by applicable legislation. In any case, the warranty provides both promotional and protective advantages.

From a promotional standpoint, the warranty is a sales tool which reduces the buyer's risk and creates goodwill. Also, from a promotional standpoint, warranties may be used to promote dealer as well as customer goodwill. From a protection standpoint, warranties may help limit the manufacturer's responsibility, thus protecting him from unjustifiable claims.

In most cases, it is wise to use warranties for both promotional and protective reasons. You can choose the warranty which best fits your needs from the following alternatives:

Promotional

There are various types of promotional warranties. Most offer either full satisfaction or one of the following remedies: refund of selling price, refund of selling price plus some penalty (e.g., double your money back), return of goods with money refunded, replacement, repair, or some combination of the above. The following are examples of warranties with promotional objectives:

ABSOLUTE SATISFACTION: completely eliminates buyer's risk; primarily for food and drug products, and sometimes for durable goods.
APPROVAL BY AUTHORITY: the use of "seals of approval" given by an organization or association creates an express warranty. Either giver or user of seal of approval must provide remedy to purchaser if product is faulty.
FREEDOM FROM HARMFUL OR DISADVANTAGEOUS RESULTS IN USE: used for products not subject to common defects familiar to potential customers.

Protective

Protective warranties generally provide for the replacement of defective parts without cost to buyer. They also protect the seller against unreasonable claims for redress on the part of unscrupulous buyers.

There is one primary protective warranty type:

MECHANICAL PERFECTION: covers products "free from defects in material and workmanship under normal use and service."

Promotional and Protective

Some warranties serve both promotional and protective objectives. They must offer the same remedies as promotional warranties.

COMPLIANCE WITH FIXED STANDARD: covers products for which minimum standards have been prescribed by law or government agencies and which have the effect of warranties.
PERFORMANCE BY TIME PERIOD OR USAGE: covers machinery and equipment which under given conditions will perform to state's specifications for a given period.

General Policy

As a matter of general ethical policy, you should fulfill all responsibilities as a warrantor and not evade obligations in dealing with a warranty holder seeking redress. Making the proper adjustment is much more important than what you say you'll do in advance. This also helps to limit legal cases that may lead to bad publicity which could damage goodwill.

Types of Warranties

A distinction is made between expressed and implied warranties. Expressed warranties result from affirmed promises and law-imposed express representations. Implied warranties are imposed by law because of the implications of certain aspects of public policy or social advantage. They include, among others, the implied warranty of fitness of a product for its intended purpose and the implied warranty of marketability.

Express Warranty

Anytime a seller affirms a fact or promises anything relating to the goods, this creates an express warranty if the buyer's reliance on such affirmation or promise tends to induce him to purchase the goods. When the seller makes a value judgment or statement of his opinion about the goods, this is not necessarily construed as a warranty (i.e., the world's best candy). On the other hand, because sellers of industrial products are expected to know their products better than sellers of consumer products, their statements of opinion can hold as a warranty.

Express warranties are legally binding in written or oral form if they were taken seriously by the buyer and he has relied on them in making his purchase.

Implied Warranty

In sale by description or by showing a sample there is an implied warranty that all goods will correspond with the description furnished or specimen shown and that the quality of the bulk of goods will correspond with the sample. In the past, there were relatively few legal actions based on implied warranties. However, the recent tendency of courts to expand the concept of warranty has created a new and viable field of potential liability. Some manufacturers have protected themselves by using exceptions and disclaimers to their carefully written and limited express warranties. Expressions like "as is," or "with all faults," are the best disclaimers.

Current Legal Position on Warranties

The Magnuson-Moss Warranty-Federal Trade Commission Improvement Act, which recently became law, gives the Federal Trade Commission (FTC) power to regulate the terms of written warranties issued on all consumer products costing $10 or more. The law does not require manufacturers to offer warranties, but if they do, the FTC can prescribe the contents of the warranty, the manner of its display, can settle disputes between the manufacturer and consumers, and can institute enforcement proceedings in which the FTC may become a class action plaintiff on behalf of all consumers.

The FTC can go into Federal District Courts to obtain temporary restraining orders or preliminary injunctions preventing any warrantor from making a deceptive warranty. They can restrain the warrantor from failing to carry out the remedies of the act, which include refunding the purchase price if the consumer will accept a refund, or repairing, or replacing the article.

Product Advertising Claims

The FTC is currently seeking the authority and resources to set testing standards for major consumer goods (appliances and other complicated products). The FTC would not dictate how products are to be designed or perform. Rather, it will strive to put the consumer in a better position to be able to compare competing brands based on performance, not on exaggerated ad claims.

Product Safety (to the Environment)

Failure to adhere to standards and legislation protecting the environment has resulted in penalties and fines levied against certain companies and the closing of many plants. Companies are being attacked on grounds ranging from polluting the environment at the production stage through selling products which are hazardous or unsafe to use.

Several key questions about the environment must be answered by all manufacturers:

Is the product contributing to depletion of a valuable material or resource? Can substitute materials be found?

Does the manufacturing process yield dangerous or offensive by-products?

Does the product itself emit dangerous or offensive products during use?

Is the product readily disposed of or recyclable after use?

Is the product's package easily disposed of (e.g., biodegradable) or recyclable?

The Government, through the Environmental Protection Agency (EPA), plans to step up its auditing of possible polluters. They even plan to investigate the small polluters, including small manufacturing firms to dry cleaning shops and filling stations. Although in recent years, complete compliance with pollution control standards has been delayed beyond set deadlines, future violators will receive the highest priority by the EPA, which may result in many firms being shut down.

Also, in this area, specific legislation, such as the *Occupational Safety and Health Act* (OSHA), have indirect effects on the marketing process. For example, OSHA limits noise levels at work stations. Therefore, machinery with noise levels exceeding a specified decibel level may no longer be sold for use in immediate areas occupied by employees. This affects equipment manufacturers who supply machines and equipment used at these work stations.

Other OSHA provisions prohibit, directly or by implication, some minor and customary aspects of OEM products. For example, certain lead additives used in lubricating oils and gasolines may have to be phased out entirely.

A copy of OSHA, including standards and record keeping requirements is offered by the nearest regional OSHA office, or from the Office of Information Services, Occupational Safety and Health Administration, U.S. Department of Labor, Washington, DC 20201.

Task 7: Review of Fair Trade Laws

History of Fair Trade Laws

Resale price maintenance (RPM) is a pricing technique which has been prevalent in the United States since the 1930s. RPM is an agreement between a manufacturer and wholesaler or retailer whereby the latter agrees to sell the manufacturer's product for not less than a stipulated minimum price. For years, the Supreme Court ruled that such agreements were in violation of the *Sherman Act;* but later implied that Congress or state legislatures may constitutionally provide for RPM.

California passed the first RPM enabling law in 1931. This legalized the signed agreement between an intrastate manufacturer and distributors concerning RPM for trademarked products. Congress passed additional interstate exemptive legislation as an amendment to the Sherman Act in 1937. This was the *Miller-Tydings Act,* which applied only in cases where manufacturers and dealers had signed an RPM agreement. The act was later expanded to include nonsigners with passage of the *McGuire Act* in 1952.

Recent fair trade laws made all wholesalers and retailers parties to an RPM agreement as long as one of them had signed the contract. The plaintiff could sue noncomplaints for breach of contract or ask for injunctions.

Repeal of Fair Trade

State-by-state, and now in Congress, fair trade laws are being repealed. This will result in increased emphasis on local planning and control of marketing activities. Other results may include:

Large chain discounters will compete against the traditional department store, variety store, and independents also carrying the previously fair-traded line.

"Suggested retail prices" will still be continued as many manufacturers want to provide a yardstick of value to the consumer. This benchmark is needed; but discounting will be encouraged.

Several branded products will concentrate their sales efforts on major store chains to reduce the amount of price discounting on their products.

Co-op advertising budgets could multiply

considerably as opportunistic retailers and manufacturers work together to maximize use of local advertising media to communicate lower prices.

Brand merchandise marketers may try to protect their "high quality" image by introducing special new discount lines.

Legal Aspects of Marketing Reference Guide

Associations

American Association For The Comparative Study of Law, % Edward D. Re, U.S. Customs Court, 1 Federal Plaza, New York, NY 10017.

American Bar Foundation, 1155 East 60th St., Chicago, IL 60637.

American Law Institute, 4025 Chestnut St., Philadelphia, PA 19104.

Practicing Law Institute, 810 Seventh Ave., New York, NY 10019.

Government Sources of Information

Code Of Federal Regulations, published by U.S. General Services Administration, National Archives Bldg., 8th & Pennsylvania N.W., Washington, DC 20408. Multivolume collection which covers administrative law, regulations and rulings, presidential proclamations and executive orders.

Congressional Record, published by United States Congress—available from U.S. Government Printing Office, Washington, DC 20402. Daily with annual cumulation. Indexes give names, subjects, and history of bills. Texts of bills not included.

Consumer Protection, Bureau of FTC, Pennsylvania Avenue and Sixth St., N.W., Washington, DC 20580.

Consumer Affairs, Office of Department of HEW, 330 Independence Ave., S.W., Washington, DC 20201.

Consumer Product Safety Commission, 1111 18th St. N.W., Washington, DC 20207.

Federal Register, National Archives Bldg., 8th & Pennsylvania Ave., N.W., Washington, DC 20408. Daily, except Sunday, Monday and day following an official federal holiday. Also included: "List Of CFR" sections affected (codification guide), monthly, cumulative quarterly, and annually. "Subject Index," monthly, cumulative quarterly, and annually.

News Summary—Effects of Laws and FTC Regulations on Business Practices, Advertising & Sales Promotion, Federal Trade Commission, Washington, DC 20580.

Public Laws, Congress, published by U.S. General Services Administration, Federal Register Office—available from U.S. Government Printing Office, Washington, DC 20402. Irregular—issued in slip form.

United States Statutes At Large, published by U.S. Office of the Federal Register—available from U.S. Government Printing Office, Washington, DC 20402. Annual—congressional acts and presidential proclamations issued during the Congressional session. For all laws in force at a specific date, refer to United States Code.

United States Code, published by United States Congress—available from U.S. Government Printing Office, Washington, DC 20402. Continual supplements. Contains permanent and general public law of the United States from 1789 to the codification date.

Periodicals and Directories

American Business Law Journal, % Dr. Gaylord Jentz, University of Texas College of Business Administration, Austin, TX 78712.

American Journal Of Comparative Law, American Association for the Comparative Study of Law, Inc., Boalt Hall, University of California, Berkeley, CA 94720.

Bar Associations, Attorneys And Judges, George E. Brand, American Judicature Society, 1155 East 60th St., Chicago, IL 60637.

Antitrust & Trade Regulation Reporter, Bureau of National Affairs, 1231 25th St., N.W., Washington, DC 20037.

Business Lawyer, American Bar Assoc., 1155 East 60th St., Chicago, IL 60637. Quarterly.

Trade Regulations Reports, Commerce Clearing House, 4025 W. Peterson Ave., Chicago, IL 60646.

Commercial Law Journal, 222 West Adams St., Chicago, IL 60606. Monthly.

Directory Of Legal Aid And Advice Facilities Available Throughout The World, International Legal Aid Assoc., 501 Fifth Avenue, New York, NY 10017.

International Directory Of Bar Associations, revised

edition, American Bar Foundation, 1155 East 60th St., Chicago, IL 60637.

Journal Of Marketing (quarterly), "Legal Developments in Marketing" (column), American Marketing Assoc., 230 North Michigan Ave., Chicago, IL 60601.

Law And Contemporary Problems, Duke University School of Law, Durham, NC 27708. Quarterly.

Marketing And The Law (semi-monthly), Man and Manager, Inc., 799 Broadway, New York, NY 10003.

Public Policy Issues In Marketing, by O. C. Ferrell and Raymond LaGarce, Lexington Books, D. C. Heath & Co., 125 Spring St., Lexington, MA 02173.

U.S. Law Week, Bureau of National Affairs, 1231 25th St., N.W., Washington, DC 20037. Weekly—two volumes.

Sources of Information on Trademarks

U.S. Trademark Association (USTA), 6 East 45th St., New York, NY 10017.

Trademark Bureau, Diamond International Corp., 133 Third Ave., New York, NY 10017.

TCR Service, Inc., 140 Sylvan Ave., P. O. Box 936, Englewood Cliffs, NJ 07632.

The Trademark Register, 422 Washington Building, Washington, DC 20005.

Index